See p. 38
Peter Wolf
p. 17
BOYD GAINES

D1573348

John Willis
Theatre World
1993-1994 SEASON

VOLUME 50

APPLAUSE
NEW YORK • LONDON
THEATRE BOOK PUBLISHERS
211 WEST 71ST STREET • NEW YORK NY • 10023

LIBRARY OF CONGRESS CATALOG CARD NO. 73-82953
ISBN 1-55783-235-8 (cloth)
ISBN 1-55783-236-6 (paper)

This silver anniversary volume is dedicated to the invaluable cooperation over fifty years of the many contributing press agents and photographers, and to the following who have given generously of their time, energy, and patience to perpetuate the 1944 dream of Daniel Blum and Norman Macdonald:

Brandt Aymar	Jay Greenberg	Virginia Maroweck	William Schelble
Linda Barry	Herbert Hayward	Gino Moya	Harold Schiff
Laura Bernay	Kevin Hickman	Don Nute	Fred Shrallow
Terence Burk	Jim Hollifield	Ruth Orkin	Martin Shwartz
Alberto Cabrera	Douglas Holmes	Louise Owens	Sally Sockwell
Constantine	Peter Howard	Darold Perkins	Jack Stauf
Jacques Crampon	Page Johnson	David Powers	Harold Stephens
Lane Cresap	Frances Keyes	Torben Prestholdt	Paul Sugarman
Dewey Dillon-Jones	Viola Kreuner	Kay Radtke	Antonio Suppa
Craig Dudley	Jerry Lacker	Stanley Reeves	Michael Viade
Patricia Elliott	Tom Lynch	Vernon Rice	Peter Warrack
Earle Forbes	Marvin Mar	Michael Riordan	Fredrika Weber
Raymond Frederick	Harry Marinsky	Evan Romero	Van Williams
Guy Gillette	Louis Melancon	Giovanni Romero	Aileen Willis
Peggy Goddard	Jorge Moctezuma	Tiko Romero	Walter Willison
Marlene Gould	Barry Monush	John Sala	Glenn Young

With immeasurable gratitude,

John Willis

John Willis
Editor

Theatre World covers volumes 3, 6, 4

Photo by Stan Schnier/ Carmen Schiavone

Jessica Stone, Sam Harris, Ricky Paull Goldin, Megan Mullally, Hunter Foster in *Grease*

Photo by William Gibson/Martha Swope

Top: Anna Deavere Smith in
Twilight: Los Angeles, 1992
Bottom: Rosemary Harris in
An Inspector Calls

Photo by Joan Marcus/Marc Bryan-Brown/Walt Disney Theatrical Productions

Burke Moses, Kenny Raskin in *Beauty and the Beast*

Photo by Martha Swope

Top: Nathan Lane in
Laughter on the 23rd Floor
Bottom: Michael Hayden
in *Carousel*

Photo by Joan Marcus

Photo by Joan Marcus

David Marshall Grant, Marcia Gay Harden
in *Angels in America: Perestroika*

Photo by Joan Marcus/ Marc Bryan-Brown

3

Jarrod Emick, Bebe Neuwirth in *Damn Yankees*

CONTENTS

EDITOR: JOHN WILLIS
ASSISTANT EDITOR: TOM LYNCH

Assistants: Herbert Hayward, Jr., Barry Monush, Stanley Reeves, John Sala
Staff Photographers: Gerry Goodstein, Michael Riordan, Michael Viade, Van Williams
Production: Bendix Anderson, Steve Ledezma, Rachel Reiss, Eric Simon,
Paul Sugarman, Andrea Whittaker

CELEBRATING
50 YEARS OF
THEATRE WORLD

Ray Bolger in *Where's Charley?*

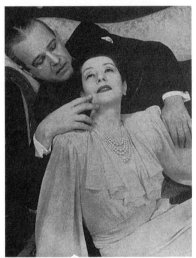

Alfred Lunt, Lynn Fontanne
in *O Mistress Mine*

6 John Gielgud in
*The Importance of
Being Earnest*

Marlon Brando, Jessica Tandy
in *A Streetcar Named Desire*

Helen Hayes
in *The Wisteria Trees*

Mae West as
Catherine of Russia

Katharine Hepburn in *As You Like It*

1944
to 1954

Photo by Zinn Arthur

Janice Rule, Ralph Meeker
in *Picnic*

Photo by Eileen Darby

Audrey Hepburn, Cathleen Nesbitt in *Gigi*

Photo by Frank Donato

James Dean in
The Immoralist

7

Carol Channing in *Hello Dolly!*

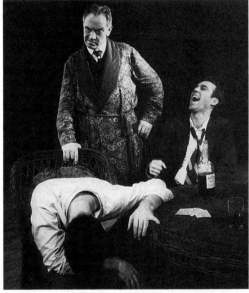

1954 to 1964

**Bradford Dillman, Fredric March, Jason Robards Jr.
in *Long Day's Journey into Night***

William Redfield, Paul Scofield in *A Man for All Seasons*

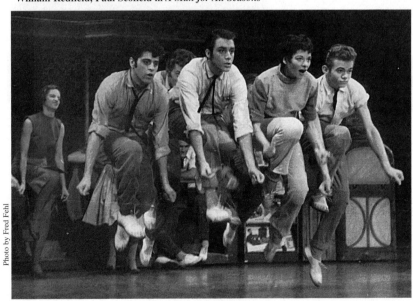

West Side Story company

**William Daniels, George Maharis
in *The Zoo Story***

Claudia McNeil, Sidney Poitier in *A Raisin in the Sun*

Barbra Streisand in *Funny Girl*

George Grizzard, Uta Hagen, Arthur Hill in
Who's Afraid of Virginia Woolf?

Julie Andrews, Richard Burton in *Camelot*

Julie Andrews, Rex Harrison
in *My Fair Lady*

9

Photo by Friedman-Abeles

Dean Jones in *Company*

1964 to 1974

Photo by Friedman-Abeles

10   **Clarence Williams III, Carolyn Daniels, George Rose
in *Slow Dance on the Killing Ground***

Photo by Martha Swope

Jack Albertson, Sam Levene in *The Sunshine Boys*

Photo by Friedman-Abeles

**Cliff DeYoung, Hector Elias, Elizabeth Wilson,
Tom Aldredge, David Selby in *Sticks and Bones***

Godspell company

Michael Maitland, Angela Lansbury in *Mame*

**Leslie Uggams, Lillian Hayman, Robert Hooks
in *Hallelujah, Baby!***

Diane Keaton, Woody Allen, Tony Roberts in *Play it Again, Sam*

**Ed Flanders, Jason Robards, Colleen Dewhurst
in *Moon for the Misbegotten***

**Albert Finney, Joan Hickson
in *A Day in the Death of Joe Egg***

11

1974 to 1984

Angela Lansbury, Len Cariou in *Sweeney Todd*

Jeremy Irons, Glenn Close in *The Real Thing*

12 **Anthony Hopkins, Peter Firth,
Everett McGill in *Equus***

**Harvey Fierstein, Susan Edwards
in *Torch Song Trilogy***

**Nancy Snyder, Jonathan Hogan, Amy Wright,
Joyce Reehling, Helen Stenborg, William Hurt,
Danton Stone, Jeff Daniels in *5th of July***

Jennifer Holiday in *Dreamgirls*

Humbert Allen Astredo, Elizabeth Taylor, Dennis Christopher,
Anthony Zerbe, Joe Ponazecki in *The Little Foxes*

Michel Stuart, Donna McKechnie, Carole Bishop, Thomas J. Walsh, Nancy Lane, Patricia Garland, Ronald Dennis, Don Percassi,
Renee Baughman, Pamela Blair, Cameron Mason, Sammy Williams in *A Chorus Line*

Andrea McArdle, Dorothy Loudon,
Janine Ruone, Robyn Finn in *Annie*

James Remar, Richard Gere, David Marshall Grant in *Bent*

13

1984 to 1994

Lily Tomlin in *The Search for Signs of Intelligent Life in the Universe*

Matthew Broderick, Alan Ruck in *Biloxi Blues*

Morgan Freeman, Dana Ivey
in *Driving Miss Daisy*

Ellen McLaughlin, Stephen Spinella in *Angels in America*

Joan Allen in *The Heidi Chronicles*

Laura Esterman, Alice Drummond
in *Marvin's Room*

Michael Crawford in *Phantom of the Opera*

Mark Nelson, Tom Hulce in
A Few Good Men

BROADWAY PRODUCTIONS
(June 1, 1993–May 31, 1994)

Brad Kane, Louis Zorich

Diane Fratantoni, Sally Mayes

Sally Mayes, Howard McGillin

Joey McKneely, Jonathan Freeman, and company

SHE LOVES ME

Music, Jerry Bock; Lyrics, Sheldon Harnick; Book, Joe Masteroff; Based on a play by Miklos Laszlo; Director, Scott Ellis; Musical Staging, Rob Marshall; Orchestrations, Frank Matosich Jr., David Krane (new), Don Walker (original); Musical Director, David Loud; Sets, Tony Walton; Costumes, David Charles, Jane Greenwood; Lighting, Peter Kaczorowski; Sound, Tony Meola; Hair/Wigs, David H. Lawrence; Cast Recording, Varese Sarabande; Production Supervisor, Jeremiah H. Harris; Stage Managers, Kathy J. Faul, Matthew T. Mundinger; Presented by Roundabout Theatre Company (Founding Director, Gene Feist; Artistic Director, Todd Haimes) joined for transfer by James M. Nederlander and Elliot Martin with Herbert Wasserman, Freddy Bienstock, and Roger L. Stevens; Press, Chris Boneau/Adrian Bryan-Brown, Susanne Tighe, John Barlow, Ellen Levine, Craig Karpel; Previewed from Saturday, May 15; Opened in the Criterion Center Stage Rights on Thursday, June 10, 1993*

CAST

Ladislav Sipos	Lee Wilkof
Arpad Laszlo	Brad Kane +1
Ilona Ritter	Sally Mayes
Steven Kodaly	Howard McGillin
Georg Nowack	Boyd Gaines —
Mr. Maraczek	Louis Zorich
1st Customer	Tina Johnson
2nd Customer	Kristi Lynes
3rd Customer	Trisha Gorman
4th Customer	Cynthia Sophiea
5th Customer	Laura Waterbury
Amalia Balash	Judy Kuhn (Roundabout)
	Diane Fratantoni (Atkinson)
Keller	Nick Corley
Headwaiter	Jonathan Freeman
Busboy	Joey McKneely
Ensemble	Bill Badolato, Peter Boynton, Mr.Corley, Ms. Gorman, Ms. Johnson, Ms. Lynes, Mr. McKneely, Ms.Sophiea, Ms. Waterbury

UNDERSTUDIES: Bill Badolato (Headwaiter), Peter Boynton (Kodaly/Georg), Nick Corley (Ladislav/Headwaiter), Mary Illes, Teri Bibb (Amalia), Kristi Lynes (Ilona), Joey McKneely (Arpad), James Clow (Georg), Peter Johl (Maraczek) SWINGS: Ms. Illes, Mason Robert

MUSICAL NUMBERS: Overture, Good Morning Good Day, Sounds While Selling, Days Gone By, No More Candy, Three Letters, Tonight at Eight, I Don't Know His Name, Perspective, Goodbye Georg, Will He Like Me?, Ilona, I Resolve, A Romantic Atmosphere, Dear Friend, Entr'acte, Try Me, Where's My Shoe?, Vanilla Ice Cream, She Loves Me, A Trip to the Library, Grand Knowing You, Twelve Days to Christmas, Finale

A new production of the musical in two acts. The action takes place in Budapest, 1934. For original 1963 Broadway production with Barbara Cook, Daniel Massey, Jack Cassidy, and Barbara Baxley, see *Theatre World* Vol. 19. Winner of 1994 "Tony" for Leading Actor in a Musical (Boyd Gaines).

Variety tallied 11 favorable and 5 mixed notices. *Times:* (Frank Rich) "...a continuously melodic evening of sheer enchantment and complete escape." (David Richards) "...a sweetheart of a musical." *News:* (Howard Kissel) "...a welcome reminder of what musical theatre ought to be." *Post:* (Clive Barnes) "...magical and faultless..." *Newsday:* (Jan Stuart) "...easily the most endearing musical ensemble between West 44th and 52nd Streets."

*After playing 61 performances and 31 previews at the Roundabout, the production re-opened Sept. 28, 1993, at the Brooks Atkinson Theatre where it played 294 performances and 11 previews before closing June 19, 1994.

+Succeeded by 1. Danny Cistone

Carol Rosegg/Martha Swope Photos

Top: Sally Mayes
Center: Joey McKneely (kneeling), Jonthan Freeman
Left: Boyd Gaines

CAMELOT

Music, Frederick Loewe; Lyrics/Book, Alan Jay Lerner; Based on *The Once and Future King* by T. H. White; Director/Choreographer, Norbert Joerder; Sets/Lighting, Neil Peter Jampolis; Costumes, Franne Lee, Tom Morse; Musical Director, John Visser; Musical Coordinator, John Monaco; General Managers, Narvin A. Krauss, Joey Parnes; Company Manager, Ken Myers; Stage Managers, Martin Gold, John C. McNamara; Executive Producer, Shelly Gross; Presented by Music Fair Productions; Press, Jeffrey Richards/Bill Schelble, Sally Frontman, Tom D'Ambrosio, Lee Solters; Previewed from Thursday, June 17; Opened in the Gershwin Theatre on Monday, June 21, 1993*

CAST

Sir Dinadan	Richard Smith
Sir Lionel	Virl Andrick
Merlyn/Pellinore	James Valentine
Arthur	Robert Goulet
Sir Sagramore	Cedric D. Cannon
Lady Anne	Jean Mahlmann
Guenevere	Patricia Kies
Nimue	Vanessa Shaw
Lancelot	Steve Blanchard
Dap	Newton R. Gilchrist
Mordred	Tucker McCrady
Tom of Warwick	Chris Van Strander
Ensemble	Mr. Andrick, Steve Asciolla, Greg Brown, Mr. Cannon, Ben Starr Coates, William Thomas Evans, Mr. Gilchrist, Lisa Guignard, Theresa Hudson, Brian Jeffery Hurst, Donald Ives, Ted Keegan, Karen Longwell, Jean Mahlmann, Raymond Sage, Barbara Scanlon, Vanessa Shaw, Richard Smith, Verda Lee Tudor, Kimberly Wells

UNDERSTUDIES: Richard Smith (Arthur), Barbara Scanlon (Guenevere), Brian Jeffery Hurst (Lancelot), Newton R. Gilchrist (Merlyn), Steve Asciolla (Pellinore), Ted Keegan (Mordred), Michael J. Novin (Tom/Sagramore), William Thomas Evans (Dinadan), Ben Starr Coates (Lionel), Theresa Hudson (Anne), Verda Lee Tudor (Nimue), Raymond Sage (Dap) SWINGS: Tina Belis, Mr. Novin

MUSICAL NUMBERS: I Wonder What the King is Doing Tonight?, Simple Joys of Maidenhood, Camelot, Follow Me, C'est Moi, Lust Month of May, How to Handle a Woman, Jousts, Before I Gaze at You Again, Madrigal, If Ever I Would Leave You, Seven Deadly Virtues, Fie on Goodness!, What Do the Simple Folk Do, I Loved You Once in Silence, Guenevere, Finale

A new production of the musical in two acts with 16 scenes. Robert Goulet played Lancelot in the original 1960 Broadway production with Richard Burton, Julie Andrews, and Roddy McDowall (see *Theatre World* Vol. 17).

Variety tallied 2 favorable, 1 mixed, and 11 negative reviews. *Times:* (Mel Gussow) "...unwisely, cuts have been made...this traveling show needs a tune-up." (Richards) "...the Gershwin stage is occupied by Mr. Goulet and a slablike construction..." *News:* (Kissel) "...all that's left here is the great score..." *Post:* (Barnes) "*Camelot* this is not." *Newsday:* (Stuart) "Goulet...gives Arthur a vocal authority heretofore unheard..." *Variety:* (Jeremy Gerard) "...dreary staging."

*Closed August 7, 1993, after 56 performances and 4 previews.

Scott Windus Photos

Top: Robert Goulet, Patricia Kies, Steve Blanchard
Center: Robert Goulet
Right: Patricia Kies, Robert Goulet

IN THE SUMMER HOUSE

By Jane Bowles; Director, JoAnne Akalaitis; Music, Philip Glass; Sets, George Tsypin; Costumes, Ann Hould-Ward; Lighting, Jennifer Tipton; Sound, John Gromada; Hairstylist, Angela Gari; Casting, Daniel Swee; General Manager, Steven C. Callahan; Production Manager, Jeff Hamlin; Stage Managers, Mireya Hepner, Mark Dobrow; Presented by Lincoln Center Theater (Artistic Director, Andre Bishop; Executive Producer, Bernard Gersten); Press, Merle Debuskey/Susan Chicoine; Previewed from Thursday, July 8; Opened in the Vivian Beaumont Theater on Sunday, August 1, 1993*

CAST

Gertrude Eastman Cuevas	Dianne Wiest
Molly	Aliana Arenal
Mr. Solares	Jaime Tirelli
Mrs. Lopez	Alma Martinez
Frederica	Karina Arroyave
Esperanza	Mary Magdelena Hernandez
Alta Gracia	Carmen De La Paz
Quintana	Carmen Rosario
Arturo	Arturo Vera
Lionel	Liev Schreiber
Figure Bearer	Robert Castro
Vivian Constable	Kali Rocha
Chauffeur/Photographer	James Puig
Mrs. Constable	Frances Conroy
Inez	Sheila Tousey

UNDERSTUDIES: Lisa Benavides (Molly/Esperanza/Alta/Quintana/Inez), James Puig (Solares), Carmen Rosario (Mrs. Lopez), Carmen De La Paz (Frederica/Arturo), John Freeman (Lionel/Figure Bearer/Chauffeur/Photographer), Katie Finneran (Vivian)

A new production of a drama in two acts with six scenes. The action takes place in Southern California, early 1950s. For original 1953 Broadway production, featuring Judith Anderson, Mildred Dunnock, and Jean Stapleton, see *Theatre World* Vol. 10.

Variety tallied 3 favorable, 2 mixed, and 5 negative reviews. *Times:* (Rich) "...odd-duck drama...seriously compromised by some poor acting and by the vast expanse of the Beaumont stage..." (Richards) "...Akalaitis has taken...an odd play, and made it odder." *News:* (Kissel) "...everything is reduced to a dumb cartoon." *Post:* (Barnes) "...a play that seems to reveal less and less as you think about it more and more." *Newsday:* (Stuart) "...beautiful, mysterious and eccentrically funny play..."

*Closed August 22, 1993, after 25 performances and 28 previews.

Martha Swope Photos

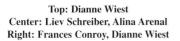

Top: Dianne Wiest
Center: Liev Schreiber, Alina Arenal
Right: Frances Conroy, Dianne Wiest

WHITE LIARS & BLACK COMEDY

Two Plays of the Sixties

By Peter Shaffer; Director, Gerald Gutierrez; Sets, John Lee Beatty; Costumes, Jess Goldstein; Lighting, Craig Miller; Sound, Douglas J. Cuomo; Stunts, Linwood Harcum; Hair/Wigs, David H. Lawrence; General Manager, Ellen Richard; Stage Managers, Jay Adler, Charles Kindl; Presented by Rondabout Theatre Company (Founding Director, Gene Feist; Artistic Director, Todd Haimes); Press, Chris Boneau/Adrian Bryan-Brown, Susanne Tighe, Ellen Levene; Previewed from Wednesday, August 11; Opened in the Criterion Center Stage Right on Wednesday, September 1, 1993*

CASTS

WHITE LIARS

Sophie: Baroness Lemberg	Nancy Marchand
Frank	Peter MacNichol
Tom	David Aaron Baker

The action takes place in a fortune teller's parlour at a run down English seaside resort, 1965.

BLACK COMEDY

Brindsley Miller	Peter MacNicol
Carol Melkett	Anne Bobby
Miss Furnival	Nancy Marchand
Colonel Melkett	Keene Curtis
Harold Gorringe	Brian Murray
Schuppanzigh	Robert Stattel
Clea	Kate Mulgrew
Georg Bamberger	Ray Xifo

The action takes place in Brindsley Miller's apartment in South Kensington, London, 1965. The action takes place in the dark though the stage is fully lit.

UNDERSTUDIES: Sybil Lines (Sophie/Furnival), Jon Patrick Walker (Frank/Tom), David Aaron Baker (Brindsley), Meg Chamberlain (Carol/Clea), Robert Stattel (Melkett), Nick Sullivan (Harold/Georg/Schuppanzigh)

A new production of two one-act comedies. For original 1967 Broadway production (titled *Black Comedy/White Lies*) with Michael Crawford, Lynn Redgrave, and Geraldine Page, see *Theatre World* Vol. 23. *White Liars* is a re-conceived and re-written version of *White Lies.*

Variety tallied 11 favorable, 2 mixed, and 1 negative review. *Times:* (Ben Brantley) "...chief pleasures come from the redoubtable Nancy Marchand and a young actress named Anne Bobby..." *News:* (Kissel) "...the stage is alive with an effervescent visual music." *Post:* (Barnes) "It is really worth the price of admission just to see and hear Brian Murray..." *Newsday:* (Stuart) "Boy-oh-boy, it feels good to laugh like this."

*Closed October 3, 1993, after 38 performances and 25 previews.

Carol Rosegg/Martha Swope Photos

**Top: David Aaron Baker, Nancy Marchand
Center: Nancy Marchand, Anne Bobby
Bottom: Anne Bobby, Peter MacNicol, Kate Mulgrew**

Anne Bobby, Brian Murray, Peter MacNicol

(on table) Peter MacNicol, Kate Mulgrew, (front) Brian Murray,
Anne Bobby, Ray Xifo, Robert Stattel, Keene Curtis

MIXED EMOTIONS

By Richard Baer; Director, Tony Giordano; Sets/Lighting, Neil Peter Jampolis; Costumes, David Murin; Sound, Dan Moses Schreier; General Manager, Gindi Theatrical Management; Casting, Pat McCorkle, Diane Silverstadt; Company Manager, Peter Bogyo; Stage Managers, Tom Aberger, John F. Weeks; Presented by Michael Maurer; Press, Shirley Herz/Miller Wright; Previewed from Tuesday, September 28; Opened in the Golden Theatre on Tuesday, October 12, 1993*

CAST

Chuck ....Vinny Capone
Ralph ....Brian Smiar
Christine Millman ....Katherine Helmond
Herman Lewis ....Harold Gould

UNDERSTUDIES: Maeve McGuire (Christine), Frank Savino (Herman/Ralph)

A comedy in two acts. The action takes place in Christine's apartment, Manhattan. A Broadway Alliance production.

Variety tallied 2 mixed and 9 unfavorable reviews. *Times:* (Brantley) "...a single note play" (Richards) "...a sex comedy about senior citizens..." *News:* (Kissel) "...the reason such comedies went out of fashion is that they relied upon the audience's squeamish, smirking attitude toward sex." *Post:* (Barnes) "...a TV sitcom placed within a proscenium arch..." *Newsday:* (Stuart) "Helmond and Gould perform with a gusto..." *Variety:* (Gerard) "...a threadbare sketch..."

*Closed November 28, 1993, after 48 performances and 17 previews.

**Top: Brian Smiar, Vinny Capone,
Katherine Helmond, Harold Gould**
Left: Harold Gould, Katherine Helmond

22

THE TWILIGHT OF THE GOLDS

By Jonathan Tolins; Director, Arvin Brown; Sets, John Iacovelli; Costumes, Jeanne Button; Lighting, Martin Aronstein; Sound, Jonathan Deans; General Manager, Marvin A. Krauss; Company Manager, Nina Skriloff; Stage Managers, Arthur Gaffin, Daniel Munson; Presented by Charles H. Duggan, Michael Leavitt; Fox Theatricals, Libby Adler Mages, Drew Dennett, Ted Snowdon; Press, Pete Sanders/Ian Rand, David Roggensack; Previewed from Friday, October 8; Opened in the Booth Theatre on Thursday, October 21, 1993*

CAST

David Gold	Raphael Sbarge
Suzanne Gold-Stein	Jennifer Grey
Rob Stein	Michael Spound
Phyllis Gold	Judith Scarpone
Walter Gold	David Groh

STANDBYS: Dean Fortunato (David/Rob), Dani Klein (Suzanne), Richard Reicheg (Walter)

A drama in two acts. The action takes place in New York, early autumn through late winter.

Variety tallied 5 mixed and 11 negative reviews. *Times:* (Brantley) "...the bridge of sympathy between actors and audience can never be fully crossed." (Richards) "...shallow theatrical goods." *News:* (Kissel) "...the play's best moments—apart from its sharp humor—are monolgues...Raphael Sbarge has an openness and sweetness..." *Post:* (Barnes) "Plays have never been good arenas in which to ventilate moral problems..." *Newsday:* (Stuart) "...a cautionary tale about genetics, homosexuality and the three original cast albums of *Gypsy*." *Variety:* (Gerard) "...ought to have a run on Broadway...provoke arguments about an issue...In a just world, that would be enough to get 'em lining up at the box office."

*Closed November 14, 1993, after 29 performances and 15 previews.

Joan Marcus Photos

**Top: Judith Scarpone, Michael Spound,
David Groh, Jennifer Grey, Raphael Sbarge
Left: Jennifer Grey, Raphael Sbarge**

WONDERFUL TENNESSEE

By Brian Friel; Director, Patrick Mason; Design, Joe Vanek; Lighting, Mick Hughes; Sound, Dave Nolan, T. Richard Fitzgerald; Production Supervisor, Jeremiah J. Harris; General Management, Joseph Harris, Thomas P. Santopietro; Stage Managers, Sally Jacobs, Judith Binus; Presented by Noel Pearson and The Shubert Organization in association with Joseph Harris and The Abbey Theatre; Press, Shirley Herz/Sam Rudy; Previewed from Thursday, October 7; Opened in the Plymouth Theatre on Sunday, October 24, 1993*

CAST

Terry ....Donal McCann
Frank ....John P. Kavanagh
Berna ....Ingrid Craigie
George..Robert A. Black
Angela ....Catherine Byrne
Trish ....Marion O'Dwyer

UNDERSTUDIES: Robert Emmet (Terry/Frank), Charlie Giordano (George), Maggie Marshall (Trish), Ellen Tobie (Angela/Berna)

A drama in two acts. The action takes place on a pier in Donegal, Ireland, August.

Variety tallied 5 favorable, 3 mixed, and 5 unfavorable reviews. *Times:* (Rich) "No one is likely to mistake it for...other Friel masterworks..." (Richards) "...beautiful and lethargic in equal parts." *News:* (Kissel) "...an arresting stop on a great journey." *Post:* (Barnes) "...there is a fantastic beauty here..." *Newsday:* (Linda Winer) "It's autumn in New York, which means Broadway has another meticulously acted, talky Irish play..." *Variety:* (Gerard) "...beautifully written and just as beautifully delivered."

*Closed October 31, 1993, after 9 performances and 20 previews.

Tom Lawlor Photos

Top: Ingrid Craigie, Donal McCann
Bottom Left: Ingrid Craigie, Catherine Byrne
Bottom Right: Marion O'Dwyer, John Kavanagh

TIMON OF ATHENS

By William Shakespeare; Director, Michael Langham; Music, Duke Ellington adapted by Stanley Silverman; Sets, Douglas Stein; Costumes, Ann Hould-Ward; Lighting, Richard Nelson; Sound, Keith Handegord; Choreography, George Faison; Fights, B. H. Barry; Casting, Liz Woodman; General Manager, Niko Associates; Special Effects, Gregory Meeh; Company Manager, Brig Berney; Stage Manager, Michael Ritchie; Executive Producer, Manny Kladitis; Presented by National Actors Theatre (Founder/Artistic Director, Tony Randall; Artistic Advisor, Michael Langham); Press, John and Gary Springer; Previewed from Tuesday, October 19; Opened in the Lyceum Theatre on Thursday, November 4, 1993*

CAST

Timon	Brian Bedford
Flavius	Jack Ryland
Flaminius	Alec Mapa
Ventidius	Tim MacDonald
Servilius	Michael Wiggins
Poet/Representative	Derek Smith
Painter/Representative	Jeffrey Alan Chandler
Jeweller/Bandit	Alec Phoenix
Merchant	Jerry Lanning
Lucius	Michael Lombard
Lucullus	Tom Lacy
Sempronius	Nicholas Kepros
State Senator	Herb Foster
Military Senator	Michael Rudko
Church Senator	Leo Leyden
Caphis/Bandit	Mark Niebuhr
Philotus	Brian Evaret Chandler
Soldiers	Kevin Shinick, Francis Henry
Old Athenian/Masseur/Bandit	Michael Stuhlbarg
Apemantus	John Franklyn-Robbins
Alcibiades	Michael Cumpsty
Alcibiades' Officer/Masseur	Jesse L. Martin
Photographer/Cupid	Rod McLachlan, Martin Kildare
Phrynia	Andi Davis
Timandra	Anette Helde
Dancers	Evelyn W. Ebo, Rebeccca Sherman, Stevi Van Meter
Hortensius	Richard Holmes
Citizens	John Dybdahl, Ted Hoffstatter, John Burton Eillson

UNDERSTUDIES: Brian Evaret Chandler (Officer/Soldier/Masseur), Andi Davis (Timandra), Annette Helde (Phrynia), Richard Holmes (Painter/Senator/Rep.), Marin Kildare (Ventidius/Messenger/Masseur/Bandit), Tim MacDonald (Flavius), Alec Mapa (Cupid/Soldier/Photographer), Jesse L. Martin (Alcibiades), Rod McLachlan (Lucius/Senator), Mark Niebuhr (Lucullus/Senator), Alec Phoenix (Poet/Rep.), Blake Robison (Merchant/Jeweller/Hortensius/Bandit), Michael Rudko (Apemantus/Sempronius), Kevin Shinick (Caphis/Bandit/Flaminius/Servilius), Derek Smith (Timon), Michael Wiggins (Philoyus/Soldier/Musician)

A drama performed in two acts. The setting is Depression-era Europe.

Variety tallied 7 favorable, 6 mixed, and 1 negative review. *Times:* (Brantley) "...combines historical scope with intense emotional intimacy...Brian Bedford delivers a landmark performance..." (Richards) "...a significant change in fortunes for the National Actors Theatre..." *News:* (Kissel) "...a solid cast..." *Post:* (Barnes) "...power, beauty and authority..." *Newsday:* (Stuart) "...a production that illuminates, surprises and hushes every last cough from the front row to the second balcony."

*Closed December 5, 1993, after 37 performances and 18 previews.

Joan Marcus Photos

Top: Tom Lacy, Nicholas Kepros, Brian Bedford, Michael Lombard
Center: Brian Bedford
Right: Brian Bedford and company

CINDERELLA

Music, Richard Rodgers; Lyrics/Original Book, Oscar Hammerstein; Book Adaptation, Steve Allen; Stage Adaptation/Director/Choreographer, Robert Johanson; Orchestrations, Robert Russell Bennett; Conductor, Eric Stern; Sets, Henry Bardon; Costumes, Gregg Barnes; Lighting, Jeff Davis; Sound, Abe Jacob; Co-Choreographer, Sharon Halley; Presented by New York City Opera; Press, Susan Woelzl/Dale Zeidman, Bert Fink; Opened in the New York State Theatre on Tuesday, November 9, 1993*

CAST

Fairy Godmother..Sally Ann Howes
Royal Herald..Ron Baker
Little Girl...Abigail Mentzer
Cinderella's Stepmother..Nancy Marchand
Stepsisters: Joy..Alix Korey
        Portia...Jeanette Palmer
Cinderella ....Crista Moore
Dog...Andrew Pacho
Cat..Debbi Fuhrman
Queen..Maria Karnilova
King ....George S. Irving
Royal Chef ....Jonathan Green
Royal Steward ....John Lankston
Prince...George Dvorsky
Youngest Fairy ....Stephanie Godino
Tiara Fairy ....Shawn Stevens

MUSICAL NUMBERS: The Prince is Giving a Ball, In My Own Little Corner, Loneliness of Evening (cut from *South Pacific*), My Best Love (cut from *Flower Drum Song*), Impossible, Gavotte, Ten Minutes Ago, Stepsister's Lament, If I Weren't King (cut from 1957 TV version), Do I Love You Because You're Beautiful, When You're Driving Through the Moonlight, A Lovely Night, Royal Wedding

A new stage version of the 1957 television musical in two acts. Performed on television by Julie Andrews (1957) and Lesley Ann Warren (1965).

Times: (Edward Rothstein) "...much of it...is pleasing for adults as well as children." *News:* (Kissel) "...comes to life whenever the songs begin..." *Post:* (Barnes) "...no great find or lost masterpiece, it has a certain wistful charm..." *Newsday:* (Stuart) "...a ramshackle event..."

*Closed November 21, 1993, after limited run of 14 performances.

Carol Rosegg Photos/Martha Swope Photos

Robert Torti in *Joseph* ...

26   **Debbi Fuhrman, Crista Moore in** *Cinderella*

Michael Damian in *Joseph* ...

JOSEPH AND THE AMAZING TECHNICOLOR DREAMCOAT

Music, Andrew Lloyd Webber; Lyrics, Tim Rice; Director, Steven Pimlott; Orchestrations, John Cameron; Musical Supervisor, Michael Reed; Musical Director, Patrick Vaccariello; Design, Mark Thompson; Choreography, Anthony Van Laast; Lighting, Andrew Bridge; Sound, Martin Levan; General Manager, Nina Lannan; Casting, Johnson-Liff Associates; Production Manager, Peter Fulbright; Company Manager, Mark Johnson; Stage Managers, Jeff Lee, J. P. Elins; Press, Chris Boneau/Adrian Bryan-Brown, John Barlow; Previewed from Tuesday, October 26; Opened in the Minskoff Theatre on Wednesday, November 10, 1993*

CAST

Joseph	Michael Damian
Narrator	Kelli Rabke
Pharaoh/Levi	Robert Torti
Jacob/Potiphar/Guru	Clifford David
Butler/Gad	Glenn Sneed
Baker/Issachar	Bill Nolte
Mrs. Potiphar/Napthali's Wife	Julie Bond +1
Reuben	Marc Kudish +2
Simeon	Neal Ben-Ari +3
Napthali	Danny Bolero
Asher	Timothy Smith
Dan	Joseph Savant
Zebulun/Apache Dancer	Tim Schulthies +4
Benjamin	Ty Taylor
Judah	Gerry McIntyre
Reuben's Wife	Michelle Murlin +5
Simeon's Wife	Mindy Franzese
Levi's Wife	Jocelyn Vodovoz Cook +6
Issachar's Wife	Jacquie Porter
Asher's Wife	Lisa Akey +7
Dan's Wife	Sarah Miles
Zebulan's Wife	Diana Brownstone
Gad's Wife	Betsy Chang
Benjamin's Wife/Apache Dancer	Tina Ou
Judah's Wife	Susan Carr George +8

Children's Choirs ....Carolabbe Chorus, La Petite Musicale, Long Island Performing Arts Center Choir, William F. Halloran Vocal Ensemble, Blessed Sacrament Chorus of Staten Island, Friends Academy Singers, Public School 39 Chorus, Righteousness Unlimited

UNDERSTUDIES: Ty Talor, Matthew Zarley (Joseph), Lisa Akey, Susan Carr George, Kelli Severson, Susan Santoro (Narrator), Bill Nolte, Glenn Sneed (Jacob/Potiphar/Guru), Marc Kudish, Joseph Savant, Bryan Batt (Pharaoh) SWINGS: Ron Kellum, Andrew Makay, Janet Rothermel, Kelli Severson, Gina Trano, Matthew Zarley, Angel Caban, Jennifer Kay Jones

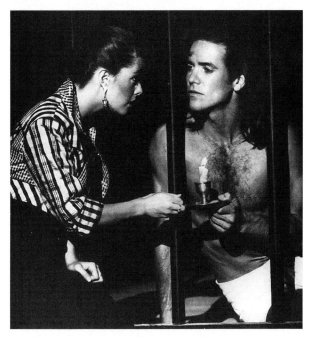

MUSICAL NUMBERS: Overture, Prologue, Any Dream Will Do, Jacob and Sons/Joseph's Coat, Joseph's Dreams, Poor Poor Joseph, One More Angel in Heaven, Potiphar, Close Every Door, Go Go Go Joseph, Entr'acte, Pharaoh Story, Poor Poor Pharaoh/Song of the King, Pharaoh's Dreams Explained, Stone the Crows, Those Canaan Days, Brothers Came to Egypt/Grovel Grovel, Who's the Thief, Benjamin Calypso, Joseph All the Time, Jacob in Egypt, Joseph Megamix

A new production of the musical based on the Biblical story of Joseph and his eleven brothers. Performed in two acts. For the 1982 Broadway production see *Theatre World* Vol. 38.

Variety tallied 3 favorable, 5 mixed, and 7 negative reviews. *Times:* (Brantley) "...a modest, tuneful little musical...grew and grew, through successive incarnations, into an oversize, glittering symbol of the Age of Hype." *News:* (Thomas M. Disch) "...this production is a steamroller..." *Post:* (Barnes) "...a bat out of showbiz hell." *Newsday:* (Winer) "...overriding goofiness...playful bad taste..." *Variety:* (Gerard) "...at once humorous and spectacular..."

*Closed May 29, 1994, after 223 performances and 17 previews.

+Succeeded by: 1. Mamie Duncan-Gibbs 2. Bryan Batt 3. Paul Harman 4. Richard Stafford, Matt Zarley 5. Jocelyn V. Cook 6. Malinda Shaffer 7. Susan Santoro 8. Kelli Severson

Craig Schwartz/Jay Thompson Photos

Top: The company
Center: Kelli Rabke, Michael Damian
Left: The company

THE KENTUCKY CYCLE

By Robert Schenkkan; Director, Warner Shook; Sets, Michael Olich; Costumes, Frances Kenny; Lighting, Peter Maradudin; Music/Sound, James Ragland; Fights, Randy Kovitz; Dramaturg, Tom Bryant; Casting, Pat McCorkle; General Management, Niko Associates; Company Manager, Alexander Holt; Production Supervisor, Bonnie Panson; Stage Managers, Joan Toggenburger, Tracy Crum; Presented by David Richenthal, Gene R. Korf, Roger L. Stevens, Jennifer Manocherian, Annette Niemtzow, Mark Taper Forum/Intiman Theatre Co., John F. Kennedy Center for the Performing Arts in association with Benjamin Mordecai; Press, Jeffrey Richards/Irene Gandy, Carol Van Keuren, Kevin Rehac, Candi Adams, Michael Cullen; Previewed from Wednesday, November 3; Opened in the Royale Theatre on Sunday, November 14, 1993*

CAST

PART ONE

Masters of the Trade - 1775
Earl Tod..Randy Oglesby
Michael Rowen ....Stacy Keach
Sam ....Tuck Milligan
Taskwan ....Ronald William Lawrence
Dragging Canoe ....John Aylward
Cherokee Warriors.....................Philip Lehl, Lee Simon, Jr., Stephen
                                        Lee Anderson, Patrick Page

Courtship of Morning Star - 1776
Michael Rowen..Stacy Keach
Morning Star ....Lillian Garrett-Groag

The Homecoming - 1792
Patrick Rowen...Scott MacDonald
Rebecca Talbert ....Katherine Hiler
Star Rowen ....Lillian Garrett-Groag
Michael Rowen ....Stacey Keach
Joe Talbert ....John Aylward
Sallie ....Gail Grate

Ties That Bind - 1819
Patrick Rowen...Scott MacDonald
Ezekiel Rowen ....Tuck Milligan
Zachariah Rowen...Ronald Hippe
Sallie Biggs ....Gail Grate
Jessie Biggs ....Ronald William Lawrence
Judge Goddard ....John Aylward
Deputy Grey ....Randy Oglesby
Deputy O'Sullivan ....Michael Hartman
Jeremiah ....Gregory Itzin
Star...Lillian Garrett-Groag
Guitar Player...James Ragland

God's Great Supper - 1861
Jed Rowen...Tuck Milligan
Ezeliel Rowen ....Stacy Keach
Patrick Rowen/Union Col./Gus Slocum........................John Aylward
Joleen Rowen ....Jeanne Paulsen
Richard Talbert ....Gregory Itzin
Randall Talbert/Carl Dawkins ....Ronald Hippe
Rose Anne Talbert ....Katherine Hiler
Julia Anne Talbert..Lillian Garrett-Groag
Sharecroppers.......................................Randy Oglesby, Philip Lehl
Rebels....................................Patrick Page, Stephen Lee Anderson
Boatman...Ronald William Lawrence
Tommy Nolan...Scott MacDonald
William Clark Quantrill.......................................Randy Oglesby
Union Soldiers.................................Michael Hartman, Lee Simon Jr.

Tuck Milligan, Stacy Keach, Ronald Hippe

PART TWO

Tall Tales - 1890
Mary Anne Rowen (younger) ....Katherine Hiler
Mary Anne Rowen (older) ....Jeanne Paulsen
J.T. Wells ....Gregory Itzin
Tommy Jackson ....Tuck Milligan
Jed Rowen ....Stacy Keach
Lallie Rowen ....Lillian Garrett-Groag

Fire in the Hole - 1920
Mary Anne Rowen Jackson...Jeanne Paulsen
Tommy Jackson ....Randy Oglesby
Joshua Rowen Jackson ....Ronald Hippe
Doctor/Preacher ....John Aylward
Andrew Talbert Winston ....Gregory Itzin
Mackie ....Patrick Page
Silus ....Scott MacDonald
Abe Steinman..Tuck Milligan
Mother Jones ....Lillian Garrett-Groag
Cassius Biggs ....Ronald William Lawrence
Sureta Biggs ....Gail Grate
Lucy ....Katherine Hiler
Man in the Woods..Michael Hartman
Gun Thugs ....Stacy Keach, Patrick Page
Banjo Player ....James Ragland

Which Side are You On? - 1954
Joshua Rowen ....Stacy Keach
Scott Rowen ....Scott MacDonald
Margaret Rowen ....Jeanne Paulsen
James Talbert Winston ....John Aylward
Franklin Biggs ....Ronald William Lawrence
Jefferson Biggs ....Lee Simon, Jr.
Lana Toller..Gail Grate
Calvin Hayes...Tuck Milligan
Chuck..Stephen Lee Anderson
Mike ....Patrick Page
Greg/Bob Smalley ....Michael Hartman
Stucky ....Randy Oglesby
Sheriff Ray Blanko ....Gregory Itzin

The War on Poverty - 1975
Steve..Randy Oglesby
Frank ....Tuck Milligan
James Talbert Winston ....John Aylward
Joshua ....Stacy Keach
Franklin Biggs ....Ronald William Lawrence

UNDERSTUDIES: Michael Hartman (for J. Aylward), Susan Pellegrino (for L. Garrett-Groag/J. Paulsen), Novel Sholars (for G. Grate), Jennifer Rohn (for K. Hiler), Philip Lehl (for R. Hippe/T. Milligan), Patrick Page (for G. Itzin/S. MacDoanld), Lee Simon Jr. (for R. W. Lawrence), Stephen Lee Anderson (for T. Milligan/R. Ogleby), Larry Paulsen (Ensemble)

A drama presented in two parts (each with one intermission). The action involves three Kentucky families over a span of 200 years. The winner of the 1992 Pulitzer Prize.

Variety tallied 6 favorable and 6 negative reviews. *Times:* (Rich) "...best enjoyed as a melodramatic pageant, and an entertaining one..." (Richards) "...a vigorous piece of popular storytelling..." *News:* (Kissel) "...six hours of mechanical, rhetorical writing and acting..." *Post:* (Barnes) "...it is the theatrical equivalent of a "good read"..." *Newsday:* (Winer) "It takes nerve to come to Broadway with a two-part, six-hour epic...enormously engrossing stuff..." *Variety:* (Gerard) "...theatregoers don't buy intention, no matter how honorable."

*Closed December 12, 1993, after 34 performances and 14 previews.

Joan Marcus Photos

**Top: Scott MacDonald,
Jeanne Paulsen, Stacy Keach
Center: Stacy Keach
Right: The company**

ANY GIVEN DAY

By Frank D. Gilroy; Director, Paul Benedict; Sets, Marjorie Bradley Kellogg; Costumes, Ann Roth; Lighting, Dennis Parichy; General Management, Marvin A. Krauss; Company Manager, Elizabeth M. Blitzer; Stage Managers, Pamela Singer, Brian Kaufman; Associate Producers, Matt Garfield, David Young; Presented by Edgar Lansbury, Everett King, and Dennis Grimaldi; Press, Keith Sherman/Jim Byk/Stuart Ginsberg; Previewed from Tuesday, November 2; Opened in the Longacre Theatre on Tuesday, November 16, 1993*

CAST

Mrs. Bendi	Sada Thompson
Carmen Benti	Andrea Marcovicci
Willis	Justin Kirk
Gus Brower	Andrew Robinson
Nettie Cleary	Lisa Eichhorn
John Cleary	Victor Slezak
Timmy Cleary	Gabriel Olds
Eddie Benti	Peter Frechette
Doctor Goldman	Stephen Pearlman

UNDERSTUDIES: Bill Cwikowski (Goldman/Gus/John), Mary Layne (Carmen/Nettie), Nick Rodgers (Eddie/Willis/Timmy)

A drama in two acts. The action takes place in The Bronx, 1941–43. A prequel of sorts to Gilroy's Pulitzer Prize-winning 1964 play *The Subject Was Roses.*

Variety tallied 5 favorable, 6 mixed, and 4 negative reviews. *Times:* (Brantley) "...as solidly constructed as the heavy, dark-wooded furniture of its set...lacks any power to surprise." *News:* (Kissel) "...the cast here does strong work..." *Post:* (Barnes) "Gilroy knows how to write, and he knows how to write for actors." *Newsday:* (Winer) "...an almost eerie time warp...belief in the verities of character development and form." *Variety:* (Gerard) "...melodramatic fare hardly seems a hot prospect for the seasonal trade..."

*Closed December 12, 1993, after 32 performances and 16 previews.

Barbara Bordnick Photos

**Top Left: Sada Thompson Top Right: The cast
Center Left: Andrea Marcovicci, Andrew Robinson
Left: Justin Kirk, Peter Frechette**

A GRAND NIGHT FOR SINGING

Music, Richard Rodgers; Lyrics, Oscar Hammerstein; Conceived/Directed by Walter Bobbie; Orchestrations, Michael Gibson, Jonathan Tunick; Musical Director/Arrangements, Fred Wells; Musical Coordinator, Seymour Red Press; Sets, Tony Walton; Costumes, Martin Pakledinaz; Lighting, Natasha Katz; Sound, Tony Meola; Cast Recording, Varese Sarabande; General Manager, Ellen Richard; Additional Staging, Pamela Sousa; Stage Manager, Lori M. Doyle; Presented by Roundabout Theatre Company (Founding Director, Gene Feist; Artistic Director, Todd Haimes) by special arrangement with Gregory Dawson and Steve Paul; Press, Chris Boneau/Adrian Bryan-Brown, Susanne Tighe; Previewed from Wednesday, October 13; Opened in the Criterion Center Stage Right on Wednesday, November 17, 1993*

CAST

Martin Vidnovic   Jason Graae   Victoria Clark
Alyson Reed   Lynne Wintersteller

STANDBYS: Rebecca Eichenberger, James Hindman

MUSICAL NUMBERS: Carousel Waltz/So Far/Grand Night for Singing, Surrey with the Fringe On Top, Stepsister's Lament, We Kiss in a Shadow, Hello Young Lovers, A Wonderful Guy, I Cain't Say No, Maria, Do I Love You Because You're Beautiful?, Honey Bun, Gentleman Is a Dope, Don't Marry Me, I'm Gonna Wash That Man Right Outa My Hair, If I Loved You, Shall We Dance?, That's the Way It Happens, All at Once You Love Her, Some Enchanted Evening, Oh What a Beautiful Mornin', Wish Them Well, The Man I Used To Be, It Might As Well Be Spring, Kansas City, When the Children Are Asleep/I Know It Can happen Again/My Little Girl, It's Me, Love Look Away, When You're Driving Through the Moonlight/A Lovely Night, Something Wonderful, This Nearly Was Mine, Impossible/I Have Dreamed

A musical revue in two acts. An expanded version of a show previously seen at Rainbow & Stars cabaret.

Variety tallied 9 favorable and 2 mixed reviews. *Times:* (Stephen Holden) "...a solidly likable show...afraid to be seen as corny and square..." *News:* (Kissel) "...pleasurable if not exhilarating." *Post:* (Barnes) "...a virtual lexicon of musical comedy gesture, movements, even grimaces..." *Newsday:* (Stuart) "Mix-and-match Rodgers and Hammerstein. Imagine the possibilities." *Variety:* (Gerard) "...a trifle that includes some of the best musical theatre songs..."

*Closed January 1, 1994, after 52 performances and 41 previews.

Carol Rosegg/Martha Swope Photos

**Top: Martin Vidnovic, Jason Graae,
Alyson Reed, Victoria Clark, Lynne Wintersteller
Left: Jason Graae, Lynne Wintersteller**

CYRANO-The Musical

Music, Ad Van Dijk; Lyrics/Book, Koen Van Dijk; English Lyrics, Peter Reeves; Additional Lyrics, Sheldon Harnick; Based on the play by Edmond Rostand; Director, Eddy Habbema; Orchestrations, Don Sebesky, Tony Cox; Musical Director, Constantine Kitsopoulos; Musical Coordinator, John Miller; Sets, Paul Gallis; Costumes, Yan Tax; Lighting, Reinier Tweebeeke; Sound, Rogier Van Rossum; Associate Director, Eleanor Fazn; Fights, Malcolm Ranson; Stage Managers, Bob Brood, David John O'Brien; Executive Producer, Robin De Levita; Presented by Joop Van Den Ende in association with Peter T. Kulok; Press, Merle Frimark & Marc Thibodeau/Erin Dunn, Colleen Brown; Previewed from Tuesday, October 19; Opened in the Neil Simon Theatre on Sunday, November 21*

CAST

Man/Capt. De Castel Jaloux	Geoffrey Blaisdell +1
Le Bret	Paul Schoeffler
Ragueneau	Ed Dixon
Christian	Paul Anthony Stewart
De Guiche	Timothy Nolen +2
Roxane	Anne Runolfsson
Valvert	Adam Pelty
Chaperone	Joy Hermalyn
Montfleury	Mark Agnes
Cyrano	Bill Van Dijk +3
	Jordan Bennett (matinees)
Mother Superior	Elizabeth Acosta
Novice	Michele Ragusa
Ensemble	Ms. Acosta, Mark Agnes, Carina Andersson, Christopher Eaton Bailey, James Barbour, Mr. Blaisdell, Michelle Dawson, Jeff Gardner, Daniel Guzman, Ms. Hermalyn, Bjorn Johnson, Joanne Lessner, Peter Lockyer, Stuart Marland, Kerry O'Malley, Mr. Pelty, Tom Polum, Ms. Ragusa, Sam Scalamoni, Robin Skye, Tami Tappan, Ann Van Cleave, Charles West, Michael Christopher Moore, Debra Wiseman

UNDERSTUDIES: Sam Scalamoni (Cyrano), Tami Tappan, Michelle Dawson (Roxane), Peter Lockyer, James Barbour (Christian), Geoffrey Blaisdell (De Guiche), Stuart Marland (Ragueneau), Jeff Gardner (Le Bret) SWINGS: Ted Keegan, Rose McGuire, Christian Nova

MUSICAL NUMBERS: Prologue, Opera Opera, Aria, One Fragment of a Moment, Confrontation, The Duel, Where's All This Anger Coming From, Loving Her, Message from Roxanne, Ragueneau's Patisserie, Roxane's Confession, What a Reward, Hate Me, Courage Makes a Man, Cyrano's Story, Letter for Roxane, I Have No Words, Two Musketeers, An Evening Made for Lovers, Balcony Scene, Poetry, Moonsong, Stay With Me!, Every Day Every Night, A White Sash, When I Write, Rhyming Menu, Even Then, Tell Her Now, The Evening, The Battle, Everything You Wrote, He Loves to Make Us Laugh, Visit from De Guiche, An Old Wound/The Letter/Moonsong

A musical in two acts. The action takes place in Paris and Arras, 1640s. In 1973, another musical *Cyrano* starred Christopher Plummer.

Variety tallied 2 favorable, 4 mixed, and 11 negative reviews. *Times:* (Brantley) "Most of the lyrics, actually, are simply functional and as unquotable as recipes." *News:* (Kissel) "Although richly orchestrated, it has no sharpness, no drive." *Post:* (Barnes) "...performances are good without being electrifying..." *Newsday:* (Stuart) "...generic, through-composed pop score...long on bombast, short on nuance." *Variety:* (Gerard) "...thundering mishmash of unspectacular spectacle..."

*Closed March 20, 1994, after 137 performances and 38 previews.

+Succeeded by: 1. Tom Polum (matinees) 2. Geoffrey Blaisdell 3. Jordan Bennett, Timothy Nolen, Robert Guillaume

Joan Marcus/Marc Bryan-Brown Photos

Top: Bill Van Dijk

Left: Bill Van Dijk, Anne Runolfsson, Paul Anthony Stewart

LAUGHTER ON THE 23RD FLOOR

By Neil Simon; Director, Jerry Zaks; Sets, Tony Walton; Costumes, William Ivey Long; Lighting, Tharon Musser; Production Supervisor, Steven Beckler; Casting, Stuart Howard/Amy Schecter, Jay Binder; General Manager, Leonard Soloway; Company Manager, Sammy Ledbetter; Stage Managers, Mr. Beckler, Frederic H. Orner; Associate Producer, Ginger Montel; Presented by Emanuel Azenberg and Leonard Soloway; Press, Bill Evans/Jim Randolph, Sandy Manley; Previewed from Tuesday, November 2; Opened in the Richard Rodgers Theatre on Monday, November 22, 1993*

CAST

Lucas	Stephen Mailer
Milt	Lewis J. Stadlen
Val	Mark Linn-Baker +1
Brian	J. K. Simmons
Kenny	John Slattery
Carol	Randy Graff
Max Prince	Nathan Lane
Helen	Bitty Schram
Ira	Ron Orbach

STANDBYS: Alan Blumenfeld (Max/Ira), Alison Martin (Carol/Helen), Mitchell Greenberg (Val/Kenny), Richard Ziman (Milt/Brian), Allan Heinberg (Lucas)

A comedy in two acts. The action takes place on the 23rd floor of a building on New York's 57th St., 1953

Variety tallied 12 favorable, 6 mixed, and 7 negative reviews. *Times:* (Rich) "...amiable, noisy, frenetically staged..." (Richards) "...allows Nathan Lane...a golden opportunity to go berserk for two hours." *News:* (Kissel) "...a stage full of such expert actors, superbly directed..." *Post:* (Barnes) "...instead of writing a play—he really is offering a succession of one liners..." *Newsday:* (Winer) "...how terrific this could have been if Simon had managed to be both true to the period and at his comic best." *Variety:* (Gerard) "...it's the funniest comedy on Broadway in years..."

*Closed August 27, 1994, after 320 performances and 24 previews.

+Succeeded by: 1. Michael Countryman

Martha Swope Photos

Bitty Schram, Stephen Mailer, J. K. Simmons, Ron Orbach, Mark Linn-Baker, Nathan Lane, Lewis J. Stadlen, Randy Graff, John Slattery

Top: (front) J. K. Simmons, John Slattery, Nathan Lane, Stephen Mailer, Bitty Schram (Back) Mark Linn-Baker, Randy Graff, Ron Orbach, Lewis J. Stadlen

Kathleen Chalfant, Stephen Spinella, Joe Mantello, Jeffrey Wright

David Marshall Grant, Ron Liebman

ANGELS IN AMERICA: PERESTROIKA

By Tony Kushner; Director, George C. Wolfe; Sets, Robin Wagner; Costumes, Toni-Leslie James; Lighting, Jules Fisher; Music, Anthony Davis; Sound, Scott Lehrer; Hair/Makeup, Jeffrey Frank; Casting, Meg Simon, Stanley Soble; Company Manager, Lisa M. Poyer; Stage Managers, Mary K. Klinger; Michael J. Passaro, Maximo Torres, Eric S. Osbun; Produced in association with the New York Shakespeare Festival; Executive Producers, Benjamin Mordecai and Robert Cole; Presented by Jujamcyn Theatres and Mark Taper Forum/Gordon Davidson with Margo Lion, Susan Quint Gallin, Jon B. Platt, Baruch-Viertel Group and Frederick Zollo in association with Herb Alpert; Press, Chris Boneau/Adrian Bryan-Brown, Bob Fennell, Jamie Morris, Ellison Scudder; Previewed from Saturday, October 23; Opened in the Walter Kerr Theatre on Tuesday, November 23, 1993*

CAST

Prelapsarianov/Hannah Pitt/Henry/
Ethel Rosenberg/Rabbi Chemelwitz ....Kathleen Chalfant +1
Angel/Emily/Mormon Mother ....Ellen McLaughlin +2
Prior Walter ....Stephen Spinella +3
Louis Ironson/Sarah Ironson ....Joe Mantello +4
Joe Pitt...David Marshall Grant +5
Harper Pitt ....Marcia Gay Harden +6
Mr. Lies/Belize...Jeffrey Wright +7
Roy Cohn..Ron Leibman +8
Council of Principalities ....The Company

UNDERSTUDIES: Larry Pine (Roy), Matthew Sussman (Louis/Roy), Daniel Zelman (Prior/Joe), Susan Bruce, Tracy Sallows (Harper/Angel), Beth McDonald (Hannah/Angel), Darnell Williams, Lance Reddick (Belize)

A drama in five acts and an epilogue. Performed with two intermissions and one pause. The action takes place in New York City and elsewhere. This play was performed in repertory with *Millenium Approaches* (see *Broadway Calendar-Opened Other Seasons*), the first play in the *Angels in America* epic. Winner of 1994 "Tonys" for Best Play, Leading Actor in a Play (Stephen Spinella) and Featured Actor in a Play (Jeffrey Wright)

Variety tallied 16 favorable, 2 mixed, and 3 negative notices. *Times:* (Rich) "...a true millenial work of art...a kiss that blesses everyone in the theatre with the promise of more life." (Richards) "...does not go out in a blaze of glory. It goes out in a blaze of compassion, which may be better." *News:* (Kissel) "...adds little to what we already know." *Post:* (Barnes) "...one of those plays defining an era... can on no account be missed." *Newsday:* (Winer) "...playful and profound, extravagantly theatrical and deeply spiritual, witty and compassionate, furious and incredibly smart." *Variety:* (Gerard) "...a monumental achievement, the work of a defiantly theatrical imagination that has no parallel on television or in the movies. It enobles Broadway..."

*Closed December 4, 1994, after 216 performances and 26 previews.

+Succeeded by: 1. Laurie Kennedy 2. Cherry Jones 3. Daniel Jenkins 4. Dan Futterman 5. Jay Goede 6. Susan Bruce, Cynthia Nixon, Megan Gallagher 7. Kevin T. Carroll 8. Larry Pine, F. Murray Abraham, David Margulies

Joan Marcus Photos

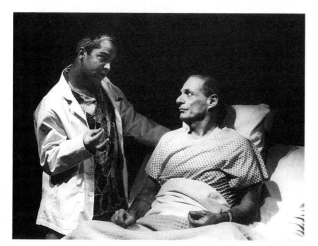

Top: Stephen Spinella, Kathleen Chalfant
Center: Ellen McLaughlin, Stephen Spinella
Left: Jeffrey Wright, Ron Liebman

GRAY'S ANATOMY

By Spalding Gray; Director, Renee Shafransky; Production Manager, Jeff Hamlin; Presented by Lincoln Center Theater (Artistic Director, Andre Bishop; Executive Producer, Bernard Gersten); Press, Merle Debuskey/Susan Chicoine; Previewed from Sunday November 7; Opened in the Vivian Beaumont Theater on Sunday, November 28, 1993*

CAST

SPALDING GRAY

Mr. Gray's fourteenth theatrical monologue, an adventure through traditional and alternative medicine.

Variety tallied 7 favorable reviews. *Times:* (Brantley) "...utterly involving piece..." *News:* (Thomas M. Disch) "...thoughtful in a way that is focused and steadily involving." *Post:* (Barnes) "...an absolutely wonderful actor." *Newsday:* (Stuart) "Revisiting Spalding Gray is catching up with an old friend." *Variety:* (Greg Evans) "...as seductive as anything he's done."

*Closed January 3, 1994, after 13 performances and 5 previews. Returned June 5–27, 1994, for 8 performances.

Nigel Dickson Photos

Spalding Gray in *Gray's Anatomy*
Top Right: Sam Waterston as Abe Lincoln
Right: Brian Reddy, Sam Waterston
in *Abe Lincoln in Illinois*

ABE LINCOLN IN ILLINOIS

By Robert E. Sherwood; Director, Gerald Gutierrez; Sets, John Lee Beatty; Costumes, Jane Greenwood; Lighting, Beverly Emmons; Music, Robert Waldman; Sound, Guy Sherman/Aural Fixation; Hairstylist, Angela Gari; Casting, Meg Simon; General Manager, Steven C. Callahan; Production Manager, Jeff Hamlin; Stage Managers, Michael Brunner, Jane E. Neufeld; Presented by Lincoln Center Theater (Artistic Director, Andre Bishop; Executive Producer, Bernard Gersten); Press, Merle Debuskey/Susan Chicoine; Previewed from Thursday, November 4; Opened in the Vivian Beaumont Theater on Monday, November 29, 1993*

CAST

Mentor Graham	George Hall
Abe Lincoln	Sam Waterston
Ann Rutledge	Marissa Chibas
Ben Mattling	Nesbitt Blaisdell
Judge Bowling Green	David Huddleston
Ninian Edwards	Robert Westenberg
Joshua Speed	Robert Joy
Trum Cogdal	Ralph Buckley
Jack Armstrong	Barton Tinapp
Bab	Charles Geyer
Feargus/Cavalry Capt.	Kevin Chamberlin
Jasp/Jed	John Michael Gilbert
Seth Gale	Tom Wiggin
Nancy Green	Joan MacIntosh
William Herndon	David Aaron Baker
Elizabeth Edwards	Ann McDonough
Mary Todd	Lizbeth Mackay
Jimmy Gale/Willie Lincoln	Jeffrey Stern
Aggie Gale	Charlotte Maier
Gobey	Bo Rucker +1
Stephen A. Douglas	Brian Reddy
Tad Lincoln	Cameron Boyd
Robert Lincoln	P. J. Ochlan
Crimmin	Peter Maloney
Barrick	John Newton
Sturveson	J. R. Horne
Phil	Resse Madigan
Kavanaugh	Charles Geyer

Soldiers/Townspeople ....Mr. Blaisdell, Robert Burke, Mr. Buckley, Mr. Chamberlin, Ms. Chibas, Bob Freschi, Jason Fuchs, Mr. Gilbert, Mr. Horne, Robert Jiminez, Ms. MacIntosh, Mr. Madigan, Ms. Maier, Mr. Maloney, David Manis, Mr. Newton, Michelle O'Neill, Bo Rucker, Carol Schultz, Barton Tinapp, Mr. Wiggin

Citizens of New Salem/Springfield ....Allan Benjamin, Melanie Boland, Scott Breitbart, Duane Butler, Stacie Chaiken, Bill Cocoran, Constance Crawford, Richard DeDomenico, Ralph Feliciello, Ralph Friar, Bill Galarno, Jeff Stuart Janus, Spencer Leuenberger, Marilyn McDonald, Nell Wade

UNDERSTUDIES: John Newton (Graham/Ben/Judge), David Manis (Lincoln), Michelle O'Neill (Ann/Aggie), Robert Burke (Ninian/Joshua/Kavanaugh), J. R. Horne (Trum/Douglas), Charles Geyer (Jack/Seth), Bob Freschi (Bab/Feargus/ Crimmin/Phil), Reese Madigan (Jasp/Robert/Capt.), Carol Schultz (Nancy/ Elizabeth), John Michael Gilbert (William), Charlotte Maier (Mary), Cameron Boyd (Jimmy/Willie), Jason Fuchs (Tad), Robert Jimenez (Gobey), Ralph Buckley (Barrick/Jed), Kevin Chamberlin (Sturveson)

A new production of the Pulitzer Prize-winning 1938 drama in three acts. The action takes place Illinois, 1830s–1861.

Variety tallied 8 favorable, 4 mixed, and 3 negative reviews. *Times:* (Richards) "...earnest but plodding play..." (Vincent Canby) "...as much about F.D.R. on the eve of World War II as it was about Lincoln facing his own call to greatness." *News:* (Kissel) "Waterston gives a genuinely heroic performance..." *Post:* (Barnes) "...I question whether *Abe Lincoln in Illinois* was worth doing..." *Newsday:* (Winer) "...play's limited point of view is outdated, the play's stage-worthiness is fairly remarkable." *Variety:* (Gerard) "...it's never boring."

*Closed January 2, 1994, after 40 performances and 27 previews.

+Succeeded by: 1. Robert Jimenez

Ken Howard Photos

Top: Jeffrey Stern, Lizbeth Mackay, Sam Waterston, Cameron Boyd

Center: Robert Westenberg, Ralph Buckley, Sam Waterston, David Huddleston

Left: Robert Joy, Sam Waterston, David Huddleston, Joan MacIntosh

MY FAIR LADY

Music, Frederick Loewe; Lyrics/Book, Alan Jay Lerner; Based on the play *Pygmalion* by Bernard Shaw; Director, Howard Davies; Choreography, Donald Saddler; Musical/Vocal Director, Jack Lee; Musical Coordinator, John Monaco; Sets, Ralph Koltai; Costumes, Patricia Zipprodt; Lighting, Natasha Katz; Sound, Peter J. Fitzgerald; Hair/Wigs, Patrik D. Moreton; Production Supervisor, Craig Jacobs; General Manager, Charlotte W. Wilcox; Company Manager, Frank Lott; Stage Managers, Maureen F. Gibson, Peter Wolf; Presented by Barry and Fran Weissler, Jujamcyn Theatres in association with Pace Theatrical Group, Tokyo Broadcasting System and Martin Rabbett; Press, Richard Kornberg/Thomas Naro; Previewed from Friday, November 26; Opened in the Virginia Theatre on Thursday, December 9, 1993*

CAST

Eliza Doolittle	Melissa Errico
Freddie Eynsford-Hill	Robert Stella
Mrs. Eynsford-Hill	Lisa Merrill McCord
Colonel Pickering	Paxton Whitehead
Professor Henry Higgins	Richard Chamberlain +1.
Bystander/George	Bill Ullman
Hoxton Man	Bruce Moore
"Loverly" Quartette	Jeffrey Wilkins, Mr. Moore, Michael Gerhart, Jamie Mackenzie
Jamie	Michael J. Farina
Harry/Zoltan Karparthy	James Young
Mrs. Pearce	Glynis Bell
Butler/Lord Boxington	Mr. Wilkins
Alfred P. Doolittle	Julian Holloway
Servants	Mr. Gerhart, Marilyn Kay Huelsman, Edwardyne Cowan, Corinne Melancon, Meg Tolin
Charles	Mr. Gerhart
Mrs. Higgins	Dolores Sutton
Lady Boxington	Marnee Hollis
Policeman	Ron Schwinn
Flower Girl	Ms. Melancon
Footman	Ben George
Queen of Transylvania	Patti Karr
Mrs. Higgins' Maid	Sue Delano

UNDERSTUDIES: Paxton Whitehead (Higgins), Meg Tolin, Edwardyne Cowan (Eliza), James Young (Doolittle), Jeffrey Wilkins, Bill Ullman (Pickering), Patti Karr (Mrs. Higgins), Michael Gerhart (Freddie), Lisa Merrill McCord (Mrs. Pearce) SWINGS: Newton Cole, Wendy Oliver, John Scott

MUSICAL NUMBERS: Overture, Why Can't the English, Wouldn't It Be Loverly, With a Little Bit of Luck, I'm an Ordinary Man, Just You Wait, Servant's Chorus, The Rain in Spain, I Could Have Danced All Night, Ascot Gavotte, On the Street Where You Live, Entr'acte, Embassy Waltz, You Did It, Show Me, Get Me to the Church on Time, Hymn to Him, Without You, I've Grown Accustomed to Her Face

A new production of the 1956 musical in two acts with eighteen scenes.

Variety tallied 8 favorable, 5 mixed, and 6 negative reviews. *Times:* (Richards) "...it would be folly to compete with the original 1956 production of *My Fair Lady*, probably the perfect expression of the perfect musical...By underscoring some of the darker implications of the fable, the show that opened last night... wants to be a brave new *My Fair Lady*..." (Canby) "This is a touring show and looks it...It lacks urgency..." *News:* (Kissel) "Its effervescent score and the resilient dialogue entertain in spite of all efforts to "improve" them. *Post:* (Barnes) "...a fresh minted staging by Howard Davies and startlingly, even radically, different scenery by Ralph Koltai." *Newsday:* (Aileen Jacobson) "...a darker heart, a '90s edge and a more socially conscious sensibility." *Variety:* (Gerard) "More a production for the age than for the ages..."

*Closed May 1, 1994, after 165 performances and 16 previews.

+Succeeded by: 1. Paxton Whitehead, Michael Moriarty

Martha Swope/Carol Rosegg Photos

Top Left: Melissa Errico, Michael Moriarty in *My Fair Lady*

GYPSY OF THE YEAR

Director, Michael Lichtefeld; Writer, Dick Scanlan; Musical Director, Phil Reno; Stage Managers, Frank Hartenstein, Perry Cline; Presented by Tom Viola and Maria Di Dia for Broadway Cares/Equity Fights AIDS; Press, Chris Boneau/ Adrian Bryan-Brown, Hillary Harrow; Presented in the St. James Theatre on Tuesday, November 30, 1993.

CAST INCLUDES

Jonathan Hadary (host)
Petula Clark, Casey Nicholaw, Hal Linden, Rex Robbins, Tom Hewitt, Stephen Stout, Lindsay Chambers, Marc Ellis Holland, Amy N. Heggins, Devanand N. Janki, Choslu Kim, Jeanine Meyers, Robb E. Morris, Rusty Mowery, Naomi Reddin, Mark Agnes, Nick Corley, Mary Illes, Joey McKneely, Mason Roberts, Leonard Joseph, Matthew Peterson, Paul Castree, John Ganun, Drew Geraci, Steve Gunderson, Nick Locilento, Ryan Perry, Richard Roland, Bobby Smith, Colton Green, Elizabeth Curtis, Jay Rogers and the companies of *Blood Brothers, Joseph and the Amazing Technicolor Dreamcoat, Crazy For You, Les Miserables, Miss Saigon, Nunsense, Guys and Dolls, Whoop-Dee-Doo, Tommy, Annie Warbucks* and *Phantom of the Opera.*

GYPSY OF THE YEAR GYPSIES

Robert Bianca	James Darrah	Melissa Haizlip
Alan Boswell	Gregory Garrison	Sharon Moore
Stephen Bourneuf	Elizabeth Green	Ken Nagy
Mindy Cooper	Paula Grider	Trina Simon

The fifth annual competition raised over $707,000 to fight AIDS.

The Ascot Gavotte

Paxton Whitehead, Julian Holloway, Richard Chamberlain

THE RED SHOES

Music, Jule Styne; Lyrics, Marsha Norman, Paul Stryker (Bob Merrill); Book, Ms. Norman; Based on the 1947 film; Director, Stanley Donen; Choreography, Lar Lubovitch; Ballet Music Arrangements, Gordon Harrell; Orchestrations, Sid Ramin, William D. Brohn; Musical Director/Vocal Arrangements, Donald Pippin; Sets, Heidi Landesman; Costumes, Catherine Zuber; Lighting, Ken Billington; Sound, Tony Meola; Hair/Makeup, Patrik D. Moreton; Flying by Foy; Musical Coordinator, Seymour Red Press; Casting, Julie Hughes, Barry Moss; General Manager, Robert Kamlot; Company Manager, Bruce Klinger; Stage Managers, Martin Gold, Frank Lombardi; Presented by Martin Starger in association with MCA/Universal and James M. Nederlander; Press, Mark Thibodeau/Merle Frimark, Erin Dunn, Colleen Brown; Previewed from Tuesday, November 2; Opened in the Gershwin Theatre on Thursday, December 16, 1993*

CAST

Grisha Ljubov ....George De La Pena
Irina Boronskaya..Leslie Brown
Ivan Boleslavsky ....Jon Marshall Sharp
Livy/Priest..Robert Jensen
Sergei Ratov..Tad Ingram
Boris Lermontov ....Steve Barton +1
Julian Craster..Hugh Panaro
Lady Ottoline Nelson..Pamela Burrell
Victoria Page ....Margaret Illmann
                                  Amy Wilder (matinees)
Marguerite ....Jamie Chandler-Torns
Jean Louis/James ....Scott Fowler
                                  Don Bellamy (Matinees)
Miss Hardiman..Lydia Gaston
Miss Lovat ....Laurie Gamache
Dr. Copelias...Daniel Wright
Angel...Jeff Lander
Ballet Company ....Jennifer Alexander, Anita Intrieri, Mr. Bellamy, Mr. Jensen, Mucuy Bolles, Christina Johnson, Mr. Chander-Torns, Mr. Lander, Geralyn Del Corso, Christina Marie Norrup, Mr. Fowler, Oscar Ruge, Antonia Franceschi, Ms. Gamache, Keith L. Thomas, Ms. Gaston, Joan Tsao, Nina Goldman, Mr. Weatherstone, Mr. Wright

UNDERSTUDIES: Robert Jensen (Lermontov/Dmitri), Amy Wilder, Christina Johnson (Vicky), Laurie Gamache (Irina/Lady Neston), Nina Goldman (Irina), Alexies Sanchez (Grisha/Ivan), James Weatherstone (Julian/Dmitri/Livy), Charles Goff (Sergei), Scott Fowler (Ivan), Christina Marie Norrup (Marguerite) SWINGS: Kellye Gordon, James Hadley, Alexies Sanchez, Catherine Ulissey, Alicecann Wilson

MUSICAL NUMBERS: Swan Lake, Audition, Corps de Ballet, When It Happens to You, Who Knows Where It Goes, Top of the Sky, Ballet Montage, It's a Fairy Tale, Be Someone, The Rag, Am I to Wish Her Love, Do Svedanya, Heart of Fire, Come Home, When You Dance for a King, Ballet of the Red Shoes DURING PREVIEWS: Alone in the Light, Impresario, I Make the Rules

A musical in two acts. The action takes place in London, Paris, and Monte Carlo, 1921–22. Stanley Donan took over the direction from Susan H. Schulman and Renee Cebellos and Tim Jerome were replaced during previews.

Times: (Richards) "...months of troubled rehearsals and previews, during which the original director, the leading man and two supporting players all got their walking papers, seem to have robbed the creators of their passion." (Canby) "With astonishing grace and wit, the ballet dramatized just about all that need be said about the sometimes obsessive nature of artists and the bargins they make with life." *News:* (Kissel) "...preserve both Lubovitch's choreography for 'the Red Shoes' ballet and Landesman's set. Otherwise, 'The Red Shoes' is forgettable." *Post:* (Barnes) "...nothing could save it." *Newsday:* (Winer) "...faceless, inappropriately saccharine music..." *Variety:* (Gerard) "Many hands cobbled 'The Red Shoes'..."

*Closed December 19, 1993, after 5 performances and 51 previews. The ballet from the show, with sets and orchestration, was resurrected by American Ballet Theatre.

+1: Roger Rees during previews.

Joan Marcus Photos

Top: Steve Barton, Margaret Illmann
Right: Hugh Panaro

CANDLES, SNOW & MISTLETOE

Music Produced and Arranged by Glen Roven; Writer, Mark Saltzman; Presented by James L. and James M. Nederlander and Stewart F. Lane in association with Nickelodeon; Press, Ellen Zeisler/Reggie Lewis, Emily Rubin; Previewed from Sunday, December 26; Opened in the Palace Theatre on Monday, December 27, 1993*

CAST

Sharon, Lois & Bram
(Sharon Hampson, Lois Lilienstein, Bram Morrison)

A musical evening for the holidays.

*Closed December 30, 1993, after limited run of 7 performances and 3 previews.

**Top Left: Margaret Illman in *The Red Shoes*
Top Right: Illmann, Jon Marshall Sharp in *The Red Shoes*
Bottom Left: George De La Pena in *The Red Shoes*
Bottom Right: Sharon, Lois and Bram in
*Candles, Snow & Mistletoe***

THE GOVERNMENT INSPECTOR

By Nikolai Gogol; Adaptation, Adrian Mitchell; American Version, Mark Vietor; Director, Michael Langham; Sets, Douglas Stein; Costumes, Lewis Brown; Lighting, Richard Nelson; Music, Stanley Silverman; Sound, Dan Moses Schreier; General Manager, Niko Associates; Casting, Liz Woodman; Company Manager, Brig Berney; Stage Manager, Michael Ritchie; Executive Producer, Manny Kladitis; Presented by National Actors Theatre (Founder/Artistic Director, Tony Randall; Artistic Advisor, Michael Langham); Press, John and Gary Springer; Previewed from Thursday, December 23, 1993; Opened in the Lyceum Theatre on Thursday, January 6, 1994*

CAST

Anton Skvoznik-Dmuchanovsky, police governor	Peter Michael Goetz
Anna, his wife	Lainie Kazan
Marya, his daughter	Nancy Hower
Mishka, household servant	Kevin Shinick
Avdotya, household servant	Elizabeth Heflin
Ammos Lyapkin-Tyapkin, judge	Jack Ryland
Artemy Zemlyanika, charities	Michael Lombard
Khristian Gibner, doctor/Rastakovsky	Leo Leyden
Ivan Shpekin, postmaster	Michael Stuhlbarg
Luka Khlopov, superintendant	Nicholas Kepros
Nastinka, his wife/Widow	Andi Davis
Bobchinsky, landowner	Derek Smith
Dobchinsky, landowner	Jefrey Alan Chandler
Police Inspector	Rod McLachlan
Svistunov, officer	Mark Niebuhr
Pugovitzin, officer	Alec Phoenix
Dherzimorda, officer/Gendarme	Jerry Lanning
Ivan Khlestakov, government clerk	Tony Randall
Osip, his servant	David Patrick Kelly
Waiter/Chernyayev, merchant	Tom Lacy
Abdulin, Merchant	Jesse L. Martin
Panteleyeva	Tim MacDonald
Locksmith's Wife/Korobkin's wife	Annette Helde
Stepan Korobkin, landowner	Herb Foster
Lyulyukov, landowner	Richard Holmes
Townspeople, Petitioners, Guests	Martin Kildare, Mr. Leyden, Mr. McLachlan, Mr. Niebuhr, Mr. Phoenix, Blake Robison, Adrienne Alitowski, John Dybdahl, Francis Henry, Ted Hoffstatter, Demetria McCain, Bruce Villineau, John Burton Willson

UNDERSTUDIES: Andi Davis (Marya), Elizabeth Heflin (Locksmith's Wife/Widow/Nastinka), Annette Helde (Anna), Richard Holmes (Superintendent/Charities), Martin Kildare (Police Governor/Rastakovsky/Doctor), Tim MacDonald (Judge/Abdulin), Jesse L. Martin (Panteleyeva), Rod McLachlan (Korobkin/Dherzimorda/Gendarme), Mark Niebuhr (Dobchinsky/Chernyayev), Alec Phoenix (Bobchinsky/Waiter), Blake Robison (Chief/Mishka/Lyulyukov/Osip), Kevin Shinick (Postmaster/Pugovitizin/Svistunov), Michael Stuhlbarg (Khlestakov)

A new production of an 1836 comedy in two acts. The action takes place in a small provincial Russian town, early 19th century.

Variety tallied 2 favorable, 2 mixed, and 5 negative reviews. *Times:* (Richards) "...Mr. Randall is...exactly 50 years too old for the part." (Canby) "...the old play just lies there..." *News:* (Kissel) "...ought to be a giddy little farce becomes a meaningless, tedious exercise." *Post:* (Barnes) "...carefully funny production..." *Newsday:* (Winer) "...each member of the large capable cast appears to be having a good time...but there is no unified style..." *Variety:* (Gerard) "...pedestrian account..."

*Closed February 6, 1994, after 37 performances and 16 previews.

Joan Marcus Photos

Top: Tony Randall, Nancy Hower
Left: Mark Niebuhr, Tony Randall

Jason Robards, Christopher Plummer

NO MAN'S LAND

By Harold Pinter; Director, David Jones; Set, David Jenkins; Costumes, Jane Greenwood; Lighting, Richard Nelson; Casting, Pat McCorkle, Richard Cole; General Manager, Ellen Richard; Stage Manager, Jay Adler; Presented by Roundabout Theatre Company (Founding Director, Gene Feist; Artistic Director, Todd Haimes); Press, Chris Boneau/Adrian Bryan-Brown, Susanne Tighe, Hillary Harrow; Previewed from Saturday, January 8; Opened in the Criterion Center Stage Right on Thursday, January 27, 1994*

CAST

Hirst ....Jason Robards
Spooner ....Christopher Plummer
Foster ....Tom Woods
Briggs ....John Seitz

STANDBYS: Kevin McClarnon (Briggs), Robert Carin (Foster)

A new production of a 1975 play in two acts. The action takes place in a large room in a house in North West London during summer. For original 1976 Broadway production with John Gielgud and Ralph Richardson see *Theatre World* Vol. 33.

Variety tallied 8 favorable, 4 mixed, and 2 negative reviews. *Times:* (Richards) "...it is Christopher Plummer whose dazzlingly witty portrayal...captures the imagination." (Canby) "...you're in the privileged position of witnessing an elegant revival of a work by the man who is possibly the greatest living playwright..." *News:* (Kissel) "...the play itself does not seem as weighty as it once did." *Post:* (Barnes) "...gorgeous and wryly funny play..." *Newsday:* (Winer) "...this less-than-ideal production's still a kick." *Variety:* (Gerard) "...a remarkable pair to watch wrangling with Pinter's elliptical, often uncrackable script."

*Closed March 20, 1994, after 61 performances and 22 previews.

Marc Bruan-Brown, Carol Rosegg/Martha Swope Photos

Tom Wood, Jason Robards, John Seitz, Christopher Plummer

Jason Robards, Christopher Plummer

43

FIORELLO!

Music, Jerry Bock; Lyrics, Sheldon Harnick; Book, Jerome Weidman and George Abbott; Adaptation, John Weidman; Director, Walter Bobbie; Orchestrations, Irwin Kostal; Musical Director, Rob Fisher; Set, John Lee Beatty; Lighting, Richard Pilbrow, Dawn Chiang; Choreography, Christopher Chadman; Sound, Scott Lehrer; Stage Manager, Perry Cline; Presented by City Center and Encores, Great American Musicals in Concert (Artistic Director, Ira Weitzman); Press, Philip Rinaldi/Dennis Crowley; Opened in City Center on Wednesday, February 9, 1994*

CAST

Fiorello	Jerry Zaks
Neil	Gregg Edelman
Mr. Lopez	Joaquin Romaguera
Mrs. Pomerantz	Marilyn Cooper
Mr. Zappatella	Paul Laureano
Morris	Adam Arkin
Dora	Liz Callaway
Marie	Faith Prince
Ben Marino	Philip Bosco
Political Hacks	Mike Burstyn, Rick Crom, Michael Goz, Philip Hoffman, James Puig, Brent Weber
Floyd	James Judy
Shirtwaist Strikers	Martha Arnold, Vanessa Ayers, Jamie Baer, Joan Barber, Andrea Green
Thea	Elizabeth Futral
Mitzi Travers	Donna McKechnie
Yoo-Hoo Yah-Hoo Dancers	Denise Faye, Mary Ann Lamb, Mary MacLeod, Leslie Stevens

The Coffee Club Orchestra

MUSICAL NUMBERS: Overture, On the Side of the Angels, Politics and Poker, Unfair, Marie's Law, The Name's LaGuardia, The Bum Won, I Love a Cop, 'Till Tomorrow, Home Again, When Did I Fall in Love, Gentleman Jimmy, Little Tin Box, The Very Next Man, Finale

A concert presentation of the 1959 Pulitzer Prize-winning musical in two acts. For original Broadway production see *Theatre World* Vol. 16.

*Closed February 12 after limited run of 4 performances.

Gerry Goodstein Photos

Stephen Bogardus, Karen Ziemba in *Allegro*

Faith Prince, Jerry Zaks in *Fiorello*

ALLEGRO

Music, Richard Rodgers; Lyrics/Book, Oscar Hammerstein II; Director, Susan H. Schulman; Orchestrations, Robert Russell Bennett; Musical Director, Rob Fisher; Set, John Lee Beatty; Lighting, Richard Pilbrow, Dawn Chiang; Choreography, Lar Lubovitch; Sound, Tony Meola; Projections, Wendall K. Harrington; Costumes, Catherine Zuber; Stage Manager, Perry Cline; Presented by City Center and Encores (Artistic Director, Ira Weitzman); Press, Philip Rinaldi/ Dennis Crowley; Opened in City Center on Wednesday, March 2, 1994*

CAST

Marjorie Taylor	Carolann Page
Dr. Joseph Taylor	John Cunningham
Grandma Taylor	Celeste Holm
Joey's Friends	Larry Hansen, Paul Laureano
Joey	Jason Danieley
Young Jenny	Gretchen Kingsley
Jenny Brinker	Donna Bullock
Hazel Skinner	Nancy Johnston
Charlie Townsend	Jonathan Hadary
Joseph Taylor, Jr.	Stephen Bogardus
Ned Brinker	John Horton
Beulah	Karen Ziemba
Minister	Robert Ousley
Millie	Sherry D. Boone
Dot	Elizabeth Green
Addie	Elizabeth Acosta
Dr. Bigby Denby	Erick Devine
Mrs. Lansdale	Susan Cella
Emily West	Christine Ebersole
Brook Lansdale	Martin Van Treuren
Dancers	Mia Babalis, Scott Rink
Ensemble	Ms. Acosta, Eric Ashcraft, Ms. Boone, Ms. Cella, Mr. Danieley, Mr. Devine, Ms. Green, Mr. Hansen, Paula Hostetter, Ms. Johnson, Ms. Kingsley, Mr. Laureano, Audrey Lavine, Mr. Ousley, Vernon Spencer, Mr. Van Treuren
Hosts	Stephen Sondheim, Christopher Reeve

The Coffee Club Orchestra

MUSICAL NUMBERS: Overture, Joseph Taylor Jr., I Know It Can Happen Again, One Foot Other Foot, Children's Dance, Winters Go By, A Fellow Needs a Girl, Freshman Dance, A Darn Nice Campus, Wildcats, So Far, You Are Never Away, What a Lovely Day for a Wedding, It May Be a Good Idea, Winters Go By/ To Have and to Hold/Wish Them Well, Entr'acte, Money Isn't Everything, Ya-Ta-Ta, The Gentleman is a Dope, Allegro, Come Home, Finale Ultimo

A concert presentation of the 1947 musical in two acts. For original Broadway production see *Theatre World* Vol. 4.

*Closed March 5, 1994, after limited run of 4 performances.

Gerry Goodstein Photos

Jarrod Emick, Bebe Neuwirth in *Damn Yankees*   45

DAMN YANKEES

Music and Lyrics, Richard Adler and Jerry Ross; Book, George Abbott and Douglas Wallop; Based on Wallop's novel *The Year the Yankees Lost the Pennant*; Director/Book Revision, Jack O'Brien; Orchestrations, Douglas Besterman; Musical Supervision/Vocal Arrangements, James Raitt; Musical Coordinator, William Meade; Choreography, Rob Marshall; Sets, Douglas W. Schmidt; Costumes, David C. Woolard; Lighting, David F. Segal; Sound, Jonathan Deans; Special Effects, Gregory Meech; Hair/Makeup, J. Roy Helland; Dance Arrangements, Tom Fay, David Krane; Production Supervisor, Alan Hall; General Manager, Charlotte W. Wilcox; Company Manager, Robb Lady; Stage Managers, Douglas Pagliotti, Cosmo P. Hanson; Presented by Mitchell Maxwell, PolyGram Diversified Entertainment, Dan Markley, Kevin McCollum, Victoria Maxwell, Fred H. Krones, Andrea Nasher, The Frankel-Viertel-Baruch Group, Paula Heil Fisher, Julie Ross in association with Jon B. Platt, Alan J. Schuster, Peter Breger; Press, Peter Cromarty/Michael Hartman; Previewed from Monday, February 14; Opened in the Marquis Theatre on Thursday, March 3, 1994*

CAST

Meg Boyd	Linda Stephens
Joe Boyd	Dennis Kelly
Applegate	Victor Garber
Sister	Susan Mansur
Joe Hardy	Jarrod Emick
Rocky	Scott Wise
Smokey	Jeff Blumenkrantz
Sohovik	Gregory Jbara
Mickey	John Ganun
Vernon	Joey Pizzi
Del	Scott Robertson
Ozzie	Michael Winther
Bubba	Cory English
Henry	Bruce Anthony Davis
Bomber	Michael Berresse
Van Buren	Dick Latessa
Gloria Thorpe	Vicki Lewis
Betty	Paula Leggett Chase
Donna	Nancy Ticotin
Kitty	Cynthia Onrubia
Photographer/Rita	Amy Ryder
Welch	Terrence P. Currier
Lola	Bebe Neuwirth

UNDERSTUDIES/STANDBYS: Patrick Quinn (Applegate), Nancy Ticotin (Lola), Michael Berresse, John Ganun (Hardy), Scott Robertson (Boyd/Van Buren/Welch), Paula Leggett Chase (Meg), Amy Ryder (Sister), Robyn Peterman (Gloria)

MUSICAL NUMBERS: Overture, Six Months Out of Every Year, Goodbye Old Girl, Blooper Ballet, Heart, Shoeless Joe from Hannibal Mo., A Little Brains a Little Talent, A Man Doesn't Know, What Ever Lola Wants (Lola Gets), Entr'acte, Who's Got the Pain, The Game, Near to You, Those Were the Good Old Days, Two Lost Souls, Finale

A revision of the 1955 musical comedy in two acts. For original Broadway production with Gwen Verdon, Ray Walston, Stephen Douglass, and Jean Stapleton, see *Theatre World* Vol. 11. Winner of 1994 "Tony" for Featured Actor in a Musical (Jarrod Emick).

Variety tallied 17 favorable, 3 mixed, and 1 negative review. *Times:* (Richards) "...a period pieces that can't quite transcend it's period..." (Canby) "...the men who play the dancing, leaping, forward-flipping members...astonish throughout." *News:* (Michael Musto) "Can a musical really be this fresh-faced...bright, jazzy..." *Post:* (Barnes) "almost sneakily artful..." *Newsday:* (Winer) "...enormously appealing, sweet and foolish..." *Variety:* (Gerard) "...good, brainless fun..."

*Closed August 6, 1995 after 510 performances and 35 previews.

Carol Rosegg/Martha Swope Photos

Top: Jarrod Emick
Center: Jeff Blumenkrantz, Scott Wise,
Gregory Jbara, Dick Latessa
Left: Victor Garber

Vicki Lewis and Washington Senators

Bebe Neuwirth, Victor Garber

A LITTLE MORE MAGIC

Conceived/Directed by Diane Lynn Dupuy, C.M.; Visual Art Effects, Mary C. Thornton; Lighting, Ken Billington; Sound, Tony Meola; General Manager, Gindi Theatrical Management; Production Supervisor, Ellis Island Entertainment; Company Manager, Peter Bogyo; Stage Manager, Phil Chart; Presented by Famous People Players; Press, Shirley Herz/Sam Rudy, Wayne Wolfe; Previewed from Tuesday, March 15; Opened in the Belasco Theatre on Thursday, March 17, 1994*

CAST

FAMOUS PEOPLE PLAYERS

Keith Albertson	Darlene Arsenault	Gord Billinger
Lesley Brown	Ronnie Brown	Else Buck
Michelle Busby	Sandra Ciccone	Charlene Clarke
Benny D'Onofrio	Jeanine Dupuy	Joanne Dupuy
Paul Edwards	Greg Kozak	Debbie Lim
Thomas O'Donnell	Debbie Rossen	Lisa Tuckwell

UNDERSTUDIES: Ginny Young, Jim Stoneburgh, Sue Ellis, Helen Lee

MUSICAL NUMBERS: A Little More Magic, Operator, Dur Dur D'etre Bebe, Dying Swan, Figaro, Meow Duet, Aquarium, If a Tree Falls, Beatles Medley, Take Five, Sing Sing Sing, What a Wonderful World, Two Hearts, Proud Mary, Crocodile Rock, Turn Me Round Polka, Bud the Spud, Flight of the Bumble Bee, Scheherazade, Jailhouse Rock, Impossible Dream

A musical entertainment with Canada's black-light theatre company featuring developmentally-handicapped young people. For the company's previous Broadway show, *A Little Like Magic*, see *Theatre World* Vol. 43.

Times: (Lawrence Van Gelder) "...an innocent pleasure for the young at heart..." *News:* (Kissel) "...more than just a show. It is a touching testament..." *Post:* (Barnes) "You'll have a surprisingly good—if totally undemanding—time." *Newsday:* (Aileen Jacobson) "Taking a child along is a good option."

*Closed April 17, 1994, after 30 performances.

A Little More Magic

THE FLOWERING PEACH

By Clifford Odets; Director, Martin Charnin; Sets, Ray Recht; Costumes, Theoni V. Aldredge; Lighting, Richard Nelson; Sound, Abe Jacobs; Music, Keith Levenson; General Manager, Niko Associates; Company Manager, Brig Berney; Stage Manager, Suzanne Prueter; Executive Producer, Manny Kladitis; Presented by National Actors Theatre (Tony Randall, Founder/Artistic Director; Michael Langham, Artistic Advisor); Press, John and Gary Springer; Previewed from Tuesday, March 8; Opened in the Lyceum Theatre on Sunday, March 20, 1994*

CAST

Noah	Eli Wallach
Esther	Anne Jackson
Japheth	David Aaron Baker
Shem	Josh Mostel
Ham	Steve Hofvendahl
Leah	Lorraine Serabian
Rachel	Joanna Going
Goldie	Molly Scott

UNDERSTUDIES: Marvin Einhorn (Noah), David Green (Shem/Ham), Danny Burstein (Japeth), Elaine Kussack (Esther/Leah), Grace Sadye Phillips (Rachel), Kaili Vernoff (Goldie)

A new production of the 1954 play in two acts. The action takes place "Then, not now." For original Broadway production see *Theatre World* Vol. 11.

Variety tallied 3 favorable, 1 mixed, and seven negative notices. *Times:* (Richards) "Time has not been gentle to Clifford Odets' 1954 play..." (Canby) "...a genial, stylish production..." *News:* (Kissel) "...may not be a profound play, but it is a sweet one..." *Post:* (Barnes) "It was better with a band...original play—without Rodgers, without Kaye and without hope." *Newsday:* (Winer) "...depends on one's whimsey threshold..." *Variety:* (Gerard) "...there's something to be said for a rep company investigating works such as this, and for a loving couple of the theatre to play a loving couple in the theatre."

*Closed April 24, 1994, after 41 performances and 7 previews.

Carol Rosegg/Martha Swope Photos

Center: Anne Jackson, Eli Wallach
Left: Lorraine Serabian, Josh Mostel, Eli Wallach

Sally Murphy, Michael Hayden in *Carousel*

CAROUSEL

Music, Richard Rodgers; Lyrics/Book, Oscar Hammerstein; Based on the play *Lilliom* by Ferenc Molnar as adapted by Benjamin F. Glazer; Director, Nicholas Hytner; Orchestrations, William David Brohn; Musical Director, Eric Stern; Choreography, Sir Kenneth MacMillan, Jane Elliott; Original Dances, Agnes DeMille; Sets/Costumes, Bob Crowley; Lighting, Paul Pyant; Sound, Steve Canyon Kennedy; Fights, David Leong; Hairstylist, Angela Gari; General Manager, Steven C. Callahan; Production Manager, Jeff Hamlin; Cast Recording, Broadway Angel; Company Manager, Edward J. Nelson; Stage Managers, Peter von Mayrhauser, Michael J. Passaro; Presented by Lincoln Center Theater by arrangement with The Royal National Theatre; Cameron Mackintosh and The Rodgers & Hammerstein Organization; Previewed from Friday, February 18; Opened in The Vivian Beaumont Theater on Thursday, March 24, 1994*

CAST

Carrie Pipperidge	Audra Ann McDonald
Julie Jordan	Sally Murphy
Mrs. Mullin	Kate Buddeke
Billy Bigelow	Michael Hayden +1
David Bascombe	Robert Breuler +2
Nettie Fowler	Shirley Verrett
Enoch Snow	Eddie Korbich
Jigger Craigin	Fisher Stevens +3
Captain/Principal/Hudson	Brian d'Arcy James
Heavenly Friend/Jenny Sanborn	Lauren Ward
Starkeeper/Dr. Seldon	Jeff Weiss
Louise	Sandra Brown +4
Louise's Friends	Robert Cary, Glen Harris, Steven Oghoa, Michael O'Donnell, Alexies Sanchez, Rocker Verastique
Fairground Boy	Jon Marshall Sharp +5
Enoch Snow Jr./Orrin Peesley	Duane Boutte
Other Snow Children	Philipp Lee Carabuena, Cece Cortes, Lovette George, Lyn Nagel, Cindy Robinson, Tiffany Sampson, Tse–Mach Washington
Robert Allen	Steven Ochoa
Hannah Bentley	Cindy Robinson
Peter Bentley Jr./Police	Tony Capone
Abbie Chase	Natascia A. Diaz
Charlie "Chip" Chase	Alexies Sanchez
Jonathan Chase	Robert Cary
Virginia Frazer	Rebecca Eichenberger
Buddy Hamlin	Devin Richards
Cyrus Hamilton/Police	Taye Diggs
Arminy Livermore	Paula Newsome
William Osgood	Rocker Verastique
Susan Peters	Linda Gabler
Myrtle Robbins	Lacey Hornkohl
Ella Sanborn	Alexia Hess
Martha Sewell	Keri Lee
Liza Sinclair	Endaylyn Taylor-Shellman
Penny Sinclair	Lovette George
Henry Sears	Jeffrey James
Abner Sperry	Michael O'Donnell
Ben Sperry	Glen Harris
Sadie Sperry	Dana Stackpole

UNDERSTUDIES: Paula Newsom (Carrie/Nettie), Lovette George (Carrie), Lauren Ward, Cindy Robinson (Julie), Rebecca Eichenberger (Mrs. Mullin/Nettie), Endalyn Taylor-Shellman (Mrs. Mullin), Duane Boutte, Tony Capone (Billy), Brian D'Arcy James (Bascombe/Jigger), Devin Richards (Bascombe/Starkeeper), Taye Diggs (Jigger), Robert Breuter (Starkeeper), Dana Stackpole, Jennifer Alexander, Donna Rubin (Louise), Glen Harris, Alexies Sanchez (Fairground Boy)

MUSICAL NUMBERS: Prologue: Carousel Waltz, You're a Queer One Julie Jordan, Mister Snow, If I Loved You, June is Bustin' Out All Over, When the Children Are Asleep, Blow High Blow Low, Soliloquy, A Real Nice Clambake, Geraniums in the Winder/Stonecutter Cut It on Stone, What's the Use of Wond'rin, You'll Never Walk Alone, Ballet, Finale

Top: Audra Ann McDonald, Fisher Stevens
Below: Eddie Korbich, Audra Ann McDonald

A new production of the 1945 musical in two acts. The action takes place in a coastal New England town, 1873. For original Broadway production with John Raitt see *Theatre World* Vol. 1. Winner of 1994 "Tonys" for Best Revival of a Musical, Featured Actress in a Musical (Audra Ann McDonald), Best Direction of a Musical, and Best Choreography.

Variety tallied 20 favorable, three mixed, and 1 negative review. *Times:* (Richards) "...the freshest, most innovative musical on Broadway...breathtaking images..." (Canby) "Forget every other *Carousel* you may have seen...one of the loveliest Broadway scores ever written..." (Frank Rich) "...until now the true *Carousel* has been supressed...we can now see clearly that it tells the truth..." *News:* (Kissel) "...most powerful score...staging throughout is astonishing." *Post:* (Barnes) "...hard-edged, imaginative and exciting." *Newsday:* (Winer) "...almost inconceivably beautiful...fearless, uncompromising power..." *Variety:* (Gerard) "...Breathtaking...beguiling beauty, explosive passion and, above all, almost unbearable intimacy."

*Closed January 17, 1995, after 322 performances and 46 previews. Winner of 1994 "Tonys" for Best Musical Revival, Best Direction, Best Choreography, Best Scenic Design, and Featured Actress in a Musical (Audra Ann McDonald).

+Succeeded by: 1. Marcus Lovett, James Barbour 2. Peter Maloney 3. David Warshofsky 4. Dana Stackpole, Sandra Brown 5. Robert Conn (during vacation)

Joan Marcus, Marc Bryan-Brown Photos

Sally Murphy, Michael Hayden

Jon Marshall Sharp, Sandra Brown

The Company

Sally Murphy, Michael Hayden

EASTER BONNET COMPETITION:

A SALUTE TO 100 YEARS OF BROADWAY

Conception/Direction, Philip Wm. McKinley; Book/Lyrics, David Levy; Musical Director, Phil Hall; Orchestrations, Michael Gibson; Costumes, Bobby Pearce; Production Supervisor, Jeff Lee; Projections, Wendall K. Harrington; Stage Managers, Joel Elins, Nancy Wernick; Presented by Suzanne Ishee and *Joseph and the Amazing Technicolor Dreamcoat;* Press, Chris Boneau/Adrian Bryan-Brown; Presented in the Minskoff Theatre on March 29 and 30, 1994

CAST INCLUDES

Bea Arthur   Raquel Welch

Larry Cahn, Adam Grupper, Tim Shew, Chita Rivera, Gary Beach, Cheryl Freeman, Sally Ann Howes, Alyson Reed, Laurie Beechman, Beth Fowler, Judy Kaye, Tony Roberts, Shaun Cassidy, David Cassidy, Lauren Gaffney, Spiro Malas, Anne Runolfsson, Petula Clark, Victor Garber, Sally Mayes, Marla Maples Trump, Jane Connell, Rita Gardner, Andrea McArdle, Gwen Verdon, Ann Crumb, Jason Graae, Bebe Neuwirth, B. D. Wong, Carmen De Lavallade, Michael Hayden, Debbie Pavelka, Carol Woods, Melissa Errico, Geoffrey Holder, John Raitt

The eighth annual Easter fund raiser for Broadway Cares/Equity Fights AIDS.

Right: Raquel Welch

JACKIE MASON: POLITICALLY INCORRECT

Written/Created by Jackie Mason; Production Design/Lighting, Neil Peter Jampolis; Sound, Bruce Cameron; Company Manager, Beth Riedmann; Stage Manager, Don Myers; Presented by Jyll Rosenfeld; Press, Robert M. Zarem; Previewed from Monday, March 21; Opened in the Golden Theatre on Tuesday, April 5, 1994*

CAST

JACKIE MASON

An evening of political comedy. Prior Mason Broadway engagements were *The World According to Me* (1986-88) and *Brand New* (1990-91).

Variety tallied 2 favorable, 1 mixed, 8 negative, and 1 inconclusive review. *Times:* (Ben Brantley) "...an often uncomfortable exercise in self-justification... real hostility." (Canby) "...one of the longest nights you'll ever spend in the theatre..." *News:* (Kissel) "...I laughed harder than I did in 1986, but not as hard as I did in 1990." *Post:* (Barnes) "...sour and dour this time around...You could hear some know-it-all loudmouth being funnier in a barroom..." *Newsday:* (Winer) "...prides himself on being an equal opportunity offender, but more than ever, his indignation is extremely selective." *Variety:* (Greg Evans) "...comic timing, vocal delivery and physical control are unflagging...mean-spirited-ness...pervasive smugness..."

*Closed June 4, 1995, after 347 performances and 13 previews.

Left: Jackie Mason

MEDEA

By Euripides; Translation, Alistair Elliot; Director, Jonathan Kent; Set, Peter J. Davison; Costumes, Paul Brown; Lighting, Wayne Dowdeswell, Rui Rita; Music, Jonathan Dove; Sound, John A. Leonard; Movement, Caroline Pope; General Manager, Stuart Thompson; Stage Managers, Dianne Trulock, Terrence J. Witter; Produced in association with The Liverpool Playhouse; Presented by Bill Kenwright and The Almeida Theatre Company; Press, Philip Rinaldi/Kathy Haberthur, Dennis Crowley, James Morrison, Bill Schelble; Previewed from Tuesday, March 29; Opened in the Longacre Theatre on Thursday, April 7, 1994*

CAST

Medea	Diana Rigg
Women of Corinth	Judith Paris, Jane Loretta Lowe, Nuala Willis
Nurse	Janet Henfrey
Tutor	John Southworth
Creon	John Turner
Jason	Tim Oliver Woodward
Aegeus	Donald Douglas
Messenger	Dan Mullane
Children	Tyler Noyes, Lucas Wiesendanger

UNDERSTUDIES: John Woodson (Jason/Messenger), Mark Hammer (Tutor/Creon/Aegus), Tanny McDonald (Women/Nurse), Blake C. Eastman (Children)

A new translation of a Greek tragedy from 431 B.C. performed without intermission. Winner of 1994 "Tony" for Leading Actress in a Play (Diana Rigg).

Variety tallied 12 favorable, 6 mixed, and 1 negative notice. *Times:* (Richards) "Diana Rigg brings a blazing intelligence and an elegant ferocity to the part." (Canby) "...makes more pronounced the feminism that is built into the Euripides text..." *News:* (Kissel) "It has a directness, a freshness that makes the play seem quite contemporary." *Post:* (Barnes) "This is classic theatre that should not be missed..." *Newsday:* (Winer) "...a tight and severe, rough and stunning new version of a very old story..." *Variety:* (Gerard) "...Rigg's performance left me cold... bypasses the heart."

*Closed June 26, 1994, after limited run of 82 performances and 9 previews.

Joan Marcus Photos

Top: Tim Oliver Woodward, Diana Rigg
Bottom: Diana Rigg

TWILIGHT: LOS ANGELES, 1992

Conceived/Written by Anna Deavere Smith; Director, George C. Wolfe; Sets, John Arnone; Costumes, Toni-Leslie James; Lighting, Jules Fisher, Peggy Eisenhauer; Sound, John Gromada; Music, Wendy Blackstone; Projections/Video, Batwin + Robin Productions; Production Supervisor, Neil A. Mazzella; General Managers, Caroline F. Turner/James Triner; Company Manager, Susan Sampliner; Stage Manager, Jane E. Neufeld; Presented by Benjamin Mordecai, Laura Rafaty, Ric Wanetik, New York Shakespeare Festival, Mark Taper Forum in association with Harriet Newman Leve, Jeanne Rizzo, James D. Stern, Daryl Roth, Jo-Lynne Worley, Ronald A. Pizzuti, The Booking Office and Freddy Bienstock; Press, Chris Boneau/Adrian Bryan-Brown, Craig Karpel, Bob Fennell, Jamie Morris; Previewed from Sunday, April 10; Opened in the Cort Theatre on Sunday, April 17, 1994*

CAST

ANNA DEAVERE SMITH

A one-woman play in two acts. The text was created out of interviews with the observers and participants of the 1992 L.A. riots.

Variety tallied 12 favorable, 2 mixed, and 1 negative review. *Times:* (Richards) "...the ultimate impressionist: she does people's souls." (Canby) "As much as it is about race relations...about language and about the inability of people to think things through without language." *News:* (Kissel) "Smith has a journalist's gift for opening up people..." *Post:* (Barnes) "Deavere Smith has virtually invented a brand-new theatrical genre..." *Newsday:* (Stuart) "Mostly, Smith gets us to listen... group therapy on a national scale..." *Variety:* (Evans) "...confirms her status as a premiere force in American theatre."

*Closed June 19, 1994, after 72 performances and 7 previews. This production played 27 Off-Broadway performances at the Public Theatre earlier in the season.

William Gibson/Martha Swope Photos

Anna Deavere Smith

Terrence Mann, Brian Press, Susan Egan in *Beauty and the Beast*

BEAUTY AND THE BEAST

Music, Alan Menken; Lyrics, Howard Ashman, Tim Rice; Book, Linda Woolverton; Director, Robert Jess Roth; Orchestrations, Danny Troob; Musical Supervision/Vocal Arrangements, David Friedman; Musical Director/Incidental Arrangements, Michael Kosarin; Choreography, Matt West; Sets, Stan Meyer; Costumes, Ann Hould-Ward; Lighting, Natasha Katz; Sound, T. Richard Fitzgerald; Hairstylist, David H. Lawrence; Illusions, Jim Steinmeyer, John Gaughan; Prosthetics, John Dods; Fights, Rick Sordelet; Cast Recording, Walt Disney Records; General Manager, Dodger Productions; Production Supervisor, Jeremiah J. Harris; Company Manager, Kim Sellon; Stage Managers, James Harker, John M. Atherlay, Pat Sosnow, Kim Vernace; Presented by Walt Disney Productions; Press, Chris Boneau/Adrian Bryan-Brown, Patty Onagan, Brian Moore, Michael Tuason; Previewed from Wednesday, March 9; Opened in the Palace Theatre on Monday, April 18, 1994*

CAST

Enchantress	Wendy Oliver
Young Prince	Harrison Beal
Beast	Terrence Mann
Belle	Susan Egan
Lefou	Kenny Raskin
Gaston	Burke Moses
Three Silly Girls	Sarah Solie Shannon, Paige Price, Linda Talbott
Maurice	Tom Bosley
Cogsworth	Heath Lamberts
Lumiere	Gary Beach
Babette	Stacey Logan
Mrs. Potts	Beth Fowler
Chip	Brian Press
Madame de la Grande Bouche	Eleanor Glockner
Monsieur D'Arque	Gordon Stanley
Townspeople/Enchanted Objects	John Barber, Roxanne Barlow, Harrison Beal, Michael-Demby Cain, Kate Dowe, David Elder, Merwin Foard, Gregory Garrison, Jack Hayes, Kim Huber, Elmore James, Rob Lorey, Patrick Loy, Barbara Marineau, Joanne McHugh, Anna McNeely, Bill Nabel, Ms. Oliver, Vince Pesce, Ms. Price, Ms. Shannon, Mr. Stanley, Ms. Talcott, Wysandria Woolsey
Prologue Narrator	David Ogden Stiers

STANDBYS/UNDERSTUDIES: Chuck Wagner (Beast/Gaston), Kate Dowe, Alisa Klein (Enchantress/Silly Girls), Gregory Garrison, Dan Mojica (Young Prince), David Elder (Beast), Kim Huber, Paige Price (Belle), Harrison Beal, Vince Pesce (Lefou), Merwin Ford (Gaston), Bill Nabel, Gordon Stanley (Cogsworth/Lumiere), Joanne McHugh, Sarah Solie Sannon (Babette), Barbara Marineau, Anna McNeely (Mrs. Potts/Wardrobe), Linda Talcott (Chip), Rob Lorey (D'Arque) SWINGS: Ms. Klein, Mr. Mojica, Ms. Dowe, Mr. Garrison, Mr. Lorey

MUSICAL NUMBERS: Overture, Prologue (Enchantress), Belle, No Matter What, Me, Home, Gaston, How Long Must This Go On?, Be Our Guest, If I Can't Love Her, Entr'acte/Wolf Chase, Something There, Human Again, Maison des Lunes, Beauty and the Beast, Mob Song, The Battle, Transformation, Finale

A musical in two acts. An expanded, live action version of the 1992 animated film musical with additional songs. Winner of 1994 "Tony" for Best Costume Design.

Variety tallied 4 favorable, 6 mixed, and 6 negative reviews. *Times:* (Richards) "...a sightseer's delight, which isn't the same thing as a theatregoer's dream." (Canby) "...over-produced..." *News:* (Kissel) "Although the musical is full of razzmatazz and old-fashioned showmanship, it lacks heart." *Post:* (Barnes) "...you can see where the money went...not...a show for critics..." *Newsday:* (Winer) "...klutzy old opera-ballet scenery with painted flats...there is magic on this stage, much of it traceable to the costumes..." *Variety:* (Gerard) "...a roar, plenty of fireworks and a fistful of lovely songs."

*Still playing May 31, 1994.

Joan Marcus/Marc Bryan-Brown/Walt Disney Theatrical Photos

Top: Terrence Mann, Susan Egan
Right: Burke Moses (center)

PICNIC

By William Inge; Director, Scott Ellis; Sets, Tony Walton; Costumes, William Ivey Long; Peter Kaczorowski; Sound, Tony Meola; Choreography, Susan Stroman; Music, Louis Rosen; Fights, David S. Leong; Hairstylist, Paul Huntley; General Manager, Ellen Richard; Stage Manager, Lori M. Doyle; Presented by Roundabout Theatre Company (Artistic Director, Todd Haimes; Founding Director, Gene Feist); Press, Chris Boneau/Adrian Bryan-Brown; Susanne Tighe, Hillary Harrow; Previewed from Wednesday, March 30; Opened in the Criterion Center Stage Right on Thursday, April 21, 1994*

CAST

Millie Owens	Angela Goethals
Helen Potts	Anne Pitoniak
Hal Carter	Kyle Chandler
Beano	W. Aaron Harpold
Madge Owens	Ashley Judd
Flo Owens	Polly Holliday
Rosemary Sydney	Debra Monk
Alan Seymour	Tate Donovan
Irma Kronkite	Audrie Neenan
Christine Schoenwalder	Charlotte Maier
Howard Bevans	Larry Bryggman

UNDERSTUDIES: Kathryn Fiore (Millie/Madge), Mary Fisher (Helen/Irma/Christine), Josh Hopkins (Hal/Beano/Alan), Charlotte Maier (Rosemary), Audrie Neenan (Flo), Michael Ouimet (Howard).

A new production of the 1953 drama performed without intermission. The action takes place in a small Kansas town, 1930s. For original Broadway production featuring Ralph Meeker, Paul Newman, Eileen Heckart, Janice Rule, and Kim Stanley, see *Theatre World* Vol. 9.

Variety tallied 8 favorable, 5 mixed, and 2 negative reviews. *Times:* (Richards) "With the passing years, William Inge gets smaller." (Canby) "...almost hopelessly dated..." *News:* (Kissel) "The play is so strong...a *Picnic* to treasure." *Post:* (Barnes) "Its sensibility towards youth and beauty, particularly the shattering effect of a nude male torso on assorted women, suggests the homosexuality of the author is at odds with the facts of heterosexual life." *Newsday:* (Winer) "...unevenly cast, pleasant-enough revival..." *Variety:* (Gerard) "...charged yet lyrical evocation of small-town despair...Monk steals the show..."

*Closed May 29, 1994, after 45 performances and 26 previews.

Carol Rosegg/Martha Swope Photos

Ashley Judd, Tate Donovan
**Bottom: Ashley Judd, Anne Pitoniak,
Kyle Chandler, Tate Donovan**

Ashley Judd, Kyle Chandler

BROKEN GLASS

By Arthur Miller; Director, John Tillinger; Sets/Costumes, Santo Loquasto; Lighting, Brian Nason; Sound, T. Richard Fitzgerald; Music, William Bolcom; General Manager, Stuart Thompson; Company Manager, Tom Santopietro; Stage Managers, Pamela Singer, Diane DiVita; Presented by Robert Whitehead, Roger L. Stevens, Lars Schmidt, Spring Sirkin, Terri & Timothy Childs in association with Herb Alpert; Press, Bill Evans/Jim Randolph, Terry M. Lilly; Previewed from Tuesday, April 12; Opened in the Booth Theatre on Sunday, April 24, 1994*

CAST

Phillip Gellburg...Ron Rifkin
Margaret Hyman ....Frances Frances Conroy
Dr. Harry Hyman..David Dukes
Sylvia Gellburg ....Amy Irving
Harriet...Lauren Klein
Stanton Case..George N. Martin

A drama performed without intermission. The action takes place in Brooklyn, November 1938.

Variety tallied 6 favorable, 10 mixed, and 4 negative reviews. *Times:* (Richards) "A kind of spiritual detective story...periodic jolts of pain and anguish." (Canby) "...a poignance so rare these days that it's almost new-fashioned." *News:* (Kissel) "...still seems more the outline for a play than the finished product." *Post:* (Barnes) "...fascinating if not entirely satisfactory or even especially illuminating." *Newsday:* (Winer) "Despite the pleasures of his probing mind, the fine cast and John Tillinger's poetic production...not likely to break the string of commercial disappointments..." *Variety:* (Gerard) "...an unfinished work whose power has only been partly realized."

*Closed June 26, 1994, after 73 performances and 15 previews.

Inge Morath/Magnum Photos

Left: Frances Conroy, Amy Irving
Bottom Left: David Dukes, Ron Rifkin
Bottom Right: David Dukes, Amy Irving

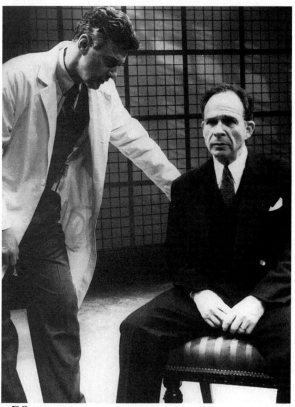

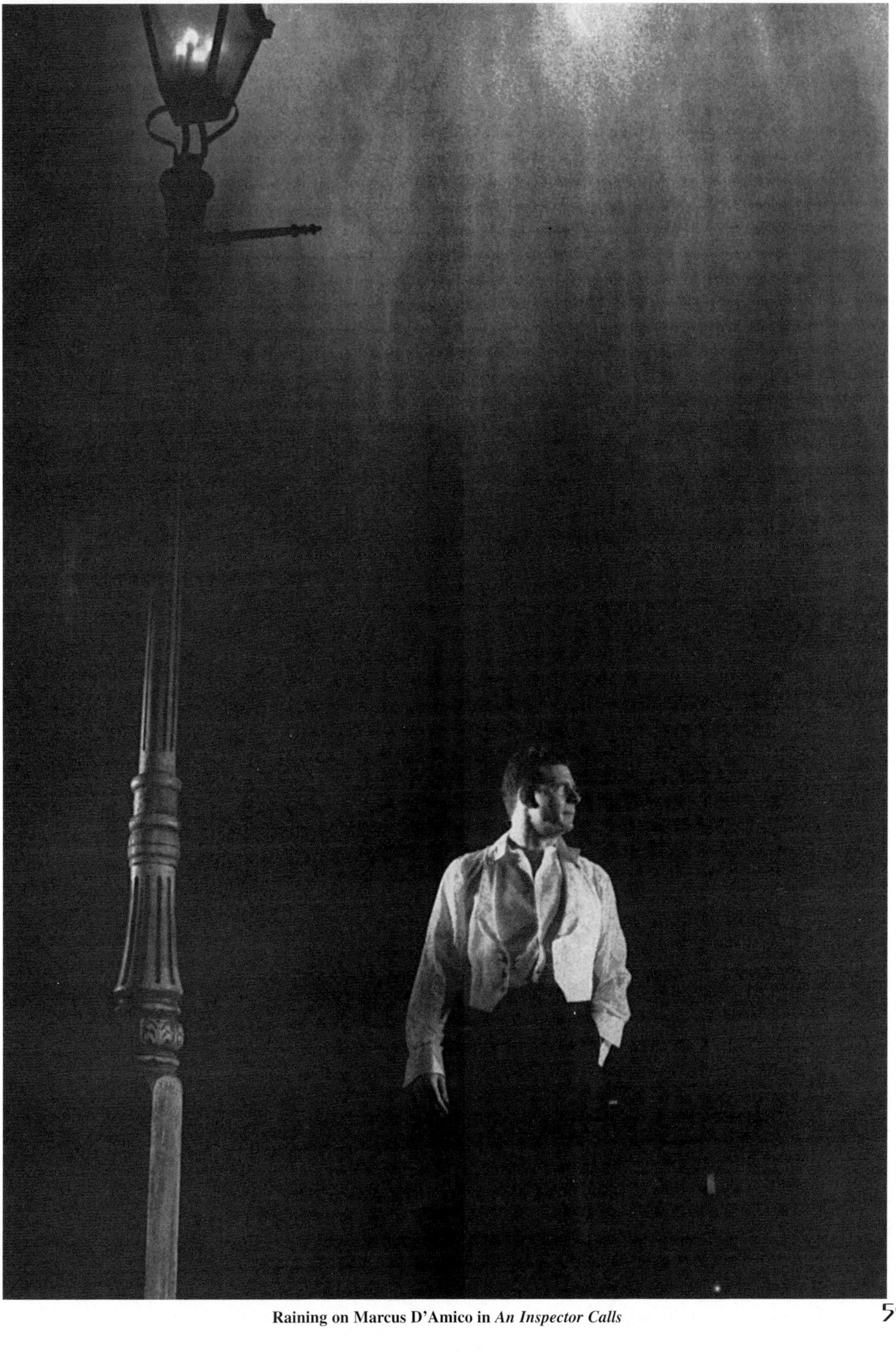

Raining on Marcus D'Amico in *An Inspector Calls*

AN INSPECTOR CALLS

By J. B. Priestley; Director, Stephen Daldry; Design, Ian MacNeil; Lighting, Rick Fisher; Music, Stephen Warbeck; Sound, T. Richard Fitzgerald; Special Effects, Gregory Meeh; Fights, B. H. Barry; Production Supervisor, Jeremiah J. Harris; Casting, Julie Hughes, Barry Moss; Company Manager, Victoria Stevenson; Stage Managers, Sally Jacobs, Judith Binus; Presented by Noel Pearson, The Shubert Organization, Capital Cities/ABC, Joseph Harris and The Royal National Theatre; Press, Alma Viator/Bill Cannon; Previewed from Thursday, April 14; Opened in the Royale Theatre on Wednesday, April 27, 1994*

CAST

Arthur Birling ....Philip Bosco
Gerald Croft ....Aden Gillett
Sheila Birling ....Jane Adams
Sybil Birling ....Rosemary Harris
Edna ....Jan Owens
Eric Birling ....Marcus D'Amico
Inspector Goole ....Kenneth Cranham
Boy ....Christopher Marquette

STANDBYS: John Lantz (Goole), Harry Carnahan (Gerald), Catherine Wolf (Sybil/Edna), Susannah Hoffman (Sheila), David E. Cantler (Boy)

A new production of a 1945 thriller performed without intermission. The action takes place in Brumley, an industrial city in the Yorkshire, spring 1912. For original 1947 Broadway production see *Theatre World* Vol. 4. Winner of 1994 "Tonys" for Best Revival of a Play, Featured Actress in a Play (Jane Adams), Best Direction of a Play, Best Scenic Design, and Best Lighting Design.

Variety tallied 15 favorable, 1 mixed, and 2 negative notices. *Times:* (Richards) "...a steadily engrossing drama and, more significantly, one of the more astonishing spectacles on Broadway right now." (Canby) "...it has the brilliant, restless imaginations of Mr. Daldry, the director, and Ian MacNeil, who's responsible for the hallucinogenic production design." *News:* (Kissel) "...a stunning piece of theatrical legerdemain." *Post:* (Barnes) "...ludicrously overheated and pompous..." *Newsday:* (Stuart) "...rekindles not just a British chestnut but the whole thrill of seeing a play..." *Variety:* (Gerard) "...an awful lot of time and talent spent making a second-rate work look good and a new director look better."

*Closed May 28, 1995, after 454 performances and 14 previews.

Joan Marcus Photos

Rosemary Harris

Christopher Marquette, Kenneth Craham

Aden Gillett, Jane Adams

Jan Owens, Christopher Marquette in the rain

Rosemary Harris, Philip Bosco, Jane Adams

THE RISE AND FALL OF LITTLE VOICE

By Jim Cartwright; Director, Simon Curtis; Sets, Thomas Lynch; Lighting, Kevin Rigdon; Costumes, Allison Reeds; Sound, Rob Milburn; Action Sequences, B. H. Barry; Music Director, June Shellene; General Manager, Leonard Soloway; Company Manager, Dana Sherman; Stage Managers, Malcolm Ewen, Alden Vasquez; Presented by James M. & Charlene Nederlander, Peggy Hill Rosenkranz, Dennis Grimaldi, PACE Theatrical Group, Kevin McCollum, Jon Platt, James L. Nederlander, Leonard Soloway, Michael Codron, and Steppenwolf Theatre; Press, Shirley Herz/Sam Rudy, Miller Wright, Wayne Wolfe; Previewed from Friday, April 15; Opened in the Neil Simon Theatre on Sunday, May 1, 1994*

CAST

Mari Hoff	Rondi Reed
Little Voice	Hynden Walch
Phone Man	John Christopher Jones
Billy	Ian Barford
Sadie	Karen Vaccaro
Ray Say	George Innes
Mr. Boo	John Christopher Jones

UNDERSTUDIES: Mary Margaret Barry (Mari/Sadie), Marci Kipnis, Fleur Phillips (Little Voice), Martin Rayner (Phone Man/Boo/Ray Say), Matthew Ross (Billy)

A drama in two acts. The action takes place in northern England, 1994.

Variety tallied 2 positive, 4 mixed, and 5 negative reviews. *Times:* (Richards) "...a kind of dim-witted grossness..." (Canby) "...acted with great zest..." *News:* (Kissel) "...a genuinely bad play...about a pathologically shy girl who has a gift for impersonating great singers (Judy Garland, Edith Piaf etc.)." *Post:* (Barnes) "The play does need a very special sleight of hand..." *Newsday:* (Winer) "...trashy, oddly entertaining, very minor English comedy..." *Variety:* (Gerard) "...it lacks a star-quality lead performance essential in making the show a must-see."

*Closed May 8, 1994, after 9 performances and 19 previews.

Michael Brosilow Photos

Ian Barford, Hynden Walch

George Innes, Rondi Reed, Hynden Walch

LADY IN THE DARK

Music, Kurt Weill; Lyrics, Ira Gershwin; Book, Moss Hart; Adaptation/Direction, Larry Carpenter; Orchestrations, Kurt Weill; Musical Director, Rob Fisher; Set, John Lee Beatty; Lighting, Richard Pilbrow, Dawn Chiang; Costumes, Lindsay W. Davis; Choreography, Daniel Pelzig; Sound, Scott Lehrer; Director of Antigravity, Christopher Harrison; Stage Manager, Robin Rumpf; Presented by City Center and Encores; Press, Philip Rinaldi/William Schelble; Opened in City Center on Wednesday, May 4, 1994*

CAST

Liza Elliott	Christine Ebersole
Dr. Brooks	Joe Morton
Alison DuBois/Sutton/Sorcerer/Gaoler	Betsy Joslyn
Russell Paxton/Beekman/Minstrel/Father of the Bride/Ringmaster	Edward Hibbert
Maggie Grant/Miss Forsythe/King/Gaoler	Carole Shelly
Charley Johnson/Marine/Jeweler/Minister/Prosecuting Attorney	Tony Goldwyn
Randy Curtis/Best Man/Defense Attorney	Patrick Cassidy
Kendall Nesbitt	Frank Converse
Little Girl	Tracy Leigh Spindler
Ben	Hank Stratton

Ensemble .... Jamie Baer, Susan Cella, John Clonts, Lisa Ericksen, Marc Heller, John Kramar, Marie Laurence-Danvers, Lori Brown Mirabal, Karen Murphy, Robert Osborne, Robert Randle, Lucy Schaufer, Daniel Shigo, Hank Stratton, Brent Weber

Antigravity .... Victor Dodonow, Debbi Fuhrman, Christopher Harrison, Tabb Nance, Kamila Zapytowska The Coffee Club Orchestra

MUSICAL NUMBERS: Oh Fabulous One in Your Ivory Tower, The World's Inamorata, One Life to Live, Girl of the Moment, Mapleton High Chorale, This is New, Princess of Pure Delight, The Woman at the Alter, Entr'acte, Greatest Show on Earth, Dance of the Tumblers, Best Years of His Life, Tschaikowsky, The Saga of Jenny, My Ship, Finale

A concert presentation of the 1941 musical. The original starred Gertrude Lawrence and Danny Kaye at the Alvin (now Neil Simon) Theatre.

*Closed May 7, 1995, after a limited run of 4 performances.

Gerry Goodstein Photos

Tony Goldwyn, Christine Ebersole in *Lady in the Dark*

Joan Rivers in *Sally Marr...*

SALLY MARR...AND HER ESCORTS

By Joan Rivers, Erin Sanders and Lonny Price; Director, Mr. Price; Set, William Barclay; Costumes, David C. Woolard, (For Joan Rivers) David Dangle; Lighting, Phil Monat; Music/Orchestrations, Tim Weil; Design, Wendall K. Harrington; Sound, Jan Nebozenko; Dance, Lynne Taylor-Corbett; General Manager, Robert Cole Productions; Company Manager, Steven H. David; Stage Managers, Martin Gold, Kenneth J. Davis; Presented by Martin Richards, Robert Cole, Ron Kastner, Sam Crothers, Dennis Grimaldi, Kenneth D. Greenblatt and 44 Productions; Press, Bill Evans/Terry M. Lilly, Jim Randolph; Previewed from Wednesday, April 13; Opened in the Helen Hayes Theatre on Thursday, May 5, 1994*

CAST

Sally Marr	Joan Rivers
Escort #1	Valerie Wright
Escort #2	Jonathan Brody
Escort #3	Ken Nagy
Young Lenny Voice	Jason Woliner

A play in two acts suggested by the life of Sally Marr, mother of comic Lenny Bruce.

Variety tallied 2 favorable, 5 mixed, and 8 negative reviews. *Times:* (Richards) "Is Ms. Rivers a great actress? No, she is not. But she is exuberant, fearless and inexhaustible." (Canby) "The text and the physical production are dreary." *News:* (Kissel) "...a tribute to the relentless drive of two amazing women, the actress and her subject." *Post:* (Barnes) "...strictly a one-on-one encounter with Joan Rivers..." *Newsday:* (Winer) "...a brave and engaging and admirable piece of work." *Variety:* (Gerard) "...Rivers...musters every ounce of her considerable comedic flamboyance..."

*Closed June 19, 1994, after 50 performances and 27 previews.

Martha Swope Photos

63

PASSION

Music/Lyrics, Stephen Sondheim; Book/Direction, James Lapine; Based on the 1981 film *Passione D'Amore*; Orchestrations, Jonathan Tunick; Musical Director, Paul Gemignani; Sets, Adrianne Lobel; Costumes, Jane Greenwood; Lighting, Beverly Emmons; Sound, Otts Munderloh; Hairstylist, Phyllis Della; Cast Recording, Broadway Angel; General Manager, Marvin A. Krauss; Company Manager, Nina Skriloff; Stage Managers, Beverley Randolph, Mireya Hepner, Frank Lombardi; Presented by The Shubert Organization, Capital Cities/ABC, Roger Berlind, Scott Rudin by arrangement with Lincoln Center Theater; Press, Philip Rinaldi/James L. L. Morrison, William Schelble, Dennis Crowley, Kathy Haberthur; Previewed from Thursday, March 24; Opened in the Plymouth Theatre on Monday, May 9, 1994*

CAST

Clara	Marin Mazzie
Giorgio	Jere Shea
Col. Ricci	Gregg Edelman
Dr. Tambourri	Tom Aldredge +1
Lt. Torasso	Francis Ruivivar
Sgt. Lombardi	Marcus Olson
Lt. Barri	William Parry
Maj. Rizzolli	Cris Groenendaal +2
Pvt. Augenti	George Dvorsky +3
Fosca	Donna Murphy
Fosca's Mother	Linda Balgord
Fosca's Father	John Leslie Wolfe +4
Ludovic	Matthew Porretta +5
Mistress	Juliet Lambert +6

UNDERSTUDIES: Matthew Porretta (Giorgio), George Dvorsky (Giorgio/Ludovic), Linda Balgord (Fosca), Colleen Fitzpatrick (Fosca/Clara/Mother/Mistress), Juliet Lambert (Clara), Gibby Brand (Tambourri/Father/Augenti), William Parry (Ricci), John Leslie Wolfe (Torasso/Rizzolli/Barri/Lombardi), Frank Lombardi (Augenti)

MUSICAL NUMBERS: Happiness, First Letter, Second Letter, Third Letter, Fourth Letter, I Read, Garden Sequence, Trio, I Wish I Could Forget You, Soldiers' Gossip, Flashback, Sunrise Letter, Is This What You Call Love?, Forty Days, Loving You, Farewell Letter, No One Has Ever Loved Me, Finale

A musical performed without intermission. The action takes place in Milan and a remote Italian military outpost, 1863. Winner of 1994 "Tonys" for Best Musical, Best Book of a Musical, Best Original Score, and Leading Actress in a Musical (Donna Murphy).

Variety tallied 8 favorable, 5 mixed, and 10 negative notices. *Times:* (Richards) "...just this side of the macabre...you have to appreciate the composer's unremitting intelligence..." (Canby) "It's heavy stuff. The only problem with the score is that there's not enough of it." *News:* (Kissel) "...I cannot imagine *Passion* without Donna Murphy...the passion she brings to the music is totally enthralling." *Post:* (Barnes) "...the first serious Broadway opera...the most thrilling piece of theatre on Broadway." *Newsday:* (Winer) "...a beautiful score is nothing to take for granted. If Broadway doesn't want it, surely the opera house will." *Variety:* (Gerard) "*Passion* is a great, great show."

*Closed January 7, 1995, after 280 performances and 52 previews.

+Succeeded by: 1. (during previews) William Duff-Griffin 2. T. J. Meyers 3. John Antony 4. Andy Umberger 5. Colleen Fitzpatrick

Joan Marcus Photos

Top: Donna Murphy
Bottom: Marin Mazzie

Marin Mazzie, Jere Shea

Jere Shea, Donna Murphy

65

THE BEST LITTLE WHORE-HOUSE GOES PUBLIC

Music/Lyrics, Carol Hall; Book, Larry L. King and Peter Masterson; Directors, Mr. Masterson and Tommy Tune; Choreography, Jeff Calhoun, Mr. Tune; Orchestrations, Peter Matz; Musical Supervision/Vocal and Dance Arrangements, Wally Harper; Musical/Vocal Director, Karl Jurman; Musical Advisor, Robert Billig; Sets, John Arnone; Costumes, Bob Mackie; Lighting, Jules Fisher, Peggy Eisenhauer; Sound, Tony Meola; Hair/Wigs, Bobby H. Grayson; Video, Batwin + Robin Productions; Cast Recording, Varese Sarabande; Casting, Stuart Howard, Amy Schecter; Production Supervisor, Gene O'Donovan; General Management, David Strong Warner; Company Manager, Lauren Singer; Stage Managers, Arturo E. Porazzi, Bonnie L. Becker; Presented by Stevie Phillips and MCA/Universal; Press, Jeffrey Richards/Irene Gandy, Kevin Rehac; Previewed from Thursday, April 14; Opened in the Lunt-Fontanne Theatre on Tuesday, May 10, 1994*

CAST

Showroom Headliner..Troy Britton Johnson
Showroom Patrons ....Gerry Burkhardt, Laurel Lynn Collins, Sally Mae Dunn, Tom Flagg, Joe Hart, Don Johanson, Mark Manley, Mary Frances McCatty, Casey Nicholaw, Louise Ruck, William Ryall, Shaver Tillitt, Jillana Urbina, Richard Vida, Theara J. Ward
Street Whores..................................Pamela Everett, Ganine Giorgione, Amy N. Heggins, Lainie Sakakura, Christina Youngman
Ralph J. Bostick ....Danny Rutigliano
Comedian ....Jim David
Las Vegas Legends ....Ms. McCatty, Mr.Johanson, Ms. Collins, Mr. Burkhardt, Ms. Dunn, Ms. Ward, Mr. Ryall
IRS Director..Kevin Cooney
Schmidt/B. S. Bullehit/U.S. President................................David Doty
Terri Clark ....Gina Torres
Mona Stangley ....Dee Hoty
Client of Whorehouse ....Joe Hart
Sam Dallas ....Scott Holmes
Sen. A. Harry Hardast..Ronn Carroll
Lotta Lovingood ....Pamela Everett
Hairdresser ....Jim David
Working Girls/Wall St. Wolves ....Mr. Burhardt, Ms. Collins, Ms. Dunn, Ms. Everett, Mr. Flagg, Ms. Giorgione, Mr. Hart, Ms. Heggins, Mr. Johanson, Mr. Johnson, Mr. Manley, Ms. McCatty, Mr. Nicholaw, Ms. Ruck, Mr. Rutigliano, Mr. Ryall, Ms. Sakakura, Mr. Tillitt, Ms. Urbina, Mr. Vita, Ms. Ward, Ms. Youngman
Pit Vocalists ....Nancy LaMott, Ryan Perry, Susannah Blinkoff

STANDBYS/UNDERSTUDIES: Lauren Mitchell (Mona), J. Mark McVey (Sam), Joe Hart (IRS/Hardast), Danny Rutigliano (Schmidt), Gerry Burkhardt (Comedian), Laurel Lynn Collins (Terri) SWINGS: Niki Harris, Vincent D'Elia

MUSICAL NUMBERS: Let the Devil Take Us, Nothin' Like a Picture Show, I'm Leavin' Texas, It's Been a While, Brand New Start, Down and Dirty, Call Me, Change in Me, Here for the Hearing, Piece of the Pie, If We Open Our Eyes

A musical comedy in two acts with 15 scenes and prologue. The action takes place in Las Vegas, Washington, D.C., Nevada, Wall Street, and on the Information Highway. A sequel to the 1978 musical *The Best Little Whorehouse in Texas* (see *Theatre World* Vol. 35).

Variety tallied 7 negative and 3 mixed, notices. *Times:* (Richards) "...too dopey to be effective as political satire, too tame to qualify as raunch and not garish enough to claim its vulgarity as a real badge of honor." (Canby) "noisy, fast-moving show-biz spectacle..." *News:* (Kissel) "...new parameters for Broadway vulgarity." *Post:* (Barnes) "...most bizarre aspect is its frenetic anxiety to be all things to all audiences..." *Newsday:* (Winer) "...moronic catastophe...unrelentingly cheesy..." *Variety:* (Gerard) "...crummiest junk to litter the district..."

*Closed May 21, 1994, after 16 performances and 29 previews.

Sonia Moskowitz Photos

Top: Dee Hoty
Left: (front) Laurel Lynn Collins (left),
Troy Britton Johnson (right)

66

Jason Opsahl, Rosie O'Donnell

GREASE

Music/Lyrics/Book by Jim Jacobs and Warren Casey; Director /Choreography, Jeff Calhoun; Orchestrations, Steve Margoshes; Musical Director/Vocal and Dance Arrangements, John McDaniel; Musical Coordinator, John Monaco; Sets, John Arnone; Costumes, Willa Kim; Lighting, Howell Binkley; Hairstylist, Patrick D. Moreton; Sound, Tom Morse; Associate Choreographer, Jerry Mitchell; Cast Recording, RCA; General Manager, Charlotte W. Wilcox; Casting, Stuart Howard, Amy Schecter; Company Manager, Scott A. Moore; Stage Managers, Craig Jacobs, Tom Bartlett; Presented in association with PACE Theatrical Group, TV Asahi; The Tommy Tune Production presented by Barry & Fran Weissler, Jujamcyn Theatres; Press, Pete Sanders/Ian Rand, Bruce Laurienzo, Meredith Oritt; Previewed from Saturday, April 23; Opened in the Eugene O'Neill Theatre on Wednesday, May 11, 1994*

CAST

Vince Fontaine ....Brian Bradley
Miss Lynch ....Marcia Lewis
Patty Simcox ....Michelle Blakely
Eugene Florczyk...Paul Castree
Jan...Heather Stokes
Marty ....Megan Mullally
Betty Rizzo ....Rosie O'Donnell
Doody ....Sam Harris
Roger..Hunter Foster
Kenickie...Jason Opsahl
Sonny Latierri..Carlos Lopez
Frenchy ....Jessica Stone
Sandy Dumbrowski ....Susan Wood
Danny Zuko ....Ricky Paull Goldin
Straight A's ....Clay Adkins, Patrick Boyd, Denis Jones
Dream Mooners...................................Patrick Boyd, Katy Grenfell
Heartbeats ....Ms. Grenfell, Janice Lorraine Holt, Lorna Shane
Cha-Cha Degregorio...Sandra Purpuro
Teen Angel ....Billy Porter
Ensemble ....Mr. Adkins, Melissa Bell, Mr. Boyd, Ms. Grenfell,
Ned Hannah, Ms. Holt, Mr. Jones, Allison Metcalf,
H. Hylan Scott II, Ms. Shane

UNDERSTUDIES: Patti D'Beck (Miss Lynch), Melissa Bell (Patty), Ned Hannah (Eugene), Katy Grenfell (Jan), Allison Metcalf (Marty), Sandra Purpuro (Rizzo), Clay Adkins (Doody/Teen Angel), Patrick Boyd (Roger), H. Hylan Scott II (Kenickie/Danny/Vince), Denis Jones (Sonny), Janice Lorraine Holt (Frenchy), Michelle Blakely (Sandy), Lorna Shane (Cha-Cha)

A new production of the 1972 musical in two acts with 13 scenes. The action takes place in and around Rydell High, 1950s. For original Broadway production see *Theatre World* Vol. 29.

Variety tallied 6 favorable, 3 mixed, and 7 negative reviews. *Times:* (Brantley) "The dilution of the original source had already begun with the...sanitized film version...current production takes the process much further..." (Canby) "...not for anyone who enjoyed the original...has been on the road since January and looks it. The energy is gone." *News:* (Lissel) "The original...was unpretentious...the revival...puts everything in overdrive." *Post:* (Barnes) "...lacks for nothing in energy. The cast busts a gut in its efforts to entertain..." *Newsday:* (Winer) "...too dumb for grown-ups and too coarse for children..." *Variety:* (Gerard) "The language in *Grease* has been somewhat retrofitted to make it even more inoffensive than it was 22 years ago...music is well played and presented."

*Still running May 31, 1994.

Stan Schnier/Carmen Schiavone Photos

**Top: Sam Harris, Jessica Stone
Center: Jason Opsahl, Rosie O'Donnell
Left: Marcia Lewis, Michelle Blakely**

Ricky Paull Goldin, Susan Wood

Carlos Lopez, Jason Opsahl, Jessica Stone, Sam Harris, Ricky Paull Goldin,
Megan Mullally, Hunter Foster, Heather Stokes, Rosie O'Donnell

SUNDAY IN THE PARK WITH GEORGE (IN CONCERT)

Music/Lyrics, Stephen Sondheim; Book/Direction, James Lapine; Orchestrations, Michael Starobin; Musical Director, Paul Gemignani; Projections, Wendall K. Harrington; Sound, Lucas Rico Corrubia; Producer, BT McNicholl; Presented by Friends In Deed; Press, Fred Nathan/Michael Borowski; 1 performance only in the St. James Theatre on Sunday, May 15, 1994*

CAST

George	Mandy Patinkin
Dot/Marie	Bernadette Peters
Old Lady/Blair Daniels	Barbara Bryne
Nurse/Mrs./Harriet Pawling	Judith Moore
Franz/Dennis	Bruce Adler
Jules/Bob Greenberg	Charles Kimbrough
Yvonne/Naomi Eisen	Dana Ivey
Boatman/Charles Redmond	William Parry
Celeste #1/Waitress	Melanie Vaughn
Celeste #2/Elaine	Mary D'Arcy
Louise	Danielle Ferland
Frieda/Betty	Nancy Opel
Louis/Billy Webster	Jeff Keller
Soldier/Alex	Howard McGillin
Man with Bicycle	John Jellison
Mr./Lee Randolph	Kurt Knudson

MUSICAL NUMBERS: Sunday in the Park with George, No Life, Color and Light, Gossip, The Day Off, Everybody Loves Louis, Finishing the Hat, We Do Not Belong Together, Beautiful, Sunday, It's Hot Up Here, Chromolume #7, Putting It Together, Children and Art, Lesson #8, Move On, Sunday

The tenth anniversary reunion concert. For original 1984 Broadway production see *Theatre World* Vol. 40.

Stephen Mosher Photos

Top: Barbara Bryne, Mandy Patinkin, Stephen Sondheim, Bernadette Peters, James Lapine, Charles Kimbrough, Dana Ivey
Right: Bernadette Peters

BROADWAY PRODUCTIONS FROM PAST SEASONS THAT PLAYED THROUGH THIS SEASON

ANGELS IN AMERICA:
MILLENNIUM APPROACHES
A Gay Fantasia On National Themes

By Tony Kushner; Director, George C. Wolfe; Sets, Robin Wagner; Costumes, Toni-Leslie James; Lighting, Jules Fisher; Original Music, Anthony Davis; Additional Music, Michael Ward; Sound, Scott Lehrer; Hair/MakeUp, Jeffrey Frank; Production Supervision, Gene O'Donovan/Neil A. Mazzella; Casting, Meg Simon, Stanley Soble; Company Manager, Lisa M. Poyer; Stage Managers, Perry Cline, Mary K. Klinger, Michael Passaro; Produced in association with The New York Shakespeare Festival; Executive Producers, Benjamin Mordecai and Robert Cole; Presented by Jujamcyn Theatres, Mark Taper Forum/Gordon Davidson, Margo Lion, Susan Quint Gallin, Jo B. Platt, The Baruch-Frankel-Viertel Group, Frederick Zollo, Herb Alpert; Press, Chris Boneau/Adrian Bryan-Brown/Bob Fennell; Previewed from Tuesday April 13, 1993; Opened in the Walter Kerr Theatre on Tuesday, May 4, 1993*

CAST

Rabbi Chemelwitz/Henry/Hannah Pitt/Ethel Rosenberg ....Kathleen Chalfant +1
Roy Cohn/Prior 2..Ron Leibman +2
Joe Pitt/Prior 1/Eskimo ....David Marshall Grant +3
Harper Pitt/Martin Heller ....Marcia Gay Harden +4
Mr. Lies/Belize ....Jeffrey Wright +5
Louis Ironson..Joe Mantello +6
Prior Walter/Man in Park ....Stephen Spinella +7
Emily/Ella Chapter/So.Bronx Woman/The Angel ....Ellen McLaughlin +8

UNDERSTUDIES: Jay Goede (Prior/Joe/Louis), Matthew Sussman (Roy Cohn/Louis), Susan Bruce (Harper/Angel), Beth McDonald, Tracy Sallows (Hannah/Angel), Darnell Williams, Lance Reddick (Belize), Daniel Zelman (Prior/Joe)

A drama in three acts. The action takes place in New York City, Salt Lake City, and Elsewhere. *Millennium Approches* is the first of two parts of *Angels In America.*

*Closed December 4, 1994 after 367 performances and 21 previews. Winner of the 1993 Pulitzer Award for Drama. Winner of 1993 "Tony" Awards for Best Play, Leading Actor in a Play (Ron Leibman), Featured Actor in a Play (Stephen Spinella), Direction of a Play. Winner of 1993 New York Drama Critics Circle for Best Play.

+Succeeded by: 1. Laurie Kennedy 2. Larry Pine, F. Murray Abraham, David Margulies 3. Jay Goede 4. Susan Bruce, Cynthia Nixon, Megan Gallagher 5. Kevin T. Carroll 6. Dan Futterman 7. Daniel Jenkins 8. Cherry Jones

Joan Marcus Photos

Top: Marcia Gay Harden
Center: David Marshall Grant, Cynthia Nixon
Right: Ron Leibman

BLOOD BROTHERS

Music/Lyrics/Book, Willy Russell; Directors, Bill Kenwright and Bob Tomson; Arrangements, Del Newman; Production Musical Director, Rod Edwards; Musical Director, Rick Fox; Musical Coordinator, Mort Silver; Sets/Costumes, Andy Walmsley; Lighting, Joe Atkins; Sound, Paul Astbury; Casting, Pat McCorkle; General Manager, Stuart Thompson; Company Manager, Bruce Klinger; Stage Managers, Mary Porter Hall, John Lucas; Associate Producer, Jon Miller; Presented by Mr. Kenwright; Press, Philip Rinaldi/Kathy Haberthur; Previewed from Wednesday, April 14; Opened in the Music Box Theatre on Sunday, April 25, 1993*

CAST

Mrs. Johnstone ....Stephanie Lawrence +1
Narrator ....Warwick Evans +2
Mrs. Lyons ....Barbara Walsh +3
Mr. Lyons ....Ivar Brogger
Mickey...Con O'Neill +4
Eddie ....Mark Michael Hutchinson +5
Sammy ....James Clow +6
Linda...Jan Graveson +7
Perkins ....Sam Samuelson
Donna Marie/Miss Jones ....Regina O'Malley +8
Policeman/Teacher/Teddy Boy ....Robin Haynes
Brenda ....Anne Torsiglieri +9
Ensemble ....Kerry Butler, Philip Lehl, John Schiappa,
Douglas Weston, Nick Cokas, Robin d'Arcy James,
Karen Quackenbush, Timothy Gulan

UNDERSTUDIES: Regina O'Malley (Mrs. Johnstone/Mrs. Lyons), Philip Lehl (Mickey/Eddie), John Schiappa, Nick Cokas (Sammy/Narrator), Sam Samuelson (Eddie), Anne Torsiglieri (Linda), Robin Haynes (Sammy/Mr. Lyons), Kerry Butler (Donna/Linda), Brian d'Arcy James (Eddie), Susan Tilson (Mrs. Johnstone/Mrs. Lyons), Karyn Quackenbush (Mrs. Lyons/Linda) SWINGS: John Soroka, Susan Tilson

MUSICAL NUMBERS: Marilyn Monroe, My Child, Easy Terms, Shoes Upon the Table, Kids Game, Prelude, Long Sunday Afternoon/My Friend, Bright New Day, That Guy, I'm Not Saying a Word, Take a Letter Miss Jones, Light Romance, Madman, Tell Me It's Not True

A musical in two acts. The action takes place in and around Liverpool. The show originally premiered in London's West End in January 1983 and was revived there in 1988.

*Closed April 30, 1995, after 839 performances and 13 previews.

+Succeeded by: 1. Petula Clark, Carole King, Helen Reddy 2. Richard Cox, Adrian Zmed 3. Regina O'Malley 4. David Cassidy, Philip Lehl 5. Shaun Cassidy, Ric Ryder 6. John Schiappa 7. Shauna Hicks 8. Kerry Butler, Jodi Jinks 9. Anne Torsiglieri, Karyn Quackenbush

Joan Marcus Photos

Top: David Cassidy
Bottom Left: Petula Clark
Below: Shaun Cassidy

CATS

Music, Andrew Lloyd Webber; Based on *Old Possum's Book Of Practical Cats* by T. S. Eliot; Orchestrations, David Cullen, Lloyd Webber; Prod. Musical Director, David Caddick; Musical Director, Edward G. Robinson; Sound, Martin Levan; Lighting, David Hersey; Design, John Napier; Choreography/Associate Director, Gillian Lynne; Director, Trevor Nunn; Original Cast Recording, Polydor/Really Useful Records; Casting, Johnson-Liff Associates; Company Manager, James G. Mennen; Stage Managers, Peggy Peterson, Tom Taylor, Suzanne Viverito; Executive Producers, R. Tyler Gatchell, Jr., Peter Neufeld; Presented by Cameron Mackintosh, The Really Useful Co., David Geffen, and The Shubert Organization; Press, Fred Nathan/Michael Borowski; Opened in the Winter Garden Theatre on Thursday, October 7, 1982*

CAST

Alonzo ....Randy Wojcik +1
Bustopher/Asparagus/Growltiger ....Jeffrey Clonts
Bombalurina..Marlene Danielle
Cassandra..Darlene Wilson +2
Coricopat..Cholsu Kim +3
Demeter..Mercedes Perez +4
Grizabella..Liz Callaway +5
Jellylorum/Griddlebone ....Nina Hennessey
Jennanydots ....Rose McGuire +6
Mistoffelees ....Lindsay Chambers +7
Mungojerrie ....Roger Kachel
Munkustrap..Dan McCoy +8
Old Deuteronomy..Ken Prymus
Plato/Macivity/Rumpus Cat..Robb Edward Morris
Pouncival..Devanand N. Janki +9
Rum Tum Tiger..B. K. Kennelly +10
Rumpleteazer..Christine DeVito
Sillabub ....Lisa Mayer +11
Skimbleshanks..George Smyros
Tantomile..Michelle Artigas
Tumblebrutus ....Marc Ellis Holland +12
Victoria..Claudia Shell +13
Cat Chorus ....John Briel, Jay Aubrey Jones, Susan Powers, Heidi Stallings

STANDBYS/UNDERSTUDIES: Marty Benn, Joe Briel, Dawn Marie Church, Colleen Dunn, Angelo H. Fraboni, Douglas Graham, James Hadley, Amy N. Heggins, Devanand N. Janki, Jay Aubrey Jones, B. K. Kennelly, Cholsu Kim, David E. Liddell, Joe Locarro, Jack Magredey, Lisa Mayer, Rusty Mowery, Mercedes Perez, Susan Powers, Jim Raposa, Naomi Reddin, Mark Santoro, Sarah Solie Shannon, Heidi Stallings, Lynn Sterling, Sally Ann Swarm, Owen Taylor, Suzanne Viverito, Leigh Webster, Darlene Wilson, Randy Wojcik, Lily-Lee Wong

MUSICAL NUMBERS: Jellicle Songs for Jellicle Cats, Naming of Cats, Invitation to the Jellicle Ball, Old Gumbie Cat, Rum Tum Tugger, Grizabella the Glamour Cat, Bustopher Jones, Mungojerrie and Rumpleteazer, Old Deuteronomy, Awful Battle of the Pekes and Pollicles, Jellicle Ball, Memory, Moments of Happiness, Gus the Theatre Cat, Growltiger's Last Stand, Skimbleshanks, Macavity, Mr. Mistoffelees, Journey to the Heavyside Layer, Addressing of Cats

A musical in two acts with 20 scenes.

*Still playing May 31, 1994. The musical celebrated its eleventh Broadway anniversary on October 7, 1993, and has now passed 4,500 performances. Winner of 1983 "Tonys" for Best Musical, Score, Book, Direction, Costumes, Lighting, and Featured Actress in a Musical (Betty Buckley as Grizabella). For original 1982 production see *Theatre World* Vol. 39.

+Succeeded by: 1. Angelo H. Fraboni 2. Darlene Wilson, Colleen Dunn, Amy N. Heggins, Leigh Webster, Sara Henry 3. James Hadley 4. Betsy Chang 5. Heidi Stallings (during vacation) 6. Carol Dilley 7. Gen Horiuchi, Lindsay Chambers 8. Keith Bernardo 9. Marty Benn (during illness) 10. David Hibbard 11. Jeanine Meyers 12. Andrew Pacho 13. Kayoko Yoshioka

Martha Swope Photos

Top: Liz Callaway
Left: Marlene Danielle

CRAZY FOR YOU

Music, George Gershwin; Lyrics, Ira Gershwin, Gus Kahn, Desmond Carter; Book, Ken Ludwig; Conception, Mr. Ludwig and Mike Ockrent, inspired by material by Guy Bolton and John McGowan; Director, Mr. Ockrent; Choreography, Susan Stroman; Orchestrations, William D. Brohn, Sid Ramin; Musical Director, Paul Gemignani; Musical Consultant, Tommy Krasker; Dance/Incidental Arrangements, Peter Howard; Sets, Robin Wagner; Costumes, William Ivey Long; Lighting, Paul Gallo; Sound, Otts Munderloh; Casting, Julie Hughes, Barry Moss; Cast Recording, Broadway Angel; Fights, B. H. Barry; Hairstylist, Angela Gari; General Manager, Gatchell & Neufeld; Prod. Manager, Peter Fulbright; Company Manager, Abbie M. Strassler; Stage Managers, Steven Zweigbaum, John Bonanni; Associate Producers, Richard Godwin, Valerie Gordon; Presented by Roger Horchow and Elizabeth Williams; Press, Bill Evans/Jim Randolph, Susan L. Schulman, Erin Dunn; Previewed from Friday, January 31, 1992; Opened in the Shubert Theatre on Wednesday, February 19, 1992*

CAST

Tess	Beth Leavel
Patsy	Stacey Logan
Bobby Child	Harry Groener
Bela Zanger	Bruce Adler
Sheila	Judine Hawkins Richard
Mitzi	Paula Legget
Susie	Ida Henry
Louise	Jean Marie
Betsy	Peggy Ayn Maas
Margie	Salome Mazard
Vera	Louise Ruck
Elaine	Pamela Everett
Irene Roth	Michele Pawk +1
Mother	Jane Connell
Perkins/Custus	Gerry Burkhardt
Moose	Brian M. Nalepka } The Manhattan
Mingo	Tripp Hanson } Rhythm
Sam	Hal Shane } Kings
Junior	Casey Nicholaw
Pete	Fred Anderson
Jimmy	Michael Kubala
Billy	Ray Roderick
Wyatt	Jeffrey Lee Broadhurst
Harry	Joel Goodness
Polly Baker	Jodi Benson +2
Everett Baker	Ronn Carroll +3
Lank Hawkins	John Hillner
Eugene	Stepehn Temperley
Patricia	Amelia White

UNDERSTUDIES: Michael Kubala (Bobby/Lank/Bela), Beth Leavel (Polly), Paula Leggett (Irene), Gerry Burkhardt (Everett), Amelia White (Mother), Casey Nicholaw (Eugene), Peggy Ayn Maas (Patsy), John Jellison (Everett/Eugene/Zangler), Ida Henry (Tess), Angelique Ilo (Patricia)

MUSICAL NUMBERS: Original sources follow in parentheses: K-ra-azy for You (*Treasure Girl,* 1928), I Can't Be Bothered Now (Film: *A Damsel in Distress,* 1937), Bidin' My Time (*Girl Crazy,* 1930), Things Are Looking Up (*A Damsel in Distress*), Could You Use Me (*Girl Crazy*), Shall We Dance (Film: *Shall We Dance,* 1937), Someone to Watch Over Me (*Oh Kay,* 1926), Slap That Bass (*Shall We Dance*), Embraceable You (*Girl Crazy*), Tonight's the Night (previously unused), I Got Rhythm (*Girl Crazy*), The Real American Folk Song is a Rag (*Ladies First,* 1918), What Causes That? (*Treasure Girl*), Naughty Baby (previously unused), Stiff Upper Lip (*A Damsel in Distress*), They Can't Take That Away From Me (*Shall We Dance*), But Not for Me (*Girl Crazy*), Nice Work If You Can Get It (*A Damsel in Distress*), Finale

A musical comedy, inspired by *Girl Grazy* (1930), in two acts with 17 scenes. The action takes place in New York City and Deadrock, Nevada, in the 1930s.

*Still playing May 31, 1994. Winer of 1992 "Tonys" for Best Musical, Best Choreography, and Best Costumes.

+Succeeded by: 1. Kay McClelland 2. Karen Ziemba 3. Carleton Carpenter

Joan Marcus Photos

Top: Karen Ziemba, Carleton Carpenter
Left: Karen Ziemba, Harry Groener, (top) Peggy Ayn Maas

74

GUYS AND DOLLS

A Musical Fable Of Broadway. Music/Lyrics, Frank Loesser; Book, Jo Swerling and Abe Burrows; Director, Jerry Zaks; Choreography, Christopher Chadman; Orchestrations, (original) George Bassman, Ted Royal, (new) Michael Starobin, Michael Gibson; Musical Supervision, Edward Strauss; Sets, Tony Walton; Costumes, William Ivey Long; Lighting, Paul Gallo; Dance Music, Mark Hummel; Sound, Tony Meola; Asst. Choreographer, Linda Haberman; Musical Coordinator, Seymour Red Press; Hairstylist, David H. Lawrence; Casting, Johnson-Liff & Zerman; Prod. Manager, Peter Fulbright; Company Manager, Marcia Goldberg; Stage Managers, Steven Beckler, Clifford Schwartz, Joe Deer; Cast Recording, RCA Victor; Executive Producer, David Strong Warner; Associate Producers, Playhouse Sq. Center, David B. Bode; Presented by Dodger Productions, Roger Berlind, Jujamcyn Theatres/TV ASAHI, Kardana Prod., and Kennedy Center for the Performing Arts; Press, Chris Boneau/Adrian Bryan-Brown, John Barlow, Jackie Green; Previewed from Monday, March 16, 1992; Opened in the Martin Beck Theatre on Tuesday, April 14, 1992*

CAST

Nicely-Nicely Johnson	Larry Cahn
Benny Southstreet	Adam Grupper
Rusty Charlie/Guy	Scott Wise +1
Sarah Brown	Josie de Guzman +2
Arvide Abernathy	Conrad McLaren
Agatha	Susan Rush +3
Calvin/Guy	Leslie Feagan
Martha	Kim Crosby +4
Harry the Horse	Ernie Sabella +5
Lt. Brannigan	Steve Ryan +6
Nathan Detroit	Jonathan Hadary +7
Angie the Ox/Joey Biltmore/Guy	Michael Brian +7
Miss Adelaide	Jennifer Allen
Sky Masterson	Tom Wopat +9
Hot Box MC/Guy	Michael Brian +10
Mimi/Doll	Tina DeLeone
Gen. Matilda B. Cartwright	Louisa Flaningam +11
Big Jule	Michael Goz +12
Drunk/Guy	Wade Williams
Waiter/Guy	Kenneth Kantor
Havana Dance Specialty	Sergio Trujillo, Nancy Lemenager
Crapshooter Dance Lead/Guy	Darren Lee
Guys	Andy Blankenbuehler, Michael Brian, Lloyd Culbreath, R. F. Daley, Randy Andre Davis, Mark Esposito, Leslie Feagan, Aldrin Gonzalez, Michael Goz, Kenneth Kantor, Darren Lee, John MacInnes, Stan Page, Michael Paternostro, Joey Pizzi, Kirk Ryder, Steven Sofia, Timothy Shew, Sergio Trujillo, Jerome Vivona, Wade Williams, Scott Wise
Dolls	Michelle Chase, Tina Marie DeLeone, Pascale Faye, Jennifer Lamberts, Nancy Lemenager, Greta Martin, Susan Misner, Holly Raye

UNDERSTUDIES: Wade Williams (Sky), Michael Brian (Nicely/Benny), Jeff Brooks (Harry/Benny/Nathan), Steve Ryan (Nathan), Leslie Feagan (Harry/Arvide), Michael Goz (Jule), Kenneth Kantor (Jule/Brannigan), Stan Page (Brannigan/Arvide), Timothy Shew (Brannigan/Nicely), Steven Sofia, Kirk Ryder (Calvin), R. F. Daley, John MacInnes (Rusty), Susan Rush (Cartwright), Susann Fletcher (Adelaide/Cartwright), Kim Crosby (Sarah/Agatha), Leah Hocking (Adelaide/Sarah/Cartwright/Agatha), Greta Martin (Mimi), Michelle Chase (Agatha/Martha), Nancy Lemenager (Martha/Mimi) SWINGS: Ms. Chase, Susan Misner, Michael Paternostro, Kirk Ryder, Mr. Sofia

MUSICAL NUMBERS: Fugue for Tinhorns, Follow the Fold, The Oldest Established, I'll Know, A Bushel and a Peck, Adelaide's Lament, Guys and Dolls, Havana, If I Were a Bell, My Time of Day, I've Never Been in Love Before, Take Back Your Mink, More I Cannot Wish You, Crapshooter's Dance, Luck Be a Lady, Sue Me, Sit Down You're Rockin' the Boat, Marry the Man Today, Finale

A new production of the 1950 musical in two acts with 17 scenes. The action takes place in "Runyonland" around Broadway and in Havana, Cuba. The original production (*Theatre World* Vol. 7) opened at the Forty-Sixth St. Theatre on Nov. 24, 1950 featuring Vivian Blaine, Robert Alda, Sam Levene, Isabel Bigley, and Stubby Kaye, running 1200 performances.

*Closed January 8, 1995 after 1,143 performances and 33 previews. Winner of 1992 "Tonys" for Best Revival, Best Actress—Musical (Faith Prince), Best Director—Musical, Best Scenic Design

+Succeeded by: 1. Dale Hensley, Tim Shew 2. Kim Crosby 3. Louisa Flaningam 4. Leslie Castay 5. Bob Amaral 6. Stephen Mendillo 7. Jamie Farr, Jeff Brooks 8. Michael Goz 9. Burke Moses, Martin Vidnovic 10. Stan Page 11. Ruth Williamson 12. Herschel Sparber, Ron Holgate

Martha Swope Photos

Burke Moses, Josie de Guzman
Top: Tom Wopat

KISS OF THE SPIDER WOMAN

Music, John Kander; Lyrics, Fred Ebb; Book, Terrence McNally; Based on the novel by Manuel Puig; Director, Harold Prince; Orchestrations, Michael Gibson; Musical Director, Jeffrey Huard; Dance Music, David Krane; Choreography, Vincent Paterson; Additional Choreography, Rob Marshall; Sets/Projections, Jerome Sirlin; Costumes, Florence Klotz; Lighting, Howell Bikley; Sound, Martin Levan; Mr. Prince's Assistant, Ruth Mitchell; Cast Recording (London), RCA; Casting, Johnson-Liff & Zerman; Company Manager, Jim Brandeberry; Stage Managers, Beverly Randolph, Clayton Phillips; Presented by Livent (U.S.); Press, Mary Bryant; Previewed from Monday, April 19, 1993; Opened in the Broadhurst Theatre on Monday, May 3, 1993*

CAST

Molina	Brent Carver +1
Warden	Herndon Lackey
Valentin	Anthony Crivello +2
Esteban	Philip Hernandez
Marcos	Michael McCormick
Spider Woman/Aurora	Chita Rivera +3
Aurora's Men/Prisoners	Keith McDaniel +4, Robert Montano, Dan O'Grady, Raymond Rodriguez
Prisoner	Darius de Haas
Molina's Mother	Merle Louise
Marta	Kirsti Carnahan
Escaping Prisoner	Colton Green
Religious Fanatic/Prisoner	John Norman Thomas
Amnesty Int'l Obserber/Prisoner Emilio	Joshua Finkel
Prisoner Fuentes	Gary Schwartz
Gabriel/Prisoner	Jerry Christakos
Window Dresser at Montoya's/Prisoner	Aurelio Padron +5

STANDBYS/UNDERSTUDIES: Nancy Hess (Spider Woman/Aurora), Juan Chioran (Molina), Barbara Andres (Mother), Judy McLane (Marta), Joshua Finkel (Molina), Philip Hernandez (Valentin), Gary Schwartz (Esteban), John Norman Thomas (Marcos), Michael McCormick (Warden), Dan O'Grady (Gabriel) SWINGS: Richard Montoya, Colton Green, David Marques

MUSICAL NUMBERS: Prologue, Her Name Is Aurora, Over the Wall, Bluebloods, Dressing Them Up/I Draw the Line, Dear One, Where You Are, Marta, Come, I Do Miracles, Gabriel's Letter/My First Woman, Morphine Tango, You Could Never Shame Me, A Visit, She's a Woman, Gimme Love, Russian Movie/Good Times, The Day After That, Mama It's Me, Anything for Him, Kiss of the Spider Woman, Only in the Movies

A musical in two acts with 19 scenes and prologue. The action takes place in a prison in Latin America, sometime in the recent past.

*Closed July 2, 1995, after 906 performances and 16 previews. Winner of 1993 "Tony" Awards for Best Musical, Leading Actor in a Musical (Brent Carver), Leading Actress in a Musical (Chita Rivera), Featured Actor in a Musical (Anthony Crivello), Book of a Musical, Costume Design, and Best Score (tie). Winner of New York Drama Critics Circle for Best Musical.

+Succeeded by: 1. Jeff Hyslop, Howard McGillin 2. Brian Mitchell 3. Carol Lawrence (during vacation), Vanessa Williams 4. Gregory Mitchell 5. Roberto Montano

Top: Jeff Hyslop, Chita Rivera, Anthony Crivello
Center: Chita Rivera
Left: Chita Rivera, Jeff Hyslop

LES MISERABLES

By Alain Boublil and Claude-Michel Schonberg; Based on the novel by Victor Hugo; Music, Mr. Schonberg; Lyrics, Herbert Kretzmer; Original French Text, Mr. Boublil and Jean-Marc Natel; Additional Material, James Fenton; Direction/Adaptation, Trevor Nunn and John Caird; Orchestral Score, John Cameron; Musical Supervisor, Robert Billig; Musical Director, Tom Helm; Design, John Napier; Lighting, David Hersey; Costumes, Andreane Neofitou; Casting, Johnson-Liff & Zerman; Original Cast Recording, Geffen; General Manager, Alan Wasser; Company Manager, Robert Nolan; Stage Managers, Marybeth Abel, Mary Fran Loftus, Gregg Kirsopp; Executive Producer, Martin McCallum; Presented by Cameron Mackintosh; Press, Marc Thibodeau/Merle Frimark; Previewed from Saturday, February 28; Opened in the Broadway Theatre on Thursday, March 12, 1987*, and moved to the Imperial Theatre on October 16, 1990.

CAST

PROLOGUE: Don Cook +1 (Jean Valjean), Chuck Wagner +2 (Javert), Rob Evan, Joel Robertson, Michael X. Martin, Ken Krugman, Matt McClanahan, Drew Eshelman, Ron Bohmer, Michael Berry, Craig Rubano (Chain Gang), Bryan Landrine (Farmer), Mr. Krugman (Labourer), Lucille DeCristofaro (Innkeeper's Wife), Gary Lynch (Innkeeper), Nicholas F. Saverine (Bishop), Tom Donoghue, Paul Avedidian (Constables)

MONTREUIL-SUR-MER 1823: Donna Kane +3 (Fantine), Mr. Robertson (Foreman), Mr. Landrine, Mr. McClanahan (Workers), Jean Fitzgibbons, Nicola Boyer, Connie Kunkle, Dianne Della Piazza (Women Workers), Jessie Janet Richards (Factory Girl), Mr. Berry, Mr. Evan, Mr. McClanahan (Sailors), Ms. DeCristofaro, Ms. Della Piazza, Ms. Kunkle, Gina Feliccia, Ms. Richards, Sarah Uriarte, Jennifer Lee Andrews, Jessica-Snow Wilson (Whores), Ms. Fitzgibbons (Old Woman), Ms. Boyer (Crone), Mr. Saverine (Pimp/Fauchelevent), Mr. Martin (Bamatabois)

MONTFERMEIL 1823: Lacey Chabert, Jessica Scholl, Savannah Wise (Young Cosette/Young Eponine), Evalyn Baron +4 (Mme. Thenardier), Drew Eshelman (Thenardier), Mr. Landrine (Drunk), Mr. Krugman, Ms. Snow-Wilson (Young Couple), Mr. Lynch (Drunk), Paul Avedisian, Ms. Della Piazza (Diners), Mr. Saverine, Mr. Martin, Mr. Evan, Ms. Fitzgibbons, Ms. Richards, Ms. DeCristofaro (Drinkers), Mr. Berry (Young Man), Ms. Kunkle, Ms. Feliccia (Young Girls), Ms. Boyer, Mr. McClanahan (Old Couple), Mr. Robertson, Mr. Donohue (Travelers)

PARIS 1832: Sean Russell, Brandon Espinoza (Gavroche), Ms. DeCristofaro (Beggar Woman), Ms. Richards (Young Prostitute), Mr. Lynch (Pimp), Tia Riebling +5 (Eponine), Mr. Krugman (Montparnasse), Mr. Donoghue (Babet), Mr. Evan (Brujon), Mr. Saverine (Claquesous), Lawrence Anderson +6 (Enjolras), Michael Sutherland Lynch +7 (Marius), Jennifer Lee Andrews (Cosette), Mr. Robertson (Combeferre), Mr. Berry (Feuilly), Mr. Landrine (Courfeyrac), Mr. McClanahan (Joly), Mr. Martin (Grantaire), Mr. Avedisian (Lesgles), Mr. Lynch (Jean Prouvaire)

UNDERSTUDIES: Joel Robertson, Bryan Landrine, Nicholas F. Saverine (Valjean), Gary Lynch, Michael X. Martin (Javert), Paul Avedisian, Joseph Kolinski, Wayne Scherzer (Bishop), Connie Kunkle, Jean Fitzgibbons (Fantine), Ken Krugman, Mr. Saverine (Thenardier), Ms. Fitzgibbons, Nicola Boyer (Mme. Thenardier), Gina Feliccia, Jessica Snow-Wilson (Eponine/Cosette), Tom Donoghue, Matt McClanahan (Marius), Mr. Avedisian, Michael Berry (Enjolras), Lacey Chabert (Gavroche) SWINGS: Mark Hardy, Christa Justus, Joseph Kolinski, Kerrianne Spellman

MUSICAL NUMBERS: Prologue, Soliloquy, At the End of the Day, I Dreamed a Dream, Lovely Ladies, Who Am I?, Come to Me, Castle on a Cloud, Master of the House, Thenardier Waltz, Look Down, Stars, Red and Black, Do You Hear the People Sing?, In My Life, A Heart Full of Love, One Day More, On My Own, A Little Fall of Rain, Drink with Me to Days Gone By, Bring Him Home, Dog Eats Dog, Soliloquy, Turning, Empty Chairs at Empty Tables, Wedding Chorale, Beggars at the Feast, Finale

A dramatic musical in two acts with 4 scenes and prologue.

*Still playing May 31, 1994. Winner of 1987 "Tonys" for Best Musical, Best Score, Best Book, Best Featured Actor and Actress in a Musical (Michael Maguire, Frances Ruffelle), Direction of a Musical, Scenic Design, and Lighting.

+ Succeeded by: 1. Craig Schulman, J. Mark McVey, David "Dudu" Fisher, Don Cook 2. Robert Cuccioli 3. Andrea McArdle 4. Diana Rogers 5. Lea Salonga, Sarah Uriarte 6. Ron Bohmer 7. Craig Rubano

Joan Marcus Photos

Top: Craig Schulman
Left: David Fisher

MISS SAIGON

Music, Claude-Michel Schonberg; Lyrics, Richard Maltby, Jr., Alain Boublil; Adapted from Boublil's French lyrics; Book, Mr. Boublil, Mr. Schonberg; Additional Material, Mr. Maltby, Jr.; Director, Nicholas Hytner; Musical Staging, Bob Avian; Orchestrations, William D. Brohn; Musical Supervisors, David Caddick, Robert Billig; Associate Director, Mitchell Lemsky; Design, John Napier; Lighting, David Hersey; Costumes, Andreane Neofitou, Suzy Benzinger; Sound, Andrew Bruce; Conductor, Dale Rieling; Stage Managers, Tom Capps, Karl Lengel, Mahlon Kruse; Cast Recording (London), Geffen; Presented by Cameron Mackintosh; Press, Fred Nathan/Marc Thibodeau, Merle Frimark; Previewed from Saturday, March 23, 1991; Opened in the Broadway Theatre on Thursday, April 11, 1991*

CAST

SAIGON - 1975
The Engineer..Herman Sebek +1
Kim...Leila Florentino +2, Annette Calud +3
Gigi...Sharon Leal
Mimi...Zoie Lam
Yvette...Imelda De Los Reyes
Yvonne..Mirla Criste
Bar Girls ....Emy Baysic, Margaret Ann Gates, Christine Langer,
                Cheri Nakamura, Melanie Mariko Tojio, Elizabeth Paw,
                                                              Roxanne Taga
Chris...Christopher Peccaro +4
John..Timothy Robert Blevins +5
Marines ....Yancey Arias, Robert Bartley, Craig Bennett, Randy Bettis,
                Tony Capone, Alvin Crawford, Matthew Dickens,
                Jay Douglas, Michael Gruber, Jamie, Eric Kunze,
                Kevin Neil McReady, Leonard Joseph, Paul Matsumoto,
                Matthew Pedersen, Jeff Reid, Bruce Winant, Welly Yang
Barmen ....Zar Acayan, Alan Ariano, Eric Chang, Ming Lee
Vietnamese Customers ....Tito Abeleda, Francis J. Cruz, Darrell Autor,
                Rob Narita, Ray Santos, Corey Smith, Nephi Jay Wimmer
Army Nurse ....Alisa Gyse Dickens +6
Thuy...Jason Ma +7
Embassy Workers, Vendors, etc. ....Company

HO CHI MINH CITY (Formerly Saigon)-April 1978
Ellen..Jane Bodle +8
Tam.....................................Kailip Boonrai, Melanie Carabuena +9
Guards...Mr. Cruz, Mr. Narita
Dragon Acrobats ....Mr. Autor, Mr. Gruber, Mr. Smith
Asst. Commissar...Mr. Arias +10
Soldiers.................Mr. Abeleda, Mr. Acayan, Mr. Ariano, Mr. Chan,
                Mr. Matsumoto, Mr. Santos, Mr. Smith, Mr. Wimmer
Citizens, Refugees ....Company

USA - September 1978
Conference Delegates..Company

BANGKOK - October 1978
Hustlers................Mr. Acayan, Mr. Arias, Mr. Chan, Mr. Matsumoto,
                Mr. Santos, Mr.Smith, Mr. Wimmer, Mr. Yang
Moulin Rouge Owner...Mr. Cruz
Inhabitants, Bar Girls, Vendors, Tourists ....Company

SAIGON - April 1975
Shultz ....Craig Bennett +11
Doc ....Eric Kunze +12
Reeves..Alvin Crawford
Gibbons...Kevin Neal McCready
Troy..Leonard Joseph
Nolen...Jamie
Huston ....Matthew Pederson
Frye ....Matthew Dickens +13
Marines, Vietnamese ....Company

BANGKOK - October 1978
Inhabitants, Moulin Rouge Customers.....................................Company

UNDERSTUDIES: Ming Lee, Paul Matsumoto, Rob Narita, Ray Santos (Engineer), Imelda de los Reyes, Elizabeth Paw, Roxanne Taga (Kim), Robert Bartley, Tony Capone, Jay Douglas (Chris), Alvin Crawford, Leonard Joseph (John), Misty Cotton, Sharon Leal (Ellen), Marc Oka, Welly Yang (Thuy) SWINGS: Sylvia Dohi, Henry Menendez, Marc Oka, Rocker Verastique, Todd Zamarripa

MUSICAL NUMBERS: The Heat is on in Saigon, Movie in My Mind, The Transaction, Why God Why?, Sun and Moon, The Telephone, The Ceremony, Last Night of the World, Morning of the Dragon, I Still Believe, Back in Town, You Will Not Touch Him, If You Want to Die in Bed, I'd Give My Life for You, Bui-Doi, What a Waste, Please, Guilt Inside Your Head, Room 317, Now That I've Seen Her, Confrontation, The American Dream, Little God of My Heart

A musical in two acts. The action takes place in Saigon, Bangkok, and the USA between 1975 and 1979.

*Still playing May 31, 1994. Winner of 1991 "Tonys" for Leading Actor in a Musical (Jonathan Pryce), Leading Actress in a Musical (Lea Salonga) and Featured Actor in a Musical (Hinton Battle). The show passed its 1000th performance during the season.

+ Succeeded by: 1. Raul Aranas 2. Rona Figueroa 3. Emy Baysic 4. Jarrod Emick, Eric Kunze 5. Keith Byron Kirk 6. Misty Cotton 7. Yancey Arias 8. Candese Marchese, Tami Tappan 9. Nicholas Chan, Keith Hong 10. Welly Yang 11. Bruce Winant 12. Tony Capone, Erik Bates 13. Jay Douglas

Joan Marcus/Michael LePoer Trench Photos

Top: Rona Figueroa, Jarrod Emick
Below: Herman Sebek

THE PHANTOM OF THE OPERA

Music, Andrew Lloyd Webber; Lyrics, Charles Hart; Additional Lyrics, Richard Stilgoe; Book, Mr. Stilgoe, Mr. Lloyd Webber; Director, Harold Prince; Musical Staging/Choreography, Gillian Lynne; Orchestrations, David Cullen, Mr. Lloyd Webber; Based on the novel by Gaston Leroux; Design, Maria Bjornson; Lighting, Andrew Bridge; Sound, Martin Levan; Musical Direction/Supervision, David Caddick; Conductor, Jack Gaughan; Casting, Johnson-Liff & Zerman; General Manager, Alan Wasser; Company Manager, Michael Gill; Stage Managers, Steve McCorkle, Bethe Ward, Richard Hester, Barbara-Mae Phillips; Presented by Cameron Mackintosh and The Really Useful Theatre Co.; Press, Merle Frimark, Marc Thibodeau; Previewed from Saturday, January 9, 1988; Opened in the Majestic Theatre on Tuesday, January 26, 1988*

CAST

The Phantom of the Opera ....Marcus Lovett
Christine Daae ....Mary D'Arcy +1
                              Luann Aronson (Mon/Thur. eves.)
Raoul, Vicomte de Chagny....................................Hugh Panaro +2
Carlotta Giudicelli..Elena Jeanne Batman
Monsieur Andre ....Jeff Keller
Monsieur Firmin ....George Lee Andrews
Madame Giry..Leila Martin +3
Ubaldo Piangi ....Gary Rideout +4
Meg Giry..Tener Brown
M. Rever ....Thomas James O'Leary
Auctioneer ....Richard Warren Pugh
Porter/Marksman ....Gary Lindemann
M. Lefevre...Kenneth Waller
Joseph Buquet...Philip Steele
Don Attilio/Passarino..Peter Atherton
Slave Master...Thomas Terry +5
Solo Dancer ....Thomas Terry
Flunky/Stagehand ....Jack Hayes
Policeman...Paul Laureano +6
Page ....Patrice Pickering
Porter/Fireman ....Maurizio Corbino
Spanish Lady ....Diane Ketchie +7
Wardrobe Mistress/Confidante ....Mary Leigh Stahl
Princess..Raissa Katona
Madame Firmin ....Dawn Leigh Stone +8
Innkeeper's Wife ....Teresa Eldh
Ballet Chorus of the Opera Populaire ....Harriet M. Clark, Alina Hernandez, Cherylyn Jones, Lori MacPherson, Tania Philip, Kate Solmssen, Christine Spizzo

UNDERSTUDIES: Jeff Keller, Ciaran Sheehan (Phantom), Raissa Katona, Laurie Gayle Stephenson (Christine), Gary Lindemann, James Romick (Raoul), Peter Atherton, Paul Laureano (Firmin), Richard Warren Pugh (Firmin/Piangi), George Lee Andrews, James Thomas O'Leary, Mr. Romick (Andre), Marcy DeGonge-Manfredi, Teresa Eldh, Melody Johnson (Carlotta), Patrice Pickering, Mary Leigh Stahl (Giry), Maurizio Corbino (Piangi), Cherilyn Jones, Kate Solmssen, Lori MacPherson (Meg), Thomas Terry (Master) Paul B. Sadler, Jr. (Dancer)

MUSICAL NUMBERS: Think of Me, Angel of Music, Little Lotte/The Mirror, Phantom of the Opera, Music of the Night, I Remember/Stranger Than You Dreamt It, Magical Lasso, Notes/Prima Donna, Poor Fool He Makes Me Laugh, Why Have You Brought Me Here?/Raoul I've Been There, All I Ask of You, Masquerade/Why So Silent?, Twisted Every Way, Wishing You Were Somehow Here Again, Wandering Child/Bravo Bravo, Point of No Return, Down Once More/Track Down This Murderer, Finale

A musical in two acts with 19 scenes and a prologue. The action takes place in and around the Paris Opera house, 1881–1911.

*Still playing May 31, 1994. Winner of 1988 "Tonys" for Best Musical, Leading Actor in a Musical (Michael Crawford), Featured Actress in a Musical (Judy Kaye), Direction of a Musical, Scenic Design, and Lighting. The title role has been played by Michael Crawford, Timothy Nolen, Cris Groendaal, Steve Barton, Jeff Keller, Kevin Gray, Marc Jacoby and Marcus Lovett as of May 1994.

+Succeeded by: 1. Tracy Shayne 2. Ciaran Sheehan 3. Kristina Marie Guiguet 4. Frederic Heringes 5. Paul B. Sadler, Jr. 6. Thomas Sandri 7. Marci DeGonge-Manfredi 8. Melody Johnson

Joan Marcus Photos

Top: Marcus Lovett
Right: The company

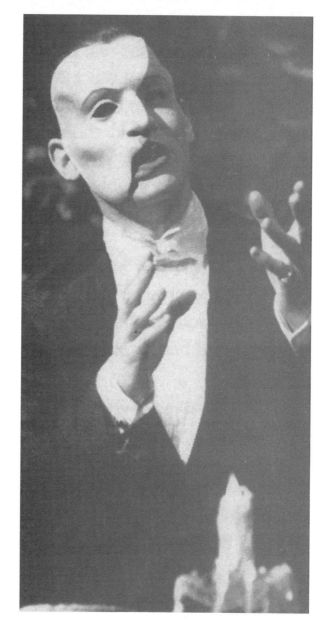

THE SISTERS ROSENSWEIG

By Wendy Wasserstein; Director, Dan Sullivan; Sets, John Lee Beatty; Costumes, Jane Greenwood; Lighting, Pat Collins; Sound, Guy Sherman/Aural Fixation; Casting, Daniel Swee; General Manager, Steven C. Callahan; Production Manager, Jeff Hamlin; Stage Managers, Roy Harris, Elise-Ann Konstantin; Produced by Lincoln Center Theater (Andre Bishop, Bernard Gersten, Directors); Press, Merle Debuskey/Susan Chicoine; Previewed from Tuesday, March 2, 1993; Opened in the Ethel Barrymore Theatre on Thursday, March 18, 1993*

CAST

Tess Goode	Julie Dretzin +1
Pfeni Rosensweig	Christine Estabrook +2
Sara Goode	Jane Alexander +3
Geoffrey Duncan	John Vickery +4
Mervyn Kant	Robert Klein +5
Gorgeous Teitelbaum	Madeline Kahn +6
Tom Valiunus	Patrick Fitzgerald +7
Nicholas Pym	John Cunningham +8

STANDBYS: Chiara Peacock (Tess), Robin Moseley (Sara/Pfeni), Lucy Martin (Gorgeous/Sara), Stephen Stout (Geoffrey/Nicholas), Stan Lachow (Mervyn/Nicholas), Jonathan Friedman (Tom)

A comedy in two acts. The action takes place in a sitting room in Queen Anne's Gate, London, during August, 1991.

*Closed July 16, 1994, after 556 performances and 18 previews at the Barrymore, preceeded by 142 performances and 29 previews Off-Broadway. Winner of 1993 "Tony" for Leading Actress in a Play (Madeline Kahn).

Succeded by: 1. Amy Ryan 2. Joanne Camp 3. Michael Learned 4. Tom Hewitt 5. Hal Linden, Tony Roberts 6. Linda Lavin 7. Brian F. O'Byrne 8. Rex Robbins

Martha Swope Photos

Top: Linda Lavin, Hal Linden, Michael Learned

Bottom Left: Julie Dretzin, Robert Klein, Patrick Fitzgerald, John Vickery

Bottom Right: Joanne Camp, Tom Hewitt

THE WHO'S TOMMY

Music/Lyrics, Pete Townshend; Book, Mr. Townshend, Des McAnuff; Director, Mr. McAnuff; Additional Music/Lyrics, John Entwistle, Keith Moon; Choreography, Wayne Cilento; Orchestrations, Steve Margoshes; Musical Supervision/Direction, Joseph Church; Musical Coordinator, John Miller; Sets, John Arnone; Costumes, David C. Woolard; Lighting, Chris Parry; Projections, Wendall K. Harrington; Sound, Steve Canyon Kennedy; Video, Batwin + Robin Productions; Hairstylist, David H. Lawrence; Special Effects, Gregory Meeh; Flying by Foy; Fights, Steve Rankin; Cast Recording, RCA; Company Manager, Sandy Carlson; Stage Managers, Frank Hartenstein, Karen Armstrong; Executive Producers, David Strong, Warner, Inc., Scott Zieger/Gary Gunas; Associate Producer, John F. Kennedy Center for the Performing Arts; Presented by PACE Theatrical Group and DODGER Productions with Kardana Productions; Press, Chris Boneau/Adrian Bryan-Brown/Susanne Tighe; Previewed from Monday, March 29, 1993; Opened in the St. James Theatre on Thursday, April 22, 1993*

CAST

Mrs. Walker ....Marcia Mitzman +1
Captain Walker...Jonathan Dokuchitz
Uncle Ernie ....Paul Kandel
Minister/Mr. Simpson ....Bill Buell
Minister's Wife ....Jody Gelb +2
Nurse ....Lisa Leguillou
Officer #1/Hawker...Michael McElroy +3
Officer #2..Timothy Warmen +4
Allied Soldier #1/1st Pinball Lad ....Donnie Kehr +5
Allied Soldier #2...Michael Arnold +6
Lover/Harmonica Player ....Lee Morgan
Tommy, Age 4 ....Carly Jane Steinborn +7,Crysta Macalush +8
                                        (alternating performances)
Tommy ....Michael Cerveris
Judge/Kevin's Father/News Vendor/DJ ....Tom Flynn +9
Tommy, Age 10 ....Buddy Smith +10
Cousin Kevin ....Anthony Barrile
Kevin's Mother...Maria Calabrese +11
Local Lads/Security Guards ....Mr. Arnold, Adrian Bailey, Paul Dobie,
              Aaron Ellis, Matthew Farnsworth, Christian Hoff, Mr. Kehr,
              Mr. McElroy, Clarke Thorell, Mr. Warmen, Matt Zarley
Local Lasses...............Ms. Calabrese, Tracy Nicole Chapman, Angela Garrison,
              Lacey Hornkohl, Pam Klinger, Lisa Leguillou,
              April Nixon, Alice Ripley, Sherie Scott
The Gypsy..Cheryl Freeman
2nd Pinball Lad ....Christian Hoff +12
Specialist ....Norm Lewis +13
Specialist's Assistant ....Alice Ripley +14
Sally Simpson ....Sherie Scott +15
Mrs. Simpson..Pam Klinger
Ensemble..........................Mr. Arnold, Mr. Buell, Ms. Calabrese, Ms. Chapman,
              Mr. Dobie, Mr. Flynn, Ms. Gelb, Mr. Hoff, Mr. Kehr,
              Ms. Klinger, Ms. Leguillou, Mr. Lewis, Mr. McElroy,
              Mr. Morgan, Ms. Ripley, Ms. Scott, Mr. Warmen SUC-
              CEEDING COMPANY: Adrian Bailey, Steven Cates,
              Aaron Ellis, Matthew Farnsworth, Angela Garrison,
              Lacey Hornkohl, Pam Klinger, Lisa Leguillou, Sara Miles,
              Jeanine Morick, April Nixon, Tom Rocco, Clarke Thorell,
              Matt Zarley

UNDERSTUDIES: Donnie Kehr, Roman Fruge, Peter Ermides, Matt Zarley (Tommy/Cousin Kevin), Ari Vernon (Tommy, 10), Alice Ripley, Jody Gelb, Angela Garrison (Mrs. Walker), Paul Dobie, Timothy Warmen, Todd Hunter, Matthew Farnsworth (Walker), Bill Buell, Tom Flynn, Tom Rocco (Ernie), Tracy Langran, Nicole Chapman, April Nixon (Gypsy) SWINGS: Victoria Lecta Cave, Roman Fruge, Todd Hunter, Tracey Langran, Joyce Chittick, Peter Ermides, Doug Friedman, Troy Myers

MUSICAL NUMBERS: Overture, Captain Walker, It's a Boy, We've Won, Twenty-One, Amazing Journey, Sparks, Christmas, See Me Feel Me, Do You Think It's Alright, Fiddle About, Cousin Kevin, Sensation, Eyesight to the Blind, Acid Queen, Pinball Wizard, Underture (Entr'act), There's a Doctor, Go to the Mirror, Listening to You, Tommy Can You Hear Me, I Believe My Own Eyes (new song), Smash the Mirror, I'm Free, Miracle Cure, Tommy's Holiday Camp, Sally Simpson, Welcome, We're Not Going to Take It, Finale

A musical in two acts with 22 scenes. The action takes place mostly in London 1941–63. *Tommy* originated as a 1969 rock opera album.

Top: Michael Cerveris, Carly Jane Steinborn
Bottom: Paul Kandel

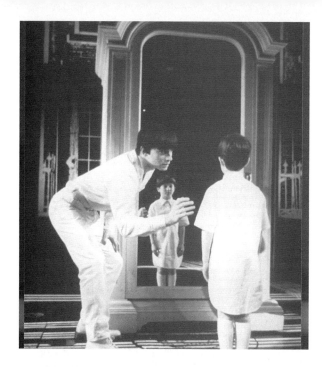

*Closed June 17, 1995, after 899 performances and 28 previews. Winner of 1993 "Tonys" for Direction of a Musical, Scenic Design, Lighting Design, Choreography, and Best Score (tie).

+Succeeded by: 1. Laura Dean 2. Jeanine Morick 3. Adrian Bailey 4. Matthew Farnsworth 5. Matt Zarley 6. Aaron Ellis 7. Kimberly Hannon 8. Nicole Zeidman 9. Tom Rocco 11. Sara Miles 12. Clarke Thorell 13. Steven Cates 14. Angela Garrison 15. Lacey Hornkohl

Marcus/Bryan-Brown Photos

OFF-BROADWAY PRODUCTIONS FROM PAST SEASONS THAT PLAYED THROUGH THIS SEASON

BEAU JEST

By James Sherman; Director, Dennis Zacek; Design, Bruce Goodrich; Costumes, Dorothy Jones; Lighting, Edward R. F. Matthews; Company Manager, Laura Heller; Stage Manager, Jana Llynn; Presented by Athur Cantor, Carol Ostrow, Libby Adler Mages; Press, Mr. Cantor; Opened at the Lambs Theatre on Wednesday, October 2, 1991*

CAST

Sara Goldman...Cindy Katz +1
Chris...William Robert Doyle
Bob...Jeffrey Edward Peters +2
Joel...Larry Fleischman +3
Miriam...Catherine Wolf +4
Abe...Bernie Landis +5

UNDERSTUDIES: Paul Amodeo (Chris/Bob/Joel), Laura Patinkin (Sarah), Paul Stolarsky (Abe), Arlene Sterne (Miriam)

A comedy in three acts. The action takes place in Sarah's apartment in the Lincoln Park area of Chicago, Illinois.

*Closed May 1, 1994, after 1077 performances.

+Succeeded by: 1. Eliza Foss 2. Sal Viviano, Jordan Leeds 3. Anthony Brienza 4. Molly Stark 5. Merwin Goldsmith

Carol Rosegg/Martha Swope Photos

Eliza Foss, Sal Viviano in *Beau Jest*

THE FANTASTICKS

Music, Harvey Schmidt; Lyrics/Book, Tom Jones; Director, Word Baker; Original Musical Director/Arrangements, Julian Stein; Design, Ed Wittstein; Musical Director, Dorothy Martin; Stage Managers, Kim Moore, James Cook, Steven Michael Daly, Christopher Scott; Presented by Lore Noto; Associate Producers, Sheldon Baron, Dorothy Olim, Jules Field, Cast Recording, MGM/Polydor; Opened in the Sullivan Street Playhouse on Tuesday, May 3, 1960*

CAST

The Boy...Richard Roland
The Girl...Debbie Pavlenka +1
The Girl's Father...William Tost
The Boy's Father...Gordon Jones
Narrator/El Gallo...Kim Moore
Mute...Christopher Scott
Old Actor...Bryan Hull
Man Who Dies...Joel Bernstein

MUSICAL NUMBERS: Overture, Try to Remember, Much More, Metaphor, Never Say No, It Depends on What You Pay, Soon It's Gonna Rain, Abduction Ballet, Happy Ending, This Plumb is Too Ripe, I Can See It, Plant a Radish, Round and Round, They Were You, Finale

A musical in two acts.

*Still playing May 31, 1994. The world's longest running musical has passed its 14,000th performance.

+Succeeded by: 1. Natasha Harper

Chuck Pulin Photo

William Tost, Gordon Jones in *Fantasticks*

FOREVER PLAID

Written/Directed/Choreographed by Stuart Ross; Music/Lyrics, Various; Musical Arrangements/Continuity/Supervision, James Raitt; Sets, Neil Peter Jampolis; Lighting, Jane Reisman; Costumes, Debra Stein; Musical Director, David Chase; Sound, Marc Salzberg; Original Cast Recording, RCA; Stage Manager, Connie Drew; Presented by Gene Wolsk in association with Allen M. Shore and Steven Suskin; Press, Shirley Herz/Miller Wright, Glenna Freedman, Sam Rudy; Opened in Steve McGraw's on Friday, May 4, 1990*

CAST

Jinx..Ryan Perry
Smudge ....Tom Cianfichi
Sparky ....Daniel Eli Friedman
Francis...Robert Lambert, Drew Geraci

ALTERNATES: Paul Castree, Drew Geraci, Steve Gunderson, Nick Locilento

MUSICAL NUMBERS: Anniversary Song, Catch a Falling Star, Chain Gang, Crazy 'bout ya Baby, Cry, Day-O, Dream Along with Me, Gotta Be This or That, Heart and Soul, Jamaica Farewell, Kingston Market, Lady of Spain (Ed Sullivan Show spoof), Love is a Many Splendored Thing, Magic Moments, Matilda, Moments to Remember, No Not Much, Papa Loves Mambo, Perfidia, Rags to Riches, Round and Round, Shangri-La, She Loves You, Sing to Me Mr. C, Sixteen Tons, Temptation, Theme from The Good The Bad The Ugly, Three Coins in the Fountain, Undecided

A musical for the "good guys" performed without intermission. The action takes place in 1964 and now.

*Closed June 12, 1994.

Jerry Dalia Photo

Robert Lambert in *Forever Plaid*

NUNSENSE

Music/Lyrics/Book/Direction by Dan Goggin; Choreography, Felton Smith; Sets, Barry Axtell; Lighting, Susan A. White; Musical Director, Michael Rice; General Manager, Roger Alan Gindi; Casting, Joseph Abaldo; Stage Managers, Paul Botchis, Nancy Wernick; Original Cast Recording, DRG; Presented by The Nunsense Theatrical Co. in association with Joseph Hoesl, Bill Crowder, & Jay Cardwell; Press, Shirley Herz/Pete Sanders, Glenna Freedman, Sam Rudy, Miller Wright, Robert Larkin; Opened in the Cherry Lane Theatre on Tuesday, December 3, 1985*, then transfered to Circle Repertory Theatre and then to the Douglas Fairbanks Theatre

1993-94 CASTS

Dody Goodman	Terri White	Denise Lor
Julie J. Hafner	Terri Mazzarella	Alvetta Guess
Jennifer Perry	Lin Tucci	Sarah Knapp
Jennifer Jay Myers	Alicia Miller	Valerie DePena

MUSICAL NUMBERS: Nunsense is Habit-Forming, A Difficult Transition, Benedicte, Biggest Ain't the Best, Playing Second Fiddle, So You Want to Be a Nun, Turn Up the Spotlight, Lilacs Bring Back Memories, Tackle That Temptation with a Time Step, Growing Up Catholic, We've Got to Clean Out the Freezer, Just a Coupl'a Sisters, Soup's On, Dying Nun Ballet, I Just Want to Be a Star, The Drive In, I Could've Gone to Nashville, Gloria in Excelsis Deo, Holier Than Thou, Finale

A musical in two acts. The action takes place in Mt. Saint Helen's School Auditorium in Hoboken, New Jersey, at the present time.

*Closed October 16, 1994, after 3,672 performances.

Carol Rosegg Photos

Denise Lor in *Nunsense*

PERFECT CRIME

By Warren Manzi; Director, Jeffrey Hyatt; Set, Chris Pickart; Costumes, Barbara Blackwood; Lighting, Patrick Eagleton; Sound, David Lawson; Stage Manager, George E. M. Kelly; Press, Michelle Vinvents, Paul Lewis, Jeffrey Clarke; Opened in the Courtyard Playhouse on April 18, 1987*, and later transferred to the Second Stage, 47th St. Playhouse, Intar, Harold Clurman Theatre, and since January 3, 1991, Theatre Four

CAST

Margaret Thorne Brent ....Catherine Russell
James Ascher...Warren Manzi
Lionel McAuley ....Trip Hamilton/J. A. Nelson
W. Harrison Brent ....Graeme Malcolm/Mark Johannes
David Breuer ....Dean Gardner

A mystery.

*Still playing May 31, 1994.

Catherine Russell in *Perfect Crime*

TONY N' TINA'S WEDDING

By Artificial Intelligence; Conception, Nancy Cassaro (Artistic Director); Director, Larry Pellegrini; Supervisory Director, Julie Cesari; Musical Director, Lynn Portas; Choreography, Hal Simons; Design/Decor, Randall Thropp; Costumes/Hairstyles/Makeup, Juan DeArmas; General Manager, Leonard A. Mulhern; Company Managers, James Hannah; Stage Managers, Bernadette McGay, W. Bart Ebbink; Presented by Joseph Corcoran & Daniel Cocoran; Press, David Rothenberg/Terence Womble; Opened in the Washington Square Church & Carmelita's on Saturday, February 6, 1988*

CAST

Valentia Lynne Nunzio, the bride ....Sharon Angela +1
Anthony Angelo Nunzio, the groom...Lee Mazzilli +2
Connie Mocogni, maid of honor...Susan Laurenzi
Barry Wheeler, best man..Timothy Monagan
Donna Marsala, bridesmaid...Susan Campanero
Dominick Fabrizzi, usher...Joseph Barbara
Marina Gulino, bridesmaid..Cheryl Giuliano
Johnny Nunzio, usher/brother of groom ....Nick Gambella
Josephine Vitale, mother of the bride...Victoria Barone
Joseph Vitale, brother of the bride ....Richard Falzone
Luigi Domenico, great uncle of the bride ....Stan Winston
Rose Domenico, aunt of the bride ....Cayte Thorpe
Sister Albert Maria, cousin of bride...Fran Gennuso
Anthony Angelo Nunzio, Sr., father of groom ....Dan Grimaldi
Madeline Monroe, Mr. Nunzio's girlfriend ....Karen Cellini
Grandma Nunzio, grandmother to groom ....Elaine Unnold
Michael Just, Tina's ex-boyfriend...Anthony T. Lauria
Father Mark, parish priest...Gary Schneider
Vinnie Black, caterer...Tom Karlya
Loretta Black, wife of the caterer...Victoria Constan
Mick Black, brother of the caterer...Robert R. Oliver
Nikki Black, daughter of the caterer...Jodi Grant
Mikie Black, son of the caterer..John Walter
Pat Black, sister of the caterer...Maria Gentile
Rick Demarco, the video man...Kerry Logan
Sal Antonucci, the photographer..Tony Patellis

An environmental theatre production. The action takes place at a wedding and reception.

*Still playing May 31, 1994, after moving to St. John's Church and Vinnie Black's Coliseum.

+Succeeded by: 1. Justine Rossi 2. Robert Cea

Linda Alaniz Photo

Sharon Angela in *Tony N' Tina's Wedding*

TUBES

Created and Written by Matt Goldman, Phil Stanton, Chris Wink; Director, Marlene Swartz; Artistic Coordinator; Caryl Glaab; Sets, Kevin Joseph Roach; Lighting, Brian Aldous; Costumes, Lydia Tanji, Patricia Murphy; Sound, Raymond Schilke; Computer Graphics, Kurisu-Chan; Stage Manager, Kevin Cunningham; Press, David Rothenberg; Opened at the Astor Place Theatre on Thursday, November 7, 1991*

CAST

Blue Man Group (Matt Goldman, Phil Stanton, Chris Wink)

An evening with the performance group, performed without intermission.

*Still playing May 31, 1994.

Martha Swope Photo

Blue Man Group

PRODUCTION	OPENED	CLOSED	PERFORMANCES
Beau Jest	10/2/91	5/1/94	1077 performances
Falsettos	4/29/92	6/27/93	487 & 23 previews
Fool Moon	2/25/93	9/5/93	207 & 15 previews
Goodbye Girl	3/4/93	8/15/93	188 & 23 previews
Jeffrey	3/6/93	1/16/94	365 performances
Jelly's Last Jam	4/26/92	9/5/93	569 & 25 previews
Oleanna	10/13/92	1/16/94	513 performances
Shakespeare For My Father	4/26/93	1/2/94	266 & 6 previews
Someone Who'll Watch Over Me	11/23/92	6/13/93	232 & 5 previews
Three Hotels	3/19/93	10/10/93	231 & 21 previews
Will Rogers Follies	5/1/91	9/5/93	983 & 34 previews

PRODUCTIONS FROM PAST SEASONS THAT CLOSED DURING THIS SEASON

OFF-BROADWAY PRODUCTIONS
(June 1, 1993-May 31, 1994)

(Carnegie Hall) Tuesday, June 1–5, 1993 (5 performances) Levon Sayan in association with Radio City Productions presents:
LIZA MINNELLI/CHARLES AZNAVOUR; Production Supervisor, Fred Ebb; Musical Director, Bill Lavorgna; Special Musical Material, Billy Stritch; Lighting, David Agress; Sound, Hank Cattaneo
 A two-act entertainment of American and French music.

(45th St. Theatre) Tuesday, June 1–20, 1993 (21 performances) The Women's Project & Production presents:
THE BROOKLYN TROJAN WOMEN by Carole Braverman; Director, Margot Breier; Set, Ted Glass; Costumes, Leslie Yarmo; Lighting, Heather Rogan; Sound, Bart Fasbender; Music, John Schaefer; Stage Manager, Randy Lawson; Press, Jonathan Slaff CAST: Adam Barnett (Luke), Ariane Brandt (Tess), Stephanie Clayman (Abigail), Joanna Merlin (Devorah), Lucille Rivin (Brenda)
 A drama in two acts. The action takes place in Brooklyn, early 1980s.

(Atlantic Theatre) Tuesday, June 1–27, 1993 (28 performances) Weissberger Theater Group presents:
DOWN THE ROAD by Lee Blessing; Director, David Dorwart; Set, E. David Cosier; Lighting, Jan Kroeze; Costumes, Therese A. Bruck; Sound, Thomas Clark; Stage Manager, Mary-Susan Gregson; Press, John and Gary Springer CAST: Lisa Eichhorn (Iris Henniman), John Dossett (Dan Henniman), Eric Stoltz (William Reach)
 A drama performed without intermission. The action takes place in a maximum security prison.

(Players Theatre) Tuesday, June 1–July 25, 1993 (56 performances and 8 previews) The Prophet Company Ltd. presents:
PRIME TIME PROPHET with Music/Lyrics/Direction by Kevin Connors; Book, Randy Buck; Musical Director/Arrangements, David Wolfson; Set, Don Jensen; Lighting, John Michael Deegan; Costumes, David Robinson; Stage Manager, James Schilling; Press, Pete Sanders, David Rothenberg CAST: Beth Glover (Ginger), Marcus Maurice (Max), David Brand (B. L./Tina Rae Tanner), Jonathan Hadley (Tim Christy), Janet Aldrich (Jennifer McCune)
MUSICAL NUMBERS: The Devil to Pay, Hot Shot, The Award, Saved!, Heavenly Party, Expect a Miracle, So Help Me God, Homesick for Hell, Leap of Faith, Step Into the Light, Diva Supreme, Tina Seeks Solace, Tips from Tina, Necessarily Evil, How Does She Do It?, Tina's Finest Hour, Armageddon, Finale
 A two-act musical satire of televangelism.

(Kaptain Banana) Tuesday, June 1, 1993–still playing May 31, 1994
LES INCROYABLES; Director, Jean Marie Riviere; Press, Terence Womble CAST: Daniel Rohou, Gilles Jean, Michael Prosper
 A musical revue featuring female impersonators.

(Theatre Off-Park) Wednesday, June 2–27, 1993 (28 performances) Stephen L. Snyder presents:
MISCONCEPTIONS by Cherie Vogelstein; Director, Josh Mostel; Set, Bill Stabile; Costumes, Sally J. Lesser; Lighting, Debra Dumas; Press, Peter Cromarty/David Bar Katz CAST: Caroline Aaron, Anne Bobby, Michael Ingram, Trish Jenkins, Lola Pashalinski, Richard Ziman, Danny Zorn
 A comedy set in Brooklyn.

(Brooklyn Academy of Music/Carey Playhouse) Wednesday, June 2–6, 1993 (7 performances) 651/Kings Majestic Corp., American Music Theatre Festival, Houston Grand Opera and Crossroads Theatre Co. present:
SHEILA'S DAY by Duma Ndlovu; Conceived/Created by Mr. Ndlovu, Mbongeni Ngema; Ruby Lee Conceived/Co-written by Ebony Jo-Ann; Director, Mr. Ngema; Set, Charles McClennahan; Lighting, Victor En Tu Yan; Costumes, Toni-Leslie James; Choreography, Thuli Dumakude; Press, Ellen Jacobs CAST: Stephanie Alston, Irene Datcher, Annelen Malebo, Valerie Jerusha Rochon, Gina Breedlove, Thuli Dumakude, Letta Mbulu, Gina Torres, Carla Brothers, Ebony Jo-Ann, Tunokwe, Khaliq Abdul Al-Rouh
A drama with music performed without intermission. The settings are South Africa and America.

Liza Minnelli, Charles Aznavour

Lisa Eichhorn, John Dossett, Eric Stoltz in *Down the Road*
(Carol Rosegg)

Ebony Jo-Ann (left) and cast in *Sheila's Day* **(Rich Pipeling)**

(Union Square Theatre) Wednesday, June 2–27, 1993 (17 performances) WonderWorks Unlimited presents:
CLASSIFIED; Written and Performed by Fred Adler; Set, Bernie Siegel; Costumes, Sama Meschel; Lighting, Michelle Bisco; Press, Peter Cromarty/Michael Hartman

Performance art in two parts: *The Job Hunter* and *The Apartment Hunter*.

(Cucaracha Theatre) Thursday, June 3–26, 1993 (15 performances) Cucaracha presents:
THE GUT GIRLS by Sarah Daniels; Director, Maria Mileaf; Sets, Vince Mountain; Lighting, Jeremy Stein; Costumes, Mary Larson; Music/Sound, Eric Lilgestrand   CAST: Joseph Fuqua, Pamela Gray, Lauren Hamilton, Deirdre Harrison, Kate Malin, Mollie O'Mara, Elizabeth Woodruff, Damian Young

A play set in a Victorian London slaughterhouse.

(P.S.122) Thursday, June 3–27, 1993 (16 performances) Purgatorio Ink and P.S. 122 present:
THE RISE AND FALL OF H. M. DICK; Written/Directed by Assurbanipal Babilla; Costumes, Audrey Fisher; Lighting, Roderick Murray; Sound, One Dream; Press, Jim Baldassare   CAST: Assurbanipal Babilla, David Cote, Leyla Ebtehadj

A "loose and leaky" adaptation of the Iranian revolution.

(St. Peter's) Thursday, June 3–20, 1993 (18 performances) St. Bart's Players present:
RUMORS by Neil Simon; Director, Tom Aberger; Set, Vicki Neal; Costumes, Estella Marie; Lighting, Karen Spahn; Press, Peter Cromarty/David Bar Katz CAST: Ken Altman, Andrea Capalaces, Susan Carlino, Tracey Cassidy, Dan Grinko, John Henderson, Jane Larkworthy, Paul Seymour

A comedy in two acts.

(Ohio Theatre) Friday, June 4–20, 1993 (16 performances) The Cheshire Company presents:
LADIES OF FISHER COVE by Allan Havis; Director, William Foeller; Set, Judy Gailen; Lighting, Adrienne Shulman; Costumes, Barbara Beccio; Sound, Matthew Schlofner; Stage Manager, Julienne Kim; Press, Jim Baldassare CAST: Anne Darragh (Judith), Kathryn Langwell (Rachel), Rebecca Nelson (Helen), Marcell Rosenblatt (Cloris), Christopher McCann (Artemus)

A drama in two acts. The action takes place in a coastal Victorian home in Northern Maine.

(William Redfield Theatre) Friday, June 4–12, 1993 (8 performances) Greensheets Productions presents:
THREE ONE-ACT PLAYS; Press, Marilyn Kirk
A CHANCE MEETING by Frederick Stroppel; Director, Paul Michael   CAST: Neal Arluck, William T. Johnson, Abigail Zealey
THE GREAT NEBULA IN ORION by Lanford Wilson; Director, Herb Ouelette CAST: Yvonne Alfano, Susan Stein
THE MIDNIGHT CALLER by Horton Foote; Director, Colin Dwyer   CAST: Colleen Brown, Tom Cahill, Joyce DeGroot, Darlene Kelley, Janet Mitchko, Ginny Stewart, Timothy Wilson

(Good Shepard Faith Church) Monday, June 7, 1993 (1 performance only) Bandwagon presents:
AFTER THE BALL with Music/Lyrics/Book by Noel Coward; *Based on Lady Windermere's Fan* by Oscar Wilde; Narrative/Scripted Continuity/Additional Staging, Sheila Smith; Musical Staging, Jerry Bell; Musical Direction, Buck Buchholz, Edward B. Gutiman, C. Colby Sachs; Gowns, Paulina Kent Dennis CAST: Mark Poppleton (Mr. Dumby), Ken Hornbeck (Mr. Graham), Mark Montalbano (Mr. Cowper-Cowper), Paul Chamlin (Lord Arthur Windermere), Margaret Burnham (Lady Margaret Windermere), Patrick Quinn (Mr. James Hopper), Paul Jackel (Lord Darlington), SuEllen Estey (Mrs. Margaret Erlynne), Paula Laurence (Lady Arabella/Narrator), Margaret Wehrle (Lady Agatha Carlisle), Elana Polin (Lady Stutfield), Julianne DiPietro (Lady Plymdale), Kent deGraffen (Lord "Tuppy" Lorton), Tammy Grimes (Introduction)
MUSICAL NUMBERS: London at Night, I Knew That You Would Be My Love, Mr. Hopper's Chantey, Sweet Day, Stay on the Side of the Angels, Creme de la Creme, Light is the Heart, May I Have the Pleasure?, I Offer You My Heart, The Woman Who Pays, Faraway Land, What Can It Mean, I Feel So Terribly Alone, Go I Beg You, Oh What a Century, Clear Bright Morning, All My Life Ago, Farewell Song, Something on a Tray, Finale

A concert musical.

Fred Adler in *Classified* (Ritch Davidson)

**David Cote, Leyla Ebtehadj, Assurbanipal Babilla in
The Rise and Fall of H.M. Dick (Thomas Ertefai)**

Rebecca Nelson, Anne Darragh, Katherine Langwell 87
in *Ladies of Fisher Cove* (Carol Rosegg)

(Theatre Arielle) Tuesday, June 8–July 3, 1993 (27 performances) transferred to the 45th St. Theatre on July 6 running through Nov. 11, 1993 Michael Ross presents:
PIAF...REMEMBERED; Conceived by Juliette Koka; Musical Director/Arrangements, John Marino; Additional Dialogue, Janet Alberti, Milli Janz; Stage Manager, Steven Jay Cohen; Press, Pete Sanders/Matthew Lenz CAST: Juliette Koka

MUSICAL NUMBERS: Padam, Bravo Pour Le Clown, L'etranger, L'accordeoniste, Mon Dieu, La Foule, L'homme A La Moto, Roulez Tambours, Mon Menage A Moi, La Vie En Rose, Hyme A L'amour, Le Trois Cloches/Sous Le Ciel de Paris/La Goulante de Pauvre Jean, Le Diable de la Bastille, C'est Toujours La Meme, Le Droit D'aimer, A Quoi Casert L'amour, Les Blouses Balnches, Milord, No Jene Regrette Rien
  A selection of Edith Piaf songs on the thirtieth anniversary of her death.

(Carnegie/Weill Hall) Wednesday, June 9–13, 1993 (6 performances) Carnegie Hall presents:
GAY DIVORCE with Music/Lyrics by Cole Porter; Book, Dwight Taylor, Kenneth Ebb, Samuel Hoffenstein; Director/Conductor, John McGlinn; Orchestrations, Hans Spialek, Robert Russell Bennett, Russell Warner CAST: Bill Moor (Robert), Simon Jones (Egbert-Teddy), Robert Westenberg (Guy), Maureen Brennan (Barbara), Nick Ulett (Waiter), Judy Kaye (Hortense), Rebecca Luker (Mimi), Kurt Ollmann (Tonetti), John Driver (Mr. Pratt), Julie Lisa Dixon (Doris), Allison Gray (Iris), Susan Pfau (Vivian), Paige Price (Claire), Sally Ann Tumas (Louella), Renee Veneziale (Betty)

MUSICAL NUMBERS: Overture, After You Who?, Why Marry Them, Salt Air, I Still Love the Red White and Blue, Night and Day, How's Your Romance?, Entr'acte, What Will Become of Our England, I've Got You on My Mind, Specialty Dance, Mister and Missus Fitch, You're in Love, Finale Ultimo
  A concert version of the 1932 musical.

(Blue Angel) Wednesday, June 9, 1993– Darren Lee Cole presents:
NOSTALGIA TROPICAL; Director, Max Ferra; Choreography, Victor Cuellar; Design, Riccardo Hernandez; Lighting, Jennifer Tipton; Press, Frimark & Thibodeau/Ian Rand CAST: Meme Solis, Merly Bordes, Aimee Cabrera, Claudina Montenegro, Marden Ramos, Ramoncito Veloz, Jr.
  An Afro-Cuban musical revue.

(Greenwich St. Theatre) Wednesday, June 16–July 17, 1993 (16 performances) Turnip Festival Company presents:
LIFE AFTER DEATH; Written/Directed by Joseph A. Massa; Set, Ed McCarthy, Stacey Tanner; Lighting, Mr. McCarthy; Stage Manager, Colleen Davis; Press, Gloria Falzer CAST: Janet Pabon (Meg), Morgan Englund (Jack)
  A drama set in a small New Hampshire town, mid-1970s.

(Actors' Playhouse) Wednesday, June 16, 1993–Feb. 20, 1994 (271 performances) The Glines and Postage Stamp Xtravaganzas present:
Howard Crabtree's WHOOP-DEE-DOO; Conceived/Created/Developed by Charles Catanese, Howard Crabtree, Dick Gallagher, Phillip George, Peter Morris, Mark Waldrop; Songs/Sketches by Mr. Gallagher, Mr. Morris, Mr. Waldrop; Additional Material, Brad Ellis, Jack Feldman, David Rambo, Bruce Sussman, Eric Schorr; Director, Phillip George; Musical Director, Fred Barton; Additional Staging/Choreography, David Lowenstein; Sets, Bill Wood; Costumes, Mr. Crabtree; Lighting, Tracy Dedrickson; Stage Manager, Michael Henderson; Press, Tony Origlio/William McLaughlin CAST: Howard Crabtree, Keith Cromwell succeeded by Keith Allen, Tommy Femia, David Lowenstein, Peter Morris, Jay Rogers, Ron Skobel, Richard Stegman, Alan Tulin
  A two-act gay musical revue.

88 Richard Stegman, Howard Crabtree, Ron Skobel in *Whoop-Dee-Doo!* (Jerry Goodstein)

Juliette Koka in *Piaf...Remembered*

Maureen Brennan, Nick Ullett, (front) John McGlinn, Rebecca Luker, Robert Westenberg in *Gay Divorce*

(Symphony Space) Thursday, June 17, 1993 (1 performance only) Friends of the Chelsea Clinton News and The Westsider present:
THE BEST OF THE WEST; Written and Supervised by Walter Willison; Staged/Choreographed by Jack Eddleman; Musical Director, Royce Twitchell; Lighting/Sound, Scot Newell; Cabaret Coordination, Bradshaw Smith; Stage Manager, Matthew G. Marholin CAST: Tovah Feldshuh, Alix Korey, Kristine Zbornik, Julie Anne Aho, Rachel Cohen, Amanda Blair Ellis, Christa Fuller, Janelle Holdren, Jason King, James Marino, Phil Zipkin
  A gala celebration featuring a tribute to Robert Wright and George Forrest.

(Manhattan Class Co.) Saturday, June 19–July 1, 1993 Manhattan Class Co. presents:
D TRAIN by James Bosley; Conceived/Choreographed by Fay Simpson; Director, Ms. Simpson, Robert LuPone; Set, Rob Odorisio; Costumes, Jeffrey Wallach; Lighting, Howard Werner; Music, Myra Melford; Press, Peter Cromarty/David Bar Katz CAST: Alyson Jackson, Bjarne Hecht, Antonia Franceschi, Nick Rodgers, Joe Knight, Fay Simpson Dance Theatre
  A dance/theatre piece set in New York City.

(Creativa) Saturday, June 19–20, 1993 (2 performances)
THE HOUR OF THE DOG by Kristina Lugn; Translation, Verne Moberg; Director, Robert Greer CAST: Elizabeth Bove, Laurie Muir, Lois Raebeck
English language premiere of a Swedish poetry play.

(Penn Yards) Tuesday, June 22–July 18, 1993 (24 performances) En Garde Arts presents:
ORESTES by Charles L. Mee, Jr.; Director, Tina Landau; Sets, Kyle Chepulis; Costumes, James Schuette; Lighting, Brian Aldous; Music/Sound, John Gromada; Stage Manager, Marjorie Goodsell Clark; Press, David Rothenberg CAST: Christopher Adams (Patient), J. Ed Araiza (William), Tiffani K. Barbour (Nurse), William Buddendorf (Patient), Jernard Burks (Nod), Jennifer Dollard (Nurse), Ramsey Faragallah (Tape Mouth Man), Gregory Gunter (Bodyguard), Jennifer Harmon (Nurse), Natalie Layne Kidd (Nurse), Jay Amelia Larson (Helen), Michael Malone (John), Sonya Martin (Nurse #1), Jefferson Mays (Orestes), Theresa McCarthy (Electra), Phaedra Philippoussis (Nurse), Elizabeth Posella (Nurse), Frank Raiter (Tyndareus), Sharon Scruggs (Forensics Expert/Nurse #2), Brendan Sexton (Apollo), Steven Skybell (Pylades), Stephen Speights (Trenchcoat Man), Jeffrey Sugarman (Menelaus), Beau Van Donkelaar (Patient), Elvin Velez (Phrygian Slave), Jean-Loup Wolfman (Patient), Stefanie Zadravec (Nurse #3)
A modern re-telling of Euripides' tragedy performed in an abandoned rail yard.

(Synchronicity Space) Friday, June 25–July 11, 1993 (13 performances) Synchronicity Theatre Group presents:
LOSING VENICE by John Clifford; Director/Sound, Bob Bowman; Set, Mark Symczak; Lighting, David Alan Comstock; Costumes, Angela Brisnovali; Stage Manager, Petra Stevens CAST: Randy Soare (Musician/Conspirator), Cap Pryor (Quevedo), John Moraitis (Pablo), Brenda Pitmon (Maria), Bill Dante (Duke), Raissa Radell (Duchess/Pirate), David Ruckman (Secretary/Conspirator), Tracy Davis (King/Conspirator), Nora Colpman (Priestess/Pirate), Sheila Sawney (Sister/Pirate/Conspirator), Jeff Kronson (Mr. Doge), Cappy Lyons (Mrs. Doge/Pirate/Woman with Baby)
A comedy set in 17th-century Venice.

(Rainbow & Stars) Tuesday, July 6–Aug. 28, 1993 (80 performances) Steve Paul and Gregory Dawson present:
THE NIGHT THEY INVENTED CHAMPAGNE...THE LERNER AND LOEWE REVUE; Director, Deborah R. Lapidus; Music Direction/Arrangements, Lawrence Yurman; Costumes, Denis Paver; Lighting, Tim Flannery; Sound, Gary Penovich; Press, David Lotz CAST: Maureen Brennan, Eddie Korbich, Juliet Lambert, Martin Vidnovic

MUSICAL NUMBERS: Follow Me, Almost Like Being in Love, It's a Bore, Simple Joys of Maidenhood, Love of My Life, C'est Moi, Heather on the Hill, My Love is a Married Man, With a Little Bit of Luck, On the Street Where You Live, You Haven't Changed at All, If Ever I Would Leave You, My Mother's Weddin' Day, Show Me, Trio, Say a Prayer for Me Tonight, A Toujours, Night They Invented Champagne, Paris is Paris Again, Come to the Ball, She is Not Thinking of Me, I've Grown Accustomed to Her Face, How Can I Wait?, There But for You Go I, Gigi, Wand'rin' Star, I'm On My Way, From This Day On

Maureen Brennan, Martin Vidnovic, Eddie Korbich, Juliet Lambert in *The Night They Invented Champagne* (Carol Rosegg)

Theresa McCarthy, Jefferson Mays in *Orestes* (William Rivelli)

(Metropolitan Opera) Tuesday, July 6–18, 1993 (16 performances) Metropolitan Opera Association presents:
DISNEY'S SYMPHONIC FANTASY; Music/Lyrics, Various; Script, Thomas E. Child; Director, Keri Keaney; Choreography, John Addis, John Charron, Sylvia Hase-Floch; Sets, Steve Bass; Lighting, Paulie Jenkins; Music Director, Bruce Healey CAST: Kimberly Andrews, Jennifer Baker, Laurel Ballard, Heather Bolton, Brian Bon, Mariah Bonner, Cate Caplin, Kimi Cochrun, Randy Connelie, Jade S. Crouch, Vicky Curry, Tony Davis, Lisa Ebeyer, Gary Franco, Patrick Garcia, Christopher Gasti, Jimmy Hippenstiel, Chris Holly, Saul Ibarra, Kimberly Jones, Robyn Kass, Tricia Lilly, Elaine Martz, Greg Martz, Cory McDaniel, Kimberly Mikesell, Kevin Moore, Stefanie Morse, Denny Newell, Keri Owens, Robert Patteri, Welton Thomas Pitchford, II, Cindy Ricalde, Tiffany Roach, Tamao M. Sato, Chris Senesac, Andi Senyel, Tom Slater, Mark Smith, Bobby Solorio, Amy Jo Stubbier, Tony Villa, Todd Williams, Kimberly Yusem
A musical variety show.

(Westbeth Theatre Center) Tuesday, July 6–25, 1993 (21 performances) The Sackett Group presents:
AWAKE AND SING by Clifford Odets; Director, Robert J. Weinstein; Set, Shawn McCrory CAST: Michael Pace (Myron), Jane B. Harris (Bessie), Kenneth Fuchs (Jacob), Laureen Lefever (Hennie), Jeff O'Malley (Ralph), Elliot Raines (Schlosser), Dan Haft (Moe), Ronald Lew Harris (Morty), Ed Chemaly (Sam), Libby Haris (Tootsie)
The 1935 drama set in the Bronx.

(Variety Arts Theatre) Tuesday, July 6, 1993–Jan. 30, 1994 (200 performances and 38 previews) Ben Sprecher, William P. Miller, Dennis Grimaldi by special arrangement with Karen Walter Goodwin present:
ANNIE WARBUCKS with Music by Charles Strouse; Lyrics/Direction, Martin Charnin; Book, Thomas Meehan; Choreography, Peter Gennaro; Musical Director/Orchestrations, Keith Levenson; Sets, Ming Cho Lee; Costumes, Theoni V. Aldredge; Lighting, Ken Billington; Sound, Tom Sorce; Stage Manager, Jeffrey M. Markowitz; Press, Jeffrey Richards CAST: Kathryn Zaremba (Annie), Harve Presnell (Oliver Warbucks), Donna McKechnie (Mrs. Sheila Kelly), Alene Robertson (Commissioner Harriet Doyle), Raymond Thorne (Franklin Delano Roosevelt), Marguerite MacIntyre (Grace Farrell), Harvey Evans (Alvin T. Paterson), Joel Hatch (Simon Whitehead), Kip Niven (Drake), Molly Scott (Ella Paterson), Jackie Angelescu (C. G. Paterson), Missy Goldberg (Pepper), Natalia Harris (Peaches), Ashley Pettet (Molly), Elisabeth Zaremba (Tessie), J. B. Adams, Brooks Almy, Colleen Fitzpatrick, Michael E. Gold, Jennifer L. Neuland, Steve Steiner, Alexis Dale Fabricant
MUSICAL NUMBERS: A New Deal for Christmas, Annie Ain't Just Annie Anymore, Above the Law, Changes, The Other Woman, That's the Kind of Woman, A Younger Man, But You Go On, When You Smile, I Got Me, Love, Somebody's Gotta Do Somethin', Leave It to the Girls, All Dolled Up, Tenement Lullaby, It Would Have Been Wonderful, Wedding Wedding, I Always Knew

   A two-act sequel to the 1977 musical *Annie*. The action takes place in New York City, Tennessee, and Washington, D.C.

Top: Harve Presnell, Kathryn Zaremba, Marguerite MacIntyre
Right: Donna McKechnie, Alene Robertson
(Carol Rosegg Photos)

90

(Village Theatre) Thursday, July 8–25, 1993 (17 performances) Village Theatre Co. presents:

EXIT MUSIC with Music by James Merillat; Lyrics, Dick Pasqual; Book, Mr. Merillat and Mr. Pasqual; Based on story *Me and the Girls* by Noel Coward; Director, Brian Meister; Musical Director, Mark Wagner; Set, James A. Bazewicz; Sound, Jim Harrington; Choreography, Karin Baker; Lighting, Betsy Adams; Costumes, Deborah Shaw; Press, Susan L. Schulman CAST: Douglas Simes (George Banks), Gardner Kyle (Harry Boy), David Young (Dr. Pierre), Lisby Larson (Mavis Edmond), Jennifer Jiles (Sally Alexander), Christie Harrington (Bonny MacIntyre), Noelle Player (Beryl Martin)

MUSICAL NUMBERS: Perfect Mate for Me, Easy Target for Love, The Grandest View, The Audition, Me and the Girls, Don't Write Any More Songs, Secrets, Never Lonely, Dancing On Air, I'll Show You How, Rest of My Life, I'm In Demand, Mezzanotte Mezzaluna, Balloon, Time to Celebrate, I Meant to Be Beautiful, Harry-Boy, Where Do We Play, You'll Get a Boot Out of Italy, A Virgin A Villain A Vamp, Consultation, To Say Goodbye
   A musical in two acts. The action takes place in Switzerland and various European locales before WWII.

(Lincoln Center) Thursday, July 8–30, 1993 (19 performances) Lincoln Center Productions present:
SERIOUS FUN; Press, Ellen Zeisler/Grant Lindsey

PROGRAMS: Reduced Shakespeare Company, Dimanda Galas, Culture Clash, Blue Gene Tyranny, Megadance, Susan Marshall, EBN, Wim Mertens, Marie Chouinard, Pomo Afro Homos, Soto and Osorio, Margaret Leng Tan, Twisted Roots, La Monte Young, Lisa Kron, Kipper Kids
   The seventh annual edition.

(Nat Horne Theatre) Tuesday, July 8–Aug. 1, 1993 (14 performances) Love Creek Productions presents:
ONE EYED VENUS AND THE BROTHERS by Le Wilhelm; Director, Diane Hoblit; Lighting, Richard Kent Green; Set, William Swartz; Stage Manager, Kirsten Walsh; Press, Chris Boneau/Adrian Bryan-Brown, Hillary Harrow CAST: George Cron (Rufus), Geoff Dawe (Ralph), Jed Dickson (Roger), Tracy Newirth (Leaetta), Merry Beamer (Patch), John Shortall (Ron)
   A drama set in the Missouri Ozarks.

(Chapter 3 Theatre) Thursday, July 15–Aug. 8, 1993 (16 performances) Joseph P. Byrne presents:
BY GEORGE! (Kelly, that is); Director, Shela Xoregos; Sets, Charles Ard; Lighting, Robert J. Perry; Sound, Kenn Dovel; Costumes, Elly Van Horne; Stage Manager, Lori A. Brown CAST: David Goodman, Rebecca Kramer, Ellen Tina Landress, Mindy Myers, Sheryl Del Prete, Princess Sandlin, David Scott, Lee Winston
   Two one-acts by George Kelly, 1916's *Finders Keepers* and 1918's *The Flattering Word*.

Mac Powell, Brian McCormack, Douglas Gibson
in *Old Flames*

Reed Martin, Adam Long, Austin Tichenor as
Reduced Shakespeare Co. (Ed Krieger)

(Playhouse 125) Friday, July 16–Aug. 29, 1993 (27 performances) Lucky Forward Productions presents:
OLD FLAMES; Written/Directed by Anthony Patton; Lighting, Jeff Glovsky; Costumes, Marcia K. McDonald; Sound, Vincent DeMarco; Fights, Eric Nottke; Music, Jon Marc Patton; Press/Producer, Floreian King CAST: Brian McCormack (Frank Dane), Leigh Patton (Lynn Dane), Douglas Gibson (Phil Sanders), Marion Killinger (Randy Patterson), Jim Maggard (Sam Chambers), Richard Jachimecki (Jim Cavens), Jay Heflin (Tony McCollough), Gary Galbraith (Charlie Cooper), Victor Verhaeghe (Tom Chandler), Mac Powell (George Harris)
   A drama in two acts. The action takes place in the "Damn Yankee" restaurant in Georgia.

(29th St. Repertory Theatre) Monday, July 19–Aug. 14, 1993 (24 performances) 29th St. Repertory/New Voices in the American Theatre presents:
THE FIFTH ANNUAL SUMMER ONE ACT FESTIVAL; Sets, Kis Knekt; Lighting, Stewart Wagner; Sound, Robert Derby; Stage Managers, Melody Ann Mora, Lisa Lyons; Press, Paula Ewin

PROGRAM A: *ALOOF* by Roger Hedden; Director, Linda June Larson CAST: Kent Heacock (Peter), Alison Lani Broda (Anna)
LOS BESOS by Richard Harland Smith; Director, Leo Farley CAST: Danna Lyons (Cal), Thomas Wehrle (Ray)
LOVE MONKEYS by Steven Sater; Director, Andrew Mutnick CAST: Richard Sacher (David), Elizabeth Elkins (Rachel)
VISITING OLIVER by Bill Nave; Director, Vera Beren CAST: Paula Ewin (Ruth), Leo Farley (Clement), David Mogentale (Oliver), Richard Larimer (Stan)

PROGRAM B: *EUKIAH* by Lanford Wilson; Director, Dan Bianchi CAST: David Mogentale (Butch), Tristan Smith (Eukiah)
COMMON GROUND by Richard Harland Smith; Director, Michael Hillyer CAST: Tim Corcoran (Frank), Elizabeth Elkins (Nell)
A LITTLE BIT OF HEAVEN by Katherine Hewett; Director, Vera Beren CAST: Richard Larimer (Gil), Suzette Breitbart (Receptionist)
VISITING OLIVER - same as above

(Samuel Beckett Theatre) Thursday, July 29–Aug. 7, 1993 Borderline Theatre Company presents:
THE FOX by D. H. Lawrence; Adaptation, Allan Miller; Director, Mark Nelson CAST INCLUDES: Joan Buddenhagen, Sharyn Jensen, Jeff Stafford
   A new production company made up of Juilliard students.

(Synchronicity Space) Friday, July 30–Aug. 15, 1993 (13 performances) Synchronicity Space and The Art & Work Ensemble present:
BABY WITH THE BATHWATER by Christopher Durang; Director, Beth Milles; Set, Rachel Raia; Lighting, David Alan Comstock; Costumes, Jed Krascella; Stage Manager, Jay Mafale CAST: Kelly Cleary (Cynthia/Another Woman in the Park/Miss Pringle/Susan), Joanne Comerford (Helen), David Frank (John), Alicia Genetski (Woman in the Park/Mrs. Willoughby), Laura Gillis (Nanny), Jimmy Hurley (Daisy)
   A 1983 comedy set in New York City.

(William Redfield Theatre) Tuesday, Aug. 3–15, 1993 Live Eyes Theatre Company presents:
THE LOVE OF THE NIGHTINGALE by Timberlake Wertenbaker; Director, Susanna Einstein; Sets, Graham Blyth; Costumes, Anne Fanganello CAST INCLUDES: Ian Kahn (Tereus), Angela Flynn (Philomele), Ryan Dunn (Procne), Susan E. Murray (Niobe), Eric Perlmutter

(Courtyard Playhouse) Wednesday, Aug. 4–Sept. 5, 1993 (25 performances) The Courtyard Playhouse Foundation, Marson Productions, Latin Images, and Calico Productions present:
LATIN LIVES by Robert Louis Maisonett and Lourdes Cuadrado; Director, Mr. Maisonett; Lighting, Bill Hubner; Art, Louanne Gilleland; Stage Manager, Ms. Cuadrado CAST: Rosa Arredondo, Guillermo Diaz, Christopher Hernandez, Gloria Herrera, Christian Jacobs, Vidal Lopez, Robert Malsonett, Evelyn Morales, Ana Veronica Munoz, Edgard Nau, Charles Santy, Lisa Tamplenizza, Tracy Vilar, Jose Manuel Yenque

PROGRAM: What is Latin?, Number 5 Train, Designing Men, La Familia, Pito's News, The Morning After, Margarita, Tito Wito's Cuchifrito, Beauty Parlor, What Being Latin Means to Me
    Comic vignettes exploring Latinos in America today.

(One Dream Theatre) Friday, Aug. 6–14, 1993 (7 performances) One Dream presents:
ROUGH FOR THEATRE II and **PLAY** by Samuel Beckett; Director, Randall Sommer; Sets/Costumes, Denise Hudson; Lighting, Sarah Sidman CAST: Judith Barcroft, Fred Burrell, Barbara Gruen, Garrison Phillips, Kevin Pinassi
    Two one-acts rarely performed together.

(City Parks) Friday, Aug. 6–29, 1993 (22 performances) Puerto Rican Traveling Theatre presents:
LOS JIBAROS PROGRESISTAS by Ramon Mendez Quinones; Director, David Crommett; Set, Daniel Ettinger; Costumes, Amparo Fuertes; Stage Manager, Fernando Quinones CAST: Bersaida Vega (Juaniya), Miriam Cruz (Chepa), Larry Ramos (Cleto), Angelo Santigo (Anton), Anibal Lleras (Bruno), Rafael Picorelli (Don Pico)
    A drama set in Puerto Rica's mountains, 1882.

(Westside Theatre/Upstairs) Monday, Aug. 9, 1993–Jan. 2, 1994 (168 performances) Steven Baruch, Richard Frankel, Thomas Viertei, The Shubert Organization, Capital Cities/ABC and Playwrights Horizons present:
LATER LIFE by A. R. Gurney; Director, Don Scardino; Set, Ben Edwards; Costumes, Jennifer Von Mayrhauser; Lighting, Brian MacDevitt; Sound, Guy Sherman/Aural Fixation; Wigs/Hairstylist, Daniel Platten; Stage Manager, Dianne Trulock; Press, Philip Rinaldi/Kathy Haberthur, Dennis Crowley CAST: Maureen Anderman (Ruth), Josef Sommer (Austin), Carole Shelley (Other Women), Anthony Heald, John C. Vennema (during vacation) (Other Men)
    A Boston-set comedy performed without intermission. Performed last season at Playwrights Horizons with Charles Kimbrough as Austin.

Later Life Photos
Top Right: Carole Shelley
Bottom Right: Anthony Heald
Below: Maureen Anderman, Josef Sommer
(T. Charles Erickson Photos)

(Theatre Row Theatre) Tuesday, Aug. 10–29, 1993 (24 performances) HAI Theatre Festival presents:
A BETTER LIFE by Louis Delgado, Jr.; Director, Max Daniels; Set, Miguel Lopez-Castillo; Costumes, Susan Ruddie; Lighting, Steven Rust; Sound, Mike Sargent; Stage Manager, Frank Laurents; Press, Terry M. Lilly/David J. Gersten CAST: Byron Utley (Marty), Rachel Follett Avidon (Norma), Lenwood Benitez (Kelvin), Sharon Hope (Nurse), Jeff Ranara (Howard), Man-ching Lorber (Pat), Tom Gerard (David)

A drama performed without intermission. The setting is a New York City hospital room and apartment, 1984.

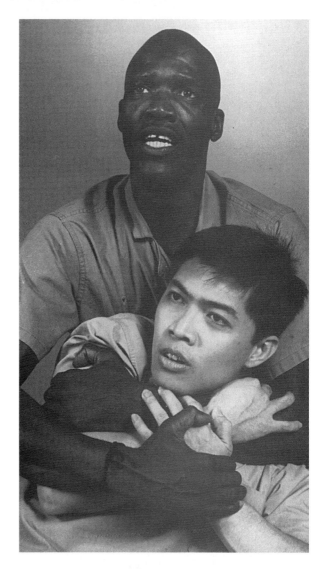

(Samuel Beckett Theatre) Wednesday, Aug. 11–15, 1993 (6 performances) Red Light District presents:
OUTWARD BOUND by Sutton Vane; Director, Marc Geller; Lighting, Matthew McCarthy; Costumes, Melissa Kalt, David Jay Smith; Stage Manager, Christina Lisi CAST: Bill Roulet (Scrubby), Karen Wexler (Ann), Christian Desmond (Henry), Marc Geller (Tom Prior), Shan Willis (Mrs. Cliveden-Banks), Stephen O'Donnell (Rev. William Duke), Helen Clark-Ziangas (Mrs. Midget), Russell Stevens (Mr. Lingley), Alan Denny (Rev. Frank Thomson)

The action takes place in the bar of an ocean liner, 1923.

(Bouwerie Lane Theatre) Friday, Aug. 20–Nov. 7, 1993 (33 performances) Jean Cocteau Repertory presents:
THE FIRST LULU by Eric Bentley; Adapted from Frank Wedekind; Director, Robert Hupp; Sets, Jim Lartin-Drake; Lighting, Giles Hogya; Costumes, Susan Soetaert; Music, Ellen Mandel; Press, Jonathan Slaff CAST: Craig Smith (Dr. Franz Schoning/Customer), John Lenartz (Edward Schwarz/Customer), T. Walker Rice (Dr. Goll/Marquis Casti-Piani), Elise Stone (Lulu), Steve Chizmadia (Alva Schoning), Harris Berlinsky (Schigolch), Kathleen Wilson (Henriette/Madelaine), Adrienne D. Williams (Countess Geschwitz), John Lynch (Rodrigo Quast/Customer), Kennedy Brown (Ferdinand/Puntschuh), Sandra Sciford (Bianetta Gazil), Monique Vukovic (Kadega di Santa Croce), Thomas Donnarumma (Bob), Michael Anduz (Customer)

The rise and fall of a femme enfante set in Berlin salons, Paris gaming houses, and Jack the Ripper's London. Performed in five acts.

(Sanford Meisner Theatre) Tuesday, Aug. 31–Oct. 3, 1993 (40 performances) reopened at the Jewel Box on Wednesday, Nov. 10, 1993
HIV Ensemble presents:
WORKING OUT WITH LEONA with Music by Paul Radelat, Michael Capece; Lyrics/Direction/Choreography, Nelson Jewell; Book, Mr. Jewell, Mary Lee Miller; Musical Director, Mr. Capece; Press, Bruce Lynn CAST: (CAST A) Carl Clayborn, Cliff Watters, Tonya Hall, Richard Navickas, Nelson Jewell, Russell Kordas, Richard Hucke (CAST B) Randall O'Neill, Pat Carlucci, Francis Blackock, Tonya Hall, David Torres Valentino, Charles Navarrette, Russell Rottkamp

MUSICAL NUMBERS: Sell Sell Sell, Doing It Every Day, Secretary Spread, Wish I Were a Beauty, Pump That Iron, Leona's Nightmare, When Will They Find Out, Yesterday Today and Tomorrow, It'll All Work Out, Yoga Song, Touch of Love, Finale

A musical comedy lampoon featuring many cast members who are HIV positive.

(Inner Space Theatre) Wednesday, Sept. 1–12, 1993 (14 performances) Group Group and Anne E. Bogoch present:
GROUP ODD/GROUP EVEN; Sets, Tim Goodmanson; Lighting, David Casteneda; Costumes, Virginia Johnson; Sound, James W. Wildman; Press, Chris Boneau/Adrian Bryan-Brown, Bob Fennell

GROUP ODD: *Proper Arrangements* by Joan Vail Thorne; Director, Frank Laurents CAST: Jill Church (Lila), Carol Anne Hansen (Ann), Jim Coyne (Hopkins)
Peephole by Shem Bitterman; Director, Nick Corley CAST: Laurence Lau (Rick), Allen Fitzpatrick (Doctor), Susanna Falcon (Alicia), Mitch Allen (Man/John#2/Deacon/Patient#3), Amelia Marshall (Sheena), Jeff Telvi (Patient #1/John #1), Scott Connell (Detective), Donald Newman (Patient#2/Appointee)

GROUP EVEN: *The Stonewater Rapture* by Doug Wright; Director, Santiago Navila CAST: Anne E. Bogoch (Carlyle), Stacy Shane (Whitney)
The Golden Bull of Boredom by Lorees Yerby; Director, Judith Searcy CAST: Doanld Newman (Slippers), Scott Connell (Shoes), Frank Laurents (Heels)
Sway; Written/Directed by Mitchell Ganem CAST: Rob Sedgwick (Daniel), Jill Church (Caroline)

Short plays in repertory.

Top: Byron Utley, Jeff Ranara in *A Better Life* **(Carol Rosegg)**
Bottom: Allen Fitzpatrick, Amelia Marshall, Laurence Lau
in *Peephole* **(William Kavanah)**

(Theatre Row Theatre) Sunday, Sept. 5–19, 1993 (16 performances) Falstaff presents:
THE TWO NOBLE KINSMEN by William Shakespeare and John Fletcher; Director, Beth F. Milles; Set, Nancy Deren; Costumes, Leslie Yarmo; Lighting, Russell H. Champa; Music, Jill Jaffee; Musical Director, Christopher Nappi; Fights, David Costabile; Stage Manager, Amy E. Ferraro CAST: Christopher Adams (Countryperson/Brother/Gentleman/Artesius), Bridgitte Barnett (3rd Queen), Buzz Bovshow (Pirithous/Doctor), Joanne Comerford (2nd Queen), Michael Edwardson (Valerius/Countryperson/Friend/Knight), China Forbes (Nell/Attendant), Kate Forbes (Emilia), Jose Garcia (Theseus), Jeremy Gold (Herald/Countryperson/Friend/Knight/Executioner), Judith Hawking (1st Queen), Peter Jacobson (Arcite), William Keeler (Jailer/Schoolmaster), Jayne Amelia Larson (Hippolyta), Kathryn Velvel (Woman/Attendant/Countryperson), Rainn Wilson (Palamon), Rebecca Waxman (Jailer's Daughter), Rex Young (Wooer)

Possibly Shakespeare's final play (1613), an adaptation of a Canterbury Tales story.

(Samuel Beckett Theatre) Wednesday, Sept. 8–26, 1993 (15 performances) The Basic Theatre presents:
THE CEREMONY OF INNOCENCE by Ronald Ribman; Director, Jessica Bauman; Set, Walt Spangler; Lighting, John-Paul Szczepanski; Costumes, Patty Burke, Jared Hammond; Sound, Matthew Schlofner; Fights, John Edmond Morgan; Stage Managers, Catherine Tarbox, Kelly Varley; Press, Sheri Delaine CAST: Steve Boles (Sweyn), Eric Brandenburg (Kent), Gary Cowling (Emma), Ellen Mareneck (Ethelred), Robert Lee Martini (Sussex), James Rutledge (Bishop), Alexandria Sage (Thula/Edmond), Ross Salinger (Monk/Thorkill/Combat), Arlene Sterne (Alfreda), Loretta Toscano (Abbot/Combat)

A drama in two acts. The action takes place on the Isle of Wight, 1013.

(Center of the Rainbow) Thursday, Sept. 9–25, 1993 (13 performances) Think It's Not When It Iz Productions presents:
CHOICES; Written/Directed by Sonya M. Hemphill; Lighting, Jeff Frazier; Press, Shirley Herz/Wayne Wolfe CAST: Sonya M. Hemphill (Alex/Flirtee), Kimberley Gilchrist (Giovanni/Dinky/Flirtee), Chachi Huesca (Marjorie/Host), Cheryl McClendon (Ashley), Celines Pimentel (Janis), Leah Rambo (Nicole), Shawn Richards (Casey), Eve Sano (Kim/Flirtee)

A lesbian soap opera in two acts.

(Nat Horne Theatre) Thursday, Sept. 9–26, 1993 (12 performances) Love Creek Productions presents:
BATS by Fred Gormley; Music, James Merillat; Lyrics, John B. Kenrick, Mr. Merillat; Director, David Ness; Lighting, Richard Kent Green; Set, William Swartz; Sound, Henry Marsden Davis; Choreography, Daryl Murphy; Press, Chris Boneau/Adrian Bryan-Brown, Hillary Harrow CAST: Cassius Allen, Francis Callahan, George Carr, Richard Kent Green, Trip Hunter, David Maxwell, Kevin Reifel, Jeff Burchfield, Carol Halstead, Kirsten Walsh, Tracy Newirth, Philip Galbraith, Vicki Weidman, Kymm Zuckert

A dark comedy with music.

Jen Gaita, Billy Hipkins, M. Lynch, Brad Von Nostrand, Jennifer Brunson, Steven Petrillo, (front) Karyn Lee in *The Make Over* (Troy Bystrom)

Rainn Wilson, Peter Jacobson in *Two Noble Kinsmen*

(Harold Clurman Theatre) Friday, Sept. 10–Oct. 3, 1993 (16 performances) Riverside Theatre Workshop presents:
THE MAKE OVER by Luigia M. Miller; Director/Choreographer, Alberto Guzman; Music, Steven Silverstein, Hershel Dwellingham; Lyrics, Bianca Miller, Ms. Miller; Musical Director, Michael Lavine; Stage Manager, Emily C. Norton; Press, Francine L. Trevens/Robert J. Weston CAST: Billy Hipkins (Swan), Jennifer Brunson (Heidi/Tamara/Mary), Jennifer Gaita (Nurse/Dreadful Rat), Corina Katt (Titwell/Lola), Karyn Lee (Chastity), Michael Lynch (Odette), Brad Van Nostrand (Dr. Hyde/Dreadful Rat), Tom Vazzana (Elmer/Ossie)
MUSICAL NUMBERS: Miracles of Change, What Fools These Mortals Be, Phantom of Avenue D, My Jolly Jelly Roll, Electrocution Rock, Let Me Sing, When You Can't See Clearly, Gotta Get Back Home, Center of the World, Brand Old Me, Silence Finds

A comedy with music in two acts.

(Village Theatre) Thursday, Sept. 9–Oct. 3, 1993 (17 performances) Village Theatre Co. presents:
COULD I HAVE THIS DANCE? by Doug Haverty; Director, Jules Aaron; Set, David Blankenship; Costumes, Marj Feenan; Lighting, Jonathan Farber; Sound, Jim Harrington; Stage Manager, Gak Kompes CAST: Alyson Reim (Monica), Toni Sawyer (Jeannette), Bob Horen (Hank), Isabel Keating (Amanda), Randell Harriss (Errol), Roger Michelson (Colin)

A drama in two acts. The action takes place in Los Angeles, 1988.

(St. Mark's Theatre) Thursday, Sept. 9–26, 1993 (12 performances) The Ark Ensemble presents:
DIVIDED TOGETHER by Girish Karnad; Director, Erin B. Mee; Lighting, Jason Boyd; Songs, Steve Gorn; Masks, Heather Foy; Stage Manager, Jessica Hall CAST: Karenjune Sanchez (Bhagavata/Kali), Michael Hazard Perry (Actor I/Devadatta), Tommy Cheng (Hayavadana), Jason McKay (Kapila/Actor II), Sakina Jaffrey (Padmini), Neera Relian (Doll I), Brian Caldwell (Doll II), Spike Appel (Child)

An adaptation of Thomas Mann's *Transposed Heads*.

(Playwrights Horizons) Tuesday, Sept. 14–Oct. 10, 1993 (33 performances) Young Playwrights Inc. in asssociation with Playwrights Horizons presents:
THE 1993 YOUNG PLAYWRIGHTS FESTIVAL; Artistic Director, Sheri M. Goldhirsch; Managing Director, Brett W. Reynolds; Sets, Allen Moyer; Costumes, Caryn Neman; Lighting, Pat Dignan; Sound, Raymond Schilke; Stage Managers, Lloyd Davis, Jr., Peter J. Davis; Board of Directors: Alfred Uhry, President; Stephen Sondheim, Executive Vice-President; Mary Rodgers, Vice-President; Press, Serino Coyne/Alan Cohen, Kris Moran

Crystal Stairs by Kim Daniel; Director, Mark Brokaw; Fights, Rick Sordelet CAST: Stacy Highsmith (Evette), Ron Brice (Ulis), Aleta Mitchell (Genesis), Curtis McClarin (Boy)
Five Visits from Mr. Whitcomb by Carter L. Bays; Director, Michael Mayer CAST: Daniel Jenkins (Tom), Robert Stanton (Whitcomb), Camryn Manheim (Sheriff), Paul Bates (Sheriff), Ramon Melindez Moses (Fed)
Sweetbitter Baby by Madeleine George; Director, Seret Scott CAST: Lucy Deakins (Malina), Michael Stuhlbarg (Sasha)
Live from the Edge of Oblivion by Jerome D. Hairston; Director, Marion McClinton CAST: Akili Prince (Johnas), Curtis McClarin (Sir Hoodlum/Frank Tuff/Mista Say No), Paul Bates (Mista Officer/Reporter/Announcer), Ramon Melindez Moses (Bobby D/Brother Wino), Lisa Louise Langford (Hood Mother/Mama/Mutha Crackhead), Lucy Deakins (Teacher)
The twelfth annual festival.

(Playhouse 91) Wednesday, Sept. 15–Oct. 17, 1993 (25 performances) INTAR Hispanic American Arts Center in association with AT&T OnStage presents:
EL GRECO with Music by William Harper; Libretto, Bernardo Solano; Director, Tom O'Horgan; Music Director, Bradford Ellis; Sets, Robin Wagner; Costumes, Donna Zakowski; Lighting, Robert Wierzel; Sound, Bob Bielecki; Masks/Props, Perry Arthur Kroeger; Stage Manager, J. Courtney Pollard; Press, Peter Cromarty/Donnalynn Wendt, David Bar Katz CAST: Daryl Henriksen (El Grecco), Sean Dooley (Child Soul), Tom Bogdan (Preboste), Selena Cantor (Jeronima), Maggi-Meg Reed (Eleni), Don Chastain (Antonio), Veronica Tyler (Teresa), Gabriel Barre (Quiroga), Steven Goldstein (Jorge Manuel), April Armstrong, Neal James Girandola, Serafina Martino, Sandra Rodriguez, Christine Sperry, Nicholas Wuehrmann
A new opera on the life of the Spanish artist, 1577–1614.

(Duo Theatre) Thursday, Sept. 16, 1993 reopened Thursday, May 5–June 26, 1994 (32 performances) Duo Theatre presents:
THE BALL with Music by Bronwen Jones; Lyrics/Book/Direction, Michael Alasa; Stage Manager, Paul Wontorek CAST: Jason Ascher (Delores Nike), Aaron Lee Battle (Mona Nike), Eric Bernat (Sandie), Sidney Myer (Livia Balenziaga), Josef Perry (Josie Fantabulous), Al Roffe (Sid), Richard Skipper (Marlene Fantabulous), Jose Manuel Yenque (Bennie Fantabulous), Jose Cortes (Emcee)
A musical performed without intermission. The action takes place in the Paradise Ballroom.

(Studio 4-A) Friday, Sept. 17–26, 1993 (8 performances) Studio e presents:
SELF TORTURE AND STRENUOUS EXERCISE and **THE FAIRY GARDEN** by Harry Kondoleon; Costumes, Keith Galluzzo; Sets, Duncan Raymond; Stage Managers, Paul Griffth, Alan Zatkow; Press, Russell Goldberg *Self Torture:* Director, Stacey-Jo Marine CAST: Matthew Boston (Carl), Joseph Andorfer (Alvin), Laura Sheaks (Bethany), Sheila Head (Adel) *Fairy Garden:* Director, Bennett Rink CAST: Andrea Maulella (aDagny), Russell Goldberg (Roman), Dana Ertischek (Fairy), Justin Kennedy (Boris), Eric Steven Mills (Mechanic)
Two one-acts.

Roger Rosenblatt in *Bibliomania* (Jonathan Slaff)

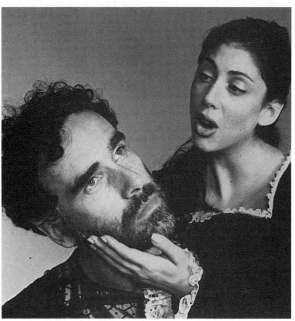
Daryl Henricksen, Selena Cantor in *El Greco*
(William Gibson)

(Village Gate) Saturday, Sept. 18, 1993—Art D'Lugoff presents:
THULI with Thuli Dumakude, Valerie Naranjo, Emma
Songs and stories of South Africa.

(Kaufman Theatre) Saturday, Sept. 18–Nov. 14, 1993 (66 performances) Martin R. Kaufman presents:
IN PERSONS; Director, Martin Charnin; Sets, Ann Keehbauch; Lighting, Ken Billington, Jason Kantrowitz; Sound, Raymond D. Schilke; Music, Keith Levenson; Stage Manager, Anne Marie Paolucci; Press, David Rothenberg CAST: Eli Wallach, Anne Jackson
Scenes from plays in which the duo has performed.

(Irish Arts Center) Tuesday, Sept. 21–Oct. 10, 1993 (14 performances and 8 previews) Irish Arts Center presents:
ONLY THE LONELY ARE FREE with William Walsh; Press, Francine L. Trevens/Robert J. Weston
Poetic insights into love and America through the eyes of Irish and British poets.

(Theatre for the New City) Wednesday, Sept. 22–Oct. 17, 1993 (20 performances) Phoenix Ensemble in association with Russian Academy of Theatre Arts presents:
THE BATHTUB by Paul Schmidt; Director, Ivan Popovsky; Sets, Felix Filshtinsky; Costumes, Cathy Small; Lighting, Paul Bartlett; Stage Manager, Elizabeth Ann Laren; Press, Shirley Herz/Sam Rudy CAST INCLUDES: Celia Arana, Edward Cunningham (Inventor), Tony Jackson, Paul Knox, Kerry Metzler, Fred Velde (Sen. Hamfat Hum), Jeremy Brisiel (Roger Rudd), Cathy Daves, Marlene Hodgdon (Secretary), Jackie Christie, Vicki Hirsch, Renee Upchurch
A new American adaptation of the 1930 Russian satire *Banya.*

(American Place Theatre) Wednesday, Sept. 22–Oct. 24, 1993 (25 performances) American Place Theatre presents:
BIBLIOMANIA; Written/Performed by Roger Rosenblatt; Director, Wynn Handman; Set, Kert Lundell; Lighting, Christopher Boll; Stage Manager, Matthew Farrell; Press, Jonathan Slaff
One man crazy about books.

(Nat Horne Theatre) Wednesday, Sept. 22, 1993– The Acting Company Studio presents:
EINSTEIN; Written/Directed by Joel Selmeier; Press, David Rothenberg/Terrence E. Womble CAST: Richard Davis Springle
One-man look at the public and private physicist. Performed at the Actor's Theatre Studio since April 1993.

(West Bank Cafe) Friday, Sept. 24–Oct. 23, 1993 (10 performances) West Bank Downstairs Theatre presents:
GAS, FOOD, TALENT; Director, Michael Schiralli; Musical Director, Doug Nervik; Lighting, Terry Van Richardson; Stage Manager, Anthony Sepulveda CAST: Jonathan Fishman, Leigh Kamioner, Jessica MacDonald, Doug Nervik, Michael Schiralli, Tom Sepulveda, Tom Shillue, Ilona Vellios
    Third return engagement of an entertainment set in the Rest Stop Lounge off the New Jersey Turnpike.

(National Shakespeare Conservatory) Friday, Sept. 24–Oct. 10, 1993 (16 performances) Chain Lightning Theatre presents:
MOURNING BECOMES ELECTRA by Eugene O'Neill; Director, Joseph Millett; Lighting, Stewart Wagner; Stage Manager, Max Faugno; Press, Jim Baldassare CAST: Susan Baum (Louisa Ames/Mrs. Borden), Burton Fitzpatrick (Peter Niles), Joel Goldes (Orin Mannon), Ginger Grace (Christine Mannon), Mark Hamlet (Everett Hills/Ira Mackel), Jamen Heisel (Dr. Blake/Abner Small), Priscilla Holbrook (Hazel Niles), Cheryl Horne (Lavinia Mannon), Kricker James (Ezra Mannon/Joe Silva), Richard Kinsey (Adam Brant), Blainie Logan (Minnie/Mrs. Hills), Frank Nastasi (Amos/Chantyman), C. T. O'Connor (Seth/Josiah Borden)
    An uncut version presented over two nights.

(Theatre Row Theatre) Saturday, Sept. 25–Oct. 10, 1993 Pulse Ensemble Theatre, Betka Productions, Laurie Sanders-Smith present:
DESERT RITES by Stephen Bittrich; Director, Will Pomerantz; Lighting, Allen Hahn; Set, Mr. Pomerantz, Mr. Hahn; Costumes, Cherie Bloodworth; Music, Dina Emerson; Sound, Andrew C. Shapiro; Stage Manager, B. Luxene Strong CAST: Stephen Bittrich (Billy Ray), Christopher Cook (John Lancaster), Karen Tsen Lee (Lulan), Stephen Xavier Lee, Michael G. Chin (Mr. Wang), Marcus Powell (Mr. Greene), Veronica Cruz (Rising Moon)
    A Vegas vision quest in two acts.

(Westbeth Theatre) Monday, Sept. 27, 1993– Joseph Traina presents:
GAMS ON THE LAM; Director, John Plummer; Costumes, Katrin Nauman; Sets, Richard Scoggins, Dennis Earle; Lighting, Peter Romaniello; Music, Leo Crandall; Press, David Lotz CAST: Patricia Buckley, Lauren Unbekant, Leslie Noble
    All-female comedy troupe.

(Brooklyn Academy of Music/Opera House) Tuesday, Sept. 28–Oct. 10, 1993 (16 performances) Brooklyn Academy of Music and Royal National Theatre of Great Britian present:
THE MADNESS OF GEORGE III by Alan Bennett; Director, Nicholas Hytner; Design, Mark Thompson; Lighting, Paul Pyant, Brian Ridley; Music, Kevin Leeman; Stage Manager, Courtney Bryant; Press, Peter Carzasty, Ben Hartley CAST: Nigel Hawthorne (King George III), Selina Cadell (Quenn Charlotte), Nick Sampson (Prince of Wales), Julian Rhind-Tutt (Duke of York), Richenda Carey (Lady Pembroke/Margaret Nicholson), Anthony Calf (Fitzroy), William Chubb (Greville), Matthew Lloyd Davies (Papandiek), William Oxborrow (Fortnum), Paul Corrigan (Braun), Juliam Wadham (Pitt), Jeffry Wickham (Lord Thurlow), Simon Scott (Henry Dundas), Collin Johnson (Sir Boothby Skrymshir), Adam Barker (Ramsden), David Verrey (Charles James Fox), Iain Mitchell (Richard Brinsley Sheridan), Roger Hammond (Sir George Baker), Robert Swann (Dr. Richard Warren), Cyril Shaps (Sir Lucas Pepys), Clive Merrison (Dr. Francis Willis), Celestine Randall (Maid), Tony Sloman (Footman)
    A two-act political comedy, based on historical fact, about the British King who lost the colonies, 1788–89.

(Westside Theatre/Downstairs) Tuesday, Sept. 28, 1993–Jan. 11, 1995 David Stone, Irene Pinn, Amy Nederlander-Case, in association with Harriet Newman Leve present:
FAMILY SECRETS by Sherry Glaser and Greg Howells; Director, Mr. Howells; Set, Rob Odorisio; Lighting, Brian MacDevitt; Costumes, Lorraine Anderson; Stage Manager, Cathy B. Blaser; Press, Pete Sanders/Ian Rand CAST: Sherry Glaser
    The story of an entire Jewish American family. Performed without intermission.

**Top: Nigel Hawthorne in *Madness of George III* (Donald Cooper)
Bottom: Sherry Glaser in *Family Secrets* (Carol Rosegg)**

(Primary Stages) Wednesday, Sept. 29–Oct. 24, 1993 (24 performances) Primary Stages presents:
BREAKING UP by Michael Cristofer; Director, Melia Bensussen; Set, Allen Moyer; Lighting, Thomas Hase; Costumes, Michael Krass; Music/Sound, Guy Sherman/Aural Fixation; Stage Manager, Kristina Schorr; Press, Anne Einhorn CAST: Kevin O'Rourke (Steve), Allison Janney (Alice)
    A drama performed without intermission.

(Atlantic Theatre) Wednesday, Sept. 29–Nov. 14, 1993 (26 performances) Atlantic Theater Company presents:
FRANK MAYA: PAYING FOR THE POOL; Director, John Masterson; Stage Manager, Chris De Camillis; Press, Jim Baldassare
    A comic remembrance of growing up and coming out.

(P.S. 122) Thursday, Sept. 30–Oct. 17, 1993 (12 performances) reopened at Downtown Art Co. and then N.Y. Theatre Workshop
P.S. 122 presents:
SOME PEOPLE; Written/Performed by Danny Hoch; Lighting, David Castaneda; Press, Tony Origlio/William McLaughlin
    A solo creation of eleven different New York characters.

(Judith Anderson Theatre) Thursday, Sept. 30–Oct. 17, 1993 (19 performances) Miranda Theatre Co. presents:
THE EYE OF THE BEHOLDER by Ira Wallach; Director, John Hickok; Sets, Kevin Joseph Roach; Lighting, Scott Griffin; Costumes, Carol Sherry; Stage Manager, Sally Frontman; Press, Peter Cromarty/Michael Hartman CAST: Kim Hunter (Aunt Sally), Jerry Mettner succeeded by John Hickok (Tod Lomax), Darby Townsend (Bea Hartz), Bob Emmett (Hansen Van Brook)
    A two-act comedy set in the art world of East Hampton and New York City.

(Ohio Theatre) Friday, Oct. 1–17, 1993 (16 performances) Watermark Theatre presents:
THE ENTHUSIASM OF THE SPECIES; Written/Performed by Michael McMurtry; Directors, Daniel Brooks, Nela Wagman; Set, Sarah Lambert; Lighting, Rob Cangemi; Stage Manager, Bernadette McGay; Press, Fred Nathan/Bill Schelble, Michael Borowski
    A solo performance.

(Samuel Beckett Theatre) Friday, Oct. 1–17, 1993 (16 performances) Gilgamesh Theatre Group in association with The WaterFront Ensemble, CTF, and TCP productions presents:
THE SHANNON DOYLE INCIDENT; Written/Directed by John Morrison; Set, George A. Allison; Lighting, Rita Ann Kogler; Costumes, Cathy Favreau; Sound, Joe Witt; Fights, Rick Sordelet; Stage Manager, Greg Skura; Press, Chris Boneau/Adrian Bryan-Brown, Bob Fennell CAST: Robert Trumbull (Fr. John McGowan), Gregory Erbach (Art Kroeger), Joe Witt (Brian Tahaney), Lori Shearer (Mary Phinney), Lynne Workinger (Shannon Doyle), Lynn Bowman (Patricia Cullen Di Santis)
    A two-act drama inspired by actual events. The action involves a rape accusation on an upstate N.Y. college campus.

(Theatre Four) Monday, Oct. 4, 1993– Wallack's Point Productions presents:
ALL THAT GLITTERS by Stephan Bullard; Director, Eleanor Reissa; Set, Harry Darrow; Lighting, Tom Sturge; Costumes, Lisa Tomczeszyn; Stage Manager, James FitzSimmons; Press, Shirley Herz/Sam Rudy CAST: Dana Vance (Clayton Maguire), Linda Cook (Barbara Reed), Barbara Gulan (Baroness Katarina von Oberdorf), Ilene Kristen (Scooter Goldberg)
    A comedy performed without intermission. The action takes place at a Park Avenue cocktail hour.

(Ubu Rep. Theatre) Tuesday, Oct. 5–24, 1993 (18 performances) Ubu Repertory presents:
FIRE'S DAUGHTERS by Ina Cesaire; Translation, Judith G. Miller; Director, Ntozake Shange; Set, Watoku Ueno; Lighting, Greg MacPherson; Costumes, Carol Ann Pelletier; Music, Mauro Regosco; Stage Manager, Bethany Ford; Press, Peter Cromarty/Michael Hartman CAST: Darlene Bel Grayson (Mama Sun), Alene Dawson (Annarose), Cee-Cee Harshaw (Roseanne), Harriet D. Foy (Sister Smoke)
    Four different Martinican women on the eve of a violent revolt during the 1800s.

(Union Square Theatre) Tuesday, Oct. 5–24, 1993 (22 performances) Richard Martini, Albert Nocciolino, Allen Spivak, Larry Magid and Center Theatre Group/Mark Taper Forum present:
HOLLY NEAR: FIRE IN THE RAIN by Holly and Timothy Near; Director, Timothy Near; Musical Director, John Bucchino; Set, Kate Edmunds; Costumes, Marianna Elliott; Lighting, Richard Winkler; Projections, Charles Rose; Press, Keith Sherman/Jim Byk/Stuart Ginsberg CAST: Holly Near
    A musical biography.

**Kevin O'Rourke, Allison Janney
in *Breaking Up* (Andrew Leynse)**

**Frank Maya in *Frank Maya:
Paying for the Pool* (Paula Court)**

**Dana Vance, Barbara Gulan, Linda Cook,
Ilene Kristen in *All That Glitters* (Gerry Goodstein)**

97

Daisy Eagan, Howard Kaye in *Little Prince* (Stephen Speliotis)

**Chelsea Altman, Robert Floyd
in *Able-Bodied Seaman* (Roya)**

(Ballroom) Wednesday, Oct. 6, 1993– The Ballroom presents:
goodbye, harry; Written/Performed by Pamela Ross; Press, David Rothenberg/
Terence Womble
A daughter's musical tribute to her father.

(28th St. Theatre) Wednesday, Oct. 6–24, 1993 (11 performances and 5 pre-
views) reopened at John Houseman Theatre Oct. 28, 1993–Jan. 2, 1994 (68 per-
formances) Chrysalis Productions presents:
THE LITTLE PRINCE with Music by Rick Cummins; Lyrics/Book, John
Scoullar; Director, William Martin; Musical Director, Alki Steriopoulos; Set,
Rob Odorisio; Lighting, Beverly Emmons; Costumes, Kristin Yungkurth; Sound,
David Meschter; Stage Manager, James Marr; Press, Peter Cromarty/Donnalynn
Wendt CAST: Daisy Eagan succeeded by Ramzi Khalaf (Little Prince), Howard
Kaye succeeded by Joseph Mahowald (Aviator), Merwin Goldsmith succeeded
by Mike Champagne (Grownup #1/Men on Planets/Fox), Natascia Diaz
(Grownup #2/Rose/Snake)

MUSICAL NUMBERS: I Fly, 44 Sunsets, Enough, Such a Lot to Do, What a
Beautiful, I Love You Goodbye, Fly Away, Admire Me, Days Go So Quickly,
The Snake, Some Otherwhere, Sunset Stories, Day After Day, This Lovely Song,
All the Stars Will Laugh
A new two-act musical version of the popular Antoine de Saint Exupery
story. Previous musical versions include John Barry and Don Black's musical
with Anthony Rapp (Alvin Theatre, Jan. 1982) and Lerner & Loewe's 1974 film
musical.

(One Dream Theatre) Thursday, Oct. 7–31, 1993 (16 performances) One Dream
and Jim Farmer present:
THE SAVAGE ROUTINE OF LIVING; Written/Directed by Jim Farmer;
Press, Chris Boneau/Adrian Bryan-Brown, Bob Fennell CAST: Cynthia Babak,
Jim Farmer, Jane Grenier, Wilbur Edwin Henry, Phillip Lombardo, Rob
McCaskill, Suzy Morris, Celia Schaefer
A musical set in a San Francisco coffee house, 1960.

(Holy Trinity) Thursday, Oct. 7–31, 1993 (20 performances) Triangle Theatre
Company presents:
PAINTING IT RED with Music by Gary Rue; Lyrics, Leslie Ball; Director,
Michael Ramach; Sets, William F. Moser; Costumes, Carol Brys; Lighting,
Nancy Collings; Stage Manager, Cathy Diane Tomlin; Press, Susan Chicoine
CAST: Tom Cayler, Lori Fischer, Allison Rice-Taylor, Andy Taylor, Joystick
A musical on the trials and travails of modern relationships.

(Manhattan Class Company) Friday, Oct. 8–30, 1993 (20 performances and 6
previews) Manhattan Class Co. presents:
THE ABLE-BODIED SEAMAN by Alan Bowne; Director, Jimmy Bohr; Sets,
Rob Odorisio; Lighting, Howard Werner; Costumes, Claudia Stephens; Sound,
Stuart J. Allyn; Stage Manager, Gail Eve Malatesta; Press, Peter Cromarty/
Michael Hatman CAST: Robert LuPone (Roy), Chelsea Altman (Fay), Anita
Gillette (Rita), Larry Attile (Manfred), Robert Floyd (Bogart), Simon Brooking
(Gamble)
A drama in two acts. The action takes place in Queens, N.Y., 1981.

(Harold Clurman Theatre) Friday, Oct. 8–31, 1993 (24 performances) Willow
Cabin Theatre Company presents:
S.S. GLENCAIRN—FOUR PLAYS OF THE SEA by Eugene O'Neill; Direc-
tor, Edward Berkeley; Set, Miguel Lopez-Castillo; Costumes, Dede Pochos,
Fiona Davis; Lighting, Michael Gottlieb; Press, Jim Baldassare CAST: John
Billeci (Scotty), John Bolger (Smitty), Paul Bolger (Paul), Thomas Borrillo (Big
Frank/Rough), Doug Broe (Cocky), Kenneth Favre (Dick/Jack), Ken Forman
(1st Mate/Ivan), Laurence Gleason (Olson), Peter Killy (Paddy/Captain/
Swanson), Charmaine Lord (Susie/Mag), Stephen Mora (Max/Mate/Rough),
Angela Nevard (Violet/Freda), Adam Oliensis (Driscoll), Linda Powell (Pearl/
Kate), Michael Rispoli (Yank/Fat Joe), Cheryl Rogers (Bella), Jonathan Sea
(Donkeyman/Nick), Craig Zakarian (Davis)
Four one-acts: *Moon of the Caribees, Bound East for Cardiff, Long Voyage
Home, In the Zone.*

(The Studio) Friday, Oct. 8–24, 1993 (14 performances) Carousel Theatre
Company presents:
THE RIMMERS OF ELDRITCH by Lanford Wilson; Director, Michael
LaPolla; Set, Charles Ard; Lighting, Denise Bourcier; Costumes, Daphne
Neiman Press, Howard and Barbara Atlee CAST INCLUDES: Howard Atlee,
Tim Connell, Lynn Evans, Pamela Dean Kenny, Tembi Locke, Harriette
Mandeville, Vicki Meisner, Angela Chale Millington, Mike Murray, Emma
Palzere, Marilyn Raphael, Zeke Rippy, Sharon Watroba, Vanessa J. Wells,
William-Kevin Young
A new production of the 1967 drama.

Craig Zakarian, John Bolger, Ken Favre, John Billeci in
S.S. Glencairn (Carol Rosegg)

R. Ward Duffy, Mark Irish in *Trophies* (William Gibson)

(Intar Theatre) Saturday, Oct. 9–Nov. 27, 1993 (48 performances) Psst! Productions presents:
SCARING THE FISH by Benjamin Bettenbender; Director, Michael Warren Powell; Set, Eric Lowell Renschler; Lighting, Deborah Constantine; Sound, Bart Fasbender; Costumes, Leslie Yarmo; Fights, Rick Sordelet; Stage Manager, Randy Lawson; Press, David Rothenberg CAST: Andrew Polk (Chris), Sheridan Crist (Dennis), Jim Bracchitta (Gene)
A New Hampshire-set drama performed without intermission.

(Theatre Row Theatre) Thursday, Oct. 14–30, 1993 (16 performances) Renegade Theatre Company presents:
ON THE WATERFRONT by Budd Schulberg in association with Stan Silverman; Director, Kelly Patton; Design, Robert Lott; Score, Edgar David Grana CAST: Adrain Pasdar (Terry Malloy), Charles Rucker (Fr. Barry), Margolite Kestin (Edie Doyle), Jack O'Connell (Johnny Friendly), Charlie Yanko (Charlie Malloy), Ed Bryce, Philip Bryce, Teddy Coluca, Jim Cronin, Tony Cucci, Ralph De Matthews, Tony Lombardi, Paul Marcazzo, Dermot McNamara, Arthur Nascarella, Bob Quinn, Jerry Rago, Bill Ray Tyson, William Winslow
A stage adapatation of the 1954 film set on the Hoboken, N.J. waterfront.

(Westbeth Theatre Center) Thursday, Oct. 14–30, 1993 (13 performances) Character Productions presents:
MASKED MEN by Anthony Cuen; Director, Tom O'Horgan CAST: Rafael Alvarez, Fay Kepperson, Doug Von Nessen
A drama involving two unlikely friends.

(American Place Theatre) Saturday, Oct. 16–Dec. 19, 1993 (47 performances) American Place Theatre presents:
JIMMY TINGLE'S UNCOMMON SENSE; Director, Larry Arrick; Press, Jonathan Slaff CAST: Jimmy Tingle
A humorist offers common wisdom.

(Bank St. Theatre) Friday, Oct. 15–30, 1993 (15 performances) Classact Productions in association with Time Vault Theatre Works presents:
THE BOYS NEXT DOOR by Tom Griffin; Director, Joseph B. Garren; Set, Elizabeth Popiel; Costumes, Jimm Halliday; Lighting, Andrew Gmoser; Stage Manager, Sue Jane Stoker CAST: Robert Colston, Mark Hardy, David Lipman, Scott McGowan, Don Stitt, Barbara Suter, Geri Tallone, Lee Teplitzky, David Titus
This production benefits Broadway Cares/Equity Fights AIDS.

(West End Gate Theatre Bar) Monday, Oct. 18–Nov. 2, 1993 (6 performances) The Matrix Theatre presents:
THREE ONE-ACT PLAYS by Tony Villela; Sets, Paul Melia; Lighting, Robert Perry; Costumes, Meghan Barr; Press, David Rothenberg

PROGRAM: *Executive Council;* Director, Nick Corley CAST: Christopher Collet, Mitchell Riggs, Michael Walker, Paul Gutrecht, Amy Sloane
Crime Scene; Director, Nancy Hancock CAST: Nancy McDoniel, Jeff Broitman, Marc Bryman
Buddy Movie; Director, Elizabeth Holder CAST: Adam Stein, John C. Havens, Lauren Bowles, John W. Kugel

(Cherry Lane Theatre) Tuesday, Oct. 19–Dec. 26, 1993 (62 performances and 16 previews) Yabadoo Productions present:
TROPHIES by John J. Wooten; Director, John Gulley; Set, Mark Cheney; Costumes, Missy West; Lighting, Mark F. O'Connor; Sound, Scott Stauffer; Music, David Brunetti; Stage Manager, Geoffrey F. Morris; Press, Shirley Herz/Glenna Freedman CAST: Marc West succeeded by R. Ward Duffy (David), John Henry Cox (Mr. Stone), Janet Nell Catt (Mrs. Stone), Mark Irish (Robert/Bobby), Christen Tassin (Laura)
A family drama.

(Cucaracha Theatre) Wednesday, Oct. 20–Nov. 13, 1993 (16 performances) Cucaracha presents:
BREMEN FREEDOM by Rainer Werner Fassbinder; Directors, Paul Lazar, Annie B. Parson; Set, Joanne Howard; Lighting, David Moodey; Costumes, Claudia Stephens; Press, Holly Becker CAST: Stephen Brantley (Johann), Stacy Dawson (M.C.), Joey Golden (Timm), Jan Leslie Harding (Geesche 1/Mother/Luisa), Deirdre Harrison (Geesche 4), Kirk Jackson (Zimmerman/Fr. Marcus), Ilyana Kadushin (Geesche 2), Susan Maginn (Geesche 3), Brennan Murphy (Gottfried), Rebecca Wisocky (Geesche 5)
A drama of a 19th-century liberated woman.

(Synchronicity Space) Thursday, Oct. 21–Nov. 7, 1993 (14 performances)
Spectrum Stage presents:
DELICATE DANGERS; Directors, Alexander Dinelaris, Stephanie Scott, Chuck Zito; Press, Kermit C. Klein   CAST: Georgia Buchanan, Nancy Jo Carpenter, Charles Derbyshire, Mark DiekmAnn, Karla Hendrick, Joan Matthiessen, Tim McCall, Charlotte Patton, Jack Poggi, Anne Popolizio, Margaret Ritchie, Frances Robertson, Darby Townsend

PROGRAM: *He Said and She Said* by Alice Gerstenberg, *The Bad Penny* by Rachel Field, *Trifles* by Susan Glaspell
   Three one-act plays, all at least 70 years old, by and about women.

(Lambs Theatre/Little) Thursday, Oct. 21–Dec. 12, 1993 (54 performances)
Lamb's Theatre Company presents:
JOHNNY PYE AND THE FOOLKILLER with Music/Lyrics by Randy Courts; Book/Lyrics, Mark St. Germain; Based on the short story by Stephen Vincent Benet; Director, Scott Harris; Musical Director, Steven M. Alper; Orchestrations, Douglas Besterman; Musical Staging, Janet Watson; Sets, Peter Harrison; Costumes, Claudia Stephens; Lighting, Kenneth Posner; Sound, David Lawson; Stage Manager, David Waggett; Press, Chris Boneau/Adrian Bryan-Brown, Hillary Harrow CAST: Daniel Jenkins (Johnny Pye), Spiro Malas (The Foolkiller), Kaitlin Hopkins (Suzy Marsh), Peter Gerety (Wilbur Wilberforce), Tanny McDonald (Mrs. Miller), Ralston Hill (Barber), Mark Lotito (Bob), Michael Ingram (Bill), Conor Gillespie (Young Johnny Pye), Heather Lee Soroka (Young Suzy Marsh)

MUSICAL NUMBERS: Another Day, Goodbye Johnny, Shower of Sparks, Occupations, Handle with Care, End of the Road, Challenge to Love, The Barbershop, Married with Children, Land Where There Is No Death, Time Passes, Never Felt Better In My Life, Epilogue(The Answer), Finale
   A musical in two acts. The action takes place in Martinsville, USA and various locations, 1928–95.

(Ohio Theatre) Friday, Oct. 22–Nov. 14, 1993 (21 performances) Arden Party presents:
THE BEGGARS' OPERA by John Gay; Music, Tony Geballe; Director/Costumes, Karin Coonrod; Set/Lighting, Darrel Maloney; Press, David Rothenberg CAST: Paula Cole (Jenny Diver/Mrs. Trapes), Kenneth Talberth (Macheath), Carolyn McDermott (Lucy Lockit), Joanna Adler, Gary Brownlee, Mary Christopher, Andrew Hubatsek, Yuri Skujins, James Urbaniak
   The 1728 play with a new score.

(Samuel Beckett Theatre) Friday, Oct. 22–Nov. 7, 1993 (15 performances) New Georges presents:
OTHER PLACES by Barbara Wiechmann; Director, Martha Banta CAST INCLUDES: Jeanne Willcoxon (Jeremiah), Frank Deal, Lynne McCollough, Mark Setlock
   A fractured fairy tale.

Kaitlin Hopkins, Spiro Malas, Daniel Jenkins in *Johnny Pye...* (Carol Rosegg)

(Folksbiene Playhouse) Saturday, Oct. 23, 1993–Jan. 17, 1994 Folksbiene Theatre presents:
STEMPENYU by Sholom Aleichem; Adaptation, Dora Wasserman; Music, Eli Rubinstein; Director, Bryna Turetsky; Musical Director, Hershey Felder; Choreography, Felix Fibush; Press, Max Eisen/Madelon Rosen CAST: Mina Bern, Zypora Spaisman, David Rogow, Hershey Felder, Richard Carlow, Norman Kruger, Miriam Greenberg, Cara L. Gaffen, Julie Alexander
   A new musical adaptation.

(Promenade Theatre) Tuesday, Oct. 26–Nov. 21, 1993 (28 performances) Drew Dennet presents:
A QUARREL OF SPARROWS by James Duff; Director, Kenneth Elliott; Set, Loren Sherman; Costumes, Debra Tennenbaum; Lighting, Donald Holder; Sound, Aural Fixation; Stage Manager, Allison Sommers; Press, Shirley Herz/Sam Rudy, Barbara Carroll CAST: Henderson Forsythe (August Ainsworth), Polly Holliday (Rosanna Ainsworth Jackson), Mitchell Lichtenstein (Paul Palmer), Jan Hooks (Angela Mercer), Andrew Weems (Lynn Waters), John C. Vennema (Martin Green)
   A comedy in two acts. The action takes place in Sag Harbor, Long Island.

(Playhouse 46) Tuesday, Oct. 26–Nov. 20, 1993 (28 performances) Pan Asian Repertory and Women's Project and Productions present:
EATING CHICKEN FEET by Kitty Chen; Director, Kati Kuroda; Lighting, Michael Chybowski; Costumes, Hugh Hanson; Set, Robert Klingelhoeffer; Sound, Jim Van Bergen; Fights, Michael G. Chin; Stage Manager, Patt Giblin; Press, Denise Roberts CAST: Liana Pai (Betty Sung), Ben Li (Dr. Sung), Wai-Ching Ho (Mrs. Sung), Steve Park (Lowell Sung), Bobby Sacher (Peter Diamond), Christine Campbell (Mrs. Barclay), Mary Lee (Diane Leong)
   A comedy in two acts. The action takes place in a hospital room.

(Madison Ave. Theatre) Wednesday, Oct. 27–Nov. 7, 1993 (10 performances) Madison Avenue Theatre in association with Robert Bryson presents:
THE QUALITY OF MERCY by David Hall; Director, Sean Howard; Press, Audrey Ross CAST: C. C. Banks, Robert Bryson, Maureen McNamara, Judith Morse, John Muntone, Eric Nielsen, Hunter Runnette, Lainie R. Siegel
   A drama involving a murder victim's parents facing her killer.

(Charles Ludlam Theatre) Thursday, Oct. 28, 1993–Jan. 16, 1994 The Ridiculous Theatre presents:
HOW TO WRITE A PLAY by Charles Ludlam; Director, Everett Quinton; Set, Tom Greenfield; Lighting, Richard Currie; Costumes, Raona Ponce; Sound, Mark Bennett; Wigs, Zsamira Ronquillo; Press Peter Cromarty/Michael Hartman CAST: Everett Quinton (Everett), Jimmy Szczepanek (Michael), Katy Dierlam (Natalie), Mel Nieves (Fed Ex Man/Orville Titwilly/Miguel), Arthur T. Acuna (Madame Wong), Chris Tanner (Mr. Poussy), Bobby Reed (Mrs. Hornblatt), Christine Weiss (Rosalie), Michael Lynch (Claudia/Emperor), Lenys Sama (Generalissimo Carragua Fanfarron), Alonia King (Empress)
   The first production of the only unproduced Charles Ludlam comedy.

Liana Pai, Wai Ching Ho in *Eating Chicken Feet* (Martha Holmes)

(American Place Theatre) Friday, Oct. 29–Nov. 21, 1993 (18 performances)
American Place Theatre presents:
COME DOWN BURNING by Kia Corthron; Director, Judyie Al-Bilali; Sets, Kert Lundell; Costumes, Judy Dearing; Lighting, Shirley Pendergast; Sound, Robert LaPierre; Stage Manager, Monique Martin; Press, Jonathan Slaff CAST: Kim Yancey (Skoolie), Serena Henry (Evie), Myra Lucretia Taylor (Tee), Tse-Mach Washington (Will-Joe), Shona Tucker (Bink)
   A drama set in a poor rural community.

(Perry St. Theatre) Wednesday, Nov. 3–20, 1993 (16 performances) Collaborative Arts Project (CAP) in association with Upstream Productions presents:
CLOUD 9 by Caryl Churchill; Director, Michael Rego; Sets, Larry Sousa; Lighting, Chris Lee; Costumes, Michael Zecker; Sound, Darron L. West; Stage Manager, Laura Fallon CAST: Beth Bogdon (Maud/Betty), Marc Geller (Joshua/Cathy), Tom Gualtieri (Betty/Gerry), Julia K. Murney (Ellen/Mrs. Saunders/Victoria), Karen O'Connell (Edward/Lin), Hugh O'Gorman (Harry/Martin), Hank Unger (Clive/Edward)
   A comedy in two acts. The action takes place in Africa, 1893, and London, 1993.

(Soho Rep) Thursday, Nov. 4–Dec. 5, 1993 (23 performances) Soho Rep presents:
CARELESS LOVE; Written/Directed by Len Jenkin; Set, John Arnone; Lighting, Don Holder; Costumes, Caryn Neman; Sound, John Kilgore; Stage Manager, Nan Strauss CAST: Arthur Aulisi, Garret Dillahunt, Deirdre O'Connell, Steve Mellor, Polly Noonan, Lorca Simons, Rocco Sisto, Colleen Werthmann
   An existential comedy.

(Judith Anderson Theatre) Friday, Nov. 5–28, 1993 (23 performances) returned Tuesday, Apr. 5, 1994– Willow Cabin Theatre Company presents:
WHO WILL CARRY THE WORD? by Charlotte Delbo; Translation, Cynthia Haft; Director, Edward Berkeley; Set, Patricia Woodbridge; Costumes, Dede Pochos, Fiona Davis; Lighting, Jane Reisman; Movement, Jessica Wolfe; Stage Manager, Cynthia Tuohy; Press, Jim Baldassare CAST: Cynthia Besterman (Reine), Sophie Comet (Monique), Fiona Davis (Yvonne), Cecil Hoffmann (Francoise), Ibi Janko (Agnes), Rebecca Killy (Hortense), Jill Kinney (Sylvie), Julie Lancaster (Madeleine), Tasha Lawrence (Mounette), Charmaine Lord (Elisabeth), Verna Lowe (Regine), Lisa Messinger (Laure/Peasant Girl), Angela Nevard (Claire), Dede Pochos (Marie), Kathy Pope (Helene), Linda Powell (Denise), Christine Radman (Berthe), Maria Radman (Gina), Cheryl Rogers (Renee), Karen Ann Welch (Dedee/Lina), Eileen Lawless, Chandra Lee-Mann
   A French Holocaust memoir.

(Manhattan Performing Arts Co.) Saturday, Nov. 6–Dec. 19, 1993 (38 performances) Ruthie Productions and Alan Phillips in association with The JCC on the Upper West Side present:
THE SURVIVOR; Written/Directed by Susan Nanus; Sets, Alexandra Rubinstein, Peter Ortel; Lighting, Steven Friedlander; Costumes, Tamara Roth; Music, Misha Segal; Stage Manager, Regina S. Guggenheim; Press, Richard Kornberg CAST: W. Aaron Harpold (Jacek), Justin Walker (Yankele), John Fairlie (Rudy), Jason Katz (Lutek), Sean Cutler (Sevek), Heather Gottlieb (Hela), Dana Chaifetz (Mala), Julie Lauren (Halina), Sam Gray (Rubinstein), Michael Oberlander (Markowsky/Franek)
   A drama in two acts based on the true story of Jack Eisner. The action takes place in the Warsaw Ghetto, 1940–43.

(Ubu Rep. Theatre) Tuesday, Nov. 9–21, 1993 (12 performances) Ubu Repertory presents:
TALK ABOUT LOVE! by Paul Emond; Translation, Richard Miller; Director, Shirley Kaplan; Set, Watoku Ueno; Lighting, Greg MacPherson; Costumes, Carol Ann Pelletier; Sound, Ephraim Kehlmann; Stage Manager, Charlotte Volage; Press, Peter Cromarty/Michael Hartman CAST: Christopher Murney (Caracala), Laurie Graff (Waitress), Jerry Ball (Man with Bloodied Face)
   A Belgian comedy set in an almost empty bar.

(Harold Clurman Theatre) Wednesday, Nov. 10–27, 1993 (17 performances) Altered Stage presents:
STRING THEORY; Director, Molly Bishop; Lighting, Jon Hill CAST: David Eggar, Reid Cottingham, Christine van Kipnis, Robby Stevens, Laurelle Rethke
   A theatrical concert.

Top: Cloud 9 *company*

Center: Fiona Davis, Tasha Lawrence
in Who Will Carry the Word? *(Carol Rosegg)*

Bottom: Michael Oberlander, Justin Walker, Heather Gottlieb,
John Fairlie, Jason Katz, Sam Gray, (front) W. Aaron Harpold,
Julie Lauren, Dana Chaifetz, Sean Cutler in Survivor
(Mickey Pantano)

(One Dream Theatre) Thursday, Nov. 11–20, 1993 (7 performances) Zena Group Theatre presents:
THE CRACKWALKER by Judith Thompson; Director, Matt Ames; Set, Sean McCarthy; Costumes, Kathleen Hardgrove; Lighting, Diana Schlenk; Press, Chris Boneau/Adrian Bryan-Brown, Bob Fennell CAST: Mark Schulte, Richard Rose, Lisa McNulty, Laine Valentino, Josh Liveright
  A drama of four "down and outers" in suburban Canada.

(Samuel Beckett Theatre) Thursday, Nov. 11–21, 1993 (12 performances) Gilgamesh Theatre Group presents:
THE RISE AND RISE OF DANIEL ROCKETT by Peter Parnell; Director, David Marcia; Set, Roger Hanna; Lighting, David B. Sislen; Costumes, Susan Scherer; Sound, Matthew Schlofner; Fights, Ron Piretti; Stage Manager, Chris Pagoota CAST: St. Clair Ripley (Jeffrey), Carlyle Owens (Roger), Brian Shnipper (Steven), Brian David Price (Daniel), Jeff Knapp (Richard), Gwen Torry-Owens (Penny), Maggie Nichols (Judy), Carol Giffen (Claudia), Suzanne von Eck (Alice), Susan Orem (Mrs. Rice)
  A dramatic comedy about growing up.

(Nat Horne Studio) Friday, Nov. 12–28, 1993 (9 performances) Aboutface Theatre Company presents:
THE ROBERT PIECES by Steve Nelson; Director, Sean Burke CAST: Colin Mitchell
  A homeless man searches for his true home.

(Charles Ludlam Theatre) Tuesday, Nov. 16–Dec. 28, 1993 (8 performances)
99% ARTFREE; Director, Carter Inskeep; Musical Director, Elizabeth Hastings; Press, Peter Cromarty/Donnalynn Wendt CAST: Bill Dyszel
  An operatic spoof.

(Metropolitan Playhouse) Saturday, Nov. 13–Dec. 12, 1993 (14 performances) The Metropolitan Playhouse presents:
THE AMERICAN CLOCK by Arthur Miller; Director, Rebecca Taylor; Musical Director, Patrick Barnes; Choreography, Lindsey Hanahan; Sets, Jim Quinlan; Lighting, Tim Stephenson; Costumes, Fran Cole; Stage Manager, Eileen Haggerty CAST: Patrick Barnes (Sidney/Matthew), David L. Carson (Robertson), Ed Chemaly (Rosman/Judge/Ryan), Luisa D'Amelio (Ensemble), Anita Davenport (Irene/Charley), David P. Dawson (Grandpa/Voice of FDR), Gino DiLorio (Bdwy Tony/Rudy/Kapush), Ron Domingo (Clayton/Ralph), Jessica Frankel (Doris/Mrs. Taylor/Miss Fowler), Kathryn Grant (Rose), Gregory Jackson (Clarence/Brewster/Toland), Danielle LaViscount (Lucy), Charisse James (Farmer), Kelly Lau (Grace/Farmer), Margaret Massman (Edie/Diana/Lucille/Harriet), Lavaughn McPherson (Waiter/Bidder), Charlene Morgan (Thief/Farmer), Michael Pace (Quinn/Sheriff/Howard), Ted Rooney (Livermore/Taylor/Dugan), Robert Ruffin (Lee), Douglas Simes (Moe), Mary Wadkins (Fanny/Isabel), Scott Wakefield (Frank/Durant/Joe/Stanislaus), J. D. Wyatt (Banks/Graham/Isaac)
  A revision of the 1980 two-act depression drama, now described as "a vaudeville."

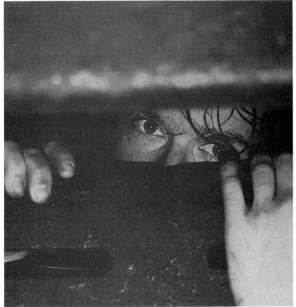

Nora Cole in *Olivia's Opus* **(Hugh Bell)**

(Madison Avenue Theatre) Wednesday, Nov. 17–21, 1993 (5 performances) Madison Avenue Theatre, Metawhateverphor Theatre and Play Producers present:
THE MAKING OF EDWARD III by James Rosenfield; Director, Becky Kemper CAST: Anthony Rapp (Edward III), Rita Crosby (Queen Isabella), Elizabeth Keiser (Phillipa), Dave Owens (Hugh Despenser), David Logan (Edward II), Adam Nelson (Roger Mortimer), Joie Jacobsen (Lady Clare), Kevin Takasato (Will Montague), Jonathan Turner (Henry Lancaster), Jon M. Ciccolini (Lord Stephen)
  A historical drama in two acts.

(Tribeca Performing Arts Center) Wednesday, Nov. 17–Dec. 19, 1993 (33 performances and 5 previews) The Negro Ensemble Company presents:
OLIVIA'S OPUS by Nora Cole; Director, Herman Leveren Jones; Set/Lighting, Ina Mayhew; Costumes, Nora Cole; Sound/Video, Hljtca Productions; Stage Manager, Femi Sarah Heggie; Press, Howard and Barbara Atlee CAST: Nora Cole (Olivia), Anastacia Baron, Alan Leach

(Holy Trinity) Thursday, Nov. 18–Dec. 12, 1993 (16 performances) Triangle Theatre Company presents:
THE CURATE SHAKESPEARE AS YOU LIKE IT by Don Nigro; Director, Robert D. Simons; Sets, William F. Moser; Costumes, Carol Brys; Lighting, Nancy Collings; Stage Manager, Cathy Diane Tomlin; Press, Susan Chicoine CAST: Frank Anderson, Peter Dinklage, Paula Wein, Robert John Metcalf, Sue-Anne Morrow, Jill Patterson, Peter Ashton Wise
  A rag-tag troupe attemps Shakespeare.

(Theatre for the New City) Thursday, Nov. 18–Dec. 12, 1994 (15 performances) Bartenieff/Fiels present:
RED CHANNELS by Laurence Holder; Director, Rome Neal; Costumes, Anita Ellis; Set, Chris Cumberbatch; Lighting, Marshall Williams; Sound, David Wright; Press, Jonathan Slaff CAST: Dennis L. Bivings (Paul Robeson), Robert F. Cole (Richard Nixon), Ed Clarkson-Farrell (Sen. McCarthy), Valentino Ferriera (Hal Porter), Elizabeth Mitchell (Sheila Harcourt), Nick Smith (W. E. B. Dubois), Daniel Tuck (Bob Burns), William Duke (Pasenger/Bartender/FBI)
  A drama in two acts. The action takes place in Washington, D.C. and New York, 1950–54.

Colin Mitchell in *The Robert Pieces* **(Aboutface)**

Charlayne Woodard in *Pretty Fire* (Gerry Goodstein)

(Brooklyn Academy of Music/Opera House) Saturday, Nov. 20–Dec. 1, 1993 (10 performances) B.A.M. and Thalia Theatre of Hamburg present:
THE BLACK RIDER by William S. Burroughs; Music/Lyrics, Tom Waits; Direction/Sets, Robert Wilson; Musical Director, Greg Cohen; Arrangements, Mr. Waits, Mr. Cohen; Costumes, Frida Parmeggiani; Lighting, Heinrich Brunke, Mr. Wilson; Sound, Gerd Bessler; Press, Ellen Zeisler/Bill Murray CAST INCLUDES: Heinz Vossbrink (Kuno/Old Forester), Dominique Horwitz (Pegleg), Annette Paulmann (Katchen), Stefan Kurt (Wilhelm/Clerk), Gerd Kunath, Jorg Holm
    A gothic pop melodrama adapted from folk tales.

(Westbeth Theatre Center) Monday Nov. 22–Dec. 13, 1993 (4 performances) Applause Books and Westbeth Theatre Center present:
THE BEST AMERICAN SHORT PLAY SERIES; Producing Director, Arnold Engelman; Program Director, Claudia Catania; Applause Producers, Glenn Young, Kay Radtke

EVENING ONE (11/22) *The Sausage Eaters* by Stephen Starosta; Director, Scott Elliott CAST: Sylvia Miles (Felicity), Everett Quinton (Norman), Roma Maffia (Gabriella), Joseph Gordon Weiss (Nilly), Pamela Blair (Mary), Richard B. Shull (Directions)
A Couple with a Cat by Tony Connor; Director, Steven Bloom CAST: Jerry Mayer (Joe), Lynn Cohen (Mary), Sean Moynihan (Dale)
Aryan Birth by Elizabeth Page; Director, Susan Einhorn CAST: Paul Provenza (David)
Pitching to the Star by Donald Margulies; Director, Rand Foerster CAST: Robert Sean Leonard (Peter Rosenthal), Lewis Black (Dick Feldman), Colleen Dodson (Dena Strawbridge), Ann Giobbe (Lauri Richards), Patricia Miller (Jennifer/Tyne)

EVENING TWO (11/29) *Show;* Written/Directed by Victor Bumbalo; CAST: Austin Pendleton (Priest), John Hollywood (Joey), Susan O'Dell (Directions)
Watermellon Rinds by Regina Taylor; Director, Leslie Lee CAST: Malik Yoba (Jes Semple), Mike Hodge (Willy), Elan Rivera (Lottie), Carmen Mathis (Liza), Stephanie Pope (Pinkie), Mary Alice (Mama Pearl), Paul Butler (Papa Tommy), Iris Little (Marva)
Jolly by David Mamet; Director, Scott Zigler CAST: Felicity Huffman (Jolly), Jim Frangone (Bob), Steven Goldstein (Carl)
The Cowboy, the Indian and the Fervent Feminist by Murray Schisgal; Director, Jack Gelber CAST: Marcia Jean Kurtz (Alicia Gerard), Bob Dishy (Stanford Gerard), Peter Basch (Dr. Bibberman)

EVENING THREE (12/6) *The Drowning of Manhattan* by John Ford Noonan; Director, Thomas Palumbo CAST: Tom Brangle (Sgt. Rock), Todd Davis (Totality Brown), Kali Rosha (Tracy Jo Kerouac), Brian Foyster (J. J. Kilbourne), William Hallmark (Charley the Lizard), Charles Gerber (Radio Voices), Robert O'Gorman (Directions)
Night Baseball by Gabriel Tissian; Director, Herman Babad CAST: Quint Von Canon (Joe), Anthony Spina (Lou), Philip Levy (Pete), Vincent Procida (Old Pete), Jim O'Hagen (Mick), Lou Sones (Sal)
The Valentine Fairy by Ernest Thompson; Director, Susanne Brinkley CAST: Julie Hagerty (Ingrid), Ernest Thompson (Rudyard)
Little Red Riding Hood by Billy Aronson; Director, Warren David Keith CAST: Trish Matthews (Red Riding Hood), Ann Mantell (Mother), Toby Wherry (Big Bad Woolf), Steve Hofvendal (Hunter), Bill Kux (Grandmother)

EVENING FOUR (12/13) *It's Our Town, Too* by Susan Miller; Director, Nela Wagman CAST: John Cameron Mitchell (Chance), Kathryn Grody (Stage Manager), Ami Brabson (Emily), Maryann Plunkett (Elizabeth), Richard Long (George), Jay O. Saunders (Louis), Lisa Gay Hamilton (Molly), Ronn Munro (Doc McAdoo), Andrienne Wilde (Angry Righteous Citizen)
Bondage by David Henry Hwang; Director, Oskar Eustis CAST: Jan Leslie Harding (Terri), Ernest Abuba (Mark)
The Tack Room by Ralph Arzoomanian; Director, Tammy Grimes CAST: Ed Setrakien (Mel), Bob Adrian (Paul), Jim Cronin (Franchy)
Dreamers by Shel Silverstein; Director, Daniel Selznick CAST: Sam Coppola (Ritchie), Tony Lo Bianco (Nick)

(Sylvia & Danny Kaye Playhouse) Tuesday, Nov. 23, 1993–Jan. 2, 1994 Manhattan Theatre Club presents:
PRETTY FIRE; Written/Performed by Charlayne Woodard; Set, Shelley Barclay; Costumes, Rita Ryack; Sound, Bruce Ellman; Lighting, Brian Nason; Stage Manager, Diane DiVita; Press, Helene Davis, Amy Lefkowitz
    Return engagement of one-woman play performed at Manhattan Theatre Club last season.

(Rainbow & Stars) Tuesday, Nov. 23, 1993–Jan. 29, 1994 (100 performances) Gregory Dawson and Steve Paul present:
THE LEONARD BERNSTEIN REVUE: A HELLUVA TOWN!; Director, Richard Sabellico; Musical Director/Arranger, Stan Freeman; Press, David Lotz CAST: Marilyn Caskey, Lauren Mitchell, J. Mark McVey, Patrick Quinn, Ruth Williamson

Ruth Wiliamson, Stan Freeman, Marilyn Caskey, Lauren Mitchell in *Leonard Bernstein Revue* (Carolyn Rosegg)

(Primary Stages) Wednesday, Nov. 24, 1993–Feb. 13, 1994 (80 performances) reopened at John Houseman Theatre on Feb. 17, 1994–May 20, 1995 (526 Houseman performances and 80 Primary Stages performances) Primary Stages and Estragon Productions present:

ALL IN THE TIMING by David Ives; Director, Jason McConnell Buzas; Sets, Bruce Goodrich; Costumes, Sharon Lynch; Lighting, Deborah Constantine; Sound, Jim van Bergen; Music, Bruce Coughlin; Stage Manager, Christine Catti; Press, Anne Einhorn; Tony Origlio/William McLaughlin CAST: Daniel Hagen succeeded by Philip Hoffman and Michael Countryman, Wendy Lawless, Ted Neustadt, Nancy Opel, Robert Stanton

PROGRAM: Sure Thing, Words Words Words, The Universal Language, Philip Glass Buys a Loaf of Bread, The Philadelphia, Variations on the Death of Trotsky

Six one-act comedies.

Right: Daniel Hagen
Bottom: Robert Stanton, Michael Countryman
(Carol Rosegg, Andrew Leynes Photos)

104

(Village Theatre) Wednesday, Nov. 24–Dec. 19, 1993 (17 performances) Village Theatre Co. in association with One World Arts Foundation presents:
LET US NOW PRAISE FAMOUS MEN by John Erlanger; Director, Alex Dmitriev; Lighting, Jerold R. Forsyth; Set, Charles E. McCarry; Costumes, Jean Brookman; Sound, Jim Harrington CAST: Kate Bushman (Laura/Via), Richard M. Davidson (Henry Luce/Hackett), James Fleming (Ingersoll/Hodgins/Weems), Christie Harrington (Auda), Randall Harris (Walker Evans), Cortez Nance, Jr. (Lucious/Earl), Samantha Reynolds (Julia), Jason Stevens (James Agee), Tim Zay (Dwight MacDonald/Barnett)

An account of James Agee and Walker Evans' Depression-era travels.

(Mint Theatre) Saturday, Nov. 27–Dec. 11, 1993 (15 performances) The Mint Theatre presents:
JEREMY RUDGE by Debbie Jones; Director, Kelly Morgan CAST: Austin Pendleton (Jeremy), Becky Ann Baker (Susan)

A drama about unexpected connections.

(Ubu Rep. Theatre) Tuesday, Nov. 30–Dec. 19, 1993 (18 performances) Ubu Repertory presents:
THE ORPHAN MUSES by Michel Marc Bouchard; Translation, Linda Gaboriau; Director, Andre Ernotte; Set, John Brown; Lighting, Greg MacPherson; Costumes, Carol Ann Pelletier; Sound, Phil Lee, Brian Hallas; Stage Manager, Bethany Ford; Press, Peter Cromarty/Michael Hartman CAST: Joyce O'Connor (Catherine), Jacqueline Lucid (Isabelle), Keith Reddin (Luc), Catherine Curtain (Martine)

A Canadian drama set in Quebec, 1965.

(One Dream Theatre) Tuesday, Nov. 30–Dec. 18, 1993 (17 performances) One Dream Theatre presents:
GODOT ARRIVES by Nathaniel C. Hutner; Director, Nancy Hancock; Set, John Wooding; Costumes, Henry Stewart; Sound, Bob Edwards; Press, David Rothenberg CAST: Jacob Harran (Godot), Jim Abele, Brennan Brown, Deborah Cresswell, Fred Harlow, Jeff Knapp, Charlotta Nutley, Michael Shelle, Garrison Phillips, David Weck

Godot finally does arrive in this new play.

(HERE) Wednesday, Dec. 1–19, 1993 HERE presents:
GENERATION X by John Augustine; Director, Bill Russell; Press, Philip Rinaldi/Kathy Haberthur CAST: Constance Shulman, Stanley Wayne Mathis, David Eigenberg, Sherry Anderson, Bellina Logan, Catherine Lloyd Burns, Gary Kimble, Gerit Queally

A collage of one-act plays about a lost generation.

(Harold Clurman Theatre/moved to Judith Anderson Theatre) Wednesday, Dec. 1, 1993–Jan. 2, 1994 Magical Eye in association with Flock Theater Company presents:
TOP GIRLS by Caryl Churchill; Director, April Shawhan; Set, Andrea Bechert; Lighting, Kay A. Albright; Stage Manager, Kyle McMurry; Press, Shirley Herz/Sam Rudy CAST: Jeannie Zusy (Marlene), Kelly Clark (Waitress/Louise/Mrs. Kidd), Irene Glezos (Isabella Bird/Joyce), Maureen Beitler (Lady Nijo/Jeanine/Win), Joanie Coyote (Dull Gret/Angie), Victoria Stern (Pope Joan/Nell), Susan Jon (Patient Griselda/Kit/Shona)

A play in two acts. The action takes place in England, early 1980s.

(John Houseman Theatre) Friday, Dec. 3, 1993–Jan. 23, 1994 (48 performances and 12 previews) Arthur Cantor and Carol Ostrow present:
GREETINGS by Tom Dudzick; Director, Dennis Zacek; Set/Costumes, Bruce Goodrich; Lighting, Deborah Constantine; Sound, One Dream; Stage Manager, Tom Aberger; Press, Mr. Cantor CAST: Gregg Edelman (Andy Gorski), Toby Poser (Randi Stein), Darren McGavin (Phil Gorski), Lenore Loveman (Emily Gorsky), Aaron Goodwin (Mickey Gorski)

A comedy in two acts. The action takes place in a working class Pittsburgh neighborhood.

(Nat Horne Theatre) Saturday, Dec. 4–19, 1993 (16 performances) Love Creek Productions presents:
BLACKBERRY FROST by Le Wilhelm; Director, Jonathan Hart; Press, Chris Boneau/Adrian Bryan-Brown, Hillary Harrow CAST: Ben Carney, George Cron, Morgan Forsey, Diane Hoblit, Jackie Jenkins, Nancy McDoniel, Tracy Newirth, Dustye Winniford

The final installment of Wilhelm's Missouri trilogy.

Austin Pendleton, Becky Ann Baker
in *Jeremy Rudge* (Stacy Honeycutt)

Keith Reddin, Jacqueline Lucid
in *Orphan Muses* (Carol Rosegg)

Toby Poser, Darren McGavin, Lenore Loveman, Gregg Edelman, Aaron Goodwin in *Greetings* (Carol Rosegg)

105

(Intar Theatre) Saturday, Dec. 4–19, 1993 (13 performances) PASSAJ Productions presents:
WHITE WIDOW with Music/Lyrics/Book by Paul Dick; Based on the play *Mafia* by Mario Fratti; Director, John Margulis; Musical Director, Christopher McGovern; Set/Lighting, Jack Mehler; Costumes, Crystal Thompson; Press, Chris Boneau/Adrian Bryan-Brown, Ellen Levene, Jamie Morris CAST: William Broderick (Don Rosario), Diana DiMarzio (Donna Raffaella), Jim Festante (Tonio), Tim Tucker (Carmelo), Anthony Razzano (Malacarne), Don Stansfield (Nesti), Mitch Poulos (Maresciallo), Carrie Wilshusen (Donna Cinzia), Kay Elise Kleinerman (Ornella), John Savarese (Peppuzzo), Jerry Rodgers (Babbio), Deborah Unger, Andrea Bianchi, Dewey Moss (Vendors)

MUSICAL NUMBERS: The Stoning, Fish Lemon Chickens, Bel Paese, The Game, The Letter, Law Order Justice, Two Young People in Love, Basic Sicilian, Music for a Murder, We Mourn, Donna Cinzia's Love, Four Proverbs, So Little Time, Don't You Understand, Not I, To Build Tomorrow, Time to Prepare For Donna Cinzia, Only Yesterday, All for You, Bel Paese
   A dramatic musical in two acts. The action takes place in Sicily.

(Samuel Beckett Theatre) Wednesday, Dec. 8, 1993–Jan. 2, 1994 (13 performances) King Spike Theatre Company presents:
WHAT YOU ARE ABOUT TO SEE IS REAL by Randy Sharp and Michael Gump; Director, Mr. Sharp; Sets, Leon Muniere; Lighting, Trad Burns; Sound, Michael Birnbaum; Press, Peter Cromarty/Michael Hartman CAST: Shari Albert, Jim Cullom, Sheryl Dold, Michael Gump, Robert Ierardi, Jon Johnson, Dee Pelltier, G. W. Rooney, Chris Swift
   Four terror plays: *Waxboy*, *Razorman*, *D.N.R.*, and *Peanut*.

(Naked Angels) Thursday, Dec. 9–23, 1993 (7 performances and 6 previews) Naked Angels presents:
CLAUS (A DARKER SIDE OF LEGEND) by Matthew Weiss; Director, Joe Gilford; Set, John Farrell; Lighting, John-Paul Szczepanski; Costumes, Ellen Cowhey; Stage Manager, Michelle Malloy McIntyre CAST: Ned Eisenberg, Timothy Britten Parker, Billy Strong, Bradley White

(Village Theatre) Monday, Dec. 13–31, 1993 (13 performances) Village Theatre Company presents:
A CHRISTMAS TWIST by Douglas Armstrong, Keith Cooper, and Maureen Morley; Music, Patric Byers; Lyrics, Scott Burkell; Director, Peter-Michael Marino; Costumes, Mary Ellen Park; Stage Manager, Terry Mac CAST: Richard Bacon, Michelle Berke, Bob Horen, Lynn Marie Hulsman, John LaLonde, Ellen McQueeney, Eric Perlmutter, Roger Seyer
   A crazy quilt of *A Christmas Carol* and *Oliver Twist*.

(Open Eye Theatre) Saturday, Dec. 18, 1993–Jan. 2, 1994 (12 performances) The Open Eyes Theatre presents:
THE WISE MEN OF CHELM by Sandra Fenichel Asher; Director, Amie Brockway; Choreography, Alice Bergman; Design, Adrienne J. Brockway; Press, Shirley Herz/Sam Rudy CAST: Alice Bergmann, John DiLeo, Judy Dodd, Scott Facher, Larry Hirschhorn, Michael Metzel
   Comic tales from Jewish folklore.

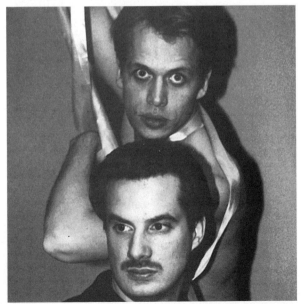

(Old Merchant's House) Thursday, Dec. 30, 1993– Mar. 27, 1994 New York Art Institute and Old Merchant's House present:
OLD NEW YORK: FALSE DAWN by Edith Wharton; Adaptation/Direction, Donald T. Sanders; Design, Vanessa James; Stage Manager, Dan Joiner; Press, David LeShay CAST: Ed Romanoff (Distant Cousin), John Anson (Mr. Halston Raycie), Nathan Smith (Lewis Raycie), Karin Wolfe (Edith Wharton/Mrs. Raycie), Elizabeth Benjamin (Treeshy Kent), Holley Stewart (Mary Adeline Raycie/Cousin Alethea), Andrea Weber (Netta Cosby), James Deloorenzo (John Ruskin/Donaldson Kent), John Selwyn, John Patterson (Robert Huzzard)
   Adaptation of Wharton's 1924 book performed in preserved 19th-century Greenwich Village home. After the drama, the audience is given a house tour.

(One Dream Theatre) Monday, Jan. 3–16, 1994 (9 performances and 3 previews) reopened Jan. 20, 1994 for late-night run
Zena Group Theatre presents:
BITCHPLATE CHARLIE; Written/Performed by Matt Ames; Director, Josh Liveright; Press, Chris Boneau/Adrian Bryan-Brown, Bob Fennell
   Three monologues: *Flow*, *Bodies*, *Monsters*.

(American Theatre of Actors) Thursday, Jan. 6–15, 1994 (6 performances)
BALLET RUSSES with Music/Lyrics by David Reiser; Book, Bernard Myers; Director, Karen Berman; Musical Director, C. Colby Sachs; Choreography, Oleg Briansky; Set, Michael Stepowany; Lighting, Kevin Lawson; Costumes, Rodney Munoz; Stage Manager, Denise S. Fabiano; Press, Fred Nathan/Michael S. Borowski CAST: Carmen DeMichael (Diaghilev), Gary Martin (Gregoriev), Petter Jacobsson (Nijinsky), Robert Maiorano (Fokine), Jenni Hjalmarson (Tata), Rachel Hennelly (Mattilda), Stephen DeLorenzo (Baron DeGunzburg), Christie Cox (Romola), Brad Menendez (Stravinsky)

MUSICAL NUMBERS: Le Dieu Bleu, Golden Slave, Something Wonderful, When You're Intimate with the Czar, When You're in Love, Les Sylphides, Afternoon of a Faun, I'm Through with You, Waltz, We Need Money, Petrouchka, Le Spectre de la Rose, He's So Near, Rite of Spring, Les Sirenes, Prayer, A Revelation, Final Dance
   A two-act musical on the love affair between Vaslav Nijinsky and Serge Diaghilev, 1909–23.

**Top Right: John Anson, Karin Wolfe, Holley Stewart
in *Old New York*: *False Dawn* (Carol Rosegg)
Bottom Left: (top) Peter Jacobsson, Carmen DeMichael
in *Ballet Russes***

Claudia Shear in *Blown Sideways Through Life* (Martha Swope)

(Symphony Space) Thursday, Jan. 6–16, 1994 (10 performances) New York Gilbert & Sullivan Players present:
THE PIRATES OF PENZANCE or *The Slave of Duty;* Music, Sir Arthur Sullivan; Libretto, Sir W. S. Gilbert; Music/Stage Director, Albert Bergeret; Choreography, Bill Fabris; Sets, Lou Anne Gilliland; Lighting, Sally Small; Costumes, Dale DiBernardo; Press, Francine L. Trevins/Robert J. Weston CAST: Noel Harrison (Major-General), Carson Church (Pirate King), Bill Fabris (Samuel), Ray Gabbard, Marc Persing (Frederic), Michael Collins, Philip Reilly (Sergeant), Kate Egan, Shelia Yates (Mabel), Karen Rich (Edith), Katie Geissinger, Dianna Sandler (Kate), Mary Lou Barber (Isabel), Elizabeth Huling (Ruth), Meredith Borden, William J. Brooke, Tyler Bunch, Christopher Carey, Charlotte Detrick, Edward Ehinger, Michael Galante, Mark L. Greenley, Katie Hershberger, Alan Hill, Suzzanne Jaffe, Monika Kendall, Mona King, Michael Meyer, Travis Messinger, Thierry Richard, Donna Sammis, Luisa Sauter, Paul Sigrist
The 1879 operetta in two acts.

(Clark Studio) Thursday, Jan. 6–16, 1994 (10 performances) Cressid Company and Survivor Productions present:
MUCH ADO ABOUT NOTHING by William Shakespeare; Director, Deloss Brown; Music, Raphael Crystal; Lighting, Wendy Luedtke; Set, Richard Kendrick; Stage Manager, Jen Moses; Press, Maya/Penny Landau CAST: John Behan (Leonardo), Don Carter (Antonio), Ethan Flower (Balthasar/Friar), John Joseph Freeman (Don John/Verges), Elizabeth Gottlieb (Margaret), Paul Griffin (Conrade), Joseph Holmgren (Claudio), Jeremy Johnson (Dogberry), Eliza Kelly (Watch), Summer Kelly (Boy), Chris Knoblock (Borachio), Cady McClain (Hero), Phil Powers (Messenger/Sexton), Mary Lou Shriber (Ursula/Watch), Gregory Sobeck (Benedick), Michael Stacy (Don Pedro), Keeley Stanley (Beatrice)
Shakespeare's comedy with new music. The action takes place in Messina, Sicily, 1500s.

(Soho Rep) Thursday, Jan. 6–16, 1994 (8 performances) Adobe Theatre Company presents:
NOTHING BUT THIS by Gil Kofman; Director, Stephen Haff; Lighting, Rick Martin; Sound, Ted Baker; Costumes, Anna R. Oliver; Stage Manager, Michele A. Kay CAST: Arthur Aulisi, Bruce Katzman, William Langan, Benjamin Lloyd, Kathryn Langwell, Frank Wood, Damian Young
Three one-act plays.

(28th St. Theatre) Thursday, Jan. 6–30, 1994 (17 performances) New Globe Productions presents:
THE COURTESAN AND THE EUNUCH by Terry Bradberry; Director, Dan McKereghan; Sets/Costumes, Kevin Lock; Lighting, Christopher Caines; Stage Manager, Sonia Belochi; Press, Peter Cromarty/Michael Hartman CAST: Elenora Kihlberg (Minette), John Marino (Emile), Jennifer Fleming (Lupe), Paolo Seganti (Leon), Blythe Baten (Corrina)
A drama in two acts. The action takes place in Tangier.

(Theatre 22) Thursday, Jan. 6–29, 1994 (9 performances) La Commedia Del Sangue: The Vampyr Theatre presents:
LET US PREY by Tony Sokol; Director, Try Acree; Special Effects/Makeup, Rick Crane; Press, Howard and Barbara Atlee CAST INCLUDES: Troy Acree (Count Grau Orlock)
A gothic vampire saga.

(St. Clement's) Thursday, Jan. 6–Feb. 19, 1994 (24 performances and 4 previews) Theatre for a New Audience presents:
AS YOU LIKE IT by William Shakespeare; Director, Mark Rylance; Set/Costumes, Jenny Tiramani; Lighting, Frances Aronson; Composer, Claire van Kampen; Choreography, Darryl Quinton; Fights, J. Allen Suddeth; Stage Manager, Alyson Augustin; Press, Shirley Herz/Miller Wright CAST: Trellis Stepter (Orlando), Leon Addison Brown (Oliver), Arthur French (Adam/Martext/William), David Dossey (Charles/1st Lord/Audrey), Erin J. O'Brien (Celia), Miriam Healy-Louie (Rosalind), Mark Rylance (Touchstone), Michael Rudko (Le Beau/Jaques), Mark Hammer (Frederick/Senior/Corin), Steven Skybell (Amiens/2nd Lord/Silvius), Melissa Ford (Phebe/Hesperia), Christine Mourand (Hymen), Bryan Webster (Jacques de Boys)
The action takes place in and around Duke Fredeick's court and the Forest of Arden.

(Cherry Lane Theatre) Friday, Jan. 7–July 17, 1994 (221 performances) James B. Freydberg, William B. O'Boyle, Sonny Everett, Evangeline Morphos, Nancy Richards, Dori Berinstein, and New York Theatre Workshop present:
BLOWN SIDEWAYS THROUGH LIFE; Written/Performed by Claudia Shear; Developed with and Directed by Christopher Ashley; Set, Loy Arcenas; Costumes, Jess Goldstein; Lighting, Christopher Akerlind; Sound, Aural Fixation; Music, Richard Peaslee; Dance, Nafisa Sharriff; Stage Manager, Kate Broderick; Press, Richard Kornberg
An autobiographical tour-de-resume of 65 jobs performed without intermission. Originated at New York Theatre Workshop in Sept. 1993.

Wallace Shawn, Karen Young in *Wifey*

(St. Mark's Theatre) Sunday, Jan. 9–Mar. 27, 1994 (56 performances) Ontological-Hysteric Theatre presents:
MY HEAD WAS A SLEDGE HAMMER; Written/Directed by Richard Foreman; Lighting, Heather Carson CAST: Jan Leslie Harding, Thomas Jay Ryan, Henry Stram

A professor with the dress and manners of a Hell's Angel is tormented by his favorite male and female students.

(Kaufman Theatre) Monday, Jan. 10–29, 1994 (16 performances) Martin R. Kaufman presents:
RIDICULOUS PRECIEUSES by Moliere; Director, Sean Pratter; Lighting, John Wooding; Design, Sally Randall; Stage Manager, Mike Hagler; Press, David Rothenberg CAST: Nancy Balbirer (Marotte), Jennifer Brown (Lucile), Edward Burke (Almanzar), Todd Butera (La Grange), Jerry Clarke (Mascarille), William Gilmore (Du Croissy), Holli Harms (Cathos), Michael Harrington (1st Carrier), Thomas McHugh (Jodelet), Peter Potter (Gorgibus), Ingrid R. Rockefeller (Magdelon), Victoria Virgin (Dancer), Dean Winters (2nd Carrier)

A 1659 comedy set on the outskirts of Paris.

(HERE) Wednesday, Jan. 12–23, 1994 (10 performances) HOME for Contemporary Theatre and Art presents:
SON OF AN ENGINEER; Written/Directed by David Greenspan; Set, Alan Glovsky; Lighting, John Lewis; Costumes, Mary Myers; Sound, Edward Cosla; Stage Manager, James Kroll; Press, Philip Rinaldi/Kathy Haberthur CAST: Thomas Pasley (Tom), Chuck Coggins (Killian Boy), Karin Levitas (Phoebe), Lisa Welti (Diane)

The action takes place in suburbia (act I) and Mars (act II).

(Samuel Beckett Theatre) Wednesday, Jan. 12–23, 1993 (12 performances) Big League Theatre Compnay presents:
BOYS' LIFE by Howard Korder; Director, Vincent Bossone; Set, Nick Falco; Lighting/Sound, Melanie S. Armer; Stage Manager, Janet Escourt; Press, Howard and Barbara Atlee CAST: Christopher Prizzi (Jack), Chance Kelly (Don), Peter Dorton (Phil), Andi Bushell (Karen), Troy Sostillio (Man), Maureen Donahue (Maggie), Sabrini Seidner (Lisa), Elissa Piszel (Girl), Jeanne Langston (Carla)

Single men in the never-ending search for single women.

Julie Hagerty, Tom Noonan in *Wifey*

(Mint Theatre) Wednesday, Jan. 12–23, 1994 (14 performances) Mint Theatre Company presents:
AMONG WOMEN by Jennie Susan Staniloff; Director, Paula Godsey; Press, Barbara Reierson CAST: Linda Ames Key (Ryann), Neil Maffin (Geoff)

A drama about friendship.

(Paradise Theatre) Wednesday, Jan. 12–Feb. 6, 1994 (24 performances) Paradise Theatre Company presents:
WIFEY; Written/Directed by Tom Noonan; Set, Dan Ouellette; Costumes, Kathryn Nixon; Lighting, Paul Clay; Stage Manager, Tony Faulkner; Press, John and Gary Springer CAST: Julie Hagerty (Rita), Tom Noonan (Jack), Karen Young (Arlie-Wifey), Wallace Shawn (Cosmo)

A black comedy about married life.

(Promenade Theatre) Friday, Jan. 14–Feb. 6, 1994 (17 performances and 13 previews) James B. Freydburg, Kenneth Feld, Dori Berinstein present:
THOSE THE RIVER KEEPS; Written/Directed by David Rabe; Set, Loren Sherman; Costumes, Sharon Sprague; Lighting, Peter Kaczorowski; Fights, David Leong; Sound, One Dream; Stage Manager, Jane Grey; Press, Chris Boneau/Adrian Bryan-Brown, Javkie Green, Jamie Morris CAST: Annabella Sciorra (Susuie), Paul Guilfoyle (Phil), Jude Ciccolella (Sal), Phyllis Lyons (Janice)

A darkly humorous drama in two acts.

(Intar Theatre) Friday, Feb. 14–Mar. 26, 1994 (63 performances) Freestyle Repertory Theatre presents:
THEATRESPORTS/SPONTANEOUS BROADWAY/OUT OF CHARACTER; Artistic Director, Laura Livingston; Press, Peter Cromarty/Michael Hartman CAST INCLUDES: Joe Anderson, Kristina Swelund, Emmy Laybourne, John Brady, Mike Durkin, Susan Murray

Improvisational theatre presented in repertory.

Jeanne Langston, Christopher Prizzi in *Boys' Life*

Paul Guilfoyle, Jude Ciccolella in *Those the River Keeps* (Joan Marcus)

(Puerto Rican Traveling Theatre) Wednesday, Jan. 19–Feb. 27, 1994 (42 performances) Puerto Rican Traveling Theatre presents:
DEATH AND THE MAIDEN by Ariel Dorfman; Director, Alba Oms; Set, Michael Sharp; Lighting, Spencer Brown; Sound, Sergio Garcia-Marruz; Stage Manager, Fernando Quinones; Press, Max Eisen CAST: Socorro Santiago (Paulina-English), Diana Volpe (Paulina-Spanish), Henry Martin Leyva (Escobar), Edouard Desoto (Miranda)
    A two-act drama. Performances in English and Spanish.

(One Dream Theatre) Thursday, Jan. 20–Feb. 6, 1994 (14 performances) Our Theatre presents:
THE STRANGE CASE OF DR. JEKYLL AND MR. HYDE by Robert Louis Stevenson; Adaptation/Direction, Graves Kiely; Press, John and Gary Springer CAST: Terry Christgau (Jekyll/Hyde), Chris McNally (Utterson), Kevin Villers (Dr. Lanyon), Emily Ellison, Mark Ellison, Whitman Filed, Joyce Kacin, Lisa McNally, David Sassoon, Joseph Travers
    Adaptation of the famous horror mystery.

(Henry St. Settlement) Thursday, Jan. 20–Feb. 13, 1994 (16 performances) New Federal Theatre presents:
IN BED WITH THE BLUES: THE ADVENTURES OF FISHY WATERS; Written/Performed by Guy Davis; Director, Shauneille Perry; Sets, Kent Hoffman; Lighting, Antoinette Tynes; Costumes, Judy Dearing; Stage Manager, Charles M. Edmonds; Press, Max Eisen/Kathryn Kinsella

MUSICAL NUMBERS: Rambling All Over, Mrs. Roley's Hobo Stew, Dust My Broom, Tight Like That, Georgia Buck, Black Man's Blues, Georgia Rag, Watch Over Me, Candy Man
    Tales from the 1920s–30s with old time acoustic blues music.

(Open Eye Theatre) Thursday, Jan. 20–Mar. 2, 1994 (18 performances and 2 previews) Open Eye presents:
FREEDOM IS MY MIDDLE NAME by Lee Hunkins; Director, Ernest Johns; Press, Shirley Herz/Sam Rudy CAST: Mary Cushman, John DiLeo, Sheryl Greene Leverett, Stephanie Marshall
    A trip back in time through African-American history.

Annabella Sciorra in *Those the River Keeps* **(Joan Marcus)**

Vicki Stuart in *Smiling Through* **(Carol Rosegg)**

(Naked Angels) Friday, Jan. 21–Feb. 7, 1994 (11 performances and 5 previews) Naked Angels presents:
THE STAND-IN by Keith Curran; Director, Ray Cochran; Set, Rob Odorisio; Lighting, John-Paul Szczepanski; Costumes, Martha Bromelmeier; Sound, Roger Raines; Choreography, Danny Herman; Stage Manager, Craig Palanker CAST: Scotty Bloch (Debbie/Edith/Woman/Ashly/Fiona/Dee Dee), T. Scott Cunningham (Kevin/Bob/Jesus/Ruffy the Clown), John Benjamin Hickey (Hal/Walter/Tom/Michael/Reporter), Amy Hohn (Bickey/Linda/Ula/Betty/Paula/A Reporter), Merrill Holtzman (Gus/Rod/Greg/Hedgehog/Leroy/Hilton), John Horton (Corbin/Man/Archer/Dan), Kristen Johnson (Festa/Gilda), David Pittu (Gordon/Harry/Sparky/Chester), Bradley White (Lester), Gareth Williams (Cody/Man/Rocko)
    The action takes place in New York City.

(Theatre Four) Friday, Jan. 21–Feb. 6, 1994 (6 performances and 15 previews) Lois Teich presents:
SMILING THROUGH by Ivan Menchell; Songs, Various; Director/Choreographer, Patricia Birch; Set, James Morgan; Costumes, Frank Krenz; Lighting, Craig Miller; Sound, Otts Munderloh; Musical Director/Arrangements, Tom Fay; Stage Manager, R. Wade Jackson; Press, Jeffrey Richards CAST: Vicki Stuart (Mavis Daily), Jeff Woodman (Arthur/Frank/Norma/Penelope)

MUSICAL NUMBERS: Don't Dilly Dally on the Way, Nobody Loves a Fairy, Underneath the Arches, All Our Tomorrows, Wish Me Luck, No One Believes, Deepest Shelter in Town, Dancing with My Shadow, I'm Gonna Get Lit Up, We'll Meet Again, White Cliffs of Dover, A Nightingale Sang in Berkeley Square
    A two-act musical set in London, 1940–44.

(Charles Ludlam Theater) Friday, Jan. 21–Feb. 25, 1994 (6 performances) Watson Arts presents:
ZORA: THE NAKED HOUSEWIFE by Zora Rasmussen and Mary Fulham; Director, Ms. Fulham; Set, Billy Gallo; Costumes, Beverly Renskers; Music, Robert Secret; Press, Bobby Reed CAST: Zora Rasmussen
    A comic monlogue.

(Circle Rep Lab) Monday, Jan. 24, 1994 (1 limited performance) Circle Repertory Co. Lab presents:
THE FAMILY ANIMAL by Mary Pope Osborne; Director, June Stein; Set, Mylene Santos; Lighting, Mal Sturchio; Costumes, Mary Myers; Sound, Melanie S. Armer; Stage Manager, Linus Lam CAST: Anthony Rapp (J. K. Abbot), Donna Davis (Lillian Abbot), Laura Hughes (Patsy Parkins), James Pritchett (Col. Abbot), Missy Yager (Annie Abbot), Lou Sumrall (Dave Parkins)
    The action takes place in the home of the president of a boys' military school in the South, 1970.

(Minetta Lane Theatre) Tuesday, Jan. 25–Apr. 24, 1994 (84 performances and 8 previews) Frederick Zollo, Nick Paleologos, Ron Kastner, Randy Finch present:
POUNDING NAILS IN THE FLOOR WITH MY FOREHEAD; Written/ Performed by Eric Bogosian; Director, Jo Bonney; Set, John Arnone; Lighting, Jan Kroeze; Sound, Raymond D. Schilke; Stage Manager, Robbie Young; Press, Philip Rinaldi/Kathy Haberthur
    Bogosian exorcises his inner demons.

(Mint Theatre) Wednesday, Jan. 26–Feb. 6, 1994 (12 performances) Mint Theatre Co. presents:
MINT CONDITION; Conceived/Directed by Peter Ratray; Written by Jack McCleland, William Mastrosimone, Robert Tamburino, Eric Bogosian, Neil Simon, Howard Korder, Lanie Robertson and Mr. Ratray; Lighting, K. T. White; Stage Manager, Francys Olivia Burch; Press, Barbara Reirson CAST: Donna DuCarme, Scott T. Thompson, Tim Goldrick, Jim Fitzpatrick, Beth Phillips, Rebecca Rosen, Andrew Chipok, Rachel C. Hoyer, Eric Rasmussen, Lauren Koff, Julia Gabor, David Beyda, Larry Ratzkin, Rosalyn Thomson, Kelley Costigan, Cynthia Lamontagne, Deloria Ruyle, Holly Maria Hudson, Joe Yates, Nancy Weiss, Stacy Honeycutt, Brandt Reiter, Kim Page, Kayla Carroll, Verna Imani Eggleston
    An urban revue.

(Synchronicity Space) Wednesday, Jan. 26–Feb. 6, 1994 (10 performances) 11th Hour Theatre Collective presents:
TALES OF THE LOST FORMICANS by Constance Congdon; Director, Douglas Hall; Lighting, Jeff Segal CAST: Michelle Benes, Thom Goff, Earle Hugens, Lara Kornitzke, Susan Peters, Chris Taylor, Ron Trenouth
    A look at American values through the eyes of space aliens.

(All Soul's) Thursday, Jan. 27–Feb. 6, 1994 (10 performances) All Souls Players present:
ERNEST IN LOVE with Music by Lee Pockriss; Lyrics/Book, Anne Croswell; Director, Jeffery K. Neill; Musical Director, Joyce Hitchcock; Sets/Lighting, Tim Callery; Costumes, Charles W. Roeder; Stage Manager, Ralph Ortiz CAST: Neal Arluck (Perkins), Joe Symon (Lane), Peter Mannion (Greengrocer), Matthew Surapine (Bootmaker), Rick Delaney (Piano Teacher), Paul W. Siebold (Tobacconist), Patrick Lleard (Rev. Chausuble/Dancing Master), Bill Scharpen (Jack), Karen Vesper (Gwendolen), Kobi Shaw (Alice), Gregory C. Watt (Algernon), Gerrianne Raphael (Lady Bracknell), Kelly Donohue (Cecily), Marlene Greene (Miss Prism), Claudia Egli (Effie)
MUSICAL NUMBERS: Come Raise Your Cup, How Do You Find the Words, The Hat, Mr. Bunbury, Perfection, A Handbag is Not a Proper Mother, A Wicked Man, Metaphorically Speaking, You Can't Make Love, Lost, My Very First Impression, Muffin Song, My Eternal Devotion, Ernest in Love
    A new production of the 1960 musical version of *Importance of Being Earnest.* Gerrianne Raphael played Cecily in the original production.

(Ohio Theatre) Friday, Jan. 28–Feb. 12, 1994 (12 performances) T.W.E.E.D. presents:
THE ART OF HANGING FIRE by Perry Souchuk; Conceived/Directed by Rebecca Holderness; Lighting, Richard Schaefer; Costumes, Loren Bevans; Score, Douglas Cuomo; Stage Manager, Karen Ott; Press, Chris Boneau/Adrian Bryan-Brown, Bob Fennell CAST: Umit Celebi, Gretchen Claggett, Gia Forakis, Peggy Gould, Raymond Lamb, Jr., Jenifer Regan, Diego Reyes, Mike Villane
    Multimedia exporation of the life of artist Eva Hesse. An original sculpture was constructed at every performance.

(Atlantic Theatre) Saturday, Jan. 29–Feb. 5, 1994 (6 performances) Motion Pictures Movement Theater Productions presents:
FALLING ANGELS; Conception Lisa Giobbi; Created/Performed by Ms. Giobbi and Tim Harling; Music, Haley Moss, G. E. Stinson; Press, Audrey Ross
    A blend of dance, physical illusion, and circus arts.

(Perry St. Theatre) Thursday, Feb. 3–26, 1994 (19 performances) The Barrow Group presents:
LONELY PLANET by Steven Dietz; Director, Leonard Foglia; Set, Michael McGarty; Costumes, Markas Henry; Lighting, Howard Werner; Sound, One Dream; Press, Shirley Herz/Wayne Wolfe CAST: Mark Shannon (Jody), Denis O'Hare (Carl)
    A drama set in Jody's Maps, a map store on the oldest street in an American city.

      Top: Eric Bogosian in *Pounding Nails...* (Joan Marcus)
    Bottom: Denis O'Hare in *Lonely Planet* (Joan Marcus)

**Charlotte Moore, Ciaran O'Reilly
in *Au Pair Man* (Carol Rosegg)**

Allison Janney in *Class 1-Acts Festival* (Roya)

**Miriam Colon, Sofia Oviedo
in *Innocent Erendira* (Gerry Goodstein)**

(28th St. Theatre) Friday, Feb. 4–Mar. 6, 1994 (32 performances) Irish Repertory Theatre and One World Arts Foundation present:
THE AU PAIR MAN by Hugh Leonard; Director, Brian Murray; Set, Alexander Solodukho; Costumes, David Toser; Lighting, Gregory Cohen; Sound, Jay DeLemos; Fights, Linwood Harkum; Stage Manager, Kathe Mull; Press, Chris Boneau/Adrian Bryan-Brown, Hillary Harrow   CAST: Charlotte Moore (Elizabeth Rogers), Ciaran O'Reilly (Eugene Hartigan)
An allegorical comedy in two acts. The action takes place in the Rogers' home in the not too distant present.

(John Houseman Theatre) Monday, Feb. 7, 1994 (1 performance only) The Acting Company presents:
SHAKESPEARE AND FRIENDS, IBSEN AND ENEMIES with Fiona Shaw; Press, Fred Nathan
Moments from the world's great plays.

(Sanford Meisner Theatre) Thursday, Feb. 10–19, 1994 (7 performances) Epoch Theatre presents:
SEARCH AND DESTROY by Howard Korder; Director, Joe Reynolds; Press, John Cantanzaro/Steve Freeman   CAST: John Mese (Martin), Phillip Hinch, Dan Sturges, James Donato, Desi Doyen, Elissa Piszel, Sean Fri, Kip Veasy, Anthony DiMaria, Joe Reynolds
An adventure story in two acts.

(Theatre for the New City) Thursday, Feb. 10–27, 1994 (12 performances) Bartenieff/Field presents:
IT IS IT IS NOT by Manuel Pereiras Garcia; Director, Maria Irene Fornes; Costumes, Carol Bailey; Set, Donald Eastman; Lighting, Ellen Bone; Press, Jonathan Slaff   CAST: Angela Chale Millington (Diana/Paula), Crystal Field (Laura/Daniel), Steve Hofvendahl (Daniel/Saul)
Two one-act plays, *Two Romantic Ladies* and *The Man Who Forgot*.

(Synchronicity Space) Friday, Feb. 11–27, 1994 (10 performances and 3 previews) No-Pants Theatre Company presents:
SUPERMAN IS DEAD; Written/Directed by Dominic Orlando; Press, Patricia Story   CAST: Donald Silva (Danny), Sean Weil, Karin Bowersock
A drama based on a true story.

(Manhattan Class Company) Sunday, Feb. 13–Mar. 12, 1994 (25 performances) Manhattan Class Co. presents:
CLASS 1-ACTS; Sets, Rob Odorisio; Lighting, Stewart Wagner; Costumes, Judy Jerald Sackhelm; Sound, John Kilgore; Stage Managers, Erica Blum, James Marr, Elaine Bayless, Jimmy Peek; Press, Peter Cromarty/Michael Hartman

PROGRAM: *I Can't Stop Thinking Today* by Annie Evans; Director, Max Mayer   CAST: Allison Janney (Stephanie)
The Amazon's Voice by Allan Heinberg; Director, Melia Benussen   CAST: Tim Blake Nelson (Spencer), Ellen Parker (Diana)
Endless Air, Endless Water by Robert Shaffron; Director, Jimmy Bohr   CAST: Bill Christ (Ditch), Scott Paetty (Fred), Bill Timoney (Control), Penny Ejke (Sheila)
Good As New; Written/Directed by Peter Hedges   CAST: Jenny O'Hara (Jan), Margaret Welsh (Maggie)

(13th St. Theatre) Sunday, Feb. 13–Aug. 1994 13th St. Repertory presents:
TIN PAN ALLEY AND THE SILVER SCREEN; Written/Directed/Performed by Wally Peterson
A one-man celebration of tunesmiths.

(Gramercy Arts Theatre) Tuesday, Feb. 15–Mar. 20, 1994 (29 performances) Repertorio Espanol and The Puerto Rican Traveling Theatre Co. present:
INNOCENT ERENDIRA by Jorge Ali Triana and Carlos Jose Reyes; Based on novella by Gabriel Garcia Marquez; Translation, Felipe Gorostiza and Rene Buch; Director, Mr. Triana; Music, German Arrieta; Lyrics, Mr. Gorostiza; Sets, Liliana Villegas; Costumes, Rosario Lozano; Lighting, Robert Weber Federico; Musical Director, Nicolas Uribe; Stage Manager, Ana Margarita Martinez-Casado; Press, Susan L. Schulman   CAST: Miriam Colon, David Johann, Sofia Oviedo, Jeffrey Rodriguez, Rene Sanchez, Tatiana Vecino
A drama of enslavement and forced prostitution.

(John Houseman Studio) Tuesday, Feb. 15, 1994– Eric Krebs presents:
LIVING IN FLAMES; Written/Performed by Todd Alcott; Director, Lee Costello; Set, Ed Morrill; Lighting, Robert Bessoir; Press, David Rothenberg
An array of people who "teeter through a Port Authority of the soul."

(American Place Theatre) Wednesday, Feb. 16, 1994– American Place Theatre presents:
THE MAYOR OF BOYS TOWN; Written/Performed by Barnaby Spring; Director, Elise Thoron; Set, Joel Reynolds; Lighting, Brian MacDevitt, Louise C. Dizon; Costumes, Emma Cairns; Stage Manager, Sue Jane Stoker; Press, Jonathan Slaff

Five characters in their post-Boys Town adult lives.

(Ohio Theatre) Wednesday, Feb. 16–Mar. 6, 1994 (33 performances) Watermark Theatre and Parallax Productions present:
WORDFIRE FESTIVAL '94; Press, Shirley Herz/Sam Rudy

PROGRAM: *My Virginia;* Written/Performed by Darci Picoult; Director, Suzanne Shepard
The Promotion/The Man in the Moon/The Sunshine's a Glorious Bird; Written/Performed by John O'Keefe
Heddy and Teddy, a Closet Drama; Written/Performed by Fred Curchack
Later That Night; with Emmett Foster, Tim Monagan, Peri Muldofsky, Eileen Myles, Dael Orlandersmith, Rohan Quine, David Simpatico, Rich Stone, Jimmy Tingle

Festival of solo performances in repertory.

(Alice's Fourth Floor) Wednesday, Feb. 16–Mar. 5, 1994 (16 performances) Alice's Fourth Floor presents:
PORTRAIT OF MY BIKINI by James Ryan; Director, William Carden; Set/Lighting, Big Deal Productions; Costumes, Julie Doyle; Sound, Aural Fixation; Stage Manager, Dave Smith; Press, Shirley Herz/Miller Wright CAST: David Burke (Andrew), Brian Tarantina (Nick), Christopher Shaw (David), Stephen Mendillo (Lori), W. T. Martin (Bobby)

A drama set on Bikini Atoll, Marshall Islands, 1987.

(29th St. Repertory Theatre) Thursday, Feb. 17–Mar. 13, 1994 (20 performances) The 29th St. Repertory Theatre presents:
BIBLE BURLESQUE by Bill Nave; Director, Vera Beren; Set, Mark Symczak; Lighting, Stewart Wagner; Costumes, Hillary Moore; Sound, Derby/Beren; Stage Manager, Gregory Dratva; Press, Tony Origlio/Stephen Murray CAST: Edward Norton (Christian Pilgrim), Leo Farley (Jesus/Leon Meggers), Alan Arenius (White/Owen/Homeless/Light Man), Leah Posey (Miss Ruby Jewell/Aunt Hayden/Whore), Paula Ewin (Harriet), Barbara Dworkin (Pandora/Bethany/Lottie Moon), Elizabeth Elkins (Le-Lah/Nurse/Sylvie/Interpreter), Tim Corcoran (Kelly Kay/Rev. Luke/Sister Ann), Peter Lewis (Member of the Right/Wayne/Crazy/Announcer/Brother Bobby/Woodenhead Woodikiah)

A two-act expose of fundamentalism.

Elizabeth Elkins, Edward Norton in *Bible Burlesque*
(Bob Diefendorf)

(Nat Horne Theatre) Thursday, Feb. 17–Mar. 11, 1994 (15 performances) Love Creek Productions present:
A MALICE IN THE WOOD by Le Wilhelm; Director, Sharon Fallon; Sets, Mr. Wilhelm, Mark Briggs; Lighting, Richard Kent Green; Stage Manager, James Gordon; Press, Chris Boneau/Adrian Bryan-Brown, Hillary Harrow CAST: Jed Dickson (C. J.), Michael Ray Martin (Clifton), Carol Halstead (Georgia), Geoff Dawe

A thriller set in Missouri.

(Village Theatre) Thursday, Feb. 17–Mar. 13, 1994 (18 performances) Village Theatre Company presents:
BLUE SKIES FOREVER—THE MYSTERY OF AMELIA EARHART by Claire Braz-Valentine; Director, Henry Fonte; Lighting, Douglas O'Flaherty; Set, Richard Crowell; Costumes, Mary Ellen Park; Sound, Rick Sirois; Stage Manager, Lisa Jean Lewis CAST: John Berg (George Palmer Putnam), Scott Michael Engler (Dan Garens), Barbara Farrar (Amy Earhart), Heidi Fischer (Jacqueline Cochran), Kimberly Schultheiss (Amelia Earhart)

A drama set in July 1937.

(Hudson Guild Theatre) Friday, Feb. 18–Mar. 26, 1994 (28 performances) Irondale Ensemble Project presents:
DANTON'S DEATH by Karl Georg Buchner; Translation, Howard Brenton; Director, Jim Niesen; Sets, Kennon Rothchild; Lighting, Hilarie Blumenthal; Costumes, Elena Pellicciaro; Choreography, Carrie Owerko; Music, Walter Thompson; Press, Peter Cromarty/Anthony Pomes CAST: Michael-David Gordon (Georges Danton), Carrie Owerko (Julie/Marion), Paul Ellis (Herault-Sechelles/Chaumette/Fouquier/LaFlotte), Terry Greiss (Philippeau/Paine/Dillon/Dumas), Joshua Taylor (Simon/LaCroix/Herman), Elena Pellicciaro (Adelaide/Simon's Wife), Nicole Potter (Robespierre/Vouland), Jeanette Horn (Collot), Terry Greiss (Legendre), Lisa Walker (Rosalie/Saint-Just/Amar), Caren LeBerre (Paris), Hilarie Blumenthal, Michael Cain, Steve Cross, Barbara McKenzie Wood, Jim Niesen, Walter Thompson, Matt Tomolanovich

A two-act drama set against the French Revolution.

112 Terry Greiss, David Lockhart in *Danton's Death*
(Gerry Goodstein)

(Orpheum Theatre) Friday, Feb. 18, 1994–still playing May 31, 1994
Columbia Artists Management, Harriet Newman Leve, James D. Stern, Morton Wolkowitz, Schuster/Maxwell, Galin/Sandler, Markley/Manocherian presents: **STOMP;** Created/Directed by Luke Cresswell and Steve McNicholas; Lighting, Mr. McNicholas, Neil Tiplady; Production Manager, Pete Donno; Press, Chris Boneau/Adrian Bryan-Brown, Jackie Green, Bob Fennell   CAST: Luke Creswell, Nick Dwyer, Sarah Eddy, Theseus Gerard, Fraser Morrison, David Olrod, Carl Smith, Fiona Wilkes

Performance art group that uses everything but conventional percussion to make rhythm and dance.

Top: Theseus Gerard, Luke Cresswell
Left: Theseus Gerard, Fiona Wilkes
(Stuart Morris Photos)

113

(Nat Horne Theatre) Thursday, Feb. 24–Mar. 20, 1994 (16 performances) Love Creek Productions presents:
WHAT'S MY LINE? by Judy Sheehan; Director, Philip Galbraith; Press, Chris Boneau/Adrian Bryan-Brown, Hillary Harrow CAST INCLUDES: Kristen Walsh (Lee Majors), Diane Hobbit, Katherine Parks
   A comedy about putting on a play in New York.

(448 W. 16th St.) Thursday, Feb. 24–Apr. 3, 1994 (22 performances) Dar A Luz presents:
QUOTATIONS FROM A RUINED CITY by Reza Abdoh and Salar Abdoh; Created/Directed by Erza Abdoh; Lighting, Jennifer Boggs; Sound, Raul Vincent Enriquez, Galen Wade; Costumes, Eddie Bledsoe; Stage Manager, Sandy Cleary; Press, David Rothenberg/Manuel Igrejas CAST: Sabrina Artel, Brendan Doyle, Anita Durst, Tom Fitzpatrick, Mario Gardner, Mel Herst, Peter Jacobs, Tom Pearl, Ken Roht, Tony Torn, John Yankee
   A meditation on the nature of ruins, physical and emotional.

(Looking Glass Theatre) Friday, Feb. 25–Mar. 21, 1994 (13 performances and 3 previews) Looking Glass Theatre presents:
MIND GAMES by Kenneth Nowell; Director, John Regis; Set, Will Crosby; Costumes, Marcia Canestrano; Press, Francine Trevens/Robert Weston CAST: Aaron Love Williams (Brian Peterson), Will Crosby (Robert Peterson), Justine Lambert (Sarah/Lucy), Marina Zenovich (Ingrid), Susan Carr (Mrs. Peterson)
   A dark comedy set in an Upper West Side living room.

(West End Theatre) Friday, Feb. 25–Mar. 21, 1994 (15 performances) Centerfold Productions present:
ROMEO AND JULIET by William Shakespeare; Director, Kate Konigisor; Choreography, Gary Slavin; Composer, Rob Tate; Fights, Steven Satta; Stage Manager, Barbara Rhodes CAST: Timothy Gulan (Romeo), Pauline Frommer (Juliet), Marni Nixon (Nurse), Keith Adams (Balthazar), Chris Charlesfields (Gregory), Tony Fross (Tybalt), Mary Grace (Lady Montague), Kate Konigisor (Prince Escalus),Cyrus Newitt (Capulet), Robin Poley (Lady Capulet), Gay Reed (Friar Lawrence), Robert Roy (Benvolio), Steven Satta (Mercutio), Adam L. Schwartz (Peter), Gregory Shultz (Servant), Allison Van Ness (Page), Donald Warfield (Montague), Joseph Will (Paris), Ann Marie Wolford (Rosaline), Danton Bankay, Allison Van Ness
   Shakespeare's drama in two acts.

(Harold Clurman Theatre) Friday, Feb. 25–Mar. 27, 1994 (20 performances) Christian Thomas Fitzgerald et al. present:
TIN & RUBBER by C. Thomas Fitzgerald; Director, Chris Fitzgerald; Set, Alice Sabo; Lighting, Rich Montero; Design, Diann Prinz-Carrajat; Stage Manager, Peg Smith CAST: Harry Patrick Christian (Bobby), Chris McGarry (John), John Flick (Kurt), Tony Rossi (Jimmy/Gargenti/Tejani), Mona Hennessy (Sue), Robert Vaccaro (Tony), Rosalind Gatto (Annie), Marcy Repp (Diane), Oscar Stokes (Stavros)
   A comedy about buying a car. The action takes place at a Brooklyn car dealership.

114 Geoffrey C. Ewing, K. Todd Freeman in *Freefall*
(Carol Rosegg)

**Stanley Earl Harrison, Jill Larson, Elaine Rinehart
in *the lost dreams...* (William Gibson)**

(Soho Rep Theatre) Saturday, Feb. 26–Mar. 6, 1994 (7 performances and 4 previews) Playwrights' Preview Productions present:
the lost dreams and hidden frustrations of every woman in brooklyn by Kathleen O'Neill; Director, Tina J. Ball; Set, Jeff Cowie; Lighting, Michael Lincoln; Costumes, Therese Bruck; Sound, Douglas J. Cuomo; Stage Manager, D. C. Rosenberg; Press, Francine L. Trevens/Robert J. Weston CAST: Stanley Earl Harrison (Old Woman/Broker/Drag Queen), Nancy Franklin (Helen), Jill Larson (Claire), Jessica Sager (Avery), Joe Taylor (Tommy), Elaine Rineheart (Tighe), Jerry Rockwood (Irv)
   A comedy in two acts.

(Village Theatre) Sunday, Feb. 27–Mar. 13, 1994 (10 performances) Village Theatre Second Stage presents:
THE MOST FAMOUS WOMAN IN THE WORLD by William Andrew Jones; Director, Kate Bushmann; Set, David Blankenship; Sound, Gak Kompes; Lighting, Doug O'Flaherty; Costumes, Kevin Draves; Video, Robert Tate; Press, Zeke Zaccaro CAST: Scott Burkell, Rhonda Christou, Anita Lento
   A comedy about fame.

(West End Gate Theater) Monday, Feb. 28–Mar. 15, 1994 (9 performances) David Rickman presents:
TWO-DOLLAR FACE by Tony Vellela; Director, Nancy Hancock; Sets, Richard Ginsburg; Costumes, Crystal Thompson; Lighting, Robert Perry; Press, Frimark & Thibodeau/Erin Dunn CAST: Desmond Devenish, Jason Duchin
   A drama set in New York.

(Church of St. Paul and St. Andrew) Monday, Feb. 28–Mar. 22, 1994 (8 performances) Theatre Gym presents:
THE BIG FUNK by John Patrick Shanley; Director, Ann Bowen; Set, Roger Mooney; Lighting/Stage Manager, Linus Lam; Costumes, Marietta Clark; Press, Howard and Barbara Atlee CAST: Eva Lowe (Jill), Margaret Inoue (Fifi), Michael Horn (Omar), Alan Shea (Austin), Robert Rowe (Gregory)
   A philosophical comedy in two acts.

(Theatre Row Theatre) Tuesday, Mar. 1–Apr. 3, 1994 (35 performances) Weissberger Theater Group presents:
FREEFALL by Charles Smith; Director, Donald Douglass; Set, Kalina Ivanov; Costumes, Toni-Leslie James; Lighting, Jan Kroeze; Sound, Darren Clark; Stage Manager, Jesse Wooden, Jr.; Press, John and Gary Springer CAST: Valarie Pettiford (Alex), Geoffrey C. Ewing (Grant), K. Todd Freeman (Monk), Eugene Fleming (Spoon)
   A Chicago-set drama about two estranged brothers.

(E.S.T. Theatre) Wednesday, Mar. 2–13, 1994 (12 performances) Quaigh Theatre presents:

THE TRAGEDY OF KING RICHARD THE SECOND by William Shakespeare; Director, Carol Bennett Gerber; Costumes, Kevin Brainerd; Sound/Lighting, Kevin Mack; Stage Manager, Melinda Kuhn; Fights, Robert John Metcalf CAST: Liz Amerly, Penelope Smith (Queen), Robert Ari (Duke of York), Michael Darden (Aumerle), Todd Davis (Northumberland), Clement Fowler (John of Gaunt/Gardner), Charles E. Gerber (Richard II), Ken Glickfeld (Green/Groom), Helen Hanft (Duchess of York), Robert John Metcalf (Bushy/Salisbury/Exton), Ted Minos (Mowbray/Carlisle), Ellen O'Mara (Duchess of Gloster), Donald Tango (Ross/Assistant), Greg Zerkle (Bolingbroke)

(Open Eyes Theatre) Thursday, Mar. 3–20, 1994 (9 performances and 3 previews)
AND THE TIDE SHALL COVER THE EARTH by Norma Cole; Director, Amie Brockway; Press, Shirley Herz/Sam Rudy CAST: Patricia Guinan, Elyzabeth Gregory Wilder, Mandy Peek, Ernest Johns, Catherine Dudley, Jeremiah Jamison, Eden Riegel
    A drama set in Kentucky's Cumberland River Gorge, 1948.

(Theatre for the New City/Cabaret) Thursday, Mar. 3–20, 1994 (12 performances) Theatre for the New City:
HE SAW HIS REFLECTION by Miranda McDermott; Director, David Willinger; Music, Arthur Abrams; Set, Clark Fidelia; Lighting, Tommy Barker; Costumes, Paula Inocent; Choreography, Oona Haaranen; Press, Jonathan Slaff CAST: Eric Brown (Jamie), Henry Afro Bradley (Crispian), Veronica King (Super), George Bartenieff (Jasper), Allie Calnan (Didi), Lisa Nicholas (Caroline), Aixa Kendrick (Young Woman), Alice White (Helen), Keith Anthony Jones (Mike Manner), Kevin Burnley (Young Man)
    A drama set in the last days of a condemned building.

(Judith Anderson Theatre) Thursday, Mar. 3–27, 1994 (24 performances) Willow Cabin Theatre Company presents:
AS YOU LIKE IT by William Shakespeare; Director, Edward Berkeley; Set, Anne C. Patterson; Costumes, Richard Shawn Dudley; Lighting, Steven Rust; Music, Wade Russo; Choreography, Nora Kasarda; Press, Jim Baldassare CAST: Cynthia Besterman (Amiens), John Billeci (Oliver), John Bolger (Orlando), Fiona Davis (Rosalind), Kenneth Favre (Dennis/Silvius), Ken Forman (Senior/Frederick/Martext/William), Laurence Gleason (Adam/Touchstone), Angela Nevard (LeBeau/Audrey/de Boys), Adam Oliensis (Jaques), Dede Pochos (Celia), Maria Radman (Phebe), Craig Zakarian (Charles/Corin)
    This version is set in America, 1930s.

(National Shakespeare Conservatory) Thursday, Mar. 3–27, 1994 (16 performances) Chain Lightning Theatre presents:
UNCLE VANYA by Anton Chekhov; Translation, Victoria Kupchinetsky and Andrei Koltanov; Director, Todd Pieper; Lighting, Stewart Wagner; Costumes, Devin Quigley; Set, Richard Kinsey, Jean Hiroshima; Stage Manager, Leslie Colucci; Press, Jim Baldassare CAST: Lyle Walford (Dr. Astrov), Constance Kane (Marina), Kricker James (Vanya), Cheryl Horne (Elena), Jack R. Marks (Serebryakov), Suzie Devoe (Sonya), Eric Russell (Telegin), Virginia Robinson (Maria), Jonathan Green (Workman)
    A new translation of the 1899 drama.

Fiona Davis, Laurence Gleason, Dede Pochos in *As You Like It*
(Carol Rosegg)

(Top-bottom) Miriam Healy-Louie, Sebastian Roche, Jean Loup Wolfman in *Titus Andronicus* **(Gerry Goodstein)**

(St. Clement's) Thursday, Mar. 3–27, 1994 (21 performances) Theatre for a New Audience presents:
TITUS ANDRONICUS by William Shakespeare; Director, Julie Taylor; Music, Elliot Goldenthal; Set, Derek McLane; Costumes, Constance Hoffman; Lighting, Donald Holder; Sound, Eric Liljestrand; Music, Richard Martinez; Fights, David Leong; Press, Shirley Herz/Miller Wright CAST: Samuel Baird (Alarbus/Goth/Sempronius), Jean Baker (Nurse), Geoffrey P. Cantor (Martinus/Publius/Goth), Curzon Dobell (Lucius), David Dossey (Clown), Ned Eisenberg (Saturninus), Miriam Healy-Louise (Lavinia), Harry Lennix (Aaron), Frank Lowe (Aemilius), Melinda Mullins (Tamora), Sebastian Roche (Demetrius), Michael Rudko (Andronicus), Darien Scott Shulman (Young Lucius), Steven Skybell (Bassianus/Goth), Robert Stattel (Titus), Adam Stein (Mutius/Caius/Goth/Servant), Bruce Turk (Quintus/Goth/Valentine), Jean Loup Wolfman (Chiron)
    Performed with one intermission.

(Brooklyn Academy of Music/Opera House) Friday, Mar. 4–5, 1994 (2 limited performances) Brooklyn Academy of Music presents:
STURM UND DRANG including **MEDEA** by Friedrich Wilhelm Gotter; Translation, Richard Luckett and Maurice Edwards CAST: Claire Bloom (Medea), Michael Cumpsty (Jason), Dina Paisner (Tutor/Nurse), Michael Foy (Younger Son), Robert Notwicz (Older Son), Brooklyn Philharmonic
    U.S. premiere of an 18th-century musical melodrama.

(Kraine Theatre) Friday, Mar. 4–20, 1994 (15 performances) Bandwagon presents:
A LOVER'S RHAPSODY with Music by Ivor Novello; Lyrics, Christopher Hassall; Staging/Continuity, Jerry Bell; Set, Dunsi Dai; Lighting, Shawn Rozsa; Costumes, Paulina Kent Dennis; Musical Director, Mark Goodman; Stage Managers, Judd Hollander, Sue Feinberg; Press, Audrey Ross CAST: Mark Calvino, Michael Dantuono, Catherine Grimshaw, Robert Mattern, Elana Polin, Margaret Shafer, Jennifer L. Welch, Gabrielle Widman, John Wilkerson

MUSICAL NUMBERS: Glamorous Night, Music in May, Gates of Paradise, Matter of Minutes, Waking or Sleeping, Man of My Heart, Easy to Live With, Love is My Reason, Manchuko, Fly Home Little Heart, Love Made the Song, What Do You Mean, Night May Have Its Sadness, When I Curtsied to the King, Dark Music, Mountain Dove/If This Were Love, Shine Through My Dreams, When It's Spring in Vienna, Singing Waltz, Paris Reminds Me of You, Fold Your Wings, Dancing Years Highlights, Wait for Me, Why Is There Ever Goodbye?, Someday My Heart Will Awake, Take Your Girl, We'll Gather Lilacs, Keep the Home Fires Burning
    Highlights from the 1935–51 musicals of English composer, writer, and actor, Ivor Novello.

(Metropolitan Playhouse) Saturday, Mar. 5–27, 1994 (14 performances) Parsifal's Productions present:
ROMEO & JULIET by William Shakespeare; Director, Mary Ethel Schmidt; Sets/Lighting, Tim Stephenson; Costumes, Susan Soetaert; Choreography, Lindsey Hanahan; Music, Michael Paris; Fights, Robert Ruffin; Stage Manager, Danielle LaViscount CAST: Nicole Parker (Juliet), Maduka Steady (Romeo), Ruqayya Abdus-Salaam, Marisa Altamura, Tara V. Cleland, Luisa D'Amelio, Nick Dantos (Gregory/Apothecary/Watchman), William Driscoll (Paris), Kurt Engstrom (Sampson/Watchman), Christopher Dansby Fisher (Escalus), Aaron James Knight (Capulet), John Kooi (Mercutio), Vincent Lamberti (Tybalt), Vincent Masterpaul (Peter), James McKnight (Abram/Page), Ira Mitchell (Friar John/Others), Cheryl Monroe (Lady Capulet), Daniel Nalbach (Friar Laurence), Jesse Ontiveros (Benvolio), Anita Outlaw (Lady Montague), Roland Sanchez (Montague), Stewart Walker (Balthasar), Collen Smith Wallnau (Nurse)

(Perry St. Theatre) Saturday, Mar. 5–Apr. 2, 1994 (26 performances) Petrashevsky Circle Productions present:
CRIME AND PUNISHMENT; Adaptation/Direction by Robert Hein; Based on the novel by Fyodor Dostoevsky; Costumes/Lighting/Set, Girogi M. Alexi; Music, Arlo McKinnon; Sound, Wendy Hedin; Stage Manager, Cathy Haig Bonjukian; Press, Peter Cromarty/Michael Hartman CAST: Daria Balling, Lilith Beitchman, Wendy Domarecki, Jaz Dorsey, David Fuhrer, Almon Grimsted, Ivana Medakovic, Nana Mukhadze, Christopher Nissley, Bernadette Pauley, Gregory Pekar, Brian Quirk, Lutz Rath, Diana Ronchini, Ken Simon, Erika Tavi, Laurie Wickens, Charles Young
   A man searches for ultimate justice.

(Naked Angels) Sunday, Mar. 6–16, 1994 (9 performances and 3 previews) Naked Angels presents:
FAT MEN IN SKIRTS by Nicky Silver; Director, Joe Mantello; Set, Steve Olson; Lighting, Howard Werner; Costumes, Laura Cunningham; Sound, Aural Fixation; Fights, Rick Sordelet; Stage Manager, Barnaby Harris CAST: Matt McGrath (Bishop Hogan), Allison Janney (Phyllis Hogan), Stanley Tucci (Howard Hogan/Dr. Nestor), Marisa Tomei (Pam/Popo Martin)
   A play in two acts.

(Courtyard Playhouse) Monday, Mar. 7, 1994– (Mon. & Tues. only)
THE LAST BRUNCH by Loud Blouse; Director, Dominic Orlando; Lighting, Marilyn Majeski; Sound, Carla Savoy; Press, Judy Jacksina CAST: Jon Kinnally, Diana Naftal, Tracy Proust, Carla Savoy, Hedda Lettuce
   Loud Blouse, a downtown comedy group, in a comic revue.

(INTAR Theatre) Tuesday, Mar. 8–Apr. 3, 1994 (28 performances) Women's Project & Productions presents:
BLACK by Joyce Carol Oates; Director, Tom Palumbo; Set, David Mitchell; Costumes, Elsa Ward; Lighting, Jackie Manassee; Sound, Bruce Ellman; Fights, Ellen Saland; Stage Manager, Patty Lyons; Press, Philip Rinaldi/Kathy Haberthur CAST: John Wojda (Jonathan Boyd), Kristin Griffith (Debra O'Donell), Jonathan Earl Peck (Lew Claybrook)
   A drama performed without intermission. The action takes place in a town off the New Jersey Turnpike.

116   **John Wojda, Kristin Griffith**
       in *Black* **(Martha Holmes)**

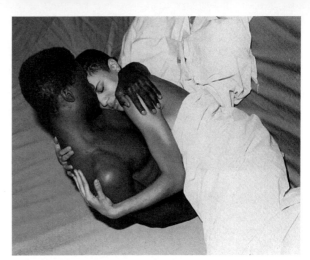

Maduka Steady, Nicole Parker in *Romeo & Juliet*

Myra Lucretia Taylor, Tom Nelis in *Marathon Dancing*
(William Rivelli)

(Masonic Hall) Tuesday, Mar. 8–Apr. 10, 1994 (32 performances) En Garde Arts presents:
MARATHON DANCING by Laura Harrington; Musical Adaptation/Supervision, Christopher Drobny; Conception/Direction, Anne Bogart; Choreography, Alison Shafer; Musical Director, Michael Rice; Sets, Kyle Chepulis; Costumes, Gabriel Berry; Lighting, Carol Mullins; Sound, Eric Lijestrand; Press, David Rothenberg CAST: P. J. Benjamin (Frankie Aragon), Steven Goldstein (Gus Wilson), Andrew Weems (Harry Miller), Jennifer Wiltsie (Jo-Jo Miller), Maureen Silliman (Juliet Bonetti), Frank Raiter (Mack MacDougle), Lauren Mitchell (Faye Lanier), Jonathan Fried (Kid Alexander), Kristen Flanders (Ingrid Anderson), Matthew Bennett (Mort Manning), Victoria Clark (Hazel Winch), Gabriel Barre (Jack Coker), Myra Lucretia Taylor (Ruby Savage), Tom Nelis (Sammy Clayton), Susann Bennett, Alan Cohen, Meredith Davidow, Allison Dubin, Peter Flamm, Abigail Gampel, Anne Hartmann, James Kampf, Lisa Monacelli, Stephen Speights, James Christopher Tracy, David Zellnik
   Site specific theatre performed in a 100-year-old ballroom. The action takes place at a 1932 dance marathon.

(SoHo Rep Theatre) Wednesday, Mar. 9–27, 1994 (15 performances) Blue Herron Theatre presents:
EXCHANGE by Yuri Trifonov; Translation/Adaptation, Michael Frayn; Director, Peter Westerhoff; Music, Brant Adams; Set, John Douglas; Lighting, Sybil Killian; Costumes, Lesley Neilson-Bowman CAST: Mark Adzick (Lena's Father), Peggy Lord Chilton (Lena's Mother), Tom Dennis (Zherekhov/Bubrik), Bill DiMichele (Viktor's Father/Felix/Snitkin), James Fleming (Viktor), Janice Johnson (Lena), Maureen Kenny (Director/Zhenya), Ruth Kulerman (Viktor's Mother), Joel Parsons (Grandfather), Madigan Ryan (Lora), Ennis Smith (Agent/Kalugin), Lynne Faljian Taylor (Tanya/Marina), Anna Vitkin (Natashka)
   The action takes place in Moscow, 1970s.

(Puerto Rican Traveling Theatre) Wednesday, Mar. 9–Apr. 17, 1994 (30 performances) Puerto Rican Traveling Theatre presents:
WRITTEN AND SEALED by Isaac Chocron; Translation, Susan J. Jones; Revised/Edited by Carmen L. Marin; Director, Miriam Colon Valle; Set/Costumes, Randy Barcelo; Lighting, Spencer Brown; Stage Manager, Roger Franklin; Press, Max Eisen CAST: Jaime Sanchez (Saul), Ramon Albino (Miguel), Rafael DeMussa (Luis), Irma-Estel LaGuerre (Carmen), Isabel Keating (Nancy)
  A two-act drama performed in English or Spanish.

(The Studio) Friday, Mar. 11–27, 1994 (9 performances each) Carousel Theatre Company presents:
BLUES FOR MISTER CHARLIE by James Baldwin; Director, William-Kevin Young and **LAST SUMMER AT BLUEFISH COVE** by Jane Chambers; Director, Deb Guston; Costumes, Catherine Anne Hayes; Lighting, Denise Bourcier; Sets, Walter A. Ulasinki CASTS: Christopher Kirk Allen, Scott Barrow, William Breedlove, Paula Eschweiler, Lynn Evans, Valentino J. Ferreira, Laura Fois, Verna O. Hobson, Dennis Horvitz, Carter Inskeep, Lawrence James, Lynellen Kagen, Pamela Dean Kenny, Peggy Lehman, Tembi Locke, James Love, Laurence Mahler, Vicki Meisner, Marilyn Raphael, Rashamella, Bonnie Rose, Teresa Rzeznik, David Sitler, Amy Stiller, Michael Walczak, Sharon Watroba, William-Kevin Young, Jude Zachary
  Two plays in repertory.

(Mint Theatre) Saturday, Mar. 12–26, 1994 (11 performances) Mint Theatre Company presents:
ANTON CHEKHOV: STORIES FROM MY YOUTH; Adaptation/Direction, Jonathan Bank; Set, Bill Kneissl; Lighting, Craig Caccamise; Costumes, Paula Godsey; Stage Manager, Gary Adamsen; Press, Barbara Reirson CAST: Eric Barkan, Lisa M. Bostnar, Stewart R. Groves, Linda Ames Key, Richard E. Long, Craig Mason, Stephen McIntyre, Hugh O'Gorman, Brandt Reiter, Joe Yates
  Selections from stories and personal letters.

(HERE) Thursday, Mar. 17–Apr. 1, 1994 (14 performances) Tiny Mythic Theatre Company presents:
PENTHESILEA by Heinrich von Kleist; Translation, Douglas Langworthy; Director, David Herskovits; Set, Denise Hudson; Costumes, David Zinn; Lighting, Lenore Doxsee; Sound, John Lewis; Stage Manager, Christine Lemme; Press, Philip Rinaldi/Kathy Haberthur CAST: Bill Blank, Carrie Boren, Linda Donald, Bradley Glenn, Jacqueline Gregg, Rinne Groff, David Haugen, Rohanna Kenin, Julie Lawrence, Joyce Lee, Sarah Long, Daniel Pardo, Scott Rabinowitz, Steven Rattazzi, Greig Sargeant, Mark Setlock, Penelope Smith, Susie Sokol, Jeanne Willcoxon
  An army of men and women at war with each other.

(Performing Garage) Thursday, Mar. 24–Apr. 9, 1994 (11 performances) The Wooster Group presents:
THE EMPEROR JONES by Eugene O'Neill; Director, Elizabeth LeCompte; Music, David Linton CAST INCLUDES: Willem Dafoe, Kate Valk
  A 1920 drama.

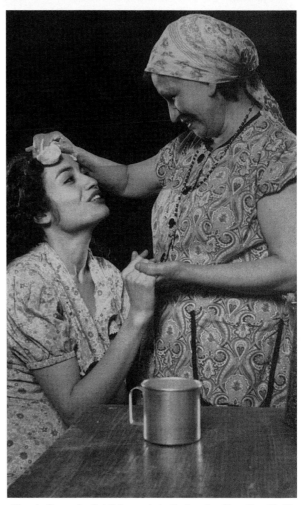

Margie Oquendo, Sol Echeverria in *Emigracion* (Jonathan Slaff)

(Theatre for the New City) Thursday, Mar. 24–Apr. 17, 1994 (16 performances) Bartenieff/Field presents:
EMIGRACION: AN AMERICAN PLAY by Yolanda Rodriguez; Director, Crystal Field; Set, Donald L. Brooks; Lighting, Kent R. Hoffman; Costumes, Jose M. Rivera; Sound, Paul Garrity; Press, Jonathan Slaff CAST: Joel Arandia, William Cruz, Joseph C. Davis, Brian DeCubellis, Sol Echeverria, Nicholas Gonzales, Ian Gordon, Bob Grimm, Zabryna Guevara, Inez I. Guzman, Patrick Lee, Terry Lee King, Raul Martinez, Tessa Morales, Margie Oquendo, Jessy Ortiz, Jose Angel Rivera, Jose Rabelo, Mira Rivera, Joyce L. Rocha E Silva, Jason Rodriguez, Al Roffe, Liana Rosario, Angelita R. Strong, Michael Vasquez, Juan Villegas, Stephen Isiah Whitley, Jimmy Walker, Barbara Wise, Benna Wise-Levine, Derek Zasky
  A drama in three acts. The action takes place in Puerto Rico and New York City.

(Synchronicity Space) Friday, Mar. 25–Apr. 10, 1994 (12 performances) Synchronicity Theatre Group presents:
FEN by Caryl Churchill; Director, Cap Pryor; Set, Mark Symczak; Lighting, David Alan Comstock CAST: Jody Barrett (Val), Samme Johnston, Brenda Pitmon, Cappy Lyons, Rachel Bones, Sheila Sawney, Bill Dante
  A drama set in an English country village.

(Charles Ludlam Theater) Friday, Mar. 25–July 10, 1994 The Ridiculous Theatrical Company presents:
MOVIELAND; Written/Performed by Everett Quinton; Director, Eureka; Set, T. Greenfield; Lighting, Richard Currie; Costumes, Toni Nanette Thompson; Wigs, Zsamira Ronquillo; Sound, Jim Van Bergen; Press, Peter Cromarty/Michael Hartman
  A comedy performed without intermission.

Irma-Estel LaGuerre, Rafael DeMussa, Jaime Sanchez in
Written and Sealed

(Samuel Beckett Theatre) Tuesday, Mar. 29–Apr. 17, 1994 (15 performances) The Basic Theatre presents:
BERTOLT BRECHT IN DARK TIMES; Conceived/Compiled by Douglas Langworthy; Director, Lester Shane; Score, Margaret R. Pine; Choreography, Susan Hefner; Musical Director, Shelly Eberhart; Set, Rick Martin; Lighting, Jeff Segal; Costumes, Patty Burke, Jared Hammond; Stage Manager, John C. Lake CAST: Eric Brandenburg, Sheri Delaine, Eureka, Jared Hammond, Ross Salinger, Tom Spivey, Elizabeth Ann Townsend
   The poems and lyrics of Brecht.

(Theatre Four) Tuesday, Mar. 29–June 10, 1994 (86 performances and 8 previews) Eric Krebs, Bobby Roberts and Roger Paglia present:
MORT SAHL'S AMERICA; Written/Performed by Mort Sahl; Lighting, Robert Bessoir; Sound, Dean Marletta; Press, David Rothenberg
   An evening with the humorist.

(Circle in the Square/Downtown) Friday, Apr. 1–May 11, 1994 (32 performances and 16 previews) Peter Holmes a Court and Rodger Hess in association with Back Row Productions present:
FALLEN ANGEL with Music/Lyrics/Book by Billy Boesky; Director, Rob Greenberg; Musical Director/Orchestrations, Steve Postell; Sets, David Birn; Lighting, Christopher Akerlind; Costumes, Wendy A. Rolfe; Murals, Adair Peck; Sound, Tom Clark; Stage Manager, Allison Sommers; Press, Chris Boneau/Adrian Bryan-Brown, Craig Karpel CAST: Jonathan Goldstein (Will), Corey Glover (Luke), Shannon Conley (Gretta), George Coe (Father/Stu Rosen), Susan Gibney (Dr. Bamberger/Alexandra)

MUSICAL NUMBERS: Coming and Going, More Than You Know, Falling in Line, Till I'm Gone, Southbound Train, Hey Lady, Silo, Fallen Angel, Unveil My Eyes, All Right
   A rock musical performed without intermission.

(Irish Arts Center) Saturday, Apr. 2–May 22, 1994 Irish Arts Center presents:
BROTHERS OF THE BRUSH by Jimmy Murphy; Director, Nye Heron; Set, David Raphel; Lighting, Maurice Saavedra Pefaur; Sound, Nico Kean; Costumes, Anne Reilly CAST: Mickey Kelly (Jack), Paul Ronan (Lar), Ronan Carr (Heno), Paul McGrane (Martin)
   A drama set at a Dublin flat being remodeled.

(Ubu Rep. Theater) Tuesday, Apr. 5–May 1, 1994 (24 performances) Ubu Repertory presents:
THE ORPHANAGE by Reine Barteve; Translation, Jill MacDougall; Director, Francoise Kourilsky; Set, Watoku Ueno; Lighting, Greg MacPherson; Costumes, Carol Ann Pelletier; Music, Mauro Refosco; Stage Manager, Teresa Conway; Press, Peter Cromarty/Michael Hartman CAST: Tanya Lopert (Mado), Chad L. Coleman (Azaf), Julie Boyd (Gwen), La Tonya Borsay (Makuma), Markita Prescott (Nesilili), Eric Coleman (Zugrako)
   An African-set drama performed without intermission.

Mort Sahl

      (front) George Coe, Jonathan Goldstein, Corey Glover, Shannon Conley, Susan Gibney, (rear) Van Romaine, Winston Roye, Derek Boshart, Allison Carnell in *Fallen Angel* **(William Gibson)**

(Promenade Theatre) Tuesday, Apr. 5–Aug. 26, 1995 (582 performances) Elizabeth I. McCann, Jeffrey Ash, Daryl Roth, in association with Leavitt/Fox/Mages and The Vineyard Theatre present:
THREE TALL WOMEN by Edward Albee; Director, Lawrence Sacharow; Set, James Noone; Costumes, Muriel Stockdale; Lighting, Phil Monat; Stage Manager, R. Wade Jackson; Press, Shirley Herz/Sam Rudy CAST: Myra Carter, Lucille Patton-matinees (A), Marian Seldes (B), Jordan Baker (C), Michael Rhodes (The Boy)
 A drama in two acts. Winner of the 1994 Pulitzer Prize and the New York Drama Critics Circle Best Play.

Marian Seldes, Myra Carter, Jordan Baker (Carol Rosegg)   119

**Marlene Hodgdon, Jeremy Brisiel,
Allan Benjamin (front) in *Black Forest* (T. L. Boston)**

**Christopher Schumann, Darynn Zimmer
in *Desert of Roses* (Carol Rosegg)**

**Richard Parent, Ken Jennings, Dale Sandish,
Jennifer Naimo, Kevin McDermott
in *Amphigorey* (Skid)**

(HERE) Wednesday, Apr. 6–17, 1994 (11 performances) Tiny Mythic Theatre Company presents:
TROILUS AND CRESSIDA by William Shakespeare; Director, Gary Schwartz; Set, Stephen Carter; Costumes, Cynthia Dumont; Lighting, Lenore Doxsee; Fights, Sasha Burdenkov; Music, Ed Ratliffe; Stage Manager, Victoria A. Epstein CAST: Nancy Balbirer, Edward Burke, Henry Caplan, Joan Chaneski, Dina Comolli, Christina Denzinger, Michael Joseph Dolan, Suzanne Ecklund, Charles Goforth, Barbara Graham, Phil Hoffman, Annette Houlihan Verdolino, Vin Knight, Jan-Peter Pedross, Beau Ruland, Gerard J. Schneider, Christian Tallman, Thaddaeus Smith, Paul Urcioli

(Vineyard Theatre/26th St.) Wednesday, Apr. 6–24, 1994 (15 performances) The Phoenix Ensemble presents:
BLACK FOREST by Jon Fraser; Director, Karen E. Lordi; Sets, Michael Sims; Lighting, Trudi Malten; Costumes, Cathy Small; Stage Manager, Diane Healy; Press, Shirley Herz/Sam Rudy, Wayne Wolfe CAST: Jeremy R. Brisiel (Hans), Allan Benjamin (Josh), Marlene Hodgdon (Greta), Blanche Cholet (Frika/Estelle), Herman O. Arbeit (Sam), Kerry Metzler (Sue)
   A drama set in Germany and America.

(Harold Clurman Theatre) Wednesday, Apr. 6–May 1, 1994 (20 performances) Quaigh Theatre presents:
THE BONDING by Hal O. Kesler; Directors, Will Lieberson and Paul Brandt; Set, Bob Phillips; Lighting, Winifred H. Powers; Set, Michael J. Kelly; Stage Manager, Jonathan Polk; Press, Francine L. Trevens/Robert J. Weston CAST: Dickson Shaw (Fred), Ken Budris (Huntley), Natasha de Vegh (Cathy)
   A drama in two acts. The action takes place in a California bungalow.

(Primary Stages) Wednesday, Apr. 6–May 1, 1994 (24 performances) Primary Stages in association with Reno Productions presents:
CRACKDANCING; Written/Directed by Joseph Hindy; Set, George Xenos; Costumes, Amanda J. Klein; Lighting, Deborah Constantine; Sound, Darren Clark; Choreography, Bridget Dengel; Press, Anne Einhorn CAST: Patricia McAneny (Mom), John Wojda (The Men)
   Satire performed without intermission about an American family gone haywire.

(Village Theatre) Thursday, Apr. 7–May 1, 1994 (17 performances) Village Theatre Company presents:
MADONNA by Don Nigro; Director, Gigi Rivkin; Set, Micael Blau; Lighting, Douglas O'Flaherty; Costumes, Alyson Hui; Stage Manager, Jennifer Creighton CAST: Pam Bennett, Jill Chamberlain, Elizabeth Daly, Marj Feenan, Mark J. Foley, Peter Husovsky, Craig Little, Lisa Littlewood, Christopher Marino, J. B. McLendon, Roger Michelson, Mike Pinney, Melanie Summerfield, Brenda Warren
   A drama about the artist Edvard Munch.

(Tribeca Performing Arts Center) Thursday, Apr. 7–24, 1994 (12 performances) Encompass Music Theatre presents:
DESERT OF ROSES with Music by Robert Moran; Libretto, Michael John LaChiusa; Director, Nancy Rhodes; Conductor, Jack Gaughan; Choreography, Judith Haskell; Set, Gary Jennings; Lighting, Marie Barrett; Costumes, Batasha Landau; Stage Manager, Tigre McMullan; Press, Richard Kornberg CAST: RoseMarie Freni (Woman), Bronwyn Thomas (Sister One), Susan Davis Holmes (Sister Two), Ron Edwards (Brother), Darynn Zimmer (Girl), Sean Baker (Father), Christopher Schumann (Monster); Rebecca Bandiere, Judd Ernster, Deana Insley, Alison Lund, Fausto Pindea, David Robeano
   A two-act chamber opera based on the *Beauty and the Beast* story.

(Perry St. Theatre) Thursday, Apr. 7–May 26, 1994 (50 performances) The Q.R.V. Company presents:
AMPHIGOREY: A MUSICALE; Written/Designed by Edward Gorey; Music, Peter Golub; Director/Choreographer, Daniel Levans; Costumes, James P. Hammer, Jr.; Lighting, Brian Nason; Set, More Than Just Scenery; Music Director, Frederick Willard; Stage Manager, Bethany Ford; Press, Keith Sherman/Jim Byk, Stuart Ginsberg CAST: Mark Baker, Allison DeSalvo, Ken Jennings, Kathleen Mahony-Bennett, Kevin McDermott, Jennifer Naimo, Richard Parent, Dale Sandish, Joyce Sozen, Clare Stollak

PROGRAM: Q.R.V., Frozen Man, Weeping Chandelier, Doubtful Guest, Deranged Cousins, Q.R.V. Too, Forty-seven Questions, Blue Aspic, Nursery Frieze, Object Lesson, Enraged Telephone, Osbick Bird, Inanimate Tragedy, Admonitory Hippopotamus, Q.R.V. Also
   A revue comprised mostly of unpublished Gorey material.

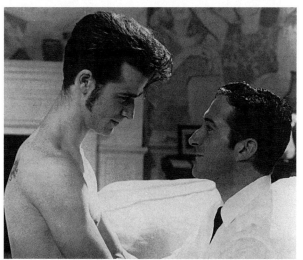

Justin Theroux, Albert Macklin
in *Hide Your Love Away* (Carol Rosegg)

Todd Weeks, Mary McCann
in *Shaker Heights* (Gerry Goodstein Photos)

Yuri Skujins, Colleen Werthmann
in *Reproducing Georgia* (Anthony Rapp)

(Theatre Row Theatre) Friday, Apr. 8–24, 1994 (16 performances) Africa Arts Theatre Company presents:
PANORAMA by Pieter-Dirk Uys; Director, George Ferencz; Set, Bill Stabile; Costumes, Sally Lesser; Lighting, Jeff Tapper; Sound, Genji Ito; Stage Manager, Jessica Hall; Press, Jonathan Slaff CAST: Margie Ryan (Karin), Bill Christ (Grobbelaar), Jacqueline Pennington (Rosa), Kim Tooks (Sibi)
    A comedy in two acts. The action takes place in South Africa.

(Altered Stages) Friday, Apr. 8–24, 1994 (15 performances) Annette Moskowitz and Alexander Racolin present:
CLOWN WANTED by Matei Visniec; Translation, Flora Papastavru; Director, Moshe Yassur; Lighting, Stewart Wagner; Music, Jacob Stern; Press, Francine L. Trevens CAST: Jonathan Teague Cook, Howard Katz, Arland Russell
    A drama from Rumania.

(Centerfold Theatre) Saturday, Apr. 9–23, 1994 (7 performances) Centerfold Productions presents:
THE BROKEN HEARTS OF EDGAR ALLEN POE by Jaz Dorsey and Phillip Beitchman; Director/Music, Jaz Dorsey; Lighting, Lucia Leon CAST: Arlene Love (Poe), Karron Haines (Signora Psyche Zenobia), Bob Hart (Imp of the Perverse), Bob Gallagher (The Lover), Mary Grace (The Muse)
    Poe's poems come to life as he dreams.

(Actors' Playhouse) Saturday, Apr. 9–May 27, 1994 (39 performances and 11 previews) Eclectic Theatre Company in association with The Liverpool Production Company and Peter Breger presents:
HIDE YOUR LOVE AWAY: *The Ballad of Brian Epstein* by Kevin Scott; Director, Leonard Foglia; Set, Michael McGarty; Costumes, Markas Henry; Lighting, Betsy Finston; Sound, One Dream; Stage Manager, Bruce Greenwood; Press, Shirley Herz/Miller Wright CAST: Albert Macklin (Brian Epstein), Sarah Long (Lynne Whelan), Justin Theroux (Teddy Baker), Stephen Singer (Clive Epstein), Amy Hohn (Cilla Black)
    Biography of the Beatles' gay manager. The action takes place in London, 1967.

(St. Clement's) Tuesday, Apr. 12–23, 1994 (16 performances) NYS Theatre Institute presents:
AMERICAN ENTERPRISE with Music/Lyrics/Book by Jeffrey Sweet; Director, Patricia Birch; Incidental Music/Arrangements, Michael Vitali; Musical Director, Betsy Riley; Set, Richard Finkelstein; Costumes, Brent Griffin; Lighting, John McLain; Sound, Matt Elie; Press, Susan L. Schulman CAST: John Romeo (George Pullman), Erol K. C. Landis (Hopkins), David Bunce (George Jr./Paymaster), Gerard Curran (Debs/Beman/McCormick/Priest), Bernard J. Tarver (Atgeld/Jackson/Clayton/Porter), Paul Villani (Stephens/Harahan/Agent), Joel Aroeste (Heathcote/Railroad Owner/Worthington), Erika Newell (Jennie/Florence), Betsy Riley, Kelly Sweeney (Soloists), John T. McGuire, III (Oggel/Field) Michael Steese (Harrison/Swift/Crosgrove/Marshall), Jack Seabury (Porter/Servant), Jason W. Bowman (Attendant), Tracey E. Madison (Secretary), Laura Roth, Alison Sharpley (Ensemble)

MUSICAL NUMBERS: Shall We Plant a Tree?, Porters on a Pullman Train, Leave a Light, It's a Trust, Columbian Exposition, Maggie Murphy, Step by Step, The Pullman Strike
    A musical biography of Chicago robber baron George Pullman.

(Atlantic Theatre) Wednesday, Apr. 13–June 5, 1994 (55 performances) Atlantic Theatre Company presents:
SHAKER HEIGHTS by Quincy Long; Director, Neil Pepe; Sets, James Wolk; Costumes, Laura Cunningham; Lighting, Howard Werner; Sound, Janet Kalas; Stage Manager, Eric Eligator; Press, Jim Baldassare CAST: Steven Goldstein (Buddy), Felicity Huffman (Gertrude), Todd Weeks (Frank), Mary McCann (Joanne), Jordan Iage (Richard), Ray Anthony Thomas (Dorsey)
    A comedy in two acts set in a house on the edge of a golf course.

(American Place Theatre) Thursday, Apr. 14–May 1, 1994
Bold Face Theatre presents:
REPRODUCING GEORGIA by Karen Hartman; Director, Dana Kirchman; Set, Peter Shevenell; Lighting, Paul Bartlett; Costumes, Karen Ngo; Sound, Matt Berman; Choreography, Katherine Profeta; Stage Manager, Susan Felber; Press, Jeffrey Richards/Kevin Rehac CAST: Colleen Werthmann (Audrey), David Herskovits (Instructor's Voice), Jeanne Dorsey (Georgia O'Keeffe), David Haugen (Alfred Stieglitz), Yuri Skujins (Victor/Man One), Malindi Fickle (Claudia/Woman One), Lauren Howard (Julia/Woman Two), Anthony Rapp (Andy/Man Two)
    A drama in two acts.

121

(Westbeth Theatre Center) Thursday, Apr. 14–May 1, 1994 (15 performances) reopened at Theatre for the New City May 11–June 5, 1994 (27 performances) Theatre for the New City in association with James Di Paola and Wind Merchant Productions presents:
THE LAST SORTIE by George Rattner; Director, Robert Landau; Set/Lighting, Fred Kolo; Costumes, Helen E. Rodgers; Sound, Gary and Timmy Harris; Stage Manager, Marybeth Ward; Press, Susan L. Schulman CAST: W. B. Brydon succeeded by Edward Seamon (Walter Karzowski), Fred Burrell (Grant Wayland), Anthony Grasso (Young Frank), Christopher Healy (Young Grant), Alan Levine (Young Joel), Kevin Martin (Young Walter), Frank S. Palmer (Constantine/Justino), David Rosenbaum (Joel Solomon), Steven Stahl (Col. McKay), Michael Twaine (Frank Lo Presti)

A drama in two acts. The action takes place in Italy, 1944–90.

(Village Theatre/Second Stage) Sunday, Apr. 17–May 1, 1994 (8 performances) Village Theatre Company presents:
2 BY STRINDBERG; Director, Norman Rhodes CAST: Michelle K. Berke, Heidi Fischer, Ruth Hackett, Christie Harrington, Catherine Hesselbach, Carol Holmes, Lynn Marie Hulsman, Julia McLaughlin, Larry Reinhardt-Meyer
Mother Love and *First Warning.*

(Brooklyn Academy of Music/Opera House) Tuesday, Apr. 19–24, 1994 (8 performances) Royal Shakespeare Company presents:
THE WINTER'S TALE by William Shakespeare; Director, Adrian Noble; Set, Anthony Ward; Lighting, Chris Parry, Mike Gunning; Music, Shaun Davey; Stage Manager, Michael Dembowicz; Press, Chris Boneau/Adrian Bryan-Brown, Bob Fennell, Ellen Zeisler, Heidi Feldman CAST: David Action (Gaoler), John Bott (Antigonus), Suzanne Burden (Hermione), Julian Curry (Polixenes), Jeffery Dench (Old Shepard), Don Gallagher (Archidamus/Servant), Emma Gregory (Dorcas), William Haden (Cleomenes), Mark Hadfield (Autolycus), Phyllinda Hancock (Perdita), Stephanie Jacob (Mopsa), Paul Jesson (Camillo), Gemma Jones (Paulina), Ruth Jones (Lady), Barnaby Kay (Florizel), Richard Long (Lord), John Nettles (Leontes), Ian Taylor (Mariner), Graham Turner (Young Shepard), Angela Vale (Emilia), James Walker (Dion), Jack Waters (Servant), Guy Williams (Lord)

Performed with one intermission.

(Playhouse on Vandam) Wednesday, Apr. 20–still playing May 31, 1994 Dana Matthow presents:
HYSTERICAL BLINDNESS *and Other Southern Tragedies That Have Plagued My Life So Far* by Leslie Jordan; Music/Lyrics, Joe Patrick Ward; Directed/Developed by Carolyne Barry; Musical Director/Vocal Arrangements, Joe Patrick Ward; Musical Staging, Mark Knowles; Musical Supervisor, Glenn Gordon; Design, Charles E. McGarry; Costumes, Wern-Ying Hwarng; Lighting, Phil Monat; Sound, Aural Fixation; Stage Manager, Sarahjane Allison; Press, John and Gary Springer CAST: Leslie Jordan succeeded by Mark Baker (Storyteller), Matthew Bennett (Preacher/Buck/Director), Mary Bond Davis (Miss Bessemer/A. D./Ethyl Mae/Nurse/Sister Shame/Bus Station Woman), Terri Girvin (Pastel Griffin/A. D./Twin/Johnnie Ruth/Dog Girl), Blair Ross (Grandma/Twin/A. D./Sister Swope/Therapist), Cordell Stahl (Grady/A. D./Specialist/Tor/Sit-Com Director), David Titus (Earl/Clerk/A. D./Master/Stepmonster/Clerk)
MUSICAL NUMBERS: Prelude/Long Long Way to Heaven, Keep Smilin' Through, God Loves the Baptist, Precious Twins, Pessimistic Voices, Come Little Children, Sing All Ye Women of the Lord, Mother May I Be Forgiven?, A Prayer for Mama, Hymn of Shame, Ace's Revelation/What a Friend We Have in Jesus, I'm Twirling, Trashy Effeminate Hoodlum, Just the Way We're Bred, Finale, Postlude

A musical comedy in two acts. The action place in Tennessee and Hollywood.

(Downtown Art Company) Thursday, Apr. 21–May 8, 1994 (12 performances) Downtown Art Co. presents:
PROMISCUOUS by David Cale and Roger Babb; Director, Brian Jucha; Lighting, Roma Flowers; Costumes, Kasia Walicka-Maimone; Choreography, Rocky Bornstein; Press, Jim Baldassare CAST: Roger Babb, David Cale, Mary Schultz, Rocky Bornstein, Hyun Yup Lee, Lenard Petit, Vicky Shick
PROGRAM: *Nightwear, English Rose of India, Table, Tro*

(Manhattan Class Co.) Thursday, Apr. 21–May 21, 1994 (24 performances) Manhattan Class Company presents:
LIAR, LIAR; Written/Performed by Dael Orlandersmith; Director, Syd Sidner; Sets, Rob Odorisio; Lighting, Howard Werner; Costumes, Karen Perry; Sound, Stuart J. Allyn; Stage Manager, Elaine Bayless; Press, Peter Cromarty/Michael Hartman

A mosaic of nine characters.

Blair Ross, Mark Baker, Terru Girvin in *Hysterical Blindness*

Mary Shultz, David Cale, Roger Babb in *Promiscuous* (Suzanne Opton)

Dael Orlandersmith in *Liar, Liar* (Roya)

(Soho Rep) Thursday, Apr. 21–May 22, 1994 (20 performances) Soho Rep presents:
DRACULA by Mac Wellman; Director, Julian Webber; Sets, Kyle Chepulis; Lighting, Brian Aldous; Sets/Costumes, James Sauli; Sound, John Kilgore; Music, Melissa Shiflett, David van Tieghem; Stage Manager, Lisa Jean Lewis CAST: Julia Gibson, Brett Rickaby, Patricia Dunnock, Christopher McCann, Tim Blake Nelson, Thomas Jay Ryan, Damian Young, Ray Xifo, House of Domination

A reworking of the famous vampire story.

Bring in the Morning company

(Variety Arts Theatre) Thursday, Apr. 21–June 5, 1994 (16 performances and 36 previews) Jeff Britton in association with Edgar M. Bronfman presents:
BRING IN THE MORNING with Music by Gary William Friedman; Lyrics/ Adaptation, Herb Schapiro; Based on writings of young people in Poets in Public Service program; Director, Sheldon Epps; Co-Director/Choreographer, Michele Assaf; Musical Director/Dance Arrangements, Louis St. Louis; Orchestrations, Dianne Adams McDowell, Michael Gibson; Vocal Arrangements, Mr. Friedman, Mr. St. Louis; Sets/Projections, Ken Foy; Costumes, Robert Mackintosh; Lighting, Ken Billington; Sound, Ivan Pokorny, Tom Clark; Stage Manager, Brian Meister; Press, Shirley Herz/Miller Wright CAST: Yassmin Alers (Sonya), Roy Chicas (Roberto), Imelda De Los Reyes (Judy), Sean Grant (Cougar), Inaya Jafa'n (Lakesha), Yvette Lawrence (Inez), Nicole Leach (Alicia), Shannon Reyshard Peters (Jamal), Raquel Polite (Mavis), Steven X. Ward (Hector), Kevin R. Wright (Nelson)
MUSICAL NUMBERS: Come Into My Jungle, Bring in the Morning, You, Not Your Cup of Tea, Ghetto of My Mind, Funky Eyes, Another Cry, I'm on My Way, Never Stop Believing, Something Is Wrong with Everyone Today, Missing Person, Light of Your Love, Hector's Dream, Trip, Glory of Each Morning, Deliver My Soul, I Want to Walk in a Garden

A musical in two acts. The setting is the ghetto of Cougar's mind.

(Ohio Theatre) Friday, Apr. 22–May 8, 1994 (12 performances and 3 previews) Arden Party in association with Annette Moskowitz and Alexander E. Racolin presents:
LEAR; Adapted by Emily Morse and Julia Listengarden from William Shakespeare; Director, Karin Coonrod; Music, Tony Geballe; Set/Lighting, Darrel Maloney; Press, Denise Roberts CAST: Kenneth Talberth (Lear), Gary Brownlee, Mary Christopher, Gretchen Krich, Randolph Curtis Rand

A highly abbreviated version of Shakespeare's drama.

Julie Dretzin, Jennifer Dundas in *...Aiken Fiction* (Martha Holmes)

(Soho Rep) Friday, Apr. 22–June 26, 1994 (29 performances) Soho Rep in association with Robert Fish presents:
HOLLYWOOD HUSTLE; Written/Performed by Jeremiah Bosgang; Director, Rob Greenberg; Lighting, Rick Martin; Stage Manager, Tim Staley; Press, Jeffrey Richards/Virginia Hunter

Monologue about making it in Hollywood, CA.

(Samuel Beckett Theatre) Tuesday, Apr. 26–May 15, 1994 (14 performances and 7 previews) Women's Project and Productions and New Georges present:
THE AUTOBIOGRAPHY OF AIKEN FICTION by Kate Moira Ryan; Director, Adrienne Weiss; Set, Narelle Sissons; Lighting, Rick Martin; Costumes, Angela Wendt; Sound, Jennifer Sharpe; Stage Manager, Warren S. Friedman; Press, Philip Rinaldi/Kathy Haberthur CAST: Jennifer Dundas (Aiken Fiction), Julie Dretzin (Jos Lubenowich), Cristine McMurdo-Wallis (Mrs. Fiction/Mother Darling), Sylvia Gassell (Gramie Lubenowich), Drew Barr (Love Child)

A drama performed without intermission. The action takes place on a road trip across America.

(Theatre for the New City) Wednesday, Apr. 27–May 1, 1994 (5 performances) Theatre for the New City and Bartenief/Field in association with U.S./ Netherlands Touring & Exchange Project present:
ROOM 5; Written/Performed/Costumed by Neville Tranter; Text Revision, Luc van Meerbeke; Design, Rene Strum, Delles Versluis

Stuffed Puppet Theatre of Amsterdam in an adult puppet show.

(John Houseman Studio) Wednesday, Apr. 27–May 22, 1994 (20 performances) The New Group presents:
THE UNDERTAKERS by Stephen Starosta; Director, Scott Elliott; Costumes, John Bartlett; Sets, Zaniz; Lighting, Francis X. Lockwood; Music, Tom Kochan; Stage Manager, Michelle Malloy McIntyre; Press, David Kratz CAST: Gordon Joseph Weiss (Barge), Lyn Fink (Janice Wizenburger), Don Leslie (Clarence/ Assistant), Reed Birney (John/Voices), Jill Bowman (Marlene/Nurse/Tap Dancer), Neal Jones (Steps), Rob Bogue (Craig), Jane Fleiss (Crazy Penny)

A black comedy in two acts.

Puppet with Neville Tranter in *Room 5* (Erwin Olaf)

(One Dream Theatre) Thursday, Apr. 28, 1994– The Working Theatre and Creation Production Company presents:
THE WINDOW MAN with Music by Bruce Barthol and Greg Pliska; Lyrics/Text, Matthew Maguire; Director, Bill Mitchelson; Musical Director, Genji Ito; Set, Mr. Maguire, Rene Wintcentsen; Lighting, Spencer Mosse; Costumes, Anne C. Patterson; Stage Manager, Christine Lemme; Press, David Rothenberg CAST: Angela Bullock (Maggie Becker), Frank Deal (Ed Wyroba), John Nesci (Jackie McCarthy), Kaipo Schwab (Tommy Kim)

A musical based on the 1982 murder of an Asian-American youth by an unemployed Detroit auto worker.

(Playhouse 46) Tuesday, May 3–28, 1994 (24 performances) Pan Asian Repertory presents:
WILDERNESS by Cao Yu; Director, Lili Liang; Set, Robert Klingelhoefer; Costumes, Helen Huang; Sound, Ty Sanders; Lighting, Richard Schaefer; Stage Manager, Lisa Ledwich CAST: Lisa Ann Li (Jinzi), Kati Kuroda, Jason Ma, James Saito, Les J. N. Mau, John Baray

A 1936 Chinese drama.

(Ensemble Studio Theatre) Wednesday, May 4–June 12, 1994 (36 performances) Ensemble Studio Theatre presents:
MARATHON '94; Artistic Director, Curt Dempster; Producer, Kevin Confoy; Sets, Michael Allen, Michael R. Smith, Kurt F. Lundell; Costumes, Julie Doyle, Lauren Press; Lighting, Greg MacPherson; Press, Shirley Herz/David Lotz

SERIES A: *Extensions* by Murray Schisgal; Director, Lee Costello CAST: Peter Maloney (Bob), Marcia Jean Kurtz (Betsy)
The Falling Man by Will Scheffer; Director, David Briggs CAST: Will Scheffer (Falling Man), Kevin Weldon (Man in Black)
I'm with Ya, Duke by Herb Gardner; Director, Jack Gelber CAST: David Margulies (Sam Margolis), Jack Koenig (Dr. Albert NacIntyre)
Paradise by Romulus Linney; Director, Christopher A. Smith CAST: David Eigenberg (Dudley), Lois Smith (Jean), Sheri Matteo (Angelina), Gretchen Walther (Linda)

SERIES B: *Lunch with Lyn* by Marsha Norman; Director, George de la Pena CAST: Polly Adams, Mary Beth Hurt, Katherine Leask, Socorro Santiago
Rosemary with Ginger by Edward Allan Baker; Director, Ron Stetson CAST: Kristin Griffith, Michaela Murphy
Dear Kenneth Blake by Jacquelyn Reingold; Director, Brian Mertes CAST: Jodi Long, Matthew Cowles
New York Actor by John Guare; Director, Jerry Zaks CAST: Kevin Confoy, Helen Eigenberg, Patrick Garner, Greg Germann, Baxter Harris, Randy Lawson, Ann McDonough, Jenny O'Hara, Joseph Siravo, Bradley Whitford
Mudtracks by Regina Taylor; Director, Woodie King, Jr. CAST: Mary Alice, Trazana Beverly, Leon Addison Brown, Clebert Ford, Frances Foster, Arthur French, Mone Walton

SERIES C: *Wasp* by Steve Martin; Director, Curt Dempster CAST: Jack Gilpin (Dad), Cecilia de Wolf (Mom), Melinda Hamilton (Sis), Josh Soboslai (Son), Jenny O'Hara (Female Voice), Richmond Hoxie (Male Voice)
The Far-Flung by Julie McKee; Director, Ethan Silverman CAST: Dolores Sutton (Mrs. Gilbert), June Ballinger (Mrs. MacWhirter), Joan Copeland (Mrs. Corban), Allison Janney (Mrs. Youngblood), Keith Reddin (Mr. Freddy Allnut)
Blood Guilty by Antoine O'Flatharta; Director, Kevin Confoy CAST: Paul Ronan (Tom), Dylan Chalfy (John), Chris O'Neill (Dan), Edward Hyland (Pat)
For Whom the Southern Belle Tolls by Christopher Durang; Director, Walter Bobbie CAST: Lizbeth Mackay (Amanda), Keith Reddin (Lawrence), David Aaron Baker (Tom), Patricia Randell (Ginny)

The seventeenth annual one-act festival.

124 Marcia Jean Kurtz, Peter Maloney
in *Marathon '94: Extensions* (Carol Rosegg)

**Gretchen Walther, David Eigenberg, Lois Smith, Sherri Matteo
in *Marathon '94: Paradise* (Carol Rosegg)**

**Greg Germann, Baxter Harris, Jenny O'Hara
in *Marathon '94: New York Actor* (Carol Rosegg)**

(Musical Theatre Works) Thursday, May 5–7, 1994 (3 performances) Musical Theatre Works presents:
BRIMSTONE with Music by Patrick Meegan; Lyrics/Book, Mary Bracken Phillips; Director, Julianne Boyd; Musical Supervisor/Arrangements, Keith Levenson; Musical Director, Christine Cadarette; Choreography, Daniel Levans; Stage Manager, Renee Lutz CAST: Patti Allison, Patrick Boll, Barclay Bulleit, Denise Cronin, Mary Beth Griffith, Jeff Gurner, Mark Horan, James Judy, John Leone, Richard Pelzman, Ed Sala, Larry Sousa, Colleen Quinn, Nick Wyman

(Madison Avenue Theatre) Thursday, May 5–22, 1994 (14 performances and 4 previews) Madison Avenue Theatre presents:
A CATERED AFFAIR by Arje Shaw and George W. George; Director, Jay Tanzi; Costumes, Margo La Zaro; Lighting, Michael Scricca; Music, Alonzo Levister; Stage Manager, David Nevarrez; Press, Francine L. Trevens CAST: Dale Stein, Ed Chemaly, Geany Masai, James Caulfield (Paul), Harley D. Faust(Charlie), Lenny Singer (Goldstein), Tony Ventura (Jimmy), Conrad Wolfson (Rabbi)

A comedy that began life under the title *The Waiters*.

(29th St. Rep. Theatre) Thursday, May 5–28, 1994 (20 performances) 29th St. Repertory Theatre presents:
CHARMER; Written/Directed by John Clancy; Lighting, Colin D. Young; Set, Tani Manfredi; Costumes, Mark D. Sorensen; Press, Tony Origlio/Stephen Murray CAST: Tim Corcoran, David Mogentale, Curtiss I. Cook, Rob Renz

A story of psychic intrigue and corrupted male bonding.

(Angel Orensanz Foundation) Friday, May 6–21, 1994 (14 performances)
Teleotheater presents:
GARBAGE, THE CITY AND DEATH by Rainer Werner Fassbinder; Translation, Brad Beckman; Director, Osiris Hertz; Movement, Steffany George; Lighting, Jason Boyd; Sets, Raul Abrego; Costumes, Derek Stenborg; Stage Manager, Mary Agnes Krell; Press, Jesse McKinley CAST: Brad Beckman (Filmmaker/Muller/Tenor), Christina Campanella (Frau Muller/Marie Antoinette), Cuman Xropper (Oscar/Muller II), James Hartling (Franz B), Eve Hartmann (Emma), Laura Ann Kachergus (Asbach-Lilly), Gregg Mulpagano (Rich Jew), John Oglevee (Peter/Jim/Achfeld/Tenor), Sam Osheroff (Dwarf/Von Gluck/Tenor), Catherine Scarboro (Frau Tau/Violet), Michelle Stern (Roma B), Antoine Vincent (Little Prince)

A controversial 1985 German drama.

(Courtyard Theatre) Wednesday, May 11, 1994– Lively Ventures I in association with New Village Productions presents:
MY LIFE AS A CHRISTIAN; Written/Performed by Jaffe Cohen; Developed/Directed by Michael Zam; Set, Daniel McDermott; Lighting, John Brian; Press, David Rothenberg

Comic journey with a young, gay Jewish male coming of age in the 1970s.

(Downtown Art Co.) Thursday, May 12–28, 1994 (15 performances) Downtown Art Co. presents:
LOVED LESS (THE HISTORY OF HELL); Conceived/Written/Directed by Brian Jucha; Set, Sarah Edkins; Lighting, Roma Flowers; Costumes, Kasia Walicka-Maimone; Press, Tony Origlio/Stephen Murray CAST: Tina Shepard (Lilith/Kitty/Leslie/Hope), Sheryl Dold (Ereshkigal/Toni), Lisa Welti (Inanna/Laurie), Kristen Lee Kelly (Lorena/Pamela/Shanda), E. William Keenan (John/Lester), Jason Butler Harner (Erik), Stephen Belber (Lyle), Tamar Kotoske (Melinda/Crawdad Lady/Jill)

Examination of media-sensationalized cased performed without intermission.

(Intar Theatre) Thursday, May 12–June 5, 1994 (16 performances) Intar Hispanic Arts Center presents:
SANCHO AND DON; Conceived by Sigfrido Aguilar and Jim Calder; Music, Andy Teirstein; Lighting, Paul Clay; Press, Peter Cromarty CAST: Sigfrido Aguilar, Jim Calder

A modern day mime and movement version of the adventures of Don Quixote.

(Metropolitan Playhouse) Thursday, May 12–June 5, 1994 (14 performances and 2 previews) Metropolitan Playhouse presents:
WENCESLAS SQUARE by Larry Shue; Director, David Zarko; Design, Susannah Hewson CAST: Steve Deighan, Louis Rabon, Robert Ruffin, Mary Ethel Schmidt

A 1985 comedy set in Czeckoslavakia, 1972.

(All Souls Players) Friday, May 13–22, 1994 (9 performances) Tran Wm. Rhodes presents:
THE OLD BOY by A. R. Gurney; Director, Steve Steiner; Set, Tran Wm. Rhodes; Costumes, Jon Michel; Lighting, David Bean; Sound, Karl Schroeder; Stage Manager, Ralph Ortiz CAST: Richard Pohlers (Dexter), Abner Genece (Bud), Rick Ross (Sam), Joanne Bayes (Harriet), Ann Russell (Alison), Daniel P. McDermott (Perry)

A drama in two acts. The action takes place at a New England prep school, now and in the past.

Francie Swift, Yusef Bulos in *Hyacinth Macaw* (Andrew Leynse)

Sheryl Dodd, Lisa Welti in *Loved Less* (Talmage Cooley)

Sigfrido Aguilar, Jim Calder in *Sancho and Don*

(Primary Stages) Saturday May 14–June 5, 1994 (23 performances) Primary Stages presents:
THE HYACINTH MACAW by Mac Wellman; Director, Marcus Stern; Sets/Lighting, Kyle Chepulis; Sound, John Huntington; Costumes, Robin Orloff; Music, David van Tieghem; Press, Tony Origlio/Stephen Murray CAST: Steven Mellor (Roy), Melissa Smith (Dora), Francie Swift (Susannah), Yusef Bulos (William Hard)

An "unofficial gloss on the apocrypha of contemporary, low-rent America."

(Public/Newman Theatre) Monday, May 16–28, 1994 (8 performances) The Acting Company presents:
THE AFRICAN COMPANY PRESENTS RICHARD III by Carlyle Brown; Director, Clinton Turner Davis; Sets, Douglas Stein; Costumes, Paul Tazewell; Lighting, Dennis Parichy; Sound, Fran Sutherland; Stage Manager, Daniel L. Bello; Press, Carol Fineman CAST: Matt Bradford Sullivan (Stephen Price), Shona Tucker (Sarah), Kelly Taffe (Ann Johnson), Allen Gilmore (James Hewlett), Chuck Patterson (Papa Shakespeare), Cedric Harris (William Henry Brown), Richard Topel (Constable)

A history-based drama set in Manhattan, 1821.

(Symphony Space) Thursday, May 19–21, 1994 (4 limited performances) Second Drama Quartet presents:
DON JUAN IN HELL by George Bernard Shaw; Director, Harris Yulin; Press, Richard Kornberg CAST: Edward Asner, Rene Auberjonois; Dianne Wiest, Harris Yulin

A concert reading.

125

(Mint Theatre) Thursday, May 19–29, 1994 (12 performances) Mint Theatre Company presents:
THE TIME OF YOUR LIFE by William Saroyan; Director, Rebecca Holderness; Set, Vicki R. Davis; Lighting, Michael Gottlieb; Costumes, Nan Young; Sound/Music, Jessica Murrow; Press, Barbara Reierson CAST: J. Bryan McMillen (Saroyan), Katie White (Newsboy), Katie Davis (Drunk), Donna DuCarme (Willie), Kelly Morgan (Joe), Hugh O'Gorman (Nick), Paula Godsey (Kitty), Doug Stuart (Dudley), Rachel C. Hoyer (Elsie), Lauren Koff (Harry), Victor Hearn (Wesley), Joan Preston (Lorene), Tim Goldrick (Tom), Tercio Bretas (Arab), Holly Maria Hudson (Mary), Joe Yates (Krupp), Stephen McIntyre (McCarthy), Rosalyn Thomson (Nick's Ma/Killer), Stewart Groves (Blick), Jennie Staniloff (Killer), Barbara Reirson (Society Lady), Craig Mason (Gentleman), Andrew Chipok (Cop/Sailor), Richard Willis (Kit Carson), Karin Anderson (Anna), Gene Silvers (Cop), Jerome Davis, Sydney Rhoads
A new production of the 1939 play. The action takes place in a San Francisco bar.

(Theatre for the New City) Thursday, May 19–June 5, 1994 (12 performances) Theatre for the New City presents:
THE HEART IS A LONELY HUNTER; Adapted/Directed by David Willinger; Based on the novel by Carson McCullers; Music, Richard Roque; Set, Clark Fidelia; Lighting, Lee Gundersheimer; Costumes, Paula Ann Inocent; Stage Manager, Colin Rudd; Press, Jonathan Slaff CAST: Bruce Hlibok (John Singer), Frederick Matzner (Biff Brannon), Ralph Navarro (Spiros), Shane Blodgett (Jake Blount), Laurel Holloman (Mick Kelly), Dennis R. Jones (Benedict), Terry Ballard (Portia), Caesar Paul Del Ray, Bryan Schany, Kimberley Myles, Scott A. Sloves, Tony Rowe, Kolawole Ogundiran
First theatre version of 1939 novel set in a small Southern city.

(Samuel Beckett Theatre) Thursday, May 19–June 5, 1994 Gilgamesh Theatre Group presents:
THE ICE-FISHING PLAY by Kevin Kling; Director, Sheldon Deckelbaum; Set, Roger Hanna; Lighting, David B. Sislen; Costumes, Jessica Grace; Sound, Matt Berman; Stage Manager, Charlene Speyerer CAST: David Weynand (Ron), Brian Shnipper (Duff), Suzanne von Eck (Irene), Bob Bender, Brian David Price, Christopher A. Russell, Raymond Munoz
A drama set on a frozen lake in Minnesota.

(Ubu Rep. Theatre) Monday, May 23–26, 1994 (4 performances) Colin MacLean presents:
THE LADY AND THE CLARINET by Michael Cristofer; Director, David Perry; Music, Stanley Silverman; Press, Lee Canaan CAST: James Waterston (Paul), Quinn Lemley (Luba), David Kener (Jack), Peter Galman (George)
A 1983 serio-comedy.

(Charles Ludlam Theatre) Monday, May 23–Aug. 9, 1994 (23 performances)
BOYS DON'T WEAR LIPSTICK; Written/Performed by Brian Belovitch; Director, Keith Greer; Lighting, Rick Belzer; Costumes, Liz McGarrity; Stage Manager, Craig Victor; Press, Pete Sanders/Ian Rand
An autobiographical monlogue.

David Weynand, Suzanne Von Eck (legs) in *Ice-Fishing Play* (Jonathan Slaff)

(Hudson Guild Theatre) Tuesday, May 24–29, 1994 (8 performances) Metropolitan Playhouse and The Post Theatre Co. presents:
THE HUSBAND; Adaptation/Direction, David Zarko; Costumes, Deborah Bergsma Otte; Music, Michael Paris; Set/Lighting, Bill Motyka CAST: Alfred Gigliati, Craig Byer, Vincent Masterpaul, Sharron Swartz, Gwendolyn McClendon, Jack Rogers, Craig Treubert, Heather Drastal, Lucy Ramos, Daniel Capalbo, Amber Ruediger, Kristen Orsini, Jodi Pulick, Joe Dos Santos, Chris Healy
Modern improvisational theatre with a touch of Italian commedia.

(Synchronicity Space) Wednesday, May 25–June 12, 1994 (15 performances) Spectrum Stage presents:
FRAYED EDGES: TWO ONE-ACT PLAYS BY JEFFREY SWEET; Sets, Paul Andrew Melia; Lighting, Maura Sheridan; Press, Kermit C. Klein

PROGRAM: *Porch;* Director, Alexander Dinelaris CAST: Nancy Jo Carpenter (Amy), Rob Quadrino (Sam), Ron Crawford (Dad)
Stops Along the Way; Director, Chuck Zito CAST: Patrick Welsh (Larry), Darby Townsend (Donna), Jamie Morris, Dennis Hearn

(SoHo Rep) Thursday, May 26–June 5, 1994 (9 performances) AAI Productions presents:
THE LOVE OF THE NIGHTINGALE by Timberlake Wertenbaker; Director, Melanie Sutherland; Lighting, Monique Millane; Sets, Lisa B. Albin CAST: Annie Bien, Buzz Bovshow, Whitney Chapman, Madison Cowan, Donna Jean Fogel, Judith Hawking, Bunky Hubbard, Gary Mink, Craig Mathers, Sharon Round, Jeff Sugarman, Lynne Taljian Taylor, Rex Young
A drama set in ancient Greece.

(Ontological St. Mark's) Thursday, May 26–June 12, 1994 Target Margin Theatre presents:
SIX SCENES by Michael Brodsky; Director, David Herskovitz; Sets, Denise Hudson; Lighting, Lenore Doxsee; Costumes, Davis Zinn; Sound, Blake Koh; Stage Manager, Meredith Palin CAST: Todd Alcott, Rinnie Groff, Charles Parnell, Jan-Peter Pedross, David Pincus, Steven Rattazzi, Yuri Skujins
An existential drama.

(Alice's Fourth Floor) Thursday, May 26–June 19, 1994 (20 performances) Miranda Theatre Company presents:
CINOMAN & REBECK; Lighting, Mahlon Kruse; Muralist, Rebecca Goyette; Costumes, Garrett Swann; Stage Manager, Rita Williams; Press, Peter Cromarty/Michael Hartman CAST: Geneva Carr, Patricia Cornell, Wayne Adam Farness, Sally Frontman, Raymond Haigler, Ibi Janko, Jerry Mettner, Patricia Migliori, Matt Mutrie, Alexander Napier, Paul O'Brien, Polly Segal, Diego Taborada
PROGRAM: (Plays by Susan Cinoman) *The Bull* Director, Valentina Fratti; *The Sineater of Cork* Director, Jan Silverman; *Hysteria* and *Truth & Sex* Director, Alison Summers
(Plays by Theresa Rebeck) *The Drinking Problem* Director, Valentina Fratti; *Does This Woman Have a Name?* Director, Jess Lynn
Six one-act plays.

(Altered Stages) Tuesday, May 31–June 5, 1994 (7 performances) AGBU Arts presents:
A NEW YORK ROMANCE; Conceived/Arranged/Written by Mary Setrakian; Director, Drew Scott Harris; Musical Director, Richard B. Evans; Lighting, Jeremy Kumin; Stage Manager, Margaret Bodriguian; Press, Tony Origlio/Michael Cullen CAST: Mary Setrakin (Maddy Madison)
A one-woman musical, performed without intermission, set in New York City.

Mary Setrakian in *New York Romance* (Beth Kelly)

OFF BROADWAY COMPANY SERIES

AMERICAN JEWISH THEATRE

Twentieth Season

Artistic Director, Stanley Brechner; Artistic Consultant, Jack Temchin; Managing Director, Ellen Rusconi; Development, Stacy Karp; Press, Jeffrey Richards/Kevin Rehac, Candi Adams

Saturday, Oct. 16–Nov. 14, 1993 (31 performances)
THE WORKROOM by Jean-Claude Grumberg; Translation, Tom Kempinski; Director, Nicolas Kent; Set, James Wolk; Costumes, Lee Austin; Lighting, David I. Taylor; Sound, Bruce Ellman CAST: Larry Block (Leon), Caroline Lagerfelt (Simone), Marcia Jean Kurtz (Helen), Jennifer Gibbs, Ruby Holbrook, Peter Jacobson, Deborah LaCoy, Jeffrey Landman, Leslie Lyles, Brent Rickaby
   A drama set in Paris, 1945–52.

Saturday, Dec. 4, 1993–Jan. 16, 1994 (44 performances)
THE ASH FIRE by Gavin Lostick; Director, Stanley Brechner; Set, Mark Fitzgibbons; Costumes, Lee Austin; Lighting, John Tissot; Sound, Bruce Ellman; Stage Manager, K. A. Smith CAST: Rosemary Fine (Cissy Katzmeir), Joseph Siravo (Nat Katzmeir), Jenny Conroy (Cait O'Shaughnessy), Michael Countryman (Rube Katzmeir), Andrew Polk (Abe Katzmeir), Terry Donnelly (Doris Hughes)
   A comedy in two acts. The action takes place in Dublin, 1935–36.

Saturday, Mar. 5–Apr. 17, 1994 (45 performances)
THE DAY THE BRONX DIED by Michael Henry Brown; Director, Gordon Edelstein; Set, Andrew Jackness, David Stein; Lighting, Christopher Akerlind; Costumes, Candice Donnelly; Sound, John Gromada; Stage Manager, James D'Asaro CAST: Leon Addison Brown (Big Mickey), Brenda Denmark (Mother), Akili Prince (Young Mickey), Luis A. Laporte, Jr. (Alexander), Kelly Neal (The Prince), Neal Huff (Billy), Ntare Mwine (Daniel), Jermaine Chambers (Odd Job), Joseph Edwards (Officer Bream), Herbert Rubens (Kornblum), Garland Whit (Butter), Glenn Herman (Silk)
   A two-act drama set on Apr. 4, 1968, the day Martin Luther King was assassinated.

Saturday, Apr. 30–June 26, 1994 (59 performances)
MILK AND HONEY with Music/Lyrics by Jerry Herman; Book, Don Appell; Director, Richard Sabellico; Musical Director, C. Lynne Shankel; Set, James Wolk; Lighting, Ed McCarthy; Costumes, Gail Baldoni; Stage Manager, James D'Asaro CAST: Jeanne Lehman (Ruth Stein), Batya Biegun (Arab Girl), Avi Hoffman (Adi Gluck), Ron Holgate succeeded by Spiro Malas (Phil Arkin), Chevi Colton (Clara Weiss), Irma Rogers (Selma Kessler), Joanne Bogart (Myra Segal), James Barbour succeeded by Michael Park (David Kaplan), Katy Selverstone (Barbara Kaplan), Lori Wilner (Zipporah Perets), Norman Golden (Cantor/Sol Horowitz)

MUSICAL NUMBERS: What They Promised Me, Shalom, Independence Day Hora, Milk and Honey, There's No Reason in the World, Chin Up Ladies, That Was Yesterday, Let's Not Waste a Moment, Like a Young Man, I Will Follow You, Hymn to Hymie, As Simple as That, Finale
   A new production of the 1961 musical in two acts. The action takes place in Israel.

Gerry Goodstein Photos

Top: Michael Countryman, Jenny Conroy in *The Ash Fire*
Center: Neal Huff, Akili Prince in *Day the Bronx Died*
Right: Jeanne Lehman, Ron Holgate in *Milk and Honey*

CIRCLE REPERTORY COMPANY

Twenty-fifth Season

Artistic Director, Tanya Berezin; Managing Director, Abigail Evans; Lab Artistic Director, Michael Warren Powell; General Manager, Meredith Freeman; Development Director, Kathleen P. McAllen; Production Manager, Jody Boese; Press, Bill Evans/Tom D'Ambrosio

(Lucille Lortel Theatre) Wednesday, Sept. 22–Nov. 28, 1993 (64 performances) THE FIERY FURNACE by Timothy Mason; Director, Norman Rene; Sets, Loy Arcenas; Costumes, Walker Hicklin; Lighting, Debra J. Kletter; Sound, Tom Clark; Stage Manager, Denise Yaney CAST: Julie Harris (Eunice), Ashley Gardner (Faith), William Fichtner (Jerry), Susan Batten succeeded by Lily Knight (Charity), Zach Grenier (Louis)
   A play in two acts. The action takes place in Chippewa Falls, Wisconsin, 1950–63.

(Lucille Lortel Theatre) Wednesday, Oct. 27–Dec. 5, 1993 (30 performances) DESDEMONA: *A Play About a Handkerchief* by Paula Vogel; Director, Gloria Muzio; Set, Derek McLane; Costumes, Jess Goldstein; Lighting, Michael Lincoln; Fights, Rick Sordelet; Music/Sound, Randy Freed; Stage Manager, Fred Reinglass CAST: Fran Brill (Emilia), J. Smith-Cameron (Desdemona), Cherry Jones (Bianca)
   A comedy performed without intermission. The action takes place in Cyprus, ages ago.

(Circle Rep. Theatre) Wednesday, Jan. 19–Mar. 12, 1994 (18 performances) A BODY OF WATER by Jenna Zark; Director, Caroline Kava; Set, Loy Arcenas; Lighting, Brian Aldous; Costumes, Thomas L. Keller; Sound, Darron L. West; Stage Manager, Denise Yaney CAST: Maggie Burke, Don T. Maseng, Bruce MacVittie, Nikki Rene, Stephanie Roth, Jodi Thelen
   Two one-acts, *White Days* and *Shooting Souls*.

in repertory with

Wednesday, Jan. 26–Mar. 13, 1994 (18 performances) ESCAPE FROM PARADISE; Written/Performed by Regina Taylor; Director, Anne Bogart; Technical Credits as above; Stage Manager, M. A. Howard
   Memories of a young women travelling the world. Performed without intermission.

(Circle Rep. Theatre) Wednesday, Apr. 20–May 29, 1994 (32 performances) MOONSHOT AND COSMOS by Lanford Wilson; Director, Marshall W. Mason; Sets, John Lee Beatty; Costumes, Walker Hicklin; Lighting, Dennis Parichy; Music, Peter Kater; Sound, Donna Riley; Stage Manager, Denise Yaney *A Poster of the Cosmos* with John Dossett (Tom); *The Moonshot Tape* with Judith Ivey (Diane)
   Two one-act monologues.

Gerry Goodstein Photos

Julie Harris in *The Fiery Furnace*

Jodi Thelen, Bruce MacVittie in *Body of Water*

Judith Ivey in *Moonshot and Cosmos*

Regina Taylor in *Escape from Paradise*

CSC REPERTORY
CLASSIC STAGE COMPANY

Twenty-seventh Season

Artistic Director, David Esbjornson; Managing Director, Patricia Taylor; General Manager, Kelley Voorhees; Production Manager, Matthew Maraffi; Development, Mary Esbjornson; Lighting Designer, Brian MacDevitt; Stage Manager, Crystal Huntington; Press, Denise Roberts

Tuesday, Sept. 21–Oct. 31, 1993 (38 performances)
THE MAIDS by Jean Genet; Translation, Bernard Frechtman; Director/Sets, David Esbjornson; Costumes, Elizabeth Fried; Sound, Dan Moses Schreier CAST: Charles Busch (Solange), Peter Francis James (Claire), Seth Gilliam (Madame)
   A new production of the 1947 drama.

Friday, Jan. 7–Feb. 13, 1994 (35 performances)
THE ILLUSION by Pierre Corneille; Adaptation, Tony Kushner; Director, David Esbjornson; Set, Karen Teneyck; Costumes, Claudia Stephens CAST: John C. Vennema (Pridamant), Dan Moran (Amanuensis/Geronte), Rocco Sisto (Alcandre), Rob Campbell (Calisto/Clindor/Theogenes), Cynthia Nixon (Melibea/Isabelle/Hippolyta), Lynn Hawley (Elicia/Lyse/Clarina), Todd Weeks (Pleribo/Adraste/Florilame), Steve Mellor (Matamore)
   A free adaptation of 1624's magical tale in two acts.

Tuesday, Mar. 29–May 8, 1994 (30 performances and 8 previews)
THE TRIUMPH OF LOVE by Marivaux; Translation, James Magruder; Director, Michael Mayer; Set, David Gallo; Costumes, Michael Krass; Music, Jill Jaffe; Fights, J. Steven White CAST: Margaret Welsh (Leonide), Camryn Manheim (Corine), Daniel Jenkins (Harlequin), Umit Celebi (Dimas), Garret Dillahunt (Agis), Randy Danson (Leontine), Thom Christopher (Hermocrate), Christine Gummere (Cellist)
   A new translation of a 1732 comedy in two acts.

T. Charles Erickson Photos

**Top: Rob Campbell, Cynthia Nixon in *The Illusion*
Bottom: Camryn Manheim, Margaret Welsh, Thom Christopher, Randy Danson in *Triumph of Love***

JEWISH REPERTORY THEATRE

Twentieth Season

Artistic Director, Ran Avni; Associate Director, Edward M. Cohen; General Management, Andrew C. McGibbon, Steven M. Levy; Production Stage Manager, D. C. Rosenberg; Press, Shirley Herz/Glenna Freedman, Wayne Wolfe

(All productions at Playhouse 91) Saturday, June 5–27, 1993 (15 performances and 9 previews)
SHOW ME WHERE THE GOOD TIMES ARE with Music/Arrangements by Kenneth Jacobson; Lyrics, Rhoda Roberts; Book, Leonora Thuna; Suggested by Moliere's *The Imaginary Invalid*; Director, Warren Enters; Musical Staging, Dennis Grimaldi; Musical Director, Darren R. Cohen; Sets, Bottari & Case; Costumes, Hal George; Lighting, Michael Baldassari; Sound, Scott Stauffer CAST: Robert Ari (Aaron), Lauren Mitchell (Rachel), Donna Ellis (Annette), Roslyn Kind (Bella), Gordon Greenberg (Maurice), Roy Alan Wilson (Kolinsky), Tim Ewing (Rothstein), Gabriel Barre (Perlman), Tom Gualtieri (Thomas), Genette Lane (Madame Schwartz), Grace Greig (Bertha)

MUSICAL NUMBERS: How Do I Feel/Bella's Plaint, He's Wonderful, Good Intentions, Is That a Woman, Show Me Where the Good Times Are, Something Special, Cafe Royal Rag, Staying Alive, One Big Happy Family, Processional/Follow Your Heart, Look Who's Throwing a Party, When Tomorrow Comes, The Test, I'm Not Getting Any Younger, Wish Me a Happy Birthday, The Examination/Finale

  A musical comedy in two acts. The action takes place in New York's Lower East Side, 1913.

Roslyn Kind, Robert Ari in *Show Me Where the Good Times Are*

David Bishins, Liz Larsen, Betsy Aidem, Steve Mellor in *Teibele and Her Demon*

Laura Esterman, Jim Abele, Irene Dailey in *Edith Stein*

Saturday, Oct. 23–Nov. 14, 1993 (23 performances)
THE CINCINNATI SAINT with Music/Orchestrations/Music Direction by Raphael Crystal; Lyrics, Richard Engquist; Book, Norman Lessing based on his play *36*; Director, Ran Avi; Set, Barbara Cohig; Costumes, Gail Cooper-Hecht; Lighting, Betsy Finston; Musical Staging, Helen Butleroff CAST: Robert Ari, Ellen Foley, Gordon Greenberg, Jonathan Hadley, Steve Sterner, Kurt Ziskie
  A two-act musical set in Cincinnati.

Saturday, Jan. 8–30, 1994 (24 performances)
EDITH STEIN by Arthur Giron; Director, Lee Sankowich; Set, Ursula Belden; Costumes, Laura Crow; Lighting, Betsy Finston; Sound, James Capenos CAST: Norman Rose (Weismann), Susan Riskin (Prioress), Laura Esterman (Edith Stein), Irene Dailey (Frau Stein), Stacie Chaiken (Hannah), Jim Abele (Karl-Heinz), Terry Serpico (Franzy), Sarah Lloyd (Clara), Naomi Riseman (Sister Prudence), Katie Finneran (Sister Ruth), Tim Lord (Bernhardt)
  A two-act drama about a woman who rediscovers her Judaism in the face of WWII atrocities.

Saturday, Apr. 9–May 1, 1994 (24 performances)
TEIBLE AND HER DEMON by Isaac Bashevis Singer and Eve Friedman; Director, Daniel Gerroll; Set/Lighting, Paul Wonsek; Costumes, Tzili Charney; Sound, Douglas J. Cuomo CAST: Steve Mellor (Alchonon), Betsy Aidem (Teible), David Bishins (Menasha), Liz Larsen (Genendel), Robert Katims (Rabbi), Tim Zay (Beadle Treitel), David Alton (Beadle Leib)
  A 1979 drama in two acts. The action takes place in Poland, 1880s.

Martha Swope/Carol Rosegg Photos

LA MAMA E.T.C.

Founder/Director, Ellen Stewart; Associate Director, Meryl Vladimer; Business Manager, James Moore; Archivist, Doris Pettijohn; Press, Jonathan Slaff

Thursday, June 17–27, 1993 (8 performances)
THE WHITE WHORE AND THE BIT PLAYER by Tom Eyen; Music, Henry Krieger; Director, Eric Concklin; Set/Lighting, David Adams; Costumes, Ellen Stewart; Sound, Tim Schellenbaum CAST: Louise Smith (Bit Player), Lois Weaver (Whore)
    A 1964 comedy with a new score.

Thursday, Sept. 30–Oct. 2, 1994 (3 performances)
HULAWOOD BABYLON OR A LITTLE HULA HELL; Directors, Ching Valdes/Aran, John Albano CAST: Robert Jon Kaena Avila, Mel Duane, Gionson, Ching Gonzalez, Nicky Paraiso, Aersli Vertido, Edwin M. Vincente, Jr.
    A Hawaiian revue.

Thursday, Sept. 30–Oct. 17, 1993 (16 performances)
GULLIVER by Lonnie Carter; Director, George Ferencz; Sets, Mr. Ferencz, Bryan Johnson; Costumes, Sally J. Lesser; Lighting, Howard Thies; Sound, Genji Ito; Stage Manager, Tom Spontelli CAST: Andre De Shields (Gulliver), Adrian Bailey (Black Hat), Fleur Phillips (White Swan), Regan Vann (Minette/Willewhinny/Media), Lia Chang (Princess Minor/Photographer), Peter Flynn (King Rolf/Sesroh/Cardinal O'Condom), Rinne Groff (Princess Major/Winne-whilly/Gubernatio), Eric Passoja (Justice Dork/Peace/Bouncer/Mayor Schmolloch)
    A very free adaptation of Gulliver's Travels.

Thursday, Oct. 7–23, 1993 (9 performances)
SUDDENLY SOMETHING RECKLESSLY GAY, OR CIRQUE DE CA-CA; Written/Performed by Assurbanipal; Costumes, Samiramis Ziyeh; Lighting, Howard Thies; Sound, One Dream
    Performance art.

Thursday, Oct. 21–31, 1994 (8 performances)
MARY by Thomas Wilson; Director, George Ferencz; Set, Esteban Fernandez Sanchez; Costumes, Sally J. Lesser; Lighting, Jeffrey Scott Taper; Music, Genji Ito; Stage Manager, Maureen McSherry CAST: Peter McCabe (Boy), Nancy Anderson (Rachael), Joanna Keyes (Michelle), Kim Tooks (Arlene/Anitra), Marilyn-Sue Perry (Gabby), Zisan Ugurlu (Irma)
    A New York-set drama performed without intermission.

Thursday, Nov. 18–Dec. 5, 1993 (11 performances)
THE CO-OP by Esteban Fernandez; Director, George Ferencz; Lighting, Jeffrey Tapper; Music, Genji Ito; Costumes, Sally Lesser; Set, Donald Eastman; Stage Manager, Jessica Hall CAST: Stewart Steinberg (Rod), Peter McCabe (Mark), Sol Echeverria (Ida), Deborah Braun (Elvsted/Uta), Dominic Marcus (Jack), Patricia Dow (Gloria), Charles Britt (Israel), Elana Polin (Delanay), Jose Manuel Yenque (Julio), Nancy Anderson (Jane), Jill Avalon (Terry/Hedda Gabler), Jonathan Goldstein (Alan), Camile de Ganon (Sissy), Alexandria Sage (Helen)
    A comedy in two acts. The action takes place in the "NoHo" section of New York City.

Andre De Shields in *Gulliver*

Louise Smith, Lois Weaver in *The White Whore and the Bit Player* (Jonothan Slaff Photo) 131

LINCOLN CENTER THEATER

Artistic Director, Andre Bishop; Executive Producer, Bernard Gersten; General Manager, Steven C. Callahan; Company Manager, Rheba Flegelman; Production Manager, Jeff Hamlin; Development Director, Hattie K. Jutagir; Marketing Director, Thomas Cott; Dramaturg, Anne Cattaneo; Musical Theatre Director, Ira Weitzman; Press, Merele Debuskey/Susan Chicoine

Wednesday, Oct. 13–Dec. 12, 1993 (71 performances)
THE LIGHTS by Howard Korder; Director, Mark Wing-Davey; Sets, Marina Draghici; Costumes, Laura Cunningham; Lighting, Christopher Akerlind; Music/Sound, Mark Bennett; Fights, David Leong; Stage Manager, Thom Widmann CAST: Tom Bloom (Ensemble), Leon Addison Brown, (Man in Chair/Scab#3), Kathleen Dennehy (Lilian), Dan Futterman (Frederic), Ileen Getz (Customer, Junk Woman/Spectator), Steven Goldstein (Overcoat Man/Man#1/Manager/Cup Man/Scab#2), Jerry Grayson (Diamond), Kristen Johnston (Rose), Jordan Lage (Spectator#2/Waiter#2/Mr. Barry), Christopher McCann (Erenhart), Andrew Mutnick (Camera Man), Neil Pepe (Young Waiter/Foreman), David Pittu (Bill/Guard/Man#2/Spectator#3/Scab#1), Herbert Rubens (Art/Waiter#1), Robin Spielberg (Passerby), Ray Anthony Thomas (Speaker/Man w/Pants), Todd Weeks (Kraus/Spectator#4)

A two-act drama set in a large city, featuring the Atlantic Theatre Company.

John Cameron Mitchell, Dennis Parlato in *Hello Again*

Thursday, Dec. 30, 1993–Mar. 27, 1994 (101 performances)
HELLO AGAIN with Music/Lyrics/Book by Michael John LaChiusa; Suggested by *La Ronde* by Arthur Schnitzler; Director/Choreographer, Graciela Daniele; Orchestrations, Michael Starobin; Musical Director, David Evans; Cast Recording, RCA; Sets, Derek McLane; Costumes, Toni-Leslie James; Lighting, Jules Fisher, Peggy Eisenhauer; Sound, Scott Stauffer; Stage Manager, Leslie Loeb CAST: Donna Murphy succeeded by Saundra Santiago (The Whore), David A. White (The Soldier), Judy Blazer (The Nurse), Michael Park (The College Boy), Carolee Carmello (The Young Wife), Dennis Parlato (The Husband), John Cameron Mitchell (The Young Thing), Malcom Gets (The Writer), Michelle Pawk (The Actress), John Dossett succeeded by Bob Stillman during illness (The Senator)

MUSICAL NUMBERS: Hello Again, Zei Gezent, I Gotta Little Time, We Kiss, In Some Other Life, Story of My Life, At the Prom, Ah Maien Zeit, Tom, Listen to the Music, Montage, Safe, The One I Love, Silent Movie, Rock with Rock, Angel of Mercy, Mistress of the Senator, The Bed Was Not My Own, Finale

A musical performed without intermission. The August 27–29, 1993 workshop performances featured Tom Hulce (The Writer), Robert Duncan McNeill (The College Boy), Barbara Walsh (The Actress), Harold Perrineau, Jr. (The Soldier), Julie Lambert (The Young Wife), and Peter Friedman (The Senator).

Kathleen Dennehy, Dan Futterman
in *The Lights*

Carolee Carmello, Donna Murphy in *Hello Again*

Michael F. Park, Judy Blazer in *Hello Again*

Donna Murphy, David A. White in *Hello Again*

Wednesday, Apr. 27–Aug. 28, 1994 (79 performances and 29 previews)
SUBURBIA by Eric Bogosian; Director, Robert Falls; Sets, Derek McLane; Costumes, Gabriel Berry; Lighting, Kenneth Posner; Sound, John Gromada; Fights, David Leong; Stage Manager, Christopher Wigle CAST: Steve Zahn succeeded by Nick Rodgers (Buff), Josh Hamilton (Jeff), Tim Guinee (Tim), Firdous E. Bamji (Norman Chaundry), Samia Shoaib (Pakeeza), Wendy Hoopes (Bee-Bee), Martha Plimpton (Sooze), Zak Orth (Pony), Babette Renee (Props)
A drama in two acts. The action takes place at a suburban "7-Eleven" store.

Joan Marcus/Marc Bryan-Brown, Gerry Goodstein Photos

For *In the Summer House*, *Abe Lincoln in Illinois*, *Gray's Anatomy*, *Carousel*, and *Sisters Rosensweig*, see BROADWAY CALENDAR section.

Martha Plimpton, Josh Hamilton in *subUrbia*

Wendy Hoopes, Steve Zahn in *subUrbia*

133

Robert Sean Leonard, Frank Whaley in *Good Evening*

MALAPARTE THEATRE COMPANY

Second Season

Artistic Director, Ethan Hawke; Producing Director, Ami Armstrong; Producers, Jason Blum, Cassandra Han, James Eaterston

(All plays at Theatre Row Theatre) Friday, Dec. 3–19, 1993 (26 performances)
WILD DOGS! by Daniel J. Rubin; Director, Ethan Hawke; Set, Rob Odorisio, Alexander Dodge; Lighting, Thomas Hague; Costumes, Laura DeFrain Yates; Stage Manager, Troy Hollar CAST: Jonathan Marc Sherman (Albert), Amelia Campbell (Trudy), Jenny Robertson (John), Isabel Gillies (Paul), Josh Hamilton (George), Steve Zahn (Ringo), Nick Phelps (Stu Sutcliffe)
  A dark comedy performed without intermission.

Tuesday, Dec. 21, 1993 (1 performance only)
ACOUSTIC NIGHT with Ethan Hawke, Robert Sean Leonard, Lisa Loeb, Frank Whaley, Jesse Harris
  A coffeehouse.

Thursday, Dec. 30–31, 1993 (4 performances) reopened at Wet Bank Cafe Feb. 9–17, 1994 (8 performances)
GOOD EVENING by Dudley Moore and Peter Cook; Director, James Waterston; Costumes, Douglas E. Huston; Original Music, Robert Sean Leonard; Choreography, Frank Whaley; Sound, Elisa Pugiliese; Stage Manager, Troy Hollar CAST: Robert Sean Leonard, Frank Whaley
  A comedy revue performed without intermission.

Friday, Jan. 7–22, 1994 (15 performances)
IT CHANGES EVERY YEAR by Jon Robin Baitz and **SONS AND FATHERS** by Jonathan Marc Sherman; Director, Nicholas Martin; Sets, Alexander Dodge; Lighting, Kenneth Posner; Costumes, Michael Krass; Music, Lisa Loeb; Sound, Roger Raines; Stage Manager, Elizabeth Timperman CASTS: *It Changes...* Linda Atkinson (Delia), Brooks Ashmanskas (Cameron), Nadia Dajani (Waitress), Dana Ivey (Sonia), Steve Zahn (Mark) *Sons and Fathers* Calista Flockhart (Joanna), Peter Frechette (Dad), Josh Hamilton (Toby), Ethan Hawke (Max), Jenny Robertson (Claudia)
  Two one-acts.

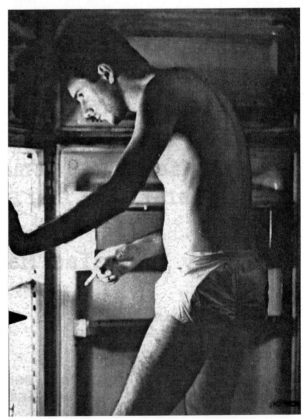

Josh Hamilton in *Sons and Fathers*

Peter Friedman, Jonathan Kaplan, Christine Baranski
in the Manhattan Theatre Club's *Loman Family Picnic*

MANHATTAN THEATRE CLUB

Twenty-second Season

Artistic Director, Lynne Meadow; Managing Director, Barry Grove; General Manager, Victoria Bailey; Associate Artistic Director, Michael Bush; Play Development Director, Kate Loewald; Development Director, Mark Hough; Company Manager, Harold Wolpert; Production Manager, Michael R. Moody; Press, Helene Davis/Amy Lefkowitz

(Stage I) Friday, June 4–Sept. 19, 1993 (123 performances)
A PERFECT GANESH by Terrence McNally; Director, John Tillinger; Sets, Ming Cho Lee; Costumes, Santo Loquasto; Lighting, Stephen Strawbridge; Sound, Scott Lehrer; Movement, Carmen de Lavallade; Stage Manager, Pamela Singer CAST: Dominic Cuskern (Ganesha), Fisher Stevens succeeded by Garret Dillahunt (Man), Frances Sterhagen succeeded by Helen Stenborg (Margaret Civil), Zoe Caldwell succeeded by Charlotte Moore (Katharine Brynne)
 A drama in two acts. The action takes place on a vacation trip to India.

(Stage II) Tuesday, Oct. 12–Dec. 5, 1993 (41 performances and 23 previews) re-opened at Lucille Lortel Theatre Dec. 9, 1993–June 26, 1994 (230 performances)
FOUR DOGS AND A BONE; Written/Directed by John Patrick Shanley; Sets, Santo Loquasto; Costumes, Elsa Ward; Lighting, Brian Nason; Sound, Bruce Ellman; Stage Manager, Donna A. Drake CAST: Mary-Louise Parker succeeded by Arabella Field (Brenda), Tony Roberts succeeded by Peter Jacobson, Adam Arkin, Grant Shaud (Bradley), Polly Draper succeeded by Ann Magnuson, Kim Zimmer (Collette), Loren Dean succeeded by Reg Rogers (Victor)
 A comedy about the movie business in two acts. The action takes place in New York City.

(Stage I) Thursday, Oct. 28, 1993–Jan. 9, 1994 (84 performances)
THE LOMAN FAMILY PICNIC by Donald Margulies; Music, David Shire; Director, Lynne Meadow; Orchestrations, Martin Erskine; Musical Staging, Marcia Milgrom Dodge; Musical Director, Seth Rudetsky; Sets, Santo Loquasto; Costumes, Rita Ryack; Lighting, Peter Kaczorowski; Sound, Otts Munderloh; Fights, Rick Sordelet; Stage Manager, William Joseph Barnes CAST: Christine Baranski (Doris), Jonathan Charles Kaplan (Mitchell), Harry Barandes (Stewie), Peter Friedman (Herbie), Liz Larsen (Marsha)
 A drama with songs. The action takes place in Brooklyn, 1965.

(Stage II) Monday, Dec. 20, 1993–Feb. 13, 1994 (64 performances)
DAY STANDING ON ITS HEAD by Philip Kan Gotanda; Director, Oskar Eustis; Sets, David Jon Hoffmann; Costumes, Lydia Tanji; Lighting, Christopher Akerlind; Sound, John Kilgore; Stage Manager, Ed Fitzgerald CAST: Keone Young (Harry Kitamura), Kiya Ann Joyce (Lillian), Stan Egi (Joe Ozu), Liana Pai (Lisa), Tamlyn Tomita (Nina), Kati Kuroda (Mother), Glenn Kubota (Fisherman), Zar Acayan (Sam)
 A city-set drama performed without intermission.

Tamlyn Tomita, Keone Young in *Day Standing On Its Head*

Alanna Ubach, Jane Kaczmarek, Dana Ivey in *Kindertransport*

(Stage I) Tuesday, Jan. 25–Mar. 27, 1994 (72 performances)
THREE BIRDS ALIGHTING ON A FIELD by Timberlake Wertenbaker; Director, Max Stafford-Clark; Sets, Sally Jacobs; Costumes, Peter Hartwell; Lighting, Rick Fisher; Sound, Bryan Bowen; Stage Manager, Thom Widmann CAST: Caitlin Clarke (Alex/Marianne), Daniel Gerroll (Jeremy/Sir Philip/Priest), Zach Grenier (Yoyo/Boreman), Deirdre O'Connell (Lady Lelouche/Fiona), Susan Pilar (Julia/Mrs. Boreman/Yoyo's Mother), Jay O. Sanders (Stephen/Mercer), Jill Tasker (Nicola/Gwen/Jean/Russet/Katerina), Harriet Walter (Biddy), Robert Westenberg (Auctioneer/David/Constantin/Ahmet)
 An art world satire in two acts. The action takes place in London, late 1980s.

(Stage II) Tuesday, Mar. 1–Apr. 10, 1994 (48 performances)
THE ARABIAN NIGHTS; Adapted/Directed by Mary Zimmerman; Set, Karen Teneyck; Costumes, Tom Broecker; Lighting, Brian MacDevitt; Stage Manager, Diane Divita CAST: Bruce Norris (Madman/Abu al-Hasan/Sage), Jenny Bacon (Scheherazade), Ellen M. Bethea (Perfect Love/Other Woman), Enrico Colantoni (Jester/Police Chief), Christopher Donahue (Shahryar/Aziz), Sara Erde (Slave/Girl/Garden Girl), Julia Gibson (Jester's Wife/Sympathy), Kathryn Lee (Dunyazad/Aziza), Jesse L. Martin (Prince of Fools/Clarinetist/Boy), Ramon Melindez Moses (Jafar/Robber/Sage), Denis O'Hare (Pastrycook/Sheik/Ishaak), Faran Tahir (Harun al-Rashid/Sheik al-Islam)

PROGRAM: Opening, Madman's Tale, Perfidy of Wives, Pastrycook's Tale/The Dream, Butcher's Tale/Contest of Generosity/Greengrocer's Tale/Wonderful Bag, Abu al-Hasan's Historic Indiscretion, Sympathy the Learned, Mock Calipha/Aziz and Aziza, Confusion of Stories, Forgotten Melody, Closing
 A new two-act adaptation of *The Book of One Thousand Nights and One Night.*

(Stage I) Tuesday, Apr. 26–June 30, 1994 (75 performances)
KINDERTRANSPORT by Diane Samuels; Director, Abigail Morris; Sets, John Lee Beatty; Costumes, Jennifer von Mayrhauser; Lighting, Don Holder; Music/Sound, Guy Sherman/Aural Fixation; Stage Manager, Thom Widmann CAST: Michael Gaston (Ratcatcher), Alanna Ubach (Eva), Jane Kaczmarek (Helga), Dana Ivey (Evelyn), Mary Mara (Faith), Patricia Kilgarriff (Lil)
 A drama in two acts. The action takes place in an outer London suburb, 1980s.

Gerry Goodstein, Martha Swope Photos

Tony Roberts, Loren Dean, Mary-Louise Parker, Polly Draper in *Four Dogs and a Bone*

Faran Tahir, Ramon Melindez Moses, Bruce Norris (center), Enrico Colantoni, Jesse L. Martin in *The Arabian Nights*

Zoe Caldwell, Dominic Cuskern, Fisher Stevens, Frances Sternhagen in *A Perfect Ganesh*

NEW YORK SHAKESPEARE FESTIVAL

Producer, George C. Wolfe; Managing Director, Jason Steven Cohen; Associate Producers, Rosemarie Tichler, Kevin Kline; Special Projects, Wiley Hausam; Play Development, Morgan Jenness; Development Director, Margaret M. Lioi; General Manager, Sally Campbell Morse; Press, Carol R. Fineman/Terence Womble, Bruce Campbell, Barbara Carroll, James Morrison, Eugenie Hero

(Central Park/Delacorte) Thursday, July 1–25, 1993
MEASURE FOR MEASURE by William Shakespeare; Director, Michael Rudman; Set, John Lee Beatty; Costumes, Toni-Leslie James; Lighting, Peter Kaczorowski; Sound, Tom Morse; Choreography, Abdel Salaam; Fights, Jamie Cheatham; Music, Andre Tanker CAST: Kevin Kline (Duke), Andre Braugher (Angelo), Karla Burns (Mistress Overdone), Ken Cheeseman (Froth), Helmar Augustus Cooper (Escalus), Hope Davis (Mariana), Lanny Flaherty (Barnardine), Johnny Garcia (1st Gentleman), Lisa Gay Hamilton (Isabella), Denise Hernandez (Juliet), Peter Francis James (Provost), Marc Johnson (2nd Gentleman), John MacKay (Friar Peter), Tom Mardirosian (Pompey Bum), Ethan Phillips (Elbow), Stuart Rudin (Abhorson), Ruben Santiago-Hudson (Lucio), Charlotte Schully (Francisca), Blair Underwood (Claudio), Brian Barnes, Brigitte Barnett, John Conlee, Enrique Cruz-DeJesus, Andi Davis, Stephen DeRosa, Megan Gleeson, Cedric Harris, Caleb Hart, Mercedes Herrero, Chris McKinney, Robert Morgan, Annette Stubbins, Stephen Turner, Dina Wright (Ensemble)
   This version takes place in the Caribbean, prior to World War II. The 22nd entry in the NYSF Shakespeare marathon.

(Central Park/Delacorte) Thursday, Aug. 5–29, 1993
ALL'S WELL THAT ENDS WELL by William Shakespeare; Director, Richard Jones; Sets/Costumes, Stewart Laing; Lighting, Mimi Jordan Sherin; Sound, Tom Morse; Music, Jonathan Dove; Movement, Daniel Banks; Stage Manager, Ron Nash CAST: Joan MacIntosh (Countess), Graham Winton (Bertram), Henry Stram (Lafeu), Miriam Healy-Louie (Helena), Michael Cumpsty (Parolles), Herb Foster (King of France), Mark Deakins, Trellis Stepter (Brothers of Dumaine/Lords), Bette Henritze (Rinalda), Rocco Sisto (Lavatch), Patricia Kilgarriff (Widow Capilet), Patrice Johnson (Diana), Vivienne Benesch (Mariana), Brett Rickaby (Interpreter), Michael Stuhlbarg (French Gentleman), Pierce Cravens (Boy), Christopher Michael Bauer, Joel de La Fuente, Enid Graham, Cedric Harris, Steven Liebhauser, Klea Scott, Stephen Turner
   Performed in two acts.

(Public/Newman Theater) Tuesday, Oct. 19–Nov. 14, 1993 (32 performances)
THE TREATMENT by Martin Crimp; Director, Marcus Stern; Set, James Schuette; Costumes, Melina Root; Lighting, Scott Zielinski; Sound, John Huntington, Darron West; Music, John Hoge, Jane Ira Bloom; Fights, David Leong; Stage Manager, Kristen Harris CAST: Rob Campbell (Simon), Randy Danson (Jennifer), Arthur French (Taxi Driver), Robert Jason Jackson (John/Police), Susan Knight (Nicky/Waitress/Movie Star/Maid/Mad Woman), David Margulies (Clifford), Angie Phillips (Anne), Daniel von Bargen (Andrew)
   A nightmare fantasy in two acts, set in New York City.

Blair Underwood, Lisa Gay Hamilton, Kevin Kline
in *Measure for Measure*

Frances McDormand, Peter Stormare in *The Swan*

(Public/Martinson Hall) Tuesday, Nov. 9–Dec. 12, 1993 (40 performances)
THE SWAN by Elizabeth Egloff; Director, Les Waters; Sets, James Youmans; Costumes, David Woolard; Lighting, Ken Posner; Music/Sound, John Gromada; Movement/Violence, David Leong; Stage Manager, Buzz Cohen CAST: Frances McDormand (Dora), David Chandler (Kevin), Peter Stormare (Bill)
   A drama performed without intermission. The action takes place in Nebraska.

(Public/Shiva Theater) Tuesday, Nov. 30–Dec. 26, 1993 (32 performances)
FIRST LADY SUITE with Music/Lyrics/Book by Michael John LaChiusa; Director, Kirsten Sanderson; Musical Director, Alan Johnson; Sets, Derek McLane; Costumes, Tom Broecker; Lighting, Brian MacDevitt; Choreography, Janet Bogardus; Stage Manager, Liz Small

PROGRAM: *Over Texas* with Carolann Page (Evelyn Lincoln), Debra Stricklin (Mary Gallagher), David Wasson (Presidential Aide), Maureen Moore (Jacqueline Kennedy), Alice Playten (Lady Bird Johnson)
   The action takes place on board Air Force One, Nov. 22, 1963.
Where's Mamie? with Alice Playten (Mamie Eisenhower), Priscilla Baskerville (Marian Anderson), David Wasson (Ike), Debra Stricklin (Ike's Chaffeur)
   The action takes place in the White House bedroom.
Olio with David Wasson (Bess Truman), Debra Stricklin (Margaret Truman)
   The action takes place at the Christian Democratic Mothers and Daughters Luncheon, 1950
Eleanor Sleeps Here with Carolann Page (Eleanor Roosevelt), Carol Woods (Lorena Hickok), Maureen Moore (Amelia Earhart)
   The action takes place on Amelia Earhart's Lockheed Electra.

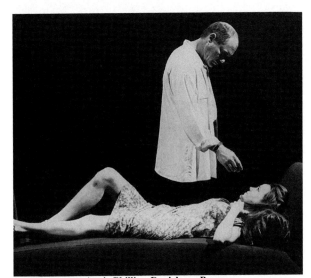

Angie Phillips, Daniel von Bargen
in *The Treatment*

(Public/Anspacher Theater) Tuesday, Jan. 4–30, 1994 (32 performances)
EAST TEXAS HOT LINKS by Eugene Lee; Director, Marion McClinton; Set, Charles McClennahan; Costumes, Toni-Leslie James; Lighting, Allen Lee Hughes; Sound, Dan Moses Schreier; Fights, David Leong; Stage Manager, Ruth Kreshka CAST: Ruben Santiago-Hudson (Roy), Curtis McClarin (XL), Loretta Devine (Charlesetta), Ed Wheeler (Columbus), Earle Hyman (Adolph), Monte Russell (Delmus), Bo Rucker (Buckshot), Willis Burks, II (Boochie)
    A drama performed without intermission. The action takes place in the Top o' the Hill Cafe, East Texas, 1955.

(Public/Shiva) Tuesday, Jan. 11–Feb. 27, 1994 (49 performances)
IRENE WORTH'S PORTRAIT OF EDITH WHARTON; From Wharton's autobiography and novels; Set, Ben Edwards; Lighting, Pat Dignan; Stage Manager, Riley Cohen CAST: Irene Worth
    A one-woman examination of Wharton.

(Public/Martinson Hall) Tuesday, Feb. 22–Mar. 27, 1994 (40 performances)
THE AMERICA PLAY by Suzan-Lori Parks; Director, Liz Diamond; Sets, Riccardo Hernandez; Costumes, Angelina Avallone; Lighting, Jeremy V. Stein; Sound, John Gromada; Stage Manager, Gwendolyn M. Gilliam CAST: Gail Grate (Lucy), Tyrone Mitchell Henderson (Men/Augusta/Asa Trenchard), Adriane Lenox (Women/Florence/Augusta), Reggie Montgomery (Founding Father as Abraham Lincoln), Michael Potts (Brazil)
    A two-act absurdist vaudeville set in "the great hole of history".

(Public/Newman) Tuesday, Mar. 8–Apr. 3, 1994 (27 performances) reopened in Broadway's Cort Theatre Apr. 10, 1994
TWILIGHT: LOS ANGELES, 1992; Conceived/Written/Performed by Anna Devere Smith; Director, George C. Wolfe; Set, John Arnone; Costumes, Toni-Leslie James; Lighting, Jules Fisher, Peggy Eisenhauer; Sound, John Gromada; Projections/Video, Batwin + Robin; Music, Wendy Blackstone; Stage Manager, William Joseph Barnes
    A one-woman panorama of the events surrounding the 1992 L.A. riots.

Anna Deavere Smith in *Twilight: Los Angeles, 1992*

Bo Rucker, Loretta Devine, Willis Burks II in
East Texas Hot Links

(Public/Anspacher Theater) Tuesday, Mar. 15–May 1, 1994 (56 performances)
THE TRAGEDY OF RICHARD II by William Shakespeare; Director, Steven Berkoff; Sets, Christine Jones; Costumes, Elsa Ward; Lighting, Brian Nason; Music, Larry Spivak; Stage Manager, Buzz Cohen CAST: Michael Stuhlbarg (Richard II), Andre Braugher (Bolingbroke), Elaina Davis (Queen), Herb Foster (Duke of York), Earle Hyman (John of Gaunt), Francis Jue (Bush/Exton's Man/Corp), Resse Madigan (Percy/Groom/Corp), Boris McGiver (Green/Duke of Surrey/Sir Pierce/Corp), T. J. Meyers (Master Gardener/Corp), Daniel Orekes (Carlisle/Corp), Patrick Page (Aumerle), Bray Poor (Bagot/Scroop/Corp), Drew Richardson (Lady), Rene Rivera (Lord Willoughby/Garderner's Man), Carole Shelley (Duchess of Gloucester/Duchess of York), Jack Stehlin (Mowbray), Darryl Theirse (Ross/Fitzwater), Sam Tsoutsouvas (Northumberland)
    Performed in five acts with one intermission.

(Public/Shiva Theater) Monday, May 2–15, 1994 (10 performances)
ALL FOR YOU; Written/Performed by John Fleck; Co-Director, David Schweizer; Lighting, Kevin Adams; Video, Adam Soch; Stage Manager, Robert Castro
    Performance art in repertory with *Airport Music*.

(Public/Shiva Theater) Friday, May 6–14, 1994 (9 performances)
AIRPORT MUSIC; Written/Performed by Jessica Hagedorn and Han Ong; Directing Consultant, Laurie Carlos; Lighting, Kevin Adams; Stage Manager, Keith Jones
    Performance art in repertory with *All for You*.

(Public/Shiva Theater) Friday, May 20–June 5, 1994 (14 performances)
BIG MOMMA 'N' EM; Conceived/Written/Performed by Phyllis Yvonne Stickney; Director, Loni Berry; Set/Costumes, Felix E. Cochren; Lighting, Kevin Adams; Sound, Carmen Whip; Stage Manager, Trevor Brown
    One-woman show featuring five characters.

Martha Swope/William Gibson, Carol Rosegg Photo

Jack Stehlin, Andre Braugher in *Richard II*

Christopher Collet, Joseph Wiseman in *Unfinished Stories*

NEW YORK THEATRE WORKSHOP

Artistic Director, James C. Nicola; Managing Director, Nancy Kassak Diekmann; Associate Artistic Director, Christopher Grabowski; Artistic Administrator, Martha Banta; General Manager, Esther Cohen; Development Director, Glen Knapp; Press, Richard Kornberg/Barbara Carroll, Tom Naro, Don Summa, Sandra Manley

Thursday, June 10–20, 1993 (10 performances)
BRAVE SMILES..._Another Lesbian Tragedy_ by The Five Lesbian Brothers; Director, Kate Stafford; Set, Jamie Leo; Costumes, Susan Young; Lighting, Diana Arecco; Sound, Peg Healy CAST: Maureen Angelos (Thalia/Martha/Reporter), Babs Davy (Millicent/Miss Gateau/Maitre 'd), Dominique Dibbell (Will/Frau von Pussenheimer/Reporter/Audrey Hepburn), Peg Healy (Babe/Miss Phillips/Soldier/Shirley MacLaine/Bum), Lisa Kron (Damwell Maxwell/Baroness)
   A comedy featuring the "Five Lesbian Brothers" as schoolgirls who meet at a strict European boarding school in the 1920s.

Wednesday, Sept. 8–Dec. 5, 1993 (89 performances) reopened at Cherry Lane Theatre on Jan. 7, 1994
BLOWN SIDEWAYS THROUGH LIFE; Written/Performed by Claudia Shear; Developed with and Directed by Christopher Ashley; Set, Loy Arcenas; Costumes, Jess Goldstein; Lighting, Christopher Akerlind; Sound, Aural Fixation; Music, Richard Peaslee; Choreography, Nafisa Sharriff; Stage Manager, Kate Broderick
   An autobiographical tour-de-resume of 65 jobs.

Elvira Colorado in *Rez Sisters*

Sunday, Dec. 12, 1993–Jan. 9, 1994 (7 performances and 19 previews)
THE REZ SISTERS by Tomson Highway; Directors, Linda S. Chapman and Muriel Miguel; Set, Anita Stewart; Costumes, Anne C. Patterson; Lighting, Christopher Akerlind; Movement, Louis Mofsie; Music, Kevin Tarrant; Stage Manager, Deborah Ratelle CAST: Kevin Tarrant (Bingo Guy), Louis Mofsie (Nanabush), Gloria Miguel (Pelajia), Muriel Miguel (Philomena), Elvira Colorado (Annie), Sheila Tousey (Marie-Adele), Lisa Mayo (Veronique), Hortensia Colorado (Zhaboonigan), Murielle Borst (Emily)
   A comedy in two acts. The action takes place on an Ontario reservation.

Friday, Feb. 4–Mar. 13, 1994 (40 performances)
UNFINISHED STORIES by Sybille Pearson; Director, Gordon Davidson; Set, Peter Wexler; Costumes, Gabriel Berry; Lighting, Ken Billington; Sound, Mark Bennett, Jon Gottlieb; Stage Manager, Terrence J. Witter CAST: Christopher Collet (Daniel), Joseph Wiseman (Walter), E. Katherine Kerr (Gaby), Laurence Luckinbill (Yves)
   A drama performed without intermission. The action takes place on the Upper West Side. Christopher Collet and Joseph Wiseman originated these roles at the Mark Taper Forum in 1992.

Sunday, May 1–June 19, 1994 (50 performances)
THE MEDIUM; Conceived/Directed by Anne Bogart; Set, Anita Stewart; Costumes, Gabriel Berry; Lighting, Michitomo Shiohara; Sound, Darron L. West; Stage Manager, Kieran Jason Hackett CAST: J. Ed Araiza, Will Bond, Ellen Lauren, Kelly Maurer, Tom Nelis
   Theatre piece based on the life and writings of Marshall McLuhan performed without intermission

Martha Swope, Joan Marcus, Dona Ann McAdams Photos

Claudia Shear in *Blown Sideways Through Life*

PEARL THEATRE COMPANY

Artistic Director, Shepard Sobel; General Manager, Parris Relkin; Development Director, Lawrence F. Swann; Set Designer, Robert Joel Schwartz; Lighting, Stephen Petrilli; Costumes, Deborah Rooney; Sound, Donna Riley; Press, Bettina Altman-Abrams

Wednesday, Sept. 8–Oct. 23, 1993 (47 performances)
OEDIPUS THE KING by Sophocles; Translation, Stephen Berg, Diskin Clay; Director, Ted Davis; Set, Stage Manager, Sandra M. Bloom CAST: Timothy Wheeler (Oedipus), Robert Hock (Priest/Choragos), Sean Pratt (Kreon/Messenger/Servant), Michael Chernov, Katherine Hill, Stefanie Zadravec (Chorus), Margo Skinner (Teiresias/Jocasta/Shepard)
   Performed without intermission. The setting is an ancient and sacred circle.

Friday, Oct. 29–Dec. 11, 1993 (45 performances)
THE GAME OF LOVE AND CHANCE by Marivaux; Translation, Adrienne and Oscar Mandel; Director, Shepard Sobel; Lighting, Russell H. Champa; Stage Manager, Mary-Susan Gregson CAST: Raye Lankford (Silvia), Margo Skinner (Lisette), Robert Hock (Organ), Andrew Sellon (Mario), Victoria Miner (Noisette), Sean Pratt (Dorante), Timothy Wheeler (Arlequin)
   A comedy in three acts. The action takes place in Paris, 1730.

Friday, Dec. 17, 1993–Jan. 29, 1994 (45 performances)
TWELFTH NIGHT by William Shakespeare; Director, John Rando; Music, Thomas Cabaniss; Stage Manager, Bill McComb CAST: Robin Leslie Brown (Viola), Raye Lankford (Olivia), Robert Hock (Malvolio), Frank Lowe (Toby Belch), Arnie Burton (Andrew Aguecheek), Michael James Reed (Orsinio), Dominic Cuskern (Feste), Bella Jarrett, Andy Paris, Sean Pratt, Stephen Price, Andrew Sellon, Mark Kenneth Smaltz
   Shakespeare's 1601 comedy.

Friday, Feb. 4–Mar. 19, 1994 (45 performances)
LITTLE EYOLF by Henrik Ibsen; Translation, William Archer; Director, Shepard Sobel; Stage Manager, Mary-Susan Gregson CAST: Robin Leslie Brown (Asta), Joanne Camp (Rita), Mark Kenneth Smaltz (Alfred Allmer), Spencer Flagg (Eyolf), Anna Minot (Rat Wife), Arnie Burton (Borgheim)
   An 1894 drama in three acts. The action takes place on Allmer's estate, 1894.

Friday, Mar. 25–May 8, 1994 (48 performances)
THE MOLLUSC by Hubert Henry Davies; Director, Anthony Cornish; Lighting, A. C. Hickox; Stage Manager, Colleen Marie Davis CAST: Robin Leslie Brown (Mrs. Baxter), Tom Bloom (Kemp), Arnie Burton (Baxter), Kathleen Christal (Miss Roberts)
   A 1907 English comedy.

Carol Rosegg/Martha Swope Photos

Sean Pratt, Margo Skinner, Timothy Wheeler in
Game of Love and Chance

Kathleen Christal, Arnie Burton in *The Mollusc*

Robin Leslie Brown, Arnie Burton in *Twelfth Night*

Robin Leslie Brown, Mark Kenneth Smaltz,
Joanne Camp in *Little Eyolf*

141

PLAYWRIGHTS HORIZONS

Twenty-third Season

Artistic Director, Don Scardino; Managing Director, Leslie Marcus; Associate Artistic Director, Nicholas Martin; General Manager, Lynn Landis; Literary Manager, Tim Sanford; Production Manager, Jack O'Connor; Development Director, Lesley J. Kranz; Press, Philip Rinaldi/Kathy Haberthur, Dennis Crowley

Tuesday, Sept. 21–Nov. 6, 1993 (54 performances)
SOPHISTRY by Jonathan Marc Sherman; Director, Nicholas Martin; Set, Allen Moyer; Costumes, Michael Krass; Lighting, Kenneth Posner; Sound, Jeremy Grody; Stage Manager, Christopher Wigle CAST: Ethan Hawke (Xavier "Ex" Reynolds), Austin Pendleton (Whitey McCoy), Steve Zahn (Willy), Jonathan Marc Sherman (Igor Konigsberg), Calista Flockhart (Robin Smith), Linda Atkinson (Quintana Matheson), Anthony Rapp (Jack Kahn), Nadia Dajani (Debbie)
 A drama in two acts. The action takes place on a small New England college campus, May 1990–June 1991.

Friday, Nov. 11–Dec. 26, 1993 (53 performances)
AN IMAGINARY LIFE by Peter Parnell; Director, Don Scardino; Sets, Loren Sherman; Costumes, Jess Goldstein; Lighting, Phil Monat; Sound, Raymond D. Schilke; Stage Manager, Dianne Trulock CAST: Chip Zien (Matt Abelman), Caroline Aaron (Maggs Morris), Reed Birney (Dr. Jeff Portnoy), Christopher Collet (Noah Abelman), Jonathan Walker (Spenser Glick), Tim Blake Nelson (Igor Fuchs), Merwin Goldsmith (Marvin Frappe)
 A drama bluring fact and fantasy in two acts. The action takes place in and around New York and Maine.

Monday, Dec. 6–13, 1993 (2 limited performances)
A CHEEVER EVENING by A. R. Gurney; Director, Don Scardino CAST: Maureen Anderman, Blair Brown, Frank Converse, Patricia Clarkson, Peter Frechette, Victor Garber, Anthony Heald, Debra Monk, Campbell Scott
 Staged reading of new play.

Friday, January 28–Apr. 3, 1994 (77 performances)
AVENUE X with Music/Lyrics by Ray Leslee; Concept/Book/Lyrics by John Jiler; Director, Mark Brokaw; Vocal Arrangements/Musical Director, Chapman Roberts; Sets, Loy Arcenas; Costumes, Ellen McCartney; Lighting, Donald Holder; Sound, Janet Kalas; Choreography, Ken Roberson; Fights, Rick Sordelet; Stage Manager, Lisa Buxbaum CAST: Ted Brunetti (Pasquale), Roger Mazzeo (Ubazz), John Leone (Chuck), Colette Hawley (Barbara), Harold Perrineau (Milton), Chuck Cooper (Roscoe), Alvaleta Guess (Julia), Keith Johnston (Winston)

MUSICAL NUMBERS: Where is Love?, A Thousand Summer Nights, Scat, Serves You Right, Waitin', Io Sono Cosi Stanco, Woman of the World, She's Fifteen, Stay with Me Baby, Where Are You Tonight?, Big Lucy, Why, Follow Me, Palermo, Command Me, Rap, Moonlight in Old Sicily, Gloria, Africa, Go There, Til the End of Time, Epilogue
 An a cappella musical in two acts. The action takes place in Brooklyn, 1963. This production played from June 3–13, 1993 (14 performances) in the Studio under the title *Avenue X, the A Cappella Musical* and with Ellis E. Williams as Roscoe.

Wednesday, Feb. 23–Mar. 6, 1994 (15 performances)
ARTS & LEISURE by Steve Tesich; Director, JoAnne Akalaitis; Costumes, Therese Bruck; Lighting, Anne M. Padien; Sound, Michael Clark; Fights, Rick Sordelet; Stage Manager, Andrea J. Testani CAST: Harris Yulin (Alex Chaney), Angela Lanza (Maria), Alice Drummond (Mother), Mary Beth Hurt (Lenore), Hope Davis (Daughter)
 A comedy about a powerful New York theatre critic.

Friday, Apr. 29–June 10, 1994 (49 performances)
MOE'S LUCKY SEVEN by Marlane Meyer; Director, Roberta Levitow; Set, Rosario Provenza; Costumes, Tom Broecker; Lighting, Robert Wierzel; Music/Sound, O-Lan Jones; Fights, Rick Sordelet; Stage Manager, William H. Lang CAST: Jodie Markell (Tiny/Divina), Steve Harris (Knuckles), Deirdre O'Connell (Patsy), Mark Margolis (Moe), Barry Sherman (Drake), Rick Dean (Drew), Jefferson Mays (Mokie), Lanny Flaherty (Kurt), Ismael Carlo (Benito), Bruce McCarty (Eggs), Phyllis Somerville (Janine), Sean San Jose Blackman (Lon)
 A comedy in two acts set in a waterfront bar.

Joan Marcus, T. Charles Erickson Photos

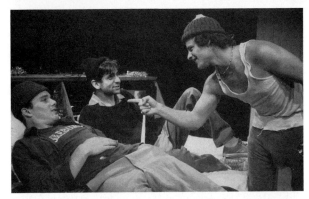

Ethan Hawke, Jonathan Marc Sherman, Steve Zahn in *Sophistry*

Austin Pendleton, Calista Flockhart in *Sophistry*

**Rick Dean, Barry Sherman, Deirdre O'Connell in
*Moe's Lucky Seven***

Patricia Kalember, Reed Birney, Constance Shulman, Tamara Tunie in *Loose Knit*

SECOND STAGE THEATRE

Fifteenth Season

Artistic Director, Carole Rothman; Producing Director, Suzanne Schwartz Davidson; Associate Producer, Carol Fishman; Marketing Director, Harold Marmon; Development Director, Lawrence Greene; Press, Richard Kornberg/ Don Summa, Tom Naro, Barbara Carroll

Friday, June 11–Aug. 1, 1993 (53 performances)
LOOSE KNIT by Theresa Rebeckl; Director, Beth Schachter; Set, Santo Loquasto; Lighting, Frances Aronson; Costumes, Elsa Ward; Sound, Mark Bennett; Stage Manager, Jess Lynn CAST: Mary B. Ward (Liz), Patricia Kalember (Lily), Tamara Tunie (Paulie), Kristine Nielsen (Gina), Constance Shulman (Margie), Reed Birney (Bob), Daniel Gerroll (Miles)
   A comedy in two acts set in New York City.

Tuesday, Nov. 9, 1993–Jan. 1, 1994 (55 performances)
LIFE SENTENCES by Richard Nelson; Director, John Caird; Set, Thomas Lynch; Lighting, Richard Nelson; Costumes, Ann Roth; Sound, Mark Bennett; Stage Manager, Marjorie Horne CAST: Edward Herrmann (Burke), Michelle Joyner (Mia)
   A comedy in two acts. The action takes place in and around New York.

Tuesday, Jan. 25–May 26, 1994 (122 performances)
RICKY JAY & HIS 52 ASSISTANTS; Written/Performed by Ricky Jay; Director, David Mamet; Set, Kevin Rigdon; Lighting, Jules Fisher; Costumes, Alan Bilzerian; Consultants, Jim Steinmeyer, Michael Weber; Stage Manager, Matthew Silver
   An evening of sleight of hand, in two acts.

Monday, Feb. 7–21, 1994 (3 limited performances)
INSOMNIA; Written/Performed by Dana Gould; Director, Mark W. Travis
   One man's escape into comedy.

Monday, Feb. 28–Mar. 14, 1994 (3 limited performances)
WAKE UP, I'M FAT; Written/Performed by Camryn Manheim; Director, Mark Brokaw
   A one-woman monologue.

Susan Cook, Brigitte Lacombe Photos

Ricky Jay

Edward Herrmann, Michelle Joyner in *Life Sentences*

143

SIGNATURE THEATRE COMPANY

Artistic Director, James Houghton; Managing Director, Thomas C. Proehl; Company Manager, Adrienne Thompson; Sets, E. David Cosier; Costumes, Teresa Snider-Stein; Lighting, Jeffrey S. Koger, Colin D. Young; Press, James Morrison

(All plays at Kampo Cultral Center) Friday, Oct. 1–31, 1993 (23 performances)
MARRIAGE PLAY by Edward Albee; Director, James Houghton; Fights, Marty Pistone; Stage Manager, Kathleen M. Nolan CAST: Kathleen Butler (Gillian), Tom Klunis (Jack)
A 1987 drama in two acts. The action takes place in suburbia.

Friday, Nov. 5–Dec. 5, 1993 (23 performances)
COUNTING THE WAYS and **LISTENING** by Edward Albee; Directors, Mr. Albee (*Counting the Ways*), Paul Weidner (*Listening*); Stage Manager, Elizabeth M. Berther CASTS: *Counting...* with Baxter Harris (Husband), Patricia Kilgarriff (Wife) *Listening* with Jacqueline Brookes (Woman), Joe Ponazecki (Man), Francie Swift (Girl), Penner (Voice)
Two one-acts.

Friday, Feb. 4–Mar. 6, 1994 (23 performances)
SAND: Three Plays Written/Directed by Edward Albee; Music, William Flanagan; Stage Manager, Bethany Ford
Box with Jacqueline Brookes' voice
The Sandbox with Aisha Benoir (Cellist), Peggy Cosgrave (Mommy), Jane Hoffman (Grandma), Earl Nash (Young Man), Edward Seamon (Daddy)
Finding the Sun with John Carter (Hendon), Brendan Corbalis (Daniel), Monique Fowler (Cordelia), Cheryl Gaysunas (Abigail), Bethel Leslie (Gertrude), Neil Maffin (Benjamin), Mary Beth Peil (Edmee), James Van Der Beek (Fergus)
Three one-acts.

Friday, Apr. 8–May 8, 1994 (23 performances)
FRAGMENTS by Edward Albee; Director, James Houghton; Stage Manager, Elliot Fox CAST: Angela Marie Bettis, John Carter, Paddy Croft, Lou Ferguson, Cheryl Gaysunas, Edward Norton, Joyce O'Connor, Scott Sowers
An experiment in dramatic structure for eight solo voices.

Suzanne Johann Photos

Francie Smith, Jacqueline Brookes, Joe Ponazecki in *Listening*

144 (clockwise from upper left) Lou Ferguson, Cheryl Gaysunas, Scott Sowers, Angela Marie Bettis, Edward Norton, Joyce O'Connor, John Carter, Paddy Croft in *Fragments*

Catherine Butterfield, Ellen Parker in *Snowing at Delphi*

Jan Horvath, Sean Dooley in *New York Rock*

WPA THEATRE
(WORKSHOP OF THE PLAYERS ART)

Seventeenth Season

Artistic Director, Kyle Renick; Managing Director, Lori Sherman; Management Associate, Barbara Crompton; Production Manager, Regan Kimmel; Press, Jeffrey Richards/Kevin Rehac, Candi Adams, Irene Gandy

Thursday, Oct. 7–Nov. 11, 1993 (33 performances)
SNOWING AT DELPHI by Catherine Butterfield; Director, Pamela Berlin; Set, Edward T. Gianfrancesco; Lighting, Jackie Manassee; Costumes, Julie Doyle; Sound, John Kilgore; Stage Manager, Karen Moore CAST: Sam Tsoutsouvas (Gary), Ray Virta (Nick), Ellen Parker (Sarah), Catherine Butterfield (Marcy), John Christopher Jones (Allan), Arabella Field (Brenda)
A play in two acts. The action takes place in upstate New York.

Tuesday, Dec. 14, 1993–Jan. 16, 1994 (35 performances)
MUSIC FROM DOWN THE HILL by John Ford Noonan; Director, Terence Lamude; Set, Edward T. Gianfrancesco; Lighting, Craig Evans; Costumes, Mimi Maxmen; Sound, Tom Gould; Stage Manager, Gail Eve Malatesta CAST: Welker White (Claire Granick), Alma Cuervo (Margot Yodakian)
A drama in two acts. The action takes place in a mental-health facility in upstate New York.

Thursday, Mar. 3–Apr. 17, 1994 (42 performances)
NEW YORK ROCK with Music/Lyrics/Book by Yoko Ono; Director, Phillip Oesterman; Orchestrations/Musical Direction, Jason Robert Brown; Choreography, Kenneth Tosti; Sets/Costumes, Terry Leong; Lighting, Craig Evans; Sound, Brian Young, Rob Stevens; Stage Manager, Mark Cole CAST: Jan Horvath (Mother), Sean Dooley (Little Bill/Boy), Pat McRoberts (Bill), Lynette Perry (Jill), Pete Herber (Ignorance), Walter O'Neil (Violence I), Paul Mahos (Violence II), Aaron Blackshear, Evan Ferrante, Peter Kim (Streetkids)
A musical in two acts set in New York City.

Thursday, May 26–July 10, 1994 (47 performances)
THE NAKED TRUTH by Paul Rudnick; Director, Christopher Ashley; Set, James Youmans; Lighting, Donald Holder; Costumes, David Woolard; Sound, Mark Bennett; Stage Manager, Karen Moore CAST: Peter Bartlett (Dan Barstow/Messenger/Fr. Middlebury), J. Smith Cameron (Sissy Bemiss Darnley), John Cunningham (Pete Bemiss), Cynthia Darlow (Bonnie Barstow/Sister Mary Loyola), Debra Messing (Lynette Marshall), Mary Beth Peil (Nan Bemiss), Valarie Pettiford (Cassandra Keefer), Victor Slezak (Alex DelFlavio)
A two-act comedy about art and censorship set in New York City.

Carol Rosegg, William Gibson/Martha Swope Photos

Welker White, Alma Cuervo in *Music from Down the Hill*

VINEYARD THEATRE

Thirteenth Season

Artistic Director, Douglas Aibel; Executive Director, Barbara Zinn Krieger; Managing Director, Jon Nakagawa; Production Manager, Mark Lorenzen; Administrative/Artistic Associate, Bob Swee; Press, Shirley Herz/Sam Rudy

Thursday, Oct. 7–Nov. 28, 1993 (54 performances)
PTERODACTYLS by Nicky Silver; Director, David Warren; Set, James Youmans; Costumes, Teresa Snider-Stein; Lighting, Donald Holder; Sound, Brian Hallas; Sculpture, Jim Gary; Fights, Rick Sordelet; Stage Manager, Karen Loftus CAST: T. Scott Cunningham (Todd Duncan), Hope Davis (Emma Duncan), Kent Lanier (Tommy McKorckle), Kelly Bishop (Grace Duncan), Dennis Creaghan (Arthur Duncan)
  A dark comedy in two acts. The action involves a main-line Philadelphia family.

Tuesday, Dec. 21, 1993–Jan. 9, 1994 (20 performances)
HIT THE LIGHTS! with Music by Jon Giluntin; Lyrics/Book, Michele Lowe; Additional Music, Chris Hajian; Director, Lisa Peterson; Musical Director, Lon Hoyt; Choreography, Lynne Taylor-Corbett; Set, Allan Moyer; Costumes, Michael Krass; Lighting, Peter Kaczorowski CAST: Annie Golden (Lucy), John Sloman, Andrea Frierson, Ann Harada, Michael Mandell, Joe Palmas, Marti Muller, Jason Danieley, Mona Wyatt, Michael O'Gorman
  A pop/rap musical fantasy.

Thursday, Jan. 27–Mar. 13, 1994 (47 performances) reopened at the Promenade Theatre on Apr. 5, 1994–still playing May 31, 1994
THREE TALL WOMEN by Edward Albee; Director, Lawrence Sacharow; Set, James Noone; Lighting, Phil Monat; Muriel Stockdale; Stage Manager, Elizabeth M. Berther CAST: Myra Carter (A), Marian Seldes (B), Jordan Baker (C), Michael Rhodes (The Boy)
  A drama in two acts. Winner of the 1994 Pulitzer Prize and New York Drama Critics Circle Best Play.

Thursday, Apr. 21–May 29, 1994 (40 performances)
CHRISTINA ALBERTA'S FATHER with Music/Lyrics/Book by Polly Pen; Based on the novel by H. G. Wells; Director, Andre Ernotte; Orchestrations, Lawrence Yurman; Musical Director, Paulette Haupt; Choreography, Lynne Taylor-Corbett; Set, William Barclay; Lighting, Michael Lincoln; Costumes, Gail Brassard; Stage Manager, Karen A. Potosnak CAST: Henry Stram (Albert Edward Preemby), Alma Cuervo (Chris Hossett), Marla Schaffel (Christina Albert Preemby), John Lathan (Teddy), Tina Johnson (Fay), Marceline Hugot (Miss Rewster), Don Mayo (Major Bone), Jane Neuberger (Mrs. Bone), Richard Holmes (Master Bone), Andy Taylor (Bobby)

MUSICAL NUMBERS: Greetings from the Paddlers on the Sheringham Front, Sleep Little Red Object, The Laundry, Court of Conscience, Alone in the World, Boarding Houses, Tunbridge Wells, A Rock and a Body, Waiting, Dance in the Studio, Early Amphibians, I am Reeling, My World, Running About, Where is the Lost and Found of London?, Uneasy Armchairs, Slow't Dow, Fricassee of Chicken, Later Amphibians, Christina Alberta and I, Tra-La-La, Daybreak, Here is Love, First Night of Summer
  A musical in two acts. The action takes place in England, 1899–1920s.

Carol Rosegg/Martha Swope Photos

Top: T. Scott Cunningham, Kent Lanier in *Pterodactyls*
Center: Jordan Baker, Marian Seldes, Myra Carter in
Three Tall Women
Bottom: Marla Schaffel, Henry Stram, Andy Taylor in
Christina Albert's Father

146

YORK THEATRE COMPANY

Twenty-fifth Season

Producing Director, Janet Hayes Walker; Managing Director, Molly Pickering Grose; Business Manager, Charles Dodsley Walker; Artistic Advisors, James Morgan, John Newton; Production Manager, Joseph V. De Michele; Press, Keith Sherman/Jim Byk, Stuart Ginsberg, Kevin McAnarney

Tuesday, Oct. 26–Nov. 21, 1993 (28 performances)
HOW THE OTHER HALF LOVES by Alan Ayckbourn; Director, Alex Dmitriev; Set, James Morgan; Costumes, Holly Hynes; Lighting, Jerold R. Forsyth; Music, Steven D. Bowen; Fights, Ricki G. Ravitts; Stage Manager, Alan Bluestone CAST: Mary Kay Adams (Fiona Foster), Susanne Marley (Teresa Phillips), James Murtaugh (Frank Foster), Woody Sempliner (Bob Phillips), Peter Bloch (William Featherstone), Tracy Thorne (Mary Featherstone).
    A 1970 two-act farce presented in the playwright's original version—the 1971 Broadway production was revised.

Wednesday, Jan. 12–Feb. 13, 1994 (34 performances)
BOOTH by Austin Pendleton; Director, David Schweizer; Sets, James Morgan; Costumes, Clifford Capone; Lighting, Mary Jo Dondlinger; Sound/Music, Jim van Bergen; Stage Manager, Mary Ellen Allison CAST: Frank Langella (Junius), Garret Dillahunt (Edwin), Frances Conroy (Mary Ann), Alexander Enberg (Johnny), Joyce Ebert (Mrs. Hill), Paul Schmidt (Mr. Page), Jan Munroe (Baxter), Molly Regan (Adelaide).
    A drama in two acts. The action takes place all over America, 1850s.

Thursday, Mar. 3–24, 1994 (4 limited performances)
A LITTLE NOON MUSIC; Presentations of New Musicals

PROGRAMS: *Acting, A Romance* by James Campodonico and Bryan D. Leys; Director, Mark-Leonard Simmons with Richard Kinscy, Kathryn Blake; *Salute to Tom Jones and Harvey Schmidt* with Jonathan Courie, Ann Brown; *Wild Swans* by Adele Ahronheim and Ben Schaechter; *Kansas* by David J. V. Meenan; Director, Mark-Leonard Simmons

Saturday, Mar. 19–Apr. 10, 1994 (9 performances)
MUSICALS IN MUFTI; Staged Concert Musicals
The Grass Harp by Claibe Richardson and Kenward Elmslie; Director, J. Randall Hugill with Lynne Wintersteller, Lillias White, Cass Morgan
A Doll's Life by Larry Grossman, Betty Comden and Adolph Green; Director, Robert Brink
Oh, Brother! by Michael Valenti and Donald Driver; Revisions, Dion Driver, Mr. Valenti; Director, Charles Abbott

Thursday, May 26–July 17, 1994 (54 performances)
MERRILY WE ROLL ALONG with Music/Lyrics by Stephen Sondheim; Book, George Furth; Based on the play by George S. Kaufman and Moss Hart; Director, Susan H. Schulman; Musical Director, Michael Rafter; Choreography, Michael Lichtefeld; Orchestral Adaptation, G. Harrell; Sets, James Morgan; Costumes, Beba Shamash; Lighting, Mary Jo Dondlinger; Projections, Wendall K. Harrington; Sound, Jim van Bergen; Stage Manager, Perry Cline CAST: Anne Bobby (Beth), Danny Burstein (Ru), Ron Butler (Bunker/Newsman), Rick Crom (Terry/Spencer), Jonathan Flanagan (Frank Jr.), Malcolm Gets (Franklin Shepard), Paul Harman (Joseph Josephson), Adam Heller (Charlie Kringas), James Hindman (Tyler), Philip Hoffman (Jerome), Adriane Lenox (Scotty), Cass Morgan (Dory/Mrs. Spencer), Michele Pawk (Gussie), Amy Ryder (Mary Flynn), Christine Toy (K. T.), Amy M. Young (Meg)

MUSICAL NUMBERS: Merrily We Roll Along, That Frank, Old Friends, Franklin Shepard Inc., Growing Up, Not a Day Goes By, Now You Know, It's a Hit!, The Blob, Good Thing Going, Bobbie and Jackie and Jack, Opening Doors, Our Time
    A new revision of the 1981 musical in two acts. The action takes place in New York City.

Carol Rosegg/Martha Swope, T. Charles Erickson Photos

Top: Frank Langella in *Booth*
Bottom: Malcolm Gets, Ann Ryder, Adam Heller
in *Merrily We Roll Along*

NATIONAL TOURING COMPANIES

ANNIE GET YOUR GUN

Music/Lyrics, Irving Berlin; Book, Herbert and Dorothy Fields; Director, Susan H. Schulman; Choreography, Michael Lichtefeld; Musical Director, Brian W. Tidwell; Orchestrations, Robert Russell Bennet, Michael Gibson, Mr. Tidwell; Sets, Heidi Landesman, Joel Reynolds; Costumes, Catherine Zuber; Lighting, Ken Billington; Stage Manager, Bryan Young; Executive Producer, George MacPherson; Presented by Tom McCoy, Tom Mallow, ATP/Dodger, Pace Theatrical Group, and Kennedy Center; Press, Laura Matalon; Opened March 3, 1993, and still touring in 1994.

CAST

Charlie Davenport ....Paul V. Ames
Doll Tate ....K. T. Sullivan
Mac ....Marty McDonough
Foster Wilson/Conductor/Pawnee...............................Mike O'Carroll
Frank Butler...Brent Barrett
Annie Oakley..Cathy Rigby
Little Jake ....Ryan Mason
Nellie ....Theresa McCoy
Jessie ....Kaitlin McCoy
Buffalo Bill ....Erick Devine
Porter ....John Walden
Cowboy/Footman ....John Anthony
Chief Sitting Bull ....Mauricio Bustamante
Stillwater ....Joe Bowerman
Indian Girl ....Catherine Gardner
Pawnee's Messenger ....Robert Preston Smith
Mrs. Sylvia Potter-Porter ....Robin Lusby
Mrs. Schuyler Adams ....Lynn Shuck
Mr. Schuyler Adams ....Bill Bateman
Mrs. Ernest Henderson...Wendy Piper
Ensemble ....Ana Maria Andricain, John Anthony, Bill Bateman,
Stephen Bourneuf, Joe Bowerman, Catherine Gardner,
Lisa Hanna, Robin Lusby, Ryan Mason, Kaitlin McCoy,
Theresa McCoy, Marty McDonough, Sharon Moore,
Wendy Piper, Hugh B. Richards, Lynn Shuck,
Roger Preston Smith, John Walden, Leigh-Anne Wencker

UNDERSTUDIES: Bill Bateman, Marty McDonough (Charlie), Lynn Shuck, Robin Lusby (Dolly), Craig Waletzko, Jow Bowerman (Mac), Mr. Bateman, Roger Preston Smith (Foster/Pawnee/Sitting Bull), John Anthony (Frank Butler/Messenger), Ana Maria Andricain (Annie Oakley/Mrs. Adams/Mrs. Henderson), Catherine Gardner (Jake/Nellie/Jessie), Mike O'Carroll (Buffalo Bill), Craig Waletzko (Porter/Conductor/Footman/Mr. Adams), Stephen Bourneuf (Cowboy), Mr. Waletzko, Hugh B. Richards (Stillwater), Ms. Shuck, Leigh Anne Wencker (Potter-Porter), Theresa McCoy (Indian Girl).

MUSICAL NUMBERS: Col. Buffalo Bill, I'm a Bad Bad Man, Doin' What Comes Natur'lly, Girl That I Marry, You Can't Get a Man with a Gun, There's No Business Like Show Business, Moonshine Lullaby, They Say It's Wonderful, Wild West Pitch Dance, My Defenses are Down, Indian Ceremonial, I Got Lost in His Arms, I Got the Sun in the Morning, Anything You Can Do, Finale

The 1946 musical in two acts.

Cathy Rigby, (front) Kaitlin McCoy, Ryan Mason, Theresa McCoy in *Annie Get Your Gun*

A CHRISTMAS CAROL

Music, Michel Legrand; Lyrics/Book, Sheldon Harnick; From the story by Charles Dickens; Director, Douglas E. Stark; Musical Director, Richard Laughlin; Choreography Doug King; Set, Tennessee Repertory Theatre; Lighting, Michael Layton; Costumes, Livingston; Stage Manager, Arden Landhuis; Presented by Zark Productions, Douglas E. Stark, Robert D. Zehr; Press, Amy Stark; Opened at Clowes Memorial Hall, Indianapolis, Indiana on Friday, December 10, 1993, and closed December 29 in Ft. Wayne, Indiana.

CAST

Ebenezer Scrooge ....Douglas E. Holmes
Fred ....Steve Hiltebrand
Bob Cratchit ....Eddie Curry
Charity Man/Ghost of Christmas Present.......................Daniel Scharbrough
Charity Woman/Laundress ....Suzanne L. Stark
Jacob Marley/Old Joe ....Brian Horton
Ghost of Christmas Past/Charwoman ....Ellen Saxton
Boy Scrooge/Albert Cratchit ....Rudy Nehrling
Fanny/Lucy Cratchit..Jana Lugar
Mr. Fezziwig/Poulterer ....Dennis Bussell
Mrs. Fezziwig ....Ginger Rittenhouse
Scrooge (Young Man)..Robert Gallagher
Belle..Tari Lynn Attoe
Fred's Wife...Marlene Dickinson
Mrs. Cratchit ....Jana Alonzo
Peter Cratchit ....David Petro
Martha Cratchit ....Heather Baker
Belinda Cratchit ....Jennifer Shuck
Tiny Tim ....Della Gillespie
Alice Cratchit ....Gia Drouzasa
Undertaker ....Douglas Edward Stark
Undertaker's Man ....Jay Emrich

MUSICAL NUMBERS: Spirit of Christmas, Icy Ebenezer, Bah! Humbug!, Thank Heaven for Christmas, Bells of Christmas Day, Christmas Eve, Partners, Penny by Penny, My Two Feet Polka, Close Were We, Yes & No, One Family, Balancing the Books, Let There Be Time, One More Chance, Finale

A musical in two acts. The action takes place in and around London, England, in Dickensian Times.

Doug E. Holmes in *A Christmas Carol*

CRAZY FOR YOU

For creative credits see *Broadway Calendar—Past Seasons*; General Managers, Gatchell & Neufeld; Press, Bill Evans; Opened in the Music Hall, Dallas, on May 13, 1993.

CAST

Tess	Cathy Susan Pyles
Bobby Child	James Brennan
Bela Zangler	Stuart Zagnit
Irene Roth	Kay McClelland
Mother	Lenka Peterson
Polly Baker	Karen Ziemba succeeded by Crista Moore
Everett Baker	Carleton Carpenter
Lank Hawkins	Christopher Council
Ensemble	Sally Boyett, Sharon Ferrol, Heather Douglas, Nora Brennan, Angie L. Schworer, Lori Hart, Laura Catalano, John Boswell, Bobby Clark, Alan Gilbert, Gary Kirsch, Frederick J. Boothe, Keith Savage, Bill Brassea, Stephen Reed, Ron DeVito, Geoffrey Wade, Jeanette Landis

A musical comedy inspired by *Girl Crazy* (1930), in two acts with 17 scenes. The action takes place in New York City and Deadrock, Nevada, in the 1930s.

Right: Karen Ziemba, Carleton Carpenter in *Crazy For You*

DRIVING MISS DAISY

By Alfred Uhry; Director, Jeff Lane; Set, Helen Pond, Herbert Senn; Costumes, Joel Vig; Lighting, Ted Mather; General Manager, Robert A. Buckley; Company Manager, Peter H. Russell; Stage Manager, Ron Nash; Opened at the Bushnell, Hartford, CT, on February 15, 1994.

CAST

Daisy Werthan	Dorothy Loudon
Hoke Coleburn	Ted Lange
Boolie Werthan	Al Hamacher

A drama performed without intermission.

Left: Dorothy Loudon

149

EVITA

Music, Andrew Lloyd Webber; Lyrics, Tim Rice; Director/Choreographer, Larry Fuller; Costumes, Jonathan Bixby; Lighting, Steve Cochrane; General Manager, Robert V. Straus; Presented by Robert L. Young and PACE Theatrical Group; Press, Smyth/Katzen, Cile Stephens; Opened in the Cashman Center, Las Vegas, Nevada, on December 27, 1993, and still touring May 31, 1994.*

CAST

Eva	Donna Marie Asbury
	(alternate) Marla Schaffel
Che	Daniel C. Cooney
Peron	David Brummel
Magaldi	Frank Mastrone
Peron's Mistress	Elisa Sagardia
Tango Couple	David Roberts, Tara Tyrrell
Company	Dominic J. Abney, Neil Badders, Rebecca Beeth, Michael Biondi, Scott Blanks, Richard Byron, Thomas E. Cunningham, Mark Dovey, Holly Evers, William Gilinsky, Scott Hayward, Tito Hernandez, Russ Jones, R. Kim Jordan, Kelli Kruger, Sherry Lee, Linda Milani, David Roberts, William Schutte, Anna Simonelli, Calvin Smith, Lauren Thompson, Tara Tyrrell SWINGS: Cynthia Leigh Heim, Timothy Hogan

MUSICAL NUMBERS: Cinema in Buenos Aires, Requiem for Evita, Oh What a Circus, On this Night of a Thousand Stars, Eva Beware of the City, Buenos Aires, Goodnight and Thank You, Art of the Possible, Charity Concert, I'd Be Surprisingly Good for You, Another Suitcase in Another Hall, Peron's Latest Flame, A New Argentina, Entr'acte, On the Balcony of the Casa Rosada, Don't Cry for Me Argentina, High Flying Adored, Rainbow High, Rainbow Tour, The Actress Hasn't Learned, And the Money Kept Rolling In, Santa Evita, Waltz for Eva and Che, She is a Diamond, Dice are Rolling, Eva's Final Broadcast, Montage, Lament

A musical drama in two acts. The action takes place in Argentina. For original 1979 Broadway production with Patti Lupone, Mandy Patinkin, and Bob Gunton, see *Theatre World* Vol. 36.

Marc Bryan-Brown Photos

Donna Marie Asbury (center) and cast

Heather Mac Rae, Barbara Walsh

150 **Barbara Walsh**

Heather Mac Rae

FALSETTOS

Music/Lyrics, William Finn; Book, Mr. Finn, James Lapine; Director, Mr. Lapine; Orchestration, Michael Starobin; Musical Director, Ben Whitely; Set, Douglas Stein; Costumes, Ann Hould-Ward; Lighting, Frances Aronson; Presented by Barry and Fran Weissler; Tour resumed Spring, 1994.

CAST

Marvin	John Herrera
Whizzer	Peter Reardon
Mendel	Adam Heller
Jason	Brett Tabisel
Trina	Barbara Walsh
Charlotte	Heather MacRae
Cordelia	Julie Prosser

MUSICAL NUMBERS: Four Jews in a Room Bitching, Tight Knit Family, Love is Blind, Thrill of First Love, Marvin at the Psychiatrist, My Father's a Homo, Everyone Tells Jason to See a Psychiatrist, This Had Better Come To a Stop, I'm Breaking Down, Please Come to My House, Jason's Therapy, Marriage Proposal, Trina's Song, March of the Falsettos, Chess Game, Making a Home, Games I Play, Marvin Hits Trina, I Never Wanted to Love You, Father to Son, Welcome to Falsettoland, Year of the Child, Miracle of Judaism, Baseball Game, Day in Falsettoland, Racquetball: How Was Your Day, The Fight, Everyone Hates His Parents, What More Can I Say, Something Bad is Happening, Holding to the Ground, Days Like This, Cancelling the Bar Mitzvah, Unlikely Lovers, Another Miracle of Judaism, You Gotta Die Sometime, Jason's Bar Mitzvah, What Would I Do

A musical in two acts. The action takes place in New York City, 1979 and 1981.

Carol Rosegg/Martha Swope Photos

GOOD NEWS

Music/Lyrics, B. G. DeSylva, Lew Brown and Ray Henderson; Original Book, Laurence Schwab, Mr. DeSylva, Frank Mandel; Adaptation, Mark Madama and Wayne Bryan; Director, Mr. Madama; Musical Director/Orchestration, Craig Barna; Choreography, Linda Goodrich; Sets, Charles O'Connor; Costumes, Peggy J. Kellner; Lighting, David Neville.

CAST

Coach Johnson	Timothy W. Robu
Patricia Bingham	Jessica Boevers
Tom Marlowe	Michael Gruber
Connie Lane	Kim Huber
Prof. Charlotte Kenyon	Linda Michele
Pooch Kearney	Steve Frazier
Babe O'Day	Ann Morrison
Beef Saunders	Edward Staudenmayer
Bobby Randall	Scott Schafer
Sylvester	Dale Lee Heidebrecht
Ticket Taker	Charles Parker

The Boys

Slats	Matt Bogart
Windy	John B. Williford
Teammates	Daniel Charon, Scott Cherry, Marshall Koop, Gene Lubas, Larry D. Mullen, Tom Pardoe, Jason Reiff, Josh Rhodes, Bob Richard, Vincent Sandoval, Brad Setser, Christopher Scott, Billy Sprague, Jr., Dennis J. Yadon

The Girls

Millie	Jamie Waggoner
Flo	Alisa Klein
Corda	Lauren Kennedy
Lucy	Carolanne Marano
Coeds	Jaci Christman, Dawn DiPasquale, Therese Friedemann, Joele Hansen, Tonya Loveday, Ashley Mortimer, Allison K. Myers, Janet Renslow, Flynn Roberts, Rhea Roberts

MUSICAL NUMBERS: Overture, Opening Chorus, Good News, He's a Ladies' Man, Football Drill, Button Up Your Overcoat, Together/My Lucky Star, On the Campus, Best Things in Life Are Free, You're the Cream in My Coffee, Varsity Drag, Lucky in Love, Today's the Day, Girl of the Pi Beta Phi, Never Swat a Fly, Tait Song, Just Imagine, Dream Ballet, Keep Your Sunny Side Up, Life is Just a Bowl of Cherries, Finale

A new revision of the 1927 musical comedy featuring interpolated songs from the same composers.

Scott Schafer, Ann Morrison

Steve Frazier and *Good News* male cast

Susan Wood, Rosie O'Donnell, Ricky Paull Goldin in *Grease*

GREASE

For creative credits and musical numbers see *Broadway Calendar*; Tour opened in the Playhouse Theatre in Wilmington, Delaware, on January 13, 1994, and subsequently toured Boston, Washington, D.C., Seattle, and Costa Mesa, California.

CAST

Miss Lynch	Marcia Lewis
Patty Simcox	Michelle Blakely
Eugene Florczyk	Paul Castree
Jan	Heather Stokes
Marty	Megan Mullally
Betty Rizzo	Rosie O'Donnell
Doody	Sam Harris
Roger	Hunter Forest
Kenickie	Jason Opsahl
Sonny Latierri	Carlos Lopez
Frenchy	Jessica Stone
Sandy Dumbrowski	Susan Wood
Danny Zuko	Ricky Paull Goldin
Vince Fontaine	Brian Bradley
Cha-Cha	Sandra Purporo
Teen Angel	Billy Porter
Company	Clay Adkins, Melissa Bell, Patrick Boyd, Daty Grenfell, Ned Hannah, Denis Jones, Janice Lorraine, Allison Metcalf, H. Hylan Scott II, Lorna Shane, Patti D'Beck, Brian Paul Mendoza

Lewis J. Stadlen, Richard Muenz

GUYS AND DOLLS

For creative credits and musical numbers see *Broadway Calendar—Past Seasons*; Production Supervisor, Steven Beckler; Musical Director, Randy Booth; Production Manager, Peter Fulbright; Executive Producer, George MacPherson; Presented by ATP/Dodger, Roger Berlind, Kardana Productions, Tom Mallow, and Kennedy Center for the Performing Arts; Tour opened in the Bushnell Theatre, Hartford, CT, on September 15, 1992, and closed July 3, 1994.

CAST

Nicely-Nicely Johnson	Kevin Ligon
Benny Southstreet	Al DeCristo
Rusty Charlie/M.C.	Jay Brian Winnick
Sarah Brown	Patricia Ben Peterson
Arvide Abernathy	MacIntyre Dixon +1
Agatha	Patricia Grace Kennedy
Calvin	Steven Bogard
Martha	Heather Lee +2
Harry the Horse	James Dybas
Lt. Brannigan	Andy Umberger +3
Nathan Detroit	David Garrison +4
Angie the Ox	Charles Cermele
Miss Adelaide	Lorna Luft +5
Sky Masterson	Richard Muenz
Joey Biltmore	David Hart +6
Mimi	Michele O'Steen +7
Gen. Matilda B. Cartwright	Joy Franz
Big Julo	Lyle Kanouse
Drunk	David Vosburgh
Guys	Andy Blankenbuehler, Steven Bogard, Mr. Cermele, John Crutchman, Chris Davis, George Dudley, Lucio Fernandez, Christopher Gattelli, David Earl Hart, Jack Hayes, Jeffrey Howard, Darren Lee, Troy P. Liddell, Rod McCune, Kenneth McMullen, George Russell, Jim Testa, Sergio Trujillo, Jerome Vivona, Mr. Vosburgh, Mr. Winnick
Dolls	Roxanne Barlow, Linda Bowen, Lisa Dawn Cave, Kyle Craig, Kriss Dias, Patricia Grace Kennedy, Heather Lee, Joanne Manning, Michelle O'Steen, Daniela Panessa

UNDERSTUDIES: Steven Bogard (Sky), Lisa Dawn Cave (Mimi), Charles Cermele (Benny/Harry), Paul DePasquale (Sky/Nicely/Nathan), David Hart, Ken McMullen (Jule/Brannigan), Patricia Grace Kennedy (Cartwright), Heather Lee (Adelaide/Sarah), Beth McVey (Adelaide/Cartwright/Agatha/Martha), Andy Umberger (Nathan), David Vosburgh (Arvide/Harry), Jay Brian Winnick (Benny/Nicely) SWINGS: Mary MacLeod, Bill Burns, Beth McVey, Paul DePasquale

A new production of the 1950 musical in two acts. The action takes place in "Runyonland" around Broadway, and in Havana, Cuba.

+Succeeded by: 1. Donald Grody 2. Dawn Spare 3. Allen Fitzpatrick 4. Philip LeStrange 5. Beth McVey 6. George Dudley 7. Kyle Craig

Martha Swope Photos

Al DeCristo, Kevin Ligon, Jay Brian Winnick

Lewis J. Stadlen, Lorna Luft

Philip LeStrange, Beth McVey

HAIR

Music, Galt MacDermot; Lyrics/Book, Gerome Ragni and James Rado; Director, Mr. Rado; Set/Lighting, Rick Belzer; Costumes, Warren Morrill; Musical Director, Keith Thompson; Choreography, Joe Donovan; Production Supervisor, Jess M. Klarnett; General Manager, Niko Associates; Opened at the Morris A. Mechanic Theatre in Baltimore, Maryland, on February 22, 1994.

CAST

Berger ....Kent Dalian
Claude ....Luther Creek
Dionne ....Catrice Joseph
Woof ....Sean Jenness
Sheila ....Cathy Trien
Jeanie ....Ali Zorlas
Crissy ....Rochele Rosenberg
M.Mead ....Matthew Ferrell
Hubert ....Eric Davis
Company ....Alexander Baez, Eric Davis, Allen Edwards,
Matthew Ferrell, Selby D. Ham, Jr., Cat Hollingsworth,
Vanessa Jones, Edward Charles Lynch,
Meredith A. Murray, Jennifer Nygard, Deidre O'Neil,
Jason Paige, Melanie May Po, James Tindel,
Mark Eugene Wilson, Julia Woloszczyk

A new production of the 1967 musical in two acts. This version features three new musical numbers.

David Bedella, Carl Anderson, Danny Zolli
in *Jesus Christ Superstar*

JESUS CHRIST SUPERSTAR

Music, Andrew Lloyd Webber; Lyrics, Tim Rice; Director/Choreographer, Tony Christopher; Asst. Director, James O'Neil; Musical Director, Michael Rapp; Sets, Bill Stabile; Costumes, David Paulin; Lighting, Rick Belzer; Sound, Jonathan Deans; Special Effects, Gregg Stephens; Stage Manager, Alan Hall; Executive Producer, Forbes Candlish; Presented by Landmark Entertainment Group, Magic Promotions, and TAP Prods.; Opened in the Morris A. Mechanic Theatre, Baltimore, on December 15, 1992.

CAST

Jesus of Nazareth ....Ted Neeley
Judas Iscariot..Carl Anderson
Mary Magdalene...Irene Cara
Caiphas ....David Bedella
Annas ....Danny Zolli
Pontius Pilate ....Dennis DeYoung
Peter ....Kevin R. Wright
King Herod...Laurent Giroux
Ensemble ....James O'Neil, Nathanial Sanders, Stephen X. Ward,
Kate L. Snyder, Amy Splitt, Kirsten Young,
David Marques, J. Steven Campbell, Dawn Feusi,
Laurie Carter, Leesa Richards Humphrey,
Steve Campanella, Curtis Clark, Michelle DeJean,
Steve Geary, Eileen Kaden, Joseph P. McDonnell,
Tracy–Lynn Neff SWINGS: Larry Vickers,
Michelle Wylie

A new production of the 1971 musical featuring Neeley and Anderson recreating their roles from the 1973 film version.

Richard Feldman Photos

Ted Neeley in *Jesus Christ Superstar*

**Jim Madden, Walter Charles,
Judith Thiergaard, Lee Roy Reams**

LA CAGE AUX FOLLES

Music/Lyrics, Jerry Herman; Book, Harvey Fierstein; Director/Choreographer, Chet Walker; Music Director, James May; Orchestrations, Jim Tyler; Set, Ken Holamon; Costumes, Theoni V. Aldredge, Tom Augustine; Lighting, Tom Sturge; General Manager, Lonn Entertainment; Stage Manager, John M. Galo; Presented by Don Gregory in association with Saul Kaufman; Press, Alma Viator/Sally Pontarelli; Opened in the Shubert Theatre in Boston on December 29, 1993, and still touring May 31, 1994.

CAST

Georges	Walter Charles
Albin	Lee Roy Reams
Jean-Michel	Robert Lambert
Les Cagelles:	
Chantal	Keith Cromwell
Dermah	Troy Lambert
Nicole	Michael Quinn
Hanna/Hercule	Scott Spahr
Mercedes	Kyle Whyte
Bitelle	Janet Bushor
Lo Singh	Shawn Ku
Angelique/Paulette	Conny Sasfai
Phaedra	Jay Poindexter
Clo-Clo	David E. Liddell
Francis	Timothy Albrecht
Jacob	Robert L. Daye, Jr.
Anne	Jennifer West
Jacqueline	Susan Cella
M. Renaud	Jim Madden
Mme. Renaud	Judith Thiergaard
Etienne/Tabarro	Dale Hensley
Babette/Mme.Dindon	Donna Monroe
Colette	Janet Bushor
Edouard Dindon	Evan Thompson

UNDERSTUDIES: Dale Hensley (Albin), Jim Madden (Dindon), Jay Poindexter (Chantal), Timothy Albrecht (Jean-Michel), Judith Thiergaard (Dindon/Jacqueline), Andrew Sakaguchi (Renaud/Francis/Tabarro/Hercule/Etienne/Lo Singh/Clo-Clo/Phaedra/Dermah/Hanna), Michelle Bruckner (Anne/Mme. Renaud/Paulette/Babette/Colette/Angelique/Bittelle/Nicole), Michael Quinn (Mercedes)

MUSICAL NUMBERS: Overture, We Are What We Are, A Little More Mascara, With Anne on My Arm, Promenade, Song on the Sand, La Cage aux Folles, I Am What I Am, Entr'acte, Masculinity, Look Over There, Cocktail Counterpoint, The Best of Times, Finale

A tenth anniversary production of the 1983 musical in two acts.

Carol Rosegg/Martha Swope Photos

Lee Roy Reams

LES MISERABLES

For creative credits and musical numbers see *Broadway—Opened Past Seasons* section; Conductor, Robert S. Gustafson; Tour opened January 12, 1994, in Pasadena (Calif.) Civic auditorium before playing Singapore.

CAST INCLUDES

Jean Valjean	Donn Cook
Javert	David Masenheimer
Fantine	Alice Ripley
Thernardier	J. P. Dougherty
Mme. Thernardier	Gina Ferrall
Eponine	Jennifer Rae Beck
Cosette	Barbara Russell
Marius	Hayden Adams
Enjolras	Gary Mauer

Donn Cook of *Les Miserables*

Davis Gaines, Dale Kristien

Michael Piontek, Dale Kristien

THE PHANTOM OF THE OPERA

For creative credits and musical numbers see *Broadway—Opened Past Seasons* section; Musical Director, Roger Cantrell; Press, Merle Frimark, Marc Thibodeau; Opened at the Ahmanson Theatre, Los Angeles, on May 31, 1989.

CAST

The Phantom of the Opera	Davis Gaines
Christine Daae	Dale Kristien
Raoul, Vicomte de Chagny	Michael Piontek
Carlotta Giudicelli	Leigh Munro
Monsieur Andre	Norman Large
Monsieur Firmin	Calvin Remsberg
Madame Giry	Barbara Lang
Ubaldo Piangi	Gualtiero Negrini
Meg Giry	Elisabeth Stringer
Monsieur Reyer	D. C. Anderson
Auctioneer	Richard Gould
Porter/Marksman	Sean Smith
Monsieur Lefevre/Don Attilio/Passarino	Gary Marshal
Joseph Buquet	Gene Brundage
Firechief	Kris Pruet
Slave Master (*Hannibal*)	David Loring
Flunky/Stagehand	Stephen Moore
Policeman	Peter Atherton
Confidante (*Il Muto*)	Rhonda Dillon
Porter/Fireman	William Scott Brown
Page (*Don Juan Triumphant*)	Candace Rogers-Adler
Wardrobe Mistress	Gail Land Hart
Princess (*Hannibal*)	Jani Neuman
Madame Firmin	Rio Hibler-Kerr
Innkeeper's Wife (*Don Juan Triumphant*)	Catherine Caccavallo
Ballet Chorus of the Opera Populaire	Leslie-Noriko Beadles, Madelyn Berdes, Mary Alyce Laubacher, Natasha MacAller, Sylvia Rico, Connie, Versteeg
Ballet Swing	Irene Cho
Swings	Karen Benjamin, Joseph Dellger, Brad Scott

UNDERSTUDIES: Norman Large (Phantom), Joseph Dellger (Phantom, Andre/Raoul), Jani Neuman (Christine), Stephen Moore (Raoul), Sean Smith (Raoul/Andre), Richard Gould, Gary Marshal (Firmin), Brad Scott (Andre), Catherine Caccavallo, Rio Hibler-Kerr (Carlotta), Rhonda Dillon (Carlotta/Madame Giry), Karen Benjamin (Madame Giry), William Scott Brown, Kris Pruet (Piangi), Irene Cho, Mary Alyce Laubacher, Natasha MacAller (Meg), Tamra Shaker (Christine Standby), Elkin Antoniou (Ballet Swing).

A musical in two acts and a prologue. For musical numbers see *Broadway Calendar*.

Joan Marcus, Michael Lamont, Robert Millard Photos

(KENNEDY CENTER COMPANY)

The Phantom	Rick Hilsabeck
Christine	Terri Bibb, Sarah Pfisterer
Raoul	Nat Chandler

also with David Huneryager, Robert DuSold, Patricia Hurd, Olga Talyn, Gale Oxley, Patricia Ward

THE SECRET GARDEN

Music, Lucy Simon; Lyrics/Book, Marsha Norman; Based on the novel by Frances Hodgson Burnett; Director, Susan H. Schulman; Musical Director, Constantine Kitsopoulos; Choreography, Michael Lichtefeld; Orchestrations, William D. Brohn; Musical Supervision, Michael Kosarin; Sets, Heidi Landesman; Costumes, Theoni V. Aldredge; Lighting, Tharon Musser; Sound, Otts Munderloh; Company Manager, John Pasinato; Stage Manager, Dan W. Langhofer; Executive Producer, George MacPherson; Presented by Heidi Landesman, Rick Steiner, Jujamcyn Theatres/TV Asahi, Tom Mallow, ATP/Dodger, Pace Theatrical Group; Press, Laura Matalon; Tour opened in the Palace Theatre, Cleveland, Ohio, on April 28, 1992, and closed May 22, 1994.

CAST

Lily	Jacquelyn Piro
Mary Lenox	Jamie Cronin
	Lydia Ooghe (alternate)
Fakir	Andy Gale
Ayah	Susan Lucia Buonincontri
Rose (Mary's mother)	Jill Patton
Capt. Albert Lennox	Kevin Dearinger
Lt. Peter Wright	James Javore
Lt. Ian Shaw	Paul Jackel
Major Holmes	Marc Mouchet
Claire/Mrs. Winthrop	Roxann Parker
Alice (Rose's friend)	Cheryl Allison
Archibald Craven(Mary's uncle)	Kevin McGuire
Dr. Neville Craven (his brother)	Peter Samuel
Mrs. Medlock (housekeeper)	Mary Fogarty
Martha (a chambermaid)	Amanda Naughton
Dickon (her brother)	Roman Fruge
Ben (the gardner)	John Carpenter, Tad Ingram
Colin	Walter Dreyer Binger, Andy Bowser
William	David Elledge
Betsy	Karen Babcock
Timothy	Skip Lackey

UNDERSTUDIES: Cheryl Allison (Lily/Rose/Ayah), Marguerite Shannon (Lily/Ayah/Claire/Winthrop/Alice/Betsy), Peter Samuel (Archibald), Marc Mouchet (Archibald/Ben), David Elledge (Neville/Lennox/Wright/Shaw/Holmes), Paul Jackel (Neville/Lennox), James Javore (Neville/Holmes), Karen Babcock (Medlock/Martha/Rose/Claire/Winthrop/Alice), Roxann Parker (Medlock), Marguerite Shannon (Martha), Skip Lackey (Dickon/Fakir/Shaw), Oliver Woodall (Dickon/Fakir/Wright/Shaw/William/Ben/Timothy), Leigh Catlett (Wright/Holmes/William/Timothy), Janet Marian Moody (Betsy), SWINGS: Marguerite Shannon, Oliver Woodall, Leigh Catlett

MUSICAL NUMBERS: Opening Dream, There's a Girl, House Upon the Hill, I Heard Someone Crying, A Fine White Horse, A Girl in the Valley, It's a Maze, Winter's on the Wing, Show Me the Key, A Bit of Earth, Storm, Lily's Eyes, Round-Shouldered Man, Final Storm, The Girl I Mean to Be, Quartet, Race to the Top of the Morning, Wick, Come to My Garden, Come Spirit Come Charm, Disappear, Hold On, Letter Song, Where in the World, How Could I Ever Know, Finale

A musical in two acts with 18 scenes and prologue. The action takes place in Colonial India and at Misselthwaite Manor, North Yorkshire, England, in 1906.

Carol Rosegg/Martha Swope Photos

Mary Fogarty, Peter Samuel, Audra Ann McDonald, Andy Gale, (Front) Lydia Ooghe, Roxann Parker in *Secret Garden*

THE SISTERS ROSENSWEIG

For creative credits see *Broadway—Opened Past Seasons* section; Company Manager, Dana Sherman; Stage Manager, Augie Mericola; Opened in Norfolk, Virginia, on January 5, 1994, and still touring May 31, 1994.

CAST

Sara Goode	Mariette Hartley
Gorgeous Teitelbaum	Caroline Aaron
Mervyn Kant	Charles Cioffi
Pfeni Rosensweig	Joan McMurtrey
Geoffrey Duncan	Richard Frank
Tess Goode	Debra Eisenstadt
Tom Valiunus	Barry McEvoy
Nicholas Pym	Ian Stuart

Carol Rosegg/Martha Swope Photos

Joan McMurtrey, Caroline Aaron, Mariette Hartley in *The Sisters Rosensweig*

THE SOUND OF MUSIC

Music, Richard Rodgers; Lyrics, Oscar Hammerstein II; Book, Howard Lindsay and Russel Crouse; Director, James Hammerstein; Musical Director, Richard Parrinello; Choreography, Joel Bishoff; Sets/Lighting, Neil Peter Jampolis; Costumes, Jonathan Bixby; General Manager, Robert V. Strauss; Presented by Robert L. Young, Nicholas C. Litrenta, Jon B. Platt, and PACE Theatrical Group; Press, Smyth/Katzen, Kelly Bukolt; Opened in Baltimore's Lyric Opera House on November 27, 1993, and still touring May 31, 1994.

CAST

Maria	Marie Osmond
Capt. Von Trapp	Keir Dullea +1
Mother Abbess	Claudia Cummings
Max	John Tillotsen
Baroness Elsa	Jane Seaman
Baron Elberfeld	Jim Oyster
The Children:	
Liesl	Vanessa Dorman
Louisa	Laura Bundy
Friedrich	Erik McCormack
Kurt	Stephen Blosil
Brigitta	Sarah Zelle
Marta	Jacy DeFilippo
Gretl	Lisbeth Zelle
Rolf	Richard H. Blake
Company	Jill Bosworth, Mary C. Sheehan, Georgia Osborne, David Barron, Elizabeth Owens, Garrett States, Richard Neilson

MUSICAL NUMBERS: Preludium, The Sound of Music, Maria, My Favorite Things, Do Re Mi, Sixteen Going on Seventeen, The Lonely Goatherd, How Can Love Survive?, So Long Farewell, Rex Admiralis, Climb Every Mountain, No Way To Stop It, Ordinary Couple, Processional, Edelweiss, Finale

A new production of the 1959 musical in two acts. The action takes place in Austria, 1938.

+Succeeded by Garrett Stakes, Laurence Guittard

Neal Preston Photos

Top: Marie Osmond, Laurence Guittard
Center: Richard H. Blake, Vanessa Dorman
Bottom: John Tillotson and "Von Trapp" children

SWING: THE BIG BAND MUSICAL

Conceived/Directed/Choreographed by Randy Skinner; Musical Director/Orchestrations, Scot Wooley; Sets, Bill Clarke; Costumes, Michael Bottari and Ronald Case; Lighting, Jeremy Kumin; Company Manager, Charlene M. Reiss; Stage Manager, Charles St. Clair; Presented by Ron Kumin; Opened at the North Carolina School of the Arts.

CAST

Margaret Whiting

Debra Ann Draper	Tina Johnson
Wendy Edmead	Marcus Neville
Robert H. Fowler	Randy Skinner
Susan M. Haefner	Tom Stuart
Frantz G. Hall	Sean Frank Sullivan
Cheryl Howard	Elizabeth Ward

A big band revue in two acts.

Margaret Whiting and *Swing* company

THE WHO'S TOMMY

For creative credits and musical numbers see *Broadway—Opened Past Seasons* section; Musical Director, Wendy Bobbitt; Company Manager, Alan Ross Kosher; Production Stage Manager, Randall Whitescarver; Presented by PACE Theatrical Group and DODGER Productions; Press, Laura Matalon, Ginny Ehrich, Tim Choy, Wayne McWorter; Opened in Dallas' Music Hall on October 12, 1993, and still touring May 31, 1994.

CAST

Mrs. Walker	Jessica Molaskey
Capt. Walker	Jason Workman
Uncle Ernie	William Youmans
Minister	Daniel Marcus
Minister's Wife	Bertilla Baker
Nurse	Aiko Nakasone
Officer #1	Destan Owens
Officer #2	Steve Dahlem
Allied Soldier #1	Chris Ghelfi
Allied Soldier #2	Darrian C. Ford
Lover/Harmonica Player	Alec Timmerman
Tommy, age 4	Kelly Mady, Caitlin Newman
Tommy	Steve Isaacs
Judge/Kevin's father/Vendor/D.J.	Tom Rocco
Tommy, age 10	Robert Mann Kayser
Cousin Kevin	Roger Bart
Kevin's Mother	Betsy Allen
Local Lads/Security Guards	Mr. Timmerman, Mr. Ford, Mr. Ghelfi, Anthony Galde, Clarke Thorell, Mr. Dahlem
Local Lasses	Hilary Morse, Ms. Nakasone, Valerie DePena, Carla Renata Williams, Cindi Klinger, Ms. Allen
Hawker/Specialist	Destam Owens
The Gypsy	Kennya Ramsey
1st Pinball Lad	Anthony Galde
2nd Pinball Lad	Clarke Thorell
Specialist's Assistant	Valerie DePena
Sally Simpson	Hilary Morse
Mrs. Simpson	Cindi Klinger
Mr. Simpson	Daniel Marcus
Other Ensemble	Bertilla Baker

UNDERSTUDIES: Chris Gelfi, Alec Timermann (Tommy/Kevin), Craig Lawlor (Tommy at 10), Bertilla Baker, Christy Tarr (Mrs. Walker), Steve Dahlem, Vincent D'Elia (Capt. Walker), Daniel Marcus, Tom Rocco (Ernie), Tracey Langran, Carla Renata Williams (Gypsy) SWINGS: Vincent D'Elia, Tracey Langran, Christy Tarr, Randy Wojcik

Marcus/Bryan Brown Photos

Center: Jason Workman, Jessica Molaskey
Bottom: The *Tommy* company

PROFESSIONAL REGIONAL COMPANIES

ACTORS THEATRE OF LOUISVILLE

Louisville, Kentucky
Thirtieth Season

Producing Director, Jon Jory; Production Manager, Frazier W. Marsh; Production Stage Manager, Debra Acquavella; Set Designs, Paul Owen, John Lee Beatty, Terry Gipson, Ming Cho Lee; Public Relations Director, James Seacat

PRODUCTIONS & CASTS

THE COCOANUTS by Irving Berlin, George S. Kaufman; Director, Jon Jory; Music Director, Tom Wojtas; Choreography, Karma Camp; Sets, John Lee Beatty; Costumes, Nanzi Adzima; Lighting, Kenneth Posner CAST: Michael Kevin (Jamison), Adale O' Brien (Mrs. Potter), V. Craig Heidenreich (Yates), Gail Benedict (Penelope), Kate Suber (Polly), Bob Kirsh (Adams), Peter Zapp (Henry W. Schlemmer), Mark Sawyer-Dailey (Silent Sam), Fred Major (Hennessey), Mark Aldrich, Rae Dawn Belt, Kevin Berdini, Myra Browning, Angel Caban, Teresa Lynn Deihl, Russell Garrett, Karen Lifshey, Jeanette Palmer, Debbie Pavelka, Neil David Seibel, Mark Edgar Stephens, Branch Woodman
AIN'T WE GOT FUN? by Val Smith; Director, Julian Webber; Costumes, Laura Peterson; Lighting, Matthew J. Reinert CAST: Bob Burrus (Hollis), Ray Fry (Man/Priest/Wilmer/Morty), Katie MacNichol (Woman/Katherine), William McNulty (Operative), Sybil Walker (Mrs. Cantor/Flapper/Angie/Ada/Woman/Billy), Time Winters (Claude/Jackson/Ledford), Adam Whisner (Lindbergh/Pole-sitter), Sheila Daniels, Lee Soroko (Staff)
TO KILL A MOCKINGBIRD by Christopher Sergel, Sr.; Director, Barry Kyle; Costumes, Laura Patterson; Lighting, Marcus Dilliard CAST: Gaia Shepard (Scout), Nick Swarts (Jem), Michael Kevin (Atticus), Stephanie Berry (Calpurnia), Jeffrey Roth (Dill), Adale O'Brien (Maudie), Gail Benedict (Stephanie), Ardeth Pappas (Mrs. Dubose), V. Craig Heidenreich (Boo), William McNulty (Heck), Ray Fry (Judge), Clark Morgan (Rev. Sykes), Kia Christina Heath (Mayella), Mark Sawyer-Dailey (Bob), Vaughn McBride (Walter), Fred Major (Gilmer), Lawrence Hamilton (Tom), Danielle L. DiDio, Joshua Dean Gordon, David Gravens, Rebecca Herman, Richard Similio, Adam Whisner, Karen Edwards-Hunter, Foster Solomon, James E. Wright, Jr.
THE GIFT OF THE MAGI by O. Henry; Adaptation/Music/Lyrics/Music Direction, Peter Ekstrom; Director, Scott Zigler; Lighting, Reinert; Costumes, Hollis Jenkins-Evans CAST: Michele Golden (Della), Lewis Cleale (Jim)
SHERLOCK HOLMES AND THE CURSE OF THE SIGN OF FOUR by Dennis Rosa; Director, Frazier W. Marsh; Costumes, Laura Patterson; Lighting, Marcus Dilliard CAST: V. Craig Heidenreich (Holmes), Patrick Husted (Watson), Corliss Preston (Mary), Jennifer Carpenter (Little Wiggins), Fred Major (Thaddeus), Michal Kevin (Lestrade), Bob Scarlett (Captain), Bob Burrus (Jonathan), Mark Sawyer-Dailey (Hindu/Police), Richard Similio (Sholto/Stoker/Police), David Gravens (Stoker)
OLEANNA by David Mamet; Director, Scott Zigler; Costumes, Hollis Jenkins-Evans; Lighting, Matthew Reinert CAST: William McNulty (John), Monica Koskey (Carol)
DEATH AND THE MAIDEN by Ariel Dorfman; Director, Matthew Wilder; Costumes, Laura Patterson; Lighting, Robert M. Wierzel CAST: Karen Grassle (Paulina), Patrick Husted (Gerardo), Mike Genovese (Roberto), Joshua Dean Gordon, David Gravens, Sarah Rachel Wolinsky (Supernumeraries)
1969; Written/Directed by Tina Landau; Costumes, Laura Patterson; Lighting, Mary Louise Geiger CAST: J. Ed Araiza (Royce), Sheila Daniels (Stefanie), Jesse Sinclair Lenat (Lester), Barney O'Hanlon (Howie), Dee Pelletier (Roz), Neil David Seibel (Robert), Timothy D. Stickney (Curtis)
MY LEFT BREAST; Written/Performed by Susan Miller; Director, Nela Wagman; Costumes, Hollis Jenkins-Evans; Lighting, Matthew Reinert
BETTY THE YETI by Jon Klein; Director, Jeff Steitzer; Costumes, Laura Patterson; Lighting, Kenneth Posner CAST: Adale O'Brien (Claire), Mary Lee (Iko), Mia Dillon (Terra), V Craig Heidenreich (Russ), Caroline Swift (Creature)
TRIP'S CINCH by Phyllis Magy; Director, Lisa Peterson CAST: Steven Culp (Trip), Barbara eda-Young (Val), Mary Shultz (Lucy)
SLAVS! by Tony Kushner; Director, Lisa Peterson; Costumes, Esther Marquis; Lighting, Mary Louise Geiger CAST: Michael Kevin (Smukov), Gerald Hiken (Serge), Ray Fry (Aleksii), Fred Major (Ippolite), Steven Culp (Yegor), Kate Goehring (Katherina), Mary Shultz (Bonfila), Barbara eda-Young (Domik)
THE SURVIVOR by Jon Lipsky; Director, Vincent Murphy; Costumes, Esther Marquis; Lighting, Kenneth Posner CAST: Peter Kwong (Haing Ngor), Yunjin Kim (Huoy), Mark W. Conklin (Pen), Eric Steinberg (Man), Midori Nakamura (Woman), Nicole Scherzinger (Girl), Sokhanarith Moeur (Dancer)

Gerald Hiken, Annie-Laurie Audenaert in *Slavs!*

Steven Culp, Mary Shultz in *Trip's Cinch*

JULIE JOHNSON by Wendy Hammond; Director, Jon Jory; Costumes, Esther Marquis; Lighting, Kenneth Posner CAST: Lily Knight (Julie), Jennifer Carpenter (Lisa), Wilder Schwartz (Frankie), Carolyn Swift (Claire), V Craig Heidenreich (Miranda)
SHOTGUN by Romulus Linney; Director, Tom Bullard; Costumes, Laura Patterson; Lighting, Kenneth Posner CAST: Tom Stechschulte (John), Michael Kevin (Fred), Jeanne Paulsen (Beth), Bob Burrus (William), Gloria Cromwell (Sarah)
STONES AND BONES; Written/Directed by Marion McClinton CAST: Timothy D. Stickney (Mister Bones), Stacy Highsmith (Sistuh Stones), Terry E. Bellamy (Bone), Fanni Green (Stony)
THE LAST TIME WE SAW HER by Jane Anderson; Director, Frazier W. Marsh; Lighting, Matthew Reinert CAST: Fred Major (Hunter), Jennifer Hubbard (Fran)
SHADOWLANDS by William Nicholson; Director, Bob Bundy; Costumes, Laura Patterson; Lighting, Kenneth Posner CAST: Edwin C. Owens (C. S. Lewis), Peter Kybart (Christopher), Mark Sawyer-Dailey (Harrington), Bob Burrus (Oakley), V. Craig Heidenreich (Gregg), Fred Major (Warnie), Ryan Haeseley (Douglas), Karen Grassle (Joy), Joshua Dean Gordon (Priest/Waiter), Adale O'Brien (Registrar/Nurse), Masha A. Obolensky (Woman/Witness)
ROMEO AND JULIET by William Shakespeare; Director, Jon Jory; Costumes, Marcia Dixcy; Lighting, Scott Zielinski CAST: Vaughn McBride (Montague), Ann Bean (Lady Montague), Neal Huff (Romeo), S. Kyle Parker (Benvolio), Lee Soroko (Balthasar), Drew Fracher (Abram), Fred Major (Capulet), Robyn Hunt (Lady Capulet), Karenjune Sanchez (Juliet), John Mossman (Tybalt), David Gravens (Petruchio), Adale O'Brien (Nurse), Jesse Sinclair Lenat (Peter), Deryl Caitlyn (Sampson), Adam Whisner (Gregory), V Craig Heidenreich (Escalus), Eric Steinberg (Mercutio), Jamie Cheatham (Paris), John Camera (Friar Lawrence), Mark Sawyer-Dailey, Bob Burrus, Brian T. Ach, Mark Rizzo, Joshua Dean Gordon, Brett Cramp, Beil David Seibel, Richard Similio, Masha A. Obolensky, Rebecca Herman, Amanda McCluskey, Danielle L. DiDio, Sarah Rachel Wolinsky, Rae Dawn Belt, Nora Newbrough, Tyler Herman, Justin Michael, Laura Herman, Ashley Michael

Richard C. Trigg Photos

159

Shirley Jones, Marty Ingels in *Love Letters*

ALLENBERRY PLAYHOUSE

Boiling Springs, Pennsylvania

Producer, John J. Heinze; Artistic Director, Michael Haney; Sets, Robert Klingelhoefer; Costumes, Jennifer Eve Flitton, Lourdes Garcia; Lighting, Richard J. Frost, Richard Schaefer, Lynette Watley; Musical Director, Robert Felstein

PRODUCTIONS & CASTS

THEY'RE PLAYING OUR SONG; Music, Marvin Hamlisch; Lyrics, Carole Bayer Sager; Book, Neil Simon; Director, Michael Haney CAST: Michael McKenzie (Vernon), Helen Hadman (Sonia), Syd Rushing, Michael Minn, Greg Edsell, Holly Cruz, Debbie Lee Jones, Jennifer Haroutounian

MY ONE AND ONLY; Music, George Gershwin; Lyrics, Ira Gershwin; Book, Peter Stone, Timothy S. Mayer; Director, Michael Haney CAST: Bob Bucci, Michael Minn, Len Pfluger (Rhythm Boys), David Wanstreet (Chandler), Debbie Lee Jones (Mickey), Dale O'Brien (Nikki), Holly Cruz (Flounder), Amber Ruediger (Sturgeon), Tina Guice (Minnow), Jessica Poirer (Prawn), Susan Celeste (Kipper), Jennifer Haroutounian (Anchovie), Pam Cecil (Edythe), Syd Rushing (Montgomery), Fern-Marie Aames, Michael Gargani, Gene Sexton, Brad Watson, Jason Graham, Greta Storace, Greg Boris, Greg Edsell, Dale O'Brien

GYPSY; Music, Jule Styne; Lyrics, Stephen Sondheim; Book, Arthur Laurents; Director, Michael Haney CAST: Gregory Boris (Jocko), Catherine Blaine, Susan Celeste, Jennifer Haroutounian (Mothers), Jason Graham (George), Zebadiah Yates (Francis), Rachel Sterner (Balloon Girl), Todd Berkich, Joe Brier, Yulia Van Doren (Contestants), Samantha Shears (Baby Louise), Ashley Shoemeker (Baby June), Adrienne Doucette (Rose), Nick Cosco, Greg Edsell, Joe Briar, Fern-Marie Aames, Dale O' Brien (Herbie), Pamela Cecil (Louise), Jessica Poirer (June), Bob Bucci (Tulsa), Len Pfluger (Yonkers), Rich Adams (Angie), Gregory Boris (LA), Holly Cruz, Jennifer Schwab, Amy Warner (Tessie), Catherine Blaine (Mazeppa), Debbie Lee Jones (Electra)

BUS STOP by William Inge; Director, Michael Haney CAST: Fern-Marie Aames (Elma), Erin Elizabeth Hunter (Grace), Bob Crawford (Will), Amy Warner (Cherie), David Coxwell (Lyman), Jason Graham (Carl), Nick Cosco (Virgil), Scott Dalton (Bo)

MURDER AT THE VICARAGE by Agatha Christie; Director, Richard J. Frost CAST: David Coxwell (Vicar), Amy Warner (Griselda), Jason Graham (Dennis), Jennifer Chaiken (Mary), Bill Eissler (Ronald), Fern-Marie Aames (Lettice), Mary Rausch (Miss Marple), Catherine Blaine (Mrs. Price Ridley), Erin Elizabeth Hunter (Anne), Scott Dalton (Redding), David Brubaker (Haydock), Dale O'Brien (Slack), Greg Edsell (Jennings)

LAST OF THE RED HOT LOVERS by Neil Simon; Director, Michael Haney CAST: Dale O'Brien (Barney), Amy Warner (Elaine/Bobbi/Jeanette)

LOVE LETTERS by A. R. Gurney; Director, Michael Haney CAST: Amy Warner, Shirley Jones (Melissa), Michael Haney, Marty Ingels (Andrew)

DON'T DRESS FOR DINNER by Marc Camoletti; Adaptation, Robin Hawdon; Director, Michael Haney CAST: Ron Wisniski (Bernard), Helen Hedman (Jaqueline), Patrick Frederic (Robert), Catherine Blaine (Suzette), Amy Warner (Suzanne), Steve Smyser (George)

JAKE'S WOMEN by Neil Simon; Director, Michael Haney CAST: David Coxwell (Jake), Amy Warner (Maggie), Catherine Blaine (Karen), Rachel Sterner (Molly, 12), Fern-Marie Aames (Molly, 21), Kathleen Conroy (Edith), Helen Hedman (Julie), Jennifer Chaiken (Sheila)

Daig Weibly Photos

Nick Cosco, Amy Warner, Scott Dalton, Fern-Marie Aames, David Coxwell in *Bus Stop*

Davis Coxwell, Helen Hedman in *Jake's Women*

Dale O'Brien, Adrienne Doucette in *Gypsy*

Pamela Cecil, David Wanstreet in *My One and Only*

AMERICAN REPERTORY THEATRE

Cambridge, Massachusetts

Artistic Director, Robert Brustein; Managing Director, Robert J. Orchard; General Manager, Jonathan Seth Miller; Press Director, Katalin Mitchell

PRODUCTIONS & CASTS

HENRY IV: Parts 1 & 2 by William Shakespeare; Director, Ron Daniels; Sets, John Conklin; Costumes, Gabriel Berry; Lighting, Frances Aronson CAST: Remo Airaldi, Mark Boyett, Bill Camp, Thomas Derrah, Herb Downer, Alvin Epstein, Benjamin Evett, James Farmer, Jeremy Geidt, Nathaniel Gundy, Christopher Mark Johnson, Karm Kernwell, Will Lebow, Robert McDonough, Royal Miller, Vontress Mitchell, Phillip Munson, Todd Peters, Maggie Rush, Noble Shropshire, Kevin Waldron, Jessica Walling, Jack Willis, William Young
WHAT THE BUTLER SAW by Joe Orton; Director, David Wheeler; Set, Derek McLane; Costumes, Catherine Zuber; Lighting, John Ambrosone CAST: Thomas Derrah (Prentice), Elizabeth Marvel (Geraldine), Margaret Gibson (Mrs. Prentice), Benjamin Evett (Nicholas), Alvin Epstein (Rance), William Young (Sgt. Match)
THE CHERRY ORCHARD by Anton Chekhov; Adaptation, Robert Brustein; Director, Ron Daniels; Set, George Tsypin; Costumes, Catherine Zuber; Lighting, Frances Aronson CAST: Maggie Rush (Dunyasha), Jack Willis (Lopakhin), Benjamin Evett (Simyon), Alvin Epstein (Firs), Claire Bloom (Lyubov), Karen Phillips (Anya), Miki Whittles (Varya), Jeremy Geidt (Leonid), Patti Allison (Carlotta), Remo Airaldi (Boris), Royal Miller (Pyotr), Ajay Naidu (Yasha), Randall Jaynes (Tramp)
A TOUCH OF THE POET by Eugene O'Neill; Director, Joe Dowling; Sets, Derek McLane; Costumes, Catherine Zuber; Lighting, Frances Aronson CAST: Royal Miller (Mickey), Jack Willis (Jamie), Elizabeth Marvel (Sara), Dearbhla Molloy (Nora), Daniel J. Travanti (Cornelius), Jeremy Geidt (Dan), Alvin Epstein (Paddy), Kevin Waldron (Patch), Margaret Gibson (Deborah), Thomas Derrah (Nicholas)
THE AMERICA PLAY by Suzan-Lori Parks; Director, Marcus Stern; Sets, Allison Koturbash; Costumes, Gail Astrid Buckley; Lighting, John Ambrose CAST: Terry Alexander (Founding Father), Kim Brockington (Lucy), Royal Miller (Brazil), Siobhan Brown (Woman), Vontress Mitchell (Man)
HOT 'N' THROBBING by Paula Vogel; Director, Anne Bogart; Set, Christine Jones; Costumes, Jenny Fulton CAST: Alexandra Loria (Voice Over), Diane D'Aquila (Woman), Amy Louise Lammert (Girl), Royal Miller (Voice), Randall Jaynes (Boy), Jack Willis (Man)
PICASSO AT THE LAPIN AGILE by Steve Martin; Director, David Wheeler; Set, Christine Jones; Costumes, Catherine Zuber; Lighting, John Ambrose CAST: Paul Benedict (Freddy), J. Slavit (Gaston), Leslie Beatty (Germaine), Thomas Derrah (Einstein), Tresha Rodriguez (Suzanne), Will LeBow (Sagot), Bill Camp (Picasso), James Farmer (Schmendiman), Sarah Newhouse (Countess), Shauna Hewrose (Admirer), Christopher Johnson (Visitor)
SHLEMIEL THE FIRST; Conceived/Adapted by Robert Brustein from play by Isaac Bashevis Singer; Music, Hankus Netsky, Zalmen Mlotek; Lyrics, Arnold Weinstein; Director/Choreographer, David Gordon; Set, Robert Israel; Costumes, Catherine Zuber; Lighting, Peter Kaczorowski CAST: Rosalie Gerut (Mrs. Shlemiel), Larry Block (Shlemiel), Marilyn Sokol (Gittel/Sender/Yenta), Remo Airaldi (Mottel/Moishe/Chaim), Vontress Mitchell (Zeinvel), Scott Cunningham (Mendel/Man), Benjamin Evett (Dopey/Zalman), Charles Levin (Gronam Ox)

Richard Feldman Photos

Jack Willis, Claire Bloom, Alvin Epstein, Jeremy Geidt in
Cherry Orchard

Thomas Derrah, Bill Camp in *Picasso at the Lapin Agile*

Shlemiel the First

Elizabeth Marvel, Dearbhla Molloy, Daniel J. Travanti in *Touch of the Poet* 161

Denis O'Hare, Kate Buddeke in *Dancing at Lughnasa*

Henry Strozier, Kathryn Meisle,
Jurian Hughes in *Twelfth Night*

Ellen Karas, Ralph Cosham in *Revenger's Comedies*

ARENA STAGE

Washington, D.C.
Forty-Third Season

Artistic Director, Douglas C. Wager; Executive Director, Stephen Richard; Founding Director, Zelda Fichandler; Press, Ann Greer, Regan Byrne

PRODUCTIONS & CASTS

TWELFTH NIGHT by William Shakespeare; Director, Douglas C. Wager; Sets/Costumes, Zack Brown; Lighting, Allen Lee Hughes CAST: Gary Slaon (Orsino), M. E. Hart (Valentine), Michael Chaban (Curio), Sharon Washington (Viola), T. J. Edwards (Capt./Priest), Jurian Hughes (Maria), David Marks (Toby Belch), Ralph Cosham (Andrew Aguecheek), Jeffery V. Thompson (Feste), Kathryn Meisle (Olivia), Henry Strozier (Malvolio), Taegle F. Bougere (Sebastian), Wendell Wright (Antonio), Michael W. Howell (Fabian), Caroline Gregg (Harp)
DANCING AT LUGHNASA by Brian Friel; Director, Kyle Donnelly; Set, Linda Buchanan; Costumes, Paul Tazewell; Lighting, Rita Pietraszek CAST: Denis O'Hare (Michael), Kate Buddeke (Maggie), Jenny Bacon (Chris), Pamela Nyberg (Agnes), Kate Goehring (Rose), Tana Hicken (Kate), Patrick Clear (Gerry), Richard Bauer (Jack)
THE PRICE by Arthur Miller; Director, Joe Dowling; Set, F. Hallinan Flood; Costumes, Paul Tazewell; Lighting, Allen Lee Hughes CAST: Stanley Anderson (Victor), Robert Prosky (Solomon), James B. Sikking (Walter), Halo Wines (Esther)
A SMALL WORLD by Mustapha Matura; Director, Kyle Donnelly; Set, Loy Arcenas; Costumes, Paul Tazewell; Lighting, Nancy Schertler CAST: Franchelle Stewart Dorn (Carol), Wendell Wright (Herman)
THE REVENGER'S COMEDIES by Alan Ayckbourn; Director, Douglas C. Wager; Sets, Thomas Lynch; Lighting, Allen Lee Hughes CAST: Richard Bauer (Lipscott), Helen Carey (Daphne/Hilary), Ralph Cosham (Henry), John Deyle (Percy/Graham), June Hansen (Winnie/Mrs. Bulley), Tana Hicken (Imogen), Michael W. Howell (Driver/Eugene), Ellen Karas (Karen), David Marks (Bruce), Jennifer Mendenhall (Norma/Tracey), Arthur S. Nordlie (Motorcyclist), Nancy Robinette (Lady Ganton/Lydia), Henry Strozier (Anthony), Jeffery V. Thompson (Jeremy), Rainn Wilson (Oliver), Halo Wines (Veronica)
A ROOM OF ONE'S OWN by Virginia Woolf; Adaptation/Direction, Patrick Garland; Set/Lighting, Bruce Goodrich CAST: Eileen Atkins (Virginia Woolf)

Joan Marcus, Carol Pratt Photos

Stanley Anderson, Halo Wines in *The Price*

ARIZONA THEATRE COMPANY

Tucson and Phoenix, Arizona

Artistic Director, David Ira Goldstein; Managing Director, Robert Alpaugh; Public Relations Director, Marion Owsnitzki

PRODUCTIONS & CASTS

SHADOWLANDS by William Nicholson; Director, David Ira Goldstein; Set, Bill Forrester; Costumes, Rose Pederson; Lighting, Robert Peterson CAST: Ken Ruta, Judith Roberts, Mitchell Edmonds, Laurence Ballard, Jeremy Lelliott, Oliver Cliff, Roberto Guajardo, Beth Cash, Ken Love, Lawrence Hecht
DREAMS FROM A SUMMER HOUSE; Music, John Pattison; Lyrics/Book, Alan Ayckbourn; Directors, Jeff Steitzer, David Ira Goldstein; Musical Director, Jerry Wayne Harkey; Sets, Tom Butsch; Costumes, Laura Crow; Lighting, Rick Paulsen CAST: Suzanne Bouchard, Rachel Coloff, David Dollase, Burt Edwards, Liz McCarthy, Darcy Pulliam, R. Hamilton Wright, Greg Zerkle
THE SEAGULL by Anton Chekhov; Translation/Adaptation, Toni Haring-Smith; Director, Olympia Dukakis; Set, Michael Miller; Costumes, Sigrid Insull; Lighting, Scott Zielinski CAST: Randy Danson, Thomas Schall, Christina Zorich, Jason Dietz, Apollo Dukakis, Maggie Abeckerly, Pamela Holden Stewart, Maury Ginsberg, Bo Brundin, Thom Keane-Koutsoukos, Phillip Connery, Bert Squire
DEATH AND THE MAIDEN by Ariel Dorfman; Director, Matthew Wiener; Set, Greg Lucas; Costumes, Tina Cantu Navarro; Lighting, Dennis Parichy CAST: Maggie Palomo, Luis Perez, Geno Silva
SOME ENCHANTED EVENING: THE SONGS OF RODGERS AND HAMMERSTEIN; Conception, Jeffrey B. Moss; Director, Marcia Milgrom Dodge; Musical Director, Jerry Wayne Harkey; Sets/Costumes, Zack Brown; Lighting, Kenneth Posner CAST: Mary Lou Barber, Frank DiPasquale, Alisa Gyse-Dickens, Gary Jackson, Cathy Wydner
LIPS TOGETHER TEETH APART by Terrence McNally; Director, Andrew J. Traister; Set, Greg Lucas; Costumes, David Kay Mickelsen; Lighting, Tracy Odishaw CAST: Robertson Dean, Linda Emond, Leslie Hendriz, Don Lee Sparks

Tim Fuller Photos

Top: **Jerry Wayne Harkey, Alisa Gyse-Dickens**
in *Some Enchanted Evening*

Center: **Don Lee Sparks, Leslie Hendrix**
in *Lips Together Teeth Apart*

Bottom: **Maggie Palomo, Geno Silva, Luis Perez**
in *Death and the Maiden*

163

CALDWELL THEATRE COMPANY

Boca Raton, Florida
Eighteenth Season

Artistic/Managing Director, Michael Hall; Company Manager, Patricia Burdett; Costume Designer, Patricia Bowes; Publicity Director, Paul Perone

PRODUCTIONS & CASTS

PICNIC by William Inge; Director, Michael Hall; Sets, Frank Bennett; Lighting, Thomas Salzman CAST: Benjamin Bedenbaugh (Bomber), April Daras (Christine), Elizabeth Dimon (Irma), Carol Emshoff (Flo), John FitzGibbon (Howard), Julia Flood (Rosemary), Joy Johnson (Mrs. Potts), Marc Kudisch (Hal), Deidre O'Neil (Madge), Carolyn Pasquantonio (Millie), Mark Schaller (Alan)

SOMEONE WHO'LL WATCH OVER ME by Frank McGuinness; Director, Michael Hall; Set, Tim Bennett; Lighting, Thomas Salzman CAST: Jeffrey Blair Cornell (Adam), John Gardiner (Michael), Neal Moran (Edward)

MY THREE ANGELS by Sam and Bella Spewack; Director, Michael Hall; Sets, Frank Bennett; Lighting, Thomas Salzman CAST: John Felix (Joseph), John FitzGibbons (Jules), Julia Flood (Emilie), John Gardiner (Henri), Peter Haig (Felix), Harriet Oser (Mme. Parole), Carolyn Pasquantonio (Marie Louise), Jim Ryan (Alfred), Tom Wahl (Paul), David Schmittou (Lieutenant)

PAPA by John deGroot; Director, John Henry Davis; Set, Tim Bennett; Lighting, F. Mitchell Dana CAST: Len Cariou (Ernest Hemingway)

LATER LIFE by A. R. Gurney; Director, Michael Hall; Set, Frank Bennett; Lighting, Thomas Salzman CAST: John FitzGibbon (Men), John Gardiner (Austin), Kathleen Huber (Ruth), Pat Nesbit (Women)

OIL CITY SYMPHONY by Mike Craver, Mark Hardwick, Debra Monk, and Mary Murfitt; Director, Ms. Murfitt; Set, Tim Bennett; Lighting, Thomas Salzman CAST: Mike Craver (Mike), Philip Cress (Mark), Mary Ehlinger (Debbie), Mary Murfitt (Mary)

Paul Perone Photos

Top: Mike Craver, Mary Ehlinger, Philip Cress, Mary Murfitt in *Oil City Symphony*
2nd Photo: Deidre O'Neil, Marc Kudisch in *Picnic*
3rd Photo: Jeffrey Blair Cornell, Neal Moran, John Gardiner in *Someone Who'll Watch Over Me*

164 John FitzGibbon, David Schmittou, Jim Ryan, John Felix in *My Three Angels*

Len Cariou in *Papa*

CENTER THEATRE GROUP

AHMANSON THEATER (AT THE JAMES A. DOOLITTLE)

Los Angeles, California
Twenty-seventh Season

Producing Director, Gordon Davidson; Managing Director, Charles Dillingham; General Manager, Douglas C. Baker; Press/Advertising Director, Tony Sherwood; Press Assistant, Nicole Gorak

PRODUCTIONS & CASTS

CONVERSATIONS WITH MY FATHER by Herb Gardner; Director, Daniel Sullivan; Set, Tony Walton; Costumes, Robert Wojewodski; Lighting, Pat Collins CAST: Judd Hirsch (Eddie), James Sutorius (Charlie), John Colicos, David Margulies (Zaretsky), Andrew Bloch, Jake Dengel (Finney), J. D. Daniels (Young Charlie), Gloria Dorson (Hannah), Mike Genovese, William Biff McGuire (Nick), Tony Gillan (Josh/Joey), Benny Grant (Young Joey), William Lucking (Blue), John Procaccino (Jimmy), Gordana Rashovich (Gusta), William H. Bassett, Robert Canaan, Rachel Davies, Alan Feinstein, Matthew McCurley, Jordan Oschin
FOOL MOON; Created by Bill Irwin and David Shiner; Set, Douglas Stein; Costumes, Bill Kellard; Lighting, Nancy Schertler CAST: David Shiner, Bill Irwin, Red Clay Ramblers
FALSETTOS; Music/Lyrics, William Finn; Book, Mr. Finn, James Lapine; Director, Mr. Lapine; Set, Douglas Stein; Costumes, Ann Hould-Ward; Lighting, Frances Aronson CAST: Michael Rupert (Marvin), Stephen Bogardus (Whizzer), Chip Zien (Mendel), Barbara Walsh (Trina), Heather MacRae (Charlotte), Carolee Carmello (Cordelia), Sivan Cotel, Brett Tabisel (Jason),Ralph Bruneau, Susan Goodman, Jay Montgomery
THE SISTERS ROSENSWEIG by Wendy Wasserstein; Director, Dan Sullivan; Sets, John Lee Beatty; Costumes, Jane Greenwood; Lighting, Pat Collins CAST: Mariette Hartley (Sara), Caroline Aaron (Gorgeous), Charles Cioffi (Mervyn), Joan McMurtrey (Pfeni), Richard Frank (Geoffrey), Debra Eisenstadt (Tess), Barry McEvoy (Tom), Ian Stuart (Nicholas), Maria Cellario, Sarah Halley, Sean Francis Howse, Albert Owens, Hal Robinson, Marsha Waterbury

Jay Thompson Photos
Marc Bryan-Brown Photos

Top: Stephen Bogardus, Chip Zien, Michael Rupert, Sivan Cotel in *Falsettos*
Center: Bill Irwin, David Shiner in *Fool Moon*
Right: Tony Gillan, Judd Hirsch in *Conversations with My Father*

165

Above: Ric Salinas, Marga Gomez, Richard Montoya,
Herbert Siguenza in *Carpa Clash*
Top Left: Howie Seago, Ben Halley, Jr. in *The Persians*
Bottom: Raphael Sbarge, Janellen Steininger in *Wood Demon*

CENTER THEATRE
GROUP/MARK TAPER FORUM

Los Angeles, California
Twenty-seventh Season

PRODUCTIONS & CASTS

THE PERSIANS by Aeschylus; Adaptation, Robert Auletta; Music, Hamza El
Din; Director, Peter Sellars; Costumes, Dunya Ramicova; Lighting, James F.
Ingalls CAST: Ben Halley, Jr., Joseph Haj, Martinus Miroto (Chorus), Cordelia
Gonzalez (Atossa), Howie Seago (Ghost), John Ortiz (Xerxes)
POUNDING NAILS IN THE FLOOR WITH MY FOREHEAD; Written/
Performed by Eric Bogosian; Director, Jo Bonney; Lighting, Paulie Jenkins
CAPRA CLASH; Written/Performed by Culture Clash (Richard Montoya, Ric
Salinas, Herbert Siguenza), Marga Gomez
MIMI'S MONOLOGUE; Written/Performed by Marga Gomez; Director, Jose
Luis Valenzuela; Set, Edward E. Haynes, Jr.; Costumes, Patssi Valdez; Lighting,
Jose Lopez
DEATH AND THE MAIDEN by Ariel Dorfman; Director, Robert Egan; Set,
Yael Pardess; Costumes, Todd Roehrman; Lighting, Martin Aronstein CAST:
Wanda De Jesus (Paulina), Tomas Milian (Roberto), Jimmy Smits (Gerardo),
Marcelo Tubert (Friend)
THE WOOD DEMON by Anton Chekhov; Translation, Nicholas Saunders and
Frank Dwyer; Director, Mr. Dwyer; Sets/Lighting, D. Martyn Bookwalter; Cos-
tumes, Holly Poe Durbin CAST: John Achorn, John Apicella, Anne Gee Byrd,
Marsha Dietlin, Nike Doukas, Frank Dwyer, Mark Harelik, Dan Kern, Eric Allan
Kramer, Jeremy Lawrence, Donald Sage Mackay, Dakin Matthews, Rose
Portillo, Lawrence Pressman, Nicholas Saunders, Raphael Sbarge, Mary Stark,
Janellen Steininger, Lorraine Toussaint, John Walcutt
BANDIDO!; Book/Lyrics, Luis Valdez; Music, Lalo Schifrin; Director, Jose Luis
Valenzuela; Sets, Victoria Petrovich; Costumes, Julie Weiss; Lighting, Geoff
Korf; Musical Director, David Holcenberg CAST: Enrique Castillo (Abdon),
Richard Coca (Chavez), Patty Holley (Kate/Mother), Lettie Ibarra (Sally),
Marabina Jaimes (Rita), Jeff Juday (Lewis/Bones), Linda Kerns (Mrs. Snyder),
Linda Lopez (Soledad/Holly B. Damn), Sal Lopez (Gonzales), Michele Mais
(Jenny), A Martinez (Tiburcio), George McDaniel (Sheriff/Snyder), Tony Perez
(Feliz), Clive Revill (Impresario/Priest), Rafael H. Robledo (Old Gabriel), Mark
Slamma (Gentleman/Minstrel), Pamela Winslow (Daisy)
THE WAITING ROOM by Lisa Loomer; Director, David Schweizer; Set,
Mark Wendland; Costumes, Deborah Nadoolman; Lighting, Anne Mitello
CAST: June Kyoko Lu (Forgiveness from Heaven), Lela Ivey (Victoria), Leah
Maddrie (Brenda), Jacalyn O'Shaughnessy (Wanda), Robert Picardo (Douglas),
Simon Templeman (Oliver), Tony Simotes (Ken), Kurt Fuller (Larry), Jim Ishida
(Blessing from Heaven), Brian Brophy, Ken Narasaki, Jason Reed (Orderlies)

Jay Thompson Photos

Marabina Jaimes, Pamela Winslow, Patty Holley, Lettie Ibarra, A Martinez, Michele Mais, Linda Lopez, Linda Kerns in *Bandido*

Jimmy Smits, Tomas Milian in *Death and the Maiden*

Eric Bogosian in *Pounding Nails...*

June Kyoko Lu, Leah Maddrie, Jacalyn O'Shaughnessy, Lela Ivey in *The Waiting Room*

CINCINNATI PLAYHOUSE IN THE PARK

Cincinnati, Ohio
Thirty-fourth Season

Producing Artistic Director, Edward Stern; Executive Director, Buzz Ward; Production Manager, Phil Rundle; Public Relations Director, Peter M. Robinson

PRODUCTIONS & CASTS

HARVEY by Mary Chase; Director, John Going; Sets, James Eolk; Costumes, Elizabeth Covey; Lighting, Kirk Bookman CAST: Tia Speros (Myrtle Mae), Polly Holliday (Veta), Walter Rhodes (Elwood), Norma Niinemets (Mrs. Chauvenet), Crista Moore (Ruth), Jack Cirillo (Duane), Dennis Ryan (Lyman Sanderson), Matt Conley (Chumley), Julia Curry (Betty), Donald Christopher (Judge), Bill Keeton (Lofgren)
DEATH AND THE MAIDEN by Ariel Dorfman; Director, Edward Stern; Sets, Paul R. Shortt; Costumes, Jeanette de Jong; Lighting, John R. Lasiter CAST: Greta Lambert (Paulina), Greg Thornton (Gerardo), Erik Frederickson (Roberto)
TO KILL A MOCKINGBIRD by Christopher Sergel; Director, Charles Towers; Sets, Bill Clarke; Costumes, Elizabeth A. Novak; Lighting, Jackie Manasee CAST: Robin Moseley (Jean), Patrick Justin Vaughn (Jem), Stevia Haller (Scout), Alan Mixon (Walter/Judge), Tom Stechschulte (Atticus), Marjorie Johnson (Calpurnia), Dixie Utter (Mrs. Dubose), Ronnie Strong (Dill), Robert Elliott (Radley/Ewell), Donald Christopher (Heck), Rodney Clark (Gilmer/Boo), Deirdre Madigan (Mayella), Reginald Madigan (Mayella), Reginald Willis (Rev. Sykes), Danny Johnson (Tom)
JACQUES BREL IS ALIVE AND WELL IN PARIS; Conception/English Lyrics, Eric Blau and Mort Shuman; Director/Choreographer, Pamela Hunt; Musical Director, Darren R. Cohen; Set, Jim Morgan; Costumes, Daniel Lawson; Lighting, Mary Jo Dondlinger CAST: Darius de Haas, Shelly Dickinson, Don Goodspeed, Jan Horvath
THE WINGFIELD TRILOGY by Dan Needles; Director, Douglas Beattie CAST: Rod Beattie (Walt Wingfield)
THE SUM OF US by David Stevens; Director, Jamie Brown; Sets, James Noone; Costumes, Randall E. Klein; Lighting, Phil Monat CAST: James Doerr (Harry), Mitchell Riggs (Jeff), Jeffrey Plunkett (Greg), Susanne Marley (Joyce)
DANCING AT LUGHNASA by Brian Friel; Director, Edward Stern; Sets, John Ezell; Costumes, Dorothy L. Marshall; Lighting, Peter E. Sargent CAST: Greg Thornton (Michael), Katherine Leask (Chris), Brooks Almy (Maggie), Mary O'Brady (Agnes), Katherine Heasley (Rose), Darrie Lawrence (Kate), Russ Jolly (Gerry), Donald Ewer (Jack)
ALCHEMY OF DESIRE/DEAD-MAN'S BLUES by Caridad Svich; Director, Lisa Peterson; Sets, Neil Patel; Costumes, Candice Donnelly; Lighting, Mimi Jordan Sherin CAST: Sheila M. Tousey (Simone), Patricia Mattick (Tirasol), Camille D'Ambrose (Caroline), Susan Barnes (Selah), Kate Malin (Miranda), Scott Ripley (Jamie)
THE MERRY WIVES OF WINDSOR, TEXAS; Music/Lyrics, Jack Herrick with Tommy Thompson, Bland Simpson, Jim Wann, John Foley; Conceived/Adapted by John L. Haber; Director, Edward Stern; Musical Director, Jack Herrick; Sets, Kevin Rupnik, Edmund A. LeFevre, Jr.; Costumes, Candice Donnelly; Lighting, Kirk Bookman CAST: Donald Christopher (Sheriff Shallow), Anthony Dodge (Preacher Hugh), Russ Jolly (Slender), Deborah Jolly (Missanne Page), Darcy Pulliam (Margaret Anne), Matt Conley (George), Noble Shropshire (Dr. Caius), Tonye Patano (Mistress Quickly), Geoffrey Simmons (Rugby), Sarah Knapp (Aggie), Rob Ladd (Host), Gary Sandy (Joe Frank), Michael Wirick (Lucas), Stephen Travis Wilson (Chester), Keith Jochim (Col. Falstaff), Mark Roberts (Bardolph), Jack Herrick (Pistol), Clay Buckner (Nym), Chris Frank (Robin the Orphan Boy), Christian Hoff (Fenton)
THE VOICE OF THE PRAIRIE by John Olive; Director, Steven Woolf; Sets, Karen TenEyck; Costumes, Jeanette De Jong; Lighting, Laura Manteuffel CAST: Joneal Joplin, Jack Cirillo, Susie Wall

Sandy Underwood Photos

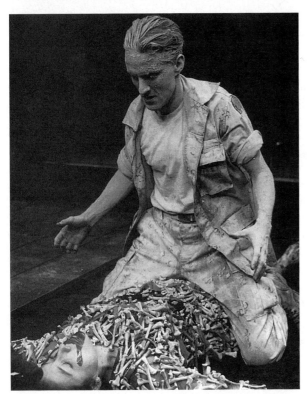

Top: Tom Stechschulte, Stevia Haller in *To Kill a Mockingbird*
Center: Scott Ripley (kneeling), Sheila M. Tousey
in *Alchemy of Desire/Dead-Man's Blues*
Left: Gary Sandy in *Merry Wives of Windsor, Texas*

DELAWARE THEATRE COMPANY

Wilmington, Delaware
Fifteenth Season

Artistic Director, Cleveland Morris; Managing Director, David Edelman; Assistant Artistic Director, Danny Peak; Production Manager, Eric Schaeffer; Marketing Director, Kevin Moore

PRODUCTION & CASTS

THE TRIP TO BOUNTIFUL by Horton Foote; Director, Cleveland Morris; Set/Lighting, Lewis Folden; Costumes, Marla Jurglanis CAST: Dorothea Hammond (Carrie Watts), Stephen Cowie (Ludie), T. Cat Ford (Jessie), Candace Dian Leverett (Thelma), Traber Burns, Danny Peak, James Doerr (Ticket Men), Will Stutts (Sheriff), Jane Beingessner, David G. Knappe, Chris Stanton (Travelers)
IMAGO: THE THEATRE MASK ENSEMBLE with Carol Triffle, James J. Peck, Shawn Sturnick, Jerry Mouawad
SHE STOOPS TO CONQUER OR THE MISTAKES OF A NIGHT by Oliver Goldsmith; Director, Cleveland Morris; Sets, Eric Schaeffer; Lighting, Rebecca G. Frederick; Costumes, Marla Jurglanis CAST: Anne MacMillan (Mrs. Hardcastle), Patrick Tull (Hardcastle), Andrew Prosky (Tony), Celeste Ciulla (Miss Hardcastle), Mary Dixie Carter (Miss Neville), John Prosky (Marlow), Jordan Lage (Hastings), Richard Thomsen (Sir Charles), Nick Santoro (Diggory), Jane Beingessner (Pimple), Gill Braswell, Sydney Davolos, Kevin Freel, Barclay Jefferis
JOE TURNER'S COME AND GONE by August Wilson; Director, L. Kenneth Richardson; Set, Donald Eastman; Lighting, Donald Holder; Costumes, Mary Mease Warren CAST: William Jay Marshall (Seth), Delores Mitchell (Bertha), Leonard Parker (Bynum), Alan Nebelthau (Selig), Troy Winbush (Jeremy), Paul Garrett (Loomis), Catherine Jean Hall (Zonia), Allison Eikeren (Matyie), Fred Mathis (Reuben), Messeret (Molly), Judy Tate (Martha)
I HATE HAMLET by Paul Rudnick; Director, Dennis Delaney; Set, Bennet Averyt; Lighting, Christopher Gorzelnik; Costumes, Marla Jurglanis CAST: Trish Hunter (Felicia), Michael Crider (Andrew), Mary Proctor (Deirdre), Frances Helm (Lillian), Martin LaPlatney (Barrymore), Ron Palillo (Gary)

Richard Carter Photos

TopLeft: Michael Crider, Martin LaPlatney in *I Hate Hamlet*
Left: Candace Dian Leverett, Dorothea Hammond in
Trip to Bountiful

CROSSROADS THEATRE COMPANY

New Brunswick, NJ
Sixteenth Season

Artistic Director, Ricardo Khan; Associate Producer, Kenneth Johnson; Press/Public Relations Director, Sandra Lanman

PRODUCTIONS & CASTS

FLYIN' WEST by Pearl Cleage; with Olivia Cole (Leah), Trazana Beverly (Sophie), Denise Burse-Mickelbury (Fannie), Count Stovall (Frank), Erika L. Heard (Minnie), Herman LeVern Jones (Wil)
TELLTALE HEARTS with Pam Grier, Amelia Marshall, Dennis Green, Jack Landron, Eugene Lee, Petronia Paley, Count Stovall, Kim Sykes
AND THE WORLD LAUGHS WITH YOU by Karimah; Director, Woodie King, Jr.; with Kalimi Baxter, Kevin Davis, Jean La Marre, Laurence Mason, Joy Moore, Ronald Brice, Sharif Rashed, Millicent Sparks, Anthony Thomas, Che J. Williams
HOME by Samm-Art Williams; with Tony Todd (Cephus), Lynda Gravatt, Melissa Maxwell
GENESIS: A CELEBRATION OF NEW VOICES IN AFRICAN AMERICAN THEATRE; Festival of new work

Rich Pipeling Photos

Top Right: Tony Todd in *Home*
Right: Olivia Cole, Herman LeVern Jones, Erika L. Heard, Count Stovall, Denise Burse-Mickelbury, Trazana Beverley in *Flyin' West*

GEORGE STREET PLAYHOUSE

New Brunswick, New Jersey

Producing Artistic Director, Gregory S. Hurst; Associate Artistic Director, Wendy Liscow; Managing Director, Diane Claussen; Production Manager, Deborah Jasien; Marketing/Public Relations Director, Rick Engler; Associate Marketing/Press Manager, Stacey Colosa

PRODUCTIONS & CASTS

BELMONT AVENUE SOCIAL CLUB by Bruce Graham; Director, Greg Hurst; Set, Deborah Jasien; Costumes, Barbara Forbes; Lighting, Donald Holder CAST: Tom Brennan (Tommy), Tony Hoty (Cholly), Bruce McCarty (Doug), Eddie Mekka (Chickie), Roger Serbagi (Frankie)
SHEER BOREDOM by John Viscardi; Director, Tom Bullard; Set, John Lee Beatty; Costumes, David M. Covach; Lighting, Jackie Manassee CAST: Matthew Arkin (Donny), Harsh Nayyar (Angel), Joel Rooks (Mike)
SUMMER FEET HEARTS by Lynn Martin; Director, Wendy Liscow; Set, Deborah Jasien; Costumes, Barbara Forbes; Lighting, Monique Millane CAST: Franchelle Stewart Dorn (Alice), Dion Graham (Tanner), Ariel Harris (Jewell), Reggie Montgomery (B. L.), Joanna Rhinehart (Jonell)
TANGENTS by Elizabeth Hansen; Director, Alyson Reed; Set, Ray Recht; Costumes, David M. Covach; Lighting, F. Mitchell Dana CAST: Kirstin Allen (Beth), Susan Cash (Dr. Ellis), Lauren Graham (Kelly), Susannah Hoffmann (Laura), Valerie Leonard (Kirsten), Deidre Madigan (Trevin), Marge Redmond (Dr. Holt)
A CRITIC AND HIS WIFE by John Ford Noonan; Director, Wendy Liscow; Set, Atkin Pace; Costumes, Barbara Forbes; Lighting, Monique Millane CAST: Robert LuPone (Len), Linda Thorson (Rebecca)
THE DIARY OF ANNE FRANK by Frances Goodrich and Albert Hackett; Director, Susan Kerner; Set, Charley Shafor; Costumes, Barbara Forbes; Lighting, Monique Millane CAST: Bibi Besch (Mrs. Frank), Elaine Bromka (Mrs. Van Daan), David S. Howard (Mr. Dussel), Timothy Jerome (Mr. Frank), Annie Meisels (Anne), Vivian Nesbitt (Meip), Kali Rocha (Margot), Nick Sullivan (Mr. Krahler), Michael Tighe (Peter), Peter Van Wagner (Mr. Van Daan)
SWINGING ON A STAR: A MUSICAL CELEBRATION OF JOHNNY BURKE; Conceived/Written/Directed by Michael Leeds; Choreography, Kathleen Marshall; Music Director, Barry Levitt; Set, Deborah Jasien; Costumes, Judy Dearing; Lighting, Richard Nelson CAST: Lisa Akey, Claire Bathe, Terry Burrell, Lewis Cleale, Kathy Fitzgerald, Michael McGrath, Alton F. White

Miguel Pagliere Photos

Top: Bruce McCarty, Tom Brennan
in *Belmont Avenue Social Club*

Center: Annie Meisels, Timothy Jerome
in *Diary of Anne Frank*

Bottom Left: Claire Bathe, Alton F. White,
Terry Burrell in *Swinging on a Star*

Bottom Right: Linda Thorson, Robert LuPone
in *A Critic and His Wife*

GOODMAN THEATRE

Chicago, Illinois

Artistic Director, Robert Falls; Associate Artistic Director, Michael Maggio; Associate Director, Frank Galati; Executive Director, Roche Schulfer; General Manager, Katherine Murphy; Press, Marlo LaCorte

PRODUCTIONS & CASTS

CRY, THE BELOVED COUNTRY; Music, Kurt Weill; Lyrics, Maxwell Anderson; Adaptation/Direction, Frank Galati; Set, Loy Arcenas; Costumes, Susan Hilferty; Lighting, James F. Ingalls; Musical Director, Edward Zelnis CAST: Ernest Perry, Jr. (Stephen), Cheryl Lynn Bruce (Grace), Brian A. Grandison (Reverend), Kingsley Leggs (Stephen's Friend), McKinley Johnson (Thief), Dathan B. Williams (Mafolo/Hlabeni), Ora Jones (Gertrude), Brandon Bush, Michael Bush (Gertrude's Son), Johnny Lee Davenport (John), JoNell Kennedy (Mrs. Mkize), Aisha de Haas (Mrs. Hlatshwayos), Ajay K. Naidu (Official), La Chanze (Absalom's Girl), William J. Norris (James), John Reeger (Captain/Judge), Darius de Haas (Absalom), J. Patrick McCormack (Harrison), Frances Limoncelli (Margaret), Michelle Elise Duffy (Barbara), Raul E. Esparza (Arthur), Deon Opperman (Announcer/Prosecutor), Tracy Hultgren, David Bonanno (police), Matthew Brennan (Arthur's Son), Kingsley Leggs, Cheryl Lynn Bruce (Chorus Leaders)
DANCING AT LUGHNASA by Brian Friel; Director, Kyle Donnelly; Set, Linda Buchanan; Costumes, Paul Tazewell; Lighting, Rita Pietraszek CAST: Denis O'Hare (Michael), Kate Buddeke (Maggie), Jenny Bacon (Chris), Pamela Nyberg (Agnes), Kate Goehring (Rose), Tana Hicken (Kate), Patrick Clear (Gerry), Richard Bauer (Jack)
RICHARD II by William Shakespeare; Director, David Petrarca; Set, Russell Metheny; Costumes, Virgil C. Johnson; Lighting, James F. Ingalls CAST: Jeffrey Hutchinson (Richard II), William J. Norris (John of Gaunt/Abbott), Martha Lavey (Duchess of Gloucester), Chuck Huber (Bolingbroke), Christopher Bauer (Mowbray), Tyress Allen (Duke of Northumberland), Nathan Anderson (Aumerle), Paul Fitzgerald, Reginald Hayes (Heralds), Kyle Colerider-Krugh (Greene), Harry Althaus (Bushy), Tim Edward Rhoze (Bagot), Mike Nussbaum (Duke of York), Larry Russo (Lord Ross), Chet Grissom (Willoughby), Gina Lo Verde (Isabel), Eric Saiet (Servingman), Clifton T. Williams (Percy), Steve Pickering (Berkeley/Gardener), John Hines (Earl of Salisbury), Eric Winzenreid (Welsh Capt.), Matt De Caro (Bishop), John Reeger (Scroope), Jacqueline Williams (Lady in Waiting), Raul E. Esparza (Fitzwater), Mary Ann Thebus (Duchess of York), Richard Wharton (Exton), Nick Offerman (Keeper)
NIGHT OF THE IGUANA by Tennessee Williams; Director, Robert Fall; Set, Loy Arcenas; Costumes, Susan Hilferty; Lighting, James F. Ingalls CAST: Cynthia Baker (Maxine), Alfredo MacDonald (Pancho), Raul Jaimes (Pedro), William Petersen (Rev. Shannon), Truda Stockenstrom (Hilda), Lawrence Woshner (Wolfgang), Dan Frick (Fahrenkopf), Betsy Freytag (Frau Fahrenkopf), Dev Kennedy (Hank), Mary Beth Fisher (Judith), Cherry Jones (Hannah), Paula Korologos (Charlotte), Lawrence McCauley (Nonno), Matt DeCaro (Jake)
I AM A MAN by OyamO; Director, Marion McClinton; Set, Scott Bradley; Costumes, Caryn Neman; Lighting, Pat Dignan CAST: Olu Dara (Bluesman), Ron O. J. Paron (Martin Luther King), Bennsy S. Cannon (Rev. Moore), Anthony Chisholm (Jones), John Cooke (Mayor), Steve Pickering (Police Chief/Rev. Weatherford/Police), Lee R. Sellars (Solicitor/Joshua), Tab Baker (Rev. Billings/Brotha Cinnamon), Ellis Foster (Councilman), Jacqueline Williams (Alice Mae), E. J. Murray (Miss Secretary), Ron O. J. Parson (Black Police), John Cooke (White Police), Clifton T. Williams (Swahili), Johnny Lee Davenport (Craig)
THE TIES THAT BIND by Regina Taylor; Director, Shirley Jo Finney; Sets, John Culbert; Costumes, Allison Reeds; Lighting, Robert Christen *Inside the Belly of the Beast* CAST: Shanesia Davis (John De Conquer), Phillip Edward VanLear (Walter), Ernest Perry, Jr. (Shoe Shine/Langley/Child), Ora Jones (Doctor), Lizan Mitchell (Ellis), Darryl Alan Reed (Malice/Sheldon/007), Felicia P. Fields (Wife), Yolanda Androzzo (Marilyn) *Watermellon Rinds* CAST: Darryl Alan Reed (Jes), Shanesia Davis (Lottie), Phillip Edward VanLear (Willie), Felicia P. Fields (Liza), Ora Jones (Pinkie), Lizan Mitchell (Mama), Ernest Perry Jnr. (Papa), Yolanda Androzzo (Marva)
BRUTALITY OF FACT by Keith Reddin; Director, Michael Maggio; Set, Linda Buchanan; Costumes, Birgit Rattenborg Wise; Lighting, Robert Christen CAST: Barbara E. Robertson (Jackie), Leslie Lyles (Maggie), Caitlin Hart (Val), Carmen Roman (Judy/Janet/Amy), Philip E. Johnson (Chris), Donna Jay Fulks (Corrine), Patrick Clear (Harold), Donna Jay Fulks (Kate), Ann Keating (Marlene)
THE NOTEBOOKS OF LEONARDO DA VINCI; Adapted/Directed by Mary Zimmerman; Set, Scott Bradley; Costumes, Allison Reeds; Lighting, T. J. Gerckens CAST: Christopher Donahue, Laura Eason, Mariann Mayberry, Christopher Pieczynski, Paul Oakley Stovall, Marc Vann, Tracy Walsh, Meredith Zinner (all Leonardo)
GRAY'S ANATOMY; Written/Performed by Spalding Gray; Director, Renee Shafransky
SOMEBODY ELSE'S HOUSE; Written/Performed by David Cale; Director, David Petrarca; Design, Michael S. Philippi
THE STATE I'M IN: A TRAVELOGUE; Written/Performed by Paula Killen; Director, Curt Columbus; Set, Sontina Reid; Costumes, Allison Reeds; Lighting, David Gipson

Liz Lauren Photos

Phillip Edward Vanlear, Ernest Perry Jr. in *Ties That Bind*

Cherry Jones, Lawrence McCauley, William Peterson in *Night of the Iguana*

Mariann Mayberry, Paul Oakley Stovall, Meredith Zinner, Christopher Piecynski in *Notebooks of Leonardo Da Vinci*

171

GOODSPEED OPERA HOUSE

East Haddam, Connecticut
Thirtieth Season

PRODUCTIONS & CASTS (1993)

ON THE TOWN; Music, Leonard Bernstein; Lyrics/Book, Betty Comden, Adolph Green; Based on idea by Jerome Robbins; Director/Choreographer, Marcia Milgrom Dodge; Musical Director, Michael O'Flaherty; Sets, Stephan Olson; Costumes, David Toser; Lighting, Michael Lincoln CAST: Joanne Baum (Lucy), Keith Bernardo (Gabey), Charlotte d'Amboise (Ivy), Frank DiPasquale (Ozzie), Donna English (Claire), Michael O'Steen (Chip), Amelia Prentice (Hildy), Maureen Sadusk (Madame Dilly), Gordon Stanley (Pitkin), Paul Cole (Tom), Kyle Craig (WAVE), Jeffrey Elsass (Poet), Cory English (Andy/Ralph), George Ewasko (Workman), Lucio Fernandez (Soldier), Ian Knauer (Prof. Figment), Kelli Kruger (Subway Lady/Diana Dream), Keri Lee (Friend), Michael McCoy (Announcer etc.), Malinda Shaffer (Flossie), Kayoko Yoshioka (WAVE)

HEARTBEATS; Music/Lyrics/Book by Amanda McBroon; Director/Choreographer, Bill Castellino; Created by McBroom and Castellino; Additional Music, Gerald Sternbach, Michael Brourman, Tom Snow, Craig Safan; Musical Director, Ann-Carol Pence; Sets, Linda Hacker; Costumes, Charlotte M. Yetman; Lighting, Richard Winkler CAST: Karen Mason (Annie), John Leslie Wolfe (Steve), Gilles Chiasson, Nicholas Cokas, Hilary James, Julie Lea Johnson

PROMISES, PROMISES; Music, Burt Bacharach; Lyrics, Hal David; Book, Neil Simon; Director/Choreographer, Ted Pappas; Musical Director, Michael O'Flaherty; Sets, James Noone; Costumes, Deborah Newhall; Lighting, Kirk Bookman CAST: P. J. Benjamin (Sheldrake), Michael Cone (Eichelberger), John Deyle (Kirkeby), Juliet Lambert (Fran), Joe Palmieri (Dreyfus), Evan Pappas (Baxter), Marilyn Pasekoff (Marge), Steve Pudenz (Vanderhof), Avery Saltzman (Dobitch), Jim Athens (Watchman), Linda Bloom (Miss Kreplinski), Paul A. Brown (Waiter), Cynthia Khoury (Ginger), Robert Roznowski (Company), Laurie Sheppard (Peggy), Elizabeth Steers (Vivien), Suzanne Van Johns (Sylvia), Mary P. Wanamaker (Nurse), Rob Woronoff (Kubelik), Koyoko Yoshioka (Miss Wong)

DAS BARBECU; Music/Conductor, Scott Warrender; Lyrics/Book, Jim Luigs; Director, Christopher Ashley; Choreography, Stephen Terrell; Sets, Eduardo Sicango; Costumes, Charlotte M. Yetman; Lighting, Kirk Bookman CAST: Anne Allgood, Alison Fraser, Gregory Jbara, Marguerite MacIntyre, Jerry McGarity

john & jen; Music/Book, Andrew Lippa; Lyrics/Book, Tom Greenwald; Director, Gabriel Barre; Musical Director, Janet Aycock; Set, Charles McCarry; Costumes, Charlotte M. Yetman; Lighting, Phil Monat CAST: Carolee Carmello (Jen), James Ludwig (John)

Diane Sobolewski Photos

Top Left: Carolee Carmello, James Ludwig in *john & jen*

2nd photo: Anne Allgood, Jerry McGarity, Alison Fraser, Gregory Jbara, Marguerite MacIntyre in *Das Barbecu*

3rd photo: Evan Pappas, Julie Lambert, P. J. Benjamin in *Promises Promises*

Bottom Left: Keith Bernardo, Charlotte d'Amboise, Frank DiPasquale, Donna English, Amelia Prentice, Michael O'Steen in *On the Town*

Bottom Right: Julie Lea Johnson, Nicholas Cokas, Karen Mason, Gilles Chiasson, Hilary James in *Heartbeats*

Michael P. Connor, David Harum in *Taming of the Shrew*
Top Left: Elizabeth Franz, Hal Holbrook in *Death of a Salesman*
Center: Noble Shropshire, Alison Bevan in *Noel and Gertie*
Bottom: Piper Laurie, James Kall in *Cherry Orchard*

GREAT LAKES THEATRE FESTIVAL

Cleveland, Ohio

Artistic Director, Gerald Freedman; Managing Director, Anne B. DesRosiers

PRODUCTIONS & CASTS

THE CHERRY ORCHARD by Anton Chekhov; Translation, Michael Frayn; Director, Gerald Freedman; Sets, John Ezell; Costumes, Lawrence Casey; Lighting, Mary Jo Dondlinger CAST: Piper Laurie (Ranyevskaya), Marin Hinkle (Anya), Tisha Roth (Varya), Reno Roop (Gayev), John Woodson (Lopakhin), Brendan Corbalis (Trofimov), Jim Hillgartner (Simeonov), Sarah Burke (Charlotta), Steve Routman (Yepikhodov), Megan Gleeson (Dunyasha), Ron Randell (Firs), James Kall (Yasha), John Buck, Jr. (Passer-by/Stationmaster), Kirk Anderson (Postmaster), Mary Bennett, William Bourquin, Chris Stuehr (Servants)

NOEL AND GERTIE: Devised by Sheridan Morley; Music/Words, Noel Coward; Director, Victoria Bussert; Musical Director, Dan Sticco; Set, John Ezell; Costumes, James Scott; Lighting, Mary Jo Dondlinger CAST: Noble Shropshire (Noel Coward), Alison Bevan (Gertrude Lawrence)

THE TAMING OF THE SHREW by William Shakespeare; Director, Michael Breault; Sets, John Ezell; Costumes, Vincent Scassellati; Lighting, Jackie Manasee CAST: Michael P. Connor (Housemaid/Grumio), David Adkins (Lucentio), Spike McClure (Tranio), Joseph Costa (Baptista), David Rogers (Gremio/Tailor), James Kall (Hortensio), Kim Sebastian (Bianca), Colleen Quinn (Katherina), James Ludwig (Biondello), David Harum (Petruchio), Sheila Heyman (Widow), Christopher Chen (Altar Boy/Gabriel), Bryan Mason (Altar Boy/Curtis/Carabiniere), Brian Pedaci (Priest/Walter/Porter), Steven Shindle (Nathaniel/Photographer), Christopher Biebelhausen (Peter), Mitchell Fields (Pedant), John Buck, Jr. (Haberdasher/Vincentio)

DEATH OF A SALESMAN by Arthur Miller; Director, Gerald Freedman; Sets, Chris Barreca; Costumes, Alfred Kohout; Lighting, Martin Aronstein CAST: Hal Holbrook (Willy), Elizabeth Franz (Linda), Steven Weber (Biff), John Speredakos (Happy), Spike McClure (Bernard), Maryann Nagel (The Woman), Howard Witt (Charley), Ron Parady (Uncle Ben), Bill Kux (Howard), Peggy Sullivan (Jenny/Letta), William P. Bourquin (Stanley), Wendy James (Miss Forsythe)

Roger Mastroianni, Jesse Epsten Photos

173

Karenjune Sanchez, Myra Lucretia Taylor, Ellen Lauren,
Karen Kandel, Kristine Nielsen in *The Women*

HARTFORD STAGE

Hartford, Connecticut
Thirtieth Season

Artistic Director, Mark Lamos; Managing Director, David Hawkanson, Stephen
J. Albert; Public Relations Director, Howard Sherman, Deborah Warren

PRODUCTIONS & CASTS

THE MERCHANT OF VENICE by William Shakespeare; Director, Mark
Lamos; Sets, John Conklin; Costumes, Martin Pakledinza; Lighting, Jennifer
Tipton CAST: Caroline Clay (Nerissa), Tim DeKay (Gratiano), Malcolm Gets
(Bassanio), Keith Glover (Prince of Morocco), Nafe Katter (Tubal), David Manis
(Launcelot), Joan McMurtrey (Portia), Ron Nakahara (Salerio), Mike Nussbaum
(Shylock), Lazaro Perez, Natacha Roi (Jessica), Michael Rupert (Antonio), Mark
Kenneth Smaltz (Solanio), Timothy D. Stickney (Lorenzo), Jacob John Albert,
Tony Bonsignore, Jean Caille, Joshua Donoghue, Timothy Huebenthal,
Christopher King, W. Scott Russell
KEELY AND DU by Jane Martin; Director, Jon Jory; Sets, Paul Owen; Cos-
tumes, Marcia Dixcy; Lighting, Mimi Jordan Sherin CAST: J. Ed Araiza (Cole),
Timothy Barone, Julie Boyd (Keely), Bob Burrus (Walter), Mary Diveny
(Guard), Anne Pitoniak (Du), Pan Riley
THE WOMEN by Claire Boothe Luce; Director, Anne Bogart; Sets, Loy
Arcenas; Costumes, Catherine Meacham Hunt; Lighting, Mimi Jordan Sherin
CAST: Sung Yun Cho (Jane), Lynn Cohen (Mrs. Morehead), Kristin Flanders
(Miriam), Hellen Gallagher (Hostess), Helen Harrelson, Karen Kandel (Sylvia),
Ellen Lauren (Mary), Kristine Nielsen (Edith), Lola Pashalinski (Countess de
Lage), Maria Porter (Olga), Laila Robins (Crystal), Karenjune Sanchez (Peggy),
Myra Lucretia Taylor (Nancy), Leecia Manning, Caitlin Mitchell (Little Mary),
Alison Russo (Euphie)
FALSE ADMISSIONS by Pierre Carlet de Marivaux; Translation, Timberlake
Wertenbaker; Director, Mark Lamos; Sets, Michael Yeargan; Costumes, Suzanne
Palmer Dougan; Lighting, Christopher Akerlind CAST: Ben Bode (Arlequin),
Olivia Birkelund (Araminte), A. Bernard Cummings (Le Comte), Jack Hannibal
(Dorante), Oni Faida Lampley (Marton), Evan Pappas (Dubois), Benjamin
Stewart (Remy), Mary Louise Wilson (Madame Argante)
BAILEY'S CAFE by Gloria Naylor; Director, Novella Nelson; Sets, Marina
Draghici; Costumes, Gabriel Berry; Lighting, Jennifer Tipton CAST: Yolande
Bavan (Sister Carrie), Cheryl Lynn Bruce (Eve), Helmar Augustus Cooper
(Daddy Jim), Michael Genet (Miss Marple); Tommy Hollis (Bailey), Renee
Joshua-Porter (Peaches), Curtis McClarin (Sugarman), Phyllis Yvonne Stickney
(Jesse), Inger Tudor (Miriam)
PRESENT LAUGHTER by Noel Coward; Director, Vivian Matalon; Sets, Rob
Odorisio; Costumes, Ann Hould-Ward; Lighting, Richard Nelson CAST: David
Birney (Garry), Michael Chernov (Fred), Katie Finneran (Daphne), Mary Layne
(Liz), Marie Lillo (Lady Saltburn), Roberta Maxwell (Monica), Mari Nelson
(Joanna), Greg Pierotti (Rolande), Count Stovall (Henry), Jack Wetherall (Morris)

T. Charles Erickson Photos

Curtis McClarin, Michael Genet in *Bailey's Cafe*

Anne Pitoniak, Julie Boyd in *Keely and Du*

Mike Nussbaum, Michael Rupert, Malcolm Gets in
Merchant of Venice

David Birney, Mari Nelson in *Present Laughter*

Reri Barrett, Juliette Marie Ferguson, Phillip Van Lear, Sandra K. Watson, Jim Jackson in *African Theatre Co. Presents Richard III*

ILLINOIS THEATRE CENTER

Park Forest, Illinois
Eighteenth Season

Artistic Director, Steve S. Billig; Managing Director, Etel Billig; Costume Design, Stephen E. Moore, Diane Moore, Pat Decker; Lighting Design, Jonathan Roark; Set Design, Wayne Adams, Jonathan Roark

PRODUCTIONS & CASTS

DON'T DRESS FOR DINNER by Marc Camoletti; Director, Steve S. Billig CAST: Iris Lieberman, Tony Dobrowolski, Steve Anders, Cynthia Huse, Shelley Crosby, Marshall Crawford
SCOTLAND ROAD by Jeffrey Hatcher; Director, Steve S. Billig; CAST: Alan Kopischke, Connie McGrail, Franette Liebow, Etel Billig
LOVE COMICS; Music, David Evans; Lyrics, Sarah Schlesinger; Book, Evans and Schlesinger; Director, Steve S. Billig; Musical Director, Jonathan Roark; Choreography, Ed Kross CAST: Michael Crafton, Barbara Helms, Matthew Orlando, Rachel Rockwell, Liz Donathan, Ed Kross
PARALLEL LIVES by Mo Gaffney and Kathy Najimy; Director, Steve S. Billig CAST: Linda Ann Waner, Cathy Bieber
THE AFRICAN COMPANY PRESENTS RICHARD THE THIRD by Carlyle Brown; Directors, Phillip Van Lear, Steve S. Billig CAST: Mr. Van Lear, Jim Jackson, Juliette Marie Ferguson, Sandra K. Watson, Reri Barrett, Mr. Billig, Edward Basden
SEPARATION by Tom Kempinski; Director, Etel Billig CAST: Gary Houston, Mierka Girten
NOT BLOODY LIKELY (OR RETURN TO RUDDIGORE) by Steve S. Billig and Jonathan Roark; Adapted from Gilbert and Sullivan; Director, Mr. Billig; Musical Director, Mr. Roark CAST: Aaron Hunt, Lynette Knapp, David Six, Keith Heimpel, Pat Fitch, Marney MacAdam, Howard Hahn, Maria Winiarski, James Braunstein, Trei M. Trefelet, Morgan Fitch
LOVE LETTERS by A. R. Gurney; Director, Wayne Adams CAST: Etel and Steve Billig

Todd Panagopolous Photos

Marshall Crawford, Cynthia Huse, Iris Lieberman, Tony Dobrowolski in *Don't Dress for Dinner*

Alan Kopischke, Connie McGrail in *Scotland Road* 175

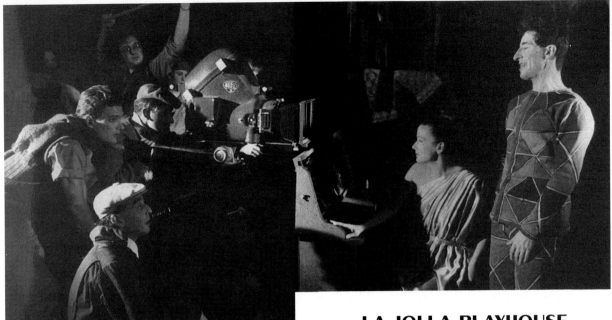

**Ben Kernan, Dominique Serrand, Felicity Jones, Steven Epp
in *Children of Paradise***

LA JOLLA PLAYHOUSE

San Diego, California

Artistic Director, Des McAnuff; Managing Director, Terrence Dwyer; Associate Artistic Director, Robert Blacker; Communications Director, Joshua Ellis

PRODUCTIONS & CASTS (1993)

CHILDREN OF PARADISE: Shooting a Dream; Collaboratively produced by Theatre de la Jeune Lune; Writers, Steven Epp, Felicity Jones, Dominique Serrand, Paul Walsh; Based on work by Marcel Carne and Jaques Prevert; Director, Dominique Serrand; Scenography, Vincent Gracieux; Music, Chandler Poling; Lighting, Fredric Desbois; Costumes, Trini Mrnak CAST: Michael Collins, Sarah Corzatt, Barbra Berlovitz Desbois, John Clark Donahue, Darcey Engen, Steven Epp, Laura Esping, Vincent Gracieux, Nancy Hogetvedt, Aimee Jacobson, Eric Jensen, Felicity Jones, Ben Kernan, Angie Lewis, Daniel Nelson, Robert Rosen, Danny Schmitz, Charles Schuminski, Luverne Seifert, Dominique Serrand, Rachel Wapnick

ARMS AND THE MAN by George Bernard Shaw; Director, Lisa Peterson; Sets, Robert Brill; Costumes, Christina Haatainen; Lighting, Chris Kortum CAST: Cynthia Nixon (Raina), Ivonne Coll (Catherine), Sevanne Kassarjian (Louka), Mark Harelik (Bluntschli), Chris Flanders (Officer), Jan Triska (Nicola), Mario Arrambide (Major Petkoff), Andrew Weems (Major Saranoff), Micha Espinoza, Maya Gurantz, Morris Pomerantz, Francine Torres, Kara Tsiaperas, Will Warren, Jonathan Winn

THE HAIRY APE by Eugene O'Neill; Director, Matthew Wilder; Sets, Robert Brill; Costumes, Cynthia Bolin; Lighting, David S. Thayer CAST: Mario Arrambide (Yank), Ivonne Coll (Aunt), Micha Espinosa (Mildred), Chris Flanders (Engineer), Mark Harelik (Long), Jan Triska (Paddy), Will Warren (Union Secretary), Andrew Weems (Voice/Cop), Trent DeLong, Johnny Evans, Joan Green, Phoebe Hyde, Sevanne Kassarjian, Elise Kuklica, Silas Neilson, Chris Pendergast, Maria Striar, Laurie Williams

LUCK, PLUCK & VIRTUE; Written/Directed by James Lapine; Based on A Cool Million by Nathaniel West; Sets, Adrianne Lobel; Costumes, Martin Pakledinaz; Lighting, Chris Parry CAST: Neil Patrick Harris (Lester), Dan Moran (Kaplan), P. J. Brown (Hoffman), Marge Redmond (Mother), George Coe (Nathan), Ming-Na Wen (Betty), Meg MacCary (Vendor), David Barrera (Wellington), Adrianne Krstansky (Talent Coordinator), Scott Corr, John Gonzalez, Teresa Kasperick, Tara Roy, David Scott, Emily Stiffler, Roland Tsui, Megan Wanlass

THE MISSION; Produced by Culture Clash; Writers, Richard Montoya, Ric Salinas, Herbert Siguenza; Director, Tony Curiel; Sets, Victoria Petrovich; Lighting, Jose Lopez; Costumes, Herbert Siguenza CAST: Richard Montoya, Ric Salinas, Herbert Siguenza

SWEET & HOT: The Songs of Harold Arlen; Conceived/Directed by Julianne Boyd; Choreography, Hope Clarke; Musical Direction, Danny Holgate; Sets, Kenneth Foy; Costumes, David C. Woolard; Lighting, Howell Binkley CAST: Terry Burell, Allen Hidalgo, Jacquey Maltby, Monica Pege, Brian Quinn, Lance Roberts

T. Charles Erickson, Eric Riel, Michal Daniel Photos

176 **Jacquey Maltby, Allen Hidalgo, Monica Pege, Lance Roberts, Brian Quinn, Terry Burrell in *Sweet & Hot***

Richard Montoya, Herbert Siguenza, Ric Salinas in *The Mission*

Andrew Weems, Cynthia Nixon in *Arms and the Man*

Mario Arrambide in *The Hairy Ape*

Adrianne Krstansky, Neil Patrick Harris in *Luck, Pluck & Virtue*

LONG WHARF THEATRE

New Haven, Connecticut
Twenty-ninth Season

Artistic Director, Arvin Brown; Executive Director, M. Edgar Rosenblum; Literary Consultant, John Tillinger; Press/Marketing Director, Robert Wildman; Press Assistant, Jeff Fickes

PRODUCTIONS & CASTS

FIRES IN THE MIRROR: Crown Heights, Brooklyn and Other Identities; Conceived/Written/Performed by Anna Deavere Smith; Design, Wendall K. Harrington; Costumes, Candice Donnelly; Lighting, John Ambrosone
THE TIMES; Music, Bradd Ross; Lyrics/Book, Joe Keenan; Conception, Mr. Keenan, Gordon Edelstein, Mr. Ross; Musical Staging, Greg Ganakas; Director, Mr. Edelstein; Musical Director, Tom Fay; Sets, Hugh Landwehr; Costumes, Jess Goldstein; Lighting, Peter Kaczorowski CAST: Ron Bohmer, Bobby Daye, Philip Hoffman, James Judy, Nora Mae Lyng, Mary Gordon Murray, Jennifer Smith, Cheryl Stern
SIGHT UNSEEN by Donald Margulies; Director, John Tillinger; Sets, James Youmans; Costumes, Jane Greenwood; Lighting, Donald Holder CAST: Jayne Atkinson, Vivienne Benesch, Michel R. Gill, Doug Stender
UNDER MILK WOOD by Dylan Thomas; Presented by National Theatre of the Deaf; Director, J Ranelli; Sets, David Hays; Costumes, Cynthia Dumont; Lighting, Frederick Geffken CAST: John Basinger, Frank L. Dattolo, Robert DeMayo, Eileen Dulen, Camille L. Jeter, Missy Keast, Mike Lamitola, Cheri Lundquist, Will Rhys, Joseph Sarpy, Andrew Vasnick
MISALLIANCE by George Bernard Shaw; Director, Arvin Brown; Sets, Michael H. Yeargan; Costumes, Jess Goldstein; Lighting, Mark Stanley CAST: Ludmila Bokievsky, Frank Converse, Tom Dunlop, Marcus Giamatti, Patrick Horgan, Jefferson Mays, Kathryn Meisle, Pamela Payton-Wright, Willis Sparks
BROKEN GLASS by Arthur Miller; Director, John Tillinger; Sets/Costumes, Santo Loquasto; Lighting, Brian Nason CAST: Frances Conroy, David Dukes, Amy Irving, Lauren Klein, George N. Martin, Ron Rifkin, Ron Silver, Doug Stender
FAITH HEALER by Brian Friel; Director, Joe Dowling; Sets, Frank Hallinan Flood; Costumes, Anne Cave; Lighting, Christopher Akerlind CAST: Ron Cook, Judy Geeson, Donal McCann
FLYIN' WEST by Pearl Cleage; Director, Kenny Leon; Set, Dax Edwards; Costumes, Jeff Cone; Lighting, Ann G. Wrightson CAST: Tom Byrd, Peter Jay Fernandez, Kimberly Hawthorne, Carol Mitchell-Leon, Sharlene Ross, Elizabeth Van Dyke
KING OF COONS by Michael Henry Brown; Director, Gordon Edelstein CAST: Beeson Carroll, Matthew Burnett, Abdul Salaam El Razzac, Ayo Haynes, Damien Leake, Martin Moran, Kelly Neal, Linda Powell, Sybil Walker
SUNDAY ON THE ROCKS by Theresa Rebeck; Director, Susann Brinkley CAST: Patricia Cornell, Kristin Flanders, Mia Korf, Jennifer Van Dyck

T. Charles Erickson Photos

Top: Philip Gellburg, Ron Silver, Amy Irving in *Broken Glass*
2nd photo: Carol Mitchell-Leon, Sharlene Ross in *Flyin' West*
3rd photo: Frank Converse, Pamela Payton-Wright in *Misalliance*

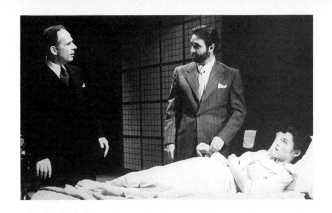

Peter Jay Fernandez, Sharlene Ross in *Flyin' West*

Doug Stender, Jayne Atkinson, Michel R. Gill in *Sight Unseen*

Ron J. Hutchins, Curt Dale Clark, Keith Jackson,
(top)Jonathan Todd Horenstein, Rob Rahn, Robert N. DeWitt,
Harrison McEldowney in *Hot Mikado*

MARRIOTT'S LINCOLNSHIRE THEATRE

Lincolnshire, Illinois

Executive Producer, Kary M. Walker; Artistic Director, Dyanne Earley; Associate Producer, Terry James; Set Design, Thomas M. Ryan; Costume Design, Nancy Missimi; Lighting Design, Diane Ferry Williams, R. Lee Kennedy; Production Assistant, Mary Thimios

PRODUCTIONS & CASTS

HOT MIKADO; Director/Choreographer, David Bell; Musical Director, Rob Bowman CAST: Robin Baxter (Petti-Sing), Stephen R. Buntrock (Nanki-Poo), Stephanie L. Burton (Stephanie), Curt Dale Clark (Pish-Tush), Deidre Dolan (Deidre), Robert N. DeWitt (Bobby), Felicia P. Fields (Katisha), LaTonya Holmes (Peep-Bo), Jonathan Todd Horenstein (Jonathan), Ron J. Hutchins (Ron), Keith Jackson (Keith), Ross Lehman (Ko-Ko), Harrison McEldowney (Harrison), Susan Moniz (Yum-Yum), Jackie J. Patterson (Mikado), Rob Rahn (Rob), Nicole Roberts (Nicole), Stanley White (Pooh-Bah)
OKLAHOMA!; Director, Dyanne Earley; Choreography, Harrison McEldowney, Eric Holt; Musical Director, Michael Duff CAST: Guy Adkins (Will), Stephen R. Buntrock (Curly), Stephen P. Full (Ali Hakim), Rita Harvey (Laurey), Andrew J. Lupp (Dream Curly), David New (Jud), Kelly Prybycien (Ado Annie), Rob Rahn (Dream Jud), Ann Whitney (Aunt Eller), Larry Wyatt (Carnes), Fred Zimmerman (Ike), Kyle Baker, Curt Dale Clark, Deidre Dolan, Jamie Dawn Gangi, Jeffrey Hancock, Philip Masterson, Tait Runnfeldt, Sheila Savage, Bill Szobody
42ND STREET; Director, Mark Hoebee; Choreography, Kenny Ingram; Musical Director, Michael Duff Deidre Dolan (Phyllis), Don Forston (Abner), Elizabeth Gelman (Maggie), Andrew J. Lupp (Billy), Brian Robert Mani (Julian), Sheila Savage (Anytime Annie), Kathy Taylor (Dorothy), Annette Thurman (Lorraine), Cindy Timms (Peggy), Jonathan Weir (Bert), Guy Adkins, Cheridah Best, Curt Dale Clark, Susan Craig, Susan Johnson, Tysh Nelson, David Nisbet, Rob Rahn, Marc Robin, Seth Swoboda, Bill Szobody, James Zager
THE GOODBYE GIRL; Directors, Joe Leonardo, David Zippel; Choreography, Eric Hoit; Musical Director, Michael Duff CAST: Madilyn A. Beck (Cynthia), Felicia P. Fields (Mrs. Crosby), Jessie Anne Fisher (Lucy), James Fitzgerald (Elliott), Pamela Harden (Jenna), Robin Kersey-Dickerson (Donna), Andrew J. Lupp (Billy), Dale Morgan (Mark/Simpson), Kathy Santen (Paula), Jamie Weisman (Melanie), Deidre Dolan, Kelly Prybycien, Rob Rahn, Chuck Saculla, Laura Schutter, Jonathan Stahl, Bill Szobody, James Zager
WINDY CITY; Director, Dyanne Earley; Choreography, Mark Hoebee; Musical Director, Michael Duff CAST: Guy Adkins (Earl), Robert Michael Baker (Hildy), Stephen P. Full (Schwartz), Joel Hatch (Walter), Kathleen Jaeck (Natalie), Ronald Keaton (Kruger), Robin Kersey-Dickerson (Mollie), John Librizzi (Sheriff), Andrew J. Lupp (Wilson), Dale Morgan (Mayor), Rob Rahn (McCue), R. C. Torri (Louie), Jonathan Weir (Egelhofer), Stanley White (Alderman/Willoughby), Larry Yando (Belsinger), Fred Zimmerman (Murphy), Jeanne Croft, Mimi Manners, Jill Walmsley

Joel Hatch, Robert Michael Baker in *Windy City*

Guy Adkins, Kelly Prybycien in *Oklahoma*

James FitzGerald, Jessie Anne Fisher, Kathy Santen in *The Goodbye Girl*

179

McCARTER THEATRE

Princeton, New Jersey

Artistic Director, Emily Mann; Managing Director, Jeffrey Woodward; Special Programming Director, W. W. Lockwood, Jr.; General Manager, Kathleen Kund Nolan; Production Stage Manager, Susie Cordon; Marketing Director, David Mayhew; Publicist, Daniel Y. Bauer

PRODUCTIONS & CASTS

THE PERFECTIONIST by Joyce Carol Oates; Director, Emily Mann; Set, Thomas Lynch; Costumes, Jennifer von Mayrhauser; Lighting, Pat Collins CAST: Josh Hamilton (Jason), Betty Buckley (Paula), Dina Spybey (Kim), David Selby (Tobias), Peter Maloney (Willy), Shareen Mitchell (Nedra)
TWILIGHT: LOS ANGELES 1992; Conceived/Written/Performed by Anna Deavere Smith; Director, Emily Mann; Set, Robert Brill; Costumes, Candice Donnelly; Lighting, Allen Lee Hughes
THE NANJING RACE by Reggie Cheong-Leen; Director, Loretta Greco; Set, Philip Creech; Costumes, Catherine Homa-Rocchio; Lighting, Christopher Gorzelnik CAST: B. D. Wong (Yu Ahn), Thom Sesma (Philip), David Chung (Bao)
HELLO & GOODBYE; Written/Directed by Athol Fugard; Associate Director/Set/Costumes, Susan Hilferty; Lighting, Dennis Parichy CAST: Zeljko Ivanek (Johnnie), Maria Tucci (Hester)
C'MON & HEAR—IRVING BERLIN'S AMERICA; Music/Lyrics, Irving Berlin; Creators, George Faison and David Bishop; Director/Choreographer, Mr. Faison; Set, Chris Barreca; Costumes, Toni-Leslie James; Lighting, Richard Nelson; Musical Director, Linda Twine CAST: Laurie Beechman (Molly), Carol Woods (Rose), James Hindman (Nathan), Mary Testa (Sophie), Ted L. Levy (Gino), Alton Fitzgerald White (Percy), Karyn Quackenbush (Anna), Stephanie Pope (Ida), John Hickok (Eric), Rodney Scott Hudson (Bruno)
CHANGES OF HEART; Adapted from *The Double Inconstancy* by Pierre Carlet de Marivaux; Adaptation/Direction, Stephen Wadsworth; Sets, Thomas Lynch; Costumes, Martin Pakledinaz; Lighting, Christopher Akerlind CAST: Robert Sean Leonard (The Prince), John Michael Higgins (Harlequin), Mary Lou Rosato (Flaminia), Natacha Roi (Silvia), Laurence O'Dwyer (Trivelin), Sheryl Taub (Lisette), Nicholas Kepros (Lord), Reid Armbruster, Michael Collins, Roberta Kastelic, Jennifer Thomas
WINTER'S TALE-One Act Play Festival; Writers, Han Ong, Deborah Tannen, Leigh Bienen, Adrienne Kennedy, Jane Anderson, Emily Mann, Russell Banks, Nicole Burdette, Gayle Pemberton, Hector Tobar, Joyce Carol Oates; Directors, Adam Arkin, Michael Kahn, Jorge Ledesma, Evan Yionoulis, Loretta Greco, Tamsen Wolff, Nikki Appino, Laura Huntsman, Jennifer Nelson CASTS: Terry Alexander, Katherine Borowitz, Jere Edmunds, Karen Garvey, Stephen Lee, Karl Light, Brandan McClain, James Morrison, James Puig, Allen Swift, Lynn Thigpen, Richard Thompson

T. Charles Erickson

Top: David Selby, Peter Maloney in *The Perfectionist*
Center: Natacha Roi, Robert Sean Leonard in *Changes of Heart*
Bottom Left: Maria Tucci, Zeljko Ivanek in *Hello and Goodbye*
Below: Stephanie Pope, Karyn Quakenbush, John Hickok, James Hindman in *C'mon & Hear*

Kraig Swartz, Jayne Houdyshell in *Broadway Bound*
Top Left: Wil Love, Alexander Webb in *The Foreigner*
2nd photo: Jayne Houdyshell as *Shirley Valentine*
3rd photo: Shirleyann Kaladjian, Peter Gregory in
You Never Can Tell
Bottom: Paul Hopper, Jeanne Arnold, Joseph Reed, Peter
Gregory in *Last Days of Mr. Lincoln*

MEADOW BROOK THEATRE

Rochester, Michigan

Artistic Director, Terence Kilburn; Managing Director, Gregg Bloomfield; Stage Managers, Terry W. Carpenter, Robert Herrle; Publicist, Michael C. Vigilant

PRODUCTIONS & CASTS

THE FOREIGNER by Larry Shue; Director, Carl Schurr CAST: James Anthony, Tamara Evans, Linde Hayen, Paul Hopper, Wil Love, Lance A. Retallick, Alexander Webb
BLACK COFFEE by Agatha Christie; Director, Terence Kilburn CAST: James Anthony, Mary Benson, Yolanda Lloyd Delgado, David Du Chene, Tamara Evans, Paul Hopper, Bill Mackenzie, Thomas D. Mahard, Joseph Reed, Lance A. Retallick, Eric Tavares, Alexander Webb
SHIRLEY VALENTINE by Willy Russell; Director, Terence Kilburn CAST: Jayne Houdyshell
YOU CAN NEVER TELL by George Bernard Shaw; Director, Carl Schurr CAST: Arthur Beer, Paul Hopper, Jayne Houdyshell, Shirleyann Kaladjian, Wil Love, Frank Polito, Carl Schurr, Deborah Staples, Peter Gregory Thomson
THE LAST DAYS OF MR. LINCOLN; Written/Directed by Charles Nolte; CAST: Jeanne Arnold, Morgan Duncan, Paul Hopper, Jayne Houdyshell, Wil Love, Joseph Reed, Carl Schurr, Peter Gregory Thomson, Alma Washington
BROADWAY BOUND by Neil Simon; Director, John Ulmer CAST: Becky Holahan, Jayne Houdyshell, Andrew Newll, Davis Regal, Kraig Swartz, Eric Tavares

Rick Smith Photos

NEW JERSEY SHAKESPEARE FESTIVAL

Drew University, Madison, New Jersey

Artistic Director, Bonnie J. Monte; Managing Director, Michael Stotts; Public Relations, Anna L. Morrone, Cat Morgan

PRODUCTIONS & CASTS

THE TAMING OF THE SHREW by William Shakespeare; Director, Dylan Baker; Set, Michael Vaughn Sims; Costumes, Susan Branch; Lighting, Scott Zielinski CAST: Patrick Morris (Lord), Peter Dinklage (Sly), Kate Schlesinger (Hostess), Bill Padilla (Page), Robert Adanto, Tom Delling, Jerry Della Salla, David James Nelson (Huntsmen/Servants), Roy Cockrum (Baptista/Tailor), Doug Mancheski (Vincento/Haberdasher), Robert Devaney (Lucento/Curtis), Thomas Schall (Petruchio), Robert Hock (Gremio), Michael Hirsch (Hortensio), Paul Mullins (Tanio), Beth Swing Harre (Biondello), James Michael Reilly (Grumio), John Wellmann (Pedant), Susan Knight (Katherina), Amanda Ronconi (Bianca), Kim Francis (Widow)

ARMS AND THE MAN by George Bernard Shaw; Director, Bonnie J. Monte; Set, Rob Odorisio; Costumes, Maggie Morgan; Lighting, Steven Rosen CAST: Laila Robins (Raina), Delphi Harrington (Catherine), Dana Reeve (Louka), James Michael Reilly (Bluntschli), Bill Padilla (Soldier), J. P. Linton (Major), Nicholas Kepros (Nicola), David Andrew Macdonald (Sergius)

MEASURE FOR MEASURE by William Shakespeare; Adapted/Directed by Mark Milbauer; Set, Matthew Hynes; Costumes, Carol Dinnean, Emily Gibbs; Lighting, Catherine Moy CAST: Patrick Morris (Angelo), Peter Hadres (Duke), Jerry Della Salla (Claudio), Deidre Harrison (Lucio), John Wellmann (Elbow/Provost), Frank Anderson (Escalus/Barnadine), Fred Burrell (Pompey/Peter), Collette Kilroy (Isabella), Amanda Ronconi (Mariana/Mistress Overdone), Kena Tangi Dorsey (Juliet)

OTHELLO by William Shakespeare; Director, Robert Walsh; Set, Shelley Barclay; Costumes, Azan King; Lighting, Bruce Auerbach CAST: Chuck Cooper (Othello), Tom Brennan (Brabantio), Michael Manuel (Cassio), Tom Tammi (Iago), Paul Mullins (Roderigo), Richard Bowden (Duke), Tom Delling (Lodovico), Keith Hampton Cobb (Montano), Peter Dinklage (Clown), Robert Devaney (Messenger), Nick Sullivan (Senator), Bill Padilla (Sailor/Servant), Robert Adanto (Herald/Officer), Melissa Bowen (Desdemona), Marya Lowry (Wmilia), Ana Munoz (Bianca)

GHOSTS by Henrik Ibsen; Translation, Michael Meyer; Director, Carlo Gabriel Sparanero; Set, Steven Capone; Costumes, Hugh Hanson; Lighting, Steve Woods CAST: Jennifer Wiltsie (Regina), Charles Cragin (Engstrand), Carrie Nye (Mrs. Alving), James Lynch (Oswald), James A. Stephens (Pastor)

THE COMEDY OF ERRORS by William Shakespeare; Director, Bonnie J. Monte; Set, Michael Ganio; Costumes, Ivan Ingerman; Lighting, Michael Gianitti CAST: James Michael Reilly (Solinus), Tom Brennan (Egeon), Christopher Yates (Antipholus of Ephesus), David Andrew Macdonald (Antipholus of Syracuse), Kevin O'Keefe (Dromio of Ephesus), Patrick Morris (Dromio of Syracuse), Bill Padilla (Balthazar/Police), Peter Dinklage (Angelo), David Mitchell (Merchant/Messenger), Doug Mancheski (Merchant), John Wellmann (Pinch), Elinor Basecu (Emilia), Laila Robins (Adriana), Dana Reeve (Luciana), Kate Schlesinger (Luce/Nell), Allison Dougherty (Courtesan), Ben Seessel (Headsman)

ELECTRA by Sophocles; Translation, John Barton, Kenneth Cavander; Director, Bonnie J. Monte; Set, Chris Muller; Costumes, Hwa Park; Lighting, Bruce Auerbach CAST: Laila Robins (Electra), Gleason Bauer (Chrysothemis), Novella Nelson (Clytemnestra), Herman Petras (Old Man), Bill Sage (Orestes), Christopher Armond (Pylades), Jamison Selby (Aegisthus)

AS YOU LIKE IT by William Shakespeare; Director, Barry Edelstein; Costumes, Daniela Kamiliotis; Lighting, Steve Woods CAST: Rodney Hudson (Duke Fredrick/Duke Senior), Daniel Travis (Amiens/Le Beau), Robert Lupone (Jacques), John Fiske (Charles), Sean Michael Dougherty (Oliver), Christopher Armond (de Boys/Martext), Dallas Roberts (Orlando), Herman Petras (Adam/Corin), Michael Gaston (Touchstone), Richard Topol (Silvius), Greg Steinbrunner (William), Jamison Selby (Hymen), Vivienne Benesch (Rosalind), Marin Hinkle (Celia), Amanda Ronconi (Phoebe), Laura Holz (Audrey), Lee Rose, Jamison Selby (Lords)

GOODNIGHT DESDEMONA, GOOD MORNING JULIET by Ann-Marie MacDonald; Director, Juliette Carillo; Set, Rob Odorisio; Costumes, Elizabeth Fried; Lighting, Scott Zielinski CAST: Caroline Clay (Desdemona), John Alban Coughlin (Othello), Deirdre Harrison (Juliet/Student), Joseph Fuqua (Romeo), Patricia Scanlon (Ledbelly), Mia Baron (Ghost/Chorus), Patrick Morris (Iago), Carolina Clay (Ramona), Federico Castelluccio (Tybalt), Ian Helfer (Mercutio/Soldier), John Alban Coughlin (Prof. Night), David Mandel (Nurse/Servant)

THE MERRY WIVES OF WINDSOR by William Shakespeare; Director, Daniel Fish; Set, Carol Bailey; Costumes, Kaye Voyce; Lighting, Scott Zielinski CAST: Jim Hillgartner (Falstaff), Berton T. Schaeffer (Fenton), Tom Brennan (Shallow), Tom Delling (Slender), Bob Kirsh (Ford), Curt Karibalis (George), Paul Mullins (Caius), Roy Cockrum (Host), David Mandel (Bardolph/Rugby), Christopher Armond (Nym/John), Ian Helfer (Pistol), Danny Hoberman (Robin), Greg Steinbruner (Simple), Melissa Gallagher (Mistress Ford), Marcia Jean Kurtz (Mistress Page), Bren McElroy (Anne), Mary Lou Rosato (Mistress Quickly), William H. Vogt, Jr. (Cabana Boy)

Paul Mullins, Elizabeth Perry, Dudley Knight in
Diary of a Scoundrel
Top: Bill Sage, Laila Robins in *Electra*

MAN TO MAN by Manfred Karge; Translation/Direction, Ulla Neuerburg; Set, Kathy Pettus; Costumes, Audrey Fisher; Lighting, Julie Martin CAST: Patrick Morris, Rebecca Ortese (Ella/Max)

DIARY OF A SCOUNDREL by Alexander Ostrovsky; Director, Bonnie J. Monte; Set, Rob Odorisio; Costumes, Ivan Ingermann; Lighting, Stephen Rosen CAST: Paul Mullins, Elizabeth Perry, Bill Padilla, Dudley Knight, Judith Roberts, Tom Brennan, James Michael Reilly, Elinor Basecu, Mia Barron, Steven Ray Dallimore, Tom Delling, Bobo Lewis, Bren McElroy, Laura Holz, Gregory Derelian, Norm Anderson

OLD GLOBE THEATRE

San Diego, California
Fifty-ninth Season

Artistic Director, Jack O'Brien; Executive Producer, Craig Noel; Managing Director, Thomas Hall; Public Relations, Charlene Baldridge

PRODUCTIONS & CASTS

BALLAD OF THE BLACKSMITH by Mercedes Rein and Jorge Curi; Translation, Raul Moncada; Director, Rene Buch; Set, Robert Weber Federico; Costumes, Andrew V. Yelusich; Lighting, Robert Peterson CAST: Rob Neukirch (Miseria), Miriam Colon (Pobreza), Daniel Faraldo (St. Peter), Quentin O'Brien (Our Lord), Coral Thuet (Dona Jesusa), John Vargas (Governor), Amy Beth Cohn (Maruchenga), Alex Fernandez (Death), Ron Campbell (Gentleman Lili)
BURNING HOPE by Douglas Michilinda; Director, Andrew J. Traister; Set, Kent Dorsey; Costumes, Andrew V. Yelusich; Lighting, Ashley York Kennedy CAST: James Greene (Padraig), Dave Florek (Chaser), Wren T. Brown (Micky), Rosina Widdowson-Reynolds (Lucia), Kim Miyori (Sisopha), Jennifer Staratman (Danielle), Dan Gunther (Larry)
KING LEAR by William Shakespeare; Director, Jack O'Brien; Sets, Ralph Funicello; Costumes, Robert Morgan; Lighting, David F. Segal CAST: Hal Holbrook (Lear), Robert Sean Leonard (Edgar), Jonathan Walker (Edmund), James R. Winker (Cornwall), Jonathan McMurtey (Albany), William Anton (Kent), Richard Easton (Gloucester), Patricia Conolly (Fool), Katherine McGrath (Goneril), Kandis Chappell (Regan), Jennifer Van Dyck (Cordelia)
THE KING OF THE KOSHER GROCERS by Joe Minjares; Director, Craig Noel; Set, Joel Fontaine; Costumes, Dona Granata; Lighting, Robert Peterson CAST: Kevin Jackson (Jamar), Kurt Knudson (Izzie), Ed Bernard (Elvis), Sam Vlahos (Joe), Michelle Breaugh (Lenora), Jeremiah Birkett (Billy), Phil Lowey (Earl)
ALL'S WELL THAT ENDS WELL by William Shakespeare; Director, Sheldon Epps; Set, Richard Hoover; Costumes, Dona Granata; Lighting, Robert Peterson CAST: James Cromwell (King), Neil Maffin (Bertram), Richard Easton (Lafew), Conan McCarty (Parolles), Jonathan McMurtry (Lavatch), Carolyn Seymour (Countess), Oni Faida Lampley (Helena), Melora Hardin (Singer), Katherine McGrath (Widow), Lyn Wright (Diana)
DAMN YANKEES; Music/Lyrics, Richard Adler and Jerry Ross; Book, George Abbott, Douglass Wallop; Revisions/Direction, Jack O'Brien; Musical Director, James Raitt; Choreography, Rob Marshall; Sets, Douglas W. Schmidt; Costumes, David C. Woolard; Lighting, David F. Segal CAST: Linda Stephens (Meg), Dennis Kelly (Joe Boyd), Victor Garber (Applegate), Jere Shea (Joe Hardy), Dick Latessa (Van Buren), Vicki Lewis (Gloria), Terrence P. Currier (Welch), Susan Mansur (Sister), Bebe Neuwirth (Lola), Scott Wise (Rocky), Jeff Blumenkrantz (Smokey), Gregory Jbara (Shohovik), Jim Borstelmann (Leonard), Scott Robertson (Stubbs), Michael Winther (Ozzie), Cory English (Bubba), Bruce Anthony Davis (Flash), Michael Berresse (Bomber), Paula Leggett Chase (Betty), Nancy Ticotin (Donna), Julia Gregory (Kitty)
MR. A'S AMAZING MAZE PLAYS by Alan Ayckbourn; Director, Craig Noel; Set, Greg Lucas; Costumes, Clare Henkel; Lighting, Michael Gilliam CAST: Ralph Elias (1st Narrator), Katherine McGrath (2nd Narrator), Jennifer Hugus (Suzy), Lynne Griffin (Mother), Sean Sullivan (Neville), Steve Jones (Father), Richard Easton (Passerby), Jonathan McMurtry (Accousticus)
BLUES IN THE NIGHT; Conception/Direction, Sheldon Epps; Musical Director, Rahn Coleman; Choreography, Patricia Wilcox; Set/Lighting, Joseph P. Tilford; Costumes, Kay Kurta CAST: Irama P. Hall (MaDear), Brenda Pressley (MayDee), Crystal Laws Green (Lola), Susan Payne (Vennie), Jurian Hughes (Raisa)
DIRT by Bruce Gooch; Director, Andrew J. Traister; Set, Ralph Funicello; Costumes, Deborah M. Dryden; Lighting, Robert Peterson CAST: James Whitmore (Sonny), John Dennis Johnston (Zac), Anette Helde (Eleanor)
MADAME MAO'S MEMORIES by Henry Ong; Director, Seret Scott; Set/Costumes, Andrew V. Yelusich; Lighting, Michael Gilliam CAST: Kim Miyori
OLEANNA by David Mamet; Director, Jack O'Brien; Set, Robert Brill; Costumes, David C. Woolard; Lighting, Ashley York Kennedy CAST: Kathleen Dennehy (Carol), William Anton (John)

Ken Howard Photos

Top: Vicki Lewis and *Damn Yankees* cast
Center: Robert Sean Leonard in *King Lear*
Bottom: James Whitmore, John Dennis Johnston in *Dirt*

PAPER MILL PLAYHOUSE

Millburn, New Jersey
Sixty-fourth Season

Executive Producer, Angelo Del Rossi; Artistic Director, Robert Johanson; General Manager, Geoffrey Cohen; Set Designer, Michael Anania; Public Relations Director, Meara Nigro

PRODUCTIONS & CASTS

PAPER MOON; Music, Larry Grossman; Lyrics, Ellen Fitzhugh, Carol Hall; Book, Martin Casella; Director, Matt Casella; Choreography, Alan Johnson; Musical Director, Steve Marzullo; Orchestrations, Michael Starobin; Costumes, Jeffrey Kurland; Lighting, Pat Collins CAST: Keith Perry (Minister/Manager), Mary Stout (Minister's Wife/Pearl/Cashier), Natalie DeLucia, Raegan Kotz (Addie Loggins), Gregory Harrison (Moses), Joe Locarro (Thompson/Dooley), John Bolton (Mechanic/Station Master/Skeeter), Roxie Lucas (Elvira/Waitress/Miss Goodwill), Ruth Gottschall (Marie), Roy Leake, Jr. (Sheriff/Barker/Floyd/Manager), Kathy Garrick (Edna/Lara/Sueleen), Christine Ebersole (Trixie Delight), Chandra Wilson (Imogene), Linda Hart (Sister Amelia Sass), John Dossett (Brother Randolph Sass), Ruth Gottschall, Rebecca Holt(Disciples), Norrice Raymaker (Beezer), Monica M. Wemitt (Crippled Woman/Disciple), Kathryn Kendall

ANIMAL CRACKERS; Music/Lyrics, Bert Kalmar, Harry Ruby; Book, George S. Kaufman, Morrie Ryskind; Director, Charles Repole; Musical Director, Keith Thompson; Choreography, Michael Lichtefeld; Costumes, David Toser; Lighting, F. Mitchell Dana CAST: Dick Decareau (Hives), Carol Swarbrick (Mrs. Rittenhouse), Hal Robinson (Roscoe), Kristin D. Chenoweth (Arabella), Jan Neuberger (Mrs. Whitehead), Karen Murphy (Grace), Michael O'Steen (Wally), John Hoshko (Horatio), Frank Ferrante (Capt. Jeffrey T. Spaulding), Robert Michael Baker (Emanuel Ravelli), Les Marsden (Professor), John Scherer (Parker), Amy M. Young (Mary), Melissa Bell, Mindy Cooper, Melissa Haizlip (Cherubs), Craig Waletzko (Capt. Henessey), James Darrah, Gregory Garrison, Paula Grider, Ken Nagy, Trina Simon

IT RUNS IN THE FAMILY; Written/Directed by Ray Cooper; Costumes, Gregg Barnes; Lighting, F. Mitchell Dana CAST: Robert Mandan (Dr. Mortimore), Kenneth L. Marks (Dr. Connolly), Anne Rogers (Rosemary), Ray Cooney (Dr. Bonney), Barbara Rosenblat (Matron), Edwin J. McDonough (Sir Willoughby), Kay Walbye (Jane), Alexandra O'Karma (Nurse), Mike Doyle (Leslie), Harry S. Murphy (Police), Eddie Bracken (Bill), Georgine Hall (Mother)

A TALE OF TWO CITIES; Writer/Director, Robert Johanson; Adapted from Charles Dickens; Costumes, Gregg Barnes; Lighting, Ken Billington CAST: Timothy Altmeyer, Nancy Bell, Steve Boles, Sabrina Boudot, Kermit Brown, William Carl, Kevin Chamberlin, Matthew D'Antuono, Jeffrey Force, Larry Grey, Margaret Hall, Verl John Hite, Christopher Innvar, Mark Irish, Stephanie Jones, John Juback, Donald S. Kilcoyne, Ken Kliban, Kathleen Mahony-Bennett, Wilma Mondi, Ron Parady, James Pritchett, John Rainer, Michael James Reed, Judith Roberts, Eliza Schlesinger, Adam Slater, Elizabeth Timperman, Suzanne Toren, Patrick Tull, Kristin Kay Wiegand

SOUTH PACIFIC; Music, Richard Rodgers; Lyrics, Oscar Hammerstein II; Book, Mr. Hammerstein, Joshua Logan; Director, Robert Johanson; Musical Director, Don Jones; Choreography, Sharon Halley; Costumes, Gregg Barnes; Lighting, F. Mitchell Dana CAST: Margueritte MacIntyre (Nellie), Ron Raines (Emile), Samantha Robyn Lee (Ngana), Jeffrey Songco (Jerome), Phillip Baltazar (Henry/Richard), Tina Fabrique (Henry), Marilyn Villamar (Liat), Gary Marachek (Luther), Billy Vitelli (Stewpot), Mo Rocca (Professor), J. Mark McVey (Lt. Cable), John Henry Cox (Brackett), Jerry Ball (Harbison), Rusty Reynolds (Buzz), John Cudia Yeoman Quale, Christopher Sieber (McCaffrey), John Bolton (O'Brien), Brian O'Brien (Hayes), Michael Stever (Mac), Bill E. Dietrich (Morton), Bradley Dean (Tony), Seth Charles Malkin (Bubba), Michael Ambrozy (Johnson), Albert Christmas (Steeves), John Wilkerson (Hassinger), Marty McDonough (MacDonald), Joe Heffernan (Patrol), Lisa Albright (Marshall), Caroline Liadakis (Murphy), M. Kathryn Quinlan (MacGregor), Tysan (Walewska), Myra Browning (Noonan)

Gerry Goodstein Photos

Top: Robert Michael Baker, Frank Ferrante, Les Marsden, John Hoshko, Carol Swarbrick in *Animal Crackers*
2nd photo: Natalie DeLucca, Roxie Lucas, Gregory Harrison in *Paper Moon*
3rd photo: Marguerite MacIntyre, Samantha Robyn Lee, Jeffrey Songco, Ron Raines in *South Pacific*
Left: Kay Walbye, Robert Mandan, Ray Cooney, Mike Doyle, Eddie Bracken in *It Runs in the Family*

PHILADELPHIA DRAMA GUILD

Philadelphia, Pennsylvania

Artistic Director, Mary B. Robinson; Managing Director, Alan Levey; Artistic Associate, Barbara Silzle; Production Stage Manager, Roy Backes; Marketing Director, Patricia Nicholson

PRODUCTIONS & CASTS

DANCING AT LUGHNASA by Brian Friel; Director, Mary B. Robinson CAST: Peter DeLaurier (Michael), Mac Orange (Chris), Alma Cuervo (Maggie), Mia Dillon (Agnes), Lisbeth Bartlett (Rose), Beth Dixon (Kate), Mark Hammer (Jack), Boris McGiver (Gerry)
INSPECTING CAROLS by Dan Sullivan and the Seattle Repertory Resident Company; Directors, Mary B. Robinson, Harriet Power CAST: Anthony Giampetro (Spike), Susan Wilder (MJ), Peter Pryor (Wayne), Janis Dardaris (Zorah), Andrew Gaspar (Luther), Douglas Wing (Sidney), Carla Belver (Dorothy), Tom Teti (Phil), Johnnie Hobbs, Jr. (Walter), Greg Wood (Kevin), Louis Lippa (Larry), Bradley Thoennes (Bart), Lisbeth Bartlett (Betty)
THE PLOUGH AND THE STARS by Sean O'Casey; Director, Shivaun O'Casey CAST: Brendan Coyle (Jack), Madeleine Potter (Nora), Des Keogh (Peter), Alan Mooney (Young Covey), Pauline Flanigan (Bessie), Helen Ryan (Mrs. Gogan), Ruth O'Briain (Mollser), Jarlath Conroy (Fluther), Peter Pryor (Langon/Stoddar), B. J. Hogg (Brennan), Mal White (Tinley), Kerry O'Malley (Rosie), Virginia Downing (Woman), M. Hayes (Figure in Window), Niall Buggy (Voice)
TWO TRAINS RUNNING by August Wilson; Director, Walter Dallas CAST: Kim Sullivan (Wolf), Johnnie Hobbs, Jr. (Memphis), Rosalyn Coleman (Risa), Lex Monson (Holloway), Vincent Yates (Hambone), Jerome Preston Bates (Sterling), Cortex Nance, Jr. (West)
OTHELLO by William Shakespeare; Director, Mary B. Robinson CAST: Bruce A. Young (Othello), Matthew Rauch (Cassio), Campbell Scott (Iago), William Leach (Brabantio), Kathleen McNenny (Desdemona), Andrew Polk (Roderigo), Pearce Bunting (Lodovico), Douglas Wing (Duke), Michael John McGuinness (Montano), Kate Skinner (Emilia), Elizabeth Meeker (Bianca), David Disbrow, Anthony M. Giampetro, Gregg Kaleck, Christopher Roberts, Stephen Sobditch, Bradley Thoennes, Marcus Weiss

Gerry Goodstein Photos

Angel Brown, Monte Russell in *Two Trains Running*

Boris McGiver, Mia Dillon, (back) Mac Orange in
Dancing at Lughnasa

PITTSBURGH PUBLIC THEATRE

Pittsburgh, Pennsylvania
Nineteenth Season

Artistic Director, Edward Gilbert; Managing Director, Dan Fallon; Marketing Director, Rosalind Ruch; Public Relations Director, Elvira DiPaolo/Kimberly Sewright

PRODUCTIONS & CASTS

DANCING AT LUGHNASA by Brian Friel; Director, Jacques Cartier; Set, Anne Mundell; Costumes, Mariann Verheyen; Lighting, Michael Baldassari CAST: Terrence Caza (Michael), Roberta Maxwell (Maggie), Laurie Kennedy (Kate), Cary Ann Spear (Agnes), Susan Wands (Rose), Jennifer Wiltsie (Chris), Philip Pleasants (Jack), Rob Gomes (Gerry)
ABSURD PERSON SINGULAR by Alan Ayckbourn; Director, Stephen Hollis; Costumes, James Wolk; Costumes, Liz Covey; Lighting, Dennis Parichy CAST: Sybil Lines (Jane), Martin Rayner (Sidney), Denis Holmes (Ronald), Jill Tanner (Marion), Suzanne Irving (Eva), Curzon Dobell (Geoffrey)
THE DYBBUK by S. Ansky; Director/Adaptor, Edward Gilbert; Sets/Costumes, Mark Negin; Lighting, Jackie Manassee CAST: Carl Don (Batalon/Minyan), Jeffrey Ware, Antone DiLeo (Batalon/Hasid), George Sperdakos (Messenger), David Bishins (Khonon), David Kener (Henek/Beggar/Hasid), Larry John Meyers (Meyer/Minyan/Judge), Shirley Tannenbaum (Hannah-Esther/Beggar/Guest), Leslie Rohland (Leah), Irma St. Paule (Frade), Colleen Delany (Gittel/Minyan), Colin Doty (Asher/Hasid), Jack Davidson (Sender), Julie Marie Paparella (Basia/Minyan), Manny Jacobs (Menashe/Student/Hasid), Alex Coleman (Nachman/Judge), Carol Ferguson (Beggar/Student), Madeline Lagattuta, Alexa Stern (Child), Paul Mochnick (Mendel/Minyan), Allan Pinsker (Mikhoel/Guest), George Morfogen (Azrielke), Joel Friedman (Shimson), Brent Peelor, Robert Scharff (Students)
WINGS, The Musical; Music, Jeffrey Lunden; Lyrics/Book, Arthur Perlman; From play by Arthur Kopit; Director, Ted Pappas; Music Director, Evans Haile; Set, Allen Moyer; Costumes, Michael Krass; Lighting, Frances Aronson CAST: Leila Martin (Emily), Wayne Hoffman (Doctor/Brambilla), Brenda Braye (Nurse/Mrs. Timmins), Barbara McCulloh (Amy), Russ Thacker (Billy)
ARMS AND THE MAN by George Bernard Shaw; Director, Edward Gilbert; Set, Dick Block; Costumes, Helen Ju; Lighting, Cindy Limauro CAST: Funda Duyal (Raina), Rosemary De Angelis (Catherine), Melissa Weil (Louka), Sheridan Crist (Capt. Bluntschli), John Hall (Officer), Ross Bickell (Nicola), Roger Serbagi (Petkoff), Christian Baskous (Saranoff)
TWO TRAINS RUNNING by August Wilson; Director, Claude Purdy; Set, James Sandefur; Costumes, Martha Hally; Lighting, Phil Donat CAST: Angel Brown (Risa), Willis Burks II (Wolf), Charles Weldon (Memphis), Sala Udin (Holloway), Ron L. Cox (Hambone), Monte Russell (Sterling), Allie Woods, Jr. (West)

Ric Evans, Gerry Goodstein, Mark Portland Photos

PLAYHOUSE ON THE SQUARE

Memphis, Tennessee

Executive Producer, Jackie Nichols; Youth Program Director, Karin Hill; Artistic Director, Wm. Perry Morgan

PRODUCTIONS: *Six Degrees of Separation, I Hate Hamlet, The Importance of Being Earnest, Smoke on the Mountain*
(Circuit Playhouse Stage) *Benched Affairs, Lips Together Teeth Apart, The Magic Mirage, The Velveteen Rabbit, For Colored Girls, Mother Hicks*

COMPANY INCLUDES: Rebecca Kolber, Carl Jay Cofield, Christopher Swan, Dave Landis, Ken Zimmerman, John Pierce, Greta Grosch, Jean McDearman, Barclay Roberts, Anne Marie Caskey, Anne Marie Thomas, Robert Neal Kwalick, Dwight Hoffman, Kristine Mason, Tracey Zerwig Ford, Vicki Edwards, Penelope Walker, Staci Shaw, Josephine Hall

Pam and John Fowler Photos

**Top Right: John Pierce, Greta Grosch, Jen McDearman
in *Smoke on the Mountain*
Bottom Right: Christopher Swan, Dave Landis in *I Hate Hamlet***

PLAYMAKERS REPERTORY COMPANY

Chapel Hill, North Carolina

Producing Director, Milly S. Barranger; Associate Producing Director, David Hammond; Administrative Director, Mary Robin Wells; Production Manager, Michael Rolleri; Sets/Costumes, Judy Adamson, Sharon K. Campbell, Bobbi Owen; Production Stage Manager, Maura J. Murphy; Communications Director, Patti Thorp

PRODUCTIONS: *The Grapes of Wrath* by John Steinbeck; Adaptation, Frank Galati; Director, David Hammond; *Marvin's Room* by Scott McPherson; Director, Ray Dooley; *Beauty and the Beast* by Tom Huey; Director, Michael Wilson; *Death of a Salesman* by Arthur Miller; Director, Jeffrey Hayden; *Arms and the Man*; Director, David Hammond; *Love Letters* by A. R. Gurney, Jr.; Director, Jeffrey Hayden; *The Winter's Tale* by William Shakespeare; Director, Charles Bewell

RESIDENT COMPANY: Patricia Barnett, Jef Betz, David M. Brooks, Thomas Carr, James Carmel, Brian Christopher, Kim Ann Clay, Dede Corvinus, Ray Dooley, Mark Eis, Barbara Eillingson, Brett Halna du Fretay, Michael Hunter, Paige Johnston, Cheryl Jones, Michael H. King, Nancy Lane, Brent Langson, Tif Luckenbill, Ronda Music, Julie Padilla, Susanna Rinehart, John Rosenfeld, Alexander Yannis Stephano, Jody Strimling, Ken Strong, Christine Suhr, Craig Turner, Ed Wagenseller, Kristine Watt
GUEST ARTISTS: (Actors) Simon Brooking, Richard Burgwin, Terrence Caza, Julie Fishell, William Griffis, George Grizzard, Judd Hirsch, Zane Lasky, Cara Duff-MacCormick, Jan Maxwell, DeAnn Mears, Joseph Murphy, Mark Niebuhr, Mary O'Brady, Sally Parrish, Stuart Rogers, Eva Marie Saint, Jeffery West, Kenneth White, Christopher Wynkoop (Directors) Michael Wison, Jeffrey Hayden, Charles Newell (Designers) Peter S. Blue, Bill Clarke, McKay Coble, Jeff Cowie, Marcus Dilliard, Mary Louise Geiger, John Gromada, Yvette Helin, Ashley York Kennedy, Sarah Lambert, Michael Lincoln, Caryn Neman, Russell Parkman

Biar Orrell, Will Owens Photos

**Top Left: Judd Hirsch, Eva Marie Saint in *Death of a Salesman*
Bottom Left: DeAnn Mears, Joseph Murphy in *Grapes of Wrath***

REMAINS THEATRE

Chicago, Illinois

Artistic Director, Neel Keller; General Manager, Janis Post; Artistic Associate, Ed Shimp; Stage Manager, Mary McAuliffe

PRODUCTIONS & CASTS

HOW COULD SUCH A MONSTER COME TO BE?; Conceived by Maestro Subgum and the Whole, Jeff Dorchen and Bryn Magnus; Sct, Eric A. Ton; Lighting, Spencer Sundell CAST: Beau O'Reilly (Lefty Fizzle), Jenny Magnus (Jenny the Magnifire), Colm O'Reilly (Clem), Michael Greenberg (Mickey da Lip), Mark Messing (Sweet Muscles Messin' with His No-Spazz Zoaz), Ned Folkerth (Red Ned, the Flame Haired Messenger of Love), Bob Jacobson (Bobby Ray)
JEFF GARLIN: UNCOMPLICATED; Written/Performed by Jeff Garlin; Director, Mick Napier
MAD FOREST by Caryl Churchill; Director, Michael Greif; Set, Michael Phillipi; Costumes, Allison Reeds; Lighting, James F. Ingalls CAST: Christine Ashe, Lance Baker, Cheryl Lynn Bruce, Thomas Carroll, Christopher Donahue, Maureen Gallagher, Kevin Hurley, Bruce Norris, Christopher Pieczynski, Michael Stumm, Lisa Tejero

Kim Soren Larsen Photos

John Pielmeier in *Willi*

Andrew Harrison Leeds, Bill Bowers in *Young Rube*

Bruce Norris, Cheryl Lynn Bruce in *Mad Forest*

REPERTORY THEATRE OF ST. LOUIS

St. Louis, Missouri

Artistic Director, Steven Woolf; Managing Director, Mark D. Bernstein; Associate Artistic Director, Susan Gregg; Public Relations Manager, Judy Andrews

PRODUCTIONS & CASTS

YOUNG RUBE; Music/Lyrics, Matthew Selman; Book, John Pielmeier; Based on play by George W. George; Director, Susan Gregg; Choreography, Donald Holdgrive; Musical Director, Albert Ahronson; Orchestrations, Michael Gibson; Sets, John Ezell; Costumes, Dorothy L. Marshall; Lighting, Dale F. Jordan CAST: Mana Allen (Tillie/Pearl), Bill Bowers (Boob), Amanda Butternaugh (Eau D'Alisque/Adenoida Sourgrapes), Frank DiPasquale (Principal/Slate/Ruef/Mike/Bartender), Susan Ericksen (Galatea de Teets/Lala Palooza), Gregory Grant (Little Rube/Mole/Mr. P/Cop/Old Man/Alf of the Alphabet/Black Bart), Steve Liebman (Christy/Bunker/Cop/Liberty Undaunted/Minister), Michael Mulheren (Max/Lucifer Gorgonzola Butts), Marcus Neville (Young Rube), Kristine Nevins (Moany Lisa/Medulla Oblongata), Russ Thacker (Woodward/Mayor/Dying Miner)
CONVERSATIONS WITH MY FATHER by Herb Gardner; Director, Jim O'Connor; Set, Michael S. Philippi; Costumes, Arthur Ridley; Lighting, Max De Volder CAST: Steve Itkin (Charlie), Chad Kraus (Josh), Joseph Costa (Eddie), Christa Germanson (Gusta), Joneal Joplin (Zaretsky), Brad Mariam (Young Joey), Zoe Vonder Haar (Hannah), Wm Daniel File (Nick), John Tyrrell (Finney), Whit Reichert (Blue), John Grassilli (Jimmy), Robert D'Haene (Joey), Mark Silverberg (Young Charlie)
DEATH AND THE MAIDEN by Ariel Dorfman; Director, Steven Woolf; Set, Gene Friedman; Costumes, Dorothy L. Marshall; Lighting, Mark Wilson CAST: Leah Maddrie (Paulina), Paul DeBoy (Gerardo), Keith Jochim (Roberto)
ONCE ON THIS ISLAND; Music, Stephen Flaherty; Lyrics/Book, Lynn Ahrens; Director/Choreographer, Eric Riley; Musical Director, Larry Pressgrove; Set, Peter Harrison; Costumes, Clyde Ruffin; Lighting, Peter E. Sargent CAST: Donnell Aarone (Daniel), Steven Cates (Papa Ge), Marcy De Nezza (Andrea), Tonya L. Dixon (Ti Moune), Lynette Du Pre (Mama), Michael James Leslie (Tonton), Brittany Noel Packnett (Little Ti Moune), John Eric Parker (Agwe), Dominic Rambaran (Armand), Fredi Walker (Erzulie), Sharon Wilkins (Asaka)
DANCING AT LUGHNASA by Brian Friel; Director, Edward Stern; Choreography, Marcia Milgram Dodge; Set, John Ezell; Costumes, Dorothy L. Marshall; Lighting, Peter E. Sargent CAST: Greg Thornton (Michael), Katherine Leask (Chris), Brooks Almy (Maggie), Mary O'Brady (Agnes), Katherine Heasley (Rose), Darrie Lawrence (Kate), Russ Jolly (Gerry), Donald Ewer (Jack)
AN ENEMY OF THE PEOPLE by Henrik Ibsen; Adaptation, Arthur Miller; Director, Susan Gregg; Set, Marie Anne Chiment; Costumes, J. Bruce Summers; Lighting, Max De Volder CAST: Ron Faber (Morten Kiil), Whit Reichert (Billing), Carol Schultz (Mrs. Stockmann), Howard Witt (Peter), R. Ward Duffy (Hovstad), Daren Kelly (Stockman), Will Delano (Morten), Sam Martin (Ejlif), Peter Ashton Wise (Horster), Alisha McKinney (Petra), Joe Palmieri (Aslaksen), R. Michael Traas (Drunk), Louis Bird, Emily Carter, Erin K. Considine, Jeffrey Cox, Teresa Doggett, David Durham, Wm Daniel File, Rob Harriell, Jennifer Jonassen, Mark La Velle, David Wassilak, Love Yascone
ROUGH CROSSING by Tom Stoppard; Music, Andre Previn; Director, Victoria Bussert; Musical Director, Diane Ceccarini; Choreography, John Sloman; Sets, John Roslevich, Jr.; Costumes, James Scott; Lighting, Mary Jo Dondlinger CAST: Edward Conery (Turai), Jonathan Bustle (Gal), Charles Tuthill (Adam), Alison Bevan (Natasha), Peter Shawn (Ivor), Steve Routman (Dvornichek)

Judy Andrews Photos

187

Darla Cash in *Three Hotels*

SAN DIEGO REPERTORY THEATRE

San Diego, California

Producing Director, Sam Woodhouse; Artistic Director, Douglas Jacobs; General Manager, John Redman; Communications Manager, Natalie Guishar

PRODUCTIONS & CASTS

BESSIE'S BLUES; Writer/Director, Thomas W. Jones II; Music/Lyrics, Mr. Jones, Keith Rawls; Choreography, Patdro Harris; Set, John P. Redman; Lighting, Brenda Berry; Costumes, Judy Watson CAST: Bernardine Mitchell (Bessie Smith), Yoshicka Betty (Woman/Dancer), Barry Bruce (Midnight), Damon Bryant (Blood), Sonya Hensley (Rhythm), Khalil Reed (Bluesman), Cheryl Renee (Passion), Harrison White (Lover/Jack)
THREE HOTELS by Jon Robin Baitz; Director, Todd Salovey; Set, Neil Patel; Costumes, Judy Watson; Lighting, Brenda Berry CAST: Douglas Jacobs (Kenneth), Darla Cash (Barbara)
BURNING DREAMS; Music/Musical Director, Gina Leishman; Libretto, Julie Herbert and Octovio Solis; Director, Ms. Herbert, Sam Woodhouse; Choreography, Deborah Slater; Sets, Robert Brill; Lighting, John Phillip Martin; Costumes, Mary Larson CAST: Alex Britton (Anselmo), Cheryl Carter (Leone), Anita De Simone (Rosaura), Rinde Eckert (Segismundo), Catalina Maynard (Midwife), Deborah Slater (Clown)
REAL WOMEN HAVE CURVES by Josefina Lopez; Director, William Alejandro Virchis; Set, John Iacovelli; Lighting, Brenda Berry; Costumes, Dione Lebhar CAST: Josefina Lopez (Ana), Lupe Ontiveros (Carmen), Coral Thuet (Pancha), Roxane Carrasco (Rosali), Lucy Rodriguez (Estela)
SLAPSTICK; Conceived/Created by Michael Fields, Donald Forrest, Joan Schirle and Jael Weisman; Director, Mr. Weisman; Set, Alain Schons; Costumes, Nancy Jo Smith; Lighting, Michael Foster CAST: Donald Forrest (Norm/Junior), Joan Schirle (Sheila/Missy), Michael Fields (Roger/Father), David Ferney (Trunker), Stephen Smith (Band)

Ken Jacques Photos

188

Joan Schirle, Donald Forrest, Michael Fields in *Slapstick*

Lupe Ontiveros, Roxane Carrasco, Lucy Rodriguez, Coral Thuet in *Real Women Have Curves*

SEATTLE REPERTORY THEATRE

Seattle, Washington

Artistic Director, Daniel Sullivan; Acting Artistic Director, Douglas Hughes; Managing Director, Benjamin Moore; Associate Artistic Director/Literary Manager, Kurt Beattie; Marketing/Public Relations Director, Karen L. Bystrom

PRODUCTIONS & CASTS

SIX DEGREES OF SEPARATION by John Guare; Director, David Saint; Set, Alexander Okun; Costumes, David Murin; Lighting, Kenneth Posner CAST: Jim Anzide, Kurt Beattie, June Christy Burch, James Chesnutt, Ray Cochran, Sara DeBoer, Barbara Dirickson, Sam Freed, Tyrone Mitchell Henderson, Hunt Holman, Peter Lohnes, Keeley Madden, David Stephen Maier, Bob Morrisey, Johanna Nemeth, Marianne Owen, Kaleo Quenzer, Branden Romans, Douglas Scholz-Carlson, Tom Spiller, Rick Tutor
HARVEY by Mary Chase; Director, Douglas Hughes; Sets, Hugh Landwehr; Costumes, Linda Fisher; Lighting, Greg Sullivan CAST: June Christy Burch, Jeannie Carson, Barbara Dirickson, Katie Forgette, Kevin C. Loomis, Glenn Mazen, Marianne Owen, Peggy Pope, Tom Spiller, Rick Tutor, Jeff Weiss, Christopher Evan Welch
OLEANNA by David Mamet; Director, Mark Wing-Davey; Set, Andrew Jackness; Costumes, Rose Pederson; Lighting, Christopher Akerlind CAST: Peter Gerety, Angie Phillips
PERICLES, PRINCE OF TYRE by William Shakespeare; Director, Douglas Hughes; Sets, Douglas Fitch; Costumes, Catherine Zuber; Lighting, Peter Maradudin CAST: Jeannie Carson, Lisa Carswell, Alene Dawson, Leslie DoQui, Anthony Lee, Kevin C. Loomis, William Biff McGuire, Bob Morrisey, Matthew Scott Olson, Marianne Owen, Kaleo Quenzer, Tom Spiller, Rick Tutor, Christopher Evan Welch, Isiah Whitlock, Jr.
A FLAW IN THE OINTMENT by Georges Feydeau; Translation/Adaptation, Lillian Garrett-Groag and William Gray; Director, Ms. Garrett-Groag; Set, Hugh Landwehr; Costumes, David Murin; Lighting, Peter Kaczorowski CAST: Jeannie Carson, Rachel Coloff, Mark Drusch, Katie Forgette, Michael Hacker, Hunt Holman, Robert Machray, William Biff McGuire, David Mong, Bob Morrisey, Gina Nagy, Marianne Owen, Rick Tutor, Christopher Evan Welch
HOLIDAY HEART by Cheryl L. West; Director/Costumes, Tazewell Thompson; Set, Riccardo Hernandez; Lighting, Jack Mehler CAST: Harriet D. Foy, LaShonda Hunt, Ron Cephas Jones, Leon Sanders, Keith Randolph Smith
NORTHEAST LOCAL by Tom Donaghy; Director, David Petrarca; Set, Linda Buchanan; Costumes, Eduardo Sicangco; Lighting, Robert Christen CAST: Kelly Coffield, Sean Cullen, Pauline Flanagan, Allen Oliver
...LOVE, LANGSTON; Conceived/Adapted/Composed/Directed by Loni Berry; Choreography, Andre De Shields; Set, Vincent Mountain; Costumes, Myrna Colley-Lee; Lighting, Andria L. Fiegel CAST: Karen-Angela Bishop, Andre De Shields, Ellia English, Grenoldo Frazier, Melody Garrett, Tommy Hollis
SILENCE, CUNNING, EXILE by Stuart Greenman; Director, Sarah Lambert; Costumes, Elizabeth Michal Fried; Lighting, Scott Zielinski CAST: Candy Buckley, Sean Cullen, Sara DeBoer, Mark Finley, Enid Graham, Hunt Holman, Joshua List, Michael MacRae, Mark Nelson, J. Smith-Cameron

Chris Bennion Photos

Top Right: Christopher Evan Welch, Katie Forgette in *Harvey*
Center Right: Keith Randolph Smith, Ron Cephas Jones in *Holiday Heart*
Bottom Right: J. Smith-Cameron, Mark Nelson in *Silence, Cunning, Exile*
Bottom Left: Tommy Hollis, Andre De Shields in *...Love, Langston*

STUDIO ARENA THEATRE

Buffalo, New York
Twenty-ninth Season

Artistic Director, Gavin Cameron-Webb; Producing Director, Raymond Bonnard

PRODUCTIONS & CASTS

MAN OF THE MOMENT by Alan Ayckbourn; Director, Gavin Cameron-Webb; Set/Costumes, G. W. Mercier; Lighting, Rachel Budin CAST: Brad Bellamy, Kelli Grey Bocock, Denia Brache, Ray Chambers, Roger Forbes, Leslie Hendrix, David Hyde-Lamb, Anne Swift, Tim White

MY CHILDREN! MY AFRICA! by Athol Fugard; Director, Seret Scott; Set, Russell Metheny; Costumes, Catherine F. Norgren; Lighting, Harry A. Feiner CAST: Nancy Bell, Stephen McKinley Henderson, Victor Mack

THE WORLD GOES 'ROUND: THE KANDER & EBB MUSICAL; Music, John Kander; Lyrics, Fred Ebb; Conception, Scott Ellis, Susan Stroman; David Thompson; Director/Choreographer, Darwin Knight; Musical Director, Randall Kramer; Set, James Kronzer; Costumes, Ann R. Emo; Lighting, William H. Grant III CAST: Peter Flynn, Lovette George, Jan Leigh Herndon, Kirk Mouser, Peggy Taphorn

MURDER BY MISADVENTURE by Edward Taylor; Director, Frederick King Keller; Set/Lighting, Paul Wonsek; Costumes, Elizabeth Haas Keller CAST: Julian Gamble (Harold), T. Ryder Smith (Paul), Nicole Orth-Pallavicini (Emma), Adrian Roberts (Egan)

DANCING AT LUGHNASA by Brian Friel; Director, Caroline FitzGerald; Set/Costumes, Bill Clarke; Lighting, Brian Mac Devitt CAST: Vincent O'Neill (Michael), Josephine Hogan (Chris), Bairbre Dowling (Maggie), Terry Donnelly (Agnes), Louise Favier (Rose), Mary Larkin (Kate), Chris O'Neill (Jack), Kevin Donovan (Gerry)

THE GAME OF LOVE AND CHANCE by Pierre Marivaux; Translation, Neil Bartlett; Director, Gavin Cameron-Webb; Set, Bob Cothran; Costumes, Laura Crow; Lighting, Frances Aronson CAST: Christopher Wynkoop (Prowde), Alexandra O'Karma (Silvia), Tim Howard (Maurice), Brad Bellamy (Arlecchino), Sue Brady (Lisette), Martin Kildare (Dorant)

ONCE ON THIS ISLAND; Music, Stephen Flaherty; Lyrics/Book, Lynn Ahrens; Director, Bob Baker; Musical Director, Don Horsburgh; Set/Costumes, Leslie Frankish; Lighting, William H. Grant III CAST: Troy Adams (Daniel), Salome Bey (Mama), Timothy Robert Blevins (Agwe), Arlene Duncan (Erzulie), China Forbes (Andrea), Tyrone Gabriel (Armand), Vanita Harbour (Ti Moune), Jeff Jones (Tonton), Nathaniel Sanders (Papa Ge), Cynthia Thomas (Asaka), Danian Vickers (Little Ti Moune)

K. C. Kratt Photos

**Top Left: Salome Bey, Danian Vickers, Jeff Jones
in *Once on this Island***
Center Left: Victor Mack, Nancy Bell in *My Children! My Africa!*

190

**Terry Donnelly, Kevin Donovan, Chris O'Neill,
Josephine Hogan in *Dancing at Lughnasa***

Anne Scurria, Phyllis Kay in *Marvin's Room*

Top Left: Timothy Crowe, Dan Welch, Cynthia Strickland in
Mrs. Sedgewick's Head

Center Left: Timothy Crowe, Anne Scurria in *The Miser*

Bottom Left: Timothy Crowe, William Damkoehler, Dan Welch in
Measure for Measure

TRINITY REPERTORY COMPANY

Providence, Rhode Island
Thirtieth Season

Artistic Director, Richard Jenkins; Associate Artistic Director, Neal Baron; Production Manager, Jeff Clark; Public Relations Director, Margaret Melozzi

PRODUCTIONS & CASTS

LADY DAY AT EMERSON'S BAR & GRILL by Lanie Robertson; Director, Neal Baron; Set, David Rotondo; Costumes, William Lane; Lighting, Jeff Clark CAST: Rose Weaver (Billie Holiday), Marc Cary (Jimmy), Kevin Morrison (Bar Owner)

MARVIN'S ROOM by Scott McPherson; Director, Michael Greif; Set, Eugene Lee; Costumes, William Lane; Lighting, Jeff Clark CAST: Anne Scurria (Bessie), Ken Cheeseman (Dr. Wally), Barbara Orson (Ruth), Fred Sullivan, Jr. (Bob), Phyllis Kay (Lee), Janice Duclos (Dr. Charlotte), Evan Andrews (Hank), Josh Joseph (Charlie), John Cady (Marvin)

MEASURE FOR MEASURE by William Shakespeare; Director, Brian McEleney; Set, Michael McGarty; Costumes, William Lane; Lighting, Dylan Costa CAST: William Damkoehler (Vincentio), Robert J. Colonna (Escalus), Ed Shea (Angelo), John Thompson (Claudio), Stephen Berenson (Lucio), Viola Davis (Isabella), Lisa Lane (Juliet), Allen Oliver (Provost), Nigel Gore (Mistress Overdone/Friar Peter), Timothy Crowe (Pompey), Rose Weaver (Francisca/Mariana), Dan Welch (Elbow), Jason Roth (Froth), Eric Evanson (Friar Thomas)

MRS. SEDGEWICK'S HEAD by Tom Griffin; Director, David Wheeler; Set/Lighting, Eugene Lee; Costumes, William Lane CAST: Joseph Hindy (Nate), Jonathan Fried (Lincoln), Christopher Byrnes (Benjamin), Richard Kneeland (Robert), Timothy Crowe (Johnny), Nance Williamson (Lindsay), Cynthia Strickland (Cara), Robert J. Colonna (Eddie), Dan Welch (Ron)

DANCING AT LUGHNASA by Brian Friel; Director, Barbara Damashek; Set, Michael McGarty; Costumes, William Lane; Lighting, Russell H. Champa CAST: Kurt Rhoads (Michael), Anne Scurria (Kate), Nance Williamson (Maggie), Phyllis Kay (Agnes), Janice Duclos (Rose), Linda Amendola (Chris), Fred Sullivan, Jr. (Gerry), Barry Press (Jack)

THE MISER by Moliere; Translation, Tori Haring-Smith; Director, Richard Jenkins; Set, Eugene Lee; Costumes, William Lane; Lighting, Russell Champa CAST: Ed Shea (Valere), William Damkoehler (Jacques), Phyllis Kay (Elise), Dan Welch (Cleante), Timothy Crowe (Harpagon), Janice Duclos (La Fleche), Allen Oliver (Simon/Officer), Anne Scurria (Simon), Chris Turner (Brindaluche), Jillian Rosenbach (Marianne), Robert J. Colonna (Anselme)

Mark Morelli Photos

WAYSIDE THEATRE

Middletown, Virginia

Producing Artistic Director, Christopher Owens; General Manager, Donna Johnson; Set Designer, Mike Heather; Costume Designer, Harriet Engler; Lighting Director, Mark T. Simpson; Stage Managers, Elizabeth Reddick, Kay Edens

PRODUCTIONS & CASTS

RUMORS by Neil Simon; Director, Christopher Owens CAST: Meg Kelly, John Little, Bruce Barton, Jen Wolfe, David Johnston, Tamara Johnson, Sally Groth, Mark Lien, Darla Frye-Moulden, Steve Hadnagy
MRS. CALIFORNIA by Doris Baizley; Director, Jonathan Michaelson CAST: Kathy Lichter, Tamara Johnson, Jen Wolfe, Sally Groth, Meg Kelly, Bruce Barton, Michelle Burd, Steve Hadnagy
LETTICE AND LOVAGE by Peter Shaffer; Director, Christopher Owens CAST: Jen Wolfe, Kathy Lichter, Bruce Barton, Michelle Burd, Steve Hadnagy, Jenny Maguire, Darla Frye-Moulden, Jeff Beam
I HATE HAMLET by Paul Rudnick; Director, Christopher Owens CAST: Ed Sala, David Chaeney, Alison Lenox, Tamara Johnson, Kathleen Huber, Joe McCullough
THE DIVINERS by Jim Leonard, Jr.; Director, Christopher Owens CAST: David Chaeney, Joe McCullough, Jenny Maguire, Jeffrey Eiche, Joseph Parra, Kathleen Huber, Tamara Johnson, Ellen Nichols, Tod Williams, Michelle Burd, Steve Hadnagy
ARMS AND THE MAN by George Bernard Shaw; Director, Christopher Owens CAST: Katherine Puma, Nick Stannard, Beth Ritson, Kathleen Huber, Joseph Parra, Jeffrey Eiche, Joe McCullough
OLEANNA by David Mamet; Director, Christopher Owens   CAST: John Michalski, Cheryl Gaysunas
A DICKENS CHRISTMAS COLLATION; Adapted/Directed by Christopher Owens CAST: Russ Cusnik, Jen Wolfe, Robin Tate, Katherine Lessner, Sally Groh, Bruce Barton, Sean Pollock

John Westervelt Photos

Top Right: David Chaeney in *The Diviners*
Below: John Michalski, Cheryl Gaysunas in *Oleanna*

WEST COAST ENSEMBLE

Los Angeles, California

Artistic Director, Les Hanson; Managing Directors, James Thomas Bailey, Sharon Lee Connors, Lori Harmon; Publicist, Anne Etue

PRODUCTIONS & CASTS

EQUUS by Peter Shaffer; Director, Jules Aaron; Set, Ramsey Avery; Lighting, Tom Ruzika, Lonnie Alcarez; Costumes, Ted C. Giammona CAST: Jack Noseworthy (Alan), Ian Buchanan (Dysart), Frank Ashmore (Frank), Gammy Singer (Dora), Karen Tarleton (Hesther), Rajia Baroudi (Jill), Tony Pandolfo (Harry), Christopher B. Duncan (Horseman/Nugget), Alison Vail (Nurse), Rex Clayton, Darnell Davis, Fred Slegers, James Ward, Jeff Davis (Horses)

THE HUMAN COMEDY; Music, Galt McDermot; Libretto, William Dumaresq; Director, David Gately; Musical Director, Darren Server; Set, Bradley Kaye; Lighting, Lawrence Oberman; Costumes, A. Jeffrey Schoenberg CAST: Tim Barber (Spangler), Leslie Becker (Diana), Leslie Bockian (Mexican Lady), Angela DeCicco (Mother), Bill Dispoto (Toby), James Geralden (Trainman), Richard Israel (Homer), Danielle Judovits, Alexys Schwartz (Ulysses), Ross Kramer (Thief/Joe), Ann LeSchander (Helen), Mary McBride (Miss Hicks), Michelle Mikesell (Bess), Scott Poland (Marcus), Henry Selvitelle (Grogan), Keith Westmoreland (Baker/Felix), Valerie Zisser (Mary), Susan Milne, Lynne Oropeza

SUDDENLY LAST SUMMER by Tennessee Williams; Director, Claudia Jaffee; Set/Lighting, Jim Barbaley; Costumes, Michael Growler CAST: Irene Roseen (Mrs. Venable), Rodger Burt (Dr. Cukrowicz), Marjorie Bowman (Foxhill), Sheila Shaw (Mrs. Holly), David Youse (George), Carol Davis (Catherine), June Silverman (Sister)

BITTER CANE by Genny Lim; Director, Tim Dang; Set, Gregory Hopkins; Lighting, David Flad; Costumes, Ken Takamoto CAST: Chris Chinn (Kam Su), Charles Chun (Lau Hing Kuo), Benjamin Lum (Fook Ming), Kei Hayashi (Wing Chun Kuo), Jo Yang (Li-Tai), Newton Kaneshiro (Kuroko)

LA MALASANGRE by Griselda Gambaro; Translation, Marguerite Feitlowitz; Director, Steven Avalos; Set, Gregory Hopkins; Lighting, David Flad; Costumes, Michael Growler CAST: Angela DeCicco (Mother), Robert Getz (Father), Robert Madrid (Fermin), Pablo Marz (Rafael), Christine Gonzalez (Dolores), Jim Krestalude (Juan)

CHARLEY'S AUNT by Brandon Thomas; Director, Dan Kern; Set/Lighting, Jim Barbaley; Costumes, Alfred E. Lehman CAST: Cleve Asbury (Jack), Michael Abrams (Brassett), Tim Barber (Charley), Peter Lavin (Babberley), Ferrell Marshall (Kitty), Karri Turner (Amy), Edmund L. Schaff (Chesney/Bart), Ben D'Aubery (Spettigue), Allison Owen (Donna), Melissa Fahn (Ela)

NINTH ANNUAL CELEBRATION OF ONE ACT PLAYS; Festival Director, Michael Donovan PROGRAMS: *Thicker Than Water* by Gary Cearlock; Director, Michael Donovan CAST: Cynthia Steele, Ramona Rhoades; *Life Support* by Max Mitchell; Director, Fred Gorelick CAST: Forest Witt; *Hubie's Best Friend* by Jules Tasca; Director, Alison Vail CAST: Jason Broad, Jonathan Bott, Melissa Fahn; *He's a Genius* by Max Mitchell; Director, Fred Gorelick CAST: Lori Harmon, Rocco Vienhage; *Old Goat Song* by Jules Tasca; Director, Toni Wilson CAST: Edmund L. Shaff, Jeanette Miller, Carol Louise, Michelle Mikesell; *Mary Harold and Fabia* by David J. Hill; Director, Marjorie Bowman CAST: Marybeth Cameron-Massett, Beth Taylor-Hart; *It's Kinda Like Math* by Charles Evered; Director, Claudia Jaffee CAST: David Mark Peterson, Kerry Haynie; *Don't Throw Bouquets at Me* by Holly Sklar; Director, Chris Hart CAST: Marjorie Bowman, Ren Hanami, Wendy Beauchamp, Michael Edelstein; *Listen to the Lightning* by Robert Canning; Director, Richard Large CAST: Sheila Shaw, Thyra Metz, Ferrell Marshall, John Marzilli

John Ballowe, Bob Bayles Photos

Top: Jack Noseworthy, Christopher B. Duncan in *Equus*
Center: Tim Barber, Ross Kramer in *The Human Comedy*
Right: Jo Yang, Benjamin Lum in *Bitter Cane*

Reggie Montgomery, Adriane Lenox in *The America Play*

YALE REPERTORY THEATRE

New Haven, Connecticut

Artistic Director, Stan Wojewodski; Managing Director, Victoria Nolan; Associate Artistic Director, Mark Bly; Marketing Director, Joan Channick; Press/Publications Director, Joyce Friedmann; Press/Marketing Assistant, Laura J. Janik

PRODUCTIONS & CASTS

OLEANNA by David Mamet; Director, Stan Wojewodski; Set, Merope Vachliotis; Costumes, Deb Trout; Lighting, Stephen Strawbridge CAST: Casey Biggs, Welker White
THE GREEN BIRD by Carlo Gozzi; Translation, Albert Bermel, Ted Emery; Director, Vincent Gracieux; Set, Henry S. Dunn; Costumes, Felicity Jones; Lighting, Frederic Desbois CAST: Kyle Acjerman, John Bolding, Sarah Corzatt, Barbara Berlovitz Desbois, Vincent Gracieux, Eric Jensen, Laura Janik, Felicity Jones, Masanari Kawahara, Angela Lewis, John Plummer, Robert de los Reyes, Robert Rosen, Dominique Serrand, Heather K. Wilson
THE AMERICA PLAY by Suzan-Lori Parks; Director, Liz Diamond; Set, Riccardo Hernanadez; Costumes, Angelina Avallone; Lighting, Jeremy V. Stein CAST: Gail Grate, Tyrone Mitchell Henderson, Adriane Lenox, Reggie Montgomery, Michael Potts
AS YOU LIKE IT by William Shakespeare; Director, Stan Wojewodski, Jr.; Music, Kim D. Sherman; Set, Dawn Robyn Petrlik; Costumes, Ilona Somogyi; Lighting, Jennifer Tipton CAST: Sarah Brown, Max Chalawsky, Michael Eaddy, Al Espinosa, Bo Foxworth, Peter Gantenbein, Paul Giamatti, Kevin Henderson, Sarah Knowlton, Elizabeth Lande, Nina Landey, Robin Dana Miles, Andrew Pang, Lance Reddick, Scott Sherman, Phillip C. Smith, Ashlee Temple, Anthony Ward
Mump and Smoot in FERNO and CAGED; Written/Created by Michael Kennard and John Turner; Director, Karen Hines; Set, Campbell Manning; Lighting, Michel Charbonneau CAST: Michael Kennard, Rick Kunst, John Turner
SCHOOL FOR WIVES by Moliere; Translation, Paul Schmidt; Director, Liz Diamond; Set, Myung Hee Cho; Costumes, Deb Trout; Lighting, Kristin Bredal CAST: Brenda Cummings, Sanaa Lathan, Adam LeFevre, David Manis, Thomas McCarthy, Jasper McGruder, James Puig, Paul Schmidt

T. Charles EricksonMichal Danie Photos

194

Barbara Berlovitz Desbois, Dominique Serrand
in *The Green Bird*

Paul Schmidt, Adam LeFevre, Jaspar McGruder
in *School for Wives*

Welker White, Casey Biggs in *Oleanna*

(back) Robin Dana Miles, Michael Eaddy, Max Chalawsky,
(front) Lance Reddick, Paul Giamatti, Kevin Henderson
in *As You Like It*

1994 THEATRE WORLD AWARD RECIPIENTS
(Outstanding New York Debut)

MARCUS D'AMICO
of *An Inspector Calls*

ARABELLA FIELD
of *Snowing at Delphi* and *4 Dogs and a Bone*

SHERRY GLASER
of *Family Secrets*

JARROD EMICK
of *Damn Yankees*

ADEN GILLETT
of *An Inspector Calls*

MARGARET ILLMAN
of *The Red Shoes*

196   **AUDRA ANN McDONALD**
of *Carousel*

MICHAEL HAYDEN
of *Carousel*

BURKE MOSES
of *Guys and Dolls* and *Beauty and the Beast*

ANNA DEAVERE SMITH
of *Twilight: Los Angeles, 1992*

HARRIET WALTER
of *3 Birds Alighting on a Field*

JERE SHEA
of *Passion*

197

THEATRE WORLD AWARDS

Presented in the Roundabout Theatre (*Picnic* set)
on Monday, May 16th, 1994.

Presenters (all previous recipients): Top: David Birney, Patricia Elliot, Adam Arkin, Andrea Martin, Victor Garber,
Dorothy Loudon; Alan Alda; Barbara Cook, John Shea, Peter Gallagher, Armelia McQueen, Rosemary Harris, Alan Alda.
Below: Audra Ann McDonald; Aden Gillett, John Shea; Barbara Cook; Adam Arkin; Margaret Illman, Victor Garber.
3rd Row: Peter Gallagher; Andrea Martin; Marcus D'Amico; Dorothy Loudon; Michael Hayden.
Bottom Row: David Birney, Patricia Elliott; Arabella Field; Jere Shea; Armelia McQueen; Sherry Glaser.
Photos by Michael Riordan, Peter Warrack, Van Williams.

**Top: Adam Arkin, Andrea Martin; Patricia Elliott; Burke Moses; Harriet Walter; David Birney; Jarrod Emick.
Below: Tovah Feldshuh, Lee Roy Reams, Dorothy Loudon, Barbara Cook; Rosetta Lenoir, Beatrice Winde; Russ
Thacker, SuEllen Estey, Harvey Evans. 3rd Row: Katharine Houghton; Rosemary Harris, Jarrod Emick; B. D. Wong,
Armelia McQueen; Cynthia Nixon; Audra Ann McDonald. Bottom: Douglas Watt (Daily News), Patricia Elliott, Susan
Browning; Jere Shea, Francis Ruivivar; Rosemary Harris, Alan Alda.
Photos: Michael Riordan, Peter Warrack, Van Williams**

199

Alan Alda

Annette Bening

Marlon Brando

Previous Theatre World Award Winners

1944-45: Betty Comden, Richard Davis, Richard Hart, Judy Holliday, Charles Lang, Bambi Linn, John Lund, Donald Murphy, Nancy Noland, Margaret Phillips, John Raitt
1945-46: Barbara Bel Geddes, Marlon Brando, Bill Callahan, Wendell Corey, Paul Douglas, Mary James, Burt Lancaster, Patricia Marshall, Beatrice Pearson
1946-47: Keith Andes, Marion Bell, Peter Cookson, Ann Crowley, Ellen Hanley, John Jordan, George Keane, Dorothea MacFarland, James Mitchell, Patricia Neal, David Wayne
1947-48: Valerie Bettis, Edward Bryce, Whitfield Connor, Mark Dawson, June Lockhart, Estelle Loring, Peggy Maley, Ralph Meeker, Meg Mundy, Douglass Watson, James Whitmore, Patrice Wymore
1948-49: Tod Andrews, Doe Avedon, Jean Carson, Carol Channing, Richard Derr, Julie Harris, Mary McCarty, Allyn Ann McLerie, Cameron Mitchell, Gene Nelson, Byron Palmer, Bob Scheerer
1949-50: Nancy Andrews, Phil Arthur, Barbara Brady, Lydia Clarke, Priscilla Gillette, Don Hanmer, Marcia Henderson, Charlton Heston, Rick Jason, Grace Kelly, Charles Nolte, Roger Price
1950-51: Barbara Ashley, Isabel Bigley, Martin Brooks, Richard Burton, Pat Crowley, James Daley, Cloris Leachman, Russell Nype, Jack Palance, William Smithers, Maureen Stapleton, Marcia Van Dyke, Eli Wallach
1951-52: Tony Bavaar, Patricia Benoit, Peter Conlow, Virginia de Luce, Ronny Graham, Audrey Hepburn, Diana Herbert, Conrad Janis, Dick Kallman, Charles Proctor, Eric Sinclair, Kim Stanley, Marian Winters, Helen Wood
1952-53: Edie Adams, Rosemary Harris, Eileen Heckart, Peter Kelley, John Kerr, Richard Kiley, Gloria Marlowe, Penelope Munday, Paul Newman, Sheree North, Geraldine Page, John Stewart, Ray Stricklyn, Gwen Verdon
1953-54: Orson Bean, Harry Belafonte, James Dean, Joan Diener, Ben Gazzara, Carol Haney, Jonathan Lucas, Kay Medford, Scott Merrill, Elizabeth Montgomery, Leo Penn, Eva Marie Saint
1954-55: Julie Andrews, Jacqueline Brookes, Shirl Conway, Barbara Cook, David Daniels, Mary Fickett, Page Johnson, Loretta Leversee, Jack Lord, Dennis Patrick, Anthony Perkins, Christopher Plummer
1955-56: Diane Cilento, Dick Davalos, Anthony Franciosa, Andy Griffith, Laurence Harvey, David Hedison, Earle Hyman, Susan Johnson, John Michael King, Jayne Mansfield, Sara Marshall, Gaby Rodgers, Susan Strasberg, Fritz Weaver

1956-57: Peggy Cass, Sydney Chaplin, Sylvia Daneel, Bradford Dillman, Peter Donat, George Grizzard, Carol Lynley, Peter Palmer, Jason Robards, Cliff Robertson, Pippa Scott, Inga Swenson
1957-58: Anne Bancroft, Warren Berlinger, Colleen Dewhurst, Richard Easton, Tim Everett, Eddie Hodges, Joan Hovis, Carol Lawrence, Jacqueline McKeever, Wynne Miller, Robert Morse, George C. Scott
1958-59: Lou Antonio, Ina Balin, Richard Cross, Tammy Grimes, Larry Hagman, Dolores Hart, Roger Mollien, France Nuyen, Susan Oliver, Ben Piazza, Paul Roebling, William Shatner, Pat Suzuki, Rip Torn
1959-60: Warren Beatty, Eileen Brennan, Carol Burnett, Patty Duke, Jane Fonda, Anita Gillette, Elisa Loti, Donald Madden, George Maharis, John McMartin, Lauri Peters, Dick Van Dyke
1960-61: Joyce Bulifant, Dennis Cooney, Sandy Dennis, Nancy Dussault, Robert Goulet, Joan Hackett, June Harding, Ron Husmann, James MacArthur, Bruce Yarnell
1961-62: Elizabeth Ashley, Keith Baxter, Peter Fonda, Don Galloway, Sean Garrison, Barbara Harris, James Earl Jones, Janet Margolin, Karen Morrow, Robert Redford, John Stride, Brenda Vaccaro
1962-63: Alan Arkin, Stuart Damon, Melinda Dillon, Robert Drivas, Bob Gentry, Dorothy London, Brandon Maggart, Julienne Marie, Liza Minnelli, Estelle Parsons, Diana Sands, Swen Swenson
1963-64: Alan Alda, Gloria Bleezarde, Imelda De Martin, Claude Giraud, Ketty Lester, Barbara Loden, Lawrence Pressman, Gilbert Price, Philip Proctor, John Tracy, Jennifer West
1964-65: Carolyn Coates, Joyce Jillson, Linda Lavin, Luba Lisa, Michael O'Sullivan, Joanna Pettet, Beah Richards, Jaime Sanchez, Victor Spinetti, Nicolas Surovy, Robert Walker, Clarence Williams III
1965-66: Zoe Caldwell, David Carradine, John Cullum, John Davidson, Faye Dunaway, Gloria Foster, Robert Hooks, Jerry Lanning, Richard Mulligan, April Shawhan, Sandra Smith, Leslie Ann Warren
1966-67: Bonnie Bedelia, Richard Benjamin, Dustin Hoffman, Terry Kiser, Reva Rose, Robert Salvio, Sheila Smith, Connie Stevens, Pamela Tiffin, Leslie Uggams, Jon Voight, Christopher Walken
1967-68: David Birney, Pamela Burrell, Jordan Christopher, Jack Crowder (Thalmus Rasulala), Sandy Duncan, Julie Gregg, Stephen Joyce, Bernadette Peters,

Peter MacNicol

Melba Moore

Ken Page

200

Faye Dunaway

John Leguizamo

Jessica Lange

Alice Playten, Michael Rupert, Brenda Smiley, Russ Thacker
1968-69: Jane Alexander, David Cryer, Blythe Danner, Ed Evanko, Ken Howard, Lauren Jones, Ron Leibman, Marian Mercer, Jill O'Hara, Ron O'Neal, Al Pacino, Marlene Warfield
1969-70: Susan Browning, Donny Burks, Catherine Burns, Len Cariou, Bonnie Franklin, David Holliday, Katharine Houghton, Melba Moore, David Rounds, Lewis J. Stadlen, Kristoffer Tabori, Fredricka Weber
1970-71: Clifton Davis, Michael Douglas, Julie Garfield, Martha Henry, James Naughton, Tricia O'Neil, Kipp Osborne, Roger Rathburn, Ayn Ruymen, Jennifer Salt, Joan Van Ark, Walter Willison
1971-72: Jonelle Allen, Maureen Anderman, William Atherton, Richard Backus, Adrienne Barbeau, Cara Duff-MacCormick, Robert Foxworth, Elaine Joyce, Jess Richards, Ben Vereen, Beatrice Winde, James Woods
1972-73: D'Jamin Bartlett, Patricia Elliott, James Farentino, Brian Farrell, Victor Garber, Kelly Garrett, Mari Gorman, Laurence Guittard, Trish Hawkins, Monte Markham, John Rubinstein, Jennifer Warren, Alexander H. Cohen (Special Award)
1973-74: Mark Baker, Maureen Brennan, Ralph Carter, Thom Christopher, John Driver, Conchata Ferrell, Ernestine Jackson, Michael Moriarty, Joe Morton, Ann Reinking, Janie Sell, Mary Woronov, Sammy Cahn (Special Award)
1974-75: Peter Burnell, Zan Charisse, Lola Falana, Peter Firth, Dorian Harewood, Joel Higgins, Marcia McClain, Linda Miller, Marti Rolph, John Sheridan, Scott Stevensen, Donna Theodore, Equity Library Theatre (Special Award)
1975-76: Danny Aiello, Christine Andreas, Dixie Carter, Tovah Feldshuh, Chip Garnett, Richard Kelton, Vivian Reed, Charles Repole, Virginia Seidel, Daniel Seltzer, John V. Shea, Meryl Streep, A Chorus Line (Special Award)
1976-77: Trazana Beverley, Michael Cristofer, Joe Fields, Joanna Gleason, Cecilia Hart, John Heard, Gloria Hodes, Juliette Koka, Andrea McArdle, Ken Page, Jonathan Pryce, Chick Vennera, Eva LeGallienne (Special Award)
1977-78: Vasili Bogazianos, Nell Carter, Carlin Glynn, Christopher Goutman, William Hurt, Judy Kaye, Florence Lacy, Armelia McQueen, Gordana Rashovich, Bo Rucker, Richard Seer, Colin Stinton, Joseph Papp (Special Award)
1978-79: Philip Anglim, Lucie Arnaz, Gregory Hines, Ken Jennings, Michael Jeter, Laurie Kennedy, Susan Kingsley, Christine Lahti, Edward James Olmos, Kathleen Quinlan, Sarah Rice, Max Wright, Marshall W. Mason (Special Award)
1979-80: Maxwell Caulfield, Leslie Denniston, Boyd Gaines, Richard Gere, Harry Groener, Stephen James, Susan Kellermann, Dinah Manoff, Lonny Price, Marianne Tatum, Anne Twomey, Dianne Wiest, Mickey Rooney (Special Award)
1980-81: Brian Backer, Lisa Banes, Meg Bussert, Michael Allen Davis, Giancarlo Esposito, Daniel Gerroll, Phyllis Hyman, Cynthia Nixon, Amanda Plummer, Adam Redfield, Wanda Richert, Rex Smith, Elizabeth Taylor (Special Award)

1981-82: Karen Akers, Laurie Beechman, Danny Glover, David Alan Grier, Jennifer Holliday, Anthony Heald, Lizbeth Mackay, Peter MacNicol, Elizabeth McGovern, Ann Morrison, Michael O'Keefe, James Widdoes, Manhattan Theatre Club (Special Award)
1982-83: Karen Allen, Suzanne Bertish, Matthew Broderick, Kate Burton, Joanne Camp, Harvey Fierstein, Peter Gallagher, John Malkovich, Anne Pitoniak, James Russo, Brian Tarantina, Linda Thorson, Natalia Makarova (Special Award)
1983-84: Martine Allard, Joan Allen, Kathy Whitton Baker, Mark Capri, Laura Dean, Stephen Geoffreys, Todd Graff, Glenne Headly, J.J. Johnston, Bonnie Koloc, Calvin Levels, Robert Westenberg, Ron Moody (Special Award)
1984-85: Kevin Anderson, Richard Chaves, Patti Cohenour, Charles S. Dutton, Nancy Giles, Whoopi Goldberg, Leilani Jones, John Mahoney, Laurie Metcalf, Barry Miller, John Turturro, Amelia White, Lucille Lortel (Special Award)
1985-86: Suzy Amis, Alec Baldwin, Aled Davies, Faye Grant, Julie Hagerty, Ed Harris, Mark Jacoby, Donna Kane, Cleo Laine, Howard McGillin, Marisa Tomei, Joe Urla, Ensemble Studio Theatre (Special Award)
1986-87: Annette Bening, Timothy Daly, Lindsay Duncan, Frank Ferrante, Robert Lindsay, Amy Madigan, Michael Maguire, Demi Moore, Molly Ringwald, Frances Ruffelle, Courtney B. Vance, Colm Wilkinson, Robert DeNiro (Special Award)
1987-88: Yvonne Bryceland, Philip Casnoff, Danielle Ferland, Melissa Gilbert, Linda Hart, Linzi Hately, Brian Kerwin, Brian Mitchell, Mary Murfitt, Aidan Quinn, Eric Roberts, B.D. Wong
1988-89: Dylan Baker, Joan Cusack, Loren Dean, Peter Frechette, Sally Mayes, Sharon McNight, Jennie Moreau, Paul Provenza, Kyra Sedgwick, Howard Spiegel, Eric Stoltz, Joanne Whalley-Kilmer, Special Awards: Pauline Collins, Mikhail Baryshnikov
1989-90: Denise Burse, Erma Campbell, Rocky Carroll, Megan Gallagher, Tommy Hollis, Robert Lambert, Kathleen Rowe McAllen, Michael McKean, Crista Moore, Mary-Louise Parker, Daniel von Bargen, Jason Workman, Special Awards: Stewart Granger, Kathleen Turner
1990-91: Jane Adams, Gillian Anderson, Adam Arkin, Brenda Blethyne, Marcus Chong, Paul Hipp, LaChanze, Kenny Neal, Kevin Ramsey, Francis Ruivivar, Lea Salonga, Chandra Wilson, Special Awards: Tracey Ullman, Ellen Stewart
1991-92: Talia Balsam, Lindsay Crouse, Griffin Dunne, Larry Fishburne, Mel Harris, Jonathan Kaplan, Jessica Lange, Laura Linney, Spiro Malas, Mark Rosenthal, Helen Shaver, Al White.
1992-93: Brent Carver, Michael Cerveris, Marcia Gay Harden, Stephanie Lawrence, Andrea Martin, Liam Neeson, Stephen Rea, Natasha Richardson, Martin Short, Dina Spybey, Stephen Spinella, Jennifer Tilly. Special Awards: John Leguizamo, Rosetta LeNoire.

Helen Shaver

Martin Short

Marisa Tomei 201

PULITZER PRIZE PRODUCTIONS

1918-Why Marry?, 1919-No award, 1920-Beyond the Horizon, 1921-Miss Lulu Bett, 1922-Anna Christie, 1923-Icebound, 1924-Hell-Bent fer Heaven, 1925-They Knew What They Wanted, 1926-Craig's Wife, 1927-In Abraham's Bosom, 1928-Strange Interlude, 1929-Street Scene, 1930-The Green Pastures, 1931-Alison's House, 1932-Of Thee I Sing, 1933-Both Your Houses, 1934-Men in White, 1935-The Old Maid, 1936-Idiot's Delight, 1937-You Can't Take It with You, 1938-Our Town, 1939-Abe Lincoln in Illinois, 1940-The Time of Your Life, 1941-There Shall Be No Night, 1942-No award, 1943-The Skin of Our Teeth, 1944-No award, 1945-Harvey, 1946-State of the Union, 1947-No award, 1948-A Streetcar Named Desire, 1949-Death of a Salesman, 1950-South Pacific, 1951-No award, 1952-The Shrike, 1953-Picnic, 1954-The Teahouse of the August Moon, 1955-Cat on a Hot Tin Roof, 1956-The Diary of Anne Frank, 1957-Long Day's Journey into Night, 1958-Look Homeward, Angel, 1959-J.B., 1960-Fiorello!, 1961-All the Way Home, 1962-How to Succeed in Business without Really Trying, 1963-No award, 1964-No award, 1965-The Subject Was Roses, 1966-No award, 1967-A Delicate Balance, 1968-No award, 1969-The Great White Hope, 1970-No Place to Be Somebody, 1971-The Effect of Gamma Rays on Man-in-the-Moon Marigolds, 1972-No award, 1973-That Championship Season, 1974-No award, 1975-Seascape, 1976-A Chorus Line, 1977-The Shadow Box, 1978-The Gin Game, 1979-Buried Child, 1980-Talley's Folly, 1981-Crimes of the Heart, 1982-A Soldier's Play, 1983-'night, Mother, 1984-Glengarry Glen Ross, 1985-Sunday in the Park with George, 1986-No award, 1987-Fences, 1988-Driving Miss Daisy, 1989-The Heidi Chronicles, 1990-The Piano Lesson, 1991-Lost in Yonkers, 1992-The Kentucky Cycle, 1993-Angels in America: Millenium Approaches, 1994-Three Tall Women

NEW YORK DRAMA CRITICS CIRCLE AWARDS

1936-Winterset, 1937-High Tor, 1938-Of Mice and Men, Shadow and Substance, 1939-The White Steed, 1940-The Time of Your Life, 1941-Watch on the Rhine, The Corn Is Green, 1942-Blithe Spirit, 1943-The Patriots, 1944-Jacobowsky and the Colonel, 1946-Carousel, 1947-All My Sons, No Exit, Brigadoon, 1948-A Streetcar Named Desire, The Winslow Boy, 1949-Death of a Salesman, The Madwoman of Chaillot, South Pacific, 1950-The Member of the Wedding, The Cocktail Party, The Consul, 1951-Darkness at Noon, The Lady's Not for Burning, Guys and Dolls, 1952-I Am a Camera, Venus Observed, Pal Joey, 1953-Picnic, The Love of Four Colonels, Wonderful Town, 1954-Teahouse of the August Moon, Ondine, The Golden Apple, 1955-Cat on a Hot Tin Roof, Witness for the Prosecution, The Saint of Bleecker Street, 1956-The Diary of Anne Frank, Tiger at the Gates, My Fair Lady, 1957-Long Day's Journey into Night, The Waltz of the Toreadors, The Most Happy Fella, 1958-Look Homeward Angel, Look Back in Anger, The Music Man, 1959-A Raisin in the Sun, The Visit, La Plume de Ma Tante, 1960-Toys in the Attic, Five Finger Exercise, Fiorello!, 1961-All the Way Home, A Taste of Honey, Carnival, 1962-Night of the Iguana, A Man for All Seasons, How to Succeed in Business without Really Trying, 1963-Who's Afraid of Virginia Woolf?, 1964-Luther, Hello Dolly!, 1965-The Subject Was Roses, Fiddler on the Roof, 1966-The Persecution and Assassination of Marat as Performed by the Inmates of the Asylum of Charenton under the Direction of the Marquis de Sade, Man of La Mancha, 1967-The Homecoming, Cabaret, 1968-Rosencrantz and Guildenstern Are Dead, Your Own Thing, 1969-The Great White Hope, 1776, 1970-The Effect of Gamma Rays on Man-in-the-Moon Marigolds, Borstal Boy, Company, 1971-Home, Follies, The House of Blue Leaves, 1972-That Championship Season, Two Gentlemen of Verona, 1973-The Hot l Baltimore, The Changing Room, A Little Night Music, 1974-The Contractor, Short Eyes, Candide, 1975-Equus, The Taking of Miss Janie, A Chorus Line, 1976-Travesties, Streamers, Pacific Overtures, 1977-Otherwise Engaged, American Buffalo, Annie, 1978-Da, Ain't Misbehavin', 1979-The Elephant Man, Sweeney Todd, 1980-Talley's Folley, Evita, Betrayal, 1981-Crimes of the Heart, A Lesson from Aloes, Special Citation to Lena Horne, The Pirates of Penzance, 1982-The Life and Adventures of Nicholas Nickleby, A Soldier's Play, no musical honored, 1983-Brighton Beach Memoirs, Plenty, Little Shop of Horrors, 1984-The Real Thing, Glengarry Glen Ross, Sunday in the Park with George, 1985-Ma Rainey's Black Bottom (no musical), 1986-A Lie of the Mind, Benefactors, no musical, Special Citation to Lily Tomlin and Jane Wagner, 1987-Fences, Les Liaisons Dangereuses, Les Misérables, 1988-Joe Turner's Come and Gone, The Road to Mecca, Into the Woods, 1989-The Heidi Chronicles, Aristocrats, Largely New York (Special), (no musical), 1990-The Piano Lesson, City of Angels, Privates on Parade, 1991-Six Degrees of Separation, The Will Rogers Follies, Our Country's Good, Special Citation to Eileen Atkins, 1992-Two Trains Running, Dancing at Lughnasa, 1993-Angels in America: Millenium Approaches, Someone Who'll Watch Over Me, Kiss of the Spider Woman, 1994-Three Tall Women, Anna Deavere Smith (Special)

AMERICAN THEATRE WING
ANTOINETTE PERRY
(TONY) AWARD PRODUCTIONS

1948-Mister Roberts, 1949-Death of a Salesman, Kiss Me, Kate, 1950-The Cocktail Party, South Pacific, 1951-The Rose Tattoo, Guys and Dolls, 1952-The Fourposter, The King and I, 1953-The Crucible, Wonderful Town, 1954-The Teahouse of the August Moon, Kismet, 1955-The Desperate Hours, The Pajama Game, 1956-The Diary of Anne Frank, Damn Yankees, 1957-Long Day's Journey into Night, My Fair Lady, 1958-Sunrise at Campobello, The Music Man, 1959-J.B., Redhead, 1960-The Miracle Worker, Fiorello! tied with The Sound of Music, 1961-Becket, Bye Bye Birdie, 1962-A Man for All Seasons, How to Succeed in Business without Really Trying, 1963-Who's Afraid of Virginia Woolf?, A Funny Thing Happened on the Way to the Forum, 1964-Luther, Hello Dolly!, 1965-The Subject Was Roses, Fiddler on the Roof, 1966-The Persecution and Assassination of Marat as Performed by the Inmates of the Asylum of Charenton under the Direction of the Marquis de Sade, Man of La Mancha, 1967-The Homecoming, Cabaret, 1968- Rosencrantz and Guildenstern Are Dead, Hallelujah Baby!, 1969-The Great White Hope, 1776, 1970-Borstal Boy, Applause, 1971-Sleuth, Company, 1972-Sticks and Bones, Two Gentlemen of Verona, 1973-That Championship Season, A Little Night Music, 1974-The River Niger, Raisin, 1975-Equus, The Wiz, 1976-Travesties, A Chorus Line, 1977-The Shadow Box, Annie, 1978-Da, Ain't Misbehavin', Dracula, 1979-The Elephant Man, Sweeney Todd, 1980-Children of a Lesser God, Evita, Morning's at Seven, 1981-Amadeus, 42nd Street, The Pirates of Penzance, 1982-The Life and Adventures of Nicholas Nickleby, Nine, Othello, 1983-Torch Song Trilogy, Cats, On Your Toes, 1984-The Real Thing, La Cage aux Folles, 1985-Biloxi Blues, Big River, Joe Egg, 1986-I'm Not Rappaport, The Mystery of Edwin Drood, Sweet Charity, 1987-Fences, Les Misérables, All My Sons, 1988-M. Butterfly, The Phantom of the Opera, 1989-The Heidi Chronicles, Jerome Robbins' Broadway, Our Town, Anything Goes, 1990-The Grapes of Wrath, City of Angels, Gypsy, 1991-Lost in Yonkers, The Will Rogers' Follies, Fiddler on the Roof, 1992-Dancing at Lughnasa, Crazy For You, Guys & Dolls, 1993-Angels in America: Millenium Approaches, Kiss of the Spider Woman 1994-Angels in America: Perestroika (play), Passion (musical), An Inspector Calls (play revival), Carousel (musical revival)

Photo by Carol Rosegg/Martha Swope

Myra Carter, Marian Seldes in *Three Tall Women*

Photo by Joan Marcus

Photo by Joan Marcus

**Philip Bosco in
*An Inspector Calls***

Marin Mazzie in *Passion*

Photo by Joan Marcus/Marc Bryan-Brown

Michael Hayden, Kate Buddeke in *Carousel*

203

Bruce Adler   Jane Alexander   Lawrence Anderson   Susan Anton   Howard Atlee   Lucie Arnaz

BIOGRAPHICAL DATA ON THIS SEASON'S CASTS

AARON, CAROLINE. Born August 7, 1954 in Richmond, VA. Graduate CatholicU. Bdwy debut 1982 in *Come Back to the 5 & Dime Jimmy Dean*, followed by *The Iceman Cometh, Social Security, I Hate Hamlet*, OB in *Flying Blind, Last Summer on Bluefish Cove, Territorial Rites, Good Bargains, The House of Bernardo Alba, Tribute, Frankie and Johnnie in the Clair de Lune, Marathon '89, Misconceptions, An Imaginary Life*.

ABELE, JIM. Born November 14, 1960 in Syracuse, NY. Graduate Ithaca Col. Debut 1984 OB in *Shepardsets*, followed by *The Cabbagehead, The Country Girl, Any Place But Here Jack, Godot Arrives, Edith Stein*.

ABRAHAM, F. MURRAY. Born October 24, 1939 in Pittsburgh, PA. Attended UTX. Debut 1967 OB in *The Fantasticks* followed by *An Opening in the Trees, 14th Dictator, Young Abe Lincoln, Tonight in Living Color, Adaptation, The Survival of St. Joan, The Dog Ran Away, Fables, Richard III, Little Murders, Scuba Duba, Where Has Tommy Flowers Gone?, Miracle Play, Blessing, Sexual Perversity in Chicago, Landscape of the Body, The Master and Margarita, Biting the Apple, The Sea Gull, The Caretaker, Antigone, Uncle Vanya, The Golem, The Madwoman of Challiot, Twelfth Night, Frankie and Johnny in the Clair de Lune, A Midsummer Night's Dream, A Life in the Theatre*, Bdwy in *The Man in the Glass Booth* (1968), *6 Rms Riv Vu, Bad Habits, The Ritz, Legend, Teibele and Her Demon, Macbeth, Waiting for Godot, Angels in America*.

ABUBA, ERNEST. Born August 25, 1947 in Honolulu, HI. Attended Southwestern La. Bdwy debut 1976 in *Loose Ends, Zoya's Apartment, Shimada*, OB in *Sunrise, Monkey Music, Station J., Yellow Fever, Pacific Overtures, Empress of China, The Man Who Turned Into a Stick, Shogun Macbeth, Three Sisters, Song of Shim Chung, It's Our Town Too*.

ACAYAN, ZAR. Born January 2, 1967 in Manila, Phil. Attended U. C. Berkley, UCLA. Bdwy debut 1991 in *Miss Saigon*, OB in *Day Standing on Its Head, Children of Eden*.

ADAMS, J. B. Born September 29, 1954 in Oklahoma City, OK. Graduate Okla. City U. Debut 1980 OB in *ELT's Plain and Fancy*, followed by *Annie Warbucks*.

ADAMS, JANE. Born April 1, 1965 in Washington, DC. Juilliard graduate. Debut 1986 OB in *The Nice and the Nasty* followed by *Young Playwrights Festival*, Bdwy in *I Hate Hamlet*, for which she received a Theatre World Award, *The Crucible, An Inspector Calls*.

ADLER, BRUCE. Born November 27, 1944 in NYC. Attended NYU. Debut 1957 OB in *It's a Funny World* followed by *Hard to be a Jew, Big Winner, The Golden Land, The Stranger's Return, The Rise of David Levinsky, On Second Avenue*, Bdwy in *A Teaspoon Every 4 Hours* (1971), *Oklahoma!* (1979), *Oh Brother!, Sunday in the Park with George, Broadway, Those Were the Days, Crazy for You*.

A'HEARN, PATRICK. Born September 4, 1957 in Chappaqua, NY. Graduate Syracuse U. Debut 1985 OB in *Pirates of Penzance* followed by *Forbidden Broadway, Bdwy in Les Miserables* (1987).

ALBINO, RAMON. Born in 1959 in Puerto Rico. Graduate UPR, Brooklyn Col., CUNY. Debut 1994 OB in *Written and Sealed*.

ALDREDGE, TOM. Born February 28, 1928 in Dayton, OH. Attended Daton U. Goodman Theatre. Bdwy debut 1959 in *The Nervous Set*, followed by *UTBU, Slapstick Tragedy, Everything in the Garden, Indians, Engagement Baby, How the Other Half Loves, Sticks and Bones, Where's Charley?, Leaf People, Rex, Vieux Carre, St. Joan, Stages, On Golden Pond, The Little Foxes, Into the Woods, Two Shakespearean Actors*, OB in *The Tempest, Between Two Thieves, Henry V, The Premise, Love's Labour's Lost, Troilus and Cressida, The Butter and Egg Man, Ergo, Boys in the Band, Twelfth Night, Colette, Hamlet, The Orphan, King Lear, The Iceman Cometh, Black Angel, Getting Along Famously, Fool for Love, Neon Psalms, Richard II, The Last Yankee*.

ALDRICH, JANET. (formerly Aldridge) Born October 16, 1956 in Hinsdale, IL. Graduate Umiani. Debut 1979 OB in *A Funny Thing Happened on the Way to the Forum* followed by *American Princess, The Men's Group, Wanted Dead or Alive, The Comedy of Errors, Prime Time Prophet*, Bdwy in

Annie (1982), *The Three Musketeers, Broadway, Starmites*.

ALEXANDER, JANE. Born October 28, 1939 in Boston, MA. Attended Sarah Lawrence Col. U. Edinburgh. Bdwy debut 1968 in *The Great White Hope*, for which she received a Theatre World Award, followed by *6 Rms Riv Vu, Find Your Way Home, Hamlet* (LC), *The Heiress, First Monday in October, Goodbye Fidel, Monday after the Miracle, Shadowlands, The Visit, Sisters Rosensweig*, OB in *Losing Time, Approaching Zanzibar*.

ALICE, MARY. Born December 3, 1941 in Indianola, MS. Debut 1967 OB in *Trials of Brother Jero* followed by *The Strong Breed, Duplex, Thoughts, Miss Julie, House Party, Terraces, Heaven and Hell's Agreement, In the Deepest Part of Sleep, Cockfight, Julius Caesar, Nongogo, Second Thoughts, Spell #7, Zooman and the Sign, Glasshouse, The Ditch, Take Me Along, Departures, Marathon '80, Richard III, Watermelon Rinds*, Bdwy in *No Place to be Somebody* (1971), *Fences*.

ALLEN, KEITH. Born February 18, 1964 in Daytona Beach, FL. Bdwy debut 1986 in *La Cage aux Folles* followed by *Whoop-dee-do*.

ALLISON, PATTI. Born June 26, 1942 in St. Louis, MO. Graduate Webster Col., IndU. Bdwy debut 1978 in *Angel* followed by *Orpheus Descending*, OB in *Brimstone*.

ALTON, DAVID. Born May 21, 1949 in Philadelphia, PA. Graduate LASalle Col. Debut 1987 OB in *Propaganda* followed by *The Cabinet of Dr. Caligari, Teibele and Her Demon, The Dream of a Ridiculous Man*.

AMBERLY, LIZ. Born October 2 in Poughkeepsie, NY. Attended Syracuse U. LAMDA. Debut 1989 OB in *Leave it to Jane* followed by *The Awakening of Spring, Richard II*.

AMBROSE, JOE. Born April 7, 1931 in Chicago, IL. Graduate Rutgers U. AADA, Columbia U. Debut 1986 OB in *Buried Child* followed by *Diary of a Scoundrel, The Crucible, Hotel Paradiso*, Bdwy in *An Inspector Calls* (1994).

ANDERSON, CHRISTINE. Born August 6 in Utica, NY. Graduate U. Wis. Bdwy debut in *I Love My Wife* (1980), OB in *I Can't Keep Running in Place, On the Swing Shift, Red Hot and Blue, A Night at Texas Guinan's, Nunsense*.

ANDERSON, LAWRENCE. Born May 18, 1964 in Poughkeepsie, NY. Graduate U. Col. Bdwy debut 1992 in *Phantom of the Opera* followed by *Les Misérables*.

ANDRES, BARBARA. Born February 11, 1939 in NYC. Graduate Catholic U. Bdwy debut 1969 in *Jimmy*, followed by *The Boy Friend, Rodgers and Hart, Rex, On Golden Pond, Doonesbury, Kiss of the Spiderwoman*, OB in *Threepenny Opera, Landscape of the Body, Harold Arlen's Cabaret, Suzanna Andler, One-Act Festival, Company, Marathon '87, Arms and the Man, A Woman without a Name. First is Supper, Fore!*.

ANDREWS, GEORGE LEE. Born October 13, 1942 in Milwaukee, WI. Debut OB in *Jacques Brel Is Alive and Well ...*, followed by *Starting Here Starting Now, Vamps and Rideouts, The Fantasticks*, Bdwy in *A Little Night Music* (1973), *On the 20th Century, Merlin, The Phantom of the Opera, A Little Night Music* (NYCO).

ANDRICK, VIRL. Born March 20, 1948 in Akron, OH. Graduate Hiram Col., Oberlin Col. Bdwy debut 1993 in *Camelot*.

ANSON, JOHN. Born June 17, 1954 in Brooklyn, NY. Graduate Queensboro Col., Hunter Col. OB in *castles* followed by *Edith Wharton, Old NY: False Dawn*.

ANTON, SUSAN. Born October 12, 1950 in Yucaipa, CA. Attended Bernardino Col. Bdwy debut 1985 in *Hurlyburly*, followed by *The Will Rogers Follies*, OB's *Xmas a Go-Go*.

ARANAS, RAUL. Born October 1, 1947 in Manilla, P.I. Graduate Pace U. Debut 1976 OB in *Savages* followed by *Yellow is My Favorite Color, 49, Bullet Headed Birds, Tooth of the Crime, Teahouse, Shepard Sets, Cold Air, La Chunga, The Man Who Turned into a Stick, Twelfth Night, Shogun Macbeth, Boutique Living, Fairy Bones, In the Jungle of Cities*, Bdwy in *Loose Ends* (1978), *Miss Saigon*.

ARBEIT, HERMAN O. Born April 19, 1925 in Brooklyn, NY. Attended CCNY, HB Studio, Neighborhood Playhouse. Debut 1939 OB in *The Golem*

followed by *Awake and Sing, A Delicate Balance, Yentl the Yeshiva Boy, A Yank in Beverly Hills, Second Avenue Rag, Taking Steam, Christopher Blake, Black Forest,* Bdwy in *Yentl* (1975).

ARCARO, ROBERT. (a.k.a. Bob), Born Aug. 9, 1952 in Brooklyn, NY. Graduate Wesleyan U. Debut 1977 OB in *New York City Street Show,* followed by *Working Theatre Festival, Man with a Raincoat, Working One-Acts, Henry Lumpur, Special Interests, Measure for Measure, Our Lady of Perpetual Danger, Brotherly Love, I Am a Man.*

ARIAS, YANCEY. Born June 27, 1971 in NYC. Attended Carnegie-Mellon U. Bdwy debut 1992 in *Miss Saigon.*

ARKIN, ADAM. Born Aug. 19, 1956 in Brooklyn, NY. Bdwy debut 1991 in *I Hate Hamlet* for which he received a Theatre World Award followed by *Guys and Dolls, Fiorello,* OB in *Sight Unseen, A Christmas Memory, Four Dogs and a Bone.*

ARNAZ, LUCIE. Born July 17, 1951 in Los Angeles, CA. Bdwy debut 1979 in *They're Playing Our Song* for which she received a Theatre World Award, followed by *Lost in Yonkers* (1992).

AROESTE, JOEL. Born April 10, 1949 in NYC. Graduate SUNY. Bdwy debut 1986 in *Raggedy Ann,* OB in *Beauty and the Beast, Slow Dance on the Killing Ground.*

ARRINDELL, LISA. Born March 24, 1969 in Bronx, NY. Juilliard graduate, Debut OB 1990 in *Richard III,* followed by *Earth and Sky, Mixed Babies, Heliotrope Bouquet.*

ASH, RANDI. Born Oct. 15, 1959 in Elmhurst, IL. Attended Central CT State Col. Debut 1977 OB in *The Comic Strip,* followed by *Elegies for Angels Punks and Raging Queens, Pageant.*

ASHFORD, ROBERT. Born Nov. 19, 1959 in Orlando, FL. Attended Washington & Lee U. Bdwy debut 1987 in *Anything Goes,* followed by *Radio City Music Hall Christmas Spectacular, The Most Happy Fella* (1992), *My Favorite Year.*

ASNER, EDWARD. Born November 15, 1929 in Kansas City, KS. Graduate U. Chicago. OB in *Threepenny Opera, Hamlet, Ivanov,* Bdwy in *Face of a Hero* (1960), *Born Yesterday* (1989), *Don Juan in Hell in Concert.*

ATLEE, HOWARD. Born May 14, 1926 in Bucyrus, OH. Graduate Emerson Col. Debut 1990 OB in *Historical Productions,* followed by *The 15th Ward, The Hells of Dante, What a Royal Pain in the Farce, Rimers of Eldrich.*

AUBERJONOIS. RENE. Born June 1, 1940 in NYC. Graduate Carnegie Inst. With LC Rep in *A Cry of Player, King Lear, and Twelfth Night,* Bdwy in *Fire* (1969), *Coco, Tricks, The Good Doctor, Break a Leg, Every Good Boy Deserves Favor, Big River, Metamorphosis, City of Angels, Don Juan in Hell in Concert,* BAM Co. in *The New York Idwa, Three Sisters, The Play's the Thing, Julius Caesar.*

AUSTRIAN, MARJORIE. Born February 3, 1934 in The Bronx, NY. Attended Syracuse U, Kansas U. OB in *Henry V, All's Well That Ends Well, Sylvia Plath, Jonah, Ivanov, Loyalties, The House of Bernarda Alba, Lucky Rita, The Diary of Anne Frank, A Day in the Death of Elizabeth, Dodger Blue, Homesick, Cole Porter's Jubilee.*

AVEDISIAN, PAUL A. Born March 1, 1962 in Detroit, MI. Graduate Hope College, Manahattan School of Music. Debut 1988 OB in *The Hired Man* followed by Bdwy in *Les Miserables* (1989).

BACON, KEVIN. Born July 8, 1958 in Philadelphia, PA Debut 1978 OB in *Getting Out,* followed by *Glad Tidings, Album, Flux, Poor Little Lambs, Slab Boys, Men without Dates, Loot, The Author's Voice, Road, Spike Heels, The Normal Heart* (Benefit reading).

BAILEY, ADRIAN. Born September 23 in Detroit, MI. Graduate U. Detroit. Bdwy debut 1976 in *Your Arms Too Short to Box with God* followed by *Prince of Central Park, Jelly's Last Jam,* OB in *A Thrill a Moment, Johnny Pye.*

BAGNERIS, VERNEL. Born July 31, 1949 in New Orleans, LA. Graduate Xavier U. Debut 1979 OB in *One Mo' Time,* followed by *Staggerlee, Further Mo', Jelly Roll Morton: A Me-Morial, Jelly Roll Morton: Hoo Dude* all of which he wrote.

BAIRD, JUDY. Born June 23, 1953 in NYC. Attended Queen's College, Pace U. Bdwy debut 1994 in *An Inspector Calls.*

BAIRD, SAMUEL. Born January 9, 1967 in Tucson, AZ. Attended UAZ, Juilliard. Debut 1993 OB in *Love's Labour's Lost* followed by *A Quarrel of Sparrows, Titus Andronicus.*

BAKER, BECKY ANN. (formerly Gelke) Born February 17, 1953 in Ft. Knox, KY. Graduate WkyU. Bdwy debut 1978 in *The Best Little Whorehouse in Texas* followed by *A Streetcar Named Desire* (1988), OB in *Altitude Sickness, John Brown's Body, Chamber Music, To Whom It May Concern, Two Gentlemen of Verona, Bob's Guns, Buzzsaw Berkeley, Colorado Catechism, Jeremy Rudge.*

BAKER, MARK. Born October 2, 1946 in Cumberland, MD. Attended Wittenberg U., Carnegie-Mellon U, Neighborhood Playhouse, AADA. Bdwy debut 1972 in *Via Galactica* followed by *Candide* for which he received a 1974 Theatre World Award, Habeas Corpus OB in *Love Me Love My Children, A Midsummer Night's Dream, From Rodgers and Hart with Love, Edgar Allan, Oh My Broken Hearts and Back, Amphigory, Hysterical Blindness.*

BAKER, DAVID AARON. Born August 14, 1963 in Durham, NC. Graduate U. Tex., Juilliard. Bdwy debut 1993 in *White Liars/Black Comedy* followed by *Abe Lincoln in Illinois, Flowering Peach,* OB in *Richard III, 110 in the Shade* (NYCO).

BAKER, ROBERT MICHAEL. Born February 28, 1954 in Boston, MA. Attended Boston U.AADA. Debut 1984 OB in *Jessie's Land* followed by

Enter Laughing, Happily Ever After, Company, The Education of Hyman Kaplan, Yiddle with a Fiddle, Carnival, Bdwy in *Guys and Dolls* (1992).

BALL, JERRY. Born December 16, 1956 in New Lexington, OH. Graduate Capitol U., NYU.

BARANSKI, CHRISTINE. Born May 2, 1952 in Buffalo, NY. Graduate Juilliard. Debut OB 1978 in *One Crack Out,* followed by *Says I Says He, The Trouble with Europe, Coming Attractions, Operation Midnight Climax, Sally and Marsha, A Midsummer Night's Dream, It's Only a Play, Marathon '86, Elliot Loves, Lips Together Teeth Apart, A Christmas Memory, Loman Family Picnic,* Bdwy in *Hide and Seek* (1980), *The Real Thing, Hurlyburly, House of Blue Leaves, Rumors, Nick & Nora.*

BARAY, JOHN. Born November 29, 1944 in San Antonio, TX. Graduate Trinity U. Debut 1981 OB in *The Red Mill* followed by *Babes in Toyland, The Mikado, The Pirates of Penzance, Pacific Overtures, Gashiram, Cambodia Agonistes, Wilderness.*

BARBOUR, JAMES. Born April 25, 1966 in Cherry Hill, NJ. Graduate HofstraU. Debut 1990 OB in *Class Clown* followed by *The Merry Wives of Windsor, Tom Sawyer, Harold and the Purple Crayon, Milk and Honey,* Bdwy in *Cyrano, The Musical* (1993) followed by *Carousel.*

BARKER, JEAN. Born December 20 in Philadelphia, PA. Attended U. PA., AM Th. Wing. Debut 1953 OB in *The Bold Soprano* followed by *Night Shift, A Month in the Country, Portrait of Jenny, Knucklebones, About Iris Berman, Goodnight Grandpa, Victory Bonds, Cabbagehead, Oklahoma Smovar, Titus Andronicus,* Bdwy in *The Innkeepers* (1956), *Prisoner of Second Avenue, Tchin Tchin, The Inspector General.*

BARNES, PATRICK. Born September 13, 1961 in Columbus, OH. Graduate Oh. State U. Debut 1987 OB in *Blue is for Boys* followed by *Soul Survivor, Them Within Us, The American Clock.*

BARNETT, EILEEN. Born May 8th in Chicago, IL. Attended Roosevelt U., U. Iowa. Debut 1972 OB in *Berlin to Broadway* followed by *Jacques Brel Is Alive...,* Bdwy in *Company, Nine.*

BARCROFT, JUDITH. Born July 6 in Washington, DC. Attended Northwestern U., Stephens Col. Bdwy debut 1965 in *The Mating Game* followed by *Dinner at 8, Plaza Suite, All God's Chillun Gots Wings, Betrayal, Elephant Man, Shimada,* OB in *M. Amilcare, Cloud 9, For Sale, Songs of Twilight, Solitaire/Double Solitaire, Breaking the Prairie Wolf Code, Rough for Theatre II/Play.*

BARON, EVALYN. Born Apr. 21, 1948 in Atlanta, GA. Graduate Northwestern U., U. Min. Debut 1979 OB in *Scrambled Feet,* followed by *Hijinks, I Can't Keep Running in Place, Jerry's Girls, Harvest of Strangers, Quilters,* Bdwy in *Fearless Frank* (1980), *Big River, Rages, Social Security, Les Miserables.*

BARRE, GABRIEL. Born August 26, 1957 in Brattleboro, VT. Graduate AADA. Debut 1977 OB in *Jabberwock* followed by *T.N.T., Bodo, The Baker's Wife, The Time of Your Life, Children of the Sun, Wicked Philanthropy, Starmites, Mistress of the Inn, Gifts of the Magi, The Tempest, Return to the Forbidden Planet, The Circle, Where's Dick?, Forever Plaid, Jacques Brel, Show Me Where the Good Times Art Marathon Dancing, El Greco,* Bdwy in *Rags* (1986), *Starmites, Anna Karenina, Ain't Broadway Grand.*

BARTENIEFF, GEORGE. Born January 24, 1933 in Berlin, Ger. Bdwy debut 1947 in *The Whole World Over,* followed by *Venus Is, All's Well That Ends Well, Quotations from Chairman Mao Tse-Tung, The Death of Bessie Smith, Cop-Out, Room Service, Unlikely Heroes,* OB in *Walking in Waldheim, Memorandum, The Increased Difficulty of Concentration, Trelawny of the Wells, Charley Chestnut Rides the IRT, Radio (Wisdom): Sophia Part I, Images of the Dead, Dead End Kids, The Blonde Leading the Blonde, The Dispossessed, Growing Up Gothic, Rosetti's Apologies, On the Lam, Samuel Beckett Trilogy, Quartet, Help Wanted, A Matter of Life and Death, The Heart That Eats Itself, Coney Island Kid, Cymbeline, Better People, Blue Heaven, He Saw His Reflection.*

BARTLETT, PETER. Born August 28, 1942 in Chicago, IL. Attended Loyola U. LAMDA. Bdwy debut 1969 in *A Patriot for Me,* followed by *Gloria and Esperanza* OB in *Boom Boom Room, I Remember the House Where I was Born, Crazy Locomotive, A Thurber Carnival, Hamlet, Buzzsaw Berkeley, Learned Ladies, Jeffrey, The Naked Truth.*

BARTLEY, ROBERT. Born October 31 in Kew Gardens, NY. Attended North Texas State U. Bdwy debut 1992 in *Miss Saigon.*

BARTOK, JAYCE. Born July 31, 1972 in Pittsburgh, PA. Debut 1989 OB in *Dalton's Back* followed by *The My House Play, Glory Girls.*

BARTON, STEVE. Born in Arkansas. Graduate U. Texas. Bdwy debut 1988 in *Phantom of the Opera* followed by *Red Shoes,* OB's *Six Wives, The Hunchback of Notre Dame.*

BASCH, PETER. Born May 11, 1956 in NYC. Graduate Columbia U. UC/Berkeley. Debut 1984 OB in *Hackers* followed by *Festival of One Acts, Marathon '92, The Cowboy The Indian and the Fervent Feminist.*

BAUM, SUSAN. Born July 12, 1950 in Miami, FL. Graduate U. FL. OB in *The Children's Hour, Holy Ghosts, Hay Fever, A Doctor in the House, Trifles, Arms and the Man, Uncle Vanya, Hedda Gabler, Close Enough for Jazz, Colette Collage, Mourning Becomes Electra.*

BEACH, DAVID. Born February 20, 1964 in Dayton, OH. Attended Darmouth Col, LAMDA. Debut 1990 OB in *Big Fat and Ugly with a Moustache* followed by *Modigliani, Octoberfest, Pets, That's Life!*

BEACH, GARY. Born October 10, 1947 in Alexandria, VA. Graduate NC Sch of Arts. Bdwy debut 1971 in *1776* followed by *Something's Afoot, Mooney Shapiro Songbook, Annie, Doonesbury, Beauty and the Beast,* OB in *Smile Smile Smile, What's a Nice Country Like You..., Ionescapade, By*

Strouse, A Bundle of Nerves.

BEAL, JOHN. Born August 13, 1909 in Joplin, MO. Graduate UPA. His many credits include *Wild Waves, Another Language, She Loves Me Not, Russet Mantle, Soliloquy, Miss Swan Expects, Liverty Jones, The Voice of the Turtle, Lend an Ear, Teahouse of the August Moon, Calculated Risk, Billy, Our Town, The Crucible, The Master Builder, A Little Hotel on the Side, The Sea Gull, Three Men on a Horse,* OB in *Wilder's Triple Bull, To Be Young Gifted and Black, Candyapple, Long Day's Journey into Night, Rivers Return.*

BEDFORD, BRIAN. Born February 16, 1935 in Morley, England. Attended RADA. Bdwy debut 1960 in *Five Finger Exercise* followed by *Lord Pengo, The Private Ear, The Astrakhan Coat, The Unknown Soldier and His Wife, The Seven Descents of Myrtle, Jumpers, The Cocktail Party, Hamlet, Private Lives, School for Wives, The Misanthrope, Two Shakespearean Actors, Timon of Athens,* OB in *The Knack, The Lunatic the Lover and the Poet.*

BEECHMAN, LAURIE. Born April 4, 1954 in Philadelphia, PA. Attended NYU. Bdwy debut 1977 in *Annie,* followed by *Pirates of Penzance, Joseph and the Amazing Technicolor Dreamcoat* for which she received a Theatre World Award, *Cats, Les Misérables,* OB in *Some Enchanted Evening, Pal Joey in Concert.*

BELL, GLYNIS. Born July 30, 1947 in London, England. Attended Oakland U., AADA. Debut 1975 OB in *The Devils* followed by *The Time of Your Life, The Robber Bridegroom, Three Sisters,* Bdwy in *My Fair Lady*(1993).

BELMONTE, VICKI. Born January 20, 1947 in U.S.A. Bdwy debut 1960 in *Bye Bye Birdie,* followed by *Subways Are for Sleeping, All American, Annie Get Your Gun* (LC), OB in *Nunsense.*

BEN-ARI, NEAL. (Formerly Neal Klein) Born March 20, 1952 in Brooklyn, NY. Graduate UPA. Bdwy debut 1981 in *The First* followed by *Roza, Chess, The Merchant of Venice, Joseph and the Amazing Technicolor Dreamcoat* (1993), OB in *La Boheme, 1-2-3-4-5.*

BENJAMIN, ALLAN. Born March 19, 1949 in Brooklyn, NY. Graduate U. Denver, U. Copenhagen. Debut 1982 OB in *A Trinity* followed by *Black Forest.*

BENJAMIN, ELIZABETH. Born June 17, Long Island, NY. Graduate NC School of Arts, Ntl Theatre Consv. Debut 1994 OB in *Edith Wharton's Old New York, False Dream* followed by *WomanKind IV.*

BENJAMIN, P.J. Born September 2, 1951 in Chicago, IL. Attended Loyola U., Columbia U. Bdwy debut 1973 in *Pajama Game,* followed by *Pippin, Sarava, Charlie and Algernon, Sophisticated Ladies, Torch Song Trilogy, Wind in the Willows, Ain't Broadway Grand,* OB in *Memories of Riding with Joe Cool, Marathon Dancing.*

BENSON, CINDY. Born October 2, 1951 in Attleboro, MA. Graduate St. Leo Col. U. IL. Debut 1981 OB in *Some Like It Cole,* followed by *Eating Raoul, Balancing Act,* Bdwy in *Les Misérables* (1987).

BENSON, JODI. Born October 10, 1961 in Rockford, IL. Attended Millkin U. Bdwy debut 1983 in *Marilyn, An American Fable* followed by *Smile, Welcome to the Club, Crazy for You,* OB in *Hurry! Hurry! Hollywood!*

BENTLEY, MARY DENISE. Born Dec. 28 in Indianapolis, IN. Graduate Ind. U. Bdwy debut 1983 in *Dreamgirls,* OB in *Little Shop of Horrors* (1987), followed by *Forbidden Broadway.*

BERGER, STEPHEN. Born May 16, 1954 in Philadelphia, PA. Attended U. Cinn. debut 1982 in *Little Me,* OB in *Nite Club Confidential, Mowgli, Isn't It Romantic, Hello Muddah Hello Fadduh, Beau Jest, That's Life!*

BERNSTEIN, DOUGLAS. Born May 6, 1958 in NYC. Amherst graduate. Debut 1982 OB in *Upstairs at O'Neal's* followed by *Backers Audition, Mayer, Showing Off, The Mayor Musicals.*

BERRESSE, MICHAEL. Born August 15, 1964 in Holyoke, MA. Bdwy debut 1990 in *Fiddler on the Roof* followed by *Guys and Dolls, Damn Yankees.*

BEVAN, ALISON. Born November 20, 1959 in Cincinnati, OH. Attended NYU. Debut 1980 OB in *Trixie True Teen Detective* followed by *Brigadoon* (LC), *Little Lies, The Mayor Musicals.*

BEVERLEY, TRAZANA. Born Aug. 9, 1945 in Baltimore, MD. Graduate NYU. Debut 1969 OB in *Rules for Running,* followed by *Les Femmes Noires, Geronimo, Antigone, The Brothers, God's Trombones, Marathon '91,* Bdwy in *My Sister, My Sister, For Colored Girls Who Have Considered Suicide* for which she received a Theatre World Award, *Death and the King's Horseman* (LC), *The Crucible.*

BIANCHI, ANDREA. Born June 5, 1965 in Tarrytown, NY. Graduate Conn. Col. Debut 1988 OB in *Italian-American Reconciliation* followed by *Lusting after Pipine's Wife, White Widow.*

BIANCHI, JAMES R. Born June 21, 1949 in Cleveland, OH. Attended Bowling Green State U. Debut 1991 OB in *Twelfth Night,* followed by *St. Joan, The Tempest, Merchant of Venice.*

BILLECI, JOHN. Born April 19, 1957 in Brooklyn, NY. Graduate Loyola Marymount U. Debut 1993 OB in *3 by Wilder* followed by *As You Like It, SSS Glencairn,* Bdwy 1993 in *Wilder Wilder Wilder.*

BIRNEY, REED. Born September 11, 1954 in Alexandria, VA. Attended Boston U. Bdwy debut 1977 in *Gemini* OB in *The Master and Margarita, Bella Figura, Winterplay, The Flight of the Earls, Filthy Rich, Lady Moonsong, Mr. Monsoon, The Common Pursuit, Zero Positive, Moving Targets, Spare Parts, A Murder of Crows, 7 Blowjobs, Loose Knot, The Undertaker, An Imaginary Life, The Family of Mann.*

BISHOP, KELLY (formerly Carole). Born Feb. 28, 1944 in Colorado Springs, CO. Bdwy debut 1967 in *Golden Rainbow,* followed by *Promises Promises, On the Town, Rachel Lily Rosenbloom, A Chorus Line, Six Degrees of Separation,* OB in *Piano Bar, Changes, The Blessing, Going to New England, Six Degrees of Separation, Pterodactyls.*

BLAIR, PAMELA. Born December 5, 1949 in Arlington, VA. Attended Ntl. Acad. Of Ballet. Bdwy debut 1972 in *Promises, Promises* followed by *Sugar, Seesaw, Of Mice and Men, Wild and Wonderful, A Chorus Lie, The Best Little Whorehouse in Texas, King of Hearts, The Nerd, A Few Good Men,* OB in *Ballad of Boris K., Split, Real Life Funnies, Double Feature, Hit Parade, 1-2-3-4-5, Sausage Eaters.*

BLAISDELL, NESBITT. Born December 6, 1928 in NYC. Graduate Amherst, Columbia U. Debut 1978 OB in *Old Man Joseph and His Family,* followed by *Moliere in Spite of Himself, Guests of the Nation, Chekov Sketch Book, Elba, Ballad of Soapy Smith, Custom of the Country, A Cup of Coffee, The Immigrant, Yokohama Duty, Quincy Blues,* Bdwy in *Cat on a Hot Tin Roof* (1990), *Abe Lincoln in Illinois.*

BLAKELY, MICHELLE. Born July 27, 1969 in Harrisonburg, VA. Graduate NYU. Debut 1992 OB in *Day Dreams,* Bdwy in *Grease* (1994).

BLAZER, JUDITH. Born October 22, 1956 in *Oh Boy!,* followed by *Roberta in concert, A Little Night Music, Company, Babes in Arms, Hello Again,* Bdwy in *Me and My Girl, A Change in the Heir.*

BLINKOFF, SUSANNAH. Born August 31, 1964 in NYC. Graduate Brown U., USCAL. Debut 1979 OB in *Sweet Main Street,* Bdwy in *The Best Little Whorehouse Goes Public* (1994).

BLOCH, SCOTTY. Born January 28 in New Rochelle, NY. Attended AADA. Debut 1945 OB in *Craig's Wife* followed by *Lemon Sky, Battering Ram, Richard III, In Celebration, An Act of Kindness, The Price, Grace, Neon Psalms, Other People's Money, Walking The Dead, EST Marathon '92, The Stand-In,* Bdwy in *Children of a Lesser God* (1980).

BLOCH, PETER. Born December 13, 1955 in Worcester, MA. Debut 1984 OB in *Paradise Lost* followed by *The Hasty Heart, How the Other Half Loves.*

BLOCK, LARRY. Born October 30, 1942, in NYC. Graduate URI. Bdwy debut 1966 in *Hail Scrawdyke,* followed by *La Turista,* OB in *Eh?, Fingernails Blue as Flowers, Comedy of Errors, Coming Attractions, Henry IV Part 2, Feuhrer Bunker, Manhattan Love Songs, Souvenirs, The Golem, Responsible Parties, Hit Parade, Largo Desolato, The Square Root of 3, Young Playwrights Festival, Hunting Cockroaches, Two Gentlemen of Verona, Yello Dog Contract, Temptation, Festival of 1 Acts, The Faithful Brethern of Pitt Street, Loman Family Picnic, One of the All-Time Greats, Pericles, Comedy of Errors, The Work Room.*

BLOOM, CLAIRE. Born February 15, 1931 in London, England. Bdwy debut 1956 with *Old Vic in Romeo and Juliet* and *Richard II* followed by *Rashomon, Vivat! Vivat! Regina,* OB in *A Doll's House, Hedda Gabler, Medea.*

BLOOM, TOM. Born Nov. 1, 1944 in Washington, D.C. Graduate Western MD Col., Emerson Col. Debut 1989 OB in *The Widow's Blind Date,* followed by *A Cup of Coffee, Major Barbara, A Perfect Diamond, Lips Together Teeth Apart.*

BLUM, MARK. Born May 14, 1950 in Newark, NJ. Graduate U. PA, U. MN. Debut 1976 OB in *The Cherry Orchard,* followed by *Green Julia, Say Goodnight Gracie, Table Settings, Key Exchange, Loving Reno, Messiah, It's Only a Play, Little Footsteps, Cave of Life, Gus & Al, Laureen's Whereabouts,* Bdwy in *Lost in Yonkers* (1991).

BLUMENKRANTZ, JEFF Born June 3, 1965 in Long Branch, NJ. Graduate Northwestern U. Debut 1986 OB in *Pajama Game* Bdwy 1987 in *Into the Woods,* followed by *3 Penny Opera, South Pacific, Damn Yankees.*

BOBBIE, WALTER. Born Nov. 18, 1945 in Scranton, PA. Graduate U. Scranton, Catholic U. Bdwy debut 1971 in *Frank Merriwell,* followed by *The Grass Harp, Grease, Tricks, Going Up, History of the American Film, Anything Goes, Getting Married, Guys and Dolls,* OB in *Drat!, She Loves Me, Up from Paradise, Goodbye Freddy, Cafe Crown, Young Playwrights '90.*

BOBBY, ANNE MARIE. Born December 12, 1967 in Paterson, NJ. Attended OxfordU. Debut 1983 OB in *American Passion* followed by *Class I Acts, Godspell, Progress, Groundhog, Misconceptions, Merrily We Roll Along,* Bdwy in *The Human Comedy* (1984), *The Real Thing, Hurlyburly, Precious Sons, Smile, Black Comedy.*

BODLE, JANE. Born Nov. 12 in Lawrence, KS. Attended U. Utah. Bdwy debut 1983 in *Cats,* followed by *Les Miserables, Miss Saigon.*

BOGARD, GUSTI. Born September 24 in San Francisco, CA. Attended UCLA, Cal Inst of Arts, HB Studio. Bdwy debut 1978 in *The King and I* OB in *Lennon, Nyuerikan Poets, Mass Transit, Our Town.*

BOGARDUS, STEPHEN. Born Mar. 11, 1954 in Norfolk, VA. Princeton graduate. Bdwy debut 1980 in *West Side Story,* followed by *Les Miserables, Falsettos, Allegro in Concert,* OB in *March of the Falsettos, Feathertop, No Way to Treat a Lady, Look on the Bright Side, Falsettoland.*

BOGOSIAN, ERIC. Born Apr. 24, 1953 in Woburn, MA. Graduate Oberlin Col. Debut 1982 OB in *Men Inside/Voices of America,* followed by *Funhouse, Drinking in America, Talk Radio, Sex Drugs Rock & Roll, Notes from Underground, The Normal Heart* (Benefit reading), *Pounding Nails in the Floor with My Forehead.*

BOND, JULIE. Born in Houston, TX. Bdwy debut 1993 in *Joseph and the Amazing Technicolor Dreamcoat.*

BOSCO, PHILIP. Born Sept. 26, 1930 in Jersey City, NJ. Graduate Catholic U. Credits: *Auntie Mame, Rape of the Belt, Ticket of Leave Man, Donnybrook, A Man for All Seasons, Mrs. Warren's Profession,* with LCRep in *A Great Career, In the Matter of J. Robert Oppenheimer, The Miser, The Time of Your Life, Camino Real, Operation Sidewinder, Amphitryon, Enemy of the People, Playboy of the Western World, Good Woman of Setzuan, Antigone, Mary Stuart, Narrow Road to the Deep North, The Crucible, Twelfth Night, Enemies, Plough and the Stars, Merchant of Venice, A*

Streetcar Named Desire, Henry V, Threepenny Opera, Streamers, Stages, St. Joan, The Biko Inquest, Man and Superman, Whose Life Is It Anyway?, Major Barbara, A Month in the Country, Bacchae, Hedda Gabler, Don Juan in Hell, Inadmissable Evidence, Eminent Domain, Misalliance, Learned Ladies, Some Men Need Help, Ah Wilderness!, The Caine Mutiny Court Martial, Heartbreak House, Come Back Little Sheba, Loves of Anatol, Be Happy for Me, Master Class, You Never Can Tell, Devil's Disciple, Lend Me a Tenor, Breaking Legs, Fiorello in Concert, An Inspector Calls.

BOSLEY, TOM. Born October 1, 1927 in Chicago, IL. Attended DePaul U. Bdwy debut 1959 in *Fiorello!* Followed by *Nowhere to go but Up, Natural Affection, A Murderer Among Us, Catch Me If You Can, Luv, Education of Hyman Kaplan, Beauty and the Beast.*

BOWMAN, LYNN. Born February 20, 1950 in Buffalo, NY. Graduate SUNY/Buffalo. Debut 1973 OB in *The Beggar's Opera, Dracula, Molly's Dream, The Shannon Doyle Incident.*

BOYD, CAMERON. Born September 6, 1984 in Carmel, NY. Bdwy debut 1992 in *Four Baboons Adoring the Sun* followed by *Abe Lincoln in Illinois.*

BOYD, JULIE. Born January 2 in Kansas City, MO. Graduate U. Utah, Yale. Bdwy debut 1985 in *Noises Off,* followed by OB in *Only You, Working Acts, Hyde in Hollywood, Nowhere, A Distance from Calcutta, The Orphanage.*

BOYD, PATRICK M. Born March 5, 1965 in Welch, WVA. Graduate W.VA.U. Bdwy debut 1994 in *Grease.*

BOYTON, PETER. Born November 4, 1955 in Damariscotta, ME. Attended U. Mass. Debut 1980 OB in *The Golden Apple,* followed by *The Wonder Years,* Bdwy in *She Loves Me* (1993).

BOYS, KENNETH. Born June 19,1960 in Seaford, DE. Attended U. Del. Debut 1976 OB in *Apple Pie* followed by *Madman and the Nun, TNT,* Bdwy 1993 in *Camelot.*

BRACCHITTA, JIM. Born February 27, 1960 in Brooklyn, NY. Graduate NYU. Bdwy debut 1989 in *Gypsy,* OB in *The Tennants of 3R, The Merchant of Venice, Rapunzel, Mock Doctor/Euridice, I Can Get it for You Wholesale, Scaring the Fish.*

BRADLEY, BRIAN. Born October 19, 1954 in Philadelphia, PA. Graduate U. Fla. Bdwy debut 1994 in *Grease.*

BRENNAN, MAUREEN. Born October 11, 1952 in Washington, DC. Attended U. Conn. Bdwy debut 1974 in *Candide* for which she received a Theatre World Award, followed by *Going Up, Knickerbocker Holiday, Little Johnny Jones, Stardust,* OB in *Shakespeare's Cabaret, The Cat and the Fiddle, Nuts and Bolts: Tightened.*

BRAND, GIBBY. Born May 20, 1946 in NYC. Graduate Ithaca Col. Debut 1977 OB in *The Castaways* followed by *The Music Man, Real Life Funnies,* Bdwy in *Little Me* (1981), *Passion.*

BRAUGHER, ANDRE. Born in 1963 in Chicago, IL. Graduate Stanford U., Juilliard. OB in *Way of the World, Twelfth Night, Much Ado About Nothing, Coriolanus, King John, Measure for Measure, Richard II.*

BRENNAN, NORA. Born Dec. 1, 1953 in East Chicago, IN. Graduate Purdue U. Bdwy debut 1980 in *Camelot,* followed by *Cats.*

BRILL, FRAN. Born Sept. 30 in PA. Attended Boston U. Bdwy debut 1969 in *Red White and Maddox,* OB in *What Every Woman Knows, Scribes, Naked, Look Back in Anger, Knuckle, Skirmishes, Baby with the Bathwater, Holding Patterns, Festival of One Acts, Taking Steps, Young Playwrights Festival, Claptrap, Hyde in Hollywood, Good Grief, Desdemona.*

BRODERICK, MATTHEW. Born Mar. 21, 1963 in New York City. Debut 1981 OB in *Torch Song Trilogy,* followed by *The Widow Claire, A Christmas Memory,* Bdwy 1983 in *Brighton Beach Memoirs* for which he received a Theatre World Award, followed by *Biloxi Blues.*

BRODERICK, WILLIAM. Born October 19, 1954 in Queens, NYC. Graduate Hunter Col. Debut 1986 OB in *Pere Goriot* followed by *The Real Inspector Hound, Iolanthe, Teasers and Tormentors, Dorian, While Fire.*

BRODY, JONATHAN. Born June 16, 1963 in Englewood, NJ. Debut 1982 OB in *Shulamith,* followed by *The Desk Set, Eating Raoul, Theda Bara and the Frontier Rabbi,* Bdwy in *Me and My Girl* (1986), *Sally Marr and Her Escorts.*

BROGGER, IVAR. Born January 10 in St. Paul, MN. Graduate U. Minn. Debut 1979 OB in *In the Jungle of Cities,* followed by *Collected Works of Billy the Kid, Magic Time, Cloud 9, Richard III, Clarence, Madwoman of Chaillot, Seascapes with Sharks and Dancer, Second Man, Twelfth Night, Almost Perfect, Up 'N' Under, Progress, Juno,* Bdwy in *Macbeth* (1981), *Pygmalion* (1987), *Saint Joan* (1983), *Blood Brothers.*

BROOKES, JACQUELINE. Born July 24, 1930 in Montclair, NJ. Graduate U. Iowa, RADA. Bdwy debut 1955 in *Tiger at the Gates,* followed by *Watercolor, Abelard and Heloise, A Meeting by the River,* OB in *The Cretan Woman* (1954) for which she received a Theatre World Award, *The Clandestine Marriage, Measure for Measure, The Duchess of Malfi, Ivanov, 8 Characters in Search of an Author, An Evening's Frost, Come Slowly Death, The Increased Difficulty of Concentration, The Persians, Sunday Dinner, House of Blue Leaves, Owners, Hallelujah, Dream of a Black-listed Actor, Knuckle, Mama Sang the Blues, Buried Child, On Mt. Chimorazo, Winter Dancers, Hamlet, Old Flames, The Diviners, Richard II, Vieux Carre, Full Hookup, Home Sweet Home/Crack, Approaching Zanzibar, Ten Blocks on the Camino Real, Listening, Sand.*

BROOKING, SIMON. Born December 23, 1960 in Edinburgh, Scot. Graduate SUNY/Fredonia, U. Wash. Debut 1989 OB in *American Bagpipes,* followed by *The Mortality Project, Prelude & Liebestod, Rough Crossing, Rumor of Glory, King Lear, Waiting at the Water's Edge, Able Bodies Seaman,* Bdwy 1993 in *Candida.*

BROOKS, JEFF. Born Apr. 7, 1950 in Vancouver, Can. Attended Portland

State U. Debut 1976 OB in *Titanic,* followed by *Fat Chances, Nature and Purpose of the Universe, Actor's Nightmare, Sister Mary Ignatius Explains It All, Marathon 84, The Foreigner, Talk Radio, Washington Heights,* Bdwy in *A History of the American Film* (1978), *Lend Me a Tenor, Gypsy, Nick & Nora, Guys & Dolls.*

BROWN, ANN. Born December 1, 1960 in Westwood, NJ. Graduate Trinity Col. Debut 1987 OB in *Pacific Overtures* followed by *Side by Side by Sondheim, Stages, The Golden Apple, 20 Fingers 20 Toes, A Salute to Tom Jones and Harvey Schmidt.*

BROWN, ANTHONY M. Born July 14, 1962 in Springfield, VA. Graduate Fla State U., Juilliard. Debut 1993 OB in *Jeffrey.*

BROWN, DARCY. Born April 7, 1968 in Poughkeepsie, NY. Graduate Brown U. Debut 1992 OB in *Cowboy in His Underwear,* followed by *Loose Ends, Arms and the Man, The Rain Always Falls.*

BROWN, BRANDY. Born in 1976 in Mobile, AL. Bdwy debut 1987 in *Les Miserables.*

BROWN, ROBIN LESLIE. Born Jan. 18, in Canandaigua, NY. Graduate LIU. Debut 1980 OB in *The Mother of Us All,* followed by *Yours Truly, Two Gentlemen of Verona, Taming of the Shrew, The Mollusc, The Contrast, Pericles, Andromache, Macbeth, Electra, She Stoops to Conquer, Berneice, Hedda Gabler, A Midsummer Night's Dream, Three Sisters, Major Barbara, The Fine Art of Finesse, 2 Schnitzler One-Acts, As You Like It, Ghosts, Chekhov Very Funny, God of Vengeance, Good Natured Man, Twelfth Night, Little Eyolf, King Lear.*

BROWN, WILLIAM SCOTT. Born Mar. 27, 1959 in Seattle, WA. Attended U. WA. Debut 1986 OB in *Juba,* Bdwy in *Phantom of the Opera* (1988).

BROWNING, SUSAN. Born Feb. 25, 1941 in Baldwin, NY. Graduate Penn. State. Bdwy debut 1963 in *Love and Kisses,* followed by *Company* for which she received a Theatre World Award, *Shelter, Goodtime Charley, Big River, Company in Concert,* OB in *Jo, Dime a Dozen, Seventeen, The Boys from Syracuse, Collision Course, Whiskey, As You Like It, Removalists, Africanus Instructus, The March on Russia.*

BROWNSTONE, DIANA. Born November 15, in NYC. Graduate High School Perf. Arts, School of Am Ballet. Debut 1992 OB in *Galina Lives,* Bdwy in *Joseph and the Amazng Technicolor Dreamcoat* (1993).

BRYANT, DAVID. Born May 26, 1936 in Nashville, TN. Attended TN State U. Bdwy debut 1972 in *Don't Play Us Cheap,* followed by *Bubbling Brown Sugar, Amadeus, Les Miserables,* OB in *Up in Central Park, Elizabeth and Essex, Appear and Show Cause.*

BRYDON, W. B. Born September 20, 1933 in Newcastle, Eng. Debut 1962 OB in *The Long the Short and the Tall,* followed by *Live Like Pigs, Sgt. Musgrave's Dance, The Kitchen, Come Slowly Eden, The Unknown Soldier and His Wife, Moon for the Misbegotten, The Orphan, Possession, Total Abandon, Madwoman of Chaillot, The Circle, Romeo and Juliet, Philadelphia Here I Come, Making History, Spinoza, Mme. MacAdam Traveling Theatre, Last Sortie,* Bdwy in *The Lincoln Mask, Ulysses in Nighttown, The Father.*

BRYGGMANN, LARRY. Born Dec. 21, 1938 in Concord, GA. Attended CCSF, Am. Th. Wing. Debut 1962 OB in *A Pair of Pairs,* followed by *Live Like Pigs, Stop You're Killing Me, Mod Donna, Waiting for Godot, Ballymurphy, Marco Polo Sings a Solo, Brownsville Raid, Two Small Bodies, Museum, Winter Dancers, Resurrection of Lady Lester, Royal Bob, Modern Ladies of Guanabacoa, Rum and Coke, Bodies Rest and Motion, Blood Sports, Class 1 Acts, Spoils of War, Coriolanus, Macbeth, Henry IV Parts 1 and 2, The White Rose, Nothing Sacred, As You Like It,* Bdwy in *Ulysses in Nighttown* (1974), *Checking Out, Basic Training of Pavlo Hummel, Richard III, Prelude to a Kiss* (also OB), *Picnic.*

BUELL, BILL. Born Sept. 21, 1952 in Paipai, Taiwan. Attended Portland State U. Debut 1972 OB in *Crazy Now,* followed by *Declassee, Lorenzaccio, Promenade, The Common Pursuit, Coyote Ugly, Alias Jimmy Valentine, Kiss Me Quick, Bad Habits, Groundhog, On the Bum,* Bdwy in *Once a Catholic* (1979), *The First, Welcome to the Club, The Miser, Taking Steps.*

BULLOCK, ANGELA. Born July 5 in NYC. Graduate Hunter Co. Debut 1993 OB in *Washington Square Moves,* followed by *John Brown, Window Man.*

BULOS, YUSEF. Born September 14, 1940 in Jerusalem. Attended American U., AADA. Debut 1965 OB in *American Savoyards* in rep, followed by *Saints, The Trouble with Europe, The Penultimate Problem of Sherlock Holmes, In the Jungle of Cities, Hermani, Bertrano, Duck Variations, Insignificance, Panache, Arms and the Man, The Promise, Crowbar, Hannah 1939, Strange Feet, Hyacinth Macaw,* Bdwy in *Indians* (1970), *Capt. Brassbound's Conversion.*

BURK, TERENCE. Born Aug. 11, 1947 in Lebanon, IL. Graduate S. IL. U. Bdwy debut 1976 in *Equus,* OB in *Religion, The Future, Sacred and Profane Love, Crime and Punishment.*

BURKE, MAGGIE. Born May 2, 1936 in Vay Shore, NY. Graduate Sarah Lawrence Col. OB in *Today is Independence Day, Lovers and Other Strangers, Jules Feiffer's Cartoons, Fog, Home is the Hero, King John, Rusty & Rico and Lena, Friends, Butterfaces, Old Times, Man with a Raincoat, Hall of North American Forests, Carla's Folks, A Betrothal, Driving Miss Daisy, The Innocents Crusade, Approaching Zanzibar, Born Guilty, Body of Water,* Bdwy in *Brighton Beach Memoirs* (1985), *Cafe Crown.*

BURKE, ROBERT. Born July 25, 1948 in Portland, ME. Graduate Boston Col. Debut 1975 OB in *Professor George* followed by *Shortchanged Review, The Arbor, Slab Boys, Gardenia, Abel & Bela/Architruc, One Act Festival,* Bdwy in *Macbeth* (1988), *Abe Lincoln in Illinois* (1993).

BURKHARDT, GERRY. Born June 14, 1946 in Houston, TX. Attended Lon Morris col. Bdwy debut 1968 in *Her First Roman,* followed by *The Best Little*

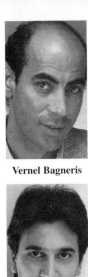

Vernel Bagneris

Laurie Beechman

Adrian Bailey

Mary Denise
Bentley

David Beach

Trazana Beverley

John Billeci

Michelle Blakely

Walter Bobbie

Maureen Brennan

W.B. Brydon

Maggie Burke

Fred Burrell

Denise Burse-
Mickelbury

Robert Canaan

Joanne Camp

David Cassidy

Kirsti Carnahan

Paul Castress

Kathleen Chalfant

Thom
Christopher

Stockard
Channing

Roy Cockrum

Sung Yun Cho

Gary Cowling

Mary Bond Davis

Keene Curtis

Diane Della
Piazza

Ed Dixon

Rebecca Downing

Whorehouse in Texas, Crazy for You, Best Little Whorehouse Goes Public, OB in *Girl Crazy, Leave it to Me.*

BURKS, WILLIS II. Born October 25, 1935 in Burmingham, AL. Attended Columbia Col. Debut 1994 OB in *East Texas Hot Links.*

BURNETT, ROBERT. Born Feb. 28, 1960 in Goshen, NY. Attended HB Studio. Bdwy debut 1985 in *Cats.*

BURNHAM, MARGARET. Born May 29 in Painsville, OH. Graduate Wooster Col. Debut 1988 OB in *A Midsummer Night's Dream* followed by *Reckonings, The Former Mrs. Meis, Pericles, Love's Labour's Lost, After the Ball.*

BURRELL, FRED. Born Sept. 18, 1936. Graduate UNC, RADA. Bdwy debut 1964 in *Never Too Late,* followed by *Illya Darling,* OB in *The Memorandum, Throckmorton, Texas, Voices in the Head, Chili Queen, The Queen's Knight, In Pursuit of the Song of Hydrogen, Unchanging Love, More Fun Than Bowling, A Woman without a Name, The Sorrows of Fredrick, The Voice of the Prairie, Spain, Democracy and Esther, Last Sortie, Rough/Play.*

BURRELL, PAMELA. Born Aug 4, 1945 in Tacoma, WA. Bdwy debut 1966 in *Funny Girl,* followed by *Where's Charley?, Strider, Sunday in the Park with George, Red Shoes,* OB in *Arms and the Man* for which she received a Theatre World Award, *Berkeley Square, The Boss, Biography: A Game, Strider: Story of a Horse, A Little Madness, Spinoza, After the Dancing in Jericho.*

BURSE-MICKLEBURY, DENISE. Born Jan. 13 in Atlanta, Ga. Graduate Spellman Col., Atlanta U. Debut 1990 OB in *Ground People* for which she received a Theatre World Award, followed by *A Worm in the Heart, Robert Johnson: Trick the Devil.*

BURSTEIN, DANNY. Born June 16, 1964 in NYC. Graduate U. Cal/San Diego. Moscow Art Theatre. Debut 1991 OB in *The Rothschilds, Weird Romance, Merrily We Roll Along,* Bdwy in *A Little Hotel on the Side* (1992), *The Sea Gull, Saint Joan, Three Men on a Horse, Flowering Peach*

BURSTYN, MIKE. (formerly Burstein) Born July 1, 1945 in the Bronx, NY. Bdwy debut 1968 in *The Megilla of Itzak Manger* followed by *Inquest, Barnum, Ain't Broadway Grand, Fiorello in Concert,* OB in *Wedding in Shtetl, Prisoner of Second Avenue, The Rothschilds.*

BURTON, ARNIE. Born Sept. 22, 1958 in Emmett, ID. Graduate U. Ariz. Bdwy debut 1983 in *Amadeus,* OB in *Measure for Measure, Major Barbara, Schnitzler One Acts, Tartuffe, As You Like It, Ghosts, Othello, Moon for the Misbegotten, Twelfth Night, Little Eyolf, Mollusc.*

BURTON, KATE. Born September 10, 1957 in Geneva, Switz. Graduate Brown U., Yale. Bdwy debut 1982 in *Present Laughter,* followed by *Alice in Wonderland, Doonesbury, Wild Honey, Some Americans Abroad, Jake's Women,* OB in *Winners* for which she received a 1983 Theatre World Award, *Romeo and Juliet, The Accrington Pals, Playboy of the Western World, Measure for Measure.*

BUSCH, CHARLES. Born Aug. 23, 1954 in Hartsdale, NY. Graduate Northwestern U. Debut OB 1985 in *Vampire Lesbians of Sodom,* followed by *Times Square Angel, Psycho Beach Party, The Lady in Question, Red Scare on Sunset,* all of which he wrote, *The Charles Busch Revue.*

BUSHMANN, KATE. Born October 6, 1961 in Ft. Smith, AR. Graduate Stephens Col. Debut 1992 OB in *Move It and It's Your's,* followed by *Roleplay, Let Us Now Praise Famous Men.*

BUTT, JENNIFER. Born May 17, 1958 in Valparaiso, IN. Stephens Col. graduate. Debut 1983 OB in *The Robber Bridegroom,* followed by *Into the Closet,* Bdwy in *Les Miserables* (1987).

BUTTERFIELD, CATHERINE. Born February 5 in NYC. Graduate SMU. Debut 1983 OB in *Marmalade Skies,* followed by *Bobo's Birthday, Joined at the Head, Snowing at Delphi.*

CAFFEY, MARION J. Born January 11, 1955 in Hempstead, TX. OB in *Come with Us, Seeds, Blackberries, Dreams of Becoming, Mayor, Queenie Pie.*

CAHN, LARRY. Born December 19, 1955 in Nassau, NY. Graduate Northwestern U. Bdwy debut 1980 in *The Music Man* followed by *Anything Goes, Guys and Dolls,* OB in *Susan B!, Jim Thorpe All American Play to Win.*

CAIN, WILLIAM. Born May 27, 1931 in Tuscaloosa, AL. Graduate U. Wash., Catholic U. Debut 1962 OB in *Red Roses for Me,* followed by *Jericho Jim Crow, Henry V, Antigone, Relatively Speaking, I Married an Angel in Concert, Buddha, Copperhead, Forbidden City, Fortinbras,* Bdwy in *Wilson in the Promise Land* (1970), *You Can't Take It with You, Wild Honey, The Boys in Autumn, Mastergate, A Streetcar Named Desire.*

CALABRESE, MARIA. Born Dec. 7, 1967 in Secone, PA. Bdwy debut 1991 in *The Will Rogers Follies, My Favorite Year.*

CALLAWAY, LIZ. Born Apr. 13, 1961 in Chicago, IL. Debut 1980 OB in *Godspell,* followed by *The Matinee Kids, Brownstone, No Way to Treat a Lady, Marry Me a Little, 1-2-3-4-5,* Bdwy in *Merrily We Roll Along* (1981), *Baby, The Three Musketeers, Miss Saigon, Cats, Fiorello in Concert.*

CALUD, ANNETTE Y. Born November 1963 in Milwaukee, WI. Graduate IL. Col. of Optometry. Bdwy debut 1991 in *Miss Saigon.*

CAMP, JOANNE. Born Apr. 4, 1951 in Atlanta, GA. Graduate Fl. Atlantic U., Geo. Wash. U. Debut 1981 OB in *The Dry Martini,* followed by *Geniuses* for which she received a Theatre World Award, *June Moon, Painting Churches, Merchant of Venice, Lady from the Sea, The Contrast, Coastal Disturbances, The Rivals, Andromache, Electra, Uncle Vanya, She Stoops to Conquer, Hedda Gabler, The Heidi Chronicles, Importance of Being Earnest, Medea, Three Sisters, A Midsummer Night's Dream, School for Wives, Measure for Measure, Dance of Death, Two Schnitzler One-Acts, Tartuffe, Lips Together Teeth Apart, As You Like It, Moon for the Misbegotten,*

Phaedra, Little Eyolf, Bdwy in *The Heidi Chronicles* (1989), *Sisters Rosensweig.*

CAMPBELL, AMELIA. Born Aug. 4, 1965 in Montreal, Can. Graduate Syracuse U. Debut 1988 OB in *Fun,* followed by *Member of the Wedding, Tunnel of Love, Five Women Wearing the Same Dress, Wild Dogs,* Bdwy in *Our Country's Good* (1991), *A Small Family Business.*

CARABUÉNA, PHILIP LEE. Born October 18, 1986 in NYC. Bdwy debut 1991 in *Miss Saigon.*

CARLO, ISMAEL (EAST). Born January 29, 1942 in Cabo Rojo, P.R. Debut 1994 OB in *Moe's Lucky Seven.*

CARMELLO, CAROLEE. Born in Albany, NY. Graduate SUNY/Albany. Bdwy debut 1989 in *City of Angels* followed by *Faslettos,* OB in *I Can Get it for You Wholesale,* (1991) *Hello Again, Goose, The Case of the Dead Flamingo Dancer.*

CARNAHAN, KIRSTI. Born June 29 in Evanston, IL. Attended U. Cinn. Bdwy debut 1983 in *Baby,* followed by *The Three Musketeers, Kiss of the Spider Woman,* OB in *Hang on to the Good Times, Mortally Fine.*

CARPENTER, CARLETON. Born July 10, 1926 in Bennington, VT. Attended Northwestern U. Bdwy debut 1944 in *Bright Boy* followed by *Career Angel, Three to made Ready, Magic Touch, John Murray Anderson's Almanac, Hotel Paradiso, Box of Watercolors, Hello Dolly!, Crazy for You,* OB in *Stage Affair, Boys in the Band, Dylan, The Greatest Fairy Story Ever Told, A Good Old Fashioned Revue, Miss Stanwyck Is Still in Hiding, Rocky Road, Apollo of Bellac, Light up the Sky, Murder at Rutherford House.*

CARR, SUSAN. Born April 19, 1940 in NYC. Attended Sarah Lawrence Col., Guildhall School/London. Bdwy debut 1964 in *The Physicists,* OB in *A Midsimmer Night's Dream, Just a Passing Fancy, The Furies, Mind Games, His Hers Mine Ours, The Marriage, Nice Girls, The Lion in Winter, The Sacred Guard, Beaux Strategem.*

CARTER, DON. Born May 29, 1933 in Hawaii. Graduate Or State U. Debut 1974 OB in *The Petrified Forest* followed by *Much Ado about Nothing.*

CARTER, MYRA. Born October 27, 1930 in Chicago, IL. Attended Glasgow U. Bdwy debut 1957 in *Major Barbara* followed by *Maybe Tuesday, Present Laughter,* OB in *Trials of Oz, Abingdon Square, Three Tall Women.*

CARVER, BRENT. Born November 17, 1951 in Cranbrook, BC, Canada. Attended UBC. Bdwy debut 1993 in *Kiss of the Spider Woman* for which he received a Theatre World Award.

CASSIDY, DAVID. Born April 12, 1950 in NYC. Bdwy debut 1969 in *Fig Leaves Are Falling,* followed by *Joseph and the Amazing Technicolor Dreamcoat, Blood Brothers.*

CASSIDY, PATRICK. Born January 4, 1961 in Los Angeles, CA. Bdwy debut 1982 in *Pirates of Penzance* followed by *Leader of the Pack* OB in *Assassins, Lady in the Dark in Concert.*

CASSIDY, SHAUN. Born September 27, 1958 in Los Angeles, CA. Bdwy debut 1993 in *Blood Brothers.*

CASTREE, PAUL. Born in Rockford, IL. Graduate U. IL. Debut 1992 OB in *Forever Plaid,* Bdwy in *Grease* (1994).

CAVISE, JOE ANTONY. Born Jan. 7, 1958 in Syracuse, NY. Graduate Clark U. Debut 1981 OB in *Street Scene,* followed by Bdwy 1984 in *Cats.*

CELEBI, UMIT. Born October 22, 1960 in Ankara, Turkey. Graduate Brown U. NYU. Debut 1984 OB in *The Golem* followed by *The Triumph of Love.*

CHAIFETZ, DANA. Born September 1, in NYC. Debut 1992 OB in *El Barrio* followed by *Somewhere, Halfway There, Resurrection, The Survivor.*

CHAIKEN, STACIE. Born December 6 in Hagerstown, MD. Graduate U. Minn., U. Cal/Berkeley. Debut 1987 OB in *A Midsummer Night's Dream* followed by *Down in the Hole, Flaming Idiots, The Wise Men of Chelm, Jack, Principia, Woman in the Second Floor Window, State of the Art, Mutiny, The Lover, Edith Stein,* Bdwy 1993 in *Abe Lincoln in Illinois.*

CHALFANT, KATHLEEN. Born January 14, 1945 in San Francisco, CA. Graduate Stanford U. Bdwy debut 1975 in *Dance with Me,* followed by *M. Butterfly, Angels in America,* OB in *Jules Feiffer's Hold Me, Killings on the Last Line, The Boor, Blood Relations, Signs of Life, Sister Mary Ignatius Explains it All, Actor's Nightmare, Faith Healer, All the Nice People, Hard Times, Investigation of the Murder in El Salvador, 3 Poets, The Crucible, The Party.*

CHAMBERLAIN, RICHARD. Born March 31, 1935 in Beverly Hills, CA. Attended Pomona Col. Bdwy debut 1976 in *Night of the Iguana* followed by *Blithe Spirit, My Fair Lady* (1993), OB in *Fathers and Sons.*

CHAMBERLIN, KEVIN. Born November 25, 1963 in Baltimore, MD. Graduate Rutgers U., Debut 1990 OB in *Neddy,* followed by *Smoke on the Mountain, My Favorite Year* (1992), *Abe Lincoln in Illinois.*

CHAMPAGNE, MICHAEL. Born April 10, 1947 in New Bedford, MA. Graduate SMU, MSU. Debut 1975 OB in *The Lieutenant,* followed by *Alinsky, The Hostage, Livingstone and Sechele, A Christmas Carol, Penelope, An Occasion of Sin, Beef, The Little Prince.*

CHANDLER, DAVID. Born February 3, 1950 in Danbury, CT. Graduate Oberlin Col. Bdwy debut 1980 in *The American Clock* followed by *Death of a Salesman, Lost in Yonkers,* OB in *Made in Heaven, Black Sea Follies, The Swan.*

CHANDLER, JEFREY ALAN. Born September 9, 1953 in Durham, NC. Graudate Carnegie Tech, AmConsvTheatre. Debut 1969 OB in *The People vs. Ranchman, Your Own Thing, Penguin Touquet,* Bdwy in *Elizabeth I* (1972), *The Dresser, Whodunit?, Two Shakespearean Actors, Timon of Athens, The Government Inspector.*

CHANDLER, KYLE. Born in 1966 in Buffalo, NY. Attended UGA. Bdwy debut 1994 in *Picnic.*

CHANG, BETSY. Born August 24, 1963 in Oakland, CA. Attended UC

209

Berkeley. Bdwy debut 1988 in *42nd Street* followed by *Cats, Joseph and the Amazing Technicolor Dreamcoat, Shogun the Musical.*

CHANNING, STOCKARD. Born Feb. 13, 1944 in NYC. Attended Radcliffe Col. Debut 1970 in *Adaptation/Next,* followed by *The Lady and the Clarinet, The Golden Age, Woman in Mind, Six Degrees of Separation,* Bdwy in *Two Gentlemen of Verona, They're Playing Our Song, The Rink, Joe Egg, House of Blue Leaves, Six Degrees of Separation, Four Baboons Adoring the Sun, Normal Heart benefit.*

CHASE, PAULA LEGGETT. Born September 2, 1961 in Evansville, IN. Graduate Ind U. Bdwy debut 1989 in *A Chorus Line* followed by *Crazy for You, Damn Yankees.*

CHENOWETH, KRISTIN D. Born July 24, 1968 in Tulsa, OK. Graduate Ok City U. Debut 1994 OB in *The Box Office of the Damned.*

CHENG, KAM. Born Mar. 28, 1969 in Hong Kong. Attended Muhlenberg Col. Bdwy debut 1991 in *Miss Saigon.*

CHIBAS, MARISSA. Born June 13, 1961 in NYC. Graudate SUNY/Purchase. Debut 1983 OB in *Asian Shade,* followed by *Sudden Death, Total Eclipse, Another Antigone, Fresh Horses,* Bdwy in *Brighton Beach Memiors* (1984), *Abe Lincoln in Illinois.*

CHIORAN, JUAN. Born June 18, 1963 in Albert, Argentina. Graduate Ualberta, York U. Bdwy debut 1994 in *Kiss of the Spider Woman.*

CHO, SUNG YUN. Born April 24, 1971 in Seoul, Korea. Graduate SUNY/Puchase. Bdwy debut 1993 in *Redwood Curtain,* OB in *Apocrypha.*

CHONG, MARCUS. Born July 8, 1967 in Seattle, WA. Attended Santa Monica City Col. Bdwy debut 1990 in *Stand-Up Tragedy* for which he received a Theatre World Award.

CHRISTAKOS, JERRY. Born September 9, 1960 in Chicago, IL. Attended U. Ariz. Bdwy debut 1993 in *Kiss of the Spider Woman.*

CHRISTOPHER, THOM. Born October 5, 1940 in Jackson Heights, NY. Attended Ithaca Col., Neighborhood Playhouse, Debut 1972 OB in *One Flew Over the Cuckoo's Nest,* followed by *Tamara, Investigation of the Murder in El Salvador, Sublime Lives, Triumph of Love,* Bdwy in *Emperor Henry IV* (1973), *Noel Coward in Two Keys* for which he received a Theatre World Award, *Caesar and Cleopatra.*

CHRYST, GARY. Born in 1959 in LaJolla, CA. Joined Joffrey Ballet in 1968. Bdwy debut 1979 in *Dancin,* followed by *A Chorus Line, Guys & Dolls,* OB in *One More Song One More Dance, Music Loves Me.*

CLARK, KELLY. Born February 26, 1970 in London, England. Attended Guilford Sch/London. Debut 1993 OB in *Top Girls* followed by *Ever After, The Good and Faithful Servant.*

CLARK, PETULA. Born November 15, 1932 in Epson, Eng. Bdwy debut 1993 in *Blood Brothers.*

CLARKE, CAITLIN. Born May 3, 1952 in Pittsburgh, PA. Graduate Mt. Holyoke Col. Yale U. Debut 1981 OB in *No One To Blame* followed by *Lorenzaccio, Summer, Quartermaine's Terms, Thin Ice, Total Exlipse, 3 Birds Alighting on a Field,* Bdwy in *Teaneck Tanzi* (1983), *Strange Interlude, Arms and the Man, Figaro.*

CLAYTON, LAWRENCE. Born Oct. 10, 1956 in Mocksville, NC. Attended NC Central U. Debut 1980 in *Tambourines to Glory,* followed by *Skyline, Across the Universe, Two by Two, Romance in Hard Times, Juba, Tapestry,* Bdwy in *Dreamgirls* (1984), *High Rollers.*

CLOW, JAMES. Born April 15, 1965 in White Plains, NY. Graduate Syracuse U. LAMDA. Debut 1992 OB in *Juno,* Bdwy in *Blood Brothers* (1993).

COCKRUM, ROY. Born June 29, 1956 in Knoxville, TN. Graduate Northwestern U. Debut 1991 OB in *The Broken Pitcher,* followed by *Vampire Lesbians of Sodom, Red Scare on Sunset, God of Vengeance.*

COHEN, LYNN. Born August 10 in Kansas City, Mo. Graduate Northwestern U. Debut 1979 OB in *Don Juan Comes Back From the Wars* followed by *Getting Out, The Arbor, The Cat and the canary, Suddenly Last Summer, Bella Figura, The Smash, Chinese Viewing Pavillion, isn't it Romatic, Total Eclipse, Angelo's Wedding, Hamlet, Love Diatribe, A Couple with a Cat,* Bdwy in *Orpheus Descending* (1989).

COHENOUR, PATTI. Born Oct. 17, 1952 in Albuquerque, NM. Attended U. NM. Bdwy debut 1982 in *A Doll's Life,* followed by *Pirates of Penzance, Big River, The Mystery of Edwin Drood, Phantom of the Opera,* OB in *La Boheme* for which she received a Theatre World Award.

COKAS, NICK. Born April 11, 1965 in San Francisco, CA. Graduate UCLA. Bdwy debut 1993 in *Blood Brothers.*

COLE, NORA. Born September 10, 1953 in Louisville, KY. Attended Beloit Col., Goodman School. Debut 1977 OB in *Movie Buff,* followed by *Cartoons for a Lunch Hour, Boogie-Woogie Rumble, Ground Hog,* Bdwy in *Your Arms Too Short to Box with God* (1982), *Inacent Black, Runaways, Jelly's Last Jam.*

COLLET, CHRISTOPHER. Born March 13, 1968 in NYC. Attended Strasberg Inst. Bdwy debut 1983 in *Torch Song Trilogy* followed OB in *Coming of Age in Soho, Spoils of War, Executive Council, Unfinished Stories, An Imaginary Life.*

COLORADO, ELVIRA. Born July 6 in Blue Island, IL. Debut 1971 OB in *The Screens* followed by *Women behind Bars, The Three Sisters, The Petrified Forest, Puerto Rican Obituary, The Dispossessed, Woman Without Borders, The Rez Sisters.*

COLTON, CHEVI. Born December 21 in NYC. Attended Hunter Col. OB in *Time of Storm, The Insect Comedy, The Adding Machine, O Marry Me, Penny Change, The Mad Show, Jacques Brel Is Alive.., Bits and Pieces, Spelling Bee, Uncle Money, Miami, Come Blow Your Horn, Almost Perfect, The Susnset Gang, Milk and Honey,* Bdwy in *Over Here, Cabaret, Grand*

Tour, Torch Song Trilogy, Roza.

CONNELL, JANE. Born Oct. 27, 1925 in Berkeley, CA. Attended U. Cal. Bdwy debut in *New Faces of 1956* followed by *Drat! The Cat!, Mame* (1966/83), *Dear World, Lysistrata, Me and My Girl, Lend a Me a Tenor, Crazy For You,* OB in *Shoestring Revue, Threepenny Opera, Pieces of Eight, Demi-Dozen, She Stoops to Conquer, Drat!, Real Inspector Hound, Rivals, Rise and Rise of Daniel Rocket, Laughing Stock, Singular Dorothy Parker, No No Nanette in Concert.*

CONNELL, TIM. Born May 3, 1961 in Philadelphia, PA. Bdwy debut 1991 in *Nick and Nora,* OB in *Anyone Can Whistle, Pets, Sharon, Rimers of Eldritch.*

CONOLLY, PATRICIA. Born Aug.29, 1933 in Tabora, E. Africa. Attended U. Sydney. With APA in *You Can't Take It With You, War and Peace, School for Scandal, Wild Duck, Right You Are, We Comrades Three, Pantagleize, Exit the King, Cherry Orchard, Misanthropre, Cocktail Party, Cock-a-doodle Dandy* followed by *Stretcar Named Desire, Importance of Being Earnest, The Circle, Small Family Business, Real Inspector Hound/15 Minute Hamlet,* OB in *Blithe Spirit, Woman in Mind.*

CONROY, FRANCES. Born in 1953 in Monroe, GA. Attended Dickinson Col., Juilliard, Neighborhood Playhouse. Debut 1978 OB with the Acting Co. in *Mother Courage, King Lear, The Other Half* followed by *All's Well That Ends Well, Othello, Sorrows of Stephen, Girls Girls Girls, Zastrozzi, Painting Churches, Uncle Vanya, Romance Language, To Gillian on Her 37th Birthday, Man and Superman, Zero Positive, Bright Room Called Day, Lips Together Teeth Apart, Booth, Last Yankee* Bdwy in *Lady from Dubuque* (1980), *Our Town, Secret Rapture* (also OB), *Some Americans Abroad* (also OB), *Two Shakespearian Actors, In the Summer House, Broken Glass*

CONVERSE, FRANK. Born May 22, 1938 in St. Louis, MO. Attended Carnegie-Mellon U. Bdwy debut 1966 in *First One Asleep Whistle* followed by *The Philadelphia Story, Brothers, Design for Living, A Streetcare Named Desire,* OB in *House of Blue Leaves, Lady in the Dark in Concert.*

CONWAY, KEVIN. Born May 29, 1941 in NYC. Debut 1968 in *Muzeeka* followed by *Saved, Plough and the Stars, One Flew Over the Cuckoo's Nest, When You Comin' Back Red Ryder, Long Day's Journey into Night, Other Places, King John, Other People's Money, Man Who Fell in Love with His Wife, Ten Below,* Bdwy in *Indians* (1969), *Moonchildren, Of Mice and Men, Elephant Man.*

COOK, LINDA. Born Juen 8 in Lubbock, TX. Attended Auburn U. Debut 1974 OB in *The Wager* followed by *Hole in the Wall, Shadow of a Gunman, Be My Father, Ghosts of the Loyal Oaks, Different People Different Rooms, Saigon Rose, Romantic Arrangements, No Time Flat, Dearly Deaprted, All That Glitters.*

COOK, JOCELYN. Born October 30, 1965 in Atlanta, GA. Attended UCSD. Bdwy debut 1993 in *Joseph and the Amazing Technicolor Dreamcoat.*

COONEY, KEVIN. Born October 2, 1945 in Houston, TX. Graduate U. St. Thomas, U. Houston. Bdwy deut 1981 in *The Best Little Whorehouse in Texas* followed by OB in *Salt Air, Rainbow Dancing.*

COOPER, CHUCK. Born November 8, 1954 in Cleveland, OH. Graduate Ohio U. Debut 1982 OB in *Colored People's Time,* followed by *Riff Raff Revue, Primary English Class, Break/Agnes/Eulogy/Lucky, Avenue X,* Bdwy in *Amen Corner* (1983), *Someone Who'll Watch Over Me.*

COOPER, MARILYN. Born December 14, 1936 in NYC. Attended NYU, Bdwy in *Mr. Wonderful, West Side Story, Brigadoon, Gypsy, I Can Get It for You Wholesale, Hallelujah Baby, Golden Rainbow, Mame, A Teaspoon Every 4 Hours, Two by Two, On the Town, Ballroom, Woman of the Year, The Odd Couple, Cafe Crown, Fiorello in Concert,* OB in *The Mad Show, Look Me Up, The Perfect Party, Cafe Crown, Milk and Honey.*

COPELAND, JOAN. Born June 1, 1922 in NYC. Attended Brooklyn Col., AADA. Debut 1945 OB in *Romeo and Juliet,* followed by *Othello, Conversation Piece, Delightful Season, End of Summer, American Clock, The Double Game, Isn't it Romantic? Hunting Cockroaches, Young Playwrights Festival, The American Plan, Rose Quartet, Another Time,* Bdwy in *Sundown Beach, Detective Story, Not for Children, Hatful of Fire, Something More, The Price, Two by Two, Pal Joey, Checking Out, The American Clock.*

COPPOLA, SAM. Born July 31, 1935 in New Jersey. Attended Actors Studio. Debut 1968 OB in *A Present from Your Old Man,* followed by *Things That Almost Happen, Detective Story, Jungle of Cities, Pals, Fore!,Dreamers,* Bdwy in *The Caine Mutiny Court Martial* (1983).

CORBALIS, BRENDAN. Born March 19, 1964 in Dublin, Ire. Graduate NYU. Debut 1988 OB in *April Snow* followed by *The Indians of Venezuela, Finding the Sun.*

CORMIER, TONY. Born November 2, 1951 in Camp Roberts, CA. Attended Pierce Col., Wash. State U. Debut 1984 in *Kennedy at Colonus,* followed by *Something Cloudy Something Clear, Three Sisters, Love's Labour's Lost, Angel in the House.*

CORTES, CECELIA. Born June 12, 1989 in Boston, MA. Bdwy debut 1994 in *Carousel.*

COSGRAVE, PEGGY. Born June 23, 1946 in San Mateo, CA. Graduate San Jose Col., Catholic U. Debut 1980 OB in *Come Back to the Five and Dime Jimmy Dean* followed by *Sandbox,* Bdwy in *The Nerd* followed by *Born Yesterday.*

COUNCIL, RICHARD E. Born October 1, 1947 in Tampa, FL. Graduate U. Fl. Debut 1973 OB in *Merchant of Venice,* followed by *Ghost Dance, Look We've Come Through. Arms and the Man, Isadora Duncan Sleeps with the Russian Navy, Arthur, The Winter Dancer, The Prevalence of Mrs. Seal, Jane Avril, Young Playwrights Festival, Sleeping Dogs, The Good Coach, Subfertile,* Bdwy in *Royal Family* (1975), *Philadelphia Story, I'm Not*

COUNTRYMAN, MICHAEL. Born Sept. 15, 1955 in St. Paul, MN. Graduate Trinity Col., AADA. Debut 1983 OB in *Changing Palettes*, followed by *June Moon, Terra Nova, Out!, Claptrap, The Common Pursuit, Woman in Mind, Making Movies, The Tempest, Tales of the Lost Formicans, Marathon '91, The Stick Wife, Lips Together Teeth Apart, All in the Timing, The Ashfire*, Bdwy in *A Few Good Men* (1990), *Face Value.*

COURIE, JONATHAN. Born October 26, 1963 in Raleigh, NC. Graduate U. Cincinnati. Debut 1986 OB in *Murder in Rutherford House* followed by *The Apple Tree, The Elephant Man, Night Games, A Frog in His Throat, 20 Fingers 20 Toes, A Salute to Tom Jones and Harvey Schmidt.*

COWAN, EDWARDYNE. Born July 23 in Queens, NYC. Graduate New Rochelle Col. Debut 1992 OB in *The Molly Maguires* followed by *Anything Goes, Lakme*, Bdwy 1993 in *My Fair Lady.*

COWLING, GARY. Born November 4, 1961 in Newport News, Va. Graduate William & Mary Col., West Va. U. Debut 1987 OB in *Spoon River*, followed by *Billy Budd, Love's Labour's Lost, Comedy of Errors, School for Scandal, Othello, Off the Beat and Path 2, Ceremony of Innocence.*

COX, RICHARD. Born May 6, 1948 in NYC. Yale U. graduate. Debut 1970 OB in *Saved* followed by *Fugs, Moonchildren, Alice in Concert, Richard II, Fishing, What a Man Weighs, The Family of Mann*, Bdwy in *The Sign in Sidney Brustein's Window, Platinum, Blood Brothers.*

CRABTREE, HOWARD. Born November 5, 1954 in Excelsior Springs, MO. Attended Maplewood Col. Debut 1987 OB in *Howard and Drew Meet the Invisible Man* followed by *Whatnot, Whoop-dee-doo.*

CRANDALL, SHELLEY. Born June 30, 1954 in Ann Arbor, MI. Graduate Carnegie-Mellon U. Debut 1986 OB in *Octoberfest* followed by *Amphytrion '38, The Search for Extraterrestrial Intelligence, Cafe Toulouse, X Train.*

CRANHAM, KENNETH. Born December 12, 1944 in Dunferline, Fife, Scotland. Graduate RADA. Bdwy debut 1968 in *Loot* followed by *An Inspector Calls* (1994).

CRAVENS, MARY ELLEN. Born June 11, 1982 in Dallas, TX. Bdwy debut 1994 in *An Inspector Calls.*

CRAVENS, PIERCE. Born January 8, 1986 in Dallas, TX. Debut 1993 OB in *All's Well that Ends Well*, Bdwy 1994 in *Beauty and the Beast.*

CREAGHAN, DENNIS. Born May 1, 1942 in London, Eng. Attended Hofstra U., HB Studio. Debut 1973 OB in *Hamlet*, followed by *The Tempest, Edward II, The Servant, Pterodactyls*, Bdwy in *The Elephant Man* (1979).

CRIST, SHERIDAN. Born December 5, 1957 in Los Angeles, CA. Graduate Redlands U., Rutgers U. Debut 1984 OB in *Orestia* followed by *The Underpants, Frankenstein, George Dandin, The Sea Gull in the Hamptons, Scaring the Fish, Jeffrey.*

CRIVELLO, ANTHONY. Born Aug. 2, 1955 in Milwaukee, WI. Bdwy debut 1982 in *Evita* followed by *The News, Les Miserables, Kiss of the Spiderwoman* OB in *Juniper Tree.*

CROFT, PADDY. Born in Worthing, England. Attended Avondale Col. Debut 1961 OB in *The Hostage* followed by *Billy Liar, Live Like Pigs, Hogan's Goat, Long Day's Journey into Night, Shadow of a Gunman, Pygmalion, The Plough and the Stars, Kill, Starting Monday, Philadephia Here I Come!, Grandchild of Kings, Fragments*, Bdwy in *The Killing of Sister George, The Prime of Miss Jean Brodie, Crown Matrimonial, Major Barbara.*

CROUSE, LINDSAY. Born May 12, 1948 in New York City. Graduate Radcliffe Col. Bdwy debut 1972 in *Much Ado About Nothing*, followed by *A Christmas Carol, The Homecoming* (1991) for which she received a Theatre World Award, OB in *The Foursome, Fishing, Long Day's Journey into Night, Total Recall, Father's Day, Hamlet, Reunion, Twelfth Night, Childe Byron, Richard II, Serenading Louie, Prairie/Shawl, The Stick Wife.*

CRUTCHFIELD, BUDDY. Born June 4, 1957 in Dallas, TX. Graduate SMU. Debut 1979 *Radio City Christmas Spectacular*, followed by OB *HMS Pinafore, Pirates of Penzance, Tent Show, A Church is Born, Senior Discretion, The Widow Clair, Six Wives*, Bdwy in *The Most Happy Fella* (1992).

CRUZ, FRANCIS J. Born Oct. 4, 1954 in Long Beach, CA. Attended F.I.D.M. Bdwy debut 1991 in *Miss Saigon.*

CUCCIOLI, ROBERT/BOB. Born May 3, 1958 in Hempstead, NY. Graduate St. John's U. Debut 1982 OB in *HMS Pinafore* followed by *Senor Discretion,Gigi, The Rothschilds, And the World Goes Round*, Bdwy in *Les Miserables.*

CUERVO, ALMA. Born August 13, 1951 in Tampa, Fl. Graduate Tulane U. Debut 1977 in *Uncommon Women and Others* followed by *A Foot in the Door, Put Them All Together, Isn't It Romantic?, Miss Julie, Quilters, The Sneaker Factor, Songs on a Shipwrecked Sofa, Uncle Vanya, The Grandma Plays, The Nest, Secret Rapture, Christine Alberta's Father, Music from Down the Hall*, Bdwy in *Once in a Lifetime, Bedroom Farce, Censored Scenes from King Kong, Is There Life After High School?, Ghetto, Secret Rapture.*

CULLITON, JOSEPH. Born January 25, 1948 in Boston, MA. Attended Cal State U. Debut 1982 OB in *Francis*, followed by *Flirtations, South Pacific* (LC) *Julius Caesar, King John, Company, On a Clear Day*, Bdwy 1987 in *Broadway.*

CULLIVER, KAREN. Born December 30, 1959 in Florida. Attended Stetson U. Bdwy debut 1983 in *Show Boat* followed by *The Mystery of Edwin Drood, Meet Me in St. Louis, Phantom of the Opera*, OB in *The Fantasticks.*

CUMPSTY, MICHAEL. Born in England. Graudate UNC. Bdwy debut 1989 in *Artist Descending a Staircase* followed by *La Bete, Timon of Athens*, OB in *The Art of Success, Man and Superman, Hamlet, Cymbeline, The Winter's Tale, King John, Romeo and Juliet, All's Well That Ends Well.*

CUNNINGHAM, JOHN. Born June 22, 1932 in Auburn, NY. Graduate Yale, Dartmouth U. OB in *Love Me a Little, Pimpernel, The Fantasticks, Love and Let Love, The Bone Room, Dancing in the Dark, Father's Day, Snapshot, Head Over Heels, Quartermaine's Terms, Wednesday, On Approval, Miami, Perfect Party, Birds of Paradise, Naked Truth*, Bdwy in *Hot Spot* (1963), *Zorba, Company, 1776, Rose, The Devil's Disciple, Six Degrees of Separation* (also OB), *Anna Karenina, The Sisters Rosensweig, Allegro in Concert*

CUNNINGHAM, T. SCOTT. Born December 15 in Los Angeles, CA. Graduate NC School of Arts. Debut 1992 OB in *Pterodactyls*, followed by *Takes on Women, Stand-In.*

CURLESS, JOHN. Born Sept. 16 in Wigan, Eng. Attended Central Schl. of Speech. NY debut 1982 OB in *The Entertainer*, followed by *Sus, Up 'n' Under, Progress, Prin, Nightingale, Absent Friends, Owners/Traps*, Bdwy in *A Small Family Business* (1992).

CURTIN, CATHERINE. Born in NYC. Graudate Pinceton U. Bdwy debut 1990 in *Six Degrees of Separation*. OB in *Gulf War, Making Book, Orphan Muses.*

CURTIS, KEENE. Born Feb. 15, 1925 in Salt Lake City UT. Graduate U. Utah. Bdwy debut 1949 in *Shop at Sly Corner*, with APA in *School for Scandal, The Tavern, Anatole, Scapin, Right You Are, Importance of Being Earnest, Twelfth Night, King Lear, Seagull, Lower Depths, Man and Superman, Judith, War and Peace, You Can't Take It with You, Pantaglieze, Cherry Orchard, Misanthrope, Cocktail Party, Cock-a-Doodle Dandy, and Hamlet, A Patriot for Me, The Rothschilds, Night Watch, Via Galactica, Annie, Division Street, La Cage aux Folles,White Liars/Black Comedy* OB in *Colette, Ride Across Lake Constance, The Cocktail Hour.*

DAILEY, IRENE. Born September 12, 1920 in NYC. Bdwy debut 1943 in *Nine Girls* followed by *Truckline Cafe, Idiot's Delight, Miss Lonelyhearts, Andorra, The Subject Was Roses, You Know I Can't Hear You When the Water's Running*, OB in *Good Woman of Setzuan, Rooms, The Loves of Cass McGuire, Edith Stein.*

DALEY, R.F. Born April 16, 1955 in Denver, Co. Attended N. Co. U. Bdwy debut 1988 in *Chess, Sweeney Todd, Guys and Dolls.*

DAMIAN, MICHAEL. (Michael Weir) Born April 26, 1962 in San Diego, CA. Bdwy debut 1993 in *Joseph and the Amazing Technicolor Dreamcoat.*

D'AMICO, MARCUS. Born December 4, 1965 in Frankfurt, Germany. Bdwy debut 1994 in *An Inspector Calls* for which he received a Theatre World Award.

DANSON, RANDY. Born April 30, 1950 in Plainfield NJ. Graduate Carnegie-Mellon U. Debut 1978 OB in *Gimme Shelter*, followed by *Big and Little, The Winter Dancers, Time Steps, Casualties, Red and Blue, The Resurrection of Lady Lester, Jazz Poets at the Grotto, Plenty, Macbeth, Blue Window, Cave Life, Romeo and Juliet, One-Act Festival, Mad Forest, Triumph of Love, The Treatment.*

DANTUONO, MICHAEL. Born July 30, 1942 in Providence, RI. Debut 1974 OB in *How to Get Rid of It* followed by *Maggie Flynn, Charlotte Sweet, Berlin to Broadway, A Lover's Rhapsody*, Bdwy in *Caesar and Cleopatra, Can-Can, Zorba, The Three Musketeers, 42nd Street.*

DARLOW, CYNTHIA. Born June 13, 1949 in Detroit, MI. Attended NCSch of Arts, Penn State U. Debut 1974 OB in *This Property Is Condemned* followed by *Portrait of a Madonna, Clytemnestra, Unexpurgated Memoirs of Bernard Morgandigler, Actor's Nightmare, Sister MaryIgnatius Explains..., Fables for Friends, That's It Folks!, Baby with the Bath Water, Dandy Dick, Prelude to a Kiss, The Naked Truth*, Bdwy in *Grease* (1976), *Rumors, Prelude to a Kiss.*

DAVID, CLIFFORD. Born June 30, 1932 in Roledo, OH. Attended U. Toledo, Actor's Studio. Bdwy debut 1960 in *Caligula* followed by *Wildcat, Aspern Papers, On a Clear Day You Can See Forever, A Joyful Noise, 1776, Joseph and the Amazing Technicolor Dreamcoat* (1993), OB in *The Boys from Sysracuse, Camino Real, Museam, Holy Places.*

DAVID, JIM. Born August 27, 1954 in Ashville, NC. Attended Furman U. SMU. Debut 1977 OB in *Wonderful Lives* followed by *Lu Ann Hampton, The Learned Ladies, The Liar, Media Messiah*, Bdwy 1994 in *The Best Little Whorehouse Goes Public.*

DAVIDSON, RICHARD M. Born May 10, 1940 in Hamilton, Ont., Can. Graduate U. Toronto, LAMDA. Debut 1978 OB in *The Beasts* followed by *The Bacchae, The Broken Pitcher, Knights Errant, The Entertainer, Lunatics and Lovers, Let Us Now Praise Famous Men*, Bdwy in *The Survivor* (1981), *The Ghetto.*

DAVIS, BRUCE ANTHONY. Born March 4, 1959 in Dayton, OH. Attended Juilliard. Bdwy debut 1979 in *Dancin'*, followed by *Big Deal, A Chorus Line, High Rollers*, OB in *Carnival.*

DAVIS, HOPE. Born March 23, 1964 in Englewood, NJ. Graduate Vassar Col. Debut 1991 OB in *Can-Can* followed by *Goodnight Desdemona, Pterodactyls, Arts and Leisure, Measure for Measure*, Bdwy in *Two Shakespearean Actors* (1991).

DAVIS, MAC. Born January 21, 1942 in Lubbock, TX. Attended Emory U. Bdwy debut 1992 in *The Will Rogers Follies.*

DAVIS, MARY BOND. Born June 3, 1958 in Los Angeles, CA. Attended Cal. State U./Northridge, LACC. Debut 1985 in *Trousers*, followed by *Hysterical Blindness*, Bdwy in *Mail* (1988), *Jelly's Last Jam.*

DAVYS, EDMUND C. Born Jan. 21, 1947 in Nashua, NH. Graduate Oberlin Col. Debut 1977 OB in *Othello*, Bdwy in *Crucifer of Blood* (1979), *Shadowlands, A Small Family Business, The Show-off, St. Joan, Three Men on a Horse.*

DAWSON, DAVID P. Born February 22, 1922 in Brooklyn, NY. Debut 1965 OB in *Hogan's Goat* followed by *Some Rain, About Face Festival, Homesick,*

Tom and Viv, American Clock, Bdwy in *The Freaking Out of Stephanie Blake*(1967).

D'BECK, PATTI. Born in Joppa MD. Graduate NYU. Bdwy debut 1970 in *Applause* followed by *Seesaw, Pippin, Chorus Line, Best Little Whorehouse in Texas, Evita, My One and Only, Will Rogers Follies, Grease* (1994).

DEAL, FRANK. Born October 7, 1958 in Birmingham, AL. Attended Duke U. Debut 1982 OB in *The American Princess* followed by *Richard III, Ruffian on the Stair, A Midsummer Night's Dream, We Shall Not All Sleep, The Legend of Sleepy Hollow, Three Sisters, The Triangle Project, One Neck, The Window Man.*

DEAKINS, LUCY. Born 1971 in NYC. Debut 1986 OB in *Hands of Its Enemy* followed by *Sweebitter Baby.*

DEAKINS, MARK. Born Nov.30, 1962 in Spokane, WA. Graduate Brigham Young U., U. Cal/San Diego. Bdwy debut 1990 in *Grapes of Wrath* followed by OB in *Henry IV, All's Well That Ends Well.*

DEAN, LAURA. Born May 27, 1963 in Smithtown, NY. Debut 1973 OB in *The Secret Life of Walter Mitty,* followed by *A Village Romeo and Juliet, Carousel, Hey Rube, Landscape of the Body, American Passion, Feathertop, Personals, Godspell, Festival of One-Acts, Catch Me If I Fall, A...My Name is Still Alice,* Bdwy in *Doonesbury* (1983), for which she received a Theatre World Award, *Tommy.*

DEAN, LOREN. Born July 31, 1969 in Las Vegas, NV. Debut 1989 OB in *Amulets Against the Dragon Forces,* for which he received a Theatre World Award, followed by *Beggars in the House of Plenty, Four Dogs and a Bone.*

deGANON, CAMILLE. Born in Springfield, OH. Appeared with several dance companies before Bdwy debut 1986 in *The Mystery of Edwin Drood* followed by *Jerome Robbins' Broadway, Brigadoon,* OB in *The Co-op.*

DeGONGÉ, MARCY. Born May 4, 1957 in Newark, NJ. Graduate Hart Col. Bdwy debut 1989 in *Cats.*

de HAAS, DARIUS. Born Sept.29, 1968 in Chicago, IL. Graduate AMDA. Bdwy debut 1994 in *Kiss of the Spiderwoman* followed by *Carousel.*

de JONG, ALEXANDER. Born Oct 2, 1962 in Holland. Attended Amsterdam Th. Sch. Bdwy debut 1993 in *My Fair Lady.*

DELAINE, SHERI. Born September 15, 1953 in Ironwood, MI. Graduate U. Wisc. Debut 1988 OB in *Tartuffe* followed by *French Gray, Pericles, The Rover, Zastrozzi, Shaviana, Off the Beat and Path 2, Bertolt Brecht in Dark Times.*

DE LA PENA, GEORGE. Born in NYC in 1956. Performed with Am. Bal. Th. before Bdwy debut 1981 in *Woman of the Year* followed by *On Your Toes, Red Shoes.*

DELLA PIAZZA, DIANE. Born Sept. 3, 1962 in Pittsburgh, PA. Graduate Cincinnati Consv. Bdwy debut 1987 in *Les Miserables.*

DeMATTHEWS, RALPH. Born April 22, 1950 in Somerville, NJ. Debut 1984 OB in *Agamemnon* followed by *Bury the Dead, A Place Called Heartbreak, Any Corner, The Strike, On the Waterfront.*

DEMPSEY, MARK J. Born Jan.29, 1936 in Hollywood, CA. Graduate U. Wash. Debut 1969 OB in *Oh! Calcutta!* followed by *Lost in the Stars, Cole Porter's Jubilee.*

DE MUSSA, RAFAEL. Born Oct.9, 1964 in Maturin, Venezuela. Graduate Parsons Sch. Debut 1984 OB in *Written and Sealed.*

DEVINE, ERIK. Born May 3, 1954 in Galveston, TX. Graduate U. Tulsa, Wayne St. U. Bdwy debut 1983 in *Cats* followed by *Sid Caesar & Co., Allegro in Concert,* OB in *Plain and Fancy, Lucky Stiff.*

DEVINE, LORETTA. Born Aug. 21 in Houston, TX. Graduate U. Houston, Brandeis U. Bdwy debut 1977 in *Hair* followed by *A Broadway Musical, Dreamgirls, Big Deal,* OB in *Godsong, Lion and the Jewel, Karma, The Blacks, Mahalia, Long Time Since Yesterday, Colored Museum, East Texas Hot Links.*

DIAZ, NATASCIA. Born Jan. 4, 1970 in Lugano, Swit. Graduate Carnegie-Mellon U. Debut 1993 OB in *Little Prince.*

DICKERSON, GEORGE. Born in Topeka, KS. Graduate Yale. Debut 1986 OB in *Shots at Fate* followed by *Lemonade.*

DIEKMANN, MARK. Born Aug.10, 1953 in Springfield, MA. Attended Clark U. Debut 1987 OB in *Misalliance* followed by *Thick Dick, Delicate Dangers.*

DIERLAM, KATY. Born July 31, 1950 in Gainesville, FL. Graduate Bennington Col., Debut 1958 OB in *Under Milkwood* followed by *Going Slow, Herd of Buffalo, Salaambo, How to Write a Play.*

DISHY, BOB. Born in Brooklyn, NYC. Graduate Syracuse U. Bdwy debut 1955 in *Damn Yankees* followed by *Can-Can, Flora the Red Menace, Something Different, Goodbye People, A Way of Life, Creation of the World and Other Business, American Millionaire, Sly Fox, Murder at Howard Johnson's, Grownups, Cafe Crown, Tenth Man,* OB in *When the Owl Screams, Wrecking Ball, By Jupiter, Unknown Soldier and His Wife, What's Wrong with This Picture?, Short Play Series, The Cowboy, The Indian and the Fervent Feminist.*

DIXON, ED. Born Sept. 2, 1948 in Oklahoma. Attended U. Okla. Bdwy in *The Student Prince,* followed by *No No Nanette, Rosalie in Concert, The Three Musketeers, Les Miserables, Cyrano: The Musical,* OB in *By Bernstein, King of the Schnorrers, Rabboni, Huncjback of Notre Dame, Moby Dick, Shylock, Johnny Pye and the Foolkiller.*

DODSON, COLLEEN. Born May 16, 1954 in Chicago, IL. Graduate U. Ill. Debut 1981 OB in *The Matinee Kids* followed by *Pal Joey, Holding Pattens, Breaks, Short Play Readings, Pitching to the Star,* Bdwy 1982 in *Nine.*

DOWE, KATE. Born December 5, 1968 in Salem, MA. Graduate Northwestern U. Bdwy debut 1994 in *Beauty and the Beast.*

DOWNING, REBECCA. Born Nov. 30, 1962 in Birmingham, AL. Graduate

Oklahoma City U. Debut 1989 OB in *Wonderful Town,* Bdwy in *The Will Rogers Follies* (1991).

DRUMMOND, ALICE. Born May 21, 1929 in Pawtucket, RI. Attended Pembroke Co. Bdwy debut 1963 in *Ballad of the Sad Cafe* followed by *Malcolm, The Chinese, Thieves, Summer Boys, Some of My Best Friends, You Can't Take it With You,* OB in *Royal Gambit, Go Show Me a Dragon, Carpenters, Charles Abbot & Son, God Says There Is No Peter Ott, Enter a Free Man, A Memory of Two Mondays, Secret Service, Boy Meets Girl, Savages, Killings on the Last Line, Knuckle, Wonderland, Endgame, Niedecker, Marvin's Room, Arts and Leisure.*

DUDLEY, CRAIG. Born Jan. 22, 1945 in Sheepshead Bay, NY. Graduate AADA, Am. Th. Wing. Debut 1970 OB in *Macbeth,* followed by *Zou, I Have Always Believed in Ghosts, Othello, War and Peace, Dial "M" for Murder, Misalliance, Crown of Kings, Trelawny of The Wells, Ursula's Permanent.*

DUNDAS, JENNIFER. Born January 14, 1971 in Boston, MA. Bdwy debut 1981 in *Grownups,* OB in *Before the Dawn, I Love You I Love You Not, The Autobiography of Aiken Fiction.*

DUNN, SALLY MAE. Born December 23, 1950 in Detroit, MI. Graduate Stephens Col. Debut 1982 OB in *The Little and the Ivy* followed by *How He Lied to Her Husband, Winners, As You Like It, Romeo and Juliet, Stopping the Desert,* Bdwy 1994 in *The Best Little Whorehouse Goes Public.*

DVORSKY, GEORGE. Born May 11, 1959 in Greensburg, PA. Attended Carnegie-Mellon. Bdwy debut 1981 in *The Best Little Whorehouse in Texas* followed by *Marilyn: An American Fable, Brigadoon. Cinderella, Passion,* OB in *Dames at Sea* (1985).

EAGAN, DAISY. Born Nov. 4, 1979 in Brooklyn, NY. Attended Neighborhood Playhouse. Debut 1988 OB in *Tiny Tim's Christmas Carol,* followed by *The Little Prince,* Bdwy in *Les Miserables* (1989), followed by *The Secret Garden.*

EBERT, JOYCE. Born June 26, 1933 in Homestead, PA. Graudate Carnegie Tech U. Deut 1956 OB in *Lilion* followed by *Sing of Winter, Asmodee, King Lear, Hamlet, Under Milk Wood, Trojan Women, White Devil, Tartuffe, Booth,* Bdwy in *Solitaire/Double Solitaire* (1971), *The Shadow Box, Watch on the Rhine, Requiem for a Heavyweight, All My Sons.*

EDELMAN, GREGG. Born Sept. 12, 1958 in Chicago, IL. Graduate Northwestern U. Bdwy debut 1982 in *Evita,* followed by *Oliver!, Cats, Cabaret, City of Angels, Falsettos, Anna Karenina, Passion, Fiorello in Concert,* OB in *Weekend, Shop on Main Street, Forbidden Broadway, She Loves Me, Babes in Arms, Make Someone Happy, Greetings.*

EGAN, SUSAN. Born February 18, 1970 in Long Beach, CA. Attended UCLA Bdwy debut in *Beauty and the Beast* (1994).

EICHHORN, LISA. Born February 4, 1952 in Reading, PA. Attended Queens Ontario U., RADA. Debut 1987 OB in *The Common Pursuit* followed by *The Summer Winds, Down the Road,* Bdwy in *The Speed of Darkness* (1991), *Any Given Day.*

EIGENBERG, DAVID M. Born May 17, 1964 in Manhasset, NY. Graduate AADA. Debut 1989 OB in *Young Playwright's Festival/Finnagan's Funeral Parlor & Ice Cream Shop,* followed by *The My House Play, EST Marathon '92, Tunnel of Love, Paradise, Generation X,* Bdwy in *Six Degrees of Separation* (1990, also OB).

EINHORN, MARVIN. Born August 30, 1920 in Philadelphia, PA. Graudate Carnegie-Tech U. Debut 1976 OB in *Othello* followed by *The Time of Your Life, Inherit the Wind, Free Fall, Second Man, Wedding of the Siamese Twins,* Bdwy in *The Flowering Peach* (1994).

EISENBERG, NED. Born January 13, 1957 in NYC. Attended Acl. Inst. of Arts. Debut 1980 OB in *The Time of the Cuckoo* followed by *Our Lord of Lynchville, Dream of a Blacklisted Actor, Second Avenue, Moving Targets, Claus, Titus Adronicus.*

ELDER, DAVID. Born July 7, 1966 in Houston, TX. Attended U. Houston. Bdwy debut 1992 in *Guys and Dolls* followed by *Beauty and the Beast.*

ELDREDGE, LYNN. Born July 25, 1953 in Holden, MA. Graduate San Fran. State U. Debut 1982 OB in *Charlotte Sweet* followed by *Hollywood Opera, Etiquette, Hysterical Blindness.*

ELLIS, BRAD. Born Oct. 5, 1960 in Lexington, MA. Attended Berklee Col. Debut 1990 OB in *Forbidden Broadway,* followed by *Forbidden Broadway 10th Anniversary, Forbidden Broadway 1993 and 1994.*

EMICK, JARROD. Born July 2, 1969 in Ft. Eustas, VA. Attended S. Dakota State U. Bdwy debut 1990 in *Miss Saigon* followed by *Damn Yankees* for which he received a 1994 Theatre World Award.

EMMETT, ROBERT/BOB. Born Sept. 28, 1921 in Monterey, CA. Attended U. Cal., Neighborhood Playhouse. Credits include Bdwy *Peter Gynt* (1951), *Two on the Aisle, Mid-Summer,* OB in *Knight of the Burning Pestle, Madam Will You Walk, Eye of the Beholder.*

ERBACH, GREGORY. Born May 10, 1961 in Teaneck, NJ. Attended Rutgers U. Debut 1987 OB in *The Irish Hebrew Lesson* followed by *Danton's Death, The Shannon Doyle Incident,*

ERDE, SARA. Born March 18, 1970 in NYC. Debut 1987 OB in *Roosters* followed by *Dancing Feet, Midsummer Night's Dream, Don Juan of Seville, Occasional Grace, Blood Wedding, Arabian Nights.*

ERRICO, MELISSA. Born March 23, 1970 in NYC. Graduate Yale U. BADA. Bdwy debut 1992 in *Anna Karenina,* OB in *After Crystal Night, Spring Awakening.*

ESHELMAN, DREW. Born October 12, 1946 in Long Beach, CA. Graduate Shimer Col., Am. Cons. Th. Broadway debut 1992 in *Les Miserables.*

ESPINOZA, BRANDON. Born August 9, 1982 in Queens, NYC. Bdwy debut 1993 in *The Will Rogers Follies* followed by *Les Miserables.*

ESTABROOK, CHRISTINE. Born September 13 in Erie, PA. OB credits include *Pastorale, Win/Lose/Draw, Ladyhouse Blues, Baby with the Bathwater, Blue Windows, North Shore Fish, The Boys Next Door, For Dear Life, The Widow's Blind Date, What a Man Weighs,* Bdwy in *I'm Not Rappaport* (1978), *The Sisters Rosensweig.*

ESTERMAN, LAURA. Born April 12 in NYC. Attended Radcliffe Col., LAMDA. Debut 1969 OB in *The Time of Your Life,* followed by *Pig Pen, Carpenters, Ghosts, Macbeth, The Sea Gull, Rubbers, Yankees 3 Detroit 0, Golden Boy, Out of Our Father's House, The Master and Margarita, Chinchilla, Dusa, Fish Stas and Vi, A Midsummer Night's Dream, The Recruiting Officer, Oedipus the King, Two Fish in the Sky, Mary Barnes, Tamara, Marvin's Room, Edith Stein,* Bdwy in *Waltz of the Toreadors, The Show-off.*

ESTEY, SUELLEN. Born Nov. 21 in Mason City, IA. Graduate Stephens Col., Northwestern U. Debut 1970 OB in *Some Other Time,* followed by *June Moon, Buy Bonds Buster, Smile Smile Smile, Carousel, Lullaby of Broadway, I Can't Keep Running, The Guys in the Truck, Stop the World..., Bittersuite— One More Time, Passionate Extremes, Sweeney Todd, Love in Two Countries, After the Ball,* Bdwy in *The Selling of the President* (1972), *Barnum, Sweethearts in Concert, Sweeney Todd* (1989).

EVANS, HARVEY. Born Jan. 7, 1941 in Cincinnati, OH. Bdwy debut 1957 in *New Girl in Town,* followed by *Annie Get Your Gun, Nash at 9, West Side Story, Redhead, Gypsy, Anyone Can Whistle, Oklahoma, Hello Dolly!, George M!, Our Town, The Boy Friend, Follies, Barnum, Damn Yankees, La Cage aux Folles,* OB in *The Rothschilds, Sextet, Annie Warbucks.*

EWING, GEOFFREY C. Born August 10, 1951 in Minneapolis, MN. Graduate U. Minn. Bdwy debut 1983 in *Guys in the Truck,* followed OB by *Cork, The Leader/The Bald Soprano, Freefall, Ali.*

EWING, J. TIMOTHY. (a.k.a. Tim) Born April 3, 1954 in Evansville, IN. Graduate Okla. State U. Debut 1972 OB in *Colette Collage* followed by *Promenade, Pacific Overtures, Good Times, Charley's Tale, Love in Two Countries, Rodgers and Hart: A Celebration, Show Me Where The Good Times Are.*

FABER, RON. Born February 16, 1933 in Milwaukee, WI. Graduate Marquette U. OB Debut 1959 in *An Enemy of the People,* followed by *The Exception and the Rule, America Hurrah, They Put Handcuffs on Flowers, Dr. Selavy's Magic Theatre, Troilus and Cressida, The Beauty Part, Woyzeck, St. Joan of the Stockyards, Jungle of Cities, Scenes from Everyday Life, Mary Stuart, 3 by Pirandello, Times and Appetites of Toulouse-Lautrec, Hamlet, Johnstown Vendicator, Don Juan of Seville, Between the Acts, Baba Goya, Moving Targets, Arturo Ui, Words Divine, Dracula,* Bdwy in *Medea* (1973), *First Monday in October.*

FAIRLIE, JOHN. Born Dec.18, 1967 on Staten Island, NY. Graduate Syracuse U. Debut 1993 OB in *The Survivor.*

FARINA, MARILYN J. Born Apr. 9, 1947 in New York City. Graduate Sacred Heart Col. Debut 1985 OB in *Nunsense.*

FARINA, MICHAEL. Born August 22, 1958 in The Bronx, NY. Attended NY Inst. of Techn., Mercy Col. Bdwy debut 1990 in *Fiddler on the Roof, My Fair Lady,* OB in *Gifts of the Magi.*

FARR, JAMIE. (Jameel Jofpeh Farah) Born July 1, 1934 in Toledo, OH. Attended Pasadena Playhouse. Bdwy debut 1994 in *Guys and Dolls.*

FAYE, PASCALE. Born January 6, 1964 in Paris, France. Bdwy debut 1991 in *Grand Hotel,* followed by *Guys and Dolls.*

FEAGAN, LESLIE. Born January 9, 1951 in Hinckley, OH. Graduate Ohio U. Debut 1978 OB in *Can-Can,* followed by *Merton of the Movies, Promises Promises, Mowgli,* Bdwy in *Anything Goes* (1978), *Guys and Dolls.*

FELDSHUH, TOVAH. Born Dec. 28, 1953 in New York City. Graduate Sarah Lawrence Col., U. Minn. Bdwy debut 1973 in *Cyrano,* followed by *Dreyfus in Rehearsal, Rodgers and Hart, Yentl* for which she received a Theatre World Award, *Sarava, Lend Me a Tenor,* OB in *Yentl the Yeshiva Boy, Straws in the Wind, Three Sisters, She Stoops to Conquer, Springtime for Henry, The Time of Your Life, Children of the Sun, The Last of the Red Hot Lovers, Mistress of the Inn, A Fierce Attachment, Custody, Six Wives, Hello Muddah Hello Faddah, Best of the West.*

FERGUSON, LOU. Born August 8, 1944 in Trinidad, W. Indies. Debut 1970 OB in *A Season in the Congo,* followed by *Night World, La Gente, Shoe Shine Parlor, The Defense, Rum'n' Coca Rola, Remembrance, Raisin in the Sun, Member of the Wedding, Playboy of the West Indies, Fragments.*

FERLAND, DANIELLE. Born Jan. 31, 1971 in Derby, CT. OB Debut 1983 in *Sunday in the Park with George,* followed by *Paradise, Young Playwrights Festival, Camp Paradox,* Bdwy in *Sunday in the Park with George* (1984), *Into the Woods* for which she received a Theatre World Award, *A Little Night Music* (NYCO/LC), *Crucible, A Little Hotel on the Side.*

FIELD, ARABELLA. Born February 5, 1970 in NYC. Graduate Fordham U. Debut 1993 OB in *Snowing at Delphi* followed by *Four Dogs and a Bone,* for which she received a Theatre World Award.

FIELD, CRYSTAL. Born December 10, 1942 in NYC. Attended Juilliard, Hunter Col., Debut 1960 OB in *A Country Scandal,* followed by *A Matter of Life and Death, The Heart That Eats Itself, Ruzzante Returns from the Wars, An Evening of British Music Hall, Ride That Never Was, House Arrest, Us, Beverly's Yard Sale, Bruno's Donuts, Coney Island Kid, Till The Eagle Hollars, The Rivalry of Dolls, Pineapple Face, It is, It is Not.*

FIGUEROA, RONA. Born March 30, 1972 in San Francisco, CA. Attended UC/Santa Cruz. Bdwy debut 1993 in *Miss Saigon.*

FINKEL, JOSHUA. Born October 29, 1963 in Los Angeles, CA. Graduate U. Cal. Bdwy debut 1993 in *Kiss of the Spider Woman.*

FISHER, DAVID. Born November 18, 1951 in Tel Aviv, Israel. Bdwy debut 1993 in *Les Miserables.*

FISHER, MARY HELEN. Born July 17 in Oklahoma City, OK. Debut 1976 OB in *Spoon River Anthology,* followed by *Aladdin, Bar Mitzvah Boy,* Bdwy in *The Most Happy Fella* (1992), *Picnic* (1994).

FITZPATRICK, ALLEN. Born January 31, 1955 in Boston, MA. Graduate U. Va. Debut 1977 OB in *Come Back Little Sheba* followed by *Wonderful Town, The Rothschilds, Group One Acts.*

FITZPATRICK, JIM. Born November 26, 1950 in Omaha, NE. Attended U. NE. Debut 1977 OB in *Arsenic and Old Lace,* followed by *Merton of the Movies, Oh Boy!, Time and the Conways, Street Scene, The Duchess of Malfi, Comedy of Errors, Much Ado about Nothing, Cinderella, Anyone Can Whistle, Mint Condition.*

FLAGG, TOM. Born March 30 in Canton, OH. Attended Kent State U., AADA. Debut 1975 OB in *The Fantasticks,* followed by *Give Me Liberty, The Subject Was Roses, Lola, Red Hot and Blue, Episode 26, Dazy, Dr. Dietrick's Process,* Bdwy in *Legend* (1976), *Shenandoah, Players, The Will Rogers Follies, Best Little Whorehouse Goes Public.*

FLANINGAM, LOUISA. Born May 5, 1945 in Chester SC. Graduate U. MD. Debut 1971 OB in *The Shrinking Bridge* followed by *Pigeons on the Walk, Etiquette, The Knife, Say It With Music, Opal,* Bdwy in *Magic Show, Most Happy Fella* (1979), *Play Me a Country Song, Guys and Dolls.*

FLEISS, JANE. Born January 28, in NYC. Graduate NYU. Debut 1979 OB in *Say Goodnight Gracie* followed by *Grace, The Beaver Coat, The Harvesting, D., Second Man, Of Mice and Men, Niedecker, The Undertakers,* Bdwy in *5th of July* (1981), *Crimes of the Heart, I'm Not Rappaport, Search and Destroy.*

FLEMING, EUGENE. Born Apr. 26, 1961 in Richmond, VA. Attended NC Sch of Arts. Bdwy in *Chorus Line* followed by *Tap Dance Kid, Black and Blue, High Rollers,* OB in *Voorhas, Dutchman, Ceremonies in Dark Old Men, Freefall.*

FOREMAN, LORRAINE. Born May 25, 1929 in Vancouver, BC, Canada. Bdwy debut 1989 in *Oklahoma,* followed by *Kiss of the Spider Woman.*

FORMAN, KEN. Born September 22, 1961 in Boston, MA. Attended NYU. Debut 1985 OB in *Measure for Measure,* followed by *Rosencrantz and Guildenstern Are Dead, Macbeth, I Stand Before You Naked, Romeo and Juliet, 3 by Wilder, As You Like It, SS Glencairn,* Bdwy in *Wilder Wilder Wilder* (1983).

FORSYTHE, HENDERSON. Born Sept.11, 1917 in Macon, MO. Attended U. Iowa. Debut 1956 OB in *Iceman Cometh* followed by *The Collection, The Room, A Slight Ache, Happiness Cage, Waiting for Godot, In Case of Accident, Not I, Evening with the Poet Senator, Museum, How Far Is It to Babylon?, Wild Life, Other Places, Cliffhanger, Broadcast Baby, After the Fall, Fridays, Quarrel of Sparrows,* Bdwy in *Cellar and the Well* (1950), *Miss Lonelyhearts, Who's Afraid of Virginia Wolf, Malcolm, Right Honorable Gentleman, Delicate Balance, Birthday Party, Harvey, Engagement Baby, Freedom of the City, Texas Trilogy, Best Little Whorehouse in Texas, Some Americans Abroad* (also OB), *110 in the Shade* (LC).

FOSTER, HERBERT. Born May 14, 1936 in Winnipeg, Can. Bdwy in *Ways and Means, A Touch of the Poet, The Imaginary Invalid, Tonight at 8:30, Henry V, Noises Off, Me and My Girl, Lettice and Lovage, Timon of Athens, Government Inspector,* OB in *Afternoon Tea, Papers, Mary Stuart, Playboy of the Western World, Good Woman of Setzuan, Scenes from American Life, Twelfth Night, All's Well That Ends Well, Richard II, Gifts of the Magi, Heliotrope Bouquet.*

FOWLER, BETH. Born November 1, 1940 in New Jersey. Graduate Caldwell Col. Bdwy debut 1970 in *Gantry* followed by *A Little Night Music, Over Here, 1600 Pennsylvania Avenue, Peter Pan, Baby, Teddy and Alice, Sweeney Todd* (1989), *Beauty and the Beast,* OB in *Preppies, The Blessing, Sweeney Todd.*

FOWLER, CLEMENT. Born December 27, 1924 in Detroit, MI. Graduate Wayne State U. Bdwy debut 1951 in *Legend of Lovers* followed by *The Cold Wind and the Warm, The Fragile Fox, The Sunshine Boys, Hamlet* (1964), *Richard II,* OB in *The Eagle Has Two Heads, House Music, The Transfiguration of Benno Blimpie, The Inheritors, Paradise Lost, The Time of Your Life, Children of the Sun, Highest Standard of Living, Cymbeline, The Chairs.*

FOWLER, SCOTT. Born Mar. 22, 1967 in Medford, MA. Debut 1989 on Bdwy in *Jerome Robbins' Broadway,* followed by *Brigadoon* (NYCO/LC), *Ain't Broadway Grand, Red Shoes.*

FOY, HARRIETT D. Born August 24, 1962 in New Bern, NC. Graduate Howard U. Debut OB 1993 in *Fire's Daughters* followed by *Mr. Wonderful, Struttin', Trinity.*

FRANCIS-JAMES, PETER. Born Sept. 16, 1956 in Chicago, IL. Graduate RADA. Debut 1979 OB in *Julius Caesar,* followed by *Long Day's Journey into Night, Antigone, Richard II, Romeo and Juliet, Enrico IV, Cymbeline, Hamlet, Learned Ladies, 10th Young Playwrights Festival, Measure for Measure.*

FRANKLIN, NANCY. Born in NYC. Debut 1959 OB in *Buffalo Skinner* followed by *Power of Darkness, Oh Dad Poor Dad..., Theatre of Peretz, 7 Days of Mourning, Here Be Dragons, Beach Children, Safe Place, Innocent Pleasures, Loves of Cass McGuire, After the Fall, Bloodletters, Briar Patch, The Lost Drums,* Bdwy in *Never Live Over a Pretzel Factory* (1964), *Happily Never After, The White House, Charlie and Algernon.*

FRANKLYN-ROBBINS, JOHN. Born December 14, 1951 in Wiltshire, Eng. Graduate U. Birmingham, RADA. Bdwy debut 1968 in *Measure for Measure,* followed by *All's Well That Ends Well, The Sea Gull, Saint Joan, 3 Men on a Horse, Timon of Athens.*

FRECHETTE, PETER. Born Oct.3, 1956 in Warwick, RI. Debut 1979 OB

Craig Dudley

Melissa Errico

David Elder

SuEllen Estey

Michael J. Farina

Pascale Faye-
Williams

Leslie Feagan

Tovah Feldshuh

Joshua Finkel

Lorraine Foreman

Jim Fitzpatrick

Toni Georgiana

Ken Forman

Joanna Glushak

Herb Foster

Kristin Griffith

John Franklyn-
Robbins

Angela Goethals

Arthur French

Julia Gibson

Joel Goodness

Julie Hagerty

Aaron Goodwin

Marcia Gay
Harden

Joel Griesemer

Lynn Hawley

Harry Groener

Ruby Holbrook

Daniel Hagen

Sharon Hope

214

in *Hornbeam Maze* followed by *Journey's End, In Cahoots, Harry Ruby's Songs My Mother Never Sang, Pontifications on Pigtails and Puberty, Scooter Thomas Makes It to the Top of the World, We're Home, Flora the Red Menace, Hyde in Hollywood, Absent Friends, And Baby Makes Seven, Destiny of Me,* Bdwy in *Eastern Standard* (1989-also OB) for which he received a Theatre World Award, *Our Country's Good, Any Given Day.*

FREEMAN, JONATHAN. Born February 5, 1950 in Bay Village, OH. Graduate Ohio U. Debut 1974 OB in *The Miser* followed by *Bil Baird Marionette Theatre, Babes in Arms, In a Pig's Valise,* Bdwy in *Sherlock Holmes* (1974), *Platinum, She Loves Me.*

FRENCH, ARTHUR. Born in New York City and attended Brooklyn Col. Debut 1962 OB in *Raisin' Hell in the Sun,* followed by *Ballad of Bimshire, Day of Absence, Happy Ending, Brotherhood, Perry's Mission, Rosalee Pritchett, Moonlight Arms, Dark Tower, Brownsville Raid, Nevis Mountain Dew, Julius Caesar, Friends, Court of Miracles, The Beautiful LaSalles, Blues for a Gospel Queen, Black Girl, Driving Miss Daisy, The Spring Thing, George Washington Slept Here, Ascension Day, Boxing Day Parade, A Tempest, The Hills of Massabielle, The Treatment, As You Like It,* Bdwy in *Ain't Supposed to Die a Natural Death, The Iceman Cometh, All God's Chillun Got Wings, The Resurrection of Lady Lester, You Can't Take It with You, Design for Living, Ma Rainey's Black Bottom, Mule Bone, Playboy of the West Indies.*

FRIED, JONATHAN. Born March 3, 1959 in Los Angeles, CA. Graduate Brown U., U. Cal/San Diego. Debut 1986 OB in *1951* followed by *Dispatches from Hell, Richard II, Marathon Dancing.*

FRIEDMAN, PETER. Born April 24, 1949 in NYC. Debut 1971 OB in *James Joyce Memorial Theatre* followed by *Big and Little, A Soldier's Play, Mr. and Mrs., And a Nightingale Sang, Dannis, The Common Pursuit, Marathon '88, The Heidi Chronicles, Hello Again, The Loman Family Picnic,* Bdwy in *The Visit, Chemin de Fer, Love for Love, Rules of the Game, Piaf!, Execution of Justice, The Heidi Chronicles, Tenth Man.*

FRUGE, ROMAIN. Born March 4, 1959 in Los Angeles, CA. Graduate Allentown Col. Bdwy debut 1986 in *Big River* followed by *The Who's Tommy.*

GAINES, BOYD. Born May 11, 1953 in Atlanta, GA. Graduate Juilliard. Debut 1978 OB in *Spring Awakening,* followed by *A Month in the Country* for which he received a Theatre World Award, BAM Theatre Co.'s *Winter's Tale, The Barbarians, and Johnny on a Spot, Vikings, Double Bass, The Maderati, The Heidi Chronicles, The Extra Man, The Comedy of Errors,* Bdwy in *The Heidi Chronicles* (1989), *Show-Off, She Loves Me.*

GALBRAITH, PHILIP. Born Decomber 12, 1950 in Toronto, Can . Graduate U. Windsor. Debut 1982 OB in *Nymph Errant* followed by *The Mast, Bats.*

GALMAN, PETER. Born Decemer 24, 1945 in Chicago, IL. Attended Purdue U., AADA. Bdwy debut 1969 in *40 Carats,* OB in *Welcome to Anfromada, The Lady and the Clarinet.*

GAMACHE, LAURIE. Born September 25, 1959 in Mayville, ND. Graduate Stephens Col. Bdwy debut 1982 in *A Chorus Line* followed by *The Red Shoes.*

GANUN, JOHN. Born Aug. 23, 1966 in Blissfield, MI. Graduate U. Mich. Bdwy debut 1991 in *The Will Rogers Follies* followed by *Damn Yankees,* OB in *Forever Plaid.*

GARBER, VICTOR. Born Mar. 15, 1949 in London, Can. Debut 1973 OB in *Ghosts* for which he received a Theatre World Award, followed by *Joe's Opera, Cracks, Wenceslas Square, Love Letters, Assassins, Christmas Memory,* Bdwy in *Tartuffe, Deathtrap, Sweeney Todd, They're Playing Our Song, Little Me, Noises Off, You Never Can Tell, Devil's Disciple, Lend Me a Tenor, Two Shakespearean Actors, Damn Yankees.*

GARDNER, JEFF. (formerly Jeffrey Holt Gardner) Born November 18, 1962 in NYC. Attended SUNY/Purchase, NYU. Bdwy debut 1982 in *The Queen and the Rebels* followed by *Jerome Robbins' Broadway, Cyrano,* OB in *The Chosen* (1987), *A Rag on a Stick and a Star.*

GARRISON, DAVID. Born June 30, 1952 in Long Branch, NJ. Graduate Boston U. Debut 1976 OB in *Joseph and the Amazing Technicolor Dreamcoat* followed by *Living at Home, Geniuses, It's Only a Play, Make Someone Happy, The Family of Mann,* Bdwy in *A History of the American Film* (1978), *A Day in Hollywood/A Night in the Ukraine, The Pirates of Penzance, Snoopy, Torch Song Trilogy, One Touch of Venus in Concert.*

GASSELL, SYLVIA. Born July 1, 1923 in NYC. Attended Hunter Col. Bdwy debut 1952 in *Time of the Cuckoo* followed by *Sunday Breakfast, Fair Game for Lovers, Inquest,* OB in *USA, Romeo and Juliet, Electra, Darker Flower, Fragments, Gos, God Bless You Harold Fineberg, Philosophy in the Boudoir, Stag Movie, The Old Ones, Where Memories are Magic, Jesse's Land, Under Milk Wood, Little Lies, Autobiography of Aiken Fiction.*

GATLIN, LARRY. Born May 2, 1948 in Seminole, TX. Attended U. Houston. Bdwy debut 1993 in *The Will Rogers Follies.*

GAYSUNIS, CHERYL. Born January 8, in Westminster, CA. Graduate Otterbein Col. Bdwy debut 1991 in *La Bete,* OB in *Finding the Sun* (1994), *An Enraged Reading, Fragments.*

GEORGE, BEN. Born June 7, 1947 in Oxford, Eng. Attended Leeds Music Col. Debut 1984 OB in *Last of the Knucklemen,* Bdwy in *The Best Little Whorehouse in Texas* (1985), *Grand Hotel, My Fair Lady.*

GEORGIANA, TONI. Born Dec. 14, 1963 in Uniontown, PA. Attended Juilliard. Bdwy debut 1991 in *The Will Rogers Follies.*

GERACI, FRANK. Born Sept. 8, 1939 in Brooklyn, NY. Attended Yale. Debut 1961 OB in *Color of Darkness,* followed by *Mr. Grossman, Balm in Gilead, The Fantasticks, Tom Paine, End of All Things Natural, Union Street,*

Uncle Vanya, Success Story, Hughie, Merchant of Venice, Three Zeks, Taming of the Shrew, The Lady from the Sea, Rivals, Deep Swimmer, The Imaginary Invalid, Candida, Hedda Gabler, Serious Co., Berenice, The Philanderer, All's Well That Ends Well, Three Sisters, A Midsummer Night's Dream, Medea, The Importance of Being Earnest, Major Barbara, Measure for Measure, The Fine Art of Finesse, Schnitzler One Acts, Peace in a Traveling Heart, Tartuffe, Widowers Houses, Good Natur'd Man, Twelfth Night, Bdwy in *Love Suicide at Schofield Barracks* (1972).

GERARD, TOM. Born October 10, 1947 in Newark, NJ. Graduate SyracuseU. Debut 1970 OB in *The Drunkard* followed by *Better Living, A Better Life,* Bdwy in *Grease* (1974).

GERBER, CHARLES. Born April 2, 1949 in Chicago, IL. Attended Wright Col., Juilliard. Bdwy debut 1981 in *Oh! Calcutta!,* followed by *Hamlet,* OB in *A Midsummer Night's Dream, One-Act Festival, Richard II, The Drowning of Manhattan.*

GERETY, PETER. Born May 17, 1940 in Providence, RI. Attended URI, Boston U. Debut 1964 OB in *In The Summer House* followed by *Othello, Baal, Six Characters in Search of an Author, Johnny Pye,* Bdwy in *The Hothouse* (1982), *Conversations with My Father.*

GERROLL, DANIEL. Born October 16, 1951 in London, England. Attended Central School of Speech. Debut 1980 OB in *Slab Boys* followed by *Knuckle/Translations* for which he received a Theatre World Award, *The Caretaker, Scences from La Vie De Boheme, The Knack, Terra Nova, Dr. Faustus, Second Man, Cheapside, Bloody Poetry, The Common Pursuit, Woman in Mind, Poet's Corner, The Film Society, Emerald City, Arms and the Man, One Shoe Off, The Holy Terror, Three Birds Alighting on a Field, Loose Knit,* Bdwy in *Plenty, The Homecoming* (1991).

GIBSON, DEBBIE. Born in 1971 in Merrick, NY. Bdwy debut 1992 in *Les Miserables.*

GIBSON, JULIA. Born June 8, 1962 in Norman, OK. Graduate U. Iowa, NYU. Debut 1987 OB in *A Midsummer Night's Dream,* followed by *Love's Labor's Lost, Crucible, The Man Who Fell in Love with His Wife, Learned Ladies, Machinal, Candide., Dracula, Arabian Nights.*

GILLETT, ADEN. Born Nov.8, 1958 in Yemen. Graduate SussexU., RADA. Bdwy debut 1994 in *An Inspector Calls* for which he received a Theatre World Award.

GILLETTE, ANITA. Born Aug.16, 1938 in Baltimore, MD. Debut 1960 OB in Russell Paterson's *Sketchbook* for which she received a Theatre World Award, followed by *Rich and Famous, Dead Wrong, Road Show, Class 1-Acts, The Blessing, Moving Targets, Juno, Able-Bodied Seaman,* Bdwy in *Carnival, Gypsy, Gay Life, All American, Mr. President, Kelly, Don't Drink the Water, Cabaret, Jimmy, They're Playing Our Song, Brighton Beach Memoirs, Chapter Two.*

GLASER, SHERRY. Born June 7, 1960 in The Bronx, NYC. Attended San Diego State U. Debut 1993 OB in *Family Secrets* for which she received a Theatre World Award.

GLEASON, LAURENCE. Born November 14, 1956 in Utica, NY. Graduate Utica Col. Debut 1984 OB in *Romance Language* follwed by *Agamemnon, A Country Doctor, The Misanthrope, The Sleepless City, Electra, Morning Sond, Like To Live, Macbeth, 3 by Wilder, As You Like It, S.S. Glencairn,* Bdwy in *Wilder Wilder Wilder* (1993).

GLENN, BETTE. Born December 13, 1946 in Atlantic City, NJ. Graduate Montpelier Col. Debut 1971 OB in *Ruddigore* followed by *Maggie Flynn, Company,* Bdwy in *Irene* (1973), *She Loves Me.*

GLEZOS, IRENE. Born June 15, in Washington, DC. Graduate Catholic U. Debut OB in *Modigliani* followed by *The Last Good Moment of Lily Baker, Antigone, The Rose Tattoo, Top Girls.*

GLUSHAK, JOANNA. Born May 27, 1958 in New York City. Attended NYU. Debut 1983 OB in *Lenny and the Heartbreakers,* followed by *Lies and Legends, Miami, Unfinished Song, A Little Night Music* (NYCO), Bdwy in *Sunday in the Park with George* (1984), *Rags, Les Miserables.*

GOETHALS, ANGELA. Born May 20, 1977 in NYC. Bdwy debut 1987 in *Coastal Disturbances* followed by *Four Baboons Adoring the Sun, Picnic,* OB in *Positive Me, Approaching Zanzibar, The Good Times are Killing Me.*

GOETZ, PETER MICHAEL. Born Decebmer 10, 1941 in Buffalo, NY. Graduate SUNY/Fredonia, So. IL U. Debut 1980 OB in *Jail Diary of Albie Sacks* followed by *Before the Dawn,* Bdwy in *Ned and Jack* (1981), *Beyond Therapy, The Queen and the Rebels, Brighton Beach Memoirs, The Government Inspector.*

GOING, JOANNA. Born July 22, 1963 in Washington, DC. Graduate Emerson Col., AADA. Bdwy debut 1994 in *The Flowering Peach,* OB in *Women and Wallace.*

GOLD, MICHAEL E. Born August 2, 1955 in Denver, CO. Graduate Loretto Heights Col. Debut 1990 OB in *Give My Regards to Broadway,* followed by *Annie Warbucks.*

GOLDBERG, RUSSELL. Born March 28, 1964 in Flushing, NY. Graduate Syracuse U. Debut 1988 OB in *All's Fair* followed by *Sherlock Holmes and the Red-Headed League, The Emperor's New Clothes, Peg O'My Heart, The High Life in Concert, Hello Muddah Hello Faddah, The Fairy Garden.*

GOLDEN, ANNIE. Born October 19, 1951 in Brooklyn, NY. Bdwy debut 1977 in *Hair* followed by *Leader of the Pack,* OB in *Dementos, Dr. Selavy's Magic Theatre, A...My Name is Alice, Little Shop of Horrors, Class of '86, Assassins, Hit the Lights!*

GOLDSMITH, MERWIN. Born Aug.7, 1937 in Detroit, MI. Graduate UCLA, Old Vic. Bdwy debut 1970 in *Minnie's Boys* followed by *The Visit, Chemin de Fer, Rex, Leda Had a Little Swan, Trelawney of the Wells, Dirty Linen, 1940's Radio Hour, Slab Boys, Me and My Girl, Ain't Broadway*

Grand, OB in *Naked Hamlet, Chickencoop Chinaman, Real Life Funnies, Wanted, Rubbers and Yanks, Chinchilla, Yours Anne, Big Apple Messengers, La Boheme, Learned Ladies, An Imaginary Life, Little Prince, Beau Jest.*

GOLDSTEIN, STEVEN. Born Oct. 22, 1963 in New York City. Graduate NYU. Debut 1987 OB in *Boy's Life*, followed by *Oh Hell, Three Sisters, Marathon '91, Angel of Death, Five Very Live, Casino Paradise, Orpheus in Love, Nothing Sacred, Jolly, Marathon Dancing, Shaker Heights, The Lights, El Greco*, Bdwy in *Our Town* (1988).

GOLDWYN, TONY. Born May 20, 1960 in Los Angeles, CA. Graduate Brandeis U., LAMDA. Debut 1985 OB in *Digby* followed by *Messiah, The Sum of Us, Spike Heels*, Bdwy in *Lady in the Dark in Concert* (1994).

GOODMAN, DODY. Born October 28, 1915 in Columbus, OH. Bdwy debut 1947 in *High Button Shoes* followed by *Miss Liberty, Call Me Madam, Wonderful Town, Fiorello!, A Rainy Day in Newark, My Daughter Your Son, Front Page, Lorelei*, OB in *Shoestring Revue, Shoestring '57, Parade, New Cole Porter Revue, Ah Wilderness!, Selling Off, Nunsense.*

GOODWIN, AARON. Born Nov. 8, 1966 in Macon, GA. Graduate Furman U. Debut 1991 OB in *Macbeth* followed by *Fridays, Tales from Hollywood, God's Country, Greetings.*

GOODNESS, JOEL. Born Jan. 22, 1962 in Wisconsin Rapids, WI. Graduate U. Wisc. Debut 1991 OB in *Custody*, followed by *Georgy*, Bdwy in *Crazy for You* (1992).

GOULD, HAROLD, Born Decebmer 10, 1923 in Schenectady, NY. Graduate SUNY/Cornell. Debut 1969 OB in *The Increased Difficulty of Concentration* followed by *Amphitryon, House of Blue Leaves, Touching Bottom*, Bdwy in *Fools* (1981), *Grownups, Artist Descending a Staircase, Mixed Emotions.*

GOULET, ROBERT. Born November 26, 1933 in Lawrence, MA. Attended Toronto's Royal Consv. of Music. Bdwy debut 1960 in *Camelot* for which he received a Theatre World Award, followed by *The Happy Time, Camelot* (1993).

GRAAE, JASON. Born May 15, 1958 in Chicago, IL. Graduate Cincinnati Consv. Debut 1981 OB in *Godspell*, followed by *Snoopy, Heaven on Earth, Promenade, Feathertop, Tales of Tinseltown, Living Color, Just So, Olympus on My Mind, Sitting Pretty in Concert, Babes in Arms, The Cat and the Fiddle, Forever Plaid, A Funny Thing Happened on the Way to the Forum, 50 Million Frenchmen, Rodgers and Hart Revue, A Grand Night for Singing, Hello Muddah Hello Faddah, All in the Timing*, Bdwy in *Falsettos* (1993), *A Grand Night for Singing.*

GRACE, EILEEN. Born July 25 in Pittsburgh, PA. Graduate Point Park Col. Bdwy debut in *42nd Street*, followed by *My One and Only, The Will Rogers Follies.*

GRACE, GINGER. Born in Beaumont, TX. Graduate U. Tex, Penn State U. Debut 1981 OB in *Peer Gynt* followed by *Wild Oats, The Ghost Sonata, The Cherry Orchard, Faust, Hamlet, The Oresteia, Mourning Becomes Electra.*

GRAFF, LAURIE. Born May 25, 1956 in NYC. Graduate SUNY/Binghamton. Debut 1985 OB in *In the Boom Boom Room* followed by *Talk about Love.*

GRAFF, RANDY. Born May 23, 1955 in Brooklyn, NY. Graduate Wagner Col. Debut 1978 OB in *Pins and Needles*, followed by *Station Joy, A...My Name Is Alice, Once on a Summer's Day*, Bdwy in *Sarava, Grease, Les Miserables, City of Angels, Falsettos, Laughter on the 23rd Floor.*

GRANT, DAVID MARSHALL. Born June 21, 1955 in New Haven, CT. Attended Conn. Col., Yale U. Debut 1978 OB in *Sganarelle*, followed by *Table Settings, The Tempest, Making Movies, Naked Rights*, Bdwy in *Bent* (1979), *The Survivor, Angels in America.*

GRANT, KATHRYN. (formerly Katie). Born January 5, 1955 in Philadelphia, PA. Graduate Juilliard. Debut OB in *A Month in the Country* (1979) followed by *Spring Awakening, Talley's Folly, The American Clock.*

GRANT, SEAN. Born July 13, 1966 in Brooklyn, NY. Attended NC School of Arts. Bdwy debut 1987 in *Starlight Express* followed by *Prince of Central Park, The Goodbye Girl*, OB in *Bring in the Morning.*

GRAVITTE, DEBBIE SHAPIRO. Born September 29, 1954 in Los Angeles, CA. Graduate LACC. Bdwy debut 1979 in *They're Playing Our Song*, followed by *Perfectly Frank, Blues in the Night, Zorba, Jerome Robbins' Broadway, Ain't Broadway Grand, Les Miserables*, OB in *They Say It's Wonderful, New Moon in Concert.*

GRAY, KEVIN. Born Feb. 25, 1958 in Westport, CT. Graduate Duke U. Debut 1982 OB in *Lola*, followed by *Pacific Overtures, Family Snapshots, The Baker's Wife, The Knife, Magdalena in Concert*, Bdwy in *The Phantom of the Opera* (1989).

GRAY, SAM. Born July 18, 1923 in Chicago, IL. Graduate Columbia U. Bdwy debut 1955 in *Deadfall* followed by *Six Fingers in a Five Finger Glove, Saturday Sunday Monday, Golda, A View from the Bridge, In the Ascent of F-6* followed by *Family Portrait, One Tiger on a Hill, Shadow of Heroes, The Recruiting Officer, The Wild Duck, Jungle of Cities, 3 Acts of Recognition, Returnings, A Little Madness, The Danube, Dr. Cook's Garden, Child's Play, Kafka Fathers and Son, Dennis, Panache, Marathon 89, Bitter Friends, Arturo Ui, Blackout, King of Carpets.*

GREEN, ANDREA. Born October 31, in NYC. Graduate Queens Col/CUNY. Bdwy debut 1980 in *They're Playing Our Song* followed by *Little Me, Fiorello in Concert*, OB in *And the World Goes Round, Yiddle with a Fiddle, Song of Singapore, Jacques Brel Is..., Fiorello! in concert.*

GREEN, DAVID. Born June 16, 1942 in Cleveland, OH. Attended Kan. State U. Bdwy debut 1980 in *Annie*, followed by *Evita, Teddy and Alice, The Pajama Game* (LC), *Flowering Peach*, OB in *Once on a Summer's Day, Miami, On the 20th Century, What About Luv?, Tom and Viv.*

GREENHILL, SUSAN. Born March 19 in NYC. Graduate U. Pa, CatholicU. Bdwy debut 1982 in *Crimes of the Heart*, OB in *Hooters, Our Lord of Lynchville, September in the Rain, Seascape with Sharks and Dancer, Murder of Crows, Better Days, Marathan '89, Tounges of Stone, Festival of One Acts.*

GRENIER, ZACH. Born February 12, 1954 in Englewood, NJ. Graduate U. Mich., Boston U. Debut 1982 OB in *Baal* followed by *Tomorrowland, Water Music, Morocco, The Cure, Birth of the Poet, Talk Radio, Marathon '90, Lilith, Arturo Ui, The Creditors, The Fiery Furnace, Three Birds Alighting on a Field*, Bdwy in *Mastergate* (1989).

GREY, JENNIFER. Born March 26, 1960 in NYC. Bdwy debut 1993 in *Twighlight of the Golds.*

GRIER, DAVID ALAN. Born June 30, 1955 in Detroit, MI. Graduate U. Mi., Yale U. Bdwy debut 1981 in *The First* for which he received a Theatre World Award, followed by *Dreamgirls*, OB in *A Soldier's Play, Richard III, The Merry Wives of Windsor.*

GRIESEMER, JOHN. Born December 5, 1947 in Elizabeth, NJ. Graduate Dickinson Col., URI. Debut 1981 OB in *Turnbuckle*, followed by *Death of a Miner, Little Victories, Macbeth, A Lie of the Mind, Kate's Diary, Little Egypt, EST Marathon 93, Woyzeck, Born Guilty*, Bdwy in *Our Town* (1989), *Abe Lincoln in Illinois.*

GRIFFITH, KRISTIN. Born September 7, 1953 in Odessa, TX. Graduate Juilliard. Bdwy debut 1976 in *Texas Trilogy*, OB in *Rib Cage, Character Lines, 3 Friends, 2 Rooms, A Month in the Country, Fables for Friends, The Trading Post, Marching in Georgia, American Garage, A Midsummer Night's Dream, Marathon '87, Bunker Reveries, On the Bench, EST Marathon '92 and '93, The Holy Terror, Black.*

GRIMES, TAMMY. Born January 30, 1934 in Lynn, MA. Attended Stephens College, Neighborhood Playhouse. Debut 1956 OB in *The Littlest Revue* followed by *Clerambord, Molly Trick, Are You Now Or..., Father's Day, A Month in the Country, Sunset, Waltz of the Toreadors, Mlle. Colombe, Tammy in Concert, After the Ball*, Bdwy in *Look After Lulu* (1959) for which she received a Theatre World Award, *The Unsinkable Molly Brown, Private Lives, High Spirits, Rattle of a Simple Man, The Only Game in Town, Musical Jubilee, California Suite, Tartuffe, Pal Joey in Concert, 42nd Street, Orpheus Descending.*

GROENENDAAL, CRIS. Born Feb. 17, 1948 in Erie, PA. Attended Allegheny Col., Exeter U. Bdwy debut 1979 in *Sweeney Todd* followed by *Sunday in the Park with George, Brigadoon, Desert Song, South Pacific* (LC), *Phantom of the Opera, Passion*, OB in *Francis, Sweethearts in Concert, Oh Boy, No No Nanette in Concert, Sitting Pretty, The Cat and the Fiddle, Broadway Classics at Carnegie Hall.*

GROENER, HARRY. Born September 10, 1951 in Augsburg, Germany, Graduate U. Washington. Bdwy debut 1979 in *Oklahoma!* for which he received a Theatre World Award, followed by *Oh, Brother!, Is There Life After High School, Cats, Harrigan 'n' Hart, Sunday in the Park with George, Sleight of Hand, Crazy for You*, OB in *Beside the Seaside.*

GROH, DAVID. Born May 21, 1939 in NYC. Graduate Brown U., LAMDA. Debut 1963 OB in *The Importance of Being Earnest* followed by *Elizabeth the Queen, The Hot 1 Baltimore, Be Happy for Me, Dead Wrong, Face to Face, Road Show, Tea with Mommy and Jack*, Bdwy in *Chapter Two, Twilight of the Golds.*

GUILLAUME, ROBERT. Born November 30, 1937 in St. Louis, MO. Bdwy debut 1961 in *Kwamina* followed by *Finian's Rainbow, Tambourines to Glory, Golden Boy, Purlie, Guys and Dolls, Cyrano the Musical*, OB in *Charlie Was Here and Now He's Gone, The Life and Times of J. Walter Smintheus, Jacques Brel Is..., Music! Music! Music!, Miracle Play, Apple Pie.*

GUINAN, PATRICIA. Born November 11 in Philadelphia, PA. Bdwy debut 1967 in *Tonight at 8:30* Followed by *Imaginary Invalid, Touch of the Poet, Deathtrap, Eccentricities of a Nightingale*, OB in *Days to Come, And the Tide Shall Cover the Earth.*

HADARY, JONATHAN. Born Oct. 11, 1948 in Chicago, IL. Attended Tufts U. Debut 1974 OB in *White Nights*, followed by *El Grande de Coca Cola, Songs from Pins and Needles, God Bless You Mr. Rosewater, Pushing 30, Scrambled Feet, Coming Attractions, Tom Foolery, Charley Bacon and Family, Road Show, 1-2-3-4-5, Wenceslas Square, Assassins, Lips Together Teeth Apart, Weird Romance, The Destiny of Me*, Bdwy in *Gemini* (1977 also OB), *Torch Song Trilogy, As Is, Gypsy, Guys and Dolls.*

HADLEY, JONATHAN. Born May 6, 1964 in Charlotte, NC. Graduate NC Sch. of Arts. Debut 1993 OB in *Theda Bara and the Frontier Rabbi* followed by *The Cincinnati Saint, Prime Time Prophet, The Mayor Musicals.*

HAGEN, DANIEL. Born September 29 in Storm Lake, IA. Graduate U. Iowa. Bdwy debut 1987 in *The Nerd*, OB in *Pillow Talk* (1988), *Variations on the Death of Trotsky, Stay Carl Stay, A Distance from Calcutta, All in the Timing.*

HAGERTY, JULIE. Born June 15, 1955 in Cincinnati, OH, Attended Juilliard. Debut 1979 OB in *Mutual Benefit Life* followed by *Wild Life, The Years, Wifey, Valentine Fairy*, Bdwy in *House of Blue Leaves* (1986-also OB) for which she recieved a Theatre World Award, *Front Page, 3 Men on a Horse.*

HALL, GEORGE. Born November 19, 1916 in Toronto, Can. Attended Neighborhood Playhouse. Bdwy debut 1946 in *Call Me Mister* followed by *Lend an Ear, Touch and Go, Live Wire, The Boy Friend, There's a Girl in My Soup, An Evening with Richard Nixon, We Interrupt This Program, Man and Superman, Bent, Noises Off, Wild Honey, Abe Lincoln in Illinois*, OB in *The Balcony, Ernest in Love, A Round with Rings, Family Pieces, Carousel, The Case Against Roberta Guardino, Marry Me!, Arms and the Man, The Old Glory, Dancing for the Kaiser, Casualties, The Sea Gull, A Stitch in Time,*

216

Mary Stuart, No End of Blame, Hamlet, Colette Collage, The Homecoming, And a Nightingale Sang, The Bone Ring, Much Ado about Nothing, Measure for Measure, The Doctor's Dilemma, The Crucible, Merry Wives of Windsor.

HALSTEAD, CAROL. Born May 17, 1952 in Hempstead, NY. Graduate Fla. State U. Debut 1992 OB in *The Mask* followed by *Bats.*

HAMILTON, LAUREN. Born Nov. 10, 1959 in Boston, MA. Graduate Bard Col., Neighborhood Playhouse. Debut 1988 OB in *Famine Plays,* followed by *Tiny Dimes, Rodents and Radios, Hunger, Homo Sapien Shuffle, A Murder of Crows, A Vast Wreck, Gut Girls.*

HAMMER, MARK. Born April 28, 1937 in San Jose, CA. Graduate Stanford U., Catholic U. Debut 1966 OB in *Jouney of the Fifth Horse* followed by *Witness for the Prosecution, Cymbeline, Richard III, The Taming of the Shrew, As You Like It,* Bdwy in *Much Ado about Nothing* (1972).

HANSEN, LARRY. Born March 11, 1952 in Anacortes, W. Va. Graduate Western Wash. U. Debut 1978 OB in *Can-Can* followed by *Box Office of the Damned, Allegro (in concert),* Bdwy in *Show Boat* (1983), *Anna Karenina.*

HARADA, ANN. Born February 3, 1964 in Honolulu, HI. Attended Brown U. Debut 1987 OB in *1-2-3-4-5* followed by *Hit the Lights!,* Bdwy in *M. Butterfly* (1988).

HARDEN, MARCIA GAY. Born August 14, 1959 in La Jolla, CA. Graduate U. MD, UTX, NYU. Debut 1989 OB in *The Man Who Shot Lincoln,* followed by *One of the Guys, The Years,* Bdwy in *Angels in America* for which she recieved a 1993 Theatre World Award.

HARDING, JAN LESLIE. Born in 1956 in Cambridge, MA. Graduate Boston U. Debut 1980 OB in *Album,* followed by *Sunday Picnic, Buddies, The Lunch Girls, Marathon '86, Traps, Father Was a Peculiar Man, A Murder of Crows, David's Red-Haired Death, Strange Feet, Impassioned Embraces, Storm Patterns, Bondage, My Head was a Sledgehammer, Bremen Freedom.*

HARDY, MARK. Born Oct. 25, 1961 in Reidsville, NC. Graduate UNC/Greensboro. Debut 1990 OB in *The Rothschilds,* followed by *Juba, Boys Next Door,* Bdwy in *Les Miserables* (1990).

HARPOLD, WILLIAM AARON. Born July 1, 1971 in Buckhannon, WV. Graduate Carnegie-Mellon U. Debut 1993 OB in *The Survivor* followed by Bdwy in *Picnic* (1994).

HARRAN, JACOB. Born July 23, 1955 in NYC. Graduate HofstraU. Debut 1984 BO in *Balm in Gilead* followed by *Awake and Sing, Crossing Delancy, Romeo and Juliet, Cabbagehead, Oklahoma Samovar, Three Sisters, Money Talks, El Dorado, Bagels and Luck, The Way of the World, Candida, Godot Arrives.*

HARRINGTON, CHRISTIE. Born in Oakland, CA. Graduate Temple U. SUNY/Fredonia. Debut 1989 OB in *You Can Never Tell* followed by *Working, The Rivers and Ravines, Anima Mundi, Exit Music, Let Us Now Praise Famous Men, 2 By Strindberg.*

HARRIS, BAXTER. Born Nov. 18, 1940 in Columbus, KS. Attended U. Kan. Debut 1967 OB in *America Hurrah,* followed by *The Serpent, Battle of Angels, Down by the River..., Ferocious Kisses, The Three Sisters, The Dolphin Position, Broken Eggs, Paradise Lost, Ghosts, The Time of Your Life, The Madwoman of Chaillot, The Reckoning, Wicked Women Revue, More Than You Deserve, Him, Pericles, Selma, Gradual Clearing, Children of the Sun, Marathon '90, Go to Ground, Marathon '92 & '93, Long Ago and Far Away,* Bdwy in *A Texas Trilogy* (1976), *Dracula, The Lady from Dubuque.*

HARRIS, JULIE. Born Dec. 2, 1925 in Grosse Pointe, MI. Yale graduate. Bdwy debut 1945 in *It's a Gift,* followed by *Henry V, Oedipus, Playboy of the Western World, Alice in Wonderland, Macbeth, Sundown Beach* for which she received a Theatre World Award, *The Young and the Fair, Magnolia Alley, Montserrat, Member of the Wedding, I Am a Camera, Mlle. Colombe, The Lark, Country Wife, Warm Peninsula, Little Moon of Alban, A Shot in the Dark, Marathon '33, Ready When You Are C. B., Hamlet* (CP), *Skyscraper, 40 Carats, And Miss Reardon Drinks a Little, Voices, The Last of Mrs. Lincoln, Au Pair Man, In Praise of Love, Belle of Amherst, Mixed Couples, Break a Leg, Lucifer's Child, A Christmas Carol,* OB in *Fiery Furnace.*

HARRIS, NIKI. Born July 20, 1948 in Pittsburgh, PA. Graduate Duquesne U. Bdwy debut 1980 in *A Day in Hollywood/A Night in the Ukraine* followed by *My One and Only, Grand Hotel, The Best Little Whorehouse Goes Public,* OB in *Leave It to Jane, No No Nanette, Berkeley Square.*

HARRIS, RONALD LEW. Born May 29, 1953 in Louisville, KY. Graduate Moorehead State U. AADA. Debut 1976 OB in *Compulsion* followed by *Between Time and Timbuktu, Going Home, A Midsummer Night's Dream, Mandrake, Three Cuckolds, Two Gentlemen of Verona, The Taming of the Shrew, Julius Caesar, Henry V, Magic Time, Awake and Sing.*

HARRIS, ROSEMARY. Born Sept.19, 1930 in Ashby, Eng. Attended RADA. Bdwy debut 1952 in *Climate of Eden* for which she received a Theatre World Award, followed by *Troilus and Cressida, Interlock, The Disenchanted, The Tumbler, with APA in The Tavern, School for Scandal, The Sea Gull, Importance of Being Earnest, War and Peace, Man and Superman, Judith and You Can't Take it with You, Lion in Winter, Old Times, Merchant of Venice, Streetcar Named Desire, Royal Family, Pack of Lies, Hay Fever, An Inspector Calls,* OB in *New York Idea, Three Sisters, The Sea Gull.*

HARRIS, SAM. Born June 4, 1961 in Cushing, OK. Attended UCLA. Bdwy debut 1994 in *Grease.*

HARRISON, STANLEY EARL. Born September 17, 1955 in Cheverly, MD. Graduate Morgan State U. Debut 1978 OB in *The Phantom* followed by *The Boogie Woogie Rumble of a Dream Deferred, The Medium, Mud, The Mighty Gents, Abyssinia, A Matter of Conscience, Morningsong, The Lost Dreams...,* Bdwy in *The King and I* (1983).

HAWKE, ETHAN. Born November 6, 1970 in Austin, TX. Debut 1991 OB in *Casanova* followed by *Sophistry, Sons and Fathers,* Bdwy in *The Sea Gull*

(1992).

HAWLEY, LYNN. Born November 12, 1965 in Sharon, CT. Graduate Middlebury Col. Debut 1992 OB in *Woyzeck* followed by *Owners, The Illusion.*

HAYDEN, MICHAEL. Born July 28 1963 in St. Paul, MN. Graduated Juilliard. Debut 1991 OB in *The Matchmaker* followed by *Hello Again, Off-Key, Nebraska,* Bdwy debut 1994 in *Carousel* for which he received a Theatre World Award.

HAYDEN, SOPHIE. Born February 23 in Miami, FL. Graduate Northwestern U. Bdwy debut 1979 in *Whoopee!,* followed by *Barnum, Comedy of Errors, The Most Happy Fella* (1992), *The Show-Off,* OB in *She Loves Me, Jessie's Land, Passover, Lies My Father Told Me, Torpedo Bra, Fun, How the Other Half Loves.*

HAYENGA, JEFFREY. Born August 13, in Sibledy, IA. Graduate U. Mn. Bdwy in *The Elephant Man* followed by *Ah! Wilderness!, Long Day's Journey into Night* OB in *King Lear, Mother Courage, The Actors' Nightmare, Burkie, Brand, Hamlet, Breaking Up, Two Rooms, Patient A, Jeffrey.*

HAYNES, ROBIN. Born July 20, 1953 in Lincoln, NE. Graduate U. Wash. Debut 1976 OB in *A Touch of the Poet* followed by *She Loves Me, Romeo and Juliet, Twelfth Night, Billy Bishop Goes to War, Max and Maxie,* Bdwy in *The Best Little Whorehouse in Texas* (1978), *Blood Brothers.*

HEARN, DENNIS. Born February 3, 1949 in Chesterland, OH. Graduate Kent State U. Deut 1973 OB in *Oh Lady! Lady!,* followed by *Frayed Edges* (1994).

HEFLIN, ELIZABETH. Born in Rockford, IL. Graduate U. Del. Bdwy debut 1993 in *The Government Inspector.*

HELDE, ANNETTE. Born November 14, in Long Beach, CA. Graduate U. Santa Barbara, U. Wash. Debut 1982 OB in *Antigone* followed by *Hamlet, Ballad of Soapy Smith, Virginia, Free Fall, A Piece of My Heart, The Merchant of Venice, As You Like It, Drowning in Loch Ness,* Bdwy in *Macbeth* (1988), *A Few Good Men, The Government Inspector, Timon of Athens.*

HELLER, ADAM. Born June 8, 1960 in Englewood, NJ. Graduate NYU. Debut 1984 OB in *Kuni-Leml,* followed by *The Special, Half a World Away, Encore!, Mererily We Roll Along,* Bdwy in *Les Miserables* (1989).

HELMOND, KATHERINE. Born in Galveston, TX. OB in *Orpheus Descending* (1959) followed by *Trip to Bountiful, Time of Your Life, Another Part of the Forest, Mousetrap, House of Blue Leaves, Karl Marx Play,* Bdwy in *Great God Brown* (1972), *Don Juan, Mixed Emotions.*

HENFREY, JANET. Born August 16, 1935 in England. Graduate Oxford U. RADA. Bdwy debut 1994 in *Medea.*

HENRITZE, BETTE. Born May 23 in Betsy Layne, KY. Graduate U. TN. OB in *Lion in Love, Abe Lincoln in Illinois, Othello, Baal, A Long Christmas Dinner, Queens of France, Rimers of Eldritch, Displaced Person, Acquisition, Crime of Passion, Happiness Cage, Henry VI, Richard III, Older People, Lotta, Catsplay. A Month in the Country. The Golem, Daughters, Steel Magnolias, All's Well That Ends Well,* Bdwy in *Jenny Kissed Me* (1948), *Pictures in the Hallway, Giants Sons of Giants, Ballad of the Sad Cafe, The White House, Dr. Cook's Garden, Here's Where I Belong, Much Ado about Nothing, Over Here, Angel Street, Man and Superman, Macbeth* (1981), *Present Laughter, The Octette Bridge Club, Orpheus Descending, Lettice and Lovage, On Borrowed Time, Hedda Gabler.*

HERNANDEZ, PHILIP. Born December 12, 1959 in Queens, NYC. Graduate SUNY. Debut 1987 OB in *The Gingerbread Lady* followed by *Ad Hock,* Bdwy in *Kiss of the Spider Woman* (1993).

HERRMANN, EDWARD. Born July 21, 1943 in Washington, DC. Graduate Bucknell U., LAMDA. Debut 1970 OB in *The Basic Training of Pavlo Hummel* followed by *A Midsummer Night's Dream, Tom and Viv, Not about Heroes ,Julius Caesar, Life Sentences,* Bdwy in *Moonchildren* (1971), *Mrs. Warren's Profession, The Philadelphia Story, Plenty.*

HIBBERT, EDWARD. Born September 9, 1955 in NYC. Attended Hurstpierpoint Col., RADA. Bdwy debut 1982 in *Alice in Wonderland* followed by *Me and My Girl, Lady in the Dark in Concert,* OB in *Candide in Concert, Dandy Dick, Privates on Parade, Lady Bracknell's Confinement, Candide, Jeffrey*

HICKOK, JOHN. Born August 31, 1957. OB in *Eye of the Beholder.*

HICKS, SHAUNA. Born January 15, 1962 in Neenah WI. Graduate American U. Debut 1987 OB in *The Gingerbread Lady* followed by *Buzzsaw Berkeley* Bdwy in *Meet Me in St. Louis* (1989), *Blood Brothers.*

HILER, KATHERINE. Born June 24, 1961 in Carson City, NV. Graduate Mt. Holyoke Col. Bdwy debut 1985 in *Hurlyburly* followed by *Kentucky Cycle,* OB in *Liebelei, Year of the Duck, A Shayna Maidel, Temptation, What a Man Weighs, Macbeth, Young Playwrights Festival, Club Soda, Sophistry.*

HILL, RALSTON. Born April 24, 1927 in Cleveland, OH. Graduate Oberlin Col. OB in *The Changeling, Streets of New York, Valmouth, Carousel, The Beggar's Opera, Colette Collage, Johnny Pye,* Bdwy 1969 in *1776.*

HILNER, JOHN. Born November 5, 1952 in Evanston, IL. Graduate Deniston U. Debut 1977 OB in *Essential Shepard,* followed by Bdwy in *They're Playing Our Song, Little Me, Woman of the Year, Crazy for You.*

HINES, MIMI. Born July 17, 1933 in Vancouver, Can. Bdwy debut 1965 in *Funny Girl* followed by *Grease* (1994), OB in *From Rodgers and Hart with Love, Little Me* (in previews).

HIPKINS, BILLY. Born May 18, 1961 in Verona, NJ. Attended AADA. Debut 1988 OB in *Alias Billy Valentine* followed by *The Makeover,* Bdwy in *Anna Karenina* (1992).

HIRSCHHORN, LARRY. Born August 31, 1958 in Oceanside, NY. Graduate Ithaca Col. Debut 1983 OB in *Promises Promises* followed by

Gingerbread Lady, The Wise Men of Chelm.

HO, WAI CHING. Born November 16, 1943 in Hong Kong. Graduate UHK, AADA. Debut 1968 OB in *The People vs Ranchman* followed by *Moon on a Rainbow Shawl, Song for Nisei Fisherman, Eating Chicken Feet.*

HOCK, ROBERT. Born May 20, 1931 in Phoenixville, PA. Yale Graduate. Debut 1982 OB in *The Caucasian Chalk Circle* followed by *Adding Machine, Romeo and Juliet, Edward II, Creditors, Two Orphans,Macbeth, Kitty Hawk, Heathen Valley, Comedy of Errors, Phaedra, The Good Natur'd Man, Oedipus the King, Game of Love and Chance, Twelfth Night,* Bdwy in *Some Americans Abroad* (1990).

HODGES, BEN. Born September 17, 1969 in Morristown, TN. Graduate Otterbein Col. Debut OB 1992 in *Loose Ends* followed by *Hysteria.*

HOFF, CHRISTIAN. Born April 21, 1968 in Berkeley, CA. Attended Stella Adler Consv. Bdwy debut 1993 in *The Who's Tommy.*

HOFFMANN, AVI. Born March 3, 1958 in The Bronx, NYC. Graduate U. Miami. Debut 1983 in *The Rise of David Levinsky,* followed by *It's Hard to Be a Jew, A Rendezvous with God, The Golden Land, Songs of Paradise, Finkel's Follies, Milk and Honey.*

HOFFMAN, JANE. Born July 24 in Seattle, WA. Graduate U. Cal. Bdwy debut 1940 in *Tis of Thee,* followed by *Crazy with the Heat, Something for the Boys, One Touch of Venus, Calico Wedding, Mermaids Singing, Temporary Island, Story for Strangers, Two Blind Mice, The Rose Tattoo, The Crucible, Witness for the Prosecution, Third Best Sport, Rhinoceros, Mother Courage and Her Children, Fair Game for Lovers, A Murderer Among Us. Murder Among Friends, Some Americans Abroad, Lost in Yonkers,* OB in *American Dream, Sandbox, Picnic on the Battlefield, Theatre of the Absurd, Child Buyer, A Corner of the Bed, Slow Memories, Last Analysis, Dear Oscar, Hocus Pocus, Lessons, The Art of Dining, Second Avenue Rag, One Tiger to a Hill, Isn't It Romantic, Alto Part, Frog Prince, Alterations, The Grandma Plays, The Mysteries.*

HOFFMAN, PHILIP. Born May 12, 1954 in Chicago, IL. Graduate U. Ill. Bdwy debut 1981 in *The Moony Shapiro Songbook,* followed by *Is There Life After High School?, Baby, Into the Woods, Falsettos,* OB in *The Fabulous 50's, Isn't It Romantic, 1-2-3-4-5, Rags, All in the Timing, The Treatment, Merrily We Roll Along.*

HOFFSTATTER, TED. Born March 10, 1969 in Freeport, NY. Graduate Eckerd Col, Neighborhood Playhouse. Bdwy debut 1993 in *Timon of Athens,* followed by *The Government Inspector.*

HOFVENDAHL, STEVE. Born September 1, 1956 in San Jose, CA. Graduate U. Santa Clara, Brandeis U. Debut 1986 OB in *A Lie of the Mind,* followed by *Ragged Trousered Philanthropists, The Miser, A Midsummer Night's Dream, Light Shining in Buckinghamshire, 10th Young Playwrights Festival, Marvin's Room, Little Red Riding Hood,* Bdwy in Mastergate (1989), *The Flowering Peach.*

HOHN, AMY. Born in Royal Oak, MI. Graduate Syracuse U. Debut 1994 OB in *The Stand-in,* followed by *Hide Your Love Away.*

HOLBROOK, RUBY. Born August 28, 1930 in St. Johns, Nfld. Attended Denison U. Debut 1963 OB in *Abe Lincoln in Illinois,* followed by *Hamlet, James Joyce's Dubliners, Measure for Measure, The Farm, Do You Still Believe the Rumor?, The Killing of Sister George, An Enemy of the People, Amulets Against the Dragon Forces, The Rose Quartet, The Workroom,* Bdwy in *Da* (1979), *5th of July, Musical Comedy Murders of 1940.*

HOLGATE, RONALD. Born May 26, 1937 in Aberdeen, SD. Attended Northwestern U., New Eng. Consv. Debut 1961 OB in *Hobo,* followed by *Hooray It's a Glorious Day, Blue Plate Special, Milk and Honey,* Bdwy in *A Funny Thing Happened..., Milk and Honey, 1776, Saturday Sunday Monday, The Grand Tour, Musical Chairs, 42nd Street, Lend Me a Tenor, Guys and Dolls* (1993).

HOLLIDAY, POLLY. Born July 2, 1937 in Jasper, AL. Attended Fla. State U. Debut 1964 OB in *Orphee,* followed by *Dinner on the Ground, Wedding Band, Girls Most Likely to Succeed, Carnival Dreams, A Quarrel of Sparrows,* Bdwy in *All over Town* (1974), *Cat on a Hot Tim Roof, Picnic* (1994).

HOLLIS, MARNEE. Born January 9 in Puyallup, WA. Graduate Pacific Luthern U. Bdwy debut 1993 in *My Fair Lady.*

HOLLOWAY, JULIAN. Born June 24, 1944 in Watlington, Eng. Graudate RADA. Bdwy debut 1993 in *My Fair Lady.*

HOLM, CÉLESTE. Born Apr.29, 1919 in NYC. Attended UCLA, U. Chicago. Bdwy debut 1938 in *Gorianna,* followed by *Time of Your Life, Another Sun, Return of the Vagabond, 8 O'Clock Tuesday, My Fair Ladies, Papa Is All, All the Comforts of Home, Damask Cheek, Oklahoma!, Bloomer Girl, She Stoops to Conquer, Affairs of State, Anna Christie, King and I, His and Hers, Interlock, Third Best Sport, Invitation to a March, Mame, Candida, Habeas Corpus, Utter Glory of Morrissey Hall, I Hate Hamlet, Allegro in Concert,* OB in *Month in the Country, Paris Was Yesterday, With Love and Laughter, Christmas Carol.*

HOLMES, RICHARD. Born March 16, 1963 in Philadelphia, PA. Graduate Gettysburg Col., NY. Debut 1990 OB in *Richard III,* followed by *Othello, Shadow of a Gunman, Mr. Parnell, Christina Alberta's Father,* Bdwy in *Saint Joan* (1993), *Timon of Athens, Government Inspector.*

HOLMES, SCOTT. Born May 30, 1952 in West Grove, PA. Graduate Catawba Col. Bdwy debut 1979 in *Grease,* followed by *Evita, The Rink, Jerome Kern Goes to Hollywood, The Best Little Whorehouse Goes Public,* OB in *Diamonds.*

HOLMES, SUSAN DAVIS. Born September 19, 1960 in Santa Barbara, CA. Graduate Manhattan School of Music. Debut 1984 OB in *Yoemen of the Guard,* followed by *Sweethears, The Drunkard, The Mikado, The*

Gondoliers,The Merry Widow, The New Moon, Pirates of Penzance, Give My Regards to Broadway, Desert of Roses.

HOLTZMAN, MERRILL. Born Sept. 1, 1959. Bdwy debut 1989 in *Mastergate,* OB in *Chelsea Walls, Nebraska, A Darker Purpose, The Stand-In.*

HOOPES, WENDY. Born Nov. 4, 1968 in Kuala Lampur , Malasia. Graduate American U., NYU. Debut 1994 OB in *SubUrbia.*

HOPE, SHARON. Born in NYC. Graduate Baruch Col. Debut 1987 OB in *A Star Ain't Nothing but a Hole in Heaven,* followed by *Black Medea, Capital Cakewalk, The Trial, Them That's Got, A Better Life, Two By David Hwang.*

HOPKINS, KAITLIN (Kate). Born Feb.1, 1964 in NYC. Attended Carnegie-Mellon U., RADA. Debut 1984 in *Come Back Little Sheba,* followed by *Take Two, My Favorite Year, Johnny Pye and the Foolkiller.*

HORAN, BOB. Born Oct.12, 1925 in Aberdeen, SD. Graduate U. Min., U. Mo. OB in *Hogan's Goat, 13th Chair, The Dropper, Christmas Twist, Could I Have This Dance?,* Bdwy in *Enemy of the People, A Minor Miracle, Great White Hope.*

HORNE, CHERYL. Born Nov.15 in Stamford, CT. Graduate SMU. Debut 1975 OB in *The Fantasticks,* followed by *Indomitable Huntresses, Andorra, Lady Windermere's Fan, Let's Get a Divorce, Mourning Becomes Electra, Uncle Vanya.*

HORVATH, JAN. Born Jan.31, 1958 in Lake Forest, IL. Graduate Cin. Consv. Bdwy debut 1983 in *Oliver,* followed by *Sweet Charity, Phantom of the Opera, 3 Penny Opera,* OB in *Sing Me Sunshine, Jacques Brel..., Chess, New York Rock.*

HOTY, DEE. Born Aug. 16, 1952 in Lakewood, OH. Graduate Otterbein Col. Debut 1979 in *The Golden Apple,* followed by *Ta-Dah!, Personals,* Bdwy in *The 5 O'Clock Girl* (1981), *Shakespeare Cabaret, City of Angels, Will Rogers Follies, Best Little Whorehouse Goes Public.*

HOWARD, LAUREN. Born May 20, 1957 in Bayonne, NJ. Graduate Franklin and Marshall Col. Debut 1993 in *Who Will Carry the Word?* followed by *Reproducing Georgia.*

HOWER, NANCY. Born May 11 in Wyckoff, NJ. Graduate Rollins Col., Juilliard. Debut 1991 OB in *Othello,* followed by *As You Like It, The Years,* Bdwy in *Government Inspector.*

HOWES, SALLY ANN. Born July 20, 1934 in London, Eng. Appeared in *My Fair Lady, Kwamina, Brigadoon, What Makes Sammy Run?, A Little Night Music, Cinderella.*

HUBER, KATHLEEN. Born March 3, 1947 in NYC. Graduaute U. Cal. Debut 1969 OB in *Scent of Flowers,* followed by *Virgin and the Unicorn, Constant Wife, Milestones, Tamara, Romeo and Juliet.*

HUFFMAN, FELICITY. Born Dec.9, 1962 in Westchesyter, NY. Graduate NYU, AADA, RADA. Debut 1988 OB in *Boys' Life,* followed by *Been Taken, Grotesque Lovesongs, Three Sisters, Shaker Heights, Jolly,* Bdwy in *Speed-the-Plow* (1988).

HUGOT, MARCELINE. Born February 10, 1960 in Hartford, CT. Graduate Brown U., U. Cal/San Diego. Debut 1986 OB in *The Maids,* followed by *Measure for Measure, Them Within Us, Gloria, Christina Albert's Father.*

HULCE, TOM. Born Dec.6, 1953 in Plymouth, MI. Graduate NC Sch of Arts. Bdwy debut 1975 in *Equus,* followed by *A Few Good Men,* OB in *Memory of Two Mondays, Julius Caesar, Twelve Dreams, Rise and Rise of Daniel Rocket, Haddock's Eyes, Hello Again.*

HUNT, ANNETTE. Born January 31, 1938 in Hampton, Va. Graduate Va. Intermont Col. Debut 1957 OB in *Nine by Six,* followed by *Taming of the Shrew, Medea, Anatomist, The Misanthrope, The Cherry Orchard, Electra, Last Resort, The Seducers, A Sound of Silence, Charades, Dona Rosita, Rhinestones, Where's Charley?, The White Rose of Memphis, M. Amilcar, The Sea Gull, Rutherford & Son, Lemonmade,* Bdwy in *All the Girls Came Out to Play* (1972).

HUNTER, KIM. Born Nov.12, 1922 in Detroit, MI. Attended Actors Studio. Bdwy debut 1947 in *Streetcar Named Desire,* followed by *Darkness at Noon, The Chase, Children's Hour, The Tender Trap, Write Me a Murder, Weekend, Penny Wars, The Women, To Grandmother's House We Go,* OB in *Come Slowly Eden, All is Bright, Cherry Orchard, When We Dead Awaken, Territorial Rites, Faulkner's Bicycle, Man and Superman, Murder of Crows, Eye of the Beholder.*

HURT, MARY BETH. Born September 26, 1948 in Marshalltown, IA. Attended U. Iowa, NYU. Debut 1972 OB in *More Than You Deserve,* followed by *As You Like It, Trelawny of the Wells, The Cherry Orchard, Love for Love, Member of the Wedding, Boy Meets Girl, Secret Service, Father's Day, Nest of the Wood Grouse, The Day Room, Secret Rapture, Othello, One Shoe Off, Arts and Leisure,* Bdwy in *Crimes of the Heart* (1981), *The Misanthrope, Benefactors.*

HYMAN, EARLE. Born Oct. 11, 1926 in Rocky Mount, NC. Attended New School, Am. Th. Wing. Bdwy debut 1943 in *Run Little Chillun,* followed by *Anna Lucasta, Climate of Eden, Merchant of Venice, Othello, Julius Caesar, The Tempest, No Time for Sergeants, Mr. Johnson,* for which he received a Theatre World Award, *St. Joan, Hamlet, Waiting for Godot, The Duchess of Malfi, Les Blancs, The Lady from Dubuque, Execution of Justice, Death of the King's Horseman, The Master Builder,* OB in *The White Rose and the Red, Worlds of Shakespeare, Jonah, Life and Times of J. Walter Smintheus, Orrin, The Cherry Orchard, House Party, Carnival Dreams, Agamemnon, Othello, Julius Caesar, Coriolanus, Pygmalion, Richard II, East Texas Hot Links.*

ILLES, MARY. Born January 20, 1962 in Dayton, OH. Graduate Ohio State U. Debut 1992 OB in *Chess,* Bdwy in *She Loves Me* (1992).

ILLMANN, MARGARET. Born in Adelaide, Australia. With Australian Ballet before joining National Ballet of Canada as principal dancer. Bdwy debut 1993 in *Red Shoes* for which she received a Theatre World Award.

IRISH, MARK. Born Dec. 18, 1963 in Hartland, ME. Graduate Dartmouth Col. Debut 1988 OB in *On Tina Tuna Walk* followed by *Good Honest Food, The Littlest Clown, Lily Wong, Trophies*.

IRVING, AMY. Born Sept. 10, 1953 in Palo Alto, CA. Attended LAMDA. Debut 1970 OB in *And Chocolate on Her Chin*, followed by *The Road to Mecca*, Bdwy in *Amadeus* (1983), *Heartbreak House, Broken Glass*.

IRVING, GEORGE S. Born Nov. 1, 1922 in Springfield, MA. Attended Leland Powers Sch. Bdwy debut 1943 in *Oklahoma!* followed by *Call Me Mister, Along Fifth Avenue, Two's Company, Me and Juliet, Can-Can, Shinbone Alley, Bells Are Ringing, The Good Soup, Tovarich, A Murderer Among Us, Alfie, Anya, Galileo, Four on a Garden, An Evening with Richard Nixon, Irene, Who's Who in Hell, All over Town, So Long 174th Street, Once in a Lifetime, I Remember Mama, Copperfield, Pirates of Penzance, On Your Toes, Me and My Girl, Cinderella*, OB in *Rosalie in Concert Pal Joey in Concert Mexican Hayride*.

IRWIN, BILL. Born April 11, 1950 in Santa Monica, CA. Attended UCLA, Clown Col. Debut 1982 OB in *The Regard of Flight* followed by *The Courtroom, Waiting for Godot*, Bdwy in *5-6-7-8 Dance* (1983), *The Accidental Death of an Anarchist, Regard of Flight, Largely New York, Fool Moon.*

ISHEE, SUZANNE. Born October 15 in High Point, NC. Graduate UNC, Manhattan School of Music. Bdwy debut 1983 in *Show Boat* followed by *Mame, La Cage aux Folles, Phantom of the Opera.*

IVES, DONALD. Born October 25, 1962 in Salem, MO. Attended Southwest MO. State, Webster Col., Southern IL. U. Bdwy debut 1993 in *Camelot.*

IVEY, DANA. Born August 12 in Atlanta, GA. Graduate Rollins Col., LAMDA. Bdwy debut 1981 in *Macbeth* (LC), followed by *Present Laughter, Heartbreak House, Sunday in the Park with George, Pack of Lies, Marriage of Figaro*, OB in *A Call from the East, Vivien, Candida in Concert, Major Barbara in Concert, Quartermaine's Terms, Baby with the Bath Water, Driving Miss Daisy, Wenceslas Square, Love Letters, Hamlet, The Subject Was Roses, Beggars in the House of Plenty, Kindertransport.*

IVEY, JUDITH. Born September 4, 1951 in El Paso, TX. Bdwy debut 1979 in *Bedroom Farce* followed by *Steaming, Hurlyburly, Blithe Spirit, Park Your Car in Harvard Yard*, OB in *Dulsa Fish Stas and Vi, Sunday Runners, Second Lady, Mrs. Dally Has a Lover, Moonshot and Cosmos.*

JACKEL, PAUL. Born June 30 in Winchester, MA. Graduate Harvard, Debut 1983 OB in *The Robber Bridegroom*, followed by *Side by Side by Sondheim, Gifts of the Magi, After the Ball*, Bdwy in *The Secret Garden* (1991).

JACKSON , ANNE. Born September 3, 1926 in Allegheny, PA. Attended Neighborhood Playhouse. Bdwy debut 1945 in *Signature* followed by *Yellow Jack, John Gabriel Borkman, The Last Dance, Summer and Smoke, Magnolia Alley, Love Me Long, Lady from the Sea, Never Say Never, Oh Men! Oh Women!, Rhinoceros, Luv, The Exercise, Inquest, Promenade All, Waltz of the Toreadors, Twice Around the Park, Cafe Crown, Lost in Yonkers, Flowering Peach*, OB in *The Tiger and the Typist, Marco Polo Sings a Solo, Diary of Anne Frank, Nest of the Wood Gouse, Madwoman of Chaillot, Cafe Crown, In Persons.*

JACKSON, KIRK. Born Feb. 8, 1956 in Albany, NY. Graduate Binghamton U., Yale U. Debut 1990 OB in *Stirrings Still* followed by *Bremen Freedom, The Secret Lives of Ancient Egyptians, Underground Soap, Heartbreak House, Untitled Lindberg, Listen to Me, Inktomi, The Almond Seller, Necropolis, Private Property, Apocrypha, Storm Patterns.*

JACOBY, MARK. Born May 21, 1947 in Johnson City, TN. Graduate GA State U., FL State U., St. John's U. Debut 1984 OB in *Bells Are Ringing*, Bdwy in *Sweet Charity* for which he received a 1986 Theatre World Award, *Grand Hotel, The Phantom of the Opera.*

JAMES, ELMORE. Born May 3, 954 in NYC. Graduate SUNY/Purchase. Debut 1970 OB in *Moon on a Rainbow Shawl* followed by *The Ups and Downs of Theopholus Maitland, Carnival, Until the Real Thing Comes Along, A Midsummer Night's Dream, The Tempest, Jacques Brel Is Alive...*, Bdwy in *But Never Jam Today* (1979), *Your Arms Too Short to Box with God, Big River, Beauty and the Beast.*

JAMES, KELLI. Born Mar. 18, 1959 in Council Bluffs, IA. Bdwy debut 1987 in *Les Miserables.*

JAMES, KRICKER. Born May 17, 1939 in Cleveland, OH. Graduate Denison U. Debut 1966 in *Winterset*, followed by *Out of Control, Rainbows for Sale, The Firebugs, Darkness at Noon, The Hunting Man, Sacraments, Trifles, Batting Practice, Uncle Vanya. Mourning Becomes Electra.*

JANKO, IBI. Born February 18, 1966 in Carmel, CA. Graduate Yale U. debut 1993 OB in *Somewhere I Have Never Travelled* followed by *Vinegar Tom, Waiting, Your Mom's a Man, Cinoman and Rebeck.*

JARRETT, BELLA. Born February 9, 1931 in Adairsville, GA. Graduate Wesleyan Col. Debut 1958 OB in *Waltz of the Toreadors* followed by *Hedda Gabler, The Browning Version, Cicero, Pequod, Welcome to Andromeda, The Trojan Women, Phaedra, The Good Natur'd Man, Twelfth Night*, Bdwy in *Once in a Lifetime* (1978), *Lolita.*

JBARA, GREGORY. Born Sept. 28, 1961 in Wayne, Michigan. Graduate U. MI., Juilliard. Debut 1986 OB in *Have I Got a Girl for You, Serious Money, Privates on Prarade, Forever Plaid*, Bdwy in *Serious Money* (1988), *Born Yesterday* (1989), *Damn Yankees* (1994).

JENKINS, DANIEL. Born Jan. 17, 1963 in NYC. Attended Columbia U. Bdwy debut 1985 in *Big River*, OB in *Feast Here Tonight, Young Playwrights Festival, The Triumph of Love, Johnny Pye and the Foolkiller.*

JENNINGS, KEN Born Oct. 10, 1947 in Jersey City, NJ. Graduate St. Peter's .Col. Bdwy debut 1975 in *All God's Chillun Got Wings*, followed by *Sweeney Todd* for which he received a 1979 Theatre World Award, *Present Laughter, Grand Hotel*, OB in *Once on a Summer's Day, Mayor, Rabboni, Gifts of the Magi, Carmilla, Sharon, The Mayor Musicals, Amphigory.*

JOHANSON, DON. Born October 19, 1952 in Rock Hill, SC. Graduate USC. Bdwy debut 1976 in *Rex* followed by *Cats, Jelly's Last Jam, The Best Little Whorehouse in Texas Goes Public*, OB in *The American Dance Machine.*

JOHN, TAYLOR. Born November 25, 1981 in NYC. Bdwy debut 1991 in *Les Miserables.*

JOHNSON, BJORN. Born May 26, 1957 in Minneapolis, MN. Graduate George Williams Col. Debut 1981 OB in *Confessional* followed by *Hamlet, Senor Discretion, Pastorale, Romantic Detachment, Charley's Tale, Wild Men*, Bdwy in *Cyrano The Musical* (1993).

JOHNSON, JEREMY. Born Oct. 2, 1933 in New Bedford, MA. Graduate CCNY, Columbia U. Debut 1975 OB in *Moby Dick* followed by *Anna Christie, Harrison Texas, Romeo and Juliet, Much Ado about Nothing, The Merchant of Venice.*

JOHNSON, PAGE. Born Aug. 25, 1930 in Welch, WV. Graduate Ithaca Col. Bdwy 1951 in *Romeo and Juliet*, followed by *Electra, Oedipus, Camino Real, In April Once* for which he received a Theatre World Award, *Red Roses for Me, The Lovers, Equus, You Can't Take It with You, Brush Arbor Revival*, OB in *The Enchanted Guitar, 4 in 1, Journey of the Fifth Horse*, APA's *School for Scandal, The Tavern*, and *The Seagull, The Odd Couple, Boys in the Band, Medea, Deathtrap, Best Little Whorehouse in Texas, Fool for Love, East Texas.*

JOHNSON, TINA. Born October 27, 1951 in Wharton, TX. Graduate N. TX State U. Debut 1979 OB in *Festival* followed by *Blue Plate Special, Christina Alberta's Father, Just So*, Bdwy in *The Best Little Whorehouse in Texas, South Pacific* (NYCO/LC).

JOHNSTON, NANCY. Born Jan. 15, 1949 in Statesville, NC. Graduate Carson Newman Col., UNC/Greensboro. Debut 1987 OB in *Olympus on My Mind*, followed by *Nunsense, Living Color, White Lies, You Can Be a New Yorker Too*, Bdwy in *The Secret Garden, Allegro in Concert.*

JOHNSTON, SAMME. Born Jan. 11, 1956 in Needham, MA. Graduate Wellesley Col. Debut 1985 OB in *A Flash of Lightining*, followed by *Theatre Olympics, Time and the Conways, Hedda Gabler, Three Sisters, Fen.*

JONES, CHERRY. Born Nov. 21, 1956 in Paris, TN. Graduate Carnegie-Mellon. Debut 1983 OB in *The Philanthropist*, followed by *He and She, The Ballad of Soapy Smith, The Importance of Being Earnest, I Am a Camera, Claptrap, Big Time, A Light Shining in Buckinghamshire, The Baltimore Waltz, Goodnight Desdemona, And Baby Makes 7, Desdemona*, Bdwy in *Stepping Out* (1986), *Our Country's Good.*

JONES, GEMMA. Born April 12, 1942 in London, Eng. Graduate RADA. Bdwy debut 1994 OB in *A Winter's Tale.*

JONES, NEAL. Born Jan. 2, 1960 in Wichita, KS. Attended Weber Col. Debut 1981 OB in *The Dear Love of Comrades*, followed by *The Tavern., Spring's Awakening, Billy Liar, Groves of Academe, A Darker Purpose, Diminished Capacity, The Undertakers*, Bdwy in *Macbeth* (1982), *The Corn Is Green* (1983).

JOSLYN, BETSY. Born April 19, 1954 in Staten Island, NY. Graduate Wagner Col. Debut 1976 OB in *The Fantasticks*, followed by *Light Up the Sky, Colette Collage*, Bdwy in *Sweeney Todd* (1979), *A Doll's Life, The Goodbye Girl, Lady in the Dark in Concert.*

JOYNER, MICHELLE. Born in California. Attended Hunter Col., Yale U. Debut 1993 OB in *Life Sentences.*

JUDD, ASHLEY. Born April 19 1968 in Los Angeles, CA. Graduate U. KT. Bdwy debut 1994 in *Picnic.*

KACZMAREK, JANE. Born Dec. 21 1955 in Milwaukee, WI. Graduate U. Wisc., Yale U. Debut 1986 OB in *Hands of the Enemy*, followed by *Loose Ends, Ice Cream/Hot Fudge, Eve's Diary, Kindertransport*, Bdwy in *Lost in Yonkers* (1991).

KALEMBER, PATRICIA. Born Dec. 30, 1956 in Schenectady, NY. Graduate Ind. U. Debut 1981 OB in *The Butler Did It*, followed by *Sheepskin, Playboy of the Western World, Poets' Corner, Loose Knit*, Bdwy in *The Nerd* (1987).

KAMPF, JAMES E. Born Oct. 24, 1962 in Chicago, IL. Attended Ball State U. Debut 1986 OB in *The Mikado*, followed by *Funny Girl, Marathon Dancing.*

KANE, CAROL. Born June 18, 1952 in Cleveland, OH. Bdwy in *The Prime of Miss Jean Brodie, The Tempest, Macbeth* (LC), *The Effect of Gamma Rays on Man-in-the-Moon Marigolds* (1978), OB in *The Lucky Spot, The Debutante Ball, In-Betweens.*

KANTOR, KENNETH. Born Apr. 6, 1949 in the Bronx, NYC. Graduate SUNY, Boston U. Debut 1974 OB in *Zorba*, followed by *Kiss Me Kate, A Little Night Music, Buried Treasure, Sounds of Rodgers and Hammerstein, Shop on Main Street, Kismet, The Fantasticks, Colette Collage, Snow White, Philemon*, Bdwy in *The Grand Tour* (1979), *Brigadoon* (1980), *Mame* (1983), *The New Moon* (NYCO/LC), *Me and My Girl, Guys and Dolls* (1992).

KAPLAN, JONATHAN. Born July 5, 1980 in Detroit, MI. Debut 1991 OB in *Rags* followed by *The Loman Family Picnic*, Bdwy in *Falsettos* (1991) for which he received a Theatre World Award.

KARNILOVA, MARIA. Born Aug. 3, 1920 in Hartford, CT. Bdwy debut 1938 in *Stars in Your Eyes*, followed by *Call Me Mister, High Button Shoes, Two's Company, Hollywood Pinafore, Beggar's Opera, Gypsy, Miss Liberty,*

Out of This World, Bravo Giovanni, Fiddler on the Roof, Zorba, Gigi, God's Favorite, Bring Back Birdie, OB in *Kaleidoscope, Cinderella* (NYCO/LC).

KARR, PATTI. Born July 10 in St. Paul, MN. Attended TCU. Bdwy debut 1953 in *Maggie*, followed by *Carnival in Flanders, Pipe Dream, Bells Are Ringing, New Girl in Town, Body Beautiful , Bye Bye Birdie, New Faces of 1962, Come on Strong, Look to the Lilies, Different Times, Lysistrata, Seesaw, Irene, Pippin, A Broadway Musical, Got to Go Disco, Musical Chairs, My Fair Lady* (1993), OB in *A Month of Sundays, Up Eden, Snapshot, Housewives Cantata, Something for the Boys, Baseball Wives, I Can Get It for You Wholesale*.

KATIMS, ROBERT. Born April 22, 1927 in Brooklyn, NYC. Attended Brooklyn Col. Debut 1953 OB in *The Penguin* followed by *The Invasion of Aratooga, Shmulnik's Waltz, On the Wing, No Conductor, Teibele and Her Demon*.

KAZAN, LAINIE. Born May 15, 1943 in Brooklyn, NYC. Attended Hofstra U. Bdwy debut in *Funny Girl*, followed by *My Favorite Year, The Government Inspector*.

KEACH, STACY. Born June 2, 1941 in Savannah, GA. Graduate U. Cal., Yale U., LAMDA. Debut 1967 OB in *MacBird*, followed by *Niggerlovers, Henry IV, Country Wife, Hamlet*, Bdwy in *Indians* (1969). *Deathtrap, Solitary Confinement, The Kentucky Cycle*.

KEATING, ISABEL. Born May 1, 1961 in Savannah, GA. Attended Lycee St. Gilles/Brussels. Debut OB 1989 in *Underground Man*, followed by *Nympho Lake, Paranoise, Major Barbara, House of Bernarda Alba, Balloonland, Could I Have This Dance?, Waiting at the Water's Edge, Written and Sealed*.

KELLNER, CATHERINE. Born Oct. 2, 1970 in NYC. Graduate Vassar Col., NYU. Debut 1994 OB in *Escape from Happiness*.

KENER, DAVID. Born May 21, 1959 in Brooklyn, NYC. Graduate NYU. Debut 1987 OB in *The Rise of David Levinsky*, followed by *Songs of Paradise, The Lady and the Clarinet*.

KEPROS, NICHOLAS. Born November 8, 1932 in Salt Lake City, UT. Graduate U. UT, RADA. Debut 1958 OB in *The Golden Six*, followed by *Wars and Roses, Julius Caesar, Hamlet, Henry IV, She Stoops to Conquer, Peer Gynt, Octaroon, Endicott and the Red Cross, The Judas Applause, The Irish Hebrew Lesson, Judgment in Havana, The Millionairess, Androcles and the Lion, The Redempter, Othello, The Times and Appetites of Toulouse-Lautrec, Two Fridays, Rameau's Nephew, Good Grief*, Bdwy in *Saint Joan* (1968/1993), *Amadeus, Execution of Justice, Timon of Athens, The Government Inspector*.

KERR, E. KATHERINE. Born April 20, 1940 in Indianapolis, IN. Graduate Ind. U., Neighborhood Playhouse. Debut 1963 OB in *Trojan Women*, followed by *The Contrast, Cloud 9, Laughing Wild, Urban Blight, Unfinished Stories*, Bdwy in *No Place to Be Somebody* (1969), *Nightwatch, Passion*.

KEY, LINDA AMES. Born Dec. 8, 1963 in NYC. Graduate Northwestern U. Debut 1989 OB in *Madame Bovary*, followed by *Shardston, Circles and Snakes, Among Women, Sunrise, The Taming of the Shrew, As You Like It, Earth Magic, Leaps of a River's Memory, Anton Chekhov: Stories of My Youth*.

KING, LARRY L. Born Jan. 1, 1929 in Putnam, TX. Attended TX. Tech. U., Harvard U., Duke U. Debut 1979 in *The Best Little Whorehouse in Texas*, followed by *The Best Little Whorehose Goes Public*, OB in *The Night Hank Williams Died*.

KINGSLEY-WEIHE, GRETCHEN. Born Oct. 6, 1961 in Washington, DC. Attended Tulane U. Debut 1985 OB in *Mowgli*, followed by *This Could Be the Start, A Backer's Audition*, Bdwy in *Les Miserables* (1987), *Sweeney Todd., Allegro in Concert*.

KINSEY, RICHARD. Born March 22, 1954. Attended Cal. State U./Fullerton, Bdwy debut 1991 in *Les Miserables*, OB in *Acting: A Romance, Mourning Becomes Electra*.

KIRBY, BRUNO. Born Apr.28,1949 in NYC. Bdwy debut 1991 in *Lost in Yonkers*, OB in *In-Betweens*.

KIRK, JUSTIN. Born May 28, 1969 in Salem, OR. Debut 1990 OB in *The Applicant*, followed by *Shardston, Loose Ends, Thanksgiving, Lovequest Live*, Bdwy in *Any Given Day* (1993)

KIRSH, BOB. Born Sept. 26, 1962 in Bristol, PA. Graduate Temple U., NYU. Debut 1990 OB in *Beautiful Soup*, followed by *Time Piece, Hyacinth Macaw, The Prince and the Pauper*.

KLEIN, ALISA. Born June 10, 1971 in Cleveland, OH. Attended Cincinnati Consv. Bdwy debut 1994 in *Beauty and the Beast*.

KLEIN, JULIA. Born April 5, 1969 in Minneapolis, MN. Graduate U. MN, NC Sch. Of Arts. Debut 1993 OB in *The Little Prince*.

KLEIN, LAUREN. Born Jan. 4, 1946 in Brooklyn, NYC. Graduate Santa Fe Col. Debut 1983 OB in *Becoming Memories*, followed by *Zastrozzi, After the Fall, Twice Shy, What's Wrong with This Picture?*, Bdwy debut 1994 in *Broken Glass*.

KLINE, KEVIN. Born Oct. 24, 1947 in St. Louis, MO. Graduate Ind. U., Juilliard. Debut 1970 OB in *War of Roses*, followed by *School for Scandal, Lower Depths, The Hostage, Women Beware Women, The Robber Bridegroom, Edward II, The Time of Your Life, Beware the Jubjub Bird, Dance on a Country Grave, Richard III, Henry V, Hamlet, Much Ado about Nothing, Measure for Measure*, Bdwy in *Three Sisters, Measure for Measure, Beggar's Opera, Scapin, On the 20th Century, Loose Ends, Pirates of Penzance, Arms and the Man*.

KLUNIS, TOM. Born in San Francisco, CA. Bdwy debut 1961 in *Gideon*, followed by *The Devils, Henry V, Romeo and Juliet, St. Joan, Hide and Seek, Bacchae, Plenty, M. Butterfly*, OB in *The Immoralist, Hamlet, Arms and the*

Man, The Potting Shed, Measure for Measure, Romeo and Juliet, The Balcony, Our Town, The Man Who Never Died, God Is My Ram, Rise Marlow, Iphigenia in Aulis, Still Life, The Master and Margarita, As You Like It, The Winter Dancers, When We Dead Awaken, Vieux Carre, The Master Builder, Richard III, A Map of the World, The Marriage Play.

KNIGHT, LILY. Born Nov. 30, 1949 in Jersey City, NJ. Graduate NYU. Debut 1980 OB in *After the Revolution*, followed by *The Wonder Years,The Early Girl, The Fiery Furnace, Musical Comedy Murders of 1940, The Holy Terror, The View from Here, Fiery Furnace*, Bdwy in *Agnes of God* (1983).

KOKA, JULIETTE. Born April 4, 1930 in Finland. Attended Helsinki Dramatic Arts school. Debut 1977 OB in *Piaf...A Remembrance*, for which she received a Theatre World Award, followed by *Ladies and Gentlemen, Jerome Kern, Salon, The Concert that Could Have Been*, Bdwy in *All Star Players Club Centennial Salute* (1989).

KOLINSKI, JOSEPH. Born June 26, 1953 in Detroit, MI. Attended U. Detroit. Bdwy debut 1980 in *Brigadoon*, followed by *Dance a Little Closer, The Human Comedy* (also OB), *The Three Musketeers, Les Miserables*, OB in *HiJinks!, Picking up the Pieces*.

KORBICH, EDDIE. Born Nov. 6, 1960 in Washington, DC. Graduate Boston Consv. Debut 1985 OB in *A Little Night Music*, followed by *Flora the Red Menace, No Frills Revue, The Last Musical Comedy, Godspell, Sweeney Todd, Assassins, Casino Paradise, Gifts of the Magi, Eating Raoul*, Bdwy in *Sweeney Todd* (1989), *Singin' in the Rain, Carousel* (1994).

KOREY, ALIX. (formerly Alexandra) Born May 14 in Brooklyn, NY. Graduate Columbia U. Debut 1976 OB in *Fiorello!*, followed by *Annie Get Your Gun, Jerry's Girls, Rosalie in Concert, America Kicks Up Its Heels, Gallery, Feathertop, Bittersuite, Romance in Hard Times, Songs You Might Have Missed, Forbidden Broadway 10th Anniversary, Camp Paradox, Cinderella* (LC), *The Best of the West*, Bdwy in *Hello Dolly* (1978), *Show Boat* (1983), *Ain't Broadway Grand*.

KRAMER, JOHN. Born July 9, 1938 in NYC. Attended Bucknell U. Debut 1966 OB in *The Kitchen*, followed by *Viet Rock, America Hurrah*, Bdwy in *Of Love Remembered, Hadrian VII, A Patriot for Me, Lady in the Dark in Concert*.

KUHN, JUDY. Born May 20, 1958 in NYC. Graduate Oberlin Col. Debut 1958 OB in *Pearls*, followed by *The Mystery of Edwin Drood, Rodgers & Hart Revue*, Bdwy in *Edwin Drood* (1985), *Rags, Les Miserables, Chess, Two Shakespearean Actors, She Loves Me*.

KUNKLE, CONNIE. Born April 4, 1958 in Memphis, TN. Graduate Ohio U. Debut 1985 OB in *Mahattan Serenade*, Bdwy in *Les Miserables*.

KURTZ, MARCIA JEAN. Born in The Bronx, NYC. Juilliard graduate. Debut 1966 OB in *Jonah*, followed by *American Hurrah, Red Cross, Muzeeka The Effect of Gamma Rays..., The Year Boston Won the Pennant, The Mirror, The Orphan, Action, The Dybbuk, Ivanov, What's Wrong with This Picture?, Today I Am a Fountain Pen, The Chopin Playoffs, Loman Family Picnic, Human Nature, When She Danced, The Workroom, The Cowboy the Indian and the Fervent Feminist, Extensions*, Bdwy in *The Chinese and Dr. Fish* (1970), *Thieves, Execution of Justice*.

KUSSACK, ELAINE. Born Dec. 30 Brooklyn, NY. Graduate Hunter Col., Columbian U. Bdwy debut 1969 in *Fiddler on the Roof*, followed by *The Flowering Peach* (1994), OB in *Boogie Room, Bargain of the Century, The Medium*.

KUX, BILL. Born June 26, 1953 in Detroit, MI. Graduate Cal. Inst. Of Arts, Yale U. Debut 1984 OB in *The Philanthropist*, followed by *Loose Ends, Absent Friends, The Mysteries?, Little Red Ridding Hood*, Bdwy in *Ain't Broadway Grand* (1993).

LaCOY, DEBORAH. (a.k.a. Debra) Born Oct. 20, 1963 in Worcester, MA. Graduate Boston U. Debut 1988 OB in *What abouth Love*, followed by *Insatiable/Temporary People, The Workroom*, Bdwy in *A Streetcar Named Desire* (1992).

LACY, TOM. Born Aug. 30, 1933 in NYC. Debut 1965 OB in *The Fourth Pig*, followed by *The Fantasticks, Shoemakers Holiday, Love and Let Love, The Millionairess, Creatures of Passion, The Real Inspector Hound, Enemies, Flying Blind, Abel & Bela/Archtruc*, Bdwy in *Last of the Red Hot Lovers* (1971), *Two Shakesperean Actors, Timon of Athens, The Government Inspector.*

LAGE, JORDAN. Born Feb. 17, 1963 in Palo Alto, CA. Graduate NYU. Debut 1988 OB in *Boy's Life*, followed by *Three Sisters, The Virgin Molly, Distant Fires, Macbeth, Yes But So What?, The Blue Hour, Been Taken, The Woods, Five Very Live, Hot Keys, As Sure as You Live, The Arrangement, The Lights, Shaker Heights*, Bdwy in *Our Town* (1989).

LAGERFELT, CAROLINE. Born September 23 in Paris, Fr.. Graduate AADA. Bdwy debut 1971 in *The Philanthropist*, followed by *4 on a Garden, Jockey Club Stakes, The Constant Wife, Otherwise Engaged, Betrayal, The Real Thing, A Small Family Business*, OB in *Look Back in Anger, Close of Play, Sea, Anchor, Quartermaine's Terms, Other Places, Phaedra Britanica, Swim Visit, Creditors*.

LAMB, MARY ANN. Born July 4, 1959 in Seattle, WA. Attended Neighborhood Playhouse. Bdwy debut 1985 in *Song and Dance*, followed by *Starlight Express, Jerome Robbins' Broadway, The Goodbye Girl, Fiorello! in Concert*.

LAMBERT, JULIET. Born Jan. 15, 1964 in MA. Graduate Middlebury Col. Debut 1989 OB in *Genesis*, followed by *Hello Again*, Bdwy in *Meet Me in St. Louis* (1989), *Passion*.

LAMBERT, ROBERT. Born Jul. 28, 1960 in Ypsilanti, MI. Graduate Wayne State U. Bdwy debut 1989 in *Gypsy*, for which he received a Theatre World Award and returned in 1991, OB in *Unfinished Song, Forever Plaid*.

Larry Hansen   Nancy Hower   Robin Haynes   Marceline Hugot   Philip Hernandez   Anette Hunt

Robert Hock   Mary Illes   Philip Hoffman   Suzanne Ishee   Earle Hyman   Dana Ivey

Bill Irwin   Ibi Janko   Ken Jennings   Bella Jarrett   Page Johnson   Cherry Jones

Robert Katims   Lanie Kazan   Stacy Keach   Gretchen Kingsley-Weihe   Brian Kerwin   Lily Knight

Philip Lehl   Alix Korey   Ron Leibman   Judy Kuhn   John Leone   Linda Lavin

LAMBERTI, VINCENT. Born Sept. 8, 1965 in Hackensack, NJ. Graduate Skidmore Col., RADA. Debut 1991 OB in *Dracula*, followed by *Romeo and Juliet*.

LaMOTT, NANCY. Born Dec 30, 1951 in Saginaw, MI. Debut 1984 OB in *It's Better with a Band*, followed by *An Evening with Dietz & Schwartz*, Bdwy in *The Best Little Whorehouse Goes Public*.

LANE, GENETTE. Born October 13, 1940 in Brooklyn, MD. Attended Peabody Consv., Am. Th. Wing. OB in *Peter Rabbit, The Adventures of High Jump, The Drunkard, Ruddigore, Wuthering Heights, Show Me Where the Good Times Are*, Bdwy 1977 in *Knickerbocker Holiday*.

LANE, NATHAN. Born Feb. 3, 1956 in Jersey City, NJ. Debut 1978 OB in *A Midsummer Night's Dream, Love, Measure for Measure, Claptrap, The Common Pursuit, In a Pig's Valise, Uncounted Blessings, The Film Society, The Lisbon Traviata, Bad Habits, Lips Together Teeth Apart*, Bdwy in *Present Laughter* (1982), *Merlin, Wind in the Willows, Some Americans Abroad, On Borrowed Time, Guys and Dolls, Laugher on the 23rd Floor.*

LANGE, ANN. Born June 24, 1953 in Pipestone, MN. Attended Carnegie-Mellon U. Debut 1979 OB in *Rats Nest*, followed by *Hunting Scenes from Lower Bavaria, Crossfire, Linda Her and the Fairy Garden, Little Footsteps, 10th Young Playwrights Festival, Jeffrey, The Family of Mann*, Bdwy in *The Survivor* (1981), *The Heidi Chronicles.*

LANGELLA, FRANK. Born Jan. 1, 1940 in Bayonne, NJ. Graduate Syracuse U. Debut 1963 OB in *The Immoralist*, followed by *The Old Glory, Good Day, The White Devil Yerma, Iphigenia in Aulis, A Cry of Players, Prince of Homburg, After the Fall, The Tempest, Booth*, Bdwy in *Seascape* (1975), *Dracula, Amadeus, Passion, Design for Living, Hurlyburly, Sherlock's Last Case.*

LANNING, JERRY. Born May 17, 1943 in Miami, FL. Graduate U. S. Cal. Bdwy debut 1966 in *Mame*, for which he received a Theatre World Award, followed by 1776, *Where's Charley?, My Fair Lady, Anna Karenina, Timon of Athens, The Government Inspector*, OB in *Memphis Store Bought Teeth, Berlin to Broadway, Sextet, Isn't It Romantic?, Paradise, Emerald City.*

LARSEN, LIZ. Born Jan. 16, 1959 in Philadelphia, PA. Attended Hofstra U. SUNY/Purchase. Bdwy debut 1981 in *Fiddler on the Roof*, followed by *Starmites, A Little Night Music*, (NYCO/LC), *The Most Happy Fella, Damn Yankees*, OB in *Kuni Leml, Hamlin, Personals, Starmites, Company, After These Messages, One Act Festival, The Loman Family Picnic, Teibele and Her Demon.*

LARSON, JILL. Born Oct. 7, 1947 in Minneapolis, MN. Graduate Hunter Col. Debut 1980 OB in *These Men*, followed by *Peep, Serious Business, It's Only a Play, Red Rover, Enter a Free Man, Scooncat, Dearly Departed, ..the Lost Dreams..,* Bdwy in *Romantic Comedy* (1980), *Death and the King's Horseman* (LC).

LARSON, LISBY. Born October 23, 1951 in Washington, DC. Graduate U. KS. Debut 1976 OB in *The Boys from Syracuse*, followed by *Some Enchanted Evening, Desire, The 5 O'Clock Girl, Eileen* (in concert), *The Firefly* (in concert), *Exit Music.*

LAUGHLIN, SHARON. Graduate U. WVA. Bdwy debut 1964 in *One by One*, followed by *The Heiress*, OB in *Henry IV, Huui Huui, Mod Donna, Subject to Fits, The Minister's Black Veil, Esther, Rag Doll, Four Friends, Heartbreak House, Marching Song, Declassee, Frozen Assets, Hamlet, Waiting at the Water's Edge.*

LAUREANO, PAUL. Born December 26 in Hartford, CT. Graduate Hartt School of Music. Debut 1988 in *Chess*, followed by *The Phantom of the Opera*, OB in *Fiorello!* (in concert), *Allegro* (in concert).

LAUREN, JULIE. Born in NYC. Graduate Dartmouth Col. *Neighborhood Playhouse*. Debut 1993 OB in *The Survivor.*

LAURENCE, PAULA. Born Jan. 25th in Brooklyn, NY. Bdwy debut 1936 in *Horse Eats Hat*, followed by *Dr. Faustus, Junior Miss, Something for the Boys, One Touch of Venus, Cyrano de Bergerac, The Liar, Season in the Sun, Tovarich, The Time of Your Life, Beggar's Opera, Hotel Paradiso, Night of the Iguana, Have I Got a Girl for You, Ivanov, Rosalie, in Concert*, OB in *7 Days of Morning, Roberta* (in concert), *One Touch of Venus, Coming of Age in SoHo, George White's Scandals, Sitting Pretty, Mexican Hayride, After the Ball.*

LAVIN, LINDA. Born October 15, 1939 in Portland, ME. Graduate Wm. & Mary Col. Bdwy debut 1962 in *A Family Affair* followed by *Riot Act, The Game Is Up, Hotel Passionata, It's a Bird It's Superman!, On a Clear Day You Can See Forever, Something Different, Cop-Out, Last of the Red Hot Lovers, Story Theatre, The Enemy Is Dead, Broadway Bound, Gypsy* (1990), *The Sisters Rosensweig*, OB in *Wet Paint* (1965) for which she received a Theatre World Award.

LAWLESS, WENDY. Born May 8, 1960 in Kansas City MO. Attended Boston U., NYU. Debut 1989 OB in *La Vie en Rose*, followed by *Midnight Rodeo, Pagan Day, Dearly Departed, The Matchmaker, All in the Timing*, Bdwy in *The Heidi Chronicles.*

LAWRENCE, CAROL. Born September 5, 1935 in Melrose Park, IL. Bdwy debut in *New Faces of 1952*, followed by *Plain and Fancy, South Pacific* (CC), *Shangri-La, Ziegfeld Follies of 1957, West Side Story* for which she received a Theatre World Award, *Saratoga, Subways Are for Sleeping, Night Life, Rockette Spectacular, Kiss of the Spider Woman.*

LAWRENCE, STEPHANIE. Born December 16, 1956 in Newcastle-upon-Tyne, England. Attended RADA. Bdwy debut 1993 in *Blood Brothers*, for which she received a Theatre World Award.

LAWRENCE, TASHA. Born January 31, 1967 in Alberta, Can. Graduate U. of Guelph. 1992 OB in *Loose Ends*, followed by *Cowboy in His Underwear,*

Ten Blocks on the Camino Real, 3 by Wilder, Who will Carry the Word? Bdwy in *Wilder Wilder Wilder* (1993).

LAWRENCE, YVETTE. Born Mar. 3, 1964 in NYC. Graduate Mt. St. Vincent Col., AADA. Bdwy debut 1991 in *Nick & Nora*, followed by OB in *Bring in the Morning.*

LAWSON, LEIGH. Born July 21, 1943 in Warwickshire, Eng. Attended RADA. Debut 1989 in *Merchant of Venice*, followed by *Macbeth.*

LEACH, NICOLE. Born May 10, 1979 in New Jersey. Debut 1994 OB in *Bring in the Morning.*

LEAVEL, BETH. Born Nov. 1, 1955 in Raleigh, NC. Graduate Meredith Col., UNC/Greensboro. Debut 1982 OB in *Applause*, followed by *Promises Promises, Broadway Juke Box, Unfinished Song*, Bdwy in *42nd Street* (1984), *Crazy for You.*

LEE, KAREN TSEN. Born in NYC. Graduate Hunter Col. OB in *Letters to a Student Revolutionary* (1991), *A Doll's House, Much Ado about Nothing, Macbeth, Desert Rites.*

LEE, KATHRYN. Born Sept. 1, 1926 in Denison, TX. Bdwy in *Helen Goes to Troy, Laffing Room Only, Are You With It?, Allegro, As the Girls Go*, OB in *Tartuffe, Arabian Nights.*

LEE, MARY. (formerly M. Lee-Aranas) Born Sept. 23, 1959 in Taipei, Taiwan. Graduate U. Ottowa. Debut 1984 OB in *Empress of China*, followed by *A State without Grace, Return of the Phoenix, Yellow Is My Favorite Color, The Man Who Turned into a Stick, The Imposter, Rosie's Cafe, Three Sisters, The Dressing Room, Eating Chicken Feet.*

LEEDS, JORDAN. Born Nov. 29,1961 in Queens, NYC. Graduate SUNY/Binghamton. Bdwy debut 1987 in *Les Miserables*, followed by OB in *Beau Jest.*

LEGUIZAMO, JOHN. Born July 22, 1965. Attended NYU. Debut 1987 OB in *La Puta Vida*, followed by *A Midsunner Night's Dream, Parting Gestures, She First Met Her Parents on the Subway, Mambo Mouth, Spic-O-Rama, House of Buggin*, 1993 recipient of Special Theatre World Award.

LEHL, PHILIP. Born April 29, 1964 in Terra Haute, IN. Graduate Drake U., Juilliard. Bdwy debut 1993 in *Blood Brothers*, followed by *The Kentucky Cycle.*

LEHMAN, JEANNE. Born September 14 in Woodland, CA. Graduate U. Cal., San Francisco. Debut 1972 OB in *The Drunkard*, followed by *Leave It to Jane, Oh Lady Lady!, Zip Goes a Million, Oh Boy!, No No Nanette, Company, Getting Married, The Mayor Musicals, Milk and Honey*, Bdwy in *Irene* (1973), *Rodgers and Hart, Going Up, A Musical Jubilee, Jerome Kern Goes to Hollywood.*

LEIBMAN, RON. Born October 11, 1937 in NYC. Attended Ohio Wesleyan Col., Actors Studio. Bdwy debut 1963 in *Dear Me the Sky is Falling*, followed by *Bicycle Ride to Nevada, The Deputy, We Bombed in New Haven* for which he received a Theatre World Award, *Cop-Out, I Ought to Be in Pictures, Doubles, Rumors, Angels in America*, OB in *The Academy, John Brown's Body, Scapin, The Premise, Legend of Lovers, Dead End, Poker Session, Transfers, Room Service, Love Two, Rich and Famous, Children of Darkness, Non Pasquale, Give the Bishop My Faint Regards.*

LENOX, ADRIANE. Born Sept. 11, 1956 in Memphis, TN. Graduate Lambuth Col. Bdwy debut 1979 in *Ain't Misbehavin*, followed by *Dreamgirls, Beehive, Merrily We Roll Along, The America Play.*

LEONARD, ROBERT SEAN. Born February 28, 1969 in Westwood, NJ. Debut 1985 OB in *Sally's Gone She Left Her Name*, followed by *Coming of Age in Soho, Beach House, Young Playwrights Festival, When She Danced, Romeo and Juliet, Pitching to the Star, Good Evening*, Bdwy in *Brighton Beach Memoirs* (1985), *Breaking the Code, The Speed of Darkness, Candida.*

LEONE, JOHN. Born April 7, 1964 in Weymouth, MA. Graduate Hofstra U. Bdwy debut 1991 in *Les Miserables*, OB in *Brimstone, Avenue X.*

LESLIE, BETHEL. Born Aug. 3, 1929 in NYC. Bdwy debut 1944 in *Snafu*, followed by *Years Ago, The Wisteria Trees, Goodbye My Fancy, Time of the Cuckoo, Mary Rose, Brass Ring, Inherit the Wind, Catch Me If You Can, But Seriously, Long Day's Journey into Night*, OB in *The Aunts, The March on Russia, Sand/Finding the Sun.*

LESSNER, JOANNE. Born September 23, 1965 in NYC. Graduate Yale U. Debut 1990 OB in *Romeo and Juliet*, followed by *You're Gonna Love Tomorrow, Company, The High Life* (in concert), *Love Life, Hamlet-The Anti-Musical, Love's Labours Lost, The Mayor Musicals, Arabian Nights.*

LEWIS, MARCIA. Born Aug. 18, 1938 in Melrose, MA. Attended U. Cinn. OB in *The Impudent Wolf, Who's Who Baby, God Bless Coney, Let Yourself Go, Romance Language, When She Danced*, Bdwy in *The Time of Your Life, Hello Dolly!, Annie, Rags, Roza, Orpheus Descending, Gypsy* (1991), *Grease.*

LEWIS, VICKI. Born March 17, 1969 in Cincinnati, OH. Graduate Cinn. Consv. Bdwy debut 1982 in *Do Black Patent Leather Shoes Really Reflect Up?*, followed by *Wind in the Willows, Damn Yankees*, OB in *Snoopy, A Bundle of Nerves, Angry Housewives, 1-2-3-4-5, One Act Festival, The Love Talker, Buzzsaw Berkeley, Marathon '90, The Crucible, I Can Get It for You Wholesale, Don Juan and the Non Don Juan.*

LEYDEN, LEO. Born January 28, 1929 in Dublin, Ireland. Attended Abbey Theatre School. Bdwy debut 1960 in *Love and Libel*, followed by *Darling of the Day, Mundy Scheme, The Rothschilds, Capt. Brassbound's Conversion, The Plough and the Stars, Habeas Corpus, Me and My Girl, The Merchant of Venice, Saint Joan Timon of Athens, The Government Inspector*, OB in *The Cat and the Fiddle.*

LI, LISA ANN. Born August 6, 1966 in Dayton, OH. Graduate Boston U. Bdwy debut 1992 in *A Little Hotel on the Side*, followed by OB in *Wilderness.*

LIN, BEN. Born Sept. 28, 1934 in Shanghai, China. Graduate U. PA.,

Temple U. Debut 1986 OB in *The Impostor,* followed by *Eating Chicken Feet.*

LINEHAN, ROSALEEN. Born Jan. 6, 1937 in Dublin, Ire. Graduate U. Dublin. Bdwy debut in *Dancing at Lughnasa* (1991), followed by *Mother of all the Behans (OB).*

LINARES, CARLOS. Born July 26, 1954 in El Salvador, C.A. Attended Lehman Col. Debut 1988 OB in *Senora Carrar's Rifles,* followed by *Tafpoletigermosquitos at Mulligan's.*

LINES, MARION SYBIL. Born Feb. 10th in London , Eng. Attended Central School. Debut 1976 OB in *The Philanderer,* followed by *Claw, The Penultimate Problem of Sherlock Holmes, The Wit to Woo, The Team, Quartermaine's Terms, Rockaby, Crimes of Vautrain,* Bdwy in *London Assurance* (1974), *Bedroom Farce, Aren't We All, Lettice and Lovage, White Liars/Black Comedy.*

LINN-BAKER, MARK. Born June 17, 1954 in St. Louis, MO. Attended Yale. Bdwy debut 1985 in *Doonesbury,* followed by *Face Value, Laughter on the 23rd Floor,* OB in *All's Well That Ends Well, Othello, Alice in Concert.*

LIPMAN, DAVID. Born May 12, 1938 in Brooklyn, NY. Graduate L. I. U., Brooklyn Col. Debut 1973 OB in *Moonchildren,* followed by *The Devil's Disciple, Don Juan in Hell, Isn't it Romantic?, Kiss Me Quick, Iron Bars,* Bdwy in *Fools* (1981), *Ain't Broadway Grand, My Favorite Year.*

LoBIANCO, TONY. Born Oct. 19, 1936 in NYC. Bdwy debut 1966 in *The Office,* followed by *Royal Hunt of the Sun, The Rose Tattoo, 90 Day Mistress, The Goodbye People, The View from the Bridge, Hizzoner,* OB in *Threepenny Opera, Answered the Flute, Camino Real, Oh Dad Poor Dad..., Journey to the Day, Zoo Story, Nature of the Crime Incident at Vichy, Tartuffe, Yankees 3 Detroit 0, Big Time, Dreamers.*

LOGAN, BELLINA. Born Sept. 28, 1966 in Los Angeles, CA. Graduate Juilliard. Debut 1988 OB in *Young Playwrights Festival,* followed by *Women and Wallace, Seniority, For Dear Life, Generation X.*

LOMBARD, MICHAEL. Born Aug. 8, 1934 in Brooklyn, NYC. Graduate Brooklyn Col., Boston U. OB in *King Lear, Merchant of Venice, Cages, Pinter Plays, La Turista, Elizabeth the Queen, Room Service, Mert and Phil, Side Street Scenes, Angelo's Wedding, Friends in High Places, What's Wrong with This Picture?, Another Time,* Bdwy in *Poor Bitos* (1964), *The Devils, Gingerbread Lady, Bad Habits, Otherwise Engaged, Awake and Sing, Nick & Nora, Timon of Athens, The Government Inspector.*

LONG, SARAH. Born in Berkeley, CA. Graduate Yale U. Debut 1994 OB in *Hide Your Your Love Away,* Bdwy in *Hedda Gabler* (1994).

LOPEZ, CARLOS. Born May 14, 1963 in Sunnyvale, CA. Attended Cal. State U./Hayward. Debut 1987 OB in *Wish You Were Here,* followed by Bdwy in *The Pajama Game* (1989), *A Chorus Line, Grand Hotel, Guys and Dolls, Grease.*

LORD, CHARMAINE. Born June 5, 1957 in Kingston, Jamaica. Graduate U. Toronto. Debut 1993 OB in *3 by Wilder,* followed by *S. S. Glencairn, Who Will Carry the Word?,* Bdwy in *Wilder Wilder Wilder* (1993)

LOREY, ROB. Born Oct. 16, 1961 in Dumont, NJ. Graduate NYU. Debut 1988 OB in *Ten Percent Revue.* followed by *The Last Days, The Cardigans, Action,* Bdwy in *Aspects of Love* (1990), *Beauty and the Beast.*

LOUDON, DOROTHY. Born Sept. 17, 1933 in Boston, MA. Attended Emerson Col., Syracuse U. Debut 1961 OB in *World of Jules Feiffer,* followed by *The Matchmaker,* Bdwy 1963 in *Nowhere to Go but Up,* for which she received a Theatre World Award, followed by *Noel Coward's Sweet Potato, Fig Leaves Are Falling, Three Men on a Horse, The Women, Annie, Ballroom, West Side Waltz, Noises Off, Jerry's Girls.*

LOUGANIS, GREGORY. Born January 29, 1960 in San Diego, CA. Graduate UMiami, UCal/ Irvine. Debut 1993 OB in *Jeffrey.*

LOVE, VICTOR. Born August 4, 1967 in Camp Lefeune, NC. Debut 1985 OB in *Jonin,* followed by *Richard II, The Colored Museum, Playboy of the West Indies,* Bdwy in *A Few Good Men* (1989).

LOVETT, MARCUS. Born in 1965 in Glen-Ellen, IL. Graduate Carnegie-Mellon U. Bdwy 1987 in *Les Miserables,* followed by *Aspects of Love, Phantom of the Opera, Carousel,* OB in *And the World Goes Round.*

LOVEMAN, LENORE. (a.k.a. Lenore Koven) Born February 23, 1934 in Brooklyn, NY. Attended Columbia U., SUNY. Debut 1954 OB in *Miss Julie,* followed by *Two by Linney, Cafe Crown, The Return, Subways Hallways Rooftops, Where Memories Are Magic and Dreams Invented, The World of Sholem Aleichem, A Backward Glance of Edith Wharton, Academy Street, Greetings,* Bdwy in *Checking Out* (1976).

LOWE, FRANK. Born June 28, 1927 in Appalachia, VA. Attended Sorbonne. Debut 1952 OB in *Macbeth,* followed by *Hotel De Breney, The Lady's Not for Burning, Fox Trot on Gardiner's Bay, As You Like it, A Sleep of Prisoners, Cymbeline, Did Elvis Cry!, Man with a Raincoat, Donkey's Years, Ring Round the Moon!, Moon for the Misbegotten , Twelfth Night, Titus Andronicus.*

LOY, PATRICK. Born Aug. 21, 1961 in Canton, OH. Graduate Cleveland State U. Bdwy debut 1994 in *Beauty and the Beast.*

LUCKINBILL, LAURENCE. Born Nov. 17. 1938 in Ft. Smith, AR. Graduate U. Ark. Catholic U. Bdwy debut 1962 in *A Man for All Seasons,* followed by *Beekman Place, Poor Murderers, A Meeting by the River, The Shadow Box, Chapter 2, Past Tense, Dancing in the End Zone,* OB in *Oedipus Rex, There's a Play Tonight, The Fantasticks, Tartuffe, Boys in the Band, Horesman Pass By, Memory Bank, What the Butler Saw, Alpha Beta, A Prayer for My Daughter, Life of Galileo, Lyndon Johnson, Unfinished Stories.*

LuPONE, ROBERT. Born July 29, 1956 in Brooklyn, NYC. Graduate Juilliard. Bdwy debut 1970 in *Minnie's Boys,* followed by *Jesus Christ Superstar, The Rothschilds, Magic Show, A Chorus Line, Saint Joan, Late Night Comic, Zoya's Apartment,* OB in *Charlie Was Here, Twelfth Night, In*

Connecticut, Snow Orchid, Lemon, Black Angel, The Quilling of Prue, Time Framed, Class 1 Acts, Remembrance, Children of Darkness, Kill, Winter Lies, The Able-Bodied Seaman.

LYLES, LESLIE. Born in Plainfield, NJ. Graduate Monmouth Col., Rutgers U. Debut 1981 OB in *Sea Marks,* followed by *Highest Standard of Living, Vanishing Act, I Am Who I Am, The Arbor, Terry by Terry, Marathon '88, Sleeping Dogs, Nebraska, My House Play, Life during Wartime, Angel of Death, Sam I Am, The Workroom,* Bdwy in *Night and Day* (1979), *Hide and Seek, The Real Thing.*

LYNCH, MICHAEL SUTHERLAND. Born November 14, 1964 in El Paso, TX. Graduate Manhattan School of Music. Bdwy debut 1989 in *Jerome Robbins' Broadway,* followed by *Fiddler on the Roof* (1990), *Starmites, Les Miserables* (1993) OB in *How to Write a Play.*

MA, JASON. Born in Palo Alto, CA. Graduate UCLA. Bdwy debut 1989 in *Chu Chem,* followed by *Prince of Central Park, Shogun: The Musical, Miss Saigon* OB in *Wilderness* (1994).

MacINTOSH, JOAN. Born November 25, 1945 in NJ. Graduate Beaver Col., NYU. Debut 1969 OB in *Dyonysus in '69,* followed by *Macbeth, The Beard, Tooth of the Crime, Mother Courage, The Marilyn Project, Seneca's Oedipus, St. Joan of the Stockyards, Wonderland in Concert, Dispatchers, Endgame, Killings on the Last Line, Request Concert, 3 Acts of Recognition, Consequence, Whispers, Cymbeline, Night Sky, A Bright Room Called Day, All's Well That Ends Well,* Bdwy in *Our Town* (1989), *Orpheus Descending, The Sea Gull, Abe Lincoln in Illinois.*

MACKAY, LIZBETH. Born Mar. 7 in Buffalo, NY. Graduate Adelphi U., Yale. Bdwy debut 1981 in *Crimes of the Heart,* for which she received a Theatre World Award, followed by *Death and the Maiden, Abe Lincoln in Illinois,* OB in *Kate's Diary, Tales of the Lost Formicans, Price of Fame, The Old Boy.*

MACKENZIE, JAMIE. Born Aug. 30, 1959 in Saginaw, MI. Attended Dartmouth Col. Bdwy debut 1993 in *My Fair Lady.*

MACKLIN, ALBERT. Born November 18, 1958 in Los Angeles, CA. Graduate StanfordU. Debut 1983 in *Doonesbury,* followed by *The Floating Light Bulb, I Hate Hamlet,* OB in *Ten Little Indians, Poor Little Lambs, Anteroom, Finding Donis Anne, The Library of Congress, Howling in the Night, Fortinbras, The Houseguests, Jeffrey, Hide Your Love Away.*

MacLEOD, MARY. Born in Vancouver, Can. Attended British Columbia U. Bdwy debut 1949 in *The Shop at Sly Corner,* followed by *The Madwomen of Chaillot, With a Silk Thread, Fiorello in Concert.*

MacNICOL, PETER. Born April 10 in Dallas, TX. Attended U. MN. Bdwy debut 1981 in *Crimes of the Heart,* for which he received a Theatre World Award, followed by *White Liars/Black Comedy,* OB in *Found a Peanut, Rum and Coke, Twelfth Night, Richard II, The Spring Thing, Human Nature.*

MacVITTIE, BRUCE. Born Oct. 14, 1956, in Providence, RI. Graduate Boston U. Bdwy debut 1983 in *American Buffalo,* followed by OB in *California Dog Fight, The Worker's Life, Cleveland and Halfway Back, Marathon '87, One of the Guys, Young Playwrights '90, A Darker Purpose, A Body of Water.*

MAHOWALD, JOSEPH. Born in Huron, SD. Attended U. SD, U. TX., U. Cinn. Debut 1990 OB in *Antigone,* followed by *The Little Prince,* Bdwy in *Les Miserables* (1992).

MAIER, CHARLOTTE. Born Jan. 29, 1956 in Chicago, IL. Graduate Northwestern U. Debut 1984 OB in *Balm in Gilead,* Bdwy in *Abe Lincoln in Illinois* (1993), *Picnic* (1984).

MAILER, STEPHEN. Born Mar. 10, 1966 in New York City. Attended Middlebury Col., NYU. Debut OB 1989 in *For Dear Life,* followed by *What's Wrong with This Picture?, Peacetime, Innocents Crusade,* Bdwy 1993 in *Laughter on the 23rd Floor.*

MALAS, SPIRO. Born Jan. 28,1933 in Baltimore, MD. Graduate Towson State U. Bdwy debut 1992 in *Most Happy Fella,* for which he received a Theatre World Award, OB in *Oklahoma!,* (NYCO/LC), followed by *Johnny Pye and the Foolkiller, Milk and Honey.*

MacDONALD, TIM. Born March 24 1962 in Washington, DC. Attended American U., Juilliard. Bdwy debut 1992 in *Two Shakespearean Actors,* followed by *Timon of Athens, The Government Inspector.*

MacINTYRE, MARGUERITE. Born in Detroit, MI. Graduate U. S. Cal., RADA. Debute 1988 OB in *Some Summer Night,* followed by *Weird Romance, The Awakening of Spring, Annie Warbucks.* Bdwy in *City of Angels* (1991).

MANTELLO, JOE. Born Dec. 27, 1962 in Rockford, IL. Debut 1986 OB in *Crackwalker,* followed by *Progress, Walking the Dead, The Baltimore Waltz,* Bdwy in *Angels in America* (1993).

MANDVIWALA, AASIF. Born March 5 1966 in Bombay, India. Gradaute U. S. Fla. Debut 1994 OB in *SubUrbia.*

MANHEIM, CAMRYN. Born March 8, 1961 in Caldwell, NJ. Graduate U. Cal./Santa Cruz, NYU. Debut 1987 OB in *Stella* followed by *Alice in Wonderland, Henry IV Parts I & II, Woyzeck, St. Joan of the Stockyards.*

MANIS, DAVID. Born Nov. 24, 1959 in Ann Arbor, MI. Graduate U. Wash. Debut 1983 OB in *Pericles,* followed by *Pieces of Eight, A New Way to Pay Old Debts, As You Like It, The Skin of Our Teeth, And They Dance Real Slow in Jackson, Rough Crossing Starting Monday, Henry IV Parts I & II,* Bdwy 1993 in *Abe Lincoln in Illinois.*

MANLEY, MARK. Born July 10, 1954 in Newark, NJ. Attended Jersey City State Col. Debut 1979 OB in *Mary,* Bdwy in *Fiddler on the Roof* (1981), *The Best Little Whorehouse in Texas Goes Public.*

MANN, TERRENCE. Born in 1951 in Kentucky. Graduate N.C. Sch. Of Arts. Bdwy debut 1980 in *Barnum,* followed by *Cats, Rags, Les Miserables,*

Jerome Robbins' Broadway, Beauty and the Beast, OB in *A Night at the Fights, The Queen's Diamond, Assassins.*

MARA, MARY. Born Sept. 21, 1960 in Syracuse, NY. Graduate Yale U. Debut 1990 OB in *Moving Targets,* followed by *Twelfth Night, Mad Forest, And Baby Makes 7, Kindertransport.*

MARCHAND, NANCY. Born June 19, 1928 in Buffalo, NY. Graduate Carnegie Tech. U. Debut 1951 in *Taming of the Shrew,* followed by *The Merchant of Venice, Much Ado about Nothing, Three Bags Full, After the Rain, The Alchemist, Yerma, Cyrano, Mary Stuart, Enemies, The Plough and the Stars, 40 Carats, And Miss Reardon Drinks a Little, Veronica's Room, Awake and Sing, Morning's at 7, The Octette Bridge Club, After the Fall, Cinderella (NYCO.LC), White Liars/Black Comedy,* OB in *The Balcony, Children, Awake and Sing, The Cocktail Hour, Love Letters, Taken in Marriage, Sister Mary Ignatius.., The End of the Day, A Darker Purpose.*

MARCUS DANIEL. Born May 26, 1955 in Redwood City, CA. Graduate Boston U. Bdwy debut 1981 in *Pirates of Penzance,* OB in *La Boheme, Kuni Leml, A Flash of Lightning, The Pajama Game, Gunmetal Blues, The Merchant of Venice.*

MARDIROSIAN, TOM. Born Dec. 14, 1947 in Buffalo, NY. Graduate U. Buffalo. Debut 1976 OB in *Gemini,* followed by *Grand Magic, Losing Time, Passione, Success and Succession, Groud Zero Club, Cliffhanger, Cap and Bells, The Normal Heart, Measure for Measure, Largo Desolato, The Good Coach, Subfertile,* Bdwy in *Happy End (1977), Magic Show, My Favorite Year.*

MARGOLIS, MARK. Born Nov. 26, 1939 in Malta. Attended Temple U. Bdwy debut 1962 in *Infidel Caesar,* followed by *The World of Sholom Aleichem,* OB in *Second Avenue Rag, My Uncle Sam, The Golem, The Big Knife, Days to Come, The Crimes of Vautrin, Balm in Gilead, Cross Dressing in the Depression, Three Americanisms, Moe's Lucky 7.*

MARGULIES, DAVID. Born Feb. 19, 1937 in NYC. Graduate CCNY. Debut 1958 OB in *Golden Six,* followed by *Six Characters in Search of an Author, Tragical Historie of Dr. Faustus, Tango, Little Murders, Seven Days of Mourning, La Analysis, An Evening with the Poet Senator, Kid Champion, The Man with the Flower in His Mouth, Old Tune, David and Paula, Cabal of Hypocrites, The Perfect Party, Just Say No, George Washington Dances, I'm with Ya Duke, The Treatment,* Bdwy in *The Iceman Cometh (1973), Zalmen or the Madness of God, Comedians, Break a Leg, West Side Waltz, Brighton Beach Memoirs, Conversations with My Father.*

MARINEAU, BARBARA. Born Aug. 22 in Detroit, MI. Graduate W. MI. U. Bdwy debut 1977 in *Shenandoah,* followed by *The Best Little Whorehouse in Texas, Beauty and the Beast,* OB in *I'm Getting My Act Together (1981), Bittersuite, Witch of Wall Street, Our American Cousin, Silas.*

MARKELL, JODIE. Born Apr. 13, 1959 in Memphis, TN. Attended Northwestern U. Debut 1984 OB in *Balm in Gilead,* followed by *Carring School Children, UBU, Sleeping Dogs, Machinal, Italian American Reconciliation, Moe's Lucky 7.*

MARKS, JACK R. Born Feb. 28, 1935 in Brooklyn, NY. Debut 1975 OB in *Hamlet,* followed by *A Midsummer Night's Dream, Getting Out, Basic Training of Pavlo Hummel, We Bombed in New Haven, Angel Street, Birthday Party, Tarzan and Boy, Goose and Tom Tom, The Carpenters, Appear and Show Cause, Uncle Vanya,* Bdwy in *The Queen and the Rebels, Ma Rainey's Black Bottom.*

MARLAND, STUART. Born Feb. 28, 1959 in Montreal, Can. Attended UCLA. Bdwy debut 1993 in *Cyrano-The Musical,* OB in *Madison Avenue, Birdwatcher, The Brass Jackal, Scoundrel.*

MARQUETTE, CHRISTOPHER. Born Oct. 3, 1984 in Stuart, FL. Bdwy debut 1994 in *An Inspector Calls.*

MARSHALL, AMELIA. Born Apr. 2, 1958 in Albany, GA. Graduate U. TX. Debut 1982 OB in *Applause,* followed by *Group One Acts,* Bdwy in *Harrigan 'n' Hart (1985), Big Deal.*

MARTIN, ANDREA. Born January 15, 1947 in Portland, ME. Graduate Stephens Col., Emerson Col., Sorbonne/Paris. Debut 1980 OB in *Sorrows of Stephen,* followed by *Hardsell, She Loves Me, The Merry Wives of Windsor,* Bdwy in *My Favorite Year (1992)* for which she received a Theatre World Award.

MARTIN, GEORGE N. Born Aug. 15, 1929 in NYC. Bdwy debut 1970 in *Wilson in the Promise Land,* followed by *The Hothouse, Plenty , Total Abandon, Pack of Lies, The Mystery of Edwin Drood, The Crucible, A Little Hotel on the Side, Broken Glass,* OB in *Painting Churches, Henry V, Springtime for Henry.*

MARTIN, W. T. Born Jan. 17 1947 in Providence, RI. Attended Lafayette Col. Debut 1972 OB in *The Basic Training of Pavlo Hummel,* followed by *Ghosts, The Caretaker, Are You Now or..., Fairy Tales of New York, We Won't Pay, Black Elk Lives, The End of the War, A Little Madness, All the Nice People, Enter a Free Man, The Other Side of Newark, Not Showing, Portrait of My Bikini.*

MARTINI, ROBERT LEE. Born July 30, 1960 in NYC. Graduate Wagner Col. Debut 1987 OB in *The Tavern,* followed by *Hamlet, Pericles, Measure for Measure, Ceremony of Innocence.*

MARTINEZ, ALMA. Born March 18, 1953 in Monclova, Coahuila, MX. Graduate Whittier Col., RADA. Debut 1988 OB in *Green Card,* followed by Bdwy 1993 in *In the Summer House.*

MASON, CRAIG. Born July 1, 1950 in Rochester, MN. Graduate Yale U. Debut 1978 OB in *Allegro,* followed by *On a Clear Day You Can See Forever, Anton Chekhov,The Time of Your Life.*

MASON, JACKIE. Born June 9, 1934 in Sheboygan, WI. Bdwy debut 1969 in *A Teaspoon Every Four Hours,* followed by *The World According to Me,*

Jackie Mason Brand New, Politically Incorrect.

MASTERS, PATRICIA. Born Dec. 8, 1952 in Washington, DC. Graduate U. MD. Debut OB 1984 in *Forbidden Broadway,* followed by *Tomfoolery, Caged Hunger.*

MASTROTOTARO, MICHAEL. Born May 17, 1962 in Albany, NY. Graduate NYU. Debut 1984 OB in Victoria Station, followed by *Submarines, Naked Truth/Name Those Names, A Darker Purpose, Hot Keys, City, Escape from Happiness.*

MATTHIESSEN, JOAN. Born Feb. 27, 1930 in Orange, NJ. Graduate Allegheny Col. Debut 1979 OB in *The Art of Dining,* followed by *The Cocktail Party, A Doll House, Summer, The Oil Well, Rutherford & Son, Delicate Dangers.*

MAYER, JERRY. Born May 12, 1941 in NYC. Debut 1968 OB in *Alice in Wonderland,* followed by *L'Ete, Marouf, Trelawny of the Wells, King of the Schnorrers, Mother Courage, You Know Al, Goose and Tom-Tom, The Rivals, For Sale, Two Gentlemen of Verona, Julius Caesar, A Couple with a Cat,* Bdwy in *Much Ado about Nothing (1972), Play Memory.*

MAYO, DON. Born Oct. 4, 1960 in Chicago, IL. Graduate Loyola U. Debut 1988 OB in *Much Ado about Nothing,* followed by *Christina Alberta's Father.*

MAYES, SALLY. Born August 3 in Livingston, TX. Attended U. Houston. Bdwy debut 1989 in *Welcome to the Club,* for which she received a Theatre World Award, followed by *She Loves Me,* OB in *Closer Than Ever.*

MAZZEO, ROGER. Born Oct. 2, 1969 in New Brunswick, NJ. Gradute Montclair State Col. Debut 1994 OB in *Avenue X.*

MAZZIE, MARIN. Born October 9, 1960 in Rockford, IL. Graduate W. MI. U. Debut 1983 OB in *Where's Charley?, And the World Goes Round,* Bdwy in *Big River (1986) Passion.*

McARDLE, ANDREA. Born Nov. 5, 1963 in Philadelphia, PA. Bdwy debut 1977 in *Annie,* for which she received a Theatre World Award, followed by *Starlight Express, Les Miserables,* OB in *They Say It's Wonderful.*

McCANN, CHRISTOPHER. Born Sept. 29, 1952 in New York City. Graduate NYU. Debut 1975 OB in *The Measures Taken,* followed by *Ghosts, Woyzeck, St. Joan of the Stockyards, Buried Child, Dwelling in Milk, Tongues, 3 Acts of Recognition, Don Juan, Michi's Blood, Five of Us, Richard III, The Golem, Kafka Father and Son, Flatbush Faithful, Black Market, King Lear, The Virgin Molly, Mad Forest, Ladies of Fisher Cove, The Lights.*

McCATTY, MARY FRANCES. Born Feb. 1 in Royal Oak, MI. Bdwy debut 1994 in *The Best Little Whorehouse in Texas Goes Public.*

McCLANAHAN, MATT. Born July 1st in Kenmore, NY. Graduate SUNY/Purchase. Debut 1988 OB in *Psycho Beach Party,* followed by *Vampire Lesbians of Sodom, A Little Night Music, Balancing Act, Forever Plaid, Hearts and Voices,* Bdwy in *Les Miserables (1992).*

McCORD, LISA MERRILL. Born March 3, 1962 in Louisville, KY. Graduate Syracuse U. Debut 1986 OB in *Two Gentlemen of Verona,* followed by *As You Like It, No No Nanette,* Bdwy in *Grand Hotel (1990), My Fair Lady (1993).*

McCORMICK, MICHAEL. Born July 24, 1951 in Gary, IN. Graduate Northwestern U. Bdwy debut 1964 in *Oliver!,* followed by *Kiss of the Spider Woman,* OB *Coming Attractions, Tomfoolery, The Regard of Flight, Charlotte's Secret, Half A World Away, In a Pig's Valise, Arturo Ui, Scapin.*

McDONALD, AUDRA ANN. Born July 3, 1970 in Berlin, Ger. Graduate Juilliard. Debut OB 1989 in *Man of La Mancha,* followed by *The Secret Garden, Carousel,* for which she received a 1994 Theatre World Award.

McDONALD, BETH. Born May 25, 1954 in Chicago, IL. Graduate Juilliard. Debut 1981 OB in *A Midsummer Night's Dream,* followed by *The Recruiting Officer, Jungle of Cities, Kennedy at Colonus, Our Own Family, Ancient History,* Bdwy 1993 in *Angels in America.*

McDONALD, TANNY. Born February 13 in Princeton, NJ. Graduate Vassar Col. Debut 1961 OB in *American Savoyards,* followed by *All in Love, To Broadway with Love, Carricknabauna, The Beggar's Opera, Brand, Goodbye, Dan Bailey, Total Eclipse, Gorky, Don Juan Comes Back from the War, Vera with Kate, Francis, On Approval, A Definite Maybe, Temptation, Titus Andronicus, Hamlet, June, Johnny Pye and the Foolkiller,* Bdwy in *Fiddler on the Roof, Come Summer, The Lincoln Mask, Clothes for a Summer Hotel, Macbeth, Man of La Mancha.*

McDONOUGH, ANN. Born Portland, ME. Graduate Towson State U. Debut 1975 OB in *Trelawney of the Wells, Secret Service, Boy Meets Girl, Scribes, Uncommon Women, City Sugar, Fables for Friends, The Dining Room, What I Did Last Summer, The Rise of Daniel Rocket, The Middle Ages, Fighting International Fat, Room Service, The Spring Thing,* Bdwy in *Abe Lincoln in Illinois (1993).*

McDORMAND, FRANCES. Born in 1958 in Illinois. Yale graduate. Debut 1983 OB in *Painting Churches,* followed by *On the Verge, The Swan,* Bdwy in *Awake and Sing (1984), A Streetcar Named Desire (1988), The Sisters Rosensweig.*

McELWEE, THERESA. Born Sept. 14, 1958 in Battle Creek, MI. Graduate E. Mich. U., Yale U. Debut 1989 OB in *Vampire Lesbians of Sodom,* followed by *Phantom Toll Booth, The Green Knight, Portfolio, Hyde in Hollywood, Jeffrey,* Bdwy in *I'm Not Rapport, The Heidi Chronicles.*

McGAVIN, DARREN. Born May 7, 1922 in Spokane, WA. Attended Col. of Pacific. Bdwy debut 1948 in *The Old Lady Says No,* followed by *Death of a Salesman, My Three Angels, The Rainmaker, The Innkeepers, The Lovers, Tunnel of Love, Blood Sweat and Stanley Poole, The King and I, Dinner at 8,* OB in *Cock-a-Doodle-Doo, The Thracian Horses, California Dog Fight, The Night Hank Williams Died, Greetings!*

McGILLIN, HOWARD. Born Nov. 5, 1953 in Los Angeles, CA. Graduate

U. Cal./Santa Barbara. Debut 1984 OB in *La Boheme*, followed by Bdwy in *The Mystery of Edwin Drood* for which he received a Theatre World Award, *Sunday in the Park with George, Anything Goes, 50 Million Frenchmen in Concert, The Secret Garden, She Loves Me, Kiss of the Spider Woman*.

McGIVER, BORIS. Born Jan. 23, 1962 in Cobleskill, NY. Graduate Ithaca Col., SUNY/Cobleskill, NYU. Debut 1994 OB in *Richard II*.

McGRATH, MATT. Born June 11, 1969 in NYC. Attended Fordham U. Bdwy debut 1978 in *Working*, followed by *A Streetcar Named Desire*, OB in *Dalton's Back* (1989), *Amulets Against the Dragon Forces, Life During Wartime, The Old Boy, Nothing Sacred, The Dadshuttle, Fat Men in Skirts*.

McGUIRE, MITCHELL. Born Dec. 26, 1936 in Chicago, IL. Attended Goodman Theatre Sch., Santa Monica City Col. OB in *The Rapists*, (1966), *Go Go God is Dead, Waiting for Lefty, The Bond, Guns to Carrar, Oh! Calcutta!, New York! New York!, What a Life!, Butter and Egg Man, Almost in Vegas, Festival of 1-Acts, Prime Time Punch Line, The Racket*.

McINTYRE, GERRY. Born May 31, 1962 in Grenada, WI. Graduate Montclair State Col. Debut 1985 OB in *Joan of Arc at the Stake* followed by *Homeseekers, Once on This Island, Broadway Jukebox*, Bdwy in *Anything Goes* (1987).

McINTYRE, STEPHEN. Born Nov. 14, 1961 in Fairbanks, AK. Graduate U. Windsor, Can. Bdwy debut 1989 in *Shenandoah*, OB 1994 in *Anton Chekov, The Time of Your Life*.

McKECHNIE, DONNA. Born in November 1944 in Detroit, MI. Bdwy debut 1961 in *How to Succeed in Business*, followed by *Promises Promises, Company, On the Town, Music! Music!, A Chorus Line*, OB in *Wine Untouched, Cut the Ribbons, Annie Warbucks, Fiorello* (in concert).

McLACHLAN, RODERICK. Born September 9, 1960 in Detroit, MI. Graduate Northwestern U. Bdwy debut 1987 in *Death and the King's Horseman* (LC) followed by *Our Town, The Real Inspector Hound, Saint Joan, Timon in Athens, The Government Inspector*, OB in *Madame Bovary, Julius Caesar, Oh Hell!, Hauptmann, Make Up Your Mind*.

McLAREN, CONRAD. Born Nov. 13 in Greenfield, IL. Graduate Ill. Wesleyan U., U. Ia. Debut 1973 OB in *Medea*, followed by *Shay, The Show-Off, Company, Time Steps, Crimes and Dreams, The Trading Post*, Bdwy in *Guys and Dolls* (1993).

McLAUGHLIN, ELLEN. Born Nov.9, 1957 in Cambridge, MA. Graduate Yale U. Debut 1991 OB in *A Bright Room Called Day*, Bdwy in *Angels in America*.

McNAMARA, DERMOT. Born Aug. 24, 1925 in Dublin, Ire. Bdwy debut 1959 in *A Touch of the Poet*, followed by *Philadelphia Here I Come!, Donnybrook, The Taming of the Shrew*, OB in *The Wise Have Spoken, 3 by Synge, Playboy of the Western World, Shadow and Substance, Happy as Larry, Sharon's Grave, A Whistle in the Dark, Red Roses for Me, The Plough and the Stars, Shadow of a Gunman, No Exit, Stephen D., Hothouse, Home Is the Hero, Sunday Morning Bright and Early, Birthday Party, All the Nice People, Roots, Grandchild of Kings, On the Waterfront*.

McNEELY, ANNA. Born June 23, 1950 in Tower Hill, IL. Graduate McKendree Col. Bdwy debut 1982 in *Little Johnny Jones*, followed by *Cats, Gypsy, Beauty and the Beast*.

McVEY, J. MARK. Born January 6, 1958 in Huntington, VA. Graduate Marshall U. Bdwy debut 1991 in *Les Miserables*, OB in *Cafe A Go-Go, Chess, Hey Love A Helluva Town*.

MEISNER, VICKI. Born Aug. 2, 1935 in NYC. Graduate Adelphi Col. Debut 1958 OB in *Blood Wedding*, followed by *The Prodigal, Shakuntala, Nathan the Wise, Decathlon, Afternoon in Las Vegas, The Beauty Part, Trelawny of the Wells, The Rimers of Eldritch*.

MELANCON, CORINNE. Born March 13 in Buffalo, NY. Attended Niagara U. Debut 1984 OB in *Up* in *Central Park*, Bdwy in *Me and My Girl* (1986), *My Fair Lady* (1993).

MELLOR, STEPHEN. Born Oct. 17, 1954 in New Haven, CT. Graduate Boston U. Debut 1980 OB in *Paris Lights*, followed by *Coming Attractions, Plenty, Tooth of the Crime, Shepard Sets, A Country Doctor, Harm's Way, Brightness Falling, Terminal Hip, Dead Mother, A Murder of Crows, Seven Blowjobs, Pericles, The Illusion, The Hyacinth Macaw, Careless Love, Teibele and Her Demon, Terminal Hip, Strange Feet*, Bdwy in *Big River* (1985).

MENDILLO, STEPHEN. Born Oct. 9, 1942 in New Haven, CT. Graduate Colo. Col., Yale U. Debut 1973 OB in *Nourish the Beast*, followed by *Gorky, Time Steps, The Marriage, Loot, Subject to Fits, Wedding Band, As You Like It, Fool for Love, Twelfth Night, Grotesque Lovesongs, Nowhere, Portrait of My Bikini, The Country Girl, The Last Yankee*, Bdwy in *National Health* (1974), *Ah! Wilderness!, A View from the Bridge, Wild Honey, Orpheus Descending, Guys and Dolls*.

METCALF, ALLISON. Born March 3, 1970 in Houston, TX. Graduate Carnegie-Mellon U. Bdwy debut 1994 in *Grease*.

METTNER, JERRY. Born Aug. 21, 1958 in Detroit, MI. Bdwy debut 1982 in *Present Laughter*, OB in *Confessional* (1983), *Look Back in Anger, Jerusalem Mountain, 3 by Wilder, Somewhere I Have Never Traveled, The Eye of the Beholder, Cinoman and Rebeck*.

METZEL, MICHAEL. Born Sept. 18 in Columbus, OH. Graduate Catholic U. Debut 1989 OB in *Wonderful Town*, followed by *Sweethearts, Alice in Wonderland, My Lord What a Morning, The Wise Men of Chelm*.

MEYERS, T. J. Born July 18, 1953 in Pittsburgh, PA. Graduate Phoenix Col., Mesa Col. Bdwy debut 1984 in *Sunday in the Park with George*, followed by *Big River, Prince of Central Park, Metamorphosis, OB in Richard II*.

MILES, SYLVIA. Born Sept. 9, 1934 in NYC. Attended Pratt Inst., Actors

Studio. Debut 1954 OB in *A Stone for Danny Fisher*, followed by *The Iceman Cometh, The Balcony, Chekhov Sketchbook, Matty Moron and Madonna, The Kitchen, Rosenbloom, Nellie Toole & Co., American Night Cry, It's Me Sylvia, American Gothic, Tea with Mommy and Jack, Ruthless!, Sausage Eaters*, Bdwy in *The Riot Act* (1963), *Night of the Iguana*.

MILLER, JUNE. Born June 10, 1934 in West Lawn, PA. Graduate Penn State. OB in *The Flies, Sunday Night Music Hall, While the Iron's Hot, Streets of Confusion, The Boy Friend, The Caller, Black Roses, The Crucible, Where People Gather*, Bdwy in *An Inspector Calls* (1994).

MILLER, PATRICIA. Born Dec. 1, 1950 in Seattle, WA. Graduate U. GA. Debut 1978 OB in *Vanities*, followed by *Pitching the Star*.

MILLIGAN, JACOB TUCK. Born March 25, 1949 in Kansas City, MO. Graduate U. KC. Bdwy debut 1976 in *Equus*, followed by *Crucifer of Blood, The Kentucky Cycle*, OB in *Beowulf, Everybody's Gettin' into the Act*.

MINOT, ANNA. Born in Boston, MA. Attended Vassar Col. Bdwy debut 1942 in *The Strings My Lord Are False*, followed by *The Russian People, The Visitor, The Iceman Cometh, An Enemy of the People, Love of Four Colonels, The Trip to Bountiful, Tunnel of Love, Ivanov, OB in Sands of the Niger, Gettin Out, Vieux Carre, State of the Union, Her Great Match, Rivals, Hedda Gabler, All's Well That Ends Well, Tarfuffe, The Good Natur'd Man, Little Eyolf*.

MITCHELL, ALETA. Born in Chicago. Graduate U. Iowa, Yale U. Bdwy debut 1984 in *Ma Rainey's Black Bottom*, OB in *Approaching Zanzibar, Night Sky, Marvin's Room, Crystal Stairs*.

MITCHELL, BRIAN. Born October 31, 1957 in Seattle, WA. Bdwy debut 1988 in *Mail*, for which he received a Theatre World Award, followed by *Oh Kay!, Jelly's Last Jam, Kiss of the Spider Woman*.

MITCHELL, GREGORY. Born December 9, 1951 in Brooklyn, NY. Graduate Juilliard, Principle with Eliot Feld Ballet before Bdwy debut 1983 in *Merlin*, followed by *Song and Dance, Phantom of the Opera, Dangerous Games, Aspects of Love, Man of La Mancha* (1992), *Kiss of the Spider Woman*, OB in *One More Song One More Dance, Tango Apasionado*.

MITCHELL, JOHN CAMERON. Born April 21, 1963 in El Paso, TX. Attended Northwestern U. Bdwy debut 1985 in *Big River*, followed by *Six Degrees of Separation, The Secret Garden*, OB in *Six Degrees of Separation, The Destiny of Me, Its Our Town Too, Hello Again*.

MOGENTALE, DAVID. Born December 28, 1959 in Pittsburgh, PA. Graduate Auburn U. Debut 1987 OB in *The Signal Season of Dummy Hoy*, followed by *The Holy Note, Killers, Battery, Necktie Breakfast, Under Control, l Act Festival, Charmer*.

MOJICA, DAN. Born June 7, 1962 in San Juan, P.R. Graduate U. Miami. Debut 1983 OB in *The Music Man*, followed by *Singin' in the Rain, Me and My Girl, Beauty and the Beast*.

MONK, DEBRA. Born February 27, 1949 in Middletown, OH. Graduate Frostburg State Col., Southern Methodist U. Bdwy debut 1982 in *Pump Boys and Dinettes*, followed by *Prelude to a Kiss, Redwood Curtain, Picnic*, OB in *Young Playwrights Festival, A Narrow Bed, Oil City Symphony, Prelude to a Kiss, Assassins, Man in His Underwear, Innocents Crusade, Three Hotels*.

MONTANO, ROBERT. Born April 22 in Queens, NYC. Attended Adelphi U. Bdwy debut 1985 in *Cats*, followed by *Chita Rivera + Two, Legs Diamond, Kiss of the Spider Woman*, OB in *The Chosen* (1987), *The Torturer's Visit, How Are Things in Costa del Fuego?, Picture Perfect*.

MOORE, BRUCE. Born Feb. 5, 1962 in Gettysburg, PA. Graduate Cin. Consv. Debut 1986 OB in *Olympus on My Mind*, followed by Bdwy in *Gypsy* (1989), *My Fair Lady* (1993).

MOORE, CHARLOTTE. Born July 7, 1939 in Herrin, IL. Attended Smith Col. Bdwy debut 1972 in *The Great God Brown*, followed by *Don Juan, The Visit, Chemin de Fer, Holiday, Love for Love, Member of the Wedding, Morning's at 7, Meet Me in St. Louis*, OB in *Out of Our Father's House, A Lovely Sunday for Creve Coeur, Summer, Beside the Seaside, The Perfect Party, The Au Pair Man, A Perfect Ganesh*.

MOORE, CRISTA. Born September 17 in Washington, DC. Attended Am. Ballet Th. Schl. Debut 1987 OB in *Birds of Paradise*, followed by Bdwy in *Gypsy* (1989) for which she received a Theatre World Award, *110 in the Shade* (LC/NYCO), *Cinderella* (LC/NYCO), *Crazy For You*, OB in *Rags, Marathon '93, Long Ago and Far Away*.

MOORE, MAUREEN. Born August 12, 1951 in Wallingford, CT. Bdwy debut 1974 in *Gypsy*, followed by *The Moonie Shapiro Songbook, Do Black Patent Leather Shoes Really Reflect Up?, Amadeus, Big River, I Love My Wife, Song and Dance, Les Misérables, Amadeus, Jerome Robbins' Broadway, A Little Night Music* (NYCO), *Falsettos*, OB in *Godspell, Unsung Cole, By Strouse, First Lady Suite*.

MOORE, MELBA. Born Oct. 29, 1945 in NYC. Graduate Montclair State Col. Bdwy debut 1968 in *Hair*, followed by *Purlie*, for which she received a 1970 Theatre World Award, *Timbuktu, Inacent Black*, OB in *Queenie Pie*.

MORAN, DAN. Born July 31, 1953 in Corcoran, CA. Graduate NYU. Debut 1977 OB in *Homebodies*, followed by *True West, Pericles, The Merchant of Venice, The Vampires, Sincerely Forever, The Illusion*.

MORATH, KATHRYN/KATHY. Born March 23, 1955 in Colorado Spirngs, CO. Graduate Brown U. Debut 1980 OB in *The Fantasticks*, followed by *Dulcy, Snapshot, Alice in concert, A Little Night Music, The Little Prince, Professionally Speaking, The Apple Tree, Prom Queens Unchained, All in the Timing*, Bdwy in *Pirates of Penzance* (1982), *Nick & Nora*.

MORFOGEN, GEORGE. Born March 30, 1933 in New York City. Graduate Brown U., Yale. Debut 1957 OB in *The Trial of D. Karamazov*, followed by *Christmas Oratorio, Othello, Good Soldier Schweik, Cave Dwellers, Once in a Lifetime, Total Eclipse, Ice Age, Prince of Homburg*,

225

Leo Leyden	Carol Lawrence	Greg Louganis	Tasha Lawrence	Robert LuPone	Beth Leavel
Michael Lynch	Jeanne Lehman	Joseph Mahowald	Joanne Lessner	Stephen Mailer	Charmaine Lord
Michael Mastrototaro	Lenore Loveman	Jordan Matter	Andrea Martin	Don Mayo	Debra Monk
Bruce Norris	Angela Nevard	Gabriel Olds	Kerry O'Malley	Hugh Panaro	Emma Palzere
Adam Pelty	Lucille Patton	Austin Pendleton	Michele Pawk	Neil Pepe	Dede Pochos

Biography: A Game, Mrs. Warren's Profession, Principia Scriptoriae, Tamara, Maggie and Misha, The Country Girl, Othello, As You Like It (CP), Bdwy in *The Fun Couple* (1962), *Kingdoms, Arms and the Man, An Inspector Calls.*

MORIARTY, MICHAEL. Born Apr. 5, 1941 in Detroit, MI. Graduate Dartmouth, LAMDA. Debut 1963 OB in *Antony and Cleopatra*, followed by *Peanut Butter and Jelly, Long Day's Journey into Night, Henry V, Alfred the Great, Our Father's Failing, G. R. Point., Love's Labour's Lost, Dexter Creed, A Special Providence, Children of the Sun*, Bdwy in *Trial of the Catonsville 9, Find Your Way Home*, for which he received a Theatre World Award, *Richard III, The Caine Mutiny Court Martial, My Fair Lady* (1994).

MORTON, JOE. Born Oct. 18, 1947 in NYC. Attended Hofstra U. Debut 1968 OB in *A Month of Sundays*, followed by *Salvation, Charlie Was Here and Now He's Gone, G. R. Point, Crazy Horse, A Winter's Tale, Johnny on a Spot, A Midsummer Night's Dream, The Recruiting Officer, Oedipus the King, The Wild Duck, Rhinestone, Souvenirs, Cheapside, King John*, Bdwy in *Hair, Two Gentlemen of Verona, Tricks, Raisin* for which he received a Theatre World Award, *Oh Brother!, Honky Tonk Nights, Lady in the Dark in Concert.*

MOSES, BURKE. Born in NYC. Graduate Carnegie-Mellon U. Debut 1986 OB in *Wasted*, followed by *The Way of the World, The Most Happy Fella* (NYC.LC), Bdwy in *Guys and Dolls* (1993), *Beauty and the Beast*, for which he received a 1994 Theatre World Award.

MOSTEL, JOSHUA. Born December 21, 1946 in NYC. Graduate Brandeis U. Debut 1971 OB in *The Proposition*, followed by *More Than You Deserve, The Misanthrope, Rocky Road, The Boys Next Door, A Perfect Diamond*, Bdwy in *Unlikely Heroes, American Millionaire, Texas Trilogy, 3 Penny Opera, My Favorite Year, Flowering Peach.*

MULLALLY, MEGAN. Born Nov. 12, 1958 in Los Angeles, CA. Attended Northwestern U. Bdwy debut 1994 in *Grease.*

MULLINS, MELINDA. Born April 20, 1958 in Clanton, AL. Graduate Mt. Holyoke Col. Juilliard. Bdwy debut 1987 in *Sherlock's Last Case*, followed by *Serious Money, Mastergate*, OB in *Macbeth, The Hideaway Hilton, Traps/Owners, Titus Andronicus.*

MURAOKA, ALAN. Born August 10, 1962 in Los Angeles, CA. Graduate UCLA. Bdwy debut 1988 in *Mail*, followed by *Shogun: The Musical, My Favorite Year, Miss Saigon.*

MURNEY, CHRISTOPHER. Born July 20, 1943 in Narragansett, RI. Graduate U. RI., Penn State U. Bdwy debut 1973 in *Tricks*, followed by *Mack and Mabel*, OB in *As You Like It, Holeville, The Lady or the Tiger, Bathroom Plays, Two Fish in the Sky, Wild Life, Making Movies, Talk about Love.*

MURPHY, DONNA. Born March 7, 1959 in Corona, NY. Attended NYU. Bdwy debut 1979 in *They're Playing Our Song*, followed by *The Human Comedy, The Mystery of Edwin Drood, Passion*, OB in *Francis, Portable Pioneer and Prairie Show, Little Shop of Horrors, A ... My Name is Alice, Showing Off, Privates on Parade, Song of Singapore, Hey Love, Hello Again.*

MURRAY, BRIAN. Born October 9, 1939 in Johannesburg, SA. Debut 1964 OB in *The Knack*, followed by *King Lear, Ashes, The Jail Diary of Albie Sachs, A Winter's Tale, Barbarians, The Purging, A Midsummer Night's Dream, The Recruiting Officer, The Arcata Promise, Candide in Concert, Much Ado about Nothing, Hamlet, Merry Wives of Windsor*, Bdwy in *All in Good Time* (1965), *Rosencrantz and Guildenstern Are Dead, Sleuth, Da, Noises Off, A Small Family Business, Black Comedy.*

MURPHY, SALLY. Born Oct. 12, 1962 in Chicago, IL. Graduate Northwestern U. Bdwy debut 1990 in *The Grapes of Wrath*, followed by *Carousel* (1994).

MURTAUGH, JAMES. Born October 28, 1942 in Chicago, IL. Debut OB in *The Firebugs*, followed by *Highest Standard of Living, Marathon '87, Other People's Money, Marathon '88, I Am a Man*, Bdwy in *Two Shakespearean Actors* (1991).

MURRAY, MIKE. Born Nov. 15, 1950 in Brooklyn, NYC. Graduate Brooklyn Col. Debut 1982 OB in *The Country Wife*, followed by *The Hostage, The Importance of Being Earnest, Uncle Vanya, Arms and the Man, Major Barbara, Deep to Center, Rimers of Eldritch.*

MUTNICK, ANDREW. Born in NYC. Graduate Colorado Col. Bdwy debut 1991 in *I Hate Hamlet*, followed by *The Lights.*

NAGY, KEN. Born Dec. 7, 1963 in Bucks County, PA. Bdwy debut 1992 in *The Most Happy Fella*, followed by *Sally Marr and Her Escorts.*

NAIMO, JENNIFER. Born Oct. 2, 1962 in Oaklawn, IL. Graduate NYU. Debut 1985 OB in *Jack and Jill*, followed by *Bachelor's Wife, Malcolm and Silverstar, Elizabeth and Essex, And the Beat Goes On, Our Lady of the Tortilla, To Whom It May Concern, Amphigory*, Bdwy in *Les Miserables.*

NALBACH, DANIEL. Born May 20, 1937 in Buffalo, NY. Graduate Canisius Col.,U. Pittsburgh. Debut 1986 OB in *Murder on Broadway*, followed by *The Thirteenth Chair, The Cellar, Romeo and Juliet.*

NASTASI, FRANK. Born Jan. 7, 1923 in Detroit, MI. Graduate Wayne U. NYU. Bdwy debut 1963 in *Lorenzo*, OB in *Avanti, OB in Bonds of Interest, One Day More, Nathan the Wise, The Chief Things, Cindy, Escurial, The Shrinking Bride, Macbird, Cakes with the Wine, Metropolitan Madness, Rockaway Boulevard, Scenes from La Vie de Boheme, Agamemnon, Happy Sunset Inc., 3 Last Plays of O'Neill, Taking Steam, Lulu, Body! Body!, Legend of Sharon Shashanova, Enrico IV, Stealing Fire, Mourning Becomes Electra.*

NEUBERGER, JAN. Born Jan. 21 1953 in Amityville, NY. Attended NYU. Bdwy debut 1975 in *Gypsy*, followed by *A Change in the Heir*, OB in *Silk Stockings, Chase a Rainbow, Anything Goes, A Little Madness, Forbidden Broadway, After These Messages, Ad Hock, Rags, Christina Alberta's Father.*

NEUSTADT, TED. Born May 28, 1954 in Baltimore, MD. Graduate NYU, Fordham U. Debut 1990 OB in *Money Talks*, followed by *Jackie, Fore!, EST Marathon 93, All in the Timing.*

NEVARD, ANGELA. Born March 19, 1963 in Montreal, Can. Graduate Skidmore Col. Debut 1988 OB in *Faith Hope and Charity*, followed by *3 by Wilder, Macbeth, The Balcony, Harm's Way, Judgment Day, Tartuffe, Morning Song, Who Will Carry the Word, 'The Sea Plays, Twelfth Night, Camino Real, As You Like It*, Bdwy in *Wilder Wilder Wilder* (1993).

NEWTON, JOHN. Born Nov. 2, 1925 in Grand Junction, CO. Graduate U. Wash. Debut 1951 OB in *Othello*, followed by *As You Like It, Candida, Candaules Commissioner, Sextet, LC Rep's, The Crucible, and A Streetcar Named Desire, The Subject was Roses, The Brass Ring, Hadrian VII, The Best Little Whorehouse in Texas, A Midsummer Night's Dream, Night Games, A Frog in His Throat, Max and Maxie, The Lark, Measure for Measure*, Bdwy in *Weekend, First Monday in October, Present Laughter, Hamlet* (1992), *Abe Lincoln in Illinois.*

NICHOLAW, CASEY. Born October 6, 1992. Attended UCLA. Debut 1986 in *The Pajama Game*, Bdwy in *Crazy for You* (1992) followed by *Best Little Whorehouse Goes Public.*

NIVEN, KIP. Born May 27, 1945 in Kansas City, MO. Graduate Kansas U. Debut 1987 OB in *Company*, followed by *The Golden Apple, Two by Two, Annie Warbucks*, Bdwy in *Chess* (1988), *Nick & Nora.*

NIXON, CYNTHIA. Born April 9, 1966 in New York City. Debut 1980 in *The Philadelphia Story* (LC) for which she received a Theatre World Award followed by *The Real Thing, Hurlyburly, The Heidi Chronicles, Angels in America*, OB in *Lydie Breeze, Hurlyburly, Sally's Gone She Left Her Name, Lemon Sky, Cleveland and Half-Way Back, Alterations, Young Playwrights, Moonchildren, Romeo and Juliet, The Cherry Orchard, The Balcony Scene, Servy-n-Bernice 4Ever, On the Bum, The Illusion.*

NIXON, MARNI. Born February 22 in Altadena, CA. Attended LACC, U.S. Cal., Pasadena Playhouse. Bdwy debut 1952 in *The Girl in Pink Tights*, followed by *My Fair Lady* (1964), OB in *Thank Heaven for Lerner and Loewe, Taking My Turn, Opal, Romeo and Juliet.*

NOLEN, TIMOTHY. Born July 9, 1941 in Rotan, TX. Graduate Trenton State, Col., Manhattan School of Music. Debut in *Sweeney Todd* (1984) with NYC Opera, Bdwy in *Grind* (1985), followed by *Phantom of the Opera, Cyrano the Musical, Bdwy Classics at Carnegie Hall.*

NOLTE, BILL. Born June 4, 1953 in Toledo, OH. Graduate Cin. Consv. Debut OB in *Wonderful Town* (1977), Bdwy in *Cats* (1985), *Me and My Girl, The Secret Garden, Joseph and the Amazing Technicolor Dreamcoat* (1993).

NOONAN, TOM. Born April 12, 1951 in Greenwich, CT. Graduate Yale U. Debut 1978 OB in *Buried Child*, followed by *The Invitational, Farmyard, The Breakers, Five of Us, Spookhouse, Marathon 88, What Happened Was..., Wifey, Careless Love*

NORRIS, BRUCE. Born May 16, 1960 in Houston, TX. Graduate Northwestern U. Bdwy debut 1985 in *Biloxi Blues*, OB in *A Midsummer Night's Dream, Wenceslas Square, The Debutante Ball, What the Butler Saw, Life During Wartime, Arabian Nights.*

NORTON, EDWARD. Born Aug. 18, 1969 in Boston, MA. Graduate Yale U. Debut 1992 OB in *Waiting for Lefty*, followed by *Lovers, Italian American Reconciliation, Bring Me Smiles, Bible Burlesque, Fragments.*

OBERLANDER, MICHAEL. Born Aug. 25, 1960 in Newark, NJ. Graduate Carnegie-Melon U. Debut 1985 OB in *The Crows*, followed by *The Misanthrope, Dracula, Georgy, Paradise Re-Lost, Promised Land, Family Obligations, The Survivor.*

O'BRIEN, ERIN J. Born October 15 in Shakopee, MN. Graduate U. Mn., NYU. Debut 1992 OB in *Juno*, followed by *As You Like It.*

O'DWYER, MARION. Born July 19, 1960 in Dublin, Ire. Attended Dublin Gate Theatre. Bdwy debut 1993 in *Wonderful Tennessee.*

O'HARA, JENNY. Born February 24 in Sonora, CA. Attended Carnegie-Tech. Bdwy debut 1964 in *Dylan*, followed by *The Odd Couple* (1985) ,OB in *Hang Down Your Head and Die, Play with a Tiger, Arms and the Man, Sambo, My House Is Your House, The Kid, The Fox, EST Marathon 93, Bed and Breakfast, Good as New.*

OLDS, GABRIEL. Born March 24 in NYC. Attended Yale U. Debut 1987 OB in *Macbeth, Any Given Day* (1993).

OLIENSIS, ADAM. Born March 22, 1960 in Passaic, NJ. Graduate U. Wisc. Debut 1985 OB in *Inside-Out*, followed by *Little Blood Brother, Macbeth, 3 by Wilder, S. S. Glencairn, As You Like It*, Bdwy in *Wilder Wilder Wilder* (1993).

OLSON, MARCUS. Born September 21, 1955 in Missoula, MT. Graduate Amherst Col. Debut 1986 OB in *Personals*, followed by *Where the Cookie Crumbles, Assassins, Them Within Us*, Bdwy in *Passion* (1994).

O'MALLEY, KERRY. Born Sept. 5, 1969, in Nashua, NH. Graduate, Duke U., Harvard U. Bdwy debut 1993 in *Cyrano: The Musical.*

O'MARA, MOLLIE. Born September 5, 1960 in Pittsburgh, PA. Attended Catholic U. Debut 1989 OB in *Rodents and Radios*, followed by *Crowbar, Famine Plays, Homo Sapien Shuffle, Vast Wreck, Gut Girls, Apocrypha.*

O'NEILL, MICHELLE. Born April 26 in Bend, OR. Graduate U. Utah, Juilliard. Bdwy debut 1993 in *Abe Lincoln in Illinois.*

ORBACH, RON. Born March 23, 1952 in Newark, NJ. Graduate Rider Col. Debut 1985 OB in *Lies and Legends*, followed by *Philistines, The Skin of Our Teeth, Mrs. Dally Has a Lover*, Bdwy in *Laughter on the 23rd Floor* (1993).

OREM, SUSAN. Born June 15, 1949 in Elizabeth, NJ. Graduate NYU. Debut 1979 OB in *Big Bad Burlesque*, followed by *Christopher Blake, The*

Rise and Rise of Daniel Rocket.

O'REILLY, CIARAN. Born March 13, 1959 in Ireland. Attended Carmelite Col., Juilliard. Debut 1978 OB in *Playboy of the Western World*, followed by *Summer, Freedom of the City,Fannie, The Interrogation of Ambrose Fogarty, King Lear, Shadow of a Gunman, The Mary Month of May, I Do Not Live Like Thee Dr. Fell, The Plough and the Stars, Yeats: A Celebration, Philadelphia Here I Come, Making History, The Mme. MacAdam Traveling Theater, The Au Pair Man.*

ORESKES, DANIEL. Born in NYC. Graduate U. PA., LAMDA. Debut 1990 OB in *Henry IV*, followed by *Othello, 'Tis Pity She's a Whore, Richard II*, Bdwy in *Crazy He Calls Me* (1992).

O'ROURKE, KEVIN. Born January 25, 1956 in Portland, OR. Graduate Williams Col. Debut 1981 OB in *Declassee*, followed by *Sister Mary Ignatius.., Submariners, A Midsummer Night's Dream, Visions of Kerouac, Self Defense, Spoils of War, The Spring Thing, Joined at the Head, Laureen's Whereabouts, Breaking Up*. Bdwy in *Alone Together* (1984), *Cat on a Hot Tin Roof, Spoils of War* .

OSCAR, BRAD. Born September 22, 1964 in Washington, DC. Graduate Boston U. Bdwy debut 1990 in *Aspects of Love*, OB in *Forbidden Broadway 1993.*

OUSLEY, ROBERT. Born July 21, 1946 in Waco, TX. Debut 1975 OB in *Give Me Liberty*, followed by *Coronation of Poppae*, Bdwy in *Sweeney Todd* (1979), *Othello* (1982), *Allegro in Concert.*

PACE, MICHAEL. Born Aug. 26, 1949 in Kansas City, MO. Graduate Carnegie-Tech U. Debut 1971 OB in *Shekina*, followed by *Marry Me a Little, Tied by the Leg, Road to Hollywood, Awake and Sing, American Clock*, Bdwy in *Rock n Roll: The First 5000 Years.*

PAETTY, SCOTT. Born April 10, 1968 in New Orleans, LA. Graduate Stanford U., LAMA. Debut 1994 OB in *Endless Air Endless Water.*

PAISNER, DINA. Born in Brooklyn, NY. OB in *The Creatan Woman, Pullman Care Hiawatha, Lysistrata, If 5 Years Pass, Troubled Waters, Sap of Life, Cave at Machpelah, Threepenny Opera, Montserrat, Gandhi, Blood Wedding, The Trial of Dr. Beck, Amidst the Gladiolas, The Long Valley, A Slight Ache, Veronica's Room, Ivanov, Medea*, Bdwy in *Andorra* (1961), *Medea* (1973).

PALMAS, JOSEPH. Born March 19, 1959 in Santiago, Cuba. Graduate U. Miami. Debut 1986 OB in *Rum & Coke*, followed by *Lovers and Keepers, Julius Caesar, The Death of Garcia Lorca, Bang Bang Blues, New York 1937, Comedy of Errors, New Hope for the Dead, The Good Mud, Hit the Lights!*

PALMER, JEANETTE. Born September 15, 1955 in Salem, MA. Attended Boston Consv. Debut 1987 OB in *Take Me Along*, followed by *Cinderella* (NYCO).

PALZERE, EMMA. Born June 15, 1962 in Manchester, CT. Graduate Emerson Col. Debut 1991 OB in *Born in the R.S.A.*, followed by *Montage, Rimers of Eldritch, Live from the Milky Way.*

PANARO, HUGH. Born February 19, 1964 in Philadelphia, PA. Graduate Temple U. Debut 1985 OB in *What's a Nice Country Like You Doing in a State Like This*, followed by *I Have Found Home, Juba, Splendora*, Bdwy in *Phantom of the Opera* (1990), *Red Shoes.*

PARK, STEVE. Born May 4, 1962 in Brooklyn, NY. Graduate SUNY/Binghamton. Debut 1987 OB in *Whai Whai a Long Time Ago*, followed by *Play Ball, Three Sisters, Shogun Macbeth, Rosie's Cafe, Distant Laughter, Timon of Athens, St. Joan, Song of Shim Chang, Eating Chicken Feet.*

PARKER, ELLEN. Born September 30, 1949 in Paris, Fr. Graduate Bard Col. Debut 1971 OB in *James Joyce Liquid Theatre*, followed by *Uncommon Women and Others, Dusa Fish Stas and Vi, A Day in the Life of the Czar, Fen, Isn't It Romantic?, The Winter's Tale, Aunt Dan and Lemon, Cold Sweat, The Heidi Chronicles, Absent Friends, Joined at the Head*, Bdwy in *Equus, Strangers, Plenty.*

PARKER, MARY-LOUISE. Born August 2, 1964 in Ft. Jackson, SC. Graduate NC School of Arts. Debut 1989 OB in *The Art of Success*, followed by *Prelude to a Kiss, Babylon Gardens, EST Marathon '92, Four Dogs and a Bone*, Bdwy in *Prelude to a Kiss* for which she received a 1990 Theatre World Award.

PARLATO, DENNIS. Born March 30, 1947 in Los Angeles, CA. Graduate Loyola U. Bdwy debut 1979 in *A Chorus Line*, followed by *The First, Chess*, OB in *Becket, Elizabeth and Essex, The Fantasticks, Moby Dick, The Knife, Shylock, Have I Got a Girl for You, Romance! Romance!, The Earl, Violent Peace, Traveler in the Dark, Hello Again.*

PARRY, WILLIAM. Born October 7, 1947 in Steubenville, OH. Graduate Mt. Union Col. Bdwy debut 1971 in *Jesus Christ Superstar*, followed by *Rockabye Hamlet, The Leaf People, Camelot* (1980), *Sunday in the Park with George, Into the Light, Passion*, OB in *Sgt. Pepper's Lonely Hearts Club Band, The Conjurer, Noah, The Misanthrope, Joseph and the Amazing Technicolor Dreamcoat, Agamemnon, Coolest Cat in Town, Dispatches, The Derby, The Knife, Cymbeline, Marathon '90.*

PATTERSON, HENRY. (formerly John) Born November 22, 1970 in NYC. Attended Hunter Col., NYU. Debut 1993 OB in *Old New York: False Dawn.*

PATTON, CHARLOTTE. Born June 12 in Danville, KY. Attended U. Cin., OB credits: *The New Living Newspaper, The Problem, The Bad Penny, The Happy Journey from Trenton to Camden, You've Changed, Montage, Delicate Dangers.*

PATTON, LUCILLE. Born in New York City. Attended Neighborhood Playhouse. Bdwy debut 1946 in *Winter's Tale*, followed by *Topaz, Arms and the Man, Joy to the World, All You Need is One Good Break, Fifth Season, Heavenly Twins, Rhinoceros, Marathon 33, The Last Analysis, Dinner at 8,*

La Strada, Unlikely Heroes, Love Suicide at Schofield Barracks, The Crucible, A Little Hotel on the Side, OB in *Ulysses in Nighttown, Failures, Three Sisters, Yes Yes No No, Tango, Mme. de Sade, Apple Pie, Follies, Yesterday is Over, My Prince My King, I Am Who I Am, Double Game, Love in a Village, 1984, A Little Night Music, Cheri, Till the Eagle Hollers, Money Talks, EST Marathon '92, Three Tall Women.*

PATTON, WILL. Born June 14, 1954 in Charleston, SC. OB in *Kingdom of Earth, Scenes from Country Life, Cops, Pedro Paramo, Limbo Tales, Tourists and Refugees, Rearrangements, Dark Ride, Salt Lake City Skyline, The Red Snake, Goose and Tomtom, Joan of Lorraine, Fool for Love, A Lie of the Mind, What Did He, See, Careless Love.*

PAWK, MICHELE. Born November 16, 1961 in Pittsburgh, PA. Graduate Cin. Consv. Bdwy debut 1988 in *Mail*, followed by *Crazy for You*, OB in *Hello Again.*

PEAHL, SUSAN. Born January 18, 1959 in Minneapolis, MN. Graduate U. Ill. Debut 1985 OB in *What's a Nice Country Like You Doing in a State Like This?* followed by *Food Gas Talent.*

PEARLMAN, STEPHEN. Born February 26, 1935 in New York City. Graduate Dartmouth Col. Bdwy debut 1964 in *Barefoot in the Park*, followed by *La Strada, Six Degrees of Separation* (also OB), *Ant Given Day*, OB in *Threepenny Opera, Time of the Key, Pimpernel, In White America, Viet Rock, Chocolates, Bloomers, Richie, Isn't It Romantic, Bloodletters, Light Up the Sky, Perfect Party, Com Blow Your Horn, A Shayna Madel, Value of Names, Hyde in Hollywood, Wrong Turn at Lunfish.*

PELLEGRINO, SUSAN. Born June 3, 1950 in Baltimore, MD. Attended C. C. San Francisco, Cal State U. Debut 1982 OB in *The Wisteria Trees*, followed by *Steel on Steel, The Master Builder, Equal Wrights, Come as You Are, Painting Churches, Marvin's Room, Glory Girls*, Bdwy in *The Kentucky Cycle* (1994).

PELTY, ADAM. Born July 31, 1967 in Chicago, IL. Graduate Purdue U. Bdwy debut 1993 in *Cyrano: The Musical.*

PENDLETON, AUSTIN. Born March 27, 1940 in Warren, OH. Debut 1962 OB in *Oh Dad Poor Dad...*, followed by *The Last Sweet Days of Isaac, Three Sisters, Say Goodnight Gracie, Office Murders, Up from Paradise, The Overcoat, Two Character Play, Master Class, Educating Rita, Uncle Vanya, Serious Company, Philoctetes, Hamlet, Richard III, What about Luv?, The Sorrows of Frederick, The Show-Off, Jeremy Rudge, Sophistry*, Bdwy in *Fiddler on the Roof, Hail Scrawdyke, The Little Foxes, American Millionaire, The Runner Stumbles, Doubles.*

PEPE, NEIL. Born June 23, 1963 in Bloomington, IN. Graduate Kenyon Col. Debut 1988 OB in *Boys' Life*, followed by *Three Sisters, Virgin Molly, Return to Sender, Five Very Live, Down the Shore, The Lights.*

PEREZ, MIGUEL. Born September 7, 1957 in San Jose, CA. Attended Natl. Shakespeare Consv. Debut 1986 OB in *Women Beware Women*, followed by *Don Juan of Seville, Cymbeline, Mountain Language, The Birthday Party, Hamlet, Henry IV Parts 1 & 2, Arturo Ui, The Merry Wives of Windsor.*

PERRY, LYNETTE. Born September 29, 1963 in Bowling Green, OH. Graduate Cin Consv. Debut 1987 OB in *The Chosen*, followed by *Lucy's Lapses, New York Rock*, Bdwy in *Grand Hotel* (1989).

PESCE, VINCE. Born December 3, 1966 in Brooklyn NY. Bdwy debut 1993 in *Guys and Dolls*, OB in *The Hunchback of Notre Dame.*

PETTET, ASHLEY. Born November 20, 1984 in Paterson, NY. Debut 1993 OB in *Annie Warbucks.*

PHILLIPS, ETHAN. Born February 8, 1950 in Rocksville Center, NY. Graduate Boston U. Cornell U. Debut 1979 OB in *Modigliani*, followed by *Eccentricities of a Nightingale, Nature and Purpose of the Universe, The Beasts, Dumb Waiter, The Indian Wants the Bronx, Last of the Red Hot Lovers, Only Kidding, Almost Perfect, Theme and Variations, Marathon '91, Lips Together Teeth Apart, Young Playwrights Festival, Measure for Measure*, Bdwy in *My Favorite Year* (1992).

PHILLIPS, GARRISON. Born October 8, 1929 in Tallahasee, Fl. Graduate U. W.Va. Debut 1956 Ob in *Eastward in Eden*, followed by *Romeo and Juliet, Time of the Cuckoo, Triptych, After the fall, Two Gentlemen of Verona, Ambrosio, The Sorrows of Frederick, La Ronde, Playing with Fire* (After Frankenstein), *Rough/Play, Godot Arrives*, Bdwy in *Clothes for a Summer Hotel* (1980).

PHOENIX, ALEC. Born Sept.9, 1964 in Bristol, Eng. Graduate Swarthmore Col., Juilliard. Debut 1992 OB in *Henry V*, followed by *Love's Labour's Lost, Merry Wives of Windsor*, Bdwy in *Timon of Athens* (1993), *Government Inspector.*

PINE, LARRY. Born March 3, 1945 in Tucson, AZ. Graduate NYU. Debut 1967 OB in *Cyrano*, followed by *Alice in Wonderland, Mandrake, Aunt Dan and Lemon, The Taming of the Shrew, Better Days, Dolphin Project*, Bdwy in *End of the World* (1984), *Angels in America.*

PINKINS, TONYA. Born May 30, 1962 in Chicago Il. Attended Carnegie-Mellon U. Bdwy debut 1981 in *Merrily We Roll Along*, followed by *Jelly's Last Jam*, OB in *Five Points, A Winter's Tale, An Ounce of Prevention, Just Say No, Mexican Hayride, Young Playwrights '90, Approximating Mother, Merry Wives of Windsor.*

PITONIAK, ANNE. Born March 30, 1922 in Westfield, MA. Attended U. NC Women's College. Debut 1982 OB in *Talking With*, followed by *Young Playwrights Festival, Phaedra, Steel Magnolias, Pygmalion, The Rose Quartet*, Bdwy in *Night, Mother* (1983) for which she received a Theatre World Award, *The Octette Bridge Club, Picnic.*

PITTU, DAVID. Born April 4, 1967 in Fairfield, CT. Graduate NYU. Debut 1987 OB in *Film is Evil: Radio is Good*, followed by *Five Very Live, White Cotton Sheets, Nothing Sacred, The Stand-In, The Lights*, Bdwy in *Tenth*

Man.

PLAYTEN, ALICE. Born August 28, 1947 in New York City. Bdwy debut 1960 in *Gypsy*, followed by *Oliver!, Hello Dolly!, Henry Sweet Henry* for which she received a Theatre World Award, *George M.!, Spoils of War, Rumors*, OB in *Promenade, The Last Sweet Days of Isaac, National Lampoon's Lemmings, Valentine's Day, Pirates of Penzance, Up from Paradise, A Visit, Sister Mary Ignatius Explains It All, An Actor's Nightmare, That's It Folks, 1-2-3-4-5, Spoils of War, Marathon '90 and '93, The Mysteries, First Lady Suite.*

PLUNKETT, MARYANN. Born in 1953 in Lowell, MA. Attended U. NH. Bdwy debut 1983 in *Agnes of God*, followed by *Sunday in the Park with George, Me and My Girl, The Crucible, The Master Builder, A Little Hotel on the Side, Saint Joan, The Sea Gull*, OB in *Aristocrats, It's Our Town Too.*

POCHOS, DEDE. Born Apr.27, 1960 in Lake Forest, IL. Graduate U. Pa. Bdwy debut 1993 in *Wilder Wilder Wilder*, OB in *Midsummer's Night Dream, Macbeth, Tomorrow Was War, Judgment Day, Tartuffe, Who Will Cary the Word?, As You LIke It.*

POGGI, JACK. Born June 14, 1928 in Oakland, CA. Graduate Harvard. U., Columbia U., Debut 1962 OB in *This Side of Paradise*, followed by *The Tavern, Dear Janet Rosenberg, House Music, The Closed Door, Ghosts, Uncle Vanya, Tiger at the Gates, Wars of Roses, The Pajama Game, Two by Horton Foote, Delicate Dangers.*

POLEY, ROBIN. Born in NYC. Graduate Oberlin Col. Debut 1988 OB in *Crystal Clear*, followed by *Love's Labour's Lost, Marie and Bruce, Trelawney of the Wells, Romeo and Juliet.*

PONAZECKI, JOE. Born January 7, 1934 in Rochester, NY. Attended Rochester U., Columbia U. Bdwy debut 1959 in *Much Ado about Nothing*, followed by *Send Me No Flowers, A Call on Kuprin, Take Her She's Mine, Fiddler on the Roof, Xmas in Las Vegas, 3 Bags Full, Love in E Flat, 90 Day Mistress, Harvey, Trial of the Catonsville 9, The Country Girl, Freedom of the City, Summer Brave, Music Is, The Little Foxes, Prelude to a Kiss*, OB in *The Dragon, Muzeeka, Witness, All Is Bright, The Dog Ran Away, Dream of a Blacklisted Actor, Innocent Pleasures, The Dark at the Top of the Stairs, 36, After the Revolution, The Raspberry Picker, A Raisin in the Sun, Light Up the Sky, EST Marathon '92, Listening.*

POPE, STEPHANIE. Born April 8, 1964 in NYC. Debut 1983 OB in *The Buck Stops Here*, followed by *Shades of Harlem, Watermellon Rinds*, Bdwy in *Big Deal* (1986), *Jelly's Last Jam, Kiss of the Spiderwoman.*

PORTER, JACQUIE. Born in 1963 in Warren, PA. Graduate Smith College. Bevut 1981 OB in *Butterflies Are Free*, followed by *Three More Sleepless Nights*, Bdwy in *Jerome Robbins' Broadway* (1990), *Joseph and the Amazing Technicolor Dream Coat.*

PORTER, BILLY. Born September 21, 1969 in Pittsburgh, PA. Graduate Carnegie-Mellon U. Debut 1989 OB in *Romance in Hard Times*, Bdwy in *Miss Saigon, Five Guys Named Moe, Grease.*

POSER, TOBY. Born April 16, 1969 in Huntingdon, PA. Graduate Tulane U. Debut 1993 OB in *Greetings!.*

POTTER, NICOLE. Born August 25, 1954 in NYC. Graduate SUNY/Purchase. Debut 1978 OB in *The Way of the World*, followed by *Danton's Death.*

PRATT, SEAN. Born December 26, 1965 in Oklahoma City, OK. Graduate Santa Fe Col. BADA. Debut OB 1993 in *The Good Natur'd Man*, followed by *Phaedra, Widowers Houses, Oedipus the King, Game of Love and Chance, Twelfth Night.*

PRESCOTT, JENNIFER. Born February 19, 1963 in Portland, OR. Graduate NYU, AMDA. Bdwy debut 1987 in *Starlight Express*, followed by *Fiddler on the Roof*, OB in *On a Clear Day You Can See Forever, 3 Americanisms, The Mayor Musicals.*

PRESNELL, HARVE. Born Sept.14, 1933. in Modesto, CA. Attended U. S. Cal. Bdwy debut 1960 in *Unsinkable Molly Brown*, followed by *Carousel, Annie Get Your Gun, Annie*, OB in *Annie Warbucks.*

PRESTON, WILLIAM. Born August 26, 1921 in Columbia, PA. Graduate Penn State U. Debut 1972 OB in *We Bombed in New Haven*, followed by *Hedda Gabler, Whisper into My Good Ear, A Nestless Bird, Friends of Mine, Iphigenia in Aulix, Midsummer, The Fantastics, Frozen Assets, The Golem, The Taming of the Shrew, His Master's Voice, Much Ado about Nothing, Hamlet, Winter Dreams, Palpitations, Rumor of Glory, Killers, Not Partners, Rumor of Glory, Great Shakes, The Bacchae*, Bdwy in *Our Town* (1988).

PRICE, BRIAN DAVID. Born March 6, 1966 in Washington, DC. Graduate Yale U. Debut OB 1989 in *Philoctetes*, followed by *Women and Wallace, Rise and Rise of Daniel Rocket, Ice-Fishing Play.*

PRICE, PAIGE. Born July 6, 1964 in Middlesex, NJ. Attended NYU. Debut 1993 OB in *Gay Divorce*, Bdwy in *Beauty and the Beast* (1994).

PRINCE, FAITH. Born August 5, 1957 in Augusta, GA. Graduate U. Cinn. Debut OB 1981 in *Scrambled Feet*, followed by *Olympus on My Mind, Groucho, Living Color, Bad Habits, Falsettoland*, Bdwy in *Jerome Robbins Broadway* (1989), *Nick & Nora, Guys and Dolls* (1992), *Fiorello in Concert.*

PROVENZA, PAUL. Born July 31, 1957 in NYC. Graduate U. Penn., RADA. Debut OB 1988 in *Only Kidding*, for which he received a Theatre World Award, followed by *Aryan Birth.*

QUINN, COLLEEN. Born April 24 in Lindenhurst, NY. Debut 1988 OB in *Borderlines*, followed by *Keeping an Eye on Louie, Octoberfest, Dutchman, Beauty Marks, Midsummer, Program for Murder, Brimstone.*

QUINN, PATRICK. Born February 12, 1950 in Philadelphia, PA. Graduate Temple U. Bdwy Debut 1976 in *Fiddler on the Roof*, followed by *A Day in Hollywood/A Night in the Ukraine, Oh, Coward!, Lend Me a Tenor*, OB in *It's Better with a Bank, By Strouse, Forbidden Broadway, The Best of Forbidden Broadway, Raft of Medusa, Forbidden Broadway's 10th Anniversary, A Helluva Town, After the Ball.*

RABKE, KELLI. Born April 6, 1967 in New Jersey. Graduate Fordham U. Bdwy debut 1993 in *Joseph and the Amazing Technicolor Dreamcoat.*

RAITER, FRANK. Born January 17, 1932 in Cloquet, MN. Yale Graduate. Bdwy debut 1958 in *Cranks*, followed by *Dark at the Top of the Stairs, J.B., Camelot, Salome*, OB in *Soft Core Pornographer, The Winter's Tale, Twelfth Night, Tower of Evil, Endangered Species, A Bright Room Called Day, Learned Ladies, 'Tis Pity She's A Whore, Othello, Comedy of Errors, Orestes, Marathon Dancing.*

RANARA, JEFF. Born August 14, 1965 in Manila, PI. Attended MIT, Yale U., AADA. Debut 1993 OB in *A Better Life*, followed by *Bocoo!*

RANDALL, TONY. Born February 26, 1920 in Tulsa, OK. Attended Northwestern, Columbia, Neighborhood Playhouse. Bdwy debut 1947 in *Antony and Cleopatra*, followed by *To Tell You the Truth, Caesar and Cleopatra, Oh Men! Oh Women!, Inherit the Wind, Oh! Captain!, UTBU, M. Butterfly, A Little Hotel on the Side, 3 Men on a Horse, Government Inspector.*

RAPHAEL, GERRIANNE. Born February 23, 1935 in NYC. Attended New School, Columbia U. Bdwy debut 1941 in *Solitaire*, followed by *A Ghost in the House, Violet, Goodbye My Fancy, Seventh Heaven, Li'l Abner, Saratoga, Man of La Mancha, King of Hearts*, OB in *Threepenny Opera, The Boy Friend, Ernest in Love, Say When, the Prime of Miss Jean Brodie, The Butler Did It, The Ninth Step, An Evening with Sid Caesar.*

REED, BOBBY. Born September 26, 1956 in NYC. Attended AMDA. Debut 1975 OB in *Boy Meets Boy*, followed by *The Hunchback of Notre Dame, Der Ring Got Farblon Jet, Big Hotel, A Christmas Carol, At Home with the TV, White Cotton Sheets, How to Write a Play.*

REED, MAGGI-MEG. Born in Columbus, OH. Graduate Harvard U. Debut 1984 OB in *She Stoops to Conquer*, followed by *Playboy of the Western World, Triangles, Beyond the Window, El Greco.*

REED, RONDI. Born October 26, 1952 in Dixon, IL. Graduate Ill State U. Bdwy debut 1990 in *The Grapes of Wrath*, OB in *The Rise and Fall of Little Voice.*

REED, VIVIAN. Born June 6, 1947 in Pittsburgh, PA. Attended Juilliard. Bdwy debut 1971 in *That's Entertainment*, followed by *Don't Bother Me I Can't Cope, Brown Sugar* for which she received a Theatre World Award, *It's So Nice to Be Civilized, High Rollers*, OB in *The End of the Day, Queenie Pie.*

REES, ROGER. Born May 5, 1944 in Wales. Graduate Glade School of Fine Art. Bdwy debut 1975 in *London Assurance*, followed by *Nicholas Nickleby* (1981), *Red Shoes* (previews only), OB in *The End of the Day.*

REEVE, CHRISTOPHER. Born September 25, 1952 in NYC. Graduate Cornell U., Juilliard. Debut 1975 OB in *Berkeley Square*, followed by *My Life, A Winter's Tale, Love Letters, Allegro* (in concert), Bdwy in *A Matter of Gravity* (1976), *5th of July, The Marriage of Figaro.*

REGAN, MOLLY. Born October 8 in Maakato, MN. Graduate Northwestern U. Debut 1979 OB in *Say Goodnight Gracie*, followed by *Personals, Etiquette, Booth*, Bdwy in *Stepping Out* (1987), *The Crucible* (1991).

RENE, NIKKI. Born May 3, 1960 in Connecticut. Attended Hartford Consv. Debut 1984 OB in *Little Shop of Horrors*, followed by *Once on This Island, A Body of Water*, Bdwy in *Smile* (1987), *High Rollers, Once on this Island.*

RICHARDSON, NATASHA. Born May 11, 1963 in London, Eng. Graduate Central School of Speech and Drama. Bdwy debut 1992 in *Anna Christie*, for which she received a Theatre World Award.

RIEGEL, EDEN. Born January 1, 1981 in Washington, DC. Bdwy debut 1989 in *Les Miserables*, followed by OB in *And the Tide Shall Cover the Earth* (1994).

RIFKIN, RON. Born October 31, 1939 in New York City. Graduate NYU. Bdwy debut 1960 in *Come Blow Your Horn*, followed by *The Goodbye People, The Tenth Man, Broken Glass*, OB in *Rosebloom, The Art of Dining, Temple, Substance of Fire, Three Hotels.*

RIGG, DIANA. Born July 20, 1938 in Doncaster, England. Attended RADA. Bdwy debut 1964 in *Comedy of Errors*, followed by *King Lear, Abelard and Heloise, The Misanthrope, Medea.*

RINEHART, ELAINE. Born August 16, 1958 in San Antonio, TX. Graduate NC Schl. Arts. Debut 1975 OB in *Tenderloin*, followed by *Native Son, Joan of Lorraine, Dumping Ground, Fairweather Friends, The Color of the Evening Sky, The Best Little Whorehouse in Texas, The Wedding of the Siamese Twins, Festival of 1 Acts, Up 'n' Under, Crystal Clear, Black Market, Festival of 1 Act Comedies, Raft of the Medusa, I Can't Stop Screaming, King of Carpets, Lost Dreams...*

RISEMAN, NAOMI. Born October 6, 1927 in Boston, MA. Graduate NYU, Columbia U. Debut 1959 OB in *Boo Hoo East Lynn*, followed by *Merry Wives of Windsor, The Lady's Not for Burning, Romeo and Juliet, Ernest in Love, Will the Mail Train Run Tonight?, Once in a Lifetime, Promenade, Heartbreak House, About Heaven and Earth, The Closed Door, Relative Values, Edith Stein*, Bdwy in *Status Quo Vadis* (1973), *How to Be a Jewish Mother, Fiddler on the Road.*

RISKIN, SUSAN. Born September 24, 1936 in Los Angeles, CA. Graduate UCLA. Debut 1974 OB in *The Sea Horse*, followed by *Edith Stein*, Bdwy in *Agnes of God* (1982).

RITCHIE, MARGARET. Born May 31 in Madison, WI. Graduate U. Wisconsin, NYU. Debut 1981 OB in *Last Summer at Bluefish Cove*, followed by *Who's There?, All Souls Day, Days and Nights of an Ice Cream Princess, Two by Horton Foote, Delicate Dangers.*

RIVERS, JOAN. Born June 8, 1933 in Brooklyn, NY. Graduate Barnard College. Bdwy debut 1971 in *Fun City,* followed by *Broadway Bound, Sally Marr and Her Escorts.*

ROBERTS, TONY. Born October 22, 1939 in NYC. Graduate Northwestern U. Bdwy debut 1962 in *Something about a Soldier,* followed by *Take Her She's Mine, The Last Analysis, Never Too Late, Barefoot in the Park, Don't Drink the Water, How Now Dow Jones, Play It Again Sam, Promises Promises, Sugar, Absurd Person Singular, Murder at the Howard Johnson's, They're Playing Our Song, Doubles, Brigadoon (LC), South Pacific (LC), Love Letters, Jerome Robbins' Broadway, The Sisters Rosensweig, The Sea Gull,* OB in *The Cradle Will Rock, Losing Time, The Good Parts, Time Framed, The Normal Heart, 4 Dogs and a Bone.*

ROBERTSON, ALENE. Born December 9 in Hartford, CT. Debut 1993 OB in *Annie Warbucks.*

ROBERTSON, SCOTT. Born January 4, 1954 in Stanford, CT. Bdwy debut 1976 in *Grease,* followed by *The Pajama Game (LC), Damn Yankees (1994),* OB in *Scrambled Feet, Applause, A Lady Needs a Change, A Baker's Audition, She Loves Me, Secrets of a Lava Lamp, Love in Two Countries.*

ROBINSON, ANDREW. Born February 14, 1942 in NYC. Graduate New School, LAMA. Debut 1967 OB in *Macbird,* followed by *Cannibals, Futz, Young Master Dante, Operation Sidewinder, Subject to Fits, Mary Stuart, Narrow Road to the Deep North, In the Belly of the Beast,* Bdwy in *Any Given Day* (1993).

ROBISON, BLAKE. Born April 2, 1966 in Falls Church, VA. Graduate Williams College, U. NC. Bdwy debut 1993 in *Timon of Athens,* followed by *The Government Inspector.*

ROCHELLE, LISA. Born March 25, 1959 in Brooklyn, NY. Bdwy debut 1973 in *Molly,* followed by *Les Miserables,* OB in *You Can't Take It with You, You're a Good Man Charlie Brown, Our Town, Christmas Rappings, Coffee Bean, Times Like These, Le Grand Cafe, Canteen, Some Summer Night, That's Life.*

RODERICK, CONNIE. Born January 7 in Dayton, OH. Attended Northwestern U., Goodman Theatre. Debut 1983 in *The Corn Is Green,* followed by *The Marriage of Figaro, Devil's Disciple, An Inspector Calls.*

RODGERS, JERRY. Born August 20, 1941 in Stockton, CA. Graduate U. Portland. Debut OB 1971 in *Miss Lizzie,* followed by *Shakuntala, Life in Bed, Rainbow Rape Trick, The Contrast, Lady Windermere's Fan, White Widow.*

ROMAGUERA, JOAQUIN. (aka Fidel Romann) Born September 5, 1932 in Key West, FL. Graduate Florida Southern College. Debut 1961 OB in *All in Love,* followed by *Mlle. Colombe,* Bdwy in *Sweeney Todd* (1979), *Fiorello in Concert.*

ROSE, NORMAN. Born June 23, 1917 in Philadelphia, PA. Graduate George Washington U. Bdwy in *Cafe Crown, St. Joan, Land of Fame, Richard III, The Fifth Season,* OB in *Career, Hemingway Hero, Wicked Cooks, Empire Builders, The Old Ones, The Wait, Edith Rose.*

ROSENBAUM, DAVID. Born in NYC. Debut 1968 OB in *America Hurrah!* followed by *The Cave Dwellers, Evenings with Chekhov, Out of the Death Cart, After Miriam, The Indian Wants the Bronx, Allergy, Family Business, Beagleman and Brackett, The Last Sortie,* Bdwy in *Oh! Calcutta!, Ghetto.*

ROSENBLATT, MARCELLE. Born July 1 in Baltimore, MD. Graduate UNC, Yale U. Debut 1979 OB in *Vienna Notes,* followed by *The Sorrows of Stephen, The Dybbuk, Twelfth Night, Second Avenue Rag, La Boheme, Word of Mouth, Twelve Dreams, Don Juan, A Midsummer Night's Dream, Mud, The Return of Pinocchio, Ladies of Fisher Cove,* Bdwy in *Stepping Out* (1986), *Our Town.*

ROTH, STEPHANIE. Born in 1963 in Boston, MA. Juilliard graduate. Bdwy debut 1987 in *Les Liaisons Dangereuses,* followed by *Artist Descending a Staircase,* OB in *The Cherry Orchard, Measure for Measure, A Body of Water.*

RUBANO, CRAIG. Born in St. Louis, MO. Graduate Yale U., Columbia U. Debut 1989 in *Pirates of Penzance,* followed by *Charlotte's Web, Ernest in Love,* Bdwy in *Les Miserables* (1993).

RUCK, LOUISE. Born April 11, 1964 in St. Louis, MO. Bdwy debut 1992 in *Crazy for You,* followed by *The Best Little Whorehouse Goes Public.*

RUCKER, BO. Born August 17, 1948 in Tampa, Fl. Debut 1978 OB in *Native Son,* for which he received a Theatre World Award, followed by *Blues for Mr. Charlie, Streamers, Forty Deuce, Dustoff, Rosetta Street, East Texas Hot Links,* Bdwy in *Joe Turner's Come and Gone, Abe Lincoln in Illinois.*

RUDIN, STUART. Born December 16, 1941 in Vancouver, WA. Graduate U. WA., East WA. State U. Debut 1974 OB in *Friends,* followed by *Great American Stickball League, Progress, Backwoods, Measure for Measure.*

RUIVIVAR, FRANCIS. Born December 21, 1960 in Hong Kong, China. Graduate Loretto Heights Col. Bdwy debut 1988 in *Chess,* followed by *Starlight Express, Shogun: The Musical,* for which he received a Theatre World Award, *Miss Saigon, Passion,* OB in *Promised Land.*

RUNOLFSSON, ANNE. Born in Long Beach, CA. Attended UCLA. Bdwy debut 1989 in *Les Miserables,* followed by *Aspects of Love, Cyrano the Musical.*

RUSSELL, ERIC. Born March 24, 1924 in Schenectady, NY. Graduate U. Chicago, CCNY. Debut 1946 OB in *Peg O' My Heart,* followed by *Cricket on the Hearth, Oedipus at Colonos, As You Like It, Sharon's Grave, Uncle Vanya.*

RUTLEDGE, JAMES. Born March 24, 1955 in Pontiac, MI. Graduate Oakland U. Debut 1993 OB in *The Ceremony of Innocence.*

RYALL, WILLIAM. Born September 18, 1954 in Binghamton, NY. Graduate AADA. Debut 1979 OB in *Canterbury Tales,* followed by *Elizabeth and Essex, He Who Gets Slapped, The Sea Gull, Tartuffe,* Bdwy in *Me and My Girl* (1986), *Grand Hotel, The Best Little Whorehouse Goes Public.*

RYAN, STEVEN. Born June 19, 1947 in New York City. Graduate Boston U., U. Minn. Debut 1978 OB in *Winning Isn't Everything,* followed by *The Beethoven, September in the Rain, Romance Language, Love's Labour's Last, Love and Anger, Approximating Mother, Merry Wives of Windsor,* Bdwy in *I'm Not Rappaport* (1986), *Guys and Dolls* (1992).

RYDER, AMY. Born January 8, 1958 in San Diego, CA. Attended San Francisco State U. Debut 1984 OB in *Options,* followed by *Falsies, Taboo in Revue, On Again, Songs in Blume, Friends and Music, Toulouse, Pretty Faces, Merrily We Roll Along,* Bdwy in *Damn Yankees,* (1994).

RYDER, RIC. Born March 31 in Baltimore, MD. Graduate U. MD. Peabody Consv. Bdwy debut 1989 in *Starmites,* followed by *Blood Brothers,* OB in *The Gifts of the Magi, Chess.*

RYLANCE, MARK. Born January 18, 1960 in Ashford, Kent, England. Graduate RADA. Debut 1993 OB in *Henry V,* followed by *As You Like It.*

RYLAND, JACK. Born July 22, 1935 in Lancaster, PA. Attended AADA. Bdwy debut 1958 in *The World of Suzie Wong,* followed by *A Very Rich Woman, Henry V, Timon of Athens, The Government Inspector,* OB in *A Palm Tree in a Rose Garden, Lysistrata, The White Rose and the Red, Old Glory, Cyrano de Bergerac, Mourning Becomes Electra, Beside the Seaside, Quartermaine's Terms, The Miracle Worker, Enrico IV, Good Grief.*

SAGE, ALEXANDRIA. Born June 25, 1968 in San Francisco, CA. Graduate Yale U. Debut 1993 OB in *A Ceremony of Innocence,* followed by *Fragments, The Co-Op.*

SAITO, JAMES. Born March 6, 1955 in Los Angeles, CA. Graduate UCLA. Debut 1988 OB in *Rashomon,* followed by *Day Standing on Its Head, Ripples in the Pond, Wilderness.*

SALINGER, ROSS. Born October 14, 1960 in Norwalk, Ct. Graduate Northwestern U. Debut 1992 OB in *On the Bum,* followed by *War of the Worlds, Bertolt Brecht: In Dark Times.*

SALLOWS, TRACY. Born April 27, 1963 in Valley Stream, NY. Graduate SNY, Purchase. Bdwy debut 1986 in *You Never Can Tell,* followed by *The Miser, Shimada,* Bdwy in *Angels in America* (1993).

SANCHEZ, JAIME. Born December 19, 1938 in Rincon, PR. Attended Actors Studio. Bdwy debut 1957 in *West Side Story,* followed by *Oh Dad Poor Dad, A Midsummer Night's Dream, Richard III,* OB in *The Toilet/Conerico Was Here to Stay* for which he received a Theatre World Award, *The Ox Cart, The Tempest, Merry Wives of Windsor, Julius Caesar, Coriolanus, He Who Gets Slapped, State without Grace, The Sun Always Shines for the Cool, Othello, Elektra, Domino, The Promise, Rising Sun Falling Star, Academy Street, Written and Sealed.*

SANDERS, JAY O. Born April 16, 1953 in Austin, TX. Graduate SUNY/Purchase. Debut 1976 OB in *Henry V,* followed by *Measure for Measure, Scooping, Buried Child, Fables for Friends, In Trousers, Girls Girls Girls, Twelfth Night, Geniuses, The Incredibly Famous Willy Rivers, Rommel's Garden, Macbeth, Heaven on Earth, 3 Birds Alighting,* Bdwy in *Loose Ends* (1979), *The Caine Mutiny Court Martial, Saint Joan.*

SANTIAGO, SAUNDRA. Born April 14, 1957 in NYC. Graduate U. Miami, SMU. Bdwy debut 1983 in *A View from the Bridge,* OB in *Road to Nirvana, Spike Heels, Hello Again.*

SANTIAGO, SOCORRO. Born July 12, 1957 in NYC. Attend Juilliard. Debut 1977 OB in *Crack,* followed by *Poets from the Inside, Unfinished Women, Family Portrait, Domino, The Promise, Death and the Maiden,* Bdwy in *The Bacchae* (1980).

SANTORO, MARK. Born January 28, 1963 in New Haven, CT. Bdwy debut 1974 in *Gypsy,* followed by *Carrie, Pajama Game (NYCO/LC), Damn Yankees* (1994).

SATTA, STEVEN. Born December 25, 1964 in The Bronx, NYC. Graduate NYU. Debut 1991 OB in *Macbeth,* followed by *Chekhov Very Funny,* Bdwy in *A Little Hotel on the Side* (1992).

SAWYER, TONI. Born October 15, 1936 in Westfield, MA. Attended Vermont College. Debut 1993 OB in *Could I Have This Dance.*

SBARGE, RAPHAEL. Born February 12, 1964 in NYC. Attended HB Studio. Debut 1981 OB in *Henry IV Part I,* followed by *The Red Snake, Hamlet, Short Change, Ghosts,* Bdwy in *The Curse of an Aching Heart, Ah Wilderness!, Twilight of the Golds.*

SCARPONE, JUDITH. Born November 6, 1942 in Jersey City, NJ. Graduate Douglass College. Debut 1984 OB in *Africanis Instructus,* followed by *Postcards, Rule of Three, Holy Heist,* Bdwy in *Twilight of the Golds* (1993).

SCHERER, JOHN. Born May 16, 1961 in Buffalo, NY. Graduate Carnegie-Mellon U. Debut 1983 OB in *Preppies,* followed by *Jass, Downriver, Ladies and Gentlemen Jerome Kern, Olympus on My Mind, Music Makes Me.*

SCHERZER, WAYNE. Born August 11 in Newark, NJ. Graduate Dartmouth College. Debut 1977 OB in *Cyrano de Bergerac,* followed by *Cohan Revue,* Bdwy in *Les Miserables* (1993).

SCHOEFFLER, PAUL. Born November 21, 1958 in Montreal, Can. Graduate U.CA/Berkley, Carnegie-Mellon, U Brussels. Debut 1988 OB in *Much Ado about Nothing,* followed by *The Cherry Orchard, Carnival,* Bdwy in *Cyrano the Musical* (1993).

SCHREIBER, LIEV. Born October 4, 1967 in San Francisco, CA. Graduate Hampshire Col., Yale U., RADA. Debut 1992 OB in *Goodnight Desdemona Good Morning Juliet,* Bdwy in *In the Summer House* (1993).

SCHULTHEISS, KIMBERLY K. Born January 4, 1962 in Mt. Pleasant, MI. Graduate Bowling Green State U. Saginaw Valley State U. Debut 1992 OB in *Roleplay,* followed by *Blue Skies Forever.*

SCHULTHEIS, TIM. Born October 22 in Chicago, IL. Graduate U. Ill. Bdwy debut 1993 in *Joseph and the Amazing Technicolor Dreamcoat.*

Miguel Perez

Stephanie Pope

David Pittu

Paige Price

Billy Porter

Kelli Rabke

Sean Pratt

Rondi Reed

Christopher
Reeve

Nikki Rene

Tony Roberts

Diana Rigg

Ric Ryder

Lisa Rochelle

Mark Santoro

Tracy Sallows

Raphael Sbarge

Carol Schultz

Gary Schwartz

Carole Shelly

Thom Sesma

Constance
Shulman

Jonathan Marc
Sherman

Alice Spivak

Nathan Smith

Elaine Stritch

Robert Stanton

Francie Swift

Mark Edgar
Stephens

Tami Tappan

231

SCHULTZ, CAROL. Born February 12 in Chicago, IL. Graduate Case Western Reserve U., U. Ill. Debut 1982 OB in *Peer Gynt*, followed by *The Cherry Orchard, King Lear, Ghost Sonata*, Bdwy in *Abe Lincoln in Illinois* (1993).

SCHWARTZ, GARY. Born November 20, 1064 in Englewood, NJ. Attended Hofstra U., Debut 1987 OB in *The Chosen*, followed by *What's a Nice Country Like You Doing in a State Like This?*, Bdwy in *Fiddler on the Roof* (1990), *Kiss of the Spider Woman.*

SCOTT, CAMPBELL. Born July 19, 1962 in NYC. Attended Lawrence U. Bdwy debut 1985 in *Hay Fever*, followed by *The Real Thing, Long Day's Journey into Night, Ah Wilderness!*, OB in *Measure for Measure, Copperhead, A Man for all Seasons, The Last Outpost, Pericles, On the Bum, A Christmas Memory.*

SCOTT, JOHN. Born July 20, 1967 in Lafayette, IN. Graduate NC School of Arts, AMDA. Debut 1989 OB in *Babes in Toyland*, Bdwy in *110 in the Shade* (NYCO/LC), *My Fair Lady* (1993).

SEAMON, EDWARD. Born April 15, 1937 in San Diego, CA. Attended San Diego State College. Debut 1971 OB in *The Life and Times*, of J. Walter Smintheus followed by *The Contractor, The Family, Fishing, Feedlot, Cabin 12, Rear Column, Devour the Snow, Buried Child, Friends, Extenuating Circumstances, Confluence, Richard II, Great Grandson of Jedediah Kohler, Marvelous Gray, Time Framed, Master Builder, Fall Hookup, Fool for Love, The Harvesting, A Country for Old Men, Love's Labour's Lost, Caligula, Mound Builders, Quiet in the Land, Talley & Son, Tomorrow's Monday, Ghosts, Or Mice and Men, Beside Herself, You Can't Think of Everything, Tales of the Last Formicans, Love Diatribe, Empty Hearts, Sandbox*, Bdwy in *The Trip Back Down* (1977), *Devour the Snow, American Clock.*

SELDES, MARIAN. Born August 23, 1928 in NYC. Attended Neighborhood Playhouse. Bdwy debut 1947 in *Media*, followed by *Crime and Punishment, That Lady, Town Beyond Tragedy, Ondine, On High Ground, Come of Age, The Chalk Garden, The Milk Train Doesn't Stop Here Anymore, The Wall, A Gift of Time, A Delicate Balance, Before You Go, Father's Day, Equus, The Merchant, Deathtrap, OB in Different, Ginger Man, Mercy Street, Isadora Duncan Sleeps with the Russion Navy, Painting Churches, Gertrude Stein and Companion, Richard II, The Milk Train Doesn't Stop…, Bright Room Called Day, Another Time, Three Tall Women.*

SELLON, ANDREW. Born November 13, 1959 in Cambridge, MA. Graduate Harvard U., NC School of Arts. Debut 1993 OB in *The Game of Love and Chance*, followed by *Twelfth Night.*

SERABIAN, LORRAINE. Born June 12, 1945 in NYC. Graduate Hofstra U. Debut OB in *Sign of Jonah* (1960) followed by *Electra, Othello, Secret Life of Walter Mitty, Bugs and Veronica, The Trojan Women, American Gothic, Gallows Humor, Company, Dorian, Deathtrap, Tonight at 8:30*, Bdwy in *Cabaret, Zorba, The Flowering Peach.*

SETRAKIAN, ED. Born October 1, 1928 in Jenkinstown, WVA. Graduate Concord Col., NYU. Debut 1966 OB *I Dreams in the Night*, followed by *Othello, Coriolanus, Macbeth, Hamlet, Baal, Old Glory, Futz, Hey Rube, Seduced, Shout across the River, American Days, Sheepskin, Inserts, Crossing the Bar, The Boys Next Door, The Mensch, Adoring the Madonna, Tack Room*, Bdwy in *Days in the Trees* (1976) *St. Joan, The Best Little Whorehouse in Texas.*

SETRAKIAN, MARY. Born in San Francisco, CA. Graduate Stanford U., New England Consv. Debut 1990 OB in *Hannah, 1939*, followed by *Colette Collage, A New York Romance.*

SHANNON, MARK. Born December 13, 1948 in Indianapolis, In. Attended U. Cin. Debut 1969 OB in *Fortune and Men's Eyes*, followed by *Brotherhood, Nothing to Report, When You Comin' Back Red Ryder?, Serenading Louie, Three Sisters, K2, Spare Parts, Lips Together Teeth Apart, Tales from Hollywood, Lonely Planet.*

SHANNON, SARAH. Born May 23, 1966 in Lacrosse, WI. Graduate U. Wisconsin. Bdwy debut 1992 in *Cats*, followed by *Beauty and the Beast.*

SHAW, CHRISTOPHER. Born October 4 in Pennsylvania. Attended NC School of Arts. Debut 1988 OB in *Romeo and Juliet*, followed by *Painted Rain, Psychoneurotic Phantasies, Angel in Las Vegas, Sunday Promenade, Boy's Play, Walking the Dead, Portrait of My Bikini.*

SHEA, JERE. Born June 14, 1965 in Boston, MA. Graduate Boston College, NYU. Debut 1992 OB in *As You Like It*, Bdwy in *Guys and Dolls*, followed by *Passion*, for which he received a 1994 Theatre World Award.

SHELLEY, CAROLE. Born August 16,1939 in London, Eng. Bdwy debut 1965 in *The Odd Couple*, followed by *The Astrakhan Coat, Loot, Noel Coward's Sweet Potato, Hay Fever, Absurd Person Singular, The Norman Conquests, The Elephant Man, The Misanthrope, Noises Off, Stepping Out, The Miser*, OB in *Little Murder, The Devil's Disciple, The Play's the Thing, Souble Feature, Twelve Dreams, Pygmalion in Concert, A Christmas Carol, Jubilee in Concert, Waltz of the Toreadors, What the Butler Saw, Maggie and Isha, Later Life, The Destiny of Me, Lady in the Dark in Concert, Richard II.*

SHERMAN, BARRY. Born November 10, 1962 in Fontina, CA. Attended Marin College, National Theatre Consv. Debut 1988 OB in *Rimers of Eldritch*, followed by *Kingfish, Love Diatribe, Chelsea Walls, The Summer Winds, Walking the Dead, Moe's Lucky 7.*

SHERMAN, JONATHAN MARC. Born October 10, 1968 in Morristown, NJ Attended Carnegie-Mellon U., AADA. Debut 1986 OB in *The Chopin Playoffs*, followed by *Sophistry, Wild Dogs.*

SHULL, RICHARD B. Born February 24, 1929 in Evanston, Il. Graduate State U. Iowa. Debut 1953 OB in *Coriolanus*, followed by *Purple Dust, Journey to the Day, American Hamburger League, Frimbo, Fade the Game, Desire under the Elms, The Marriage of Betty and Boo, The Front Page* (LC),

One of the All-Time Greats, Sausage Eaters, Bdwy in *Black-eyed Susan* (1954), *Wake Up Darling, Red Roses for Me, I Knock at the Door, Pictures in the Hallway, Have I Got a Girl for You, Minnie's Boys, Goodtime Charley, Fools, Oh, Brother!, Ain't Broadway Grand.*

SHULMAN, CONSTANCE. (aka Connie). Born April 4, 1958 in Johnson City, TN. Graduate U. Tenn. Debut 1985 OB in *Walking Through*, followed by *Windfall, Pas de Deux, Steel Magnolias, Desire, Generation X, Loose Knit.*

SILLIMAN, MAUREEN. Born December 3 in New York City. Attended Hofstra U. Bdwy debut 1975 in *Shenandoah*, followed by *I Remember Mama, Is There Life After High School?*, OB in *Umbrellas of Cherbourg, Two Rooms, Macbeth, Blue Window, Three Postcards, Pictures in the Hall, The Voice of the Prairie, Picking Up the Pieces, Democracy and Esther, Marathon Dancing.*

SILVA, DONALD. Born February 7, 1949 in Gloucester, MA. Graduate Brandies U. Debut 1985 OB in *Loose Connections*, followed by *Bodega, Superman is Dead.*

SILVER, RON. Born July 2, 1946 in NYC. Graduate SUNY, St. John's U. Debut OB in *El Grande de Coca-Cola*, followed by *Lotta, Kaspar, More Than You Deserve, Emperor of Late Night Radio, Friends, Hunting Cockroaches*, Bdwy in *Hurlyburly* (1984), *Social Security.*

SIMES, DOUGLAS. Born April 21, 1949 in New Salem, NY. Graduate Lehigh U, Yale U. Debut 1974 OB in *The Lady's Not for Burning*, followed by *The Dumbwaiter, The Revenger's Tragedy, The Lady from the Sea, Between Time and Timbuktu, A Chaste Maid and Cheapside, Measure for Measure, Exit Music, The American Clock.*

SISTO, ROCCO. Born February 8, 1953 in Bari, Italy. Graduate U. Ill., NYU. Debut 1982 OB in *Hamlet*, followed by *The Country Doctor, The Times and Appetites of Toulouse-Lautrec, The Merchant of Venice, What Did He See, A Winter's Tale, The Tempest, Dream of a Common Language, Tis Pity She's a Whore, Mad Forest, Careless Love, All's Well That Ends Well, The Illusion, Merry Wives of Windsor.*

SIMMONS, J.K. (formerly Jonathan). Born January 9, 1955 in Detroit, MI. Graduate U. Minn. Debut 1987 OB in *Birds of Paradise*, followed by *Dirty Dick*, Bdwy in *A Change in the Heir* (1990), *A Few Good Men, Peter Pan* (1990/1991), *Guys and Dolls, Laughter on the 23rd Floor.*

SITLER, DAVID. Born April 7, 1957 in Harrisburg, PA. Graduate Franklin-Marshall College, Catholic U. Debut 1991 OB in *Necktie Breakfast*, followed by *Blues for Mr. Charlie*, Bdwy in *An Inspector Calls* (1994).

SKINNER, MARGO. Born January 3, 1950 in Middletown, OH. Graduate Boston U. Debut 1980 OB in *Missing Persons*, followed by *The Dining Room, Mary Barnes, The Perfect Party, Spare Parts, Oedipus the King, The Game of Love and Chance.*

SLEZAK, VICTOR. Born July 7, 1957 in Youngstown, OH. Debut 1979 OB in *Electra Myth*, followed by *The Hasty Heart, Ghosts, Alice and Fred, The Window Claire, The Miracle Worker, Talk Radio, Marathon '88, One Act Festival, Briar Patch, Appointment with a High Wire Lady, Sam I Am, The White Rose, Born Guilty, The Naked Truth*, Bdwy in *Any Given Day* (1993).

SLOMAN, JOHN. Born June 23, 1954 in Rochester, NY. Graduate SUNY/Genasco. Debut 1977 OB in *Unsung Cole*, followed by *The Apple Tree, Romance in Hard Times, The Waves, An Elephant Never Forgets, Hit the Lights!*, Bdwy in *Whoopee!* (1979), *1940's Radio Hour, A Day in Hollywood/A Night in the Ukraine, Mayor.*

SMIAR, BRIAN. Born August 27, 1937 in Cleveland, OH. Graduate Kent State U., Emerson College. Debut 1982 OB in *Edmund*, followed by *3X3, True to Life, Young Playwrights Festival, Marathon '90, Winter's Tale*, Bdwy in *Mixed Emotions* (1993).

SMITH, ANNA DEAVERE. Born September 18, 1950 in Baltimore, MD. Graduate Beaver College, American Consv. Theatre. Debut 1980 OB in *Mother Courage*, followed by *Mercenaries, Fires in the Mirror, Twilight: Los Angeles 1992*, Bdwy in *Twilight: Los Angeles 1992* for which she received a 1994 Theatre World Award.

SMITH, DEREK. Born December 4, 1959 in Seattle, WA. Juilliard Graduate. Debut 1986 OB in *Cruise Control*, followed by *Ten by Tennessee, Traps, Hyde in Hollywood*, Bdwy in *Timon of Athens* (1993), *The Government Inspector.*

SMITH, LOIS. Born November 3, 1930 in Topeka, KS. Attended U. W.V. Bdwy debut 1952 in *Time Out for Ginger*, followed by *The Young and the Beautiful, The Wisteria Trees, The Glass Menagerie, Orpheus Descending, Stages, The Grapes of Wrath*, OB in *A Midsummer Night's Dream, Non Pasquale, Promenade, LaBoheme, Bodies Rest and Motion, Gus and Al, Measure for Measure, Spring Thing, Beside Herself, Sam I Am, Dog Logic, Paradise.*

SMITH, NATHAN. Born May 2 in Wichita Falls, TX. Graduate U. Oklahoma, National Theatre Consv. Debut 1994 OB in *Old New York: False Dawn.*

SMITH, NICK. Born January 13, 1932 in Philadelphia, PA. Attended Boston U. Debut 1963 OB in *The Blacks*, followed by *Man is Man, The Connection, Blood Knot, No Place to be Somebody, Androcles and the Lion, So Nice They Named it Twice, In the Recovery Lounge, Liberty Call, Raisin in the Sun, Boogie Woogie and Booker T, The Balm Years, Red Channels.*

SMITH, TIMOTHY. Born May 4, 1955 in Gaylord, MI. Attended HB Studio. Bdwy debut 1976 in *My Fair Lady*, followed by *A Chorus Line, Joseph and the Amazing Technicolor Dreamcoat* (1993).

SMITH-CAMERON, J. Born September 7 in Louisville, KY. Attended Florida State U. Bdwy debut 1982 in *Crimes of the Heart*, followed by *Wild Honey, Lend Me a Tenor, Our Country's Good, The Real Inspector Hound, 15 Minute Hamlet*, OB in *Asian Shade, The Knack, Second Prize: Two Weeks in*

Leningrad, The Great Divide, The Voice of the Turtle, Women of Manhattan, Alice and Fred, Mi Vida Loca, Little Egypt, On the Bum, Traps/Owners, Desdemona, The Naked Truth.

SNEED, GLENN. Born July 30, 1962 in Springfield, MO. Graduate SMSU. Bdwy debut 1993 in Joseph and the Amazing Technicolor Dreamcoat.

SOCKWELL, SALLY. Born June 14 in Little Rock, AR. Debut 1976 OB in Vanities, followed by Double Awareness.

SOUTHWORTH, JOHN. Born November 8, 1929 in Blackpool, England. Attended Old Vic School. Debut 1950 OB in Henry IV, and Bdwy in Medea (1994).

SOZEN, JOYCE. Born in Springfield, IL. Graduate U. Ill. Debut 1980 OB in Mrs. Warren's Profession, followed by The Rug of Identity, The Beggar's Opera, Lady Windermere's Fan, Amphigory, All's Well That Ends Well.

SPAISMAN, ZYPORA. Born January 2, 1920 in Lublin, Poland. Debut 1955 OB in Lonesome Ship, followed by My Father's Court, A Thousand and One Nights, Eleventh Inheritor, Enchanting Melody, Fifth Commandment, Bronx Express, The Melody Lingers On, Yoshke Musikant, Stempenya, Generation of Green Fields, Ship, A Play for the Devil, Broome Street America, The Flowering Peach, Riverside Drive, Big Winner, The Land of Dreams, Father's Inheritance, At the Crossroads, Stempenyu.

SPENCER, VERNON. Born December 1, 1955 in Brooklyn, NY. Attended Queens College. Debut 1976 OB in Panama Hattie, followed by Happy with the Blues, Street Jesus, Amahl and the Night Visitors, Dreams of the Sea, Allegro in Concert, Bdwy in The Human Comedy (1984), Dreamgirls (1987).

SPIELBERG, ROBIN. Born November 20, 1962 in New Jersey. Attended Mich. State U., NYU. Debut 1988 OB in Boys' Life, followed by Marathon '90, Three Sisters, 5 Very Live, Cocktails and Camp, Nothing Sacred, The Lights.

SPINELLA, STEPHEN. Born October 11, 1956 in Naples, Italy. Graduate NYU. Debut 1982 OB in The Age of Assassins, followed by Dance for Me Rosetta, Bremen Coffee, The Taming of the Shrew, L'Illusion, Burrhead, Bdwy 1993 in Angles in America, for which he received a Theatre World Award.

SPIVAK, ALICE. Born August 11, 1935 in Brooklyn, NY. Debut 1954 OB in Early Primrose, followed by Of Mice and Men, Secret Concubine, Port Royal, Time for Bed, House of Blue Leaves, Deep Six the Briefcase, Selma, Ferry Tales, Temple, A Backer's Audition, Group One Acts.

SPIVEY, TOM. Born January 28, 1951 in Richmond, VA. Graduate WM & Mary, Penn State. Debut 1989 OB in The Thirteenth Chair, followed by The Rover, Off the Beat and Path 2, Bertolt Brecht: In Dark Times.

SPORE, RICHARD. Born March 23, 1948 in Chicago, IL. Debut 1982 OB in The Frances Farmer Story, followed by Counselor-at-Law, Troilus and Cressida, Motions of History, Henry IV, Comedy of Errors, Woyzeck, Under the Kerosene Moon.

SPOUND, MICHAEL. Born April 8, 1957 in Concord, MA. Graduate Northwestern U. Bdwy debut 1993 in Twilight of the Golds.

STACKPOLE, DANA. Born February 25, 1966 in Misawa, Japan. Bdwy debut 1994 in Carousel.

STADLEN, LEWIS J. Born March 7, 1947 in Brooklyn, NY. Attended Stella Adler Studio. Bdwy debut 1970 in Minnie's Boys, for which he received a Theatre World Award, followed by The Sunshine Boys, Candide, The Odd Couple, Laughter on the 23rd Floor, OB in The Happiness Cage, Heaven on Earth, Barb-A-Que, Don Juan and Non Don Juan, Olympus on My Mind, 1-2-3-4-5, S. J. Perelman in Person, The My House Play.

STANLEY, GORDON. Born December 20, 1951 in Boston, MA. Graduate Brown U., Temple U. Debut 1977 OB in Lyrical and Satirical, followed by Allegro, Elizabeth and Essex, Red Hot and Blue, Two on the Isles, Moby Dick, Johnny Pye and the Foolkiller, The Golden Apple, Gifts of the Magi, Big Fat and Ugly with a Moustache, Lightin' Out, Bdwy in Onward Victoria (1980), Joseph and the Amazing Technicolor Dreamcoat, Into the Light, Teddy and Alice, Beauty and the Beast.

STANTON, ROBERT. Born March 8, 1963 in San Antonio, TX. Graduate George Mason U., NYU. Debut 1985 OB in Measure for Measure, followed by Rum and Coke, Cheapside, Highest Standard of Living, One Act Festival, Best Half-Foot Forward, Sure Thing, Emily, Ubu, Casanova, Owners/Traps, Visits from Mr. Whitcomb, All in the Timing, Bdwy in A Small Family Business (1992).

STARK, MOLLY. Born in NYC. Graduate Hunter College. Debut 1969 OB in Sacco-Vanzetti, followed by Riders to the Sea, Medea, One Cent Plain, Elisabeth and Essex, Principally Pinter, Toulouse, Winds of Change, The Education of Hyman Kaplan, The Land of Dreams, Beau Jest, Bdwy in Molly (1973).

STATTEL, ROBERT. Born November 20, 1937 in Floral Park, NY. Graduate Manhattan College. Debut 1958 in Heloise, followed by When I Was a Child, Man and Superman, The Storm, Don Carlos, The Taming of the Shrew, Titus Andronicus, Henry IV, Peer Gynt, Hamlet, Danton's Death, The Country Wife, The Caucasian Chalk Circle, King Lear, Iphigenia in Aulis, Ergo, The Persians, Blue Boys, The Minister's Black Veil, Four Friends, Two Character Play, The Merchant of Venice, Cuchulain, Oedipus Cycle, Guilles de Rais, Woyzeck, The Feuhrer Bunker, Learned Ladies, Domestic Issues, Great Days, The Tempest, Brand, A Man for All Seasons, Bunker Reveries, Enrico IV, Selling Off, Titus Andronicus, Bdwy in Zoya's Apartment (1990), Black Comedy.

STAUFFER, BLAIRE. Born in Terre Haute, IN. Graduate Hunter Col. Debut 1960 OB in The Fantasticks, followed by Twelfth Night, As You Like It, Fortuna, Bdwy in An Inspector Calls (1995).

STEHLIN, JACK. Born June 21, 1936 in Allentown, PA. Graduate Julliard.

Debut 1984 OB in Henry V, followed by Gravity Shoes, Julius Caesar, Romeo and Juliet, Phaedra Britannica, Don Juan of Seville, Uncle Vanya, Henry IV Part I, Life off Earth, Danton's Death, Casanova, Washington Square Moves, Richard II.

STEINER, STEVE. Born November 30, 1951 in Chicago, IL. Graduate Webster University. Debut 1986 OB in Two Blind Mice, followed by Hot Sake, Return to the Forbidden Planet, Annie Warbucks, Bdwy in Anything Goes.

STENBORG, HELEN. Born January 24, 1925 in Minneapolis, MN. Attended Hunter College. OB in A Doll's House, A Month in the Country, Say Nothing, Rosmersholm, Rimers of Eldritch, Trial of the Catonsville 9, The Hot 1 Baltimore, Pericles, Elephant in the House, A Tribute to Lili Lamont, Museum, 5th of July, In the Recovery Lounge, The Chisholm Trail, Time Framed, Levitation, Enter a Free Man, Talley and Son, Tomorrow's Monday, Niedecker, Heaven on Earth, Daytrips, A Perfect Ganesh, Bdwy in Sheep on the Runway (1970), Da, A Life.

STERN, CHERYL. Born July 1, 1956 in Buffalo, NY. Graduate Northwestern U. Debut 1984 OB in Daydreams, followed by White Lies, Pets, That's Life!

STERN, JEFFREY. Born May 21, 1983 in Manhasset, NY. Bdwy debut 1992 in The Will Rogers Follies.

STERNE, ARLENE. Born March 23 in Boston, MA. Graduate Northwestern University. Debut 1986 OB in The First Night of Pygmalion, followed by Final Curtain, Papa's Violin, Pericles, Ceremony of Innocence.

STERNE, VICTORIA. Born December 30, 1962 in Washington, DC. Graduate Smith College. Debut 1993 OB in Top Girls, followed by Survival of the Species.

STERNER, STEVE. Born May 5, 1951 in NYC. Attended NYCC. Bdwy debut 1980 in Clothes for a Summer Hotel, followed by Oh Brother!, OB in Lovesong, Vagabond Stars, My Heart is in the East, Mandrake, The Special, Let It Ride, Encore!, Yiddle with a Fiddle, That's Life!, The Cincinnati Saint.

STEVENS, FISHER. Born November 27, 1963 in Chicago, IL. Attended NYU. Bdwy debut 1982 in Torch Song Trilogy, followed by Brighton Beach Memoirs, Carousel, OB in A Darker Purpose, A Perfect Ganesh.

STEVENS, JASON. Born February 27, 1969 in Los Angeles, CA. Attended London Drama Center. Debut 1993 OB in Let Us Now Praise Famous Men, followed by Not about Heroes.

STEWART, HOLLEY. Born in NYC. Graduate Harvard University. Debut 1994 OB in Old New York: False Dawn.

STITT, DON. Born January 25, 1956 in NYC. Graduate San Francisco State University. Bdwy debut 1982 in Do Black Patent Leather Shoes Really Reflect Up?, followed by Late Nite Comic, OB in The Boy Next Door.

STOLTZ, ERIC. Born in 1961 in California. Attended U.S. Cal, Debut 1987 OB in The Widow Claire, followed by The American Plan, Down the Road, Bdwy in Our Town, for which he received a 1989 Theatre World Award, Two Shakespearean Actors.

STONE, JESSICA. Born July 30, 1970 in Rochester, NY,. Attended Barnard College. Bdwy debut 1994 in Grease.

STORMARE, PETER. Born August 27, 1953 in Arbro, Sweden. Attended Royal Dramatic Theatre. Debut OB in Hamlet, followed by Rasputin, The Swan.

STRAM, HENRY. Born September 10, 1954 in Lafayette, IN. Attended Juilliard. Debut 1978 OB in King Lear, followed by Shout and Twist, The Cradle Will Rock, Prison-made Tuxedos, Cinderella/Cendrillon, The Making of Americans, Black Sea Follies, Eddie Goes to Poetry City, A Bright Room Called Day, The Mind King, On the Open Road, My Head was a Sledge Hammer, Christina Alberta's Father, All's Well that Ends Well.

SULLIVAN, NICK. Born February 23, 1968 in Oak Ridge, TN. Graduate University of the South, Rutgers University. Bdwy debut 1993 in White Lies/Black Comedy, OB in Merry Wives of Windsor (1994).

SUSSMAN, MATTHEW. Born March 8, 1958 in NYC. Graduate Brown U., Yale U. Debut 1981 OB in Steel on Steel, Bdwy in Angels in America (1993).

SUTTON, DOLORES. Born in NYC. NYU Graduate. Bdwy debut 1962 in Rhinoceros, followed by General Seeger, My Fair Lady (1993), OB in Man with the Golden Arm, Machinal,-Career, Brecht on Brecht, To Be Young Gifted and Black, The Web and the Rock, My Prince My King, Our Own Family, What's Wrong with this Picture?

SWARTZ, DANNY. Born July 5, 1964 in Dowagiac, MI. Graduate Fresno State University, New York University. Debut 1993 OB in The Game of Love and Chance, followed by Twelfth Night.

SWIFT, FRANCIE. Born March 27, 1969 in Amarillo, TX. Graduate SUNY/Purchase. Debut 1993 OB in Listening, followed by The Hyacinth Macaw.

TALBERTH, KENNETH. Born June 22, 1956 in Boston, MA. Graduate New York University. Debut 1981 OB in Total Eclipse, followed by Henry IV Part I, The Misanthrope, Stray Dog Story, A Winter's Tale, After the Rain, King Lear.

TALCOTT, LINDA. Born July 5, 1960 in Edwards AFB, CA. Attended San Diego State University. Bdwy debut 1989 in Jerome Robbins' Broadway, followed by The Goodbye Girl, Beauty and the Beast.

TAPPAN, TAMI. Born September 24, 1969 in Silver Spring, MD. Graduate Carnegie-Mellon University. Bdwy debut 1993 in Cyrano the Musical, followed by Miss Saigon.

TARADASH, LAUREE. Born June 4, 1959 in New York City. Debut 1984 OB in The Emperor of My Baby's Heart, followed by Harvest of Strangers, Milk and Honey.

TARANTINA, BRIAN. Born March 27, 1959 in New York City. Debut 1980 OB in *Innocent Thoughts and Harmless Intentions*, followed by *Time Framed, Fables for Friends, Balm in Gilead, V & V Only, Portrait of My Bikini*, Bdwy in *Angels Fall*, for which he received a 1983 Theatre World Award, *Biloxi Blues, Boys of Winter*.

TASSIN, CHRISTEN. Born January 2, 1979 in Spartanburg, SC. Bdwy debut 1989 in *Gypsy*, followed by *Radio City Christmas Spectacular*, OB in *Trophies*.

TATE, ROBERT. Born April 30, 1964 in Albuquerque, New Mexico. Graduate Yale University. Debut 1988 OB in *Ten Percent Revue* followed by *Harold and the Purple Dragon, Nefertiti, Rags, Lightin' Out, Blocks*.

TAYLOR, ANDY. Born October 3 in Eugene, OR. Graduate Oberlin Col., U. Mon. Debut 1990 OB in *Romeo and Juliet*, followed by *Rodgers and Hart, On The Open Road, Juno, Painting it Red, Christina Alberta's Father*.

TAYLOR, MYRA. Born July 9, 1960 in Ft. Motte, SC. Graduate Yale U. Debut 1985 OB in *Dennis*, followed by *The Tempest, Black Girl, Marathon 86, Phantasie, Walking the Dead, I Am a Man, Marathon Dancing, Come Down Burning*, Bdwy in *A Streetcar Named Desire, Mule Bone*.

THELIN, JODI. Born June 12, 1962 in St. Cloud, MN. Bdwy debut 1983 in *Brighton Beach Memoirs*, OB in *Before the Dawn, Springtime for Henry, Largo Desolato, The Nice and the Nasty, Dream of a Blacklisted Actor, A Body of Water*.

THOMAS, JOHN NORMAN. Born May 13, 1961 in Detroit, MI. Graduate U. Cincinnati Consv. Bdwy debut 1987 in *Les Miserables*, followed by *The Merchant of Venice, Kiss of the Spider Woman*.

THOMAS, RAYMOND ANTHONY Born December 19, 1956 in Kentwood, LA. Graduate U. Tex/El Paso. Debut 1981 OB in *Escape to Freedom*, followed by *The Sun Gets Blue, Blues for Mr. Charlie, The Hunchback of Notre Dame, Ground People, The Weather Outside, One Act Festival, Caucasian Chalk Circle, The Virgin Molly, Black Eagles, Distant Fires, Shaker Heights, The Lights*.

THOMPSON, ERNEST. Born November 6, 1949 in Bellow Falls, VT. Attended Catholic U., U. Md., American U. Bdwy debut 1975 in *Summer Brave*, OB in *The Valentine Fairy*.

THORNE, RAYMOND. Born November 27, 1934 in Lackawanna, NY. Graduate U. Connecticut. Debut 1966 OB in *Man with a Load of Mischief*, followed by *Rose, Dames at Sea, Love Course, Blue Boys, Jack and Jill, Annie Warbucks*, Bdwy in *Annie* (1977), *Teddy and Alice*.

THORNE, TRACY. Born in NYC. Graduate Smith College, LAMA. Debut 1986 OB in *I Shaw*, followed by *Burrhead, All for Charity, How the Other Half Loves*.

TICOTIN, NANCY. Born September 4, 1957 in NYC. Bdwy debut 1980 in *West Side Story*, followed by *Jerome Robbins' Broadway, Damn Yankees*, OB in *The King and I*, (CC), *A.. My Name is Alice*.

TILLITT, SHAVER. Born March 4, 1957 in Beardstown, IL. Graduate U. Illinois. Bdwy debut 1994 in *Best Little Whorehouse Goes Public*, OB in *Lola*.

TIRELLI, JAIME. Born March 4, 1945 in NYC. Attended U. Mundial, AADA. Debut 1975 OB in *Rubbers, Yanks 3 Detroit 0, followed by The Sun Always Shines on the Cool, Body Bags, Bodega*, Bdwy in *In the Summer House* (1993).

TOLIN, MEG. Born November 11, 1966 in Wheatridge, CO. Attended Indiana U. Bdwy debut 1990 in *Grand Hotel*, followed by *My Fair Lady* (1993)

TOMEI, MARISA. Born December 4, 1964 in Brooklyn, NY. Attended Boston U., NYU. Debut 1986 OB in *Daughters*, for which she received a Theatre World award, followed by *Class 1 Acts, Evening Star, What the Butler Saw, Marathon '88, Sharon and Billy, Chelsea Walls, The Summer Winds, Comedy of Errors, Fat Men in Skirts*.

TOMPOS, DOUG. Born January 27, 1962 in Columbus, OH. Graduate Syracuse U., LAMA. Debut 1985 OB in *Very Warm for May*, followed by *A Midsummer Night's Dream, Mighty Fine Music, Muzeeka, Wish You Were Here, Vampire Lesbians of Sodom, Jeffrey*, Bdwy in *City of Angels*.

TOWNSEND, ELIZABETH. Born in Jackson, MI. Graduate Columbia U. Debut 1989 OB in *Pericles Prince of Tyre*, followed by *Bertolt Brecht: In Dark Times*.

TOY, CHRISTINE. Born December 26, 1959 in Scarsdale, NY. Graduate Sarah Lawrence Col. Debut 1982 OB in *Oh Johnny!*, followed by *Pacific Overtures, Genesis, Festival of One Acts, Balancing Act, Merrily We Roll Along*.

TRANO, GINA. Born January 16, 1964 in Clovis, NMx. Graduate Boston Conservatory. Bdwy debut 1986 in *Singin' in the Rain*, followed by *Joseph and the Amazing Technicolor Dreamcoat*, OB in *The Gay Divorcee* (1987).

TRAVERS, JOSEPH. Born January 2, 1960 in NYC. Graduate SUNY/Albany. Debut 1987 OB in *The Jew of Malta*, followed by *The Witch, The Strange Case of Dr. Jekyll and Mr. Hyde*.

TRUE, JIM. Born July 31, 1966 in Greenwich, CT. Attended Northwestern U. Bdwy debut 1990 in *Grapes of Wrath*, followed by *Philadelphia Here I Come!*

TRUJILLO, ROBERT. Born February 8, 1938 in San Rafael, CA. Graduate U. Toronto. Bdwy debut 1989 in *Jerome Robbins' Broadway*, followed by *Guys and Dolls*.

TRUMBULL, ROBERT. Born February 8, 1938 in San Rafael, CA. Graduate U. California/Berkley. *Bradley and Beth, Othello, The Shannon Doyle Incident, Hers and His, Carbondale Dreams, Asian Shade, Oedipus at Colonus*.

TSOUTSOUVAS, SAM. Born August 20, 1948 in Santa Barbara, CA.

Attended U. Cal., Juilliard. Debut 1969 OB in *Peer Gynt*, followed by *Twelfth Night, Timon of Athens, Cymbeline, School for Scandal, The Hostage, Women Beware Women, Lower Depths, Emigre, Hello Dali, The Merchant of Venice, The Leader, The Bald Soprano, The Taming of the Shrew, Gus & Al, Tamara, The Man Who Shot Lincoln, Puppetmaster of Lodz, Richard III, Snowing at Delphi, Richard II*, Bdwy in *Three Sisters, Measure for Measure, Beggar's Opera, Scapin, Dracula, Our Country's Good, The Misanthrope*.

TUCKER, SHONA. Born in Louisville, KY. Graduate Northwestern U., NYU., Debut 1989 OB in *The Investigation of the Murder of El Salvador* followed by *A Light from the East, Diary of an African American, A Light Shining in Buckinghamshire, Caucasian Chalk Circle, Greeks, Marvin's Room, From the Mississippi Delta, Come Down Burning*.

TURK, BRUCE. Born December 27, 1962 in California. Graduate Northwestern U. Debut 1994 OB in *Titus Andronicus*.

TWAINE, MICHAEL. Born November 1, 1936 in Lawrence, NY. Graduate Ohio State U. Bdwy debut 1956 in *Mr. Roberts*, OB in *Kill the One-Eyed Man, The Duchess of Malfi, Recess, The Empire Builders, Pictures at an Exhibition, Holy Heist, The Seagull: The Hamptons, As You Like It, The Last Sortie*.

UBACH, ALANNA. Born October 3, 1975 in Downey, CA. Debut 1991 OB in *Club Soda*, followed by *Kindertransport*.

ULISSEY, CATHERINE. Born August 4, 1961 in NYC. Attended Natl.. Academy of Arts. Bdwy debut 1986 in *Rags*, followed by *The Mystery of Edwin Drood, Phantom of the Opera, Red Shoes*.

ULLMAN, BILL. Born March 5, 1965 in Park Ridge, NJ. Graduate Syracuse U. LAMA. Debut 1991 in *Home Fires*, followed by *Body Game, As You Like It*, Bdwy in *My Fair Lady* (1993).

UNDERWOOD, BLAIR. Born Aug.25, 1964 in Tacoma, WA. Attended Carnegie-Mellon U. OB debut 1993 in *Measure for Measure*.

UNGER, DEBORAH. Born July 2, 1953 in Philadelphia, PA. Graduate U. Pittsburgh, Florida State U. Debut 1981 OB in *Seesaw*, followed by *The Rise of David Levinsky, Henry the 8th at the Grand Ole Opry, White Widow*.

UTLEY, BYRON. Born November 4, 1954 in Indianapolis, IN. Attended UDC. Bdwy debut 1977 in *Hair*, followed by *Reggae, Big Deal*, OB in *Bones, The Trojan Women, Sweet Will Shakespeare, Transposed Heads, Death and the King's Horseman, A Better Life*.

VALENTINE, JAMES. Born February 18, 1933 in Rockford, IL. Attended U. London, Central School in London. Bdwy debut 1958 in *Cloud 7*, followed by *Epitaph for George Dillon, Duel of Angels, Ross, Caesar and Cleopatra, The Importance of Being Earnest, Camelot*, (1980,1981,1993), *Alice in Wonderland*.

VANCE, DANA. Born June 23, 1952 in Steubenville, OH. Graduate U. WV. Debut 1981 OB in *An Evening with Sheffman and Vance*, followed by *A Backers Audition, CBS Live, All That Glitters*, Bdwy in *Teaneck Tanzi*.

VAN DER BEEK, JAMES. Born March 8, 1977 in Cheshire, CT. Debut 1993 OB in *Finding the Sun*, followed by *Sand*.

VAN DIJK, BILL. Born December 22, 1947 in Rotterdam, Netherlands. Attended Amsterdam Theatre School. Bdwy debut 1993 in *Cyrano the Musical*.

VAN TREUREN, MARTIN. Born December 6, 1952 in Hawthorne, NJ. Graduate Montclair State College. Debut 1978 OB in *Oklahoma!* Followed by *The Miser, Allegro in Concert*.

VENNEMA, JOHN C. Born August 24, 1948 in Houston, TX. Graduate Princeton U., LAMA. Bdwy debut 1976 in *The Royal Family*, followed by *The Elephant Man, Otherwise Engaged*, OB in *Loot, Statements after an Arrest, The Biko Inquest, No End of Blame, In Celebration, Custom of the Country, The Basement, A Slight Ache, Young Playwrights Festival, Danday Dick, Nasty Little Secrets, Mountain, Light Up the Sky, Joined at the Head, A Quarrel of Sparrows, The Illusion*.

VERRETT, SHIRLEY. Born May 31, 1931 in New Orleans, LA. Juilliard Graduate. International opera star before Bdwy debut 1993 in *Carousel*.

VIDA, RICHARD. Born March 15, 1963 in Hartford, CT. Graduate S. Ct. State U. Bdwy debut 1994 in *The Best Little Whorehouse Goes Public*.

VIVONA, JÉROME. Born March 7, 1967 in Bayville, Long Island, NY. Attended Quinipiac College, Indiana U., Nassau County College. Bdwy debut 1994 in *Guys and Dolls*.

VIDNOVIC, MARTIN. Born January 4, 1948 in Falls Church, VA. Graduate Cinn. Consv. Of Music. Debut 1972 OB in *The Fantasticks*, followed by *Lies and Legends, Some Enchanted Evening*, Bdwy in *Home Sweet Homer* (1976), *The King and I, Oklahoma* (1979), *Brigadoon* (1980), *Baby, Some Enchanted Evening, Guys and Dolls* (1994).

VIRTA, RAY. Born June 18, 1958 in L'Anse, MI. Debut 1982 OB in *Twelfth Night*, followed by *The Country Wife, The Dubliners, Pericles, Tartuffe, The Taming of the Shrew, No One Dances, Jacques and His Master, Progress, Snowing at Delphi, The Eye of the Beholder*.

VON BARGEN, DANIEL. Born June 5, 1950 in Cincinnati, OH. Graduate Purdue U. Debut 1981 OB in *Missing Persons*, followed by *Macbeth, Beggars in the House of Plenty, Angel of Death, The Treatment*, Bdwy debut in *Mastergate* (1989) for which he received a Theatre World Award.

WAGNER, CHUCK. Born June 20, 1958 in Nashville, TN. Graduate U. S. Cal. Bdwy debut 1985 in *The Three Musketeers*, followed by *Into the Woods, Les Miserables, Beauty and the Beast*.

WALKER, DIANA. Born June 28, 1942 in NYC. Bdwy debut 1966 in *Mame*, OB in *Fourth Pig, The Cat and the Canary, Allergy, Broadway Classics at Carnegie Hall*.

WALKER, MICHAEL. Born March 11, 1950 in Kenya. Bdwy debut 1974 in *Sherlock Holmes*, OB in *Open Admission, Executive Council*.

WALKER, THOMAS. Born May 12, 1947 in Torrington, CT. Graduate Yale U. Debut 1985 OB in *A Beckett Trilogy*, followed by *The Tablets, VKTMS: Orestes in Scenes, Anarchia*.

WALLACH, ELI. Born December 7, 1915 in Brooklyn, NY. Graduate U. Texas, CCNY. Bdwy debut 1945 in *Skydrift*, followed by *Henry VIII, Androcles and the Lion, Alice in Wonderland, Yellow Jack, What Every Woman Knows, Antony and Cleopatra, Mr. Roberts, Lady from the Sea, The Rose Tattoo*, for which he received a 1951 Theatre World Award, *Mlle. Colombe, Teahouse of the August Moon, Major Barbara, The Cold Wind and the Warm, Rhinoceros, Luv, Staircase, Promenade All, Waltz of the Toreadors, Saturday Sunday Monday, Every Good Boy Deserves Favor, Twice Around the Park, Cafe Crown, The Price, The Flowering Peach*, OB in *The Diary of Anne Frank, Nest of the Wood Grouse, Cafe Crown, In Persons*.

WALLNAU, COLLEEN SMITH. Born June 28, 1948 in Trenton, NJ. Graduate Trenton State College, Rutgers U. Debut 1993 OB in *Through Darkest Ohio*, Bdwy in *Crazy for You* (1994).

WALSH, BARBARA. Born June 3, 1955 in Washington, DC. Attended Montgomery Col. Bdwy debut 1982 in *Rock 'n' Roll: The First 5000 Years*, followed by *Nine, Falsettos, Blood Brothers*, OB in *Forbidden Broadway, Hello Again*.

WALTER, HARRIET. Born September 24 in London, England. Graduate LAMA. Bdwy debut 1983 in *All's Well That Ends Well* (With Royal Shakespeare Co.), OB in *Three Birds Alighting on a Field*, for which she received a 1994 Theatre World Award.

WALTHER, GRETCHEN. Born March 8, 1938 in NYC. Attended Northwestern U. Bdwy debut 1962 in *Something about a Soldier*, OB in *Innocent Pleasures, The Novelist, Paradise*.

WARD, LAUREN. Born June 19, 1970 in Lincoln, NE. Graduate NC School of Arts. Bdwy debut 1994 in *Carousel*.

WARFIELD, DONALD. Born August 25 in Rhinelander, WI. Graduate Brown U., Yale U. Debut 1968 OB in *People vs Ranchman*, followed by *War Games, Saved, Love Your Crooked Neighbor, Mystery Play, The Children's Mass, G.R. Point, Romeo and Juliet*, Bdwy in *Watercolor*.

WATERSTON, SAM. Born November 15, 1940 in Cambridge, MA. Graduate Yale U. Bdwy debut 1963 in *Oh Dad Poor Dad...*, followed by *First One Asleep Whistle, Halfway Up the Tree, Indians, Hay Fever, Much Ado about Nothing, A Meeting by the River, Lunch Hour, Benefactors, A Walk in the Woods, Abe Lincoln in Illinois*, OB in *As You Like It, A Thistle in My Bed, The Knack, The Ritz, Biscuit, La Turista, Posterity for Sale, Ergo, Muzeeka, Red Cross, Henry IV, Spitting Image, I Met a Man, Brass Butterfly, Trial of the Catonsville 9, Cymbeline, Hamlet, The Tempest, A Doll's House, Measure for Measure, Chez Vous, Waiting for Godot, Gardenia, The Three Sisters, An Evening of Primo Levi*.

WEBER, ANDREA. Born in Midland, MI. Graduate Ind. U., Hunter Col. Julliard. Debut 1981 OB in *Inadmissible Evidence*, followed by *Childhood, Festival of One Acts, Comedy of Errors, Macbeth, Entre Chats, Linda Her, Old New York: False Dawn*, Bdwy in *Anna Karenina* (1992).

WEEMS, ANDREW. Born July 18, 1961 in Seoul, S. Korea. Graduate Brown U., U. California. Debut 1993 OB in *A Quarrel of Sparrows*, followed by *Marathon Dancing, Mud Angel, A Midsummer Night's Dream, The Dolphin Position*.

WEIL, SEAN. Born May 28, 1961 in The Bronx, NYC. Attended Sienna College. Debut 1991 in *Nebraska*, followed by *Heart of Earth, Dalton's Back, Superman is Dead*.

WEISS, JEFF. Born in 1940 in Allentown, PA. Debut 1986 OB in *Hamlet*, followed by *The Front Page, Casanova*, Bdwy in *Macbeth*, (1988), *Our Town, Mastergate, Face Value, The Real Inspector Hound/15 Minute Hamlet, Carousel* (1994).

WEISS, GORDON JOSEPH. Born June 16, 1949 in Bismarck, ND. Attended Moorhead College. Bdwy debut 1974 in *Jumpers*, followed by *Goodtime Charley, King of Hearts, Raggedy Ann, Ghetto, Jelly's Last Jam*, OB in *A Walk on the Wild Side* (1988), *Ragtime Blues, Andorra, Tourists of the Mindfield, God in Bed, The Undertakers, Sausage Eaters*.

WELLS, CRAIG. Born July 2, 1955 in Newark, NJ. Graduate Albion Col. Debut 1985 OB in *Forbidden Broadway*, followed by *The Best of Forbidden Broadway, Closer Than Ever, Colette Collage, Balancing Act*, Bdwy in *Chess* (1988), *Les Miserables*.

WESTENBERG, ROBERT. Born October 26, 1953 in Miami Beach, FL. Graduate U. California/Fresco. Debut 1981 OB in *Henry IV Part I*, followed by *Hamlet, The Death of von Richthofen, 3 Birds Alighting on a Field*, Bdwy in *Zorba* (1983), for which he received a Theatre World Award, *Sunday in the Park with George, Into the Woods, Les Miserables, The Secret Garden, Abe Lincoln in Illinois*.

WESTON, DOUGLAS. Born January 13, 1960 in London, England. Graduate Princeton U. RADA. Debut 1991 OB in *Whitestones*, followed by Bdwy in *Blood Brothers* (1993).

WHALEY, FRANK. Born July 20, 1963 in Syracuse, NY. Graduate SUNY/Albany. Debut 1986 OB in *Tigers Wild*, followed by *The Years, Good Evening*.

WHEELER, TIMOTHY. Born July 21, 1957 in Waterville, ME. Bevut 1993 OB in *Oedipus the King*, followed by *The Game of Love and Chance*.

WHITE, ALICE. Born January 6, 1945 in Washington, DC. Graduate Oberlin College. Debut 1977 OB in *The Passion of Dracula*, followed by *La Belle au Bois, Zoology, Show Leopards, Fridays, Candida, He Saw His Reflection*.

WHITE, AMELIA. Born September 14, 1954 in Nottingham, England. Attended London Central School. Debut 1984 OB in *The Accrington Pals*, for

which she received a Theatre World Award, followed by *American Bagpipes*, Bdwy in *Crazy for You* (1992).

WHITE, DAVID A. Born June 26, 1960 in West Virginia. Graduate Ashland College. Debut 1986 OB in *Olympus on My Mind*, followed by *Hello Again*.

WHITE, JULIE. Born June 4, 1962 in San Diego, CA. Attended Fordham U. Debut 1988 OB in *Lucky Stiff*, followed by *Just Say No, Early One Evening, Stick Wife, Marathon '91, Spike Heels, The Family of Mann*.

WHITEHEAD, PAXTON. Born in Kent, England. Attended Webber-Douglas Acad. Bdwy debut 1962 in *The Affair*, followed by *Beyond the Fringe, Candida, Habeas Corpus, Crucifer of Blood, Camelot, Noises Off, Run for Your Wife, Artist Descending A Staircase, Lettice and Lovage, A Little Hotel on the Side, My Fair Lady*, OB in *Gallows Humor, One Way Pendulum, A Doll's House, Rondelay*.

WHITTON, MARGARET. (formerly Peggy). Born November 30 in Philadelphia, PA. Debut 1973 OB in *Baba Goya*, followed by *Arthur, Nourish the Beast, Another Language, Chinchilla, Othello, The Art of Dining, One Tiger to a Hill, Henry IV Parts 1 and 2, Don Juan, My Uncle Sam, Aunt Dan and Lemon, Ice Cream and Hot Fudge, The Merry Wives of Windsor*, Bdwy in *Steaming* (1982).

WIEST, DIANNE. Born March 28, 1948 in Kansas City, MO. Attended U. MD. Debut 1976 OB in *Ashes*, followed by *Leave it to Beaver is Dead, The Art of Dining*, for which she received a 1980 Theatre World Award, *Bonjour La Bonjour, The Three Sisters, Serenading Louie, Other Places, Hunting Cockroaches, After the Fall, Square One, Don Juan in Hell* (in concert), Bdwy in *Frankenstein* (1981), *Othello, Beyond Therapy, In the Summer House*.

WILLIAMS, L. B. Born May 7, 1949 in Richmond, VA. Graduate Albion College. Bdwy debut 1976 in *Equus*, OB in *Spa, Voices, 5 on the Blackhand Side, Chameleon, Forbidden Copy, Song of Solomon, G.R. Point, New Works '87, X Train*.

WILLIAMSON, NANCE. Born October 22 in Clintonville, WI. Graduate State Olaf College, Trinity U. Debut 1992 OB in *Marvin's Room*, followed by *Two Gentlemen of Verona*, Bdwy in *Broken Glass* (1994).

WILLIAMSON, RUTH. Born January 25, 1954 in Baltimore, MD. Graduate U. Md. Bdwy debut 1981 in *Annie*, followed by *Smile, Guys and Dolls*, OB in *Preppies, Bodo, A Helluva Town*.

WILLIS, RICHARD. Born in Dallas, TX. Graduate Cornell U., Northwestern U. Debut 1986 OB in *Three Sisters*, followed by *Nothing to Report, The Rivalry of Dolls, The Time of Your Life*.

WILLIS, SHAN. Born in USA. NY U. Graduate. Bdwy debut 1992 in *The Real Inspector Hound/15 Minute Hamlet*, OB in *Voices, As You Like It, The Taming of the Shrew, Dark of the Moon, A Midsummer Night's Dream*.

WILLISON, WALTER. Born June 24, 1947 in Monterey Park, CA. Bdwy debut 1970 in *Norman Is That You?*, followed by *Two by Two*, for which he received a Theatre World Award, *Wild and Wonderful, A Celebration of Richard Rodgers, Pippin, A Tribute to Joshua Logan, A Tribute to George Abbott, Grand Hotel*, OB in *South Pacific in Concert, They Say It's Wonderful, Broadway Scandals of 1928* and *Options*, both of which he wrote, *Aldersgate '88*.

WILLS, RAY. Born September 14, 1960 in Santa Monica, CA. Graduate Wichita State U., Brandeis U. Debut 1988 OB in *Side by Side by Sondheim*, followed by *Kiss Me Quick, The Grand Tour, The Cardigans, The Rothschilds, Little Me, A Backers Audition, All in the Timing*, Bdwy in *Anna Karenina* (1993).

WILLSON, JOHN BURTON. Born July 26, 1966 in Garland, TX. Graduate U. Texas, Neighborhood Playhouse. Bdwy debut 1993 in *Timon of Athens*, followed by *The Government Inspector*.

WILNER, LORI. Born July 17, 1959 in NYC. Graduate SUNY/Binghamton. Debut 1985 OB in *Hannah Senesh*, followed by *The Witch, Hannah 1939, Milk and Honey*, Bdwy 1990 in *Those Were the Days*.

WILSON, ROY ALAN. Born January 5, 1945 in Portland, OR. Graduate U. Puget Sound, U. W. V. Debut 1957 in *The Music Man*, followed by *1776, Fiddler on the Roof*, OB in *Robin Hood, Show Me Where the Good Times Are*.

WINTERSTELLER, LYNNE. Born September 18, 1955 in Sandusky, OH. Graduate Umd. Bdwy debut 1982 in *Annie*, followed by *Grand Night for Singing*, OB in *Gifts of the Magi* (1984), *The Rise of David Levinsky, Nunsense, Closer Than Ever*.

WISEMAN, JOSEPH. Born May 15, 1919 in Montreal, Canada. Attended CCNY. Bdwy in *Journey to Jerusalem, Abe Lincoln in Illinois, Candle in the Wind, The Three Sisters, Storm Operation, Joan of Lorraine, Anthony and Cleopatra, Detective Story, That Lady, King Lear, Golden Boy, The Lark, Zalmen or the Madness God, The Tenth Man* OB in *Marco Cillions, Incident at Vichy, In the Matter of Robert Oppenheimer, Enemies, The Duchess of Malfi, The Last Analysis, The Lesson, The Golem, Unfinished Stories*.

WOJDA, JOHN. Born February 19, 1957 in Detroit, MI. Attended U. Michigan. Bdwy debut *Two Shakespearean Actors*, OB in 1982 in *Macbeth*, followed by *The Merchant of Venice, Natural Disasters, The Merchant of Venice, The Coming of Mr. Pine, Henry IV Parts 1 & 2, Crackdancing, Black*.

WOLF, CATHERINE. Born May 25 in Abington, PA. Attended Carnegie-Tech U., Neighborhood Playhouse. Bdwy debut 1976 in *The Innocents*, followed by *Otherwise Engaged, An Inspector Calls*, OB in *A Difficult Burning, I Can't Keep Running in Place, Cloud 9, The Importance of Being Earnest, Miami*.

WOLFE, KARIN. Born in Dallas, TX. Attended HB Studio. Bdwy debut 1960 in *Bye Bye Birdie*, followed by *Gigi*, OB in *Best Foot Forward, Jo, Autumn's Here, Old New York: False Dawn*.

WOOD, TOM. Born Apr.19, 1963 in Long Beach, CA. Graduate Carnegie-

Nick Sullivan	Myra Taylor	Andy Taylor	Nancy Ticotin	Jim True	Gina Trano

Robert Trumball	Shona Tucker	Bruce Turk	Shirley Verrett	Byron Utley	Colleen Smith Wallnau

Jerome Vivona	Andrea Weber	Chuck Wagner	Dianne Wiest	Jake Weber	Nance Williamson

Robert Westenberg	Lynne Wintersteller	Frank Whaley	Wysandria Woolsey	Walter Willison	Irene Worth

Nicholas Wyman	Mona Wyatt	Harris Yulin	Kim Yancey	Kurt Ziskie	Karen Ziemba

Mellon U. Debut 1988 OB in *Palace of Amateurs*, Bdwy in *No Man's Land* (1994).

WOODARD, CHARLAYNE. Born December 29, in Albany, NY. Graduate Goodman Theatre School, SUNY. Debut 1975 OB in *Don't Bother Me I Can't Cope*, followed by *Dementos, Under Fire, A..My Name is Alice, Twelfth Night, Hang on to the Good Times, Paradise, Caucasian Chalk Circle, Pretty Fire*, Bdwy in *Hair* (1977), *Ain't Misbehavin'*(1978/1988).

WOODS, CAROL. Born November 13, 1943 in Jamaica, NY. Graduate Ithaca Col. Debut 1980 OB *One Mo' Time*, followed by *Blues in the Night*, Bdwy in *Grind* (1985), *Big River, Stepping Out, The Crucible, A Little Hotel on the Side, The Goodbye Girl*.

WOOLSEY, WYSANDRIA. Born May 9, 1960 in Little Rock, AR. Graduate Loretto Heights College. Debut 1985 OB in *Surf City*, Bdwy in *Chess* (1988) followed by *Cats, Phantom of the Opera, Aspects of Love, Beauty and the Beast*.

WORKMAN, JASON. Born October 9, 1962 in Omaha, Neb. Attended U. Ky., Goodman School. Bdwy debut 1989 in *Meet Me in St. Louis*, for which he received a Theatre World Award followed by *Damn Yankees*, OB in *Haunted Host, Safe Sex*.

WORTH, IRENE. Born June 23, 1916 in Nebraska. Graduate UCLA. Bdwy debut 1943 in *The Two Mrs. Carrolls*, followed by *The Cocktail Party, Mary Stuart, Toys in the Attic, King Lear, Tiny Alice, Sweet Bird of Youth, The Cherry Orchard, The Lady from Dubuque, John Gabriel Borkman*, OB in *Happy Days, Letters of Love and Affection, Chalk Garden, The Golden Age, Coriolanus, Edith Wharton*.

WRIGHT, JEFFREY. Born in Washington, DC. Attended Amherst College. Bdwy debut 1993 in *Angels in America*.

WYATT, MONA. Born January 31 in Ft. Monmouth, NJ. Attended Shenandoah Consv. Debut 1984 in *Radio City Christmas Spectacular*, followed by Bdwy in *Oh Kay!* (1990), *High Rollers, Black and Blue*, OB in *Manhattan Serenade, Hit the Lights*

WYMAN, NICHOLAS. Born May 18, 1950 in Portland, ME. Graduate Harvard U. Bdwy debut 1975 in *Very Good Eddie*, followed by *Grease, The Magic Show, On the 20th Century, Whoopee!, My Fair Lady* (1981), *Doubles, Musical Comedy Murders of 1940, Phantom of the Opera*, OB in *Paris Lights, When We Dead Awaken, Charlotte Sweet, Kennedy at Colonus, Once on a Summer's Day, Angry Housewives, The Hunchback of Notre Dame, Brimstone*.

XIFO, RAYMOND. Born September 3, 1942 in Newark, NJ. Graduate Don Bosco College. Debut 1974 OB in *The Tempest*, followed by *Frogs, My Uncle Sam, Shlemiel the First, A Murder of Crows, Dracula, Threepenny Opera*, Bdwy in *City of Angels* (1989), *3 Penny Opera, Black Comedy*.

YANCEY, KIM. Born September 25, 1959 in NYC. Graduate CCNY. Debut 1978 OB in *Why Lillie Won't Spin*, followed by *Escape to Freedom, Dacha, Blues for Mr. Charlie, American Dreams, Ties That Bind, Walking Through, Raisin in the Sun, Don Juan of Seville, Heliotrope Bouquet, Come Down Burning*.

YOUNG, DAVID. Born July 14, 1947 in Kansas City, MO. Graduate U. Kansas. Debut 1973 OB in *The Raree Show*, followed by *Inexhaustible Banquet, Time Like These, The Night Boat, Rabboni, Madison Avenue, Exit Music*, Bdwy in *Into the Light* (1986).

YOUNG, KAREN. Born September 29, 1958 in Pequonnock, NJ. Attended Douglas Col., Rutgers U. Debut 1982 OB in *Three Acts of Recognition*, followed by *A Lie of the Mind, Dog Logic, Wifey*.

YOUNGMAN, CHRISTINA. Born September 14, 1963 in Philadelphia, PA. Attended Point Park Col. Debut 1983 OB in *Emperor of My Baby's Heart*, followed by *Carouselle des Folles*, Bdwy in *Starlight Express* (1987), *Largely New York, The Will Rogers Follies, My Favorite Year, The Best Little Whorehouse Goes Public*.

YULIN, HARRIS. Born November 5, 1937 in California. Attended USC. Debut 1963 OB in *Next Time I'll Sing to You*, followed by *A Midsummer Night's Dream, Troubled Waters, Richard III, King John, The Cannibals, A Lesson from Aloes, Hedda Gabler, Barnum's Last Life, Hamlet, Mrs. Warren's Profession, Don Juan in Hell* (in concert), *Art and Leisure*, Bwdy in *Watch on the Rhine* (1980), *The Visit*.

ZAKARIAN, CRAIG. Born September 17, 1960 in Kent Island, MD. Graduate Shepherd Col. Debut 1993 OB in *3 by Wilder*, followed by *SS Glencairn, As You Like It*, Bdwy in *Wilder Wilder, Wilder* (1993).

ZAKS, JERRY. Born September 7, 1946 in Germany. Graduate Dartmouth, Smith College. Bdwy debut 1973 in *Grease*, followed by *Once in a Lifetime, Fiorello in Concert*, OB in *Death Story, Dream of a Blacklisted Actor, Kid Champion, Golden Boy, Marco Polo, One Crack Out, Tintypes*.

ZAREMBA, KATHRYN. Born September 10, 1982 in Broken Arrow, OK. Debut 1993 OB in *Annie Warbucks*.

ZAY, TIM. Born August 13, 1952 in Cleveland, OH. Graduate U. Cincinnati. Debut 1988 OB in *Moby Dick*, followed by *This One Thing I Do, The Rover, Teibele and Her Demon, Let Us Now Praise Famous Men*.

ZERKLE, GREG. Born August 19, 1957 in Wisconsin. Graduate U. Wisconsin. U. Washington. Debut 1986 OB in *Sherlock Holmes and the Redheaded League*, followed by *Bittersuite, Juba, Richard II*, Bdwy in *Into the Woods* (1988), *Grand Hotel*.

ZIEMBA, KAREN. Born November 12 in St. Joseph, MO. Graduate U. Akron, Debut 1981 OB in *Seesaw*, followed by *I Married an Angel, Sing for Your Supper, 50 Million Frenchmen, And the World Goes Round, 110 in the Shade* (NYCO/LC), *A Grand Night for Singing*, Bdwy in *Crazy for You* (1994), *Allegro in Concert*.

ZIEN, CHIP. Born March 20, 1947 in Milwaukee, WI. Attended U. Penn. OB in *You're a Good Man Charlie Brown*, followed by *Kadish, How to Succeed ..., Dear Mr. G., Tuscaloosa's Calling, Hot L Baltimore, El Grande de Coca Cola, Split, Real Life Funnies, March of the Falsettos, Isn't It Romantic, Diamonds, Falsettoland, Imaginary Life*, Bdwy in *All Over Town* (1974), *The Suicide, Into the Woods, Grand Hotel, Falsettos*.

ZISKIE, KURT. Born April 16, 1956 in Oakland, CA. Graduate Stanford U., Neighborhood Playhouse. Debut 1985 OB in *A Flash of Lightning*, followed by *Ulysses in Nighttown, Three Sisters, EST Marathon '92*, Bdwy in *Broadway* (1987).

ZUSY, JEANNIE. Born in Washington, DC. Graduate SMU. Debut 1993 OB in *Top Girls*

Don Ameche

Leon Ames

Bill Arlen

Harry Bellaver

OBITUARIES
(June 1, 1993-May 31, 1994)

CHARLES AIDMAN, 68, Indianapolis-born actor died November 7, 1993 in Beverly Hills of cancer. Debut 1957 in Off Bdwy's *Career,* followed by Broadway in *Spoon River Anthology* and *Zoot Suit* .

ADRIANNE ALLEN, 86, English-born actress, died September 14, 1993 in Montreux, Switzerland of cancer. New York debut 1931 in *Cyranara,* followed by *The Shining Hour, Pride and Prejudice, Love for Love, Edward My Son,* and *The Reluctant Debutante* (1956). Survived by her children Anna and Daniel, both performers.

DON AMECHE, 85, Wisconsin-born actor and noted 1930s and 40s film star, died December 6, 1993 in Scotsdale Arizona of cancer. Bdwy debut 1929 in *Jerry-for-Short,* followed by *Silk Stockings, Holiday for Lovers, Goldilocks, 13 Daughters, Henry Sweet Henry,* and *Our Town.* He won a 1985 Oscar for the film *Cocoon* . Survived by four sons, two daughters, two sisters, a brother, and grandchildren.

LEON AMES, 91, Indiana-born actor, died October 12, 1993 in Laguna Beach, California of complications from a stroke. Bdwy debut 1933 in *It Pays to Sin,* followed by *Bright Honor, House in the Country, Thirsty Soil, Male Animal, The Land is Bright, Guest in the House, Little Darling, The Russian People, Slightly Married, Paradise Question, Winesburg Ohio, Howie* and *Life with Father* (CC). Survived by his wife, son and daughter, and two grandchildren.

BILL ARLEN (formerly Christopher Cole), 41, New York-born producer and actor, died June 8, 1993 in Studio City, California. Off-Bdwy performances included 1973's *Call Me Madam,* followed by *The Boy Friend,* before producing West Coast musicals. Survived by his companion, mother, sister and two brothers.

LUCINDA BALLARD (Lucinda Davis Goldsborough), 87, New Orleans-born costume dseigner, died Aug.19, 1993 in Manhattan of cancer. Design debut with 1937's *As You Like It* . Miss Ballard won the first Tony award for Costumes in 1947 for her work on five plays: *Happy Birthday, Another Part of the Forest, Street Scene, John Loves Mary,* and *Chocolate Soldier.* Other notable credits include *I Remember Mama, The Gay Life, Streetcar Named Desire* and her last work 1985's *Night of the Iguana.* Survived by a son, stepdaughter and grandchildren.

EVAN BELL, 43, actor, died October 21, 1993 in NYC of a heart attack. He appeared in Bdwy's *Ain't Misbehavin,* and subsequently appeared in that show all over the world. Many regional credits include playing the Lion in Paper Mill Playhouse's 1992 *Wizard of Oz* .

HARRY BELLAVER, 88. Illinois-born actor, died Aug. 8, 1993 in Nyack, NY of pneumonia. Bdwy debut 1931 in *House of Connelly,* followed by *Night Over Taos, Carry Nation, We the People, Threepenny Opera, The Sellout, Page Miss Glory, Noah, Black Pitt, How Beautiful with Shoes, Russet Mantle, St. Helena, To Quito and Back, Tortilla Flat, Johnny 2 x 4, Mr. Sycamore, The World's Full*

of Girls, Annie Get Your Gun and *That Championship Season.* Survived by two daughters and grandchildren.

STEVE BELLIN, 43, Milwaukee-born actor/singer/dancer, died April 14, 1993 of AIDS. Bdwy credits include *No No Nanette, Sarava, Chorus Line,* and *42nd St.* Survived by his mother and brother.

ERIC BERRY, 80, London-born actor, died Sept. 2, 1993 in Laguna Beach, Calif. of cancer. NY debut in 1954's *The Boy Friend,* followed by *Family Reunion, Power and the Glory, Beaux Stratagem, Broken Jug, Pictures in the Hallway, Peer Gynt, Great God Brown, Henry IV, The White House, White Devil, Charley's Aunt, The Homecoming, Capt. Brassbound's Conversation, Tiny Alice,* and the entire Bdwy run of *Pippin.* Survived by a sister.

JACK BITTNER, 76, Omaha-born actor/singer died June 26, 1993 in Manhattan of a heart attack. Best known as a Shakespearean actor, he performed at the American Shakespeare Festival and Antioch Shakespeare Festival. NY credits include *Nathan the Wise* (1942), *Land of Fame, Beggar's Holiday, All the King's Men, Room Service, Witness for the Prosecution, Tiger at the Gates, Rip Van Winkle, Dear Oscar, What Every Woman Knows, By Bernstein, Philanderer, Enemy of the People, Harold and Maude,* and *Little Johnny Jones.* Survived by his wife.

BILL BIXBY, 59, San Francisco-born actor, died Nov.21, 1993 in Century City Calif. Best known for his tv series work, he appeared in 1967's *The Paisley Convertible* on Bdwy. Survived by his wife.

JAY BLACKTON (Jay Schwartzdorf), 84, conductor, died Jan.8, 1994 in Los Angeles of a heart attack. The conductor of *Oklahoma,* has Bdwy credits including *Annie Get Your Gun, Miss Liberty, Call Me Madam, Mr. President, Wish You Were Here, Happy Hunting,* among others. Survived by his wife, son, daughter and grandson.

SORRELL BOOKE, 64, Buffalo-born actor, died Feb.11, 1994 in Sherman Oaks, Calif. of cancer. Known for his character work on tv, he debuted in 1956's *Sleeping Prince,* followed by *Nature's Way, Heartbreak House, Caligula, Finian's Rainbow, Purlie Victorious, Fiorello, The White House, Come Live with Me,* and *Morning Noon and Night.* Survived by his son, daughter and brother.

REIZL BOZYK, 79, Polish-born actress, died Sept. 30, 1993 in NYC. Star of the Yiddish theatre for over 60 years, she made her Bdwy debut 1966 in *Let's Sing Yiddish,* followed by work on and off-Bdwy in *Sing Israel Sing, Mirele Efros, The Jewish Gypsy, Light Lively and Yiddish, Rebecca the Rabbi's Daughter, Wish Me Mazel-Tov, Roumanian Wedding, The Showgirl, Match Made in Heaven,* and *Dividends.* She had success in the film version of *Crossing Delancey.* Survived by her daughter and grandchildren.

LORAYNE BROX, 94, singer, died June 14, 1993 in LA. She was the eldest member of the singing trio the *Brox Sisters,* who appeared in *Music Box Revue* editions in 1921, 23 and 24. The sisters appeared with the Marx Bros. in *The Cocoanuts,* and in the 1927 *Ziegfeld Follies.* Survived by a daughter and sister, Bobbie.

RAYMOND BURR, 76, Canadian-born actor, died Sept. 12, 1993 in Dry Creek Valley, Calif. of metastatic cancer. Though best known for his starring role as tv's Perry Mason and numerous film parts, he appeared on Bdwy in 1941's *Crazy with the Heat,* and 1944's *The Duke in Darkness.* Survived by his sister.

Eric Berry

Jack Bittner

Bill Bixby

Reizl Bozyk

BRUCE CAMPBELL, 42, press agent, died June 18, 1993 in NYC from a self-inflicted gunshot wound to the head. He was under treatment for manic-depression and was diagnosed as HIV-positive. At his death he was chief press officer for the New York Shakespeare Festival, and had worked for Merle Debuskey/Lincoln Center Theater, La Jolla Playhouse, Disney East Coast Productions and others. He was active in the fight against AIDS. Survived by his father, mother and sister.

MACDONALD CAREY, 81, Iowa-born actor, died March 21, 1994 in Beverly Hills of cancer. In addition to his Emmy Award-winning tv and film work, he appeared on Bdwy in *Lady in the Dark* (1941) and *Anniversary Waltz* (1944). Survived by three daughters, three sons and six grandchildren.

FRAN CARLTON, 80, actress, died Oct. 4, 1993 in Manhattan of cancer. Bdwy credits include *Sunrise at Campobello* and *Men of Distinction.* Survived by her husband, daughter, son, sister and two grandchildren.

MICHAEL CLARKE, 31, stage manager, died Feb.12, 1994 in Manhattan of AIDS. Bdwy credits include *She Loves Me, Prince of Central Park,* and *O! Calcutta!* Survived by his companion, mother and stepfather.

E.P.CONKLE, 94, Nebraska-born playwright and teacher, died Feb.18, 1994 in Austin, TX of a lung infection. Bdwy plays include *200 Were Chosen* (1936) and *Prologue to Glory* (1938). Survived by his wife, daughter, two brothers, and six grandchildren.

JOSEPH COTTEN, 88, Virginia-born actor, died Feb. 6, 1994 in Westwood, Calif. of pneumonia. Starting as an understudy for David Belasco's *Dancing Partner,* he appeared in *Absent Father, Accent on Youth, Jezebel, Postman Always Rings Twice, Julius Caesar, Shoemaker's Holiday, Horse Eats Hat, Danton's Death, The Philadelphia Story, Sabrina Fair, Once More with Feeling,* and *Calculated Risk.* After working for Orson Welles Mercury Theatre, he appeared in Welles' films including *Citizen Kane.* Survived by his second wife, actress Patricia Medina.

JOHN CURRY, 44, Alabama-born skater and actor, died April 15, 1994 in Stratford-upon-Avon, England of AIDS. A 1976 Olympic champion, he made his Bdwy debut in 1980's *Brigadoon,* followed by *Ice Dancing, John Curry's Skaters,* and the 1989 *Privates on Parade.* Survived by his mother.

KEVIN DALY, actor/singer/dancer, died Oct 26, 1993 in Las Vegas after a long illness. Bdwy credits include *Show Me Where the Good Times Are, No No Nanette, Rodgers and Hart,* and the nat'l tour of *42nd Street.*

ROYAL DANO, 71, NYC-born actor, died May 15, 1994 in Los Angeles of a heart attack. Bdwy debut in 1947's *Finian's Ranibow,* followed by *Mrs. Gibbons Boys, Metropole, She Stoops to Conquer, Four Twelves Are 48,* and *Three Wishes for Jamie.* He appeared in many films and is survived by his wife and son.

MACK DAVID, 81, NYC-born composer/lyricist, died Dec. 30, 1993 in Rancho Mirage, Calif. of a heart attack. Best known for his film work, he wrote lyrics to the 1973 musical *Molly.*

RICHARD DeFABEES, 46, New Jersey-born actor, died Nov.18, 1993 of AIDS. He debuted OB 1973 in *Creeps,* followed by *Monsters* (Sideshow), *36, Skin of Our Teeth, Whose Life Is It Anyway,* and he alternated in the lead role in *Torch Song Trilogy.* Survived by his parents and sister.

AGNES deMILLE, 88, NYC-born choreographer/writer, died Oct. 6, 1993 in Manhattan. Her choreography for 1943's *Oklahoma* and *One Touch of Venus* and 1945's *Carousel* transformed musical theatre. Other notable shows include *Brigadoon* (Tony), *Allegro, Hooray for What, Swingin' the Dream, Bloomer Girl, Gentlemen Prefer Blondes, Paint Your Wagon, Girl in the Pink Tights, Goldilocks, Juno, Kwamina* (Tony), *110 in the Shade, Come Summer.* In addition to her ballet credits, she associated with the direction of *Out of This World* (1950). Survived by her son.

Raymond Burr

MacDonald Carey

Joseph Cotten

Royal Dano

Richard DeFabees

Agnes de Mille

Franc Geraci

Ruth Gillette

MICHAEL DEWELL, 62, Connecticut-born producer/writer/translator, died March 3, 1994 in Los Angeles of lung cancer. A co-founder of the National Repertory Theatre, which received a Tony in 1965, his Broadway productions include *The Crucible, The Seagull, Tonight at 8:30, Touch of the Poet,* and *The Imaginary Invalid.* The repertory company toured classical theatre all over the United States. In 1973 Mr. Dewell founded the Los Angeles Free Theatre project. Divorced from actress Nina Foch, he is survived by a sister.

PATRICIA DRYLIE, 69, Toronto-born dancer/actress, died Nov.11, 1993 in NYC of lung cancer. She danced in *On Your Toes* (1950), *My Fair Lady,* and 1978's *Ballroom.* Survived by a sister.

EDWARD DUKE, 40, English-born actor, died Jan. 8, 1994 in London of AIDS. Recently in the 1992 Bdwy *Private Lives,* with Joan Collins, he was well known for his show *Jeeves Takes Charge* on both sides of the Atlantic. At his death he was set to open in the West End's *Relative Values.*

JEAN ECKART (Levy), 72, set/lighting/costume designer, died Sept. 6, 1993 in Dallas, TX of lung cancer. With her husband William, she worked on *Fiorello!, Damn Yankees, Golden Apple, Li'l Abner, She Loves Me, Mame,* and *Once Upon a Mattress* which they co-produced. Survived by her husband, brother, son, daughter, half-sister and grandson.

BERNARD EVSLIN, 77, playwright/mythologist, died June 4, 1993 in Hawaii of cardiac arrest. He wrote 1959's *The Geranium Hat,* followed by *Step on a Crack,* starring Rita Hayworth, which lasted 1 performance only. Survived by his wife, two sons, two daughters and fourteen grandchildren.

JOHN M. FALABELLA, 40, designer, died July 6, 1993 in NYC of AIDS. He designed fourteen Bdwy shows including *Safe Sex, Lady from Dubuque, Harry Connick Jr. on Bdwy,* and *Tango Passion.* Survived by his companion, parents and brother.

JOSEPH A. FALLON, 51, child actor and later, attorney, died Nov. 11, 1993 of pancreatic cancer. Stage credits include *Design on a Stained Glass Window, Sundown Beach, Anniversary Waltz,* and *On Borrowed Time.* As an adult he was prominent in Gotham Democratic politics. Survived by his companion, her son and daughter.

RALPH FARNSWORTH, 71, actor/singer, died Feb. 24, 1994 in NYC. Bdwy include *Bells are Ringing, Most Happy Fella, Destry, Unsinkable Molly Brown, Milk and Honey, Drat the Cat,* the entire run of Man of *La Mancha* (as the Padre), and *1600 Pennsylvania Avenue.* Survived by his wife, and three sons.

ARDEN FINGERHUT, 48, lighting designer, died May 13, 1994 in North Adams, Mass. of breast cancer. Bdwy and Off-Bdwy designs include *Da, Bent,Hay Fever, Plenty, Driving Miss Daisy, Julius Caesar,* and *King John,* and much regional work. Survived by her husband and a daughter.

TOM FUCCELLO, 56, New Jersey-born actor, died Aug. 16, 1993 in Van Nuys, Calif. of AIDS. NYC credits include *Butterflies Are Free, Unknown Soldier and His Wife,* and *Are You Now...?* . Often seen on tv, he is survived by his mother and a brother.

TYLER GATCHELL, 50, Princeton-born general manager/producer, died July 1, 1993 in NYC of a heart attack. Composer Andrew Lloyd Webber dedicated *Sunset Boulevard* to Gatchell's memory. With partner Peter Neufeld, he founded Gatchell & Neufeld Ltd. in 1969 and subsequently was involved with more than 100 shows including *Jesus Christ Superstar, Evita, Cats, Song and Dance, Starlight Express, Aspects of Love, No No Nanette, Annie, Sweeney Todd, Talley's*

Folly, March of the Falsettos, Hurlyburly, Chess, Shirley Valentine, Lettice and Lovage, and most recently *Joseph and the...Dreamcoat, Crazy For You,* and *Sunset Boulevard.* Survived by his companion, father, mother, two brothers and two sisters.

FRANK GERACI, 54, Brooklyn-born actor/teacher, died Feb. 24, 1994 in NYC of AIDS. An original Pear Theatre resident company member, he also appeared in *The Fantasticks* and many regional theatres. Survived by his father and brother.

RUTH GILBERT, 71, actress, died Oct. 12, 1993 in Manhattan of brain cancer. Bdwy debut in 1932's *Girls in Uniform* brought her to Eugene O'Neill's attention. O'Neill cast her in *Ah Wilderness,* and later *Iceman Cometh* (1946). Other shows include *Processional* and *Detective Story.* After radio roles she worked with Milton Berle on his tv show. Survived by her husband, brother, daughter and two grandchildren.

RUTH GILLETTE, 89, Chicago-born actress/singer, died May 13, 1994 in Los Angeles of cancer. Bdwy debut in 1925's *Gay Paree.* Her many shows include *Pajama Game, The Gazebo, How Now Dow Jones, Mame, 70 Girls 70,* and many regional shows and film and tv work. A brother survives.

STEWART GRANGER, 80, London-born actor, died Aug. 16, 1993 in Santa Monica, Calif. of cancer. Starting with English repertory stage work, he became a film actor in Britain and the U.S. before finally appearing in Bdwy's 1989 *The Circle,* for which he received a special Theatre World Award. He took the play to London after it's NYC closing. Three times divorced, he is survived by three daughters and a son.

JOHN GRIGAS, 71, Pennsylvania-born actor, died March 6, 1994 of a heart attack. Bdwy debut 1956 in *Plain and Fancy,* followed by *My Fair Lady, Milk and Honey, Baker Street, It's Superman, Man of La Mancha, Dear World, Follies, A Little Night Music,* and *Pacific Overtures.*

MOSES GUNN, 64, St. Louis-born actor, died Dec.17, 1993 in Connecticut of asthma. Co-founder of the Negro Ensemble Company, his NYC credits include *Measure for Measure, Bohikee Creek, Day of Absence, Happy Ending, Baal, Hard Travelin', Lonesome Train, In White America, The Blacks, Titus Andronicus, Song of the Lusitanian-Bogey, Summer of the 17th Doll, Kongi's Harvest, Daddy Goodness, Cities in Bezique, Perfect Party, To Be Young Gifted and Black, Sty of the Blind Pig, Twelfth Night, American Gothic, Tapman, King John, Coriolanus, Hand Is on the Gate, Othello, First Breeze of Summer, Poison Tree,* and *I Have a Dream.* He won several Obie awards and also worked in film and tv. Survived by his wife, son, daughter, brother and three sisters.

FRED GWYNNE, 66, NYC-born actor, died July 2, 1993 in Taneytown, MD. of pancreatic cancer. He debuted in 1952's *Mrs. McThing,* followed by *Love's Labour's Lost, Frogs of Spring, Irma La Douce, Here's Love, Lincoln Mask, More Than You Deserve, Fair Game, Grand Magic, Salt Lake City Skyline, Cat on a Hot Tin Roof* (1974),*Texas Trilogy, Angel, Players and Whodunnit* (1983). Well known for the tv series *The Munsters* and *Car 54 Where Are You. He* was a versatile stage performer in both plays and musicals. Survived by his second wife and four children.

ADELAIDE HALL, 92, Brooklyn-born singer, died Nov. 7, 1993 in London after a fall. Bdwy debut in 1921's *Shuffle Along,* followed by *Runnin' Wild,* and *Blackbirds of 1928,* where she introduced "I Can't Give You Anything But Love." After success as a jazz singer with Duke Ellington, she starred in several West End shows. She returned to Bdwy in 1957's *Jamaica* and performed in clubs and concerts till her death.

240

Stewart Granger

Moses Gunn

Mark Hardwick

Tiger Haynes

NATALIE HALL (ROWE), 89, Rhode Island-born actress/singer, died March 4, 1994 in Edgecomb, Maine of heart failure. Bdwy debut in 1926's *Iolanthe*, follwed by *Three Little Girls, Through the Years, Music in the Air, Music Hath Charms, Otello, Nights of Song,* and several operatic roles in New York and London. Survived by her daughter and sister.

JAMES LEE HANSEN, JR., 36, playwright, died Dec. 1, 1993 in New York after a long illness. His play *What's a Girl to Do* was produced at Second Stage (1987) and other work was produced in Chicago.

MARK HARDWICK, 39, Texas-born actor/pianist/writer, died Nov. 17, 1993 in New York after an extended illness. He co-created and performed in *Pump Boys and Dinettes* (1982), followed by *Oil City Symphony*. He was musical director for *Smoke on the Mountain*. Survived by longtime companion Mike Craver, his mother and three brothers.

MICHAEL HARVEY, 49, producer, died Sept.23, 1993 in Manhattan of AIDS. He produced on and off-Broadway including *The Grass Harp* (1971), *Why Hannah's Skirt Won't Stay Down, Four Friends, Kennedy's Children, Sweet Bird of Youth* (1976), *Happy Ending,* and *The First.* Survived by his companion, step-mother, brother, sister and stepsisters.

TIGER HAYNES (GEORGE HAYNES), 79, St. Croix-born actor/musician, died Feb.15, 1994 in NYC of cardiac arrest. Bdwy debut in *New Faces of 1956,* followed by *Finian's Rainbow, Fade-Out Fade-In, Pajama Game, The Wiz, A Broadway Musical, Comin' Uptown, My One and Only;* Off-Bdwy includes *Turns, Bags, Louis and Taking My Turn.* Survived by his wife, daughter and grandson.

TERRY HELBING, 42, Illinois-born critic/producer/actor, died March 28, 1994 in NYC of AIDS. As an actor he worked in *Pines '79, Prisoner of the Invisible Kingdom, Franny the Queen of Provincetown, Demolition of Harry Fay* and *Street Theatre.* He presented and published many gay plays and wrote criticism for Theatre Week among others. Survived by a sister.

SPENCER HENDERSON 3D, 44, Texas-born dancer/choreographer, died Nov. 14, 1993 in Ft. Worth. Bdwy includes *Promises Promises, Jesus Christ Superstar,* and *Liza at the Winter Garden,* in addition to many tours and film and tv choreography. Survived by his mother and stepfather.

JAMES LEO HERLIHY, 66, Detroit-born novelist/playwright, died Oct. 10, 1993 in Los Angeles of an overdose of sleeping pills. Best known for his novels including *Midnight Cowboy* and *All Fall Down* he also co-wrote *Blue Denim* (1958) with William Noble for Bdwy. Off-Bdwy plays include *Moon in Capricorn* (1953) and *Stop You're Killing Me* (1970). He wrote and acted in West Coast productions and is survived by a brother.

SEYMOUR HERSCHER, 82, general manager, died Feb. 12, 1994 in NYC. His 60 Bdwy shows include Richard Burton's *Hamlet, Anna Christie* (Liv Ullmann), and *Evening with Nichols and May.* He worked with Alexander H. Cohen's producing organization and is survived by his wife, daughter, son and two grandchildren.

BOB HIGGINS, 40, Florida-born actor, died Nov.14, 1993 in NYC of AIDS. Debut OB 1979 in *Teeth 'n' Smiles,* followed by *Holding Patterns* and several regional shows including *Ford's Theatre's Christmas Carol.*

ROBERT HOREN, 68, South Dakota-born actor, died Jan.12, 1994 in NYC from cancer. Bdwy credits include *Great White Hope, Raisin, Minor Miracle,*

Borstal Boy; Off-Bdwy includes *Hogan's Goat,* and many tours. Survived by a brother, nieces and nephews.

GUSTI HUBER, 78, Austrian-born actress, died July 12, 1993 in Mount Kisco, NY of heart failure. One of Vienna's leading actresses, she came to Bdwy with 1952's *Flight Into Egypt,* followed by *Dial M for Murder* and *Diary of Anne Frank.* She retired in 1961 and is survived by her husband, three daughters (including actress Bibi Besch), a son and four grandchildren (including actress Samantha Mathis).

LAWRENCE HUGO, 76, California-born actor, died March 2, 1994 in Charlottesville, VA, of Alzheimer's disease. Bdwy debut 1941 in *Distant City,* followed by 50 roles on and off-Bdwy including *Skin of Our Teeth* (replacing Monty Clift during illness), *I'll Take the High Road, Decision, Born Yesterday, Stalag 17, Double in Hearts, Bird Cage Decision, There's a Girl in My Soup, Hamlet ,U.S.A.,* and *Enclave.* Survived by a son, daughter and grandchildren.

LETITIA IDE, 84, Illinois-born dancer, died Aug.29, 1993 in Hastings-on-Hudson, NY of cancer. Noted for modern dance, she did appear on Bdwy in 1930's *Lysistrata,* followed by *As Thousands Cheer, Life Begins at 8:40,* and *Americana.*

EUGENE IONESCO, 84, Romanian-born playwright, died March 28, 1994 in Paris. Known for changing theatre with his absurdist masterpieces, his plays were frequently controversial. They include *The Bald Soprano* (1950), *The Lesson, The Chairs, Rhinoceros, Jack or the Submission, Victims of Duty, Amedee, The New Tennant, Exit the King, The Killer, Man with the Suitcases, Pedestrian (A Stroll) in the Air, Hunger and Thirst, Killing Game, Macbeth, Man with Bags, Ce Formidable Bordel,* and *Journey Among the Dead* (1980).

STERLING JENSEN, 68, San Diego-born actor/mime, died Dec.8, 1993 in New Orleans. NY credits include 1955's *Desk Set,* followed by *Mime Theatre, The Father, The Miser, Pelias and Melisande, The Bond, King Lear, Journey's End, Dance of Death, Trumpet's and Drums, Macbeth, Oedipus, Lady from Maxim's, Uncle Vanya, Master Builder,* and *Taming of the Shrew.* In 1965 he helped found the Roundabout Theatre and taught writing and acting in NYC schools. Survived by his wife.

ZITA JOHANN, 89, Hungarian-born actress, died Sept 24, 1993 in Nyack, NY of pneumonia. Bdwy debut in 1924 in *Man and the Masses,* followed by *Machinal, Tomorrow and Tomorrow,* among others. Films include playing the love interest in Boris Karloff's *Mummy* (1932).

RICHARD JORDAN, 56, NYC-born actor, died Aug 27, 1993 in LA of a brain tumor. Bdwy debut in 1961's *Take Her She's Mine,* followed by *Bicycle Ride to Nevada, War and Peace, Generation, A Patriot for Me;* Off-Bdwy in *Judith, All's Well That Ends Well, Trail of the Catonsville 9, Three Acts of Recognition, A Private View, Protest* (1983 Obie) and *Measure for Measure.* He directed 1990's *Macbeth,* with Raul Julia and often worked in film and tv Divorced from actress Kathleen Widdoes, he is survived by a son Robert Jordan, whose mother is actress Blair Brown, his mother, a brother and three sisters.

RITA KARIN, 73, Polish-born actress, died Sept.10, 1993 in New York after a brief illness. Bdwy debut in 1960's *The Wall,* followed by *Call on Kuprin, Penny Wars, Yentl* (also OB); Off-Bdwy in *Pocket Watch, Scuba Duba, House of Blue Leaves, World of Sholom Aleichem, Poets from the Inside, Sharon Shashanovah,* and *I Love You I Love You Not.* Survived by a daughter, son and five grandchildren.

241

Bob Higgins

Bob Horen

Laurence Hugo

Richard Jordan

STEVEN KEATS, 48, NYC-born actor, died in Manhattan on May 8, 1994, a suicide. Debut Off-Bdwy in 1970's *One Flew Over the Cuckoo's Nest*, followed by *We Bombed in New Haven, Awake and Sing, Rose Tattoo, I'm Getting My Act Together … , Sunday Runners in the Rain, Who They Are and How It Is with Them, Other People's Money, Raft of the Medusa*, and *Rags*; Bdwy in 1971 cast of *Oh Calcutta!* Active in film and tv, he is survived by two sons, two daughters and a sister.

ED KERRIGAN, 58, dancer/choreographer, died Jan.12, 1994 of AIDS. Bdwy include *On Your Toes, My Fair Lady,* and *Camelot*. He danced in tours, film and tv. Survived by a brother.

LOIS KIBBEE, 71, West Virginia-born actress, died Oct.18, 1993 of a brain tumor. Known for her tv work, she appeared in many plays including Bdwy's *A Man for All Seasons* and *Venus Is*. Survived by her mother, two brothers and a sister.

PHIL KILLIAN, 47, North Carolina-born actor/director, died Aug.14, 1993 in Los Angeles of melanoma. NY credits include *The Fantasticks* (1972), *Scapino and The Rothschilds,* and *Tamara,* on which he served as associate director in NY and LA. Survived by his father and brother.

HARRY KONDOLEON, 39, playwright/novelist, died March 16, 1994 in Manhattan of AIDS. Plays include *Christmas on Mars, Anteroom, Zero Positive, Love Diatribe,* and a one-act collection *Self Torture and Strenuous Exercise*. An Obie award winner in 1983 (Most Promising Playwright) and 1993, he is survived by his parents and a sister.

ROBERT (DIRK) KOOIMAN, 64, actor, died March 7, 1994 in L.A. He acted Off-Bdwy in the early 1950s, including *Ulysses in Nighttown* and *Summer of the 17th Doll*. Survived by his companion, a brother and a sister.

WILLIAM LANTEAU, 70, Vermont-born actor, died Nov.3, 1993 after heart surgery. Bdwy credits include *At War with the Army, Mrs. McThing, Remarkable Mr. Pennypacker, What Every Woman Knows, The Matchmaker,* and *Li'l Abner*. He appeared in many L.A. productions including *On Golden Pond* for which he re-created his role on film. Survived by a brother.

JOE LAYTON, 64, NYC-born director/producer/choreographer/dancer, died May 5, 1994 in Key West Florida after a long illness. Bdwy debut at 16 in *Oklahoma,* followed by dance roles in *High Button Shoes, Gentlemen Prefer Blondes,* and *Wonderful Town*. He started choreographing with 1959's *On the Town,* followed by *Once Upon a Mattress, Sound of Music, Greenwillow, Tenderloin and Sail Away*. He became director as well as choreographer with *No Strings* (Tony, Choreography) followed by many productions including *George M!* (Tony, Choreography), *Dear World, Two By Two, Bette Midler's Clams on the Halfshell, Diana Ross at the Palace, Platinum, Rock 'n' Roll: The First 500 Years, Woman of the Year, Barnum, Three Musketeers* (1984) and *Harry Connick Jr. on Bdwy* (1990). He directed notable tv specials for Barbra Streisand and others and directed a musical *Gone With the Wind* in London (1972). Survived by a son.

EDWINA LEWIS (MARGARET KLENCK), 42, Detroit-born actress, died Aug 23, 1993 in Augusta, Mich. of a heart attack. Bdwy credits include recent productions of *Cat on a Hot Tin Roof* and *Streetcar Named Desire* as well as *Mule Bone*.

LEON LIEBGOLD, 83, Poland-born actor, a member of the Yiddish theatre for 50 years, died on Sept. 3, 1993 in New Hope, PA. His credits include many productions of *The Dybbuk, Mazel Tov Molly, The Wedding March,* and his last, *Riverside Drive,* in 1987. Survived by a brother.

ROY LONDON, 50, New York City-born actor, writer and director died at his home in Los Angeles of lymphoma on Aug. 8, 1993. He debuted on Broadway in *Little Murders* in 1967, after which he appeared in *The Birthday Party* and

Rita Karin

Steven Keats

Phil Killian

William Lanteau

Roy London

Myrna Loy

Janet Margolin

Winston May

Gingham Dog, and Off-Bdwy in *Three by de Ghelderode, Once in a Lifetime, Viet Rock, America Hurrah, Monopoly, New York! New York!, End of Summer,* and *Ballymurphy.* His play *Mr. Murray's Farm* was produced by Circle Rep in 1976. He is survived by his companion, producer Tim Healey, his mother, and a brother.

MYRNA LOY, 88, Montana-born actress, one of the legendary movie stars of the 1930's and 40's, died on Dec. 14, 1993 in surgery at Lennox Hill Hospital in Manhattan following a long illness. Best known for her movie roles in the *Thin Man* comedies as well as such dramas as *The Best Years of Our Lives,* Ms. Loy made her long-delayed legitimate stage debut in 1962's *There Must Be a Pony,* which closed out of town. Following a tour of *Barefoot in the Park* and stock appearance in *The Marriage Go Round* she had her one and only Broadway role in the 1973 revival of *The Women.* No survivors.

JANET MARGOLIN, 50, Manhattan-born stage, screen and tv actress, perhaps best known for co-starring in the movies *David and Lisa* and *Take the Money and Run,* died of ovarian cancer on Dec. 17, 1993 at her home in Los Angeles. She received a Theatre World Award for her 1961 Broadway debut in *Daughter of Silence.* Survived by her husband, actor Ted Wass, two children, and three sisters.

SHERRY MATHIS, 44, stage and tv actress, who appeared for 7 years on the daytime tv drama *Search for Tomorrow,* died of cancer on Jan. 23, 1994 in Memphis. On Broadway she was seen in *A Little Night Music* (debut, 1971) and *Music Is.* Survived by two brothers, and her mother.

WINSTON MAY, 57, Arkansas-born stage actor died of AIDS on Apr. 29, 1994 in Manhattan. Following his 1978 Off-Bdwy debut in *The Man Who Washed His Hands,* he appeared in *King Lear, Candida, Trumpets and Drums, Otho the Great, Uncle Vanya, Servant of Two Masters, The Play's the Thing, Autumn Garden, Madmen,* and *Villager.* Survived by a brother.

ALDYN McKEAN, 45, singer-actor whose credits include the Broadway musical *The Robber Bridegroom,* died at his Manhattan home of AIDS in late February of 1994. Survived by his parents and two brothers.

JOHN McLIAM (John Williams), 76, stage, film and tv actor, died of melanoma and Parkinson's disease on Apr. 16, 1994 at his home in Woodland Hills, CA. After his 1951 Broadway debut in *Barefoot in Athens,* he was seen in *One More River, Desire Under the Elms, Saint Joan,* and *Tiger at the Gates.* Survived by his wife, daughter, two brothers, and a granddaughter.

CLAUDIA McNEIL, 77, Baltimore-born actress, best remembered for her role as the mother in the original Broadway production of *A Raisin in the Sun,* which she repeated in the screen version, died on Nov. 25, 1993 in Englewood, NJ from complications of diabetes. She also performed on Broadway in *The Crucible* (debut, 1952), *Simply Heavenly, Tiger Tiger Burning Bright, Something Different, Her First Roman,* and *Wrong Way Light Bulb.* Off-Bdwy she was seen in *Contributions* and *Raisin.* No reported survivors.

EDITH MEISER, 95, Detroit-born stage and film actress-writer, died of a heart attack in New York on Sept. 26, 1993. She debuted on Broadway in 1923 in *The New Way,* followed by *Fata Morgana, The Guardsman, Garrick Gaieties, The Chief Thing, Peggy-Ann, Greater Love, He, Strangler Fig, Let's Face It, Mexican Hayride, Round Trip, Rich Full Life, I Gotta Get Out, Getting Married, Sabrina Fair, The Magic and the Loss, Happy Hunting, The Unsinkable Molly Brown,* and Off-Bdwy in *Airways Inc., Carefree Tree,* and *Pygmalion.* She wrote the play *The Wooden O.* No reported survivors.

MELINA MERCOURI, 68 or 71, Greek actress who came to prominence in the 1960 film *Never on Sunday,* then made her Broadway debut in the 1967 musical adaptation, *Ilya Darling,* died on March 6, 1994 in Manhattan of complications from lung cancer. She made one other NY stage appearance, in *Lysistrata.* Later she served as the Greek Minister of Culture. Survived by her husband, director Jules Dassin, and a brother.

ANITA MORRIS, 50, North Carolina-born stage, screen and tv actress-dancer, who came to fame with her provocative performance in the 1982 Broadway musical *Nine,* died of cancer on March 3, 1994 at her home in Los Angeles. Debuting in the chorus of *Jesus Christ Superstar* in 1972 she later appeared in *Seesaw, Rachel Lily Rosenbloom, The Magic Show, Sugar Babies,* and *The Best Little Whorehouse in Texas.* Survived by her husband, director Grover Dale, a son, her parents, and two brothers.

JEFF MORROW, 86, New York-born stage, screen and tv actor, died on Dec. 26, 1993 in Canoga Park, CA. His many Broadway appearances include *Billy Budd, Macbeth,* and *Romeo and Juliet.* Survived by his wife and daughter.

KENNETH NELSON, 63, North Carolina-born stage, screen and tv actor, who created two of Off-Broadway's most notable roles, the Boy in *The Fantasticks* and Michael in *The Boys in the Band,* died of AIDS on Oct. 7, 1993 in London. Following his 1951 Broadway debut in *Seventeen,* he was seen in the musicals *Stop the World I Want to Get Off, Half a Sixpence,* and *Lovely Ladies Kind Gentlemen,* then moved to England. Survived by a sister.

CLAIRE NICHTERN, 73, New York theatre producer died of cancer on March 26, 1994 in New York City. Her credits include *The Typist, The Tiger, Luv* (for which she won a Tony Award), *The Banker's Daughter, Jimmy Shine, Crimes of the Heart, Cold Storage, God Bless You Mr. Rosewater, Mass Appeal, Piaf,* and *The Dresser.* Survived by a daughter and a son.

PATRICK J. O'HARA, 55, singer and dancer died on June 11, 1993 in Burbank following a long illness. His Broadway credits include *Promises Promises* and *Seesaw.*

Sherry Mathis

John McLiam 245

Claudia McNeil

Edith Meiser

Melina Mercouri

Anita Morris

GEORGE PEPPARD, 65, Detroit-born stage, screen and theatre actor died of pneumonia on May 8, 1994 in Los Angeles. He debuted on Broadway in 1956 in *Girls of Summer*, followed by *The Pleasure of His Company*. Notable film credits include *Breakfast at Tiffany's* and *The Carpetbaggers*. He was best known to tv audiences from the series *Banacek* and *The A-Team*. Survived by his fifth wife, three children, and three grandchildren.

BRUCE PEYTON, 44, playwright whose works included *Mother and Son Inc.* and *Feathertop* died of AIDS on Dec. 25, 1993 at his Manhattan home. Survived by his father and a step-sister.

VINCENT PRICE, 82, St. Louis-born actor who became noted for his horror movie roles in such films as *House of Wax, The Fly, The Pit and the Pendulum*, and *Theatre of Death*, died of lung cancer on Oct. 25, 1993 at his home in Los Angeles. He made his Broadway debut in the 1935 production *Victoria Regina*, followed by *Shoemaker's Holiday, Heartbreak House, The Lady Has a Heart, Outward Bound, Angel Street, Richard III, Black-Eyed Susan, Darling of the Day*, and *Diversions and Delights*. He is survived by a son and a daughter. His third wife, actress Coral Browne, died in 1991.

JAMES RAITT, 41, musical director for such shows as the Broadway revival of *Damn Yankees* and the Off-Brodaway revue *Forever Plaid*, died of AIDS at his Manhattan home on Apr. 25, 1994. He was a cousin to singers John Raitt and his daughter Bonnie. Survived by three sisters, and a brother.

RENE RAY, 81, British actress who made her sole Broadway appearance in the 1947 production of *An Inspector Calls*, died on Aug. 28, 1993 in the Channel Islands of unreported causes. Survived by a sister.

ALICE REINHEART, 83, stage, tv and screen actress, whose Broadway appearances include *The Wooden Slipper* and *Journey to Jerusalem*, died on June 10, 1993 in Avon, CT. No reported survivors.

HAROLD ROME, 85, Broadway composer-lyricist died at his Manhattan home on Oct. 26, 1993 of complications from a stroke. His credits include *Pins and Needles, Call Me Mister, I Can Get It for You Wholesale, Wish You Were Here*, and *Fanny*. He was inducted into the Songwriters' Hall of Fame in 1981, and the Theatre Hall of Fame in 1991. Survived by his wife, a son, a daughter, two sisters, and two grandchildren.

CESAR ROMERO, 86, New York City-born stage, screen and tv actor, who became known for his Hollywood roles as the suave Latin, died on Jan. 1, 1994 in Los Angeles from complications related to a blood clot after being hospitalized with bronchitis and pneumonia. Before his long movie career he danced in several choruses and acted in such plays as *Strictly Dishonorable, Stella Brady, All Points West, Social Register*, and *Dinner at Eight*. Survivors include a brother, three nieces, and a nephew.

FRED SADOFF, 68, Brooklyn-born stage, tv and film actor died of AIDS on May 6, 1994 in Los Angeles. Following his 1949 debut in the original production of *South Pacific*, he was seen on Broadway in *Wish You Were Here* and *Camino Real*, and Off-Bdwy in *The Collyer Brothers at Home, Period Piece*, and *Hannah*. Survived by a brother, two nieces and two nephews.

SCOTT SALMON, 51, stage dancer-choreographer-director died on July 17, 1993 in Northridge, CA, from injuries received in an automobile accident. In addition to staging the *Radio City Music Hall Christmas* and *Easter Shows* since 1990 he also choreographed *La Cage aux Folles* and danced in such shows as *Mame* and *George M*. Survived by a daughter, a son, and his mother.

PETER MARK SCHIFTER, 44, theatre and opera director died of AIDS on Sept. 10, 1993 in New York. His New York stage work included the Broadway productions of *Gemini* and *Welcome to the Club*, and the Off-Bdwy shows *History of the American Film* and *Das Lusitania Songspiel*. Survived by his father and a sister.

Kenneth Nelson

George Peppard

Vincent Price

Cesar Romero

Fred Sadoff

Hilda Simms

Alexis Smith

Jeremiah Sullivan

IRENE SHARAFF, 83, notable costume designer for stage and film, died of congestive heart failure on Aug. 16, 1993 in Manhattan. She created her first Broadway designs for *Alice in Wonderland* in 1932 and thereafter worked on dozens of shows including *As Thousands Cheer, Lady in the Dark, A Tree Grows in Brooklyn, Idiot's Delight, The King and I* (Tony Award) and *Jerome Robbins' Broadway*. She won 5 Academy Awards for her film creations. No reported survivors.

HILDA SIMMS (HILDA MOSES), 75, Minneapolis-born stage, tv and film actress, best known for playing the title role in the 1944 Broadway production of *Anna Lucasta*, died of cancer of the pancreas on Feb. 6, 1994 in Buffalo, NY. She also appeared on the New York stage in *Cool World, Tambourines to Glory, and The Madwoman of Chaillot* (Off-Bdwy). Survived by her husband, three sisters, and two brothers.

ALEXIS SMITH, 72, Canada-born actress who, following a long career on screen and temporary retirement, made her Broadway debut in *Follies* in 1971 and won a Tony Award, died of cancer in Los Angeles on June 9, 1993. Her subsequent Broadway roles were in *The Women, Summer Brave,* and *Platinum*. Survived by her husband of 49 years, actor Craig Stevens.

OLIVER SMITH, 75, one of the theatre's most notable set designers, died of emphysema on Jan. 23, 1994 at his home in Brooklyn Heights. His many Broadway credits include *A Clearing in the Woods, Candide, My Fair Lady* (Tony Award), *Auntie Mame, Eugenia, Visit to a Small Planet, West Side Story* (Tony Award), *Camelot, Becket* (Tony Award), *Hello Dolly!* (Tony Award), *Baker Street* (Tony Award), and *The Odd Couple*. Survived by two brothers.

MARK STEVENSON, 44, actor and agent who appeared in such solo pieces as *A Visitation From John Keats* and *Shedding Light on Shakespeare*, died of AIDS on March 16, 1994. Survived by his parents and three brothers.

EZRA STONE, 76, Massachusetts-born actor and director, best known for his starring role as Henry Aldrich on radio, died on March 3, 1994 in an automobile accident near Perth Amboy, NJ. His Broadway credits as an actor include *Three Men on a Horse, Brother Rat,* and *What a Life* (where he first played Henry Aldrich), and his directorial credits include *See My Lawyer, Me and Molly, At War With the Army,* and *January Thaw*. Survived by a son, a daughter, a sister, and four grandchildren.

SAINT SUBBER, 76, Broadway producer whose credits include *Kiss Me Kate, House of Flowers, Come Blow Your Horn, Barefoot in the Park,* and *The Odd Couple,* died of heart failure at his home in Berkeley, CA, on Apr. 19, 1994. Survived by a niece.

JEREMIAH SULLIVAN, 58, stage, film and tv actor, and professional astrologer, died of AIDS on Dec. 12, 1993 in New York City. Following his 1957 Broadway debut in *Compulsion,* he appeared in *The Astrakhan Coat, Philadelphia Here I Come!, Lion in Winter, House of Blue Leaves, Gogol, The Master and Margarita, Breakfast Conversations in Miami, Life Is a Dream,* and *Legend of Sharon Shashanova*. No reported survivors.

DONALD SWANN, 70, Welsh composer and entertainer, best known for teaming with lyricist Michael Flanders for the revues *At the Drop of a Hat* and *At the Drop of Another Hat,* died of prostate cancer on March 23, 1994 in London. Both shows played in London prior to coming to Broadway. Survived by his wife, and two daughters.

SWEN SWENSON, 63, Broadway actor-dancer died of AIDS on June 23, 1993 in Los Angeles. He was perhaps best remembered for performing the song "I've Got Your Number" in the 1962 musical *Little Me,* for which he received a Theatre World Award. His other Broadway appearances were in *Great to Be Alive!* (debut, 1950), *Bless You All, As I Lay Dying, Destry Rides Again, Wildcat, Golden Apple, Molly, Ulysses in Nigttown,* and *Can-Can*. Survived by two sisters.

JEROME THOR, 69, star of the 1950's tv series "Foreign Intrigue," died of cardiac arrest on Aug. 12, 1993 in Westwood, CA. His Broadway credits include *The Marriage Proposal, He Who Gets Slapped, Get Away Old Man,* and *Golden Boy*. He is survived by his wife and "Foreign Intrigue" co-star actress Synda Scott.

ALFRED TOIGO, 59, Broadway actor-singer died on Apr. 22, 1994 at his home in Ossining, NY following a brief illness. His NY credits include *Zorba, Cabaret, Kean, Kismet,* and *Annie*. Survived by his wife, choreographer Mary Jane Houdina, three children, a brother, and two grandchildren.

KATE TOMLINSON, theatre actress whose Broadway credits include *Eastward in Eden, Minor Miracle, Guys and Dolls,* and *A Day in the Death of Joe Egg*. Survived by her husband and a nephew.

LOUISE TROY, 60, New York City-born stage, screen and tv actress, died of breast cancer on May 5, 1994 at her home in Manhattan. After debuting Off-Broadway in 1955 in *The Infernal Machine,* she was seen in *Merchant of Venice, Conversation Piece, Salad Days, O Oysters!, A Doll's House, Last Analysis, Judy and Jane, Heartbreak House,* and *Rich Girls*; also on Broadway in *Pipe Dream, A Shot in the Dark, Tovarich, High Spirits, Walking Happy, Equus, Woman of the Year, Design for Living,* and *42nd Street*. She is survived by her second husband, actor Douglas Seale.

Swen Swenson

Alfred Toigo

Paula Trueman

Joseph Warren

Sam Wanamaker

PAULA TRUEMAN, 96, stage and film actress whose career in the New York theatre spanned sixty years, died on March 23, 1994 in Manhattan. After her Broadway debut in 1922 in *Thunderbird,* she appeared in *Grand Street Follies, Sweet and Low, Grand Hotel, You Can't Take It With You, George Washington Slept Here, Kiss and Tell, Violet, For Love or Money, Gentlemen Prefer Blondes, Solid Gold Cadillac, Mrs. McThing, Wake Up Darling, Family Affair, Wonderful Town, Sherry!,* and *The Chinese.* Off-Bdwy she was seen in *Sunday Man, Wilder's Triple Bill, Postcards,* and *The Chisholm Trail Went Through Here.* Survived by a stepson.

VIRGINIA TURGEON, 70, dancer with the Agnes de Mille Company, died on Sept. 21, 1993 in Amagansett, NY, after a long illness. Her Broadway credits include *One Touch of Venus* and *Brigadoon.* Survived by her husband, actor Peter Turgeon, a son, a daughter, and five grandchildren.

RON VAWTER, 45, stage and screen actor died on Apr. 16, 1994 of a heart attack while flying from Zurich to New York; he had AIDS. A founder of the *Performing Garage* as well as actor with the Wooster Group his NY stage credits include *LDS (Just the High Points), Frank Dell's Temptation of St. Anthony, Three Sisters,* and the one-man show *Roy Cohn/Jack Smith.* He is survived by his companion, director Greg Mehrten, his mother, and two sisters.

EVELYN VENABLE, 80, stage and screen actress, died of cancer on Nov. 16, 1993 in Post Falls, ID. Her stage credits include *Dear Brutus, Cyrano de Bergerac, Hamlet,* and *Romeo and Juliet.* She was the widow of cinematographer Hal Mohr.

PAUL WALKER, 41, theatre actor-director-teacher, died of AIDS on Dec. 5, 1993 in Manhattan. A member of the Acting Company his stage appearances include *Hamlet* with the NY Shakespeare Festival. For the Music Theatre Group of Manhattan he directed such works as *Ladies, Legacy,* and *Short Takes.* Survived by two brothers.

SAM WANAMAKER, 74, Chicago-born actor-director, died of cancer on Dec. 18, 1993 at his home in England. He appeared on Broadway in *Cafe Crown, Counterattack, This Too Shall Pass, Joan of Lorraine, Goodbye My Fancy,* and *Arms and the Man.* After being blacklisted in the early 1950's he spent most of his subsequent career in England. His life-long dream of rebuilding Shakespeare's Globe Theatre in London was finally coming to fruition at the time of his death. Survived by his wife, and three daughters, one of whom is actress Zoe Wanamaker.

JOSEPH WARREN, 77, Massachusetts-born stage and screen actor, died of respiratory failure on Oct. 1, 1993 in Manhattan. His NY stage credits include *Barefoot in Athens* (Broadway debut, 1951), *One Bright Day, The Hidden River, The Advocate, Philadelphia Here I Come!, Borstal Boy, The Lincoln Mask, Monday Day After the Miracle,* as well as many appearances with the NY Shakespeare Festival (*Measure for Measure, Hamlet,* etc.). He is survived by his wife, two sons, a stepson and several grandchildren.

MURIAL WILLIAMS (HART), 80, stage and tv actress whose Broadway credits include the original 1934 production of *Merrily We Roll Along,* died of cancer in Manhattan on Feb. 10, 1994. Survived by a stepdaughter, a sister, a brother, and a stepson.

TOMMY WONDER, 78, Montana-born stage and film actor-dancer, died of heart failure on Dec. 11, 1993 in New York City. His NY theatre appearances include *Ziegfeld Follies of 1943, Two for the Show,* and *Banjo Eyes.* Survivors include a niece.

CHARLES WOODWARD, 70, theatre producer, died of cancer on Feb. 23, 1994 in New York. His many NY credits include *The Boys in the Band, What the Butler Saw, All Over, The Grass Harp, The Last of Mrs. Lincoln, Noel Coward in Two Keys, P.S. Your Cat Is Dead, Seascape,* and *Sweeney Todd.* Survived by a brother and a sister.

INDEX

Crawford, Bob, 160
Crawford, Constance, 37
Crawford, Marshall, 175
Crawford, Michael, 15, 20, 79
Crawford, Ron, 126
Crazy For You, 38, 74, 149, 202
Creaghan, Dennis, 146, 211
Creation Production Company, 124
Creech, Philip, 180
Creek, Luther, 153
Creighton, Jennifer, 120
Cress, Philip, 164
Cressid Company, 107
Cresswell, Deborah, 105
Cresswell, Luke, 113
Crider, Michael, 169
Crime and Punishment, 116
Crime Scene, 99
Crimp, Martin, 138
Crist, Sheridan, 99, 185, 211
Cristofer, Michael, 97, 126, 201
Critic and His Wife, A, 170
Crivello, Anthony, 76, 211
Croft, Jeanne, 179
Croft, Paddy, 144, 211
Crom, Rick, 44, 147
Cromarty, Peter, 46, 86-88, 95, 97-98, 100-102, 105-108, 111-112, 116-118, 122, 125-126
Crommett, David, 92
Crompton, Barbara, 145
Cromwell, Gloria, 159
Cromwell, James, 183
Cromwell, Keith, 88, 154
Cron, George, 91, 105
Cronin, Denise, 124
Cronin, Jamie, 156
Cronin, Jim, 99, 103
Crosby, Rita, 102
Crosby, Shelley, 175
Crosby, Will, 114
Cross, Steve, 112
Crossroads Theatre Co., 86
Croswell, Anne, 110
Crothers, Sam, 63
Crouch, Jade S., 89
Crouse, Lindsay, 201, 211
Crouse, Russel, 157
Crow, Laura, 130, 163, 190
Crowe, Timothy, 191
Crowell, Richard, 112
Crowley, Bob, 50
Crowley, Dennis, 44, 53, 64, 92, 142
Crum, Tracy, 28
Crumb, Ann, 52
Crutchfield, Buddy, 211
Crutchman, John, 152
Cruz, Francis J, 78, 211
Cruz, Holly, 160
Cruz, Miriam, 92
Cruz, Veronica, 96
Cruz, William, 117

Cruz-DeJesus, Enrique, 138
Cry, the Beloved Country, 171
Crystal Stairs, 95
Crystal, Raphael, 107, 130
CSC Repertory, 129
Cuadrado, Lourdes, 92
Cucaracha, 87, 99
Cucci, Tony, 99
Cuccioli, Robert, 77, 211
Cudia, John, 184
Cuellar, Victor, 88
Cuen, Anthony, 99
Cuervo, Alma, 145-146, 185, 211
Culbert, John, 171
Cullen, Michael, 28, 126
Cullen, Sean, 189
Culliton, Joseph, 211
Culliver, Karen, 211
Cullom, Jim, 106
Culp, Steven, 159
Culture Clash, 91, 166, 176
Cumberbatch, Chris, 102
Cummings, A. Bernard, 174
Cummings, Brenda, 194
Cummings, Claudia, 157
Cummins, Rick, 98
Cumpsty, Michael, 25, 115, 138, 211
Cunningham, Edward, 95
Cunningham, John, 44, 80, 145, 211
Cunningham, Laura, 116, 121, 132
Cunningham, Scott, 109, 146, 161
Cunningham, T. Scott, 109, 146, 211
Cunningham, Thomas E., 150
Cuomo, Douglas J., 20, 110, 114, 130
Curate Shakespeare As You Like It, The, 102
Curchack, Fred, 112
Curi, Jorge, 183
Curiel, Tony, 176
Curless, John, 211
Curran, Gerard, 121
Curran, Keith, 109
Currie, Richard, 100, 117
Currier, Terrence P., 46, 183
Curry, Eddie, 148
Curry, John, 240
Curry, Julia, 168
Curry, Julian, 122
Curry, Vicky, 89
Curtin, Catherine, 105, 211
Curtis, Elizabeth, 38
Curtis, Keene, 20-21, 208, 211
Curtis, Simon, 62
Cushman, Mary, 109
Cuskern, Dominic, 136-137, 141
Cusnik, Russ, 192
Cutler, Sean, 101
Cwikowski, Bill, 30
Cyrano-The Musical, 32

D Train, 88

d'Amboise, Charlotte, 172
D'Ambrose, Camille, 168
D'Ambrosio, Tom, 18, 128
D'Amelio, Luisa, 102, 116
D'Amico, Marcus, 59-60, 195, 198, 211
D'Antuono, Matthew, 184
D'Aquila, Diane, 161
D'Arcy, Mary, 70, 79
D'Asaro, James, 127
D'Aubery, Ben, 193
D'Beck, Patti, 68, 151, 212
D'Elia, Vincent, 66, 158
D'Haene, Robert, 187
D'Onofrio, Benny, 48
Dafoe, Willem, 117
Dahlem, Steve, 158
Dai, Dunsi, 115
Dailey, Irene, 130, 211
Dajani, Nadia, 134, 142
Daldry, Stephen, 60
Daley, R. F., 75, 211
Dalian, Kent, 153
Dallas, Walter, 185
Dallimore, Steven Ray, 182
Dalton, Scott, 160
Daly, Elizabeth, 120
Daly, Kevin, 240
Damashek, Barbara, 191
Damian, Michael, 26-27, 211
Damkoehler, William, 191
Damn Yankees, 4, 45-46, 183, 195, 202
Dana, F. Mitchell, 164, 170, 184
Dancing at Lughnasa, 162, 168, 171, 185, 187, 190-191, 202
Dang, Tim, 193
Dangle, David, 63
Daniel, Kim, 95
Daniele, Graciela, 132
Danieley, Jason, 44, 146
Daniels, J. D., 165
Daniels, Max, 93
Daniels, Ron, 161
Daniels, Sarah, 87
Daniels, Sheila, 159
Dano, Royal, 239-240
Danson, Randy, 129, 138, 163, 211
Dante, Bill, 89, 117
Danton's Death, 112
Dantos, Nick, 116
Dantuono, Michael, 115, 211
Dar A Luz, 114
Dara, Olu, 171
Daras, April, 164
Dardaris, Janis, 185
Darden, Michael, 115
Darlow, Cynthia, 145, 211
Darragh, Anne, 87
Darrah, James, 38, 184
Darrow, Harry, 97
Das Barbecu, 172

Datcher, Irene, 86
Dattolo, Frank L., 178
Davenport, Anita, 102
Davenport, Johnny Lee, 171
Daves, Cathy, 95
Davey, Shaun, 122
David, Clifford, 27, 211
David, Hal, 172
David, Jim, 66, 211
David, Mack, 240
David, Steven H., 63
Davidow, Meredith, 116
Davidson, Gordon, 35, 71, 140, 165
Davidson, Jack, 185
Davidson, Richard M., 105, 211
Davidson, Suzanne Schwartz, 143
Davies, Howard, 38
Davies, Hubert Henry, 141
Davies, Matthew Lloyd, 96
Davies, Rachel, 165
Davis, Andi, 25, 42, 138
Davis, Anthony, 35, 46, 71, 183
Davis, Bruce Anthony, 46, 183, 211
Davis, Carol, 193
Davis, Chris, 152
Davis, Clinton Turner, 125
Davis, Colleen, 88, 141
Davis, Darnell, 193
Davis, Donna, 109
Davis, Elaina, 139
Davis, Eric, 153
Davis, Fiona, 98, 101, 115
Davis, Guy, 109
Davis, Helene, 103, 136
Davis, Henry Marsden, 94
Davis, Hope, 138, 142, 146, 211
Davis, Jeff, 26, 193
Davis, Jerome, 126
Davis, John Henry, 164
Davis, Joseph C., 117
Davis, Katie, 126
Davis, Kenneth J., 63
Davis, Kevin, 169
Davis, Lindsay W., 63
Davis, Lloyd, Jr., 95
Davis, Mac, 211
Davis, Mary Bond, 122, 208, 212
Davis, Peter J., 95
Davis, Shanesia, 171
Davis, Ted, 141
Davis, Todd, 103, 115
Davis, Tony, 89
Davis, Tracy, 89
Davis, Vicki R., 126
Davis, Viola, 191
Davison, Peter J., 53
Davolos, Sydney, 169
Davy, Babs, 140
Davys, Edmund C, 212
Dawe, Geoff, 91, 112
Dawson, Alene, 97, 189
Dawson, David P., 102, 212

Gilchrist, Newton R., 18
Gilford, Joe, 106
Gilgamesh Theatre Group, 97, 102, 126
Gilinsky, William, 150
Gill, Michel R., 178
Gillan, Tony, 165
Gilleland, Louanne, 92
Gillespie, Conor, 100
Gillespie, Della, 148
Gillett, Aden, 60, 196, 198, 215
Gillette, Anita, 98, 200, 215
Gillette, Ruth, 240-241
Gilliam, Gwendolyn M., 139
Gilliam, Michael, 183
Gilliam, Seth, 129
Gillies, Isabel, 134
Gilliland, Lou Anne, 107
Gillis, Laura, 91
Gilmore, Allen, 125
Gilmore, William, 108
Gilpin, Jack, 124
Gilroy, Frank D., 30
Giluntin, Jon, 146
Gindi Theatrical Management, 22, 48
Ginsberg, Maury, 163
Ginsberg, Stuart, 30, 97, 120, 147
Ginsburg, Richard, 114
Giobbe, Ann, 103
Giobbi, Lisa, 110
Giordano, Charlie, 24
Giordano, Tony, 22
Giorgione, Ganine, 66
Gipson, David, 171
Gipson, Terry, 159
Girandola, Neal James, 95
Giron, Arthur, 130
Giroux, Laurent, 153
Girten, Mierka, 175
Girvin, Terri, 122
Glaser, Sherry, 96, 195, 198, 215
Glaspell, Susan, 100
Glass, Philip, 19, 104
Glass, Ted, 86
Glazer, Benjamin F., 50
Gleason, Laurence, 98, 115, 215
Gleeson, Megan, 138, 173
Glenn, Bette, 215
Glenn, Bradley, 117
Glezos, Irene, 105, 215
Glickfeld, Ken, 115
Glines, 88
Glockner, Eleanor, 55
Glover, Beth, 86
Glover, Corey, 118
Glover, Keith, 174
Glovsky, Alan, 108
Glovsky, Jeff, 91
Glushak, Joanna, 214-215
Gmoser, Andrew, 99
Godino, Stephanie, 26

Godot Arrives, 105
Godsey, Paula, 108, 117, 126
Godspell, 11
Goede, Jay, 35, 71
Goehring, Kate, 159, 162, 171
Goethals, Angela, 56, 214-215
Goetz, Peter Michael, 42, 215
Goff, Charles, 40
Goff, Thom, 110
Goforth, Charles, 120
Gogol, Nikolai, 42
Going, Joanna, 48, 215
Going, John, 168
Gold, Jeremy, 94
Gold, Martin, 18, 40, 63
Gold, Michael E., 90, 215
Goldberg, Missy, 90
Goldberg, Russell, 95, 215
Golden Bull of Boredom, The, 93
Golden, Annie, 146, 216
Golden, Joey, 99
Golden, Michele, 159
Golden, Norman, 127
Goldenthal, Elliot, 115
Goldes, Joel, 96
Goldhirsch, Sheri M., 95
Goldin, Ricky Paull, 3, 68-69, 151
Goldman, Nina, 40
Goldrick, Tim, 110, 126
Goldsmith, Merwin, 82, 98, 142, 216
Goldsmith, Oliver, 169
Goldstein, David Ira, 163
Goldstein, Jess, 20, 107, 128, 140, 142, 178
Goldstein, Jonathan, 118, 131
Goldstein, Steven, 95, 103, 116, 121, 132, 216
Goldwyn, Tony, 63, 216
Golub, Peter, 120
Gomes, Rob, 185
Gomez, Marga, 166
Gonzales, Nicholas, 117
Gonzalez, Ching, 131
Gonzalez, Christine, 193
Gonzalez, Cordelia, 166
Gonzalez, John, 176
Gooch, Bruce, 183
Good As New, 111
Good Evening, 134
Good News, 151
Goodbye Girl, The, 179, 190
goodbye, harry, 98
Goodman, David, 91
Goodman, Dody, 83, 216
Goodman, Mark, 115
Goodman, Susan, 165
Goodmanson, Tim, 93
Goodness, Joel, 74, 214, 216
Goodnight Desdemona, Good Morning Juliet, 182
Goodrich, Bruce, 82, 104-105, 162
Goodrich, Frances, 170

Goodrich, Linda, 151
Goodspeed, Don, 168
Goodwin, Aaron, 105, 214, 216
Goodwin, Karen Walter, 90
Gorak, Nicole, 165
Gordon, David, 159, 161
Gordon, Glenn, 122
Gordon, Ian, 117
Gordon, James, 40, 112
Gordon, Joshua Dean, 159
Gordon, Kellye, 40
Gordon, Michael-David, 112
Gore, Nigel, 191
Gorelick, Fred, 193
Gorey, Edward, 120
Gorman, Trisha, 17
Gormley, Fred, 94
Gorn, Steve, 94
Gorostiza, Felipe, 111
Gorzelnik, Christopher, 169, 180
Gotanda, Philip Kan, 136
Gotter, Friedrich Wilhelm, 115
Gottlieb, Elizabeth, 107
Gottlieb, Heather, 101
Gottlieb, Jon, 140
Gottlieb, Michael, 98, 126
Gottschall, Ruth, 184
Gould, Dana, 143
Gould, Harold, 22, 216
Gould, Peggy, 110
Gould, Richard, 155
Gould, Tom, 145
Goulet, Robert, 18
Government Inspector, The, 42
Goyette, Rebecca, 126
Goz, Michael, 44, 75
Gozzi, Carlo, 194
Graae, Jason, 31, 52, 216
Grabowski, Christopher, 140
Grace, Eileen, 216
Grace, Ginger, 96, 216
Grace, Jessica, 126
Grace, Mary, 114, 121
Gracieux, Vincent, 176, 194
Graff, Laurie, 101, 216
Graff, Randy, 33, 216
Graham, Barbara, 120
Graham, Bruce, 170
Graham, Dion, 170
Graham, Enid, 138, 189
Graham, Jason, 160
Graham, Lauren, 170
Grana, Edgar David, 99
Granata, Dona, 183
Grand Night For Singing, A, 31
Grandison, Brian A., 171
Granger, Stewart, 201, 241
Grant, Benny, 165
Grant, David Marshall, 3, 13, 34-35, 71, 216
Grant, Gregory, 187
Grant, Kathryn, 102, 216

Grant, Sean, 123, 216
Grant, William H., III, 190
Grapes of Wrath, The, 186
Grass Harp, The, 147
Grassilli, John, 187
Grassle, Karen, 159
Grasso, Anthony, 122
Grate, Gail, 28-29, 139, 194
Gravatt, Lynda, 169
Gravens, David, 159
Gravitte, Debbie Shapiro, 216
Gray's Anatomy, 36, 133, 171
Gray, Allison, 88
Gray, Kevin, 79, 216
Gray, Pamela, 87
Gray, Sam, 101, 216
Gray, Spalding, 36, 171
Gray, William, 189
Grayson, Bobby H., 66
Grayson, Darlene Bel, 97
Grayson, Jerry, 132
Grease, 3, 68, 151
Great American Musicals in Concert, 44
Great Nebula In Orion, The, 87
Greco, Loretta, 180
Green Bird, The, 194
Green, Adolph, 147, 172
Green, Andrea, 44, 216
Green, Colton, 38, 76
Green, Crystal Laws, 183
Green, David, 37, 48, 76, 216
Green, Dennis, 169
Green, Elizabeth, 38, 44
Green, Fanni, 159
Green, Jackie, 75, 108, 113
Green, Joan, 37, 176
Green, Jonathan, 26, 115
Green, Richard Kent, 91, 94, 112
Greenberg, Gordon, 130
Greenberg, Michael, 187
Greenberg, Miriam, 100
Greenberg, Mitchell, 33
Greenberg, Rob, 118, 123
Greenblatt, Kenneth D., 63
Greene, James, 183
Greene, Lawrence, 143
Greene, Marlene, 110
Greenfield, Tom, 100, 117
Greenhill, Susan, 216
Greenley, Mark L., 107
Greenman, Stuart, 189
Greensheets Productions, 87
Greenspan, David, 108
Greenwald, Tom, 172
Greenwood, Bruce, 121
Greenwood, Jane, 17, 37, 43, 64, 80, 165, 178
Greer, Ann, 162
Greer, Keith, 126
Greer, Robert, 89
Greetings, 105

276

Ryan, Thomas Jay, 108, 123
Ryan, Thomas M., 179
Ryder, Amy, 46, 147, 230
Ryder, Ric, 72, 230-231
Rylance, Mark, 107, 230
Ryland, Jack, 25, 42, 230
Ryskind, Morrie, 184
Rzeznik, Teresa, 117

S.S.Glencairn-Four Plays of the Sea, 98
Sabellico, Richard, 103, 127
Sabo, Alice, 114
Sacharow, Lawrence, 119, 146
Sacher, Bobby, 100
Sacher, Richard, 91
Sachs, C. Colby, 87, 106
Sackett Group, The, 89
Sackhelm, Judy Jerald, 111
Saculla, Chuck, 179
Saddler, Donald, 38
Sadoff, Fred, 245-246
Sadusk, Maureen, 172
Safan, Craig, 172
Sagardia, Elisa, 150
Sage, Alexandria, 94, 131, 230
Sage, Bill, 182
Sage, Raymond, 18
Sager, Carole Bayer, 160
Sager, Jessica, 114
Sahl, Mort, 118
Saiet, Eric, 171
Saint, David, 189
Saint, Eva Marie, 186, 200
Saito, James, 124, 230
Sakaguchi, Andrew, 154
Sakakura, Lainie, 66
Sala, Ed, 124, 192
Salaam, Abdel, 138
Saland, Ellen, 116
Salinas, Ric, 166, 176-177
Salinger, Ross, 94, 118, 230
Sallows, Tracy, 35, 71, 230-231
Sally Marr And Her Escorts, 63
Salmon, Scott, 246
Salovey, Todd, 188
Saltzman, Avery, 172
Saltzman, Mark, 41
Salute to Tom Jones and Harvey Schmidt, 147
Salzman, Thomas, 164
Sama, Lenys, 100
Sammis, Donna, 107
Sampliner, Susan, 54
Sampson, Nick, 96
Sampson, Tiffany, 50
Samuel, Peter, 156
Samuels, Diane, 136
Sanchez, Alexies, 40, 50
Sanchez, Esteban Fernandez, 131
Sanchez, Jaime, 117, 200, 230
Sanchez, Karenjune, 94, 159, 174

Sanchez, Rene, 111
Sanchez, Roland, 116
Sancho and Don, 125
Sand: Three Plays, 144
Sandbox, The, 144
Sande, Michael, 172
Sandefur, James, 185
Sanders, Donald T., 106
Sanders, Erin, 63
Sanders, Jay O., 103, 136, 230
Sanders, Leon, 189
Sanders, Nathaniel, 153, 190
Sanders, Pete, 23, 68, 83, 86, 88, 96, 126
Sanders, Ty, 124
Sanders-Smith, Laurie, 96
Sanderson, Kirsten, 138
Sandish, Dale, 120
Sandler, Dianna, 107
Sandlin, Princess, 91
Sandoval, Vincent, 151
Sandy, Gary, 168
Sanford, Tim, 142
Sankowich, Lee, 130
Sannon, Sarah Solie, 55
Sano, Eve, 94
Santen, Kathy, 179
Santiago, Saundra, 132, 230
Santiago, Socorro, 109, 124, 230
Santiago-Hudson, Ruben, 138-139
Santigo, Angelo, 92
Santopietro, Tom, 24, 58
Santoro, Mark, 73, 230-231
Santoro, Nick, 169
Santoro, Susan, 27
Santos, Mylene, 109
Santy, Charles, 92
Sarabande, Varese, 17, 31, 66
Sargeant, Greig, 117
Sargent, Mike, 93
Sargent, Peter E., 168, 187
Saroyan, William, 126
Sarpy, Joseph, 178
Sasfai, Conny, 154
Sassoon, David, 109
Sater, Steven, 91
Sato, Tamao M., 89
Satta, Steven, 114, 230
Sauli, James, 123
Saunders, Nicholas, 166
Sausage Eaters, The, 103
Sauter, Luisa, 107
Savage Routine of Living, The, 98
Savage, Keith, 149
Savage, Sheila, 179
Savant, Joseph, 27
Savarese, John, 106
Savino, Frank, 22
Savoy, Carla, 116
Sawney, Sheila, 89, 117
Sawyer, Toni, 94, 230
Sawyer-Dailey, Mark, 159

Saxton, Ellen, 148
Sayan, Levon, 86
Sbarge, Raphael, 23, 166, 230-231
Scalamoni, Sam, 32
Scanlan, Dick, 38
Scanlon, Barbara, 18
Scanlon, Patricia, 182
Scarboro, Catherine, 125
Scardino, Don, 92, 142
Scaring the Fish, 99
Scarlett, Bob, 159
Scarpone, Judith, 23, 230
Scassellati, Vincent, 173
Schachter, Beth, 143
Schaechter, Ben, 147
Schaefer, Celia, 98
Schaefer, John, 86
Schaefer, Richard, 110, 124, 160
Schaeffer, Berton T., 182
Schaeffer, Eric, 169
Schafer, Scott, 151
Schaffel, Marla, 146, 150
Schall, Thomas, 163, 182
Schaller, Mark, 164
Schany, Bryan, 126
Schapiro, Herb, 123
Scharff, Robert, 185
Scharpen, Bill, 110
Schaufer, Lucy, 63
Schecter, Amy, 33, 66, 68
Scheffer, Will, 124
Schelble, William, 2, 18, 53, 63-64, 97
Schellenbaum, Tim, 131
Schenkkan, Robert, 28
Scherer, John, 184, 232
Scherer, Susan, 102
Schertler, Nancy, 162, 165
Scherzer, Wayne, 77, 232
Scherzinger, Nicole, 159
Schifrin, Lalo, 166
Schifter, Peter Mark, 246
Schilke, Raymond D., 85, 95, 110, 142
Schilling, James, 86
Schiralli, Michael, 96
Schirle, Joan, 188
Schisgal, Murray, 103, 124
Schlenk, Diana, 102
Schlesinger, Eliza, 184
Schlesinger, Kate, 182
Schlesinger, Sarah, 175
Schlofner, Matthew, 87, 94, 102
Schmidt, Douglas W., 46, 183
Schmidt, Lars, 58
Schmidt, Mary Ethel, 116, 125
Schmidt, Paul, 95, 147, 194
Schmittou, David, 164
Schmitz, Danny, 176
Schneider, Gerard J., 120
Schnitzler, Arthur, 132
Schoeffler, Paul, 32, 232
Schoenberg, A. Jeffrey, 193
Scholz-Carlson, Douglas, 189

Schons, Alain, 188
School For Wives, 194
Schorr, Eric, 88
Schorr, Kristina, 97
Schram, Bitty, 33
Schreiber, Liev, 19, 232
Schreier, Dan Moses, 22, 42, 129, 139
Schroeder, Karl, 125
Schuette, James, 89, 138
Schulberg, Budd, 99
Schulfer, Roche, 171
Schully, Charlotte, 138
Schulman, Susan H., 40, 44, 147-148, 156
Schulman, Susan L., 74, 91, 111, 121-122
Schulte, Mark, 102
Schultheiss, Kimberly K, 112, 232
Schulthies, Tim, 27, 230
Schultz, Carol, 37, 187, 231-232
Schultz, Mary, 122, 159
Schumann, Christopher, 120
Schuminski, Charles, 176
Schurr, Carl, 181
Schuster, Alan J., 46
Schutte, William, 150
Schutter, Laura, 179
Schwab, Jennifer, 160
Schwab, Kaipo, 124
Schwab, Laurence, 151
Schwartz, Adam L., 114
Schwartz, Alexys, 193
Schwartz, Gary, 76, 120, 231-232
Schwartz, Robert Joel, 141
Schwartz, Wilder, 159
Schweizer, David, 139, 147, 166
Schwinn, Ron, 38
Schworer, Angie L., 149
Sciford, Sandra, 93
Sciorra, Annabella, 108-109
Scoggins, Richard, 96
Scotland Road, 175
Scott, Brad, 155
Scott, Campbell, 142, 185, 232
Scott, Christopher, 82, 151
Scott, David, 91, 176
Scott, H. Hylan, II, 68, 151
Scott, James, 40, 173, 187
Scott, John, 38, 232
Scott, Kevin, 121
Scott, Klea, 138
Scott, Molly, 48, 90
Scott, Seret, 95, 183, 190
Scott, Simon, 96
Scott, Stephanie, 100
Scoullar, John, 98
Scricca, Michael, 124
Scruggs, Sharon, 89
Scudder, Ellison, 35
Scurria, Anne, 191
Sea, Jonathan, 98
Seabury, Jack, 121